THE RECORD SOCIETY OF LANCASHIRE AND CHESHIRE

FOUNDED TO TRANSCRIBE AND PUBLISH
ORIGINAL DOCUMENTS RELATING TO THE TWO COUNTIES

VOLUME CXXVII

The Society wishes to acknowledge with gratitude
the assistance given towards the cost of publication by
Greater Manchester County Council and Residuary Body
Cheshire County Council
Lancashire County Council
Mrs D. Powell
Miss J. M. D. Prescott
Major L. W. Prescott

ISBN 0 902593 16 1

Produced by Alan Sutton Publishing Limited, Gloucester
Printed in Great Britain

THE DIARY OF HENRY PRESCOTT, LL.B., DEPUTY REGISTRAR OF CHESTER DIOCESE

Edited by
John Addy, M.A., Ph.D.

Volume 1, 28 March 1704–24 March 1711

PRINTED FOR THE SOCIETY
1987

COUNCIL AND OFFICERS FOR THE YEAR 1987

President

Professor A. Harding, B.Litt., M.A., F.S.A., F.R.Hist.S.

Hon. Council Secretary

Dorothy J. Clayton, M.A., Ph.D., A.L.A., c/o John Rylands University Library of Manchester, Oxford Road, Manchester, M13 9PP

Hon. Membership Secretary

Miss M. Patch, B.A., D.A.A., c/o Greater Manchester County Record Office, 56 Marshall Street, Manchester, M4 5FU

Hon. Treasurer

B.W. Quintrell, M.A., Ph.D., F.R.Hist.S., c/o School of History, Liverpool University, 8 Abercromby Square, Liverpool 7

Hon. General Editor

P. McNiven, M.A., Ph.D., c/o John Rylands University Library of Manchester, Oxford Road, Manchester, M13 9PP

Other Members of Council

J.J. Bagley, M.A., F.R.Hist.S.
Miss E.A. Danbury, B.A.
R.N. Dore, M.A., F.R.Hist.S.
F.I. Dunn, B.A., D.A.A.
K. Hall, B.A., D.A.A.
B.E. Harris, M.A., Ph.D.
Mrs J.I. Kermode, B.A.
P.J. Morgan, B.A., Ph.D.
M.A. Mullett, B.A., M.Litt., Ph.D.
C.B. Phillips, B.A., Ph.D.
J.R. Studd, B.A., Ph.D., F.R.Hist.S.
A.T. Thacker, M.A., D.Phil.

CONTENTS

INTRODUCTION

HENRY PRESCOTT, 1649–1719

It is known that the Prescott family lived at Ayrfield, Upholland, not far from Wigan. William Prescott had supported the ill-fated seventh earl of Derby by assisting him to raise troops for the Royalist cause in the Civil War. The earl was executed, and William was ruined, by their support for the Royalist cause. In 1655 Ayrfield had to be sold to pay William's debts. By 1686 Henry was able to redeem Ayrfield for the family. William's son Thomas lived at Rough Park, in which house Henry was born on 9 June 1649.

Henry, so far as we know, was the only member of the family to have kept a diary, which is complete, with certain exceptions, from 1704 to 1719, when Henry died. For the earlier period there is one volume covering the years 1689–1690, in Latin, and there are a few loose sheets for the years 1693–1696. The folios of the diary are now fragile due to age and poor conservation.[1]

Henry Prescott had two sisters; Jane, who married Peter Winstanley of Billinge in 1677, and Margaret, who married John Birchal of Warrington on 20 October 1674. Margaret never appears in the diary, but Peter Winstanley and his problems do. He lived at Yately Lane near Bispham Hall, and Henry, who was generous with his assistance, lodged there during his visits to Wigan. Their only son Thomas was employed as a clerk in the diocesan registry, but by 1702 both Thomas and his parents were dead.

When Charles Stanley succeeded to the estates of his executed father he appears to have remembered those who had supported the family, and Henry Prescott, nephew of William, was one of these. The earl, being in reduced circumstances, lived in Deeside, Chester, in a small house that had been built by the sixth earl. One family seat, Lathom, had been 'spoiled' by parliamentary forces and the other at Knowsley was too expensive to maintain. So, in all probability, Henry was taken to Chester, where a situation was found for him in the diocesan registry around 1677.

On 26 February 1677, William Wilson, deputy registrar, and Henry's employer, with his son-in-law John Massie, purchased Ayrfield for £400, a house they retained until Henry redeemed it in 1686 for the same sum.

William Wilson encouraged Henry to go to Trinity College, Dublin to read law and qualify for the registry. There was a close link between Lancashire, Cheshire and Ireland through Chester's status as a port. For some reason, Henry had been educated at Winwick school rather than at Rivington, Wigan or Heskin, the nearest schools to Rough Park. Winwick school had a close

1 Cheshire Record Office (C.R.O.), MS. Diary of Henry Prescott, on loan from Miss J. Prescott, Bourton on the Hill.

connection with the Stanleys, and Henry was probably educated with the Stanley children at Winwick.

For some unknown reason, Henry did not graduate until the summer of 1682, when he married Lydia Peake, widow of John Williamson, in St. Patrick's Cathedral, Dublin. They had one son Thomas, who lived fourteen days, both child and mother dying on 18 May 1685 at Wigan. Henry never entered the room where Lydia died for twenty years, but he recalls the date of her death.[2]

On 18 September 1686 William Wilson, the deputy registrar, died, and on the same day Henry Prescott was made a notary public, which enabled him to continue the work of the registry. Not until 29 November was Henry officially appointed as deputy registrar.[3] At that time the see was vacant, and Bishop Pearson's successor, Thomas Cartwright, dean of Ripon, was not enthroned until 30 November 1686. The new bishop and Henry Prescott became close friends even after Bishop Cartwright went to Dublin to join James II.[4]

Securely established in the registry, Henry married a second time on 11 August 1687. His bride was Susanna Puleston, daughter of Sir John Puleston of Havod-y-Wern, and a very happy marriage it turned out to be. Susanna was eighteen years younger than Henry, and bore him eleven children. Of these, only Jack, Harry and Ken, and one daughter, Margaret survived. Will, Susy, Arabella and Lydia, who are mentioned in the diary, died in childhood or as infants.[5]

Susanna Puleston had good family connections that brought Henry many influential and valuable friends in Chester. These were useful when Henry was appointed registrar of St. Asaph in February 1711, though Bishop Fleetwood appeared anxious to placate Henry, who had openly criticised the bishop for refusing to present Dr. Sacheverell to the benefice of Sallatyn in April 1710.[6]

Susanna's cousin was Sir Henry Bunbury of Stanney, whose father had married Mary, daughter of Sir Kenrick Eyton of Eyton (Denbigh) and sister of Helen, wife of Sir John Puleston, all of whom are mentioned in the diary. Sir Henry Bunbury represented Chester as M.P. from 1700 until 1727, and had married Susanna Hanmer of Hanmer, a family connected to the Pulestons.[8]

Henry took a keen interest in the Ayrfield property. By 1704 he owned the Hall Green, or Green House as he calls it, and also Whitely farm. He soon became involved with the financial problems of William Whalley of the Bank. From 1705 onwards Henry had periods of financial difficulty. Whalley had

2 30 November 1711: 'Lady Cornwallis' birthday, I remember it with affection to my Lydia'. Also 9 July 1705.

3 C.R.O., Bishop's Register, EDA2/3 f.185.

4 *Ibid.*, Correspondence of Henry Prescott.

5 S. Harrison, *Early Pulestons* (Whitchurch, 1975). Bangor Parish Registers: 11 August 1687, Henry Prescott to Susanna Puleston, daughter of John Puleston.

6 C.R.O., Prescott correspondence, letter from Bishop Fleetwood concerning Dr. Sacheverell. This will be reproduced in an appendix to Vol. II.

8 Sir Henry Bunbury of Stanney, 3rd Baronet, who lived at Bryn y Fynnon House until 1699, when he removed to Chester.

borrowed large sums of money from Henry on the security of the Bank estate. By 1708 his borrowings had become so large that Henry had to take over the estate, now valued at 960^{li}.

He found himself faced with repayment of a mortgage to Mr Gillebrand of Chorley, and with the distasteful task of sheltering Whalley from his creditors, the most persistent and implacable being Whalley's brother. Finally, Whalley, who had taken temporary residence in Chester, was compelled to escape hurriedly, dressed in his wife's clothes as a disguise, and Henry was left to provide for the family. All efforts to find employment for Whalley failed, and he disappears from the diary.[9]

The above properties Henry rented out at an annual rent which was collected by John Cross, the village blacksmith, who acted as rent collector and steward for forty shillings per annum. Henry was keen to develop the estate and, at intervals in the diary, he records details of tree planting and also his plans to enlarge Ayrfield House, but there is no evidence that this ever took place.

At this period the river Douglas ran below Ayrfield and the Bank. It was a considerable stream always liable to flood the land. In order to control the floodwaters, Henry planned a dam and sluices to adjust the flow of water. He also erected a water mill and improved the supply of fresh water to the house. On one occasion he consulted a Mr Cumberbatch for advice on tree pruning.

As frequently as his official duties permitted, Henry visited Wigan. Here he lodged with his sister Jane Winstanley at Gately Lane or else at his cousin Holt's in Standishgate, which gave him the opportunity to walk or ride the six miles to Ayrfield. After an inspection of the property he would drink a pint or two of claret or special ale. If time permitted, Henry would spend a day at Upholland, calling upon his godmother Rigby, a sprightly old lady of ninety at the last reference to her, then call upon his neighbour Halliwell, his cousin Finch, and lastly the curate. On Sunday he would sit in his new pew in the chancel of the church and later visit the Ashursts of Ashurst or the Banks at Winstanley. On those occasions when Henry stayed in Wigan he attended the parish church, occupying his seat in the gallery, and later visited Edward Finch the rector, whose brother Henry was dean of York. Later he called upon Alderman Markland and Sir Richard Bradshaigh at Haigh, ending the day in congenial company at Nanny Tottel's ale house the *Owl in the Ivy Bush,* which stood near the old Court House.

Henry was devoted to the House of Derby, and when the tenth earl was placed in a difficult situation by his two sisters, who both claimed dowries, Henry records his anxiety. The earl was compelled to sell the contents of the houses at Deeside and Lathom, and a portion of the Knowsley property. Between April and December 1705, Henry was greatly troubled by events, especially the auction sale of the goods on 27 August 1705.

When the tenth earl came to Chester in 1707, Henry rode out to Dunham to

9 See Prescott's Diary, especially August-December 1708.

meet him and was invited to dinner. Henry travelled to Lancaster when the case between the earl and his sisters came up for hearing. The earl lost, and on his way to the Isle of Man, he called in Chester to say farewell to Susanna Prescott.

Another friend of Henry was James Butler, 2nd duke of Ormonde and brother-in-law to the earl of Derby. The duke appears for the first time in the diary on 7 June 1690, where he records, 'The Duke of Ormonde is my guest'.[10]

The duke was then twenty-five years of age and had given his support to William of Orange, who at that time was on his way to take command of the Life Guards at the Battle of the Boyne. The duke spent a few days as Henry's guest before embarking with William's troops at Hoylake on the 10th. Henry records this in his diary: 'Laribus valedicit meis'.[11]Not until 1711 is the duke mentioned again, when he visited Chester and was entertained at the Pentice. On this occasion Henry records

> 'His Grace there takes me by the hand with kind enquiry after my Family & invites me to see him at Sir H[enry] B[unbury]'s'.[12]

This friendship could have arisen when Henry and the duke were at one of the Derby houses. Henry must have been so impressed by the duke's career that eventually it influenced his political attitude in a decisive manner.

As one would expect of the nephew of a cavalier, Henry was a keen admirer of Charles I and never failed to observe the anniversary of his execution.

> [30 Jan. 1704/5] 'King Charles 1st his Martyrdom. The 56 year celebrated. . . Apply to the History of that Glorious Martyr read by Jack.'

That enthusiasm never extended to Charles II or James II, and he accepted William of Orange without any enthusiasm. There is no evidence before 1714 to indicate that Henry was disloyal to the Crown, for he religiously observed both Queen Anne's birthday and her accession.

> [1 Jan 1711/12] 'After dinner the Church and Queen remembered in Q. Elizabeth's Glass and then a smaller glass goes freely round.'[13]

Following the Jacobite rising of 1715, Lord Charles Murray and a large number of men were captured at Preston on 13 November, all of whom were brought to Chester Castle. The severity of the weather, accompanied by an outbreak of gaol fever, caused a number of prisoners to die, so the survivors were shipped out to the plantations. Lord Charles Murray was known to Henry,

10 For translations and extracts from this Latin Diary see Vol. II.

11 Trans.:'he bids farewell to my home'. See G. V. Bennett, *Tory Crisis in Church and State 1688–1730* (Oxford 1975), for the career of the duke of Ormonde.

12 Diary, 18 June 1711.

13 The Queen Elizabeth glass came from the workshop of Jacob Vezelini and was engraved by Anthony de Lyste of London 1586. The glass came into the Prescott family from the Pulestons on Henry's marriage to Susanna. The initials R.P. and M.P. can only refer to Roger Puleston of Emral (Flint) and Maud, or Mawdlin, daughter of Sir Thomas Hanmer.

for his grandfather had married Lady Amelia Stanley, and Henry's sister Elizabeth had gone with her to Scotland, so he was a frequent visitor at Henry's and Sir Henry Bunbury's.

The misfortunes of the Old Pretender after 1715 were a source of anxiety to Henry who, until it was denied, believed that

> 'King James 3rd was arrested and imprisoned in Milan'.

The barbaric treatment of the prisoners of 1715, and his sympathy for the duke of Ormonde, an exiled and secret Jacobite who had openly assisted the rising, may have been contributory factors in Henry's conversion to Jacobitism. On 10th June 1716, he records

> 'Mr Midleton and Mr Lloyd came over to celebrate this Birthday of K. James 3. The health is not drunk by name we invent the toast within the compass of good manners.'

The greater part of Henry's life was spent in Chester. Almost every morning he took a number of turns on the Roodee; the exact number varied with the state of his health after the previous evening spent drinking at the Fountain, the Falcon, the Pied Bull, or one or other of the many inns in the city. Mornings, and frequently evenings, saw Henry involved in work at the registry, visiting the bishop and chancellor, or engaged in the Consistory Court. Occasionally he would ride out in the afternoon to visit a friend at one of the country houses, and conclude the evening in the company of the chancellor and a few close friends.

Henry travelled to visit places of interest. In August 1708, he went with the bishop and a few friends to Buxton, Bakewell, and Chatsworth House, where the duke refused to see them (he being a staunch Whig and they high Tories), travelling on via country houses to Nottingham and returning via Derby.

On 1 September 1711 Henry travelled to see his son Jack at Christ Church, Oxford. He records in detail the places he visited, including an account of Blenheim Palace, of which he does not wholeheartedly approve. In addition to these private tours. Henry accompanied the chancellor and the bishop on visitation tours and frequently complains about the poor quality of food provided.

Henry was a keen collector of Roman artefacts and coins, recording his acquisitions in some detail. He was an avid reader of books, not only the Latin classical authors, but a wide range of publications that were of interest to him.[14]

Through the efforts of Canon Stratford, formerly Archdeacon Stratford, Jack obtained a place at Christ Church, Oxford as an undergraduate. In 1714 Jack had an offer of Orders from Archbishop Dawes, who also promised him presentation to the benefice of Waverton. On 18 October 1714, Jack was made

14 See C. Leigh, *Natural History of Lancashire, Cheshire and the Peak with an Account of the Antiquities in those Parts*(Oxford, 1700), Vol.iii pp.21,31,81; J. Horsley, *Britannia Romana* (London, 1732), p.314. See the appendix in Vol. II for details of the books that Henry read.

deacon, and was ordained priest on 24 December in the Savoy Chapel by Archbishop Dawes. The archbishop also promised Jack the prebendal stall of Dr Blake when vacant. This occurred on 10 January 1715. Jack had failed to become the academic scholar his father expected.

Harry, the second son, was a problem. In 1711, while still a pupil at King's School, he was patronising tippling houses, raking and drinking to excess. Henry was disturbed by reports he received upon Harry's conduct, and on 27 November 1711 decided to send him to sea. By November the following year Harry joined his ship at Liverpool, where he managed to pile up debts and worries for his father. Evidently he was taught navigation, and the last reference in the diary to Harry is on 2 December 1717, when he sailed for Virginia.

The youngest son Ken was, at fourteen years of age, elected to a place at the Charterhouse through the effort and nomination of the duke of Ormonde. In later years the governors of Charterhouse appointed Ken as master of St. Catherine's College, Cambridge.

During the time of the financial troubles that Harry had brought upon Henry, his friend John Massie, who had married as his third wife a daughter of John Puleston of Pickhill, came to his aid. Henry's improvements at Ayrfield had burdened him with heavy interest charges which absorbed a large proportion of estate revenue. This meant that he had to surrender a considerable proportion of the registry profits. In addition he had Jack at Oxford and Ken and a daughter at home.

Normally, he borrowed money from his cousin Holt who, being a business man, charged 6% interest. To Henry's surprise, in November 1716, John Massie insisted on lending Henry £100 interest free and on the Lady Day next following a further £500 on the same terms. When in October 1717 he went to Ormskirk, he heard the news about the proposed sale of the lordship of Holland. In Wigan, he arranged for enquiries to be made about the estate and the value of the manor. The opportunity to purchase never came, and in September of the following year, he learned from the carrier Thomas Naylor of, 'the melancholy history of the fate of Upholland which affects me.'

Henry never saw Upholland again, for the severe winter weather of January 1719 prevented his journey. He died quite suddenly on 9 June 1719 while undertaking a visitation of St. Asaph diocese at Wrexham. His body was taken to Upholland and buried there.

THE REGISTRY

The office of diocesan registrar was in the gift of the bishop, but at this period in Chester diocese the registrar deputed the administration to a deputy in return for a proportion of the fees. Hence the entry in the diary from time to time of 'paid to Dr. Pope 40.^{li}' Registrar's fees, like those of the chancellor, arose from a variety of sources, such as probate, letters of administration, marriage licences, executors' bonds, visitation fees, admission of church wardens, the induction and institution of clergy to benefices, faculties to make changes in churches, clergy resignation deeds, and fees that arose in the cases being conducted in the Consistory Court. All these items provided a considerable source of revenue for diocesan officials.

Although Dr. O'Day, in her book *Continuity and Change,* laments the lack of detailed knowledge of the part played by registrars in the daily administration of a diocese, Henry Prescott's diary does provide valuable clues. It records the daily working life in the registry with comments on political, social and economic life as they affected the diocese.

The registrar at this date was Dr. Walter Pope, step-brother to Bishop Wilkins (1668–1672). He was professor of Astronomy at Oxford, but resided permanently in Epsom. Dr. Pope was appointed registrar in 1668 and held the office for many years, far too many for Henry's peace of mind, since Bishop Dawes had promised Henry the reversion of the registry when Dr. Pope died.

In the meantime, Bishop Fleetwood appointed Henry as registrar of his diocese of St. Asaph in 1712. Doubtless this was partly a means of pacifying Henry following his complaints because the bishop refused to present Dr. Sacheverell to the benefice of Sallatyn.[15] Reading between the lines, Suzy's relatives were also bringing some pressure upon Bishop Fleetwood over the registry. The fees from this office did augment Henry's income, but not to any great extent. Unfortunately, Bishop Dawes was transferred to York following the death of Archbishop Sharp in 1713. As a result of this, Henry felt insecure, for Dr. Pope still lived on. Furthermore, Henry was disturbed upon the receipt of a letter from Canon Stratford of Christ Church, Oxford, that the new bishop Francis Gastrell might appoint someone else to the office of registrar.

Early in 1714, Dr. Pope died and Bishop Gastrell appointed his brother-in-law, Dr. Mapletoft, who was at that time in France, as registrar. Less than eighteen months later Dr. Mapletoft died in Cambridge, so once again Henry expected the reversion of the registry – but, alas, in vain. The bishop granted the registry to a Mr. Smith in trust for the bishop's son, and Henry now had to account for his annual profits to the bishop in order that he might assess the proportion to be paid to the titular holder of the office.

In December 1716 the bishop's son died, so the registry was transferred to Mr. Smith. In January 1716/17, the new registrar lessened the severity of the bishop's treatment of Henry by surrendering to him the rights of the registry of Chester archdeaconry. Unfortunately this came too late, for Henry died within eighteen months of the grant. It is not apparent that Dr. Pope ever visited Chester, but he remained at Epsom drawing his fees. Therefore, the deputy registrar appears to have exercised the duties of the registrar in the diocese. Dr. C. Kitching has expressed the view that it is impossible for the historian to estimate the number of hours registrars or their deputies spent in homework.[16] Nevertheless, the diary does yield a certain amount of information on this point.

15 C.R.O., Correspondence between Bishop Fleetwood and Henry Prescott. See Diary 1710–17ll for the case of Dr. Sacheverell.

16 R. O'Day & F. Heal, *Continuity & Change* (Leicester, 1976), pp.77ff.

> [13 Sept. 1704]'I turn Berty Geographiam, apply to enter the presentments, dispatch 5 Deanaries, recollect this Diary for the last month vidt. since Aug. 15th.'

The following day appears to have been spent chiefly in entering up the churchwardens' presentments.

> [14th Sept.] At early prayers proceed in the Deanaries, pay Hen. Maddock on Mr. Vaudrey's order 15^{li} In the Evening at the Falcon with ArchDeacons Booth and Stratford, Mrs Cowper, Wells &c very cheerfully.'

Just as the work of the registrar was frequently undertaken by a deputy in many dioceses, so with the work of the chancellor. This was not the custom in Chester, where the chancellor was also Vicar General and Official Principal with oversight of the archdeaconry of Chester. The diary indicates quite clearly that the chancellor, John Wainwright, worked closely with Prescott, and the relationship between them was close and friendly. On 21 September 1704, Prescott records

> 'St. Matthews day at early prayers, then to busienes, the Bishop of Mann and his Lady call on and sitt with us. I go with him to Mr. Harper's, after I am at the Chancellors at his entertainment of the ArchDeacons, where Mr Egerton, Dr. Thane, Mr Boucher; wee stay freely and late.' [17]

The organisation of the registry left a great deal to be desired. An orderly filing system appears to have been totally absent, which may, to some extent, account for the confused state of the surviving records, especially the court files. Henry spent some days searching for the Correction Court book for 1637, which he failed to find, and also the register of parish clerks in connection with a dispute at Wigan in 1709.[18] A good illustration concerning the organisation of the office is revealed in a case concerning the right of presentation to the benefice of Wycliffe on Tees. The first entry occurred on 13 June 1704.

> 'Wait on my Lord with the Chancellor about a Commission de Iure patronatus of Wycliffe to which Mr. Smales by the University of Cambridge, Mr. Gilpin by Mr. Hodgson is presented . . .'[19]

The next entry is dated 18 June 1706, and following a comment about the weather and the news, continues with the Wycliffe case.

> '. . .with my Lord in search of a verdict in Iure patronatus Wycliffe about 2 years ago but do not (since not deliver'd into the Registry) find it . . .call'd over by Sir H.B., drink a Glass or 2 of Claret with him . . .After at the Office in Dust, continue till 8.'

17 For biographical references see the appendix in Vol. II.
18 C.R.O., Consistory Court files EDC.5 (1709) No.3, Wigan.
19 Leeds District Archives, Wycliffe Parish Papers, CD/PP/9. This bundle contains a full report of the enquiry into the patronage in 1704.

Four days later the missing document is found only with the assistance of the bishop.

> 'After my Lord and myself had searcht near 3 daies I find the Commission and Verdict in Iure Patronatus Wycliffe.'[20]

The patronage belonged to the University of Cambridge and not to Hodgson.

The first indication that the deputy registrar had about an impending vacancy in a benefice was the entry of a caveat to protect the rights of the patron, where this right may or could be disputed, but it was not a common practice to do this as the Eccleston case reveals.

> [15 April 1704] 'My Lord hears the controversy about the Rectory of Eccleston laid open by Mr Birkenhead & Hulse, a hardship on the one and Cheat on the other side, laid open . . .'

Three weeks later, on 6 May, the matter of the presentation was raised again.

> 'I am with my Lord about the Institution to Eccleston, hee hesitates tho Mr Egerton only presented and no Caveats in force . . .'

Henry then went to supper with Mr Holland on a leveret and a bottle of port.

Resignations of benefices are always recorded, but many of these did not take place in the registry office, but elsewhere. Egerton remained rector of Eccleston for two years, and on 12 November 1706 he resigned his benefice.

> '. . .After prayers to the Ship where in a full little room Mr Egerton reads his resignation of Eccleston.'[21]

This was followed by a session with Dr. Thane and Mr Lancaster, rector of Tarporley and canon of Chester, at claret, after which he returned to the office where he records, 'I go slow on the returns.'

Henry was involved for the greater part of his time with the clergy and the exercise of patronage, including the alienation of right of presentation to a benefice and the sales of advowsons, which took place fairly frequently. On 15 November 1704 he was involved in one such sale.

> '. . . In the Evening at Lady Otways where I am wittnes to her sealing a Deed of Sale of the Advowson of Windermere to Dr. Fenton for which the consideration seems to bee to her 130^{li}. Sir Christopher Phillipson joining in the same Deed.'

On 26 January 1704/5 he was again a witness to three deeds by Lady Otway concerning the sale of lands in Hawkshead.

To what extent was the deputy registrar able to influence presentations to

20 C.R.O., EDA2/4 f.58.
21 *Ibid.*, f.6, Eccleston.

livings? We may never obtain the whole truth on the workings of patronage and influence, but it is clear from the entries in the diary that Henry was involved in the lives of the clergy and able to plead the case of a client with a patron who had a vacant benefice to fill. This seems to have operated in the case of Bowden during a voidance of the see in 1707. During the time the see was vacant, Archbishop Sharp exercised the bishop's patronage, so on 14 May 1707 one finds this entry.

> 'I write to the Commissary about the ArchBishop's Option of Bowden and my own Gratitude to his Grace.'

What favour Henry had been granted we do not know, but he records that a Mr. Wood was eventually instituted to Bowden.

Not all attempts at complying with the requests from patrons were successful. On two occasions he failed to obtain the consent of the bishop when he wrote

> [9 June 1704] '. . . wait on the Bishop on account of Licences to serve the Cure of Whitegate & Denton at the request (not directly) of Mr. Cholmley and Sir John Egerton but do not succeed.'

The vacancy in the benefice of Holy Trinity, Chester reveals, in all probability, the influence the registry could exercise on patronage. On 11 July 1707 the rector of Holy Trinity died.

> '. . . upon the death of Mr. Wright of Trinity yesterday, Mr. Adams desires my interest to the E. of Derby for Mr. Swinton, I prefer Mr. Oliver to him . . .'

Henry then left Chester to spend a few days with Sir Thomas Hanmer at Hanmer Hall, so nothing further was undertaken in the matter until the 20th when he records

> '. . . I speak to the recorder about Mr.Oliver, hee agrees with me and promises to write to Mr.Oliver . . . I call on Alderman Allen communicate my design to serve Mr. Oliver, hee approves and encourages, tho hee signed with others of the parish an Address to my Lord Derby in behalf of Mr.Kirkes.'

On 28 August, Henry went to Lancaster to hear the case of a disputed dowry between the earl of Derby and his two sisters. Whilst in the town he took the opportunity to call at the Mermaid and discuss the matter of the living of Trinity. A further move was made on 12 September when Henry went to meet the recorder at Dr. Norris's.

> '. . . here I meet with him and tell him of my Applicacions to Lord Derby on Mr.Oliver's part, and the Event.'

In the end it was Christopher Sudell who was presented to the living through the efforts of Arthur Fogge, son of the Dean. However, John Oliver was not forgotten and by the efforts of Henry he was preferred from the living of Audlem to that of St. Peter's, Chester in 1710.

One feature of Chester diocese was the number of chapels where the freeholders had acquired the patronage and the incumbents were appointed by means of an election. These public elections of incumbents were a source of irritation to the diocesan bishops, who attempted to suppress them in favour of a single patron. From time to time the bishops were successful, especially in cases where the election was disputed, in getting the freeholders to surrender their rights. The vacancy at Holt chapel provides an excellent example. On 16 August 1705, Henry wrote to the bishop about the dispute over the election of a new incumbent. The bishop decided to hear the case himself, so on the 22nd the parties presented themselves at the palace.

> '. . . About 2 the Holt Candidates attend my Lord.Mr.Adams with Mr.Peck the Mayor and about 80 others on his,Mr.Clutten and about 7 on his part. My Lord is offended at the number and reprehends it. The matter is discust with confusion, my Lord blames the popular Election and is prepossest against the major side . . .'

In the end three alternatives were proposed; to refer the choice to a further meeting of the parishioners appointed by the bishop, to allow the election by the mayor and corporation, or to accept the bishop's power to admit an incumbent.

On the 24th the mayor of Holt, Mr. Homerston, and Mr. Adams came to hear the decision. In the meantime, Henry went to see the chancellor with a request that he would see the bishop on behalf of the mayor. The chancellor succeeded, so Henry drew up a deed giving the bishop the patronage. The next day, the bishop insisted that the mayor and Mr. Homerston subscribe their names to the document nominating Mr. Adams, whereupon, the two having signed the deed, the bishop licensed Adams to the cure of Holt.

The election at Hindley proved to be an involved case, since the parties who asserted that they had the right of presentation produced a decree from the Duchy Court confirming that the custom of electing an incumbent had operated for the previous seven presentations.

> [27 August 1708] 'The Chancellor and myself appear averse to popular Elections. My Lord blames the remissnes of his predecessors, who were also Rectors of Wigan, especially the last in complying with the Election of Mr.Jackson by the Inhabitants.'

The bishop decided the issue in favour of Edward Finch, the then rector of Wigan.

From time to time, the diary records, often in some detail, the consecration of new churches., On 29 June, 1704, Henry records the consecration of St. Peter's, Liverpool. Two halberdiers head the procession, followed by the deputy registrar, the dean of Chester, the preacher, Mr. Styth, the mayor of Liverpool, the bishop, attended by several maces, then the chancellor, forty-two clergy, the gentry and others. He records a detailed account of the consecration service. Afterwards, a dinner was held at the Talbot which was followed by Evening Prayer attended by the bishop and the corporation. In his sermon the preacher stressed the need to rebuke both papists and dissenters. He commended Liverpool on building so magnificent a church at a time of heavy taxation and war.[22]

During his primary visitation in the summer of 1709, the bishop was asked to consecrate Selside chapel. Henry agreed to draw up the consecration deed and petition, 'tho very much indispos'd'. This task was completed on 4 July so that the consecration could take place on the following day. The offertory, about three pounds, the bishop ordered to be spent on a silver chalice and salver. On 19 September the bishop came to Warrington to consecrate the new church. The patron and others entertained him at the Golden Lion, and the consecration followed next day. In this case the offertory was ordered to be spent on a chalice and paten. On their return journey the chancellor and deputy registrar took the opportunity to inspect the dilapidated church and churchyard wall at Backford, preparatory to issuing orders for their repair.[23]

Henry was involved, as deputy registrar, in the licensing of schoolmasters and the settling of disputes that arose from time to time between the feoffees and the masters of a school. The churchwardens of Nantwich had presented their schoolmaster, Mr. Okes, for using the church as a school. Henry records that

> [22 January 1704/5] 'Met Mr. Okes . . . at Sandyway . . . tells me . . . his Offence at teaching children to write in the Chancel of Namptwich Church, ita etiam absolvit Animam . . . Wee dine on Hen and Bacon, are cheerfull.'

The case against the schoolmaster at Goostrey was more serious, for it was alleged that he, Matthew Holford, had neglected his school, was illiterate in Latin, kept an alehouse, spent Sunday tippling with company and never attended church. The case was heard in the Consistory Court.[24] A similar case from Rainford, concerning the behaviour of Roger Walthew and the accusation that he neglected his school, came into the Consistory in 1705.[25] Similar cases arose at Preston and Blackrod.[26]

The licensing of a schoolmaster was an occasion for celebration. On 4 May 1705, Henry was present at the licensing of Robert Wright, B.A., to Winwick school on the nomination of Mr. Legh.

> 'My Lord admitts and Licences him . . . About 6 Mr. Colly . . . and I go to the Fountain where we join Dr. Thane and Mr. Fogge. After our civil pints wee part about 9.'

A dispute between the master and usher of the King's School, Chester, caused the bishop to revise the statutes. He gave the master complete control of the school, the usher to act as his deputy during the master's absence. A register of

22 *Ibid.*, f.8,Liverpool St. Peter.
23 *Ibid.*, f.95, Selside; f.109, Warrington (Holy Trinity).
24 C.R.O., EDC.5(1705) No.5, Goostrey.
25 *Ibid.*, EDC.5(1704) No.6, Rainford.
26 *Ibid.*, EDC.5 (1701) No.13, and (1702) No.7.

attendances and absences of the boys was to be kept and recorded daily. Since there were only 50 boys in the upper school and 70 in the lower, the numbers were to be divided equally to encourage the master to develop the school.[27] The foundation of the S.P.C.K., in 1698, led to an interest in the provision of education for the children of the lower orders. The intention behind this was to train boys to be God-fearing apprentices and the girls to be dutiful domestic servants. Out of this came the Charity School movement, and Henry records the foundation of the Blue Coat School, on All Saints Day 1706, by Bishop Stratford.

> 'After Dinner, at the palace where a publique meeting about the Charity School, my Lord subscribes 100^{li}, Nine others 20^{li} a peece by which benefacion their annual payments end, but they their heirs and Assigns, to be Trustees, and to have their Election of Boys in their Turns for ever . . .'

Mrs Stratford was instrumental in founding the Grey Coat School for girls. From these beginnings there were some thirty-two Charity Schools founded in Cheshire alone.[28]

The duties attached to his office involved Henry in attendance at the Consistory Court presided over by the chancellor. Each case involved a number of documents, beginning with the appointment of proctors to represent the parties. Then followed the libel or list of charges, the interrogations to be put to the plaintiff and his witnesses, the responsions, the depositions of witnesses and the equivalent for the defence. Since all the evidence was taken down verbatim, a great deal of time had to be spent in preparing the files.

Ned Roberts was Henry's clerk in the registry office, but the Act Books were written up by Henry himself, and he also prepared several court files which are signed by him. During the law terms he attended the court, but the examination of witnesses required a great deal of time.

> [28 Sept. 1704] 'First Court this Term . . . I examine 8 wittnesses for Harrison and Nixon. Step into the town, and at the Fountain find the wine bad.'

The Consistory Court dealt with a wide variety of cases ranging from moral offences to pew disputes, dilapidated churches, schools and schoolmasters, and tithe causes.

Two interesting cases that involved the clergy arose at Maghull and Cartmel. Thomas Tyrer brought a charge against George Burches, curate, for committing adultery, cruelty to his wife, drinking to excess, keeping bad company, marrying Alexander Hesketh to Elizabeth Birch in an alehouse and involvement in the sale of Betty Gregson to a Virginian planter. The hearing was lengthy and involved, commencing in 1703. The sentence was not issued until 18 May 1704,

27 Diary, 1 September 1709.
28 J. Addy, 'Two Eighteenth Century Bishops and their Diocese of Chester, 1771–1787', Leeds Ph.D. thesis, pp.174–9.

when Burches was suspended from the benefice and refused admission to priest's orders.[29]

Burches was also involved in an allegation that he had entered into a simoniacal contract with Robert Janny, the rector of Woodchurch. The case was heard before the bishop on 1 September 1705, and two days later the bishop decreed that the allegation warranted a new presentation by the Crown.[30]

Thomas Proddy, vicar of Cartmel, appeared on a charge of drunkenness, negligence of his cure, preaching no sermons, beating his wife and cutting up her bed. At his first appearance on 10 November 1704, he was obstinate and denied the charges rather than confess to them. By the 14th, he had become more amenable. However, the final decision was made on 27 September 1705, when the bishop ordered the sequestration of the living of Cartmel for the incumbent was found to be totally incapable of serving the cure since his mental state was unstable [31] due to the pain caused by gravel and dropsy.

Pew ownership was a constant source of litigation, and these cases always involved some travelling with overnight accommodation.

On 22 July 1706, Henry went to Farnworth to inspect a disputed pew between the families of Hirst and Blundell.

> 'I observe the seat in controversy betwixt Hurst and Blundel on the back of which the Letters W.C. & E.C. and Figures 1602 relateing only to the seat . . .[32]

A pew dispute in Wigan church involved the bishop in addition to the deputy registrar and the chancellor. On 10 July 1705 a Court was held in church to determine whether Rigby of Aspull or the rector owned the pew. Evidence was produced that in 1622 Sir George Booth and Sir Piers Legh judged that it belonged to the Rigbys, but the bishop had permission to use it. The churchwardens produced evidence that they sat in the first seat by Rigby's permission in 1634. Further inspection revealed that Bishop Bridgman had carved the initials I..B. on the seat, which had been altered by a penknife into I.R., signifying Joseph Rigby. The bishop also commented that the arrangement of the seats showed that part of the church was formerly the chancel. However, it was agreed that until the rector produced further evidence, the Rigby family could occupy the seat in question.[33]

From time to time one finds a personal note about a pew dispute. On 2 August 1705 there was a hearing at Wigan into a seat disputed by Mrs Pilkington and Mr. Herle. She claimed the right to occupy the seat belonging to the house now owned by Mr. Herle. He acknowledged that he had given her permission to sit in

29 C.R.O., EDC.5 (1703) No.12, (1704) No.5.
30 Diary, September 1705.
31 C.R.O., EDC.5 (1704) No.4, (1705) No.6.
32 *Ibid.*, EDC.5 (1706) No.4, marked 1705-1.
33 The court files on this case are missing.

the seat occupied by his servants until she disturbed them. Then in court she revealed her temper.

> '. . . shee in a passion returns, vilifies the servants, scorns to sit with 'em, my Lord rebukes her pride and passion. As Mr. Walmesley & my cozen Holt interpose, shee indevors to represse 'em, the most malitious words and reflecions are us'd. Mr. Herle saies her Father used to call her Brandy Whore, and adds hee knew her to sell potts of Ale. Shee replies shee never sold pins Incle &c tells him of a whore hee had and mencions him as of the brood of the rebellion. . .'

The bishop pointed out she had no right to sit in Mr. Herle's seat but she could sit in that for the bishop's servants so long as she behaved herself.

The inspection of dilapidations in church and parsonage was part of the deputy registrar's duty. So, on the 11 July, the bishop went to Croston to be joined later by the chancellor and Henry Prescott. Accordingly, an inspection of the church was made and Mr. Hesketh's chancel at Becconsall was also ordered to be demolished, since the bishop considered it to be a 'crazy member of the church'. From Croston the party went to Eccleston, where they inspected the dilapidations of the parsonage. The rector resided in Chester, so the house was rented to a tenant, who offered the party access to the cellar.

> '. . . wee meet with good Ale and Beer in Bottles, make bold with them. I by stricter search discover some wine, bring out 2 pints, find it right French . . . My Lord well pleas'd with the Expedition . . .'

In a similar manner, applications for major faculties also involved an inspection. On 8 October 1706 they went to Shotwick to inspect the church after receiving a petition to reseat it.

> 'The Chancellor and I take Horse before 11 come to Shotwick Hall about 12 are liberally entertaind by Mr. Hockenhall with a good dinner and good Claret, wee see the Church and the Necessity of Uniformity of Seates . . .'

The visit concluded with a dram of brandy at Madocks inn. Later the diary records the issue of a faculty to reseat the church.[34]

Henry's advice was sought in connection with building projects. On 3 August 1711 Sir Thomas Hanmer consulted him about building a chancel on Hanmer church, asking for his assistance in that and also in matters relating to the tithes of the parish. Tithe disputes are common cases in the Consistory Court, and there are numerous references to these in the diary.

One case of interest is that involving Peter Slaynehead's attack on the Church. The accused, it appears, had not only written a book, but had also placed a handbill on the church door at Warrington in which he openly attacked the

34 C.R.O., EDA2/4 f.34, Shotwick.

Church and the chancellor in particular. The case against Slaynehead was heard at Quarter Sessions before eleven justices, on 17 July 1711 at Wigan. Slaynehead confessed to the charges but was evasive on those relating to the chancellor. He was sentenced to pay a fine of 200^{li} and then

> '. . . to stand in the pillory in 5 market Towns, Leverpool, Prescot, Ormskirk, Warrington, and Wigan, to find security for good behaviour for 7 years and to be in custody till hee do that and pay the 200^{li} fine.

The decision was most acceptable to the Church, and at the end the officials drank, 'a glass congratulatory'.

The period between the departure of a diocesan bishop and the news of his successor is one of speculation reported in the press and other means. It was no different in Henry Prescott's day, as the diary reveals.

On 16 February 1706/7 news reached Chester that Bishop Stratford had died on the 10th. On the 18th Henry records that he had received letters of condolence from the bishop of Meath and 'my coz. Parr', adding a comment of a 'hazard to my Circumstances', for his job could be at risk if the new bishop should have another deputy registrar in mind. The funeral took place on the 21st; Henry records it in great detail,[35] commenting that, 'the singing was not commended.'

Two days later speculation was rife about the new bishop, though Mr. Egerton stated he was not one of the diocesan candidates. Early in March came more reports, including a letter that Archdeacon Booth would be the new bishop. Both Henry and the dean offered him their congratulations, but it appeared that the archdeacon had received no notice of it. The news of 7 March named Archdeacon Booth, but Henry went to the White Talbot with the warden of Manchester, where they discussed the possible candidates for bishop. On the 11th, Archdeacon Booth said his interest was insufficient to procure his election to the see, but added the unwelcome news that Dr. S. Freeman would be the next bishop. This gave Henry 'fresh uneasiness and concern, Lament and refresh in domestic Quota.'

The next day Dr. Stratford informed Henry and the other officials that Dr. Freeman would be bishop. Henry added to his account that, 'He is said to ly under a worse Character than any of his Coat'. By the 14th it was certain that Dr. Freeman would be bishop, so a deep gloom descended on all, especially when they heard the contents of Lady Crewe's letter to her sister. Henry fervently adds

> '. . . May God . . . avert this, this still magnifies our fears. I visit the Chancellor about 7 and find him under the same impressions.'[36]

What Henry and the Cathedral chapter did not know of, however, was the fierce

35 Diary, 21 February 1706/7.
36 *Ibid.*, 12 March 1706/7.

political struggle taking place at Westminster between Whigs and Tories for the right to appoint candidates of their own side to vacant sees. Dr. Samuel Freeman was a Whig and a pluralist who had been tutor to Lord Treasurer Sunderland, and was not only rector of St. Paul's, Covent Garden but held a prebend at Canterbury and in the deanery of Peterborough.

By 26 May the name of Sir William Dawes as bishop pleased both Henry and the chancellor, who went to the Rose and Crown to drink two bottles of claret 'in votes for Sir Wm. Dawes'. The matter dragged on until 16th October, when the death of Dr. Freeman was announced. This news was received in Chester with great rejoicing, and the announcement of Sir William Dawes as the new bishop was eagerly awaited. At this point the diary breaks, and when it recommences in May 1708 it is clear that Sir William Dawes and the deputy registrar were firm friends. A High Church and High Tory bishop was what Chester expected and received.[37] The election of Bishop Gastrell, who succeeded Sir William Dawes, is not recorded since there is a break once again at this point.

One of the first duties placed upon a new bishop was to hold his primary visitation of his diocese. Bishop Dawes undertook his visitation, in company with the chancellor and deputy registrar, in May and June 1709. On 22 May the directions for confirmation candidates were sent out to the parishes, for it was the custom to hold confirmations during the visitation. It is, however, clear that Bishop Dawes had held some confirmations in the Chester deaneries in 1708.[38]

The bishop commenced his visitation in the Cathedral on 24 May, when he delivered his charge to the clergy and churchwardens. On this occasion the clergy were advised to see that their parishioners were not affected by Atheism or Socinianism, and to warn them of the dangers from popish and protestant dissenters, and that schism was still schism. They were to acknowledge the Royal Supremacy, to preach against immoralities, observe the state holy days, especially 5 November (commemorating the Revolution of 1688), and to live sober and pious lives. On the Saturday the party went to Nantwich, and on Sunday the bishop attended Acton church, where, 'Mr. Edgley reads the prayers and preaches, both stiffly and imperfectly.'

At Preston the party were entertained by the corporation, but at Lancaster they received 'a mean pittiful dinner' while the bishop was entertained in the vicarage by the corporation. The bishop was entertained at Dalton Towers, Holker Hall, and Conishead Priory, and concluding the visitation tour at Rose Castle where they were entertained by the bishop of Carlisle. The visitation had taken forty-five days to complete. The bishop and his party travelled to Newcastle and then to Durham, where they left the bishop at Auckland Castle while the rest returned to Chester via Halifax.

From time to time details concerning the election of churchwardens are recorded which were by no means orderly. Henry spent Easter 1709 at Wigan,

37 R.V.H. Burne, *Chester Cathedral* (London, 1958), pp.116–17, 178.
38 Diary, August 1708, for the bishop's itinerary.

where as a parishioner he had a pew and a vote. He attended the nomination of the churchwardens and approved the account of the retiring wardens. After this the party, about twenty electors, retired to feast upon ale, buns and cheese. Next day the annual vestry meeting took place. An argument developed between the rector and the mayor, who said that the corporation had chosen Sir Roger Bradshaigh, which the rector as chairman ruled out of order. When Canons 89 and 90 were ordered to be read, Mr. Walmsley objected but he was overruled, whereupon

> '. . . Mr. Walmsley makes a motion with his head and hand and forces a Cough or Screatum loud to the party or Mobb, who imediately make a nauseous and rude noise, the Clerk is not heard . . . the Mayor calls Silence, which succeeds . . .'

In the end Mr. Markland was chosen people's warden and Sir Roger rejected. The business completed, the new wardens, with the rector and Henry, retired to the clerk's house for ale, simlins and cheese.[39]

Henry, as a High Churchman and Tory, was interested in the sermons he heard preached in the Cathedral and in parish churches. Often he will quote the text and comment upon the preacher's delivery and the structure of his sermon. On 29 March 1704, Mr. Legh, vicar of High Legh, preached, upon whose sermon Henry commented

> '. . . a florid and ingenious discourse . . . 'Strive to enter in at the straight Gate', is much applauded. I admire the redundancy both of words and Invencion . . .'

Again, on 7 May, Mr. Newton 'has a long prayer, a loose and incoherent Harangue . . . tis much observd and censur'd.' On 11 March 1704/5, when Philip Egerton preached on Joel 2 v13, Henry commented:- 'indifferent oratory, worse elocucion a great auditory.'

During the visitation tour of 1707, Henry disliked the sermon at Ormskirk, for he records that

> 'The Curate (Hull) in a desultory and immusical Cant, is scandalous and almost intollerable in the prayers, the Vicar mean & perfunctory in his Sermon . . .'

Henry was very critical of the sermons delivered by the warden of Manchester Collegiate Church, for on one occasion he commented after hearing one of his sermons, on 30 April 1710

> 'The Warden of Manchester has a grave, stout and substancial Discourse . . . on 1 Peter 3:15, the sermon is condemn'd justly, and the different phrase from the last hee had in that place is admir'd, but not by all . . .'

39 *Ibid.*, April 1709.

On the other hand, he had a great respect for Mr. Oliver of St. Peter's, Chester. On 8 January 1709/10 he noted

> '. . . hear with difficulty Mr. Oliver's very excellent discourse on St. John 1:12. Hee has a deep and musical voice, but do's not exert it and is not heard by half the Congregacon . . . I tell Mr. Oliver of his insuccess in the morning, and desire him to advance his voice.'

Henry was a regular communicant, and as a High Churchman records the dates on which he made his communion in Latin, as though English was an unworthy language to convey what the sacrament meant for him.

> 'Post sanctissimae Eucharistiae particeps sumus.Det D.O.M. vitam puriorem.'

Although matters ecclesiastical were of prime importance in Henry's life, yet as a High Tory he was also concerned with the political situation both in county and town. He took part in elections, and records details of the voting. He associated with those who shared his interests, education and politics, and took a keen interest in civic matters. Throughout the diary, Henry's cousin by marriage, Sir Henry Bunbury, represented Chester as one of its M.P.s. Henry had little respect for the Whigs whom he describes as 'fanatics'.

The General Election of 1705 was fiercely contested, and Whig propaganda led to a Tory defeat. Henry recorded his impression of this election as it concerned Chester. At the same time, the clergy met to elect a proctor to represent them in Convocation, an event in which Henry was involved.

The voting took place in the Shire Hall at five tables. The crowd of voters at the Golden Talbot proved to be too much for Henry, so he, with a few companions, went to the Fountain and, joined by a few others, continued drinking until midnight. Henry, Mr. Cholmondeley of Holford and Sir Peter Soames remained drinking until 3 a.m. The next day he rose, with an aching head, but attended the Visitation Court, afterwards going to the Shire Hall. Relieved that the majority appeared to be with the old candidates, he waited until the court adjourned at 7.00 pm.

> [24 May] 'the Court adjourns and the 2 old Candidates are carry'd to the Golden Talbot in a vast and from quality, laudable Corona of exulting Freinds. Indispos'd . . . I . . . sculk home. Here alarm'd with unexpected ill News that the Young Candidates are 400 superior in Votes. This strikes a damp on that side . . .'

So the night was spent in attempts to draw more votes from the country.

Next day, the old candidates were afraid they would lose and the young ones sensed victory. Mr. Cholmondeley and others left the city in some haste. Henry went to the Talbot to await the result of the election which he records.

> 'The poll ends in these Numbers, Offley 3165, Booth 3088, Warburton 2878, Mostyn 2665. The Minority of Booth, hee not being of age till 8th June next is here. The Corrupcion of voteing men, the makeing of 1000 fraudulent Freehold Leases, and double trebles and more voteing of many will in parliament bee objected. A Ball is made by the fortunate Offley, many decline to bee there. In the night the windows of the Cathedral and St. Marys are especially batter'd, concluded to bee done by the party which cry'd all the Week, Down with the Church . . .'

The conduct of this election had all the marks of the corruption of the pre-1832 elections.

Since Henry owned some freehold property in Liverpool, he had attended the election on the 14th at the Exchange, where he voted for the Tory candidate.

> '. . . thence to the Theatre of Action. Wee attend till near 6 when the Election finisht. Norris has 393, Clayton 453, Johnson abov 500 votes, a good Event . . .'

Clayton was one of the Tory candidates, so naturally Henry was pleased. On his return to Chester, he narrated an account of the Liverpool election to the chancellor over pints at the Fountain.

> 'I acquaint him with our Leverpool expedicion, and particularly how the best Quality were on Clayton, the meaner & Fanatics on Norris's part.'

He also comments upon the same election at Lancaster on 19 May when Stanley and Fleetwood were returned with large majorities for the Tory cause.

Henry played a full part in the social life of the city and county. Daily he called at one of the many inns in Chester to meet friends and deal with clients over a bottle or two of claret. On 15 June 1704, he went with the bailiff of Liverpool to see Bishop Stratford. After dinner with the bishop, Henry, the bailiff and Mr. Woodward of Shevington the party went to the Fountain,' cheerfully we bring the matter to 17 pints of claret.' Not surprisingly, the entry for the following day is

> 'Extremely indispos'd from the Claret, the Good repose most of the day.'

During his visitation tour of 1709, while staying at the Queen's Arms in Kendal, he records that on Sunday evening, 3 July

> 'Mr.Fryth treats the Chancellor, Commissary and myself at Duke Lamberts with a Bowl of Punch. Wee part about 10, the Chancellor slips down in the street.'

Naturally, Henry was indisposed the following day.

The great events in the life of the city always saw Henry present. On 13 October 1704 he went to the mayor-making, when his brother-in-law Alderman Partington was elected and his friends Peck and Houghton made sheriffs. The event concluded, 'very cheerfully and late at the Ship.'

On 8 March 1708/9 he went to celebrate the Queen's birthday, an event that was solemnly observed in the city, with the mayor at the Pentice. The diary records this event.

> '. . . Mr Chancellor, my coz. Kendric and I go to the Pentice. Here with the Mayor a Company about 30 in number, each has his Bottle before him which is exhausted by these Healths viz. The Queen, to the Church, her Majesties Forces, her Allyes, the Dukes of Hanover, Marlborough, Prince Eugene, Lord High Admiral, Lord Treasurer, Lord Bishop, Lord Lieftenant of the County, prosperity to the City, begun by the Mayor . . .' .

Fond of horse racing, he often attended the Farndon races and was frequently asked to draw articles to be observed by the parties. On 21 April 1704 he records

> 'The Night . . . spent in Jocky discourse. I draw Articles for a race to be run betwixt Mr. Warburton's mare & Mr. Colly's horse at Farndon Hey, Tuesday 20th of June, wee part about 3 in the morning.'

The following day he was very sick from the 'Jocky wine,' so he slept most of the day.

Henry enjoyed and appreciated gracious living. On Ascension Day (25 May) 1704 he, the chancellor and Mr. Boucher went to Shrigley where they were entertained by Mr. Legh. Later they went to Lyme where they

> 'sit down to a magnificent supper serv'd all in plate. After solace in variety of Ale and Wine till 3 in the morning.
> 26 Rise indispos'd about 10. The Chancellor and myself . . . sit to a Breakfast like the supper about 11. Here Moselle wine go's about. Mr. Legh in all things great & generous . . .'

At noon they left for Stockport to hold a visitation.

Taken as a whole, it is possible to extract from the diary a day-by-day account of the operation of diocesan administration, a great deal of which was transacted in one or other of the better inns in Chester. It is clear that Henry worked in close cooperation with the chancellor, and they frequently initiated policy and decided how it should be implemented. There were checks on Henry's influence, but since Henry and the chancellor had channels of power and patronage, such checks were not always effective. Neither does it appear that the bishop's secretary posed any threat to Henry. Certainly, during the period covered by the diary, it is clear that the deputy registrar at Chester held an important and coveted position in diocesan administration, in addition to a place in the society of city, county and diocese. Hopefully, this diary may lead to the study of an area of diocesan administration which has long been overlooked by those who work in the field of administration.

****

In due course the diary was handed down until it passed into the hands of the Revd. Charles Kenric Prescott, great grandson of Henry, who transcribed it. Unfortunately, Charles held some of the folios 'too near the flame of the candle', and these were lost. He also acquired his great grandfather's library, but this was subsequently dispersed. The diary eventually came into the possession of Brigadier C. P. Prescott of Bourton on the Hill, who requested the editor to transcribe it for eventual publication. The present volume covers the period 28 March 1704 to 24 March 1711; Volume II will continue the diary to 1719. It will also contain the more fragmentary entries for the years 1689–96, and the index to the two volumes. A number of appendices in Volume II will include biographical details of important people mentioned in the diary; details of the books which Prescott read; and notes on the various references to medical remedies.

NOTE ON THE DIOCESAN RECORDS

The Consistory Court Act Books were written up after a court session by Henry's clerk, Ned Roberts. Henry added his comments on various cases. Few details are given beyond the names of the parties and the parish concerned. The majority of the causes were testamentary. These Court Books are difficult to use, since they were not foliated, and the manner of entering causes was to add subsequent hearings under the date on which the cause commenced.

The bishop's register contains details about church alterations and the issue of faculties, although these are noted in the Consistory Court Books, which state whether there were objectors to a petition for a faculty.

The Institution Act Books for 1688–1752 are lost, and the only way to trace clergy is by reference to the Call Books, or to the Parish Papers, which contain details of institution. However, these are not always complete, and great gaps appear from time to time. I have attempted to fill in details of as many clergy as possible and identify the various bishops, deans, and others of the hierarchy who are referred to by title only.

John Addy 1987

EDITORIAL CONVENTIONS AND NOTES ON ABBREVIATIONS

Henry Prescott abbreviated the entries in the diary very heavily. The abbreviations which he used when dealing with legal documents have been extended in full, e.g. 'certe' for certificate and 'comm^{on}' for commission, as also his use of 'chell' for chapel and 'admon' for administration. The use of '-con' for the modern '-tion' has been retained, as well as his use of 'Mrs' to denote 'Messrs' or 'Mistress' according to context.

In order that the modern reader can interpret the entries more easily, some modifications have been made in punctuation, e.g. by inserting a colon in place of a comma, or by breaking down long sentences. Prescott's use of upper and lower case has been standardised in the case of proper names where the Christian name appears in lower case, e.g. 'peter'. His peculiar spelling of 'busienes' has been retained.

Those Consistory Court cases for which no precise files remain have been noted as summarised in the Consistory Court Books, which are unfortunately not yet foliated.

Prescott followed the traditional style of dating the year, e.g. from 25 March 1704 to 24 March 1704/5, which continued to be in use until the calendar was standardised in 1752. However, the new practice of dating from 1 January to 31 December was creeping in at this time, so one finds material dated as 1700/1 or 170½.

Where possible, the short entries which Prescott made in his sometimes obscure Latin have been translated in the footnotes. In certain instances, longer portions of the diary in Latin have been translated in an appendix to this volume.

General abbreviations

Coz, cozen – cousin
E. Term – Easter Term (Law)
Fr. Ch. – Francis Cholmondeley
Mrs – Mrs *or* Messrs
Mrs A. G. – Mrs Anne Gerard
N. R. – Ned Roberts
Q.Qs – questions
S – Suzy
vidt. – videlicet
10m – 10 miles

Abbreviations of Latin phrases include:

Deus O.M. – Deus Optimus Maximus
D.G. – Deo Gratia
D.L. – Deo Laus

D.V. – Deo Volente
D.O.M.G. – Deo Optimo Maximo Gratia
D.O.M.G.E.H. – Deo Optimo Maximo Gratia et Honor
D.O.M.L.E.G. – Deo Optimo Maximo Laus Et Gratia (also D.O.M.G.E.L.)
D.O.M.L. et. G. – Deo Optimo Maximo Laus Et Gratia
Q.B.E. – Qui Beatus Est
Q.E.B. – Qui Beatus Est

The following remain to be identified:

F.F.F.
Q.B.E.P.E
Q.D.A
Q.F.F.E.F.S
Q.F.F.Q.E.
Q.F.F.F.Q.S
S.D.P.

Editorial abbreviations in footnotes:

C.R.O. – Cheshire Record Office
L.D.A. – Leeds District Archives
L.R.O. – Lancashire Record Office

THE DIARY OF HENRY PRESCOTT, 28 MARCH 1704 – 24 MARCH 1711

1704

MARCH 28 After a Walk of 4 Turns apply to Busienes, thence to the News yet tardy. Recreate in Spanhemius.[1] After Evening prayer, Mr. Boyer and I take 3 Turns on roody, thence I go to the Fountain where I stay with Sir Hen. B.[2] Drs Entwisle, Thane, Mr. Legh the Clerk of High Legh Mr. Ian Egerton till past 9.
29 A fine morning invite mee to roody where a walk of 4 Turns refreshes. I write to Mrs. Maddison, Gorst, Seaman. Mr. Legh has a florid and ingenious discourse in the Quire on 'Strive to enter in at the straight Gate', is much applauded. I admire the redundancy both of works and Invencion. I dine with him, his brother in Law Egerton, invited at Dr. Entwisles, stay there till prayers. In the Evening the Chancellor, Dr. Thane and myself are treated by Mr. Bouchier at his chambers with 4 Bottles of true French Claret. I write after this to Mr. Cholmley of Holford on behalf of Thos. Bellin who is to carry the Letter.
30 A moist morning. Mr. Styth pays mee for 20 Licences.[3] Court day, I examin 3 Wittnesses on Ackers Will. Receive by Mr. Bellin, Mr. Cholmleys answer, write to Sir Wm. Parsons about providing a lodging for his son here in Chester.
31 A brisk cool morning. I take a walk of 5 Turns, apply to Busienes, see the News yet not active. At Mr. Bouchiers after Noon. My sister Jones comes in the Evening and staies with us.

APRIL 1 A brisk cold morning. I write to Mr. Peirson, Holt, Meredith of Eccleston, John Cross. Afternoon repose, in the Evening at Mr. Hollands late with Mrs Bowyer, Minshall, Hodgson.
2 Dr Thane has a grave discourse on 5 Eph. v. 6. The new of the Lords addressing the Queen to alter the Commission of Peace. In the Evening wee take leave of Sir H. Bry,[4] designing to set out towards Bath tomorrow.
3 A brisk cool morning. I take a walk of 5 Turns, in Beveridge his Chronology. Mr. Bavands third son is buried at Christleton. I(Mr Minshal and Topping with mee)after dinner go to Boughton to see little Mr. Bunbury, in our return, call on Mr. Dennis and Mr. Rieves, stay and drink Ale roundly for the Time. In the Even wee wait on Lady Bry. Shee treats us with a Bottle of Claret.

1 See appendix in Vol.II for details of the books read by Henry Prescott.
2 Sir Henry Bunbury was M.P. for Chester.
3 These were marriage licences which were issued by a surrogate of the Commissary of Chester, in this case Mr. Styth. Testamentary disputes were frequent, and these cause papers have been removed from series EDC.5 and placed with the original Wills. See also Consistory Court Books EDC.1/100–105.
4 W.C. Costin & J. Watson, *The Law and Working of the Constitution* (London, 1952).

4 A brisk morning, take a walk of 5 Turns. The News barren of forrain Affairs;after Evening prayer at the Fountain with Aldermen Allen and Bennet, maritime & merchant matters talkt & how Wilson of the Custom house went for London after noon Thursday came thither Friday about **5** afternoon, did busienes and returnd Monday morn last about 5 very well.

5 A very sharp Frost and Snow, surprizeing weather. I write to Sam. Prescott & John Cross. Mr Markland pays mee providentially D. G. 39 li for Licences. Hee and Mr. Foxcroft now of Ireland sit with mee. Pay Mr. Hodgson for Books 2li;10s;0, with him and Mr. Foxcroft late at Mr. Hollands. Much of the Irish Bishops, severely of the Archbishop of Tuam and Sir Tho. Vesey his son.

6 A wett cool morning. I write to Sir Wm. Gerard & desire whether the 20th or 25th current will be a convenient day to attend him about the finishing my Assignment. The last Court this Term. I examin 4 Witt, Houghton contra Cash. Mr. Leftwich visits us at Night hee has complaint of Mr. Harpers partiality in teaching. Much of Lady Calvleys affairs.

7 A dull wett day at home in Books particularly Craigh of Homages. At the Coffee house where the News of the parliament prorogu'd till July, little els of moment. After prayers with my Lord about Archdeacon Stratfords Dispensacion.[5] After with Alderman Allen at the Ship where each a Bottle of good wine with very free and freindly discourse.

8 Not well, take a very sharp walk of 5 Turns. Write to Dr. Pope and inclose a Bill of 30^{li} and to Mr. Trotter. A dull day in Books and recesse.

9 A warm day to surprise. The Bishop preaches in the Quire. The News still very lean from abroad. The prayers and sermon return to the repair'd parish church, prayers to the Quire at 4. After which in Antonius Le Grand his Historia sacra dispatcht the 5th Book.

10 A very warm and springy morning. At early prayers. Write to Archdeacon Stratford and Mr. Trotter, draw ten ounces of Blood, begin to enter the Deaneries.[6] In the Evening at Mr. Bench with Mr Vaudry, see the Judges Jekell and Lovel come in attended by the Sheriff Baskervile, then the Court sett about 8 the Justices call'd over.

11 A very hott morning and day, at early prayers, take the compound scurvy dropps.[7] Mr Peake sees and stays with us 2 hours. Mr. Cowper preaches before the Judges yet I hear him not. See the indifferent news, proceed in and end the Deaneries. In the Evening at the Fountain with Mrs. Peake and Hulton, the later shows usual vanity and ostentation and particularly on the subject of his kinsman Coll. Daniel.

12 A glowing morning and day. I take the golden spirit of scurvy, it has effect. Tom Gorst calls on us, hee walks with mee about roody. The Bishop of Cloyn return'd from London sees us;with him at Dr. Entwisle, after prayers thence to

5 Archdeacon Stratford, the son of Bishop Stratford, was about to become a canon of Christ Church, Oxford.

6 A reference to the churchwardens' presentments made prior to the annual visitation.

7 See Appendix in Vol.II for comments on medicine and Prescott's remedies.

the Walls with Mr. Ashurst, Dr. Worthington &c at the chang Coffee house, lastly wee wait on Lady Bunbury.

13 Another glowing day a walk of 4 Turns on roody with the Bishop of Cloyn to the hindrance of my own Busienes. In the Evening, call at the Talbot to inquire after Mr. Cowper, am lead to my surprize up the narrow stair Case to the top of the Eastgate where I find the High Sheriff, Mrs. Cowper, Partington, Puleston, Fletcher, Walley &c. I make hast down by the same candle, meet the other elder Mr. Cowper at Mr. Hollands, stay there cheerfully till 10.

14 Good Friday, the same vidt. Midsummer weather continues, take a walk of 4 Turns go to church where Dr Challenor a Canon of Lichfield, preaches, much of the vacant time with the Bishop of Cloyn, the rest at home and in Books.

15 The same weather, after a walk apply to draw a Declaracion for Mr. Clegge. My Lord hears the controversy about the Rectory of Eccleston laid open by Mr. Birkenhead & Hulse, a hardship on the one and Cheat on the other side, laid open. Pay John 30s, lend John Savage 1^{li}, Mrs Worger 2 Guineas. After prayers, at Mr. Hollands with Alderman Allen Mr. Fogge and Mr Allen freely and freindly till 10, hear of Gilbert Hulmes death.

16 Easter Day a glorious and warm morning. I take 4 Turns pretty early on Roody, The Dean preaches, Sanctissimae Cenae in coetu frequenti sum particeps Det Deus O. M. vitam puriorem.[8] In the Evening take a Turn out of Norgate with the Bishop of Cloyn, retreat after to my Corner and reading.

17 At early prayers repeat the Golden Spirit, take a walk, indizpos'd almost all the Day, the weather cooler with wind. The Bishop of Cloyn in the Evening sitts with us, I treat him with the last Bottle of my wine sent by the Bishop of Man.

18 A windy day but dry, a short walk on roody, indispos'd in Books and Busienes perfunctorie. After prayers in the Evening the Bishop of Cloyn hastens with his compnay to Neston, hee leaves with mee a paper of Moment. Fill some processes for the Visitacion.

19 The wind continues brisk the weather dry. After early prayers a walk. I pay my sister Partington 10 Guineas on Account and to Mr Hoil for Mr. Vaudrey 10 Guineas likewise, on the Account. Apply to busienes draw a peticion and Declaracion for Mrs Watson.

20 A calmer yet a cool day take a walk of 4 Turns, with my Lord about Archdeacon Stratfords Dispensacion draw it and a peticion and Declaracion for Mrs. Watson. After dinner with Alderman Allen, Bennet, Mrs. Fogg, Allen &c at the Falcon. After prayers waite with the Recorder in the Vice Chamber, at Mr Bennets an hour or 2 thence to the Chancellor sup there on fine Beef and suffer for it.

21 The weather still cool and windy. I take a walk on roody a small one – thence to Books and repose. After Evening prayer in my way to Alderman Allens fall into Mr. Collys Cellar and Mrs. Egerton, Done and Warburton

8 Trans: 'I partake of the most Holy Supper in a crowded congregation. May God the best and greatest grant [me] a purer life.'

company. After the wine tryd and fixt on, Mr. Colly takes us up into his street chamber, treats plentifully with good wine, the Night is wholly spent in Jocky discourse. I draw Articles for a race to be run betwixt Mr Warburtons Mare & Mr. Collys horse at Farndon Hey, Tuesday 20th of June, wee part about 3 in the morning.

22 Excessive sick of Jocky wine and company, ly and repose all day unfit for busienes or any Applicacion.

23 By help of Elixir, recover at Home and repose, read in Chronicles le Grand. The 2nd Coronacion day, a wind all day to a Storm, the day celebrated not very warmly, Lady Bunbury and Mrs. Anne Eyton come over to us.

24 A cool and windy morning, perform yet a walk of above 4 Turns on roodee. Write to the Honble Mr. Fran. Godolphin and Mr. Vernatty from Sir H. B. to Mr. Peirson & Mr. Meredith. People crowd down to the race, that for St. George plate omitted to the next, because Mr. Egerton's horse (Godolphin) meets with no competitor. A small plate of 5^{li} run for by little scandalous Horses wherein Mr. Gammul's Victor. After this, at Golden Lyon pretty late with Mr. Farrington of Minshall and Mr. Edmundson.

25 A dry windy morning, after golden spirits, a short walk of 4 Turns on roody. The News tells of Earl Nottingham laid down his office of principal Secretary,[9] and a prospect of other changes at Court, acceptable to Dissenters, melancholy to others. Dispatch the Deaneries of Blackburn and Lealand, write to Mr. Price, dispatch Midlewich and Macclesfield Deaneries, receive from Mr. Bouchier 7^{li}; 10^{s}, on Harrison's Commission. And upon the Accounts take a Glass of Claret, at night with him and Mr. Boyer at the Fountain.

26 Repeat the golden spirit, take a walk after with in the walls, the weather very dry and windy, write to my cozn Parre about his and my cozn Fleetwood's kind mencion of my Son Jack. Pay Mr. Foulks upon Accounts 30^{li}, examine 2 Wittnesses against Nixon, 1 against Alderman Ince. Mr. Topping going tomorrow for Oxford sees and takes leave with us.

27 First Court E. Term, busienes competent, examine 1 Witnes for Hurleston 2 on Stonehew's Will. The Chancellor disturb'd about Smith and Johnson's Commutacion.[10] In the Evening at Mr. Pickmer's with Mr. Hodgson.

28 Repeat the golden Spirit. A soft and warm and welcome rain falls till Noon. The Letters mencion new and surprizeing Changes at Court, of no good Aspect. Apply to Busienes with the Bishop about a process against Lealand, intrudeing Clark of Wigan, draw a Citacion against him.

29 After early prayers a rambling walk in the Fields. Mr. Taylor with mee about the process against Lealand.[11] Hee tells mee an unwelcome Story of an accident suspected to have hapn'd to Mr. Holland of Winstanley (Q. D. A.)and

9 J.R. Jones, *Country and Court 1658–1714* (London, 1978), pp.316ff.

10 Commutation of a penance for a money payment was by no means rare, but such acts often came close to a breach of the law.

11 Cheshire Record Office (C.R.O.), Cause Papers EDC.5(1709) No.3. The case against Lealand, parish clerk of Wigan, began in 1704.

of small hopes of yong Mr. Bank's recovery. I write to Mr. James Close, pay Mr. Chapman on Account 5^{s}. Receive a Letter and 11 Coins from Mr. Gandy, find out 7 of the coins, send him in an answer, an Account of their Age vidt. about 265.

30 After a rainy night such a morning, repeat the golden drops. After early prayers in books captim. Stay at home till Evening prayers, after them with Mr. Bunbury on the same journy, dispatch the 7th and begin the 8th Book of Le Grand.

MAY 1 A warm and moist morning, write to Mr. Newman of Drs. Commons with a copy of Wickstead's Will inclosd 4^{s}:6^{d}. At church where Mr. Taylor preaches on, "Hee that over cometh the world is born of God." Collect shortly the presentacion to Melsonby for Mr. Denison of University College,[12] write to John Cross. Apply something to busienes. After prayers meet Mr. James Boucher at his uncles chamber where with Capt. Tichburn a Bottle of good wine, pay Mr. Morrey for an end (100^{li}wt.) of Hops 3^{li}:15^{s}:6^{d}. Write in hast to the Bishop of Man.

2 A delicate warm and springy morning. After early prayers a walk of above 4 Turns in which read the case of the prodigious Imposter Arnold Tilly. See the news silent almost tam domi quam foris.[13] Apply to busienes and particularly to inspect the writeings and Accounts sent mee by Mr. Willis belonging to the Ayrfield, matters of very melancholy reflection.

3 After early prayers 3 Turns on roody, pay John Bousey for my little Mare 12 weeks, 12^{s}, for her running this summer on Trafford Moor 11^{s}. A Court for the Deaneries of Chester & Wirrall held & dispatcht easily.[14] After prayers and some busienes, meet Alderman Allen, Alderman Bennet and Mr. Mainwaring, at the Fountain where wee drink our Bottles of mixt wine.

4 Indispos'd from the wine. A Court day of slender busienes. In the Evening return to the writings involv'd in, and make mee more doubtfull as to my cozn. Walthews Account.

5 A delicate day. Wee set for Frodsham about ½ hour after nine, haveing read the little News first, come there before 12 dispatch the small busienes with ease. Mr. Hinchman meets us here. I first hear of my old Friend Mr. Jonathon Hales death as dying about a week ago. It readily brings melancholy recollections of my first Acquaintance at Warrington. I always esteemd him a good Clerk in his way and a true Freind. Wee come hence (the Chancellor going to Crewood) before 5, reach home easily before 7 (D. G.) . I rid my Gray horse the first and am well pleas'd with him. My Lord comes to mee about Dr. Flemming's

12 Leeds District Archives (L.D.A.), CD/PP/6, Melsonby Parish Papers.

13 Trans: 'as much at home as abroad'.

14 The annual courts of visitation for the archdeaconry of Chester were held by the Chancellor as commissary of the rural deaneries. Those for Richmond archdeaconry were held by the commissary of Richmond. The presence of the deputy registrar was required to administer the oath to the new churchwardens.

peevishness in refuseing to pay for Fast books &c. I tell my Lord of the Custom here.[15]
6 I am with my Lord about the Institucion to Eccleston, hee hesitates tho Mr. Egerton only presented and no Caveats in force. I write to Mr. Lawton about Letter ad colligendum &c my late Lord Derby Goods, and to my cozn. Parr about Alderman Allen &c case. After Evening prayer with Mr. Cowper and Mr. Sherwin at Mr. Hollands where wee solace in a yong Leporet and a Bottle of port.
7 Hott from the supper and the day, Mr. Newton has a long prayer, a loose and incoherent Harangue on 'My son give mee thine Heart'&c. Prov: tis much observd and censur'd. After see the news almost dumb. After prayers write to Sam. Prescott, inter scribendum:receive a Letter of Feb. 15 from him. I wait on the Chancellor, am excusd from going to Malpas tomorrow. Wee wait on Lady B. stay past 10.
8 Mr Boucher, Hulton and Ned Roberts go to Malpas. I write to Mr. Watchking about my Shell. The Bishop comes over to mee about the Consecracion of Liverpool Church design'd about Midsummer and about the presentacions talkt of to Melsonby. The rest of the day is taken up in sorting Deeds and writeings relateing to the Ayrfield. I pay Mr. Whitehead for a load of Coales 9^{s}.
9 About 9 after the little news read, sett out in a cool breeze, call at Mr. Huxley's and in his absence leave the History of the Calves head Clubb for him, come to Namptwich at dinner about 1. Apply to Busienes, about 6 Mr. Philip Egerton calls on us, I go with him for an hour to Mr. Bradshaws. After this Mr. Bradshaw and I go to see Dr. Bullen (ill of his Eye) here Mr. Bradshaw is teazing with his Questions about Herbage and discourse on Tom Stringer printed, yet wee stay past 10. I find Mr. Stringer and Chamberlain together, wee drink a pint of white wine. I go to bed about 12.
10 Indispos'd from last night, Mr. Boucher and myself stay till a shower over, are treated by Mr. Bradshaw with Tea and Usqebagh. After see Mr. Wettenhall's home and Garden about 10 m. A cool day, set forward call on Mr. Huxley, drink on Horseback one bottle of his strong Beer, thence wee go to Bunbury, see the well modell'd church, Sir Calveley's monument in the last year Queen Mary. Sir Raufe Egerton of Ridley, his noble Chapel and monument of the Beestons, walk about, drink sage Tea with Mrs. Brock lately come from Winstanley, her mother & sister. Sett hence about 4 in a sweet Evening come safe D. G. before 7.
11 Court day easy of Busienes and this of dispatch. I divert in Mr. Salamanaasaar's the Formosan Indian his Book and at Night in Tully de Finibus.
12 A severe hot day, take up the Fore noon with Mr. Minshall in stateing our Account, after see the News speaking of Accion and readiness to it, in all parts. In the evening with my Lord about the Consecracion of the Church of Leverpool

15 These were official printed orders of Divine Service appointed for use on national fast or thanksgiving days. The custom in Chester diocese was to issue them free.

and new informacion from Mr. Taylor against Mr. Clegge. After a walk round roody with J. Stringer, a Tankard of Ale and return to Tully.
13 After Elixir, cool and easy in Books and papers. Sir Henry Bunbury returns about noon from the Bath, wee wait on him. After prayers agen with my Lord about Leverpool Church. After a Turn on roody call on Alderman Allen, sit 2 hours and drink a Glass of good wine with him.
14 A glowing day, Mr. Subdean Wright preaches in the Quire on The Spirit of God-witnesseth with our Spirit that wee are his children Rom. 8, gravely & soundly. The news yet dull in Portugal. After Evening prayer with the Chancellor, drink a Bottle of good Claret with him only in his Garden, after wee are late at Sir Hen. Bunbury's.
15 After early prayers a walk of 4 Turns on roodey. Write to Sir Wm. Gerard about my resignment, to Mr. Styth about the Consecracion of the church of Leverpool, about 12 set out, come to Eaton Boat before one, here Mr. Mather by the Chancellor's appointment has the Anniversary Feast[16]. Sir Hen. Bunbury is my Guest, wee have a polite dinner, good Ale and cheerfull diversion, wee stay past 6 and come home before 7.
16 Not without effects of the Ale yesterday, helpt by Elixir, write to Mr. Mawdesley the Governor of the Isle of Man with a Cheese I send him. The News is favorable to Portugal and expects revolt of Spain – a walk to Boughton in the Evening.
17 Write to Mr. Watchking about my Box, with the Bishop about the Sentence against Burches which I draw, apply to Account of my Saxon Coins. In the Evening go to the Falcon with Mr. Egerton, Birkenhead, Mercer, drink our Bottles cheerfully, stay till 11 the hot weather alters to rain.
18 Indispos'd, the last Court day of this Term, slender busienes, the Bishop reads the Sentence against Burches, praepare for a journy, write to Mr. Maddison by Mr. Minshall and deliver 21 coins in a Box to him. In the Evening at Sir Hen. Bunbury's cheerfully with bro. & sister Jones.
19 A cool but not rainy day, prepare matters for my journy. See the News dull agen and suspending. Mr. Lawton is here upon the Commission ad colligendum but the further progress referr'd to the 2^{d} June at Wigan. After dinner the matter of a seat in St. Osward's church betwixt Mrs. Swift and Mr. Coker is heard before the Bishop & Chancellor, the Dean and prebendarys come in pro interceptio. My Lord determines oratinus and for peace sake that they enjoy the seat, as formerly promiscuously shee refunding to Mr. Coker half the charge of the late repairs of it. The Dean and Chapter pray even this may be so determin'd with a salvo their right, this is don, a proposal is made by the Dean, that the parishioners instead of Contribucions, pay certain annuall rates for their seats, to the Vicar;this is approv'd, but has no effect till propos'd to & concluded on, by the parishioners. I write to Mrs Holt about her cozn Kenyon's incestuous

16 This anniversary feast is referred to as Chad Feast, and was held at Eaton Boat, but little is known about its origin.

marriage, deliver directions to Mr. Minshall about my Shell. At the Fountain cheerfully with Mr. Egerton, Aldersey, Boyer past about 10.

20 Write to Mr. Parre and inclose a Sequestracion[17] to the Churchwardens of Woodchurch,[18] waite on the Bishop and Chancellor and receive their commands, pay Mr. Coker for the Cheese to the Governor of Man 8^s: 6^d. I wait on the Bishop and Chancellor. After dinner in a fine cool day set out about 2 come to Sandiway about 5, meet Mr. Edw. Massie there, stay an hour proceed and come to Holford about 8, find him very warm parting with company. Hee receives mee very kindly, I sup and drink with him and Mr. Tho. Walley a Bottle of wine and to bed before 12.

21 Refresht and easy walk in the Feilds towards the Meadow, observe good full grown Okes. After dinner Mr. Cumberbach comes invited. I acquaint him with my desire of his seeing my patrimony and directing a plantacion at Ayrfeild, hee promises to come with my cozn. Peake & I shall appoint him. After supper wee go up to the Summerhouse. I drink my Bottle of good Claret. Mr. Cholmley and Mr. Walley, 3 of Ale, Mr. Cholmley is very kind free and cheerfull, wee part about 11 so to bed.

22 I set hence about nine in a fine sweet morning, see the plants about Tabley, come to Knutsford about 10, meet with Mrs. Wall, Cowper, Hulton about the Commission. I examine 4 Wittnesses on Mr. Peake's part against Sam. Leadbeater.[19] In the Evening my cozn. Peake and I drink a glass of Ale together. I lodg at his house, am very decently receiv'd, the rest of the Company to Midlewich.

23 A delicate day, stay and relax at Knutsford. Mr. Leigh the Non Juror Clergy Man comes to my cozn. Peake's. I perceive they differ in their notions of the present doubts betwixt them and the Clergy conforming to the Government. Mr. Leigh maintains that the church is in the conforming Clergy, Mr. Peake seems to deny it, adhering to Mr. Dodwell's schisma Anglicanum. Mr. Cumberbach comes invited on my account, wee fix the time to meet at Ayrfeild on Tuesday in Whitsunweek. Wee dine and divert the afternoon. About 6, set hence in a sweet Evening, in a fine road and country, come to Macclesfield about 8.

24 The company comes from Hulms Chapell about 10, wee set to busienes, which proves considerable for the place. I examine Wittnesses on Mrs. Stanley's Will. In the Evening The Chancellor and I walk up the Hill to the Cistern which supplies the Town with water, thence to Alderman Johnson's where with the Mayor Mr. Phillips and Mr. Hulme wee sitt till 11.

25 Holy Thursday a delicate and cool day, the Chancellor, Mr. Boucher and myself set hence before 11, come to Shrigley about 12 a decent house, accomodated with Fish, Fowl, Venison, adorn'd with Gardens, Water &c. Lyme in Epitome. Wee are neatly and fully treated. Mr. Legh meets us here at dinner.

17 Sequestration took place when a benefice became vacant. The custody of the church goods, the parsonage house and the revenues were entrusted to the care of the churchwardens for the time being.

18 C.R.O., EDPI/306, Woodchurch Parish Papers.

19 *Ibid.*, EDC.5(1704) No.11, Knutsford.

After which in a Cool Bottle home, wee divert some hours, hence thro a fine prospect and the part wee advance to Lym, come there thoro the walks & over the Cascade, about 9;presently sit down to a magnificent supper serv'd all in plate. After solace in variety of Ale and Wine till 3 in the morning.

26 Rise indispos'd about 10. The Chancellor and my self staying behind sit to a Breakfast like the supper about 11. Here Moselle wine go's about. Mr Legh in all things great & generous, about 12 set hence, reach Stockport about 2 where competent busiens, after that see Mr. Shawcrosse where Dr. Thane is with us. I give Mr. Swetenham a Faustina for his daughter Margaret. Wee set hence about 8, come to Manchester about ½ hour past 9. As I am writeing to my S. in my chamber am disturb'd by one Ed. Harris a Drugster of London, hee breaks in as a mad man, swears hee'l stay and lodg there, but is carry'd out by James the Hostler. Hee is furious calls mee names, threatens to fight mee, I go down to him, hee is after some time calmer. The Hostler and maid sit up with him to prevent any insidious design against Mee.

27 Harris, early in the morning, attempts to throw a stone into my chamber but is prevented by James the Hostler, then gos away. After Elixir and good rest, well recover'd, wee set to the considerable busienes (about 30) dispatch in good time. In the Evening we visit the Warden.

28 Wee go to Church where yong Mr. Moreley a moderate Orator, preaches. Invited wee walk to Hulme, dine elegantly with Sir John Bland who receives liberally. About 5 wee return. I visit Mr. Pigot at his home, wee drink our pints of wine freindly, thence about 9, in bed about 11.

29 In a warm day set out after 10, go by and call at Ratcliffe Bridge, find little or no Advantage this way, come to Blackburn about 3, very thirsty and weary, sup on Mr. Price's good Mutton and fatt Capon about 6.[20]

30 After Elixir and secure repose, recover'd, apply to Busienes which proves competent to the place. After that the same supper repeated, after Conversacion to bed about 11.

31 I like at first and try but return Mr. Price's horse, wee go hence after Coffee about 9, come to Chorley about 11 meet here Mr. Meredith, the busienes indifferent and the Conversacion considerable. Sir Tho. Standish, Mr. Pilkington, Haydock &c. Wee sent hence about 4 Mr. Ashurst and Mrs Crispe with us to Parbold where wee call and drink base Ale. The Chancellor walks hence to the bottom of the Hill, I to Newbrough, I call on Harry Prescott and bring him thither, wee drink a cheerfull Glass, the Chancellor is well pleas'd with Harry's humor, wee set hence and in a sweet Evening come to Ormskirk about 10. I ly at Mrs Dods.

JUNE 1 Apply to the Busienes which is considerable, the company so, especially from Leverpoole. The 2 Mr. Ashtons come in the Evening. Mr. Peter inseasonably mentions our Busienes as being complain'd of in parliament and

20 Mr. Price was vicar of Blackburn and surrogate for the deanery.

under consideration once to bee reformed, this said unseasonably makes the Chancellor Chagrin, puts mee to difficulty to manage.

2 A gentle rain falls, the rest before, the Chancellor and I go about 9, halt a while at Holland, reach Wigan about 11. the Busienes is very considerable. Mr. Taylor in a heat comes into the church, gives an unadvisd presentment against Sir Roger Bradshaigh. The rest of the company go to Warrington. I stay in the divided place, write to Mr. Walker about my Shell about 9 go to my cozn. Walmisleys.

3 I expect Sir Wm. Gerard's servant, hee himself comes about 11. After dinner wee aply with Mr. Holland to Accounts and satisfacion of all the Debts, wee finish the matter, I seal the Assigment and receive my Bond cancelld, togeather with 9^{li} for Margaret Hulme and about 6^{li} in consideracion of my Expenses. After a Bottle of white wine wee part in good Freindship. Mr. Holland and I go to Nanny's near the Church Gate, hee desires my advice in the disposal of his son. I promise to try his Learning then to advise. I visit my cozn. Carter and his wife a Gentile person sister to Mr. Davenport of Bramhal, thence to my Lodging.

4 A rainy day, Whitsunday, I sit in my own Seat. Mr. Taylor preaches, but with difficulty. Indisposicion makes him end abruptly and with an Apology to prorogue the Sacrament. After church see the dull News, the place frequented by rejoiceing papists at it. After dinner I repose and in the Evening visit Mr. Holland, who renews his applicacion to mee about his son. I hence suspect hee has a desire to place him with mee tho hee speaks not plain. Wee visit Mr Taylor and after Mr. Johnson.

5 About 10 sett out come to Ayrfeild before 12, it proves favorable and fair. I walk about the ridded Ground see the wrecking and approve it, design what Okes are to stand in the place, treat the workmen at the house with 18^{d} in Ale, sent for, Give Margaret Hulme a note for her 9^{li} and Interest, see old Jane tell her of repairs wanting, shee promises them. I receive the Bible I gave Gilbert in 1677 leave it with John Cross. I am hansomly treated by Wm. Whaley. I call on Sam. Prescott and for his pains &c in setting Gateley &c give him Half a Guinea, it pleases. Hee brings mee to Tho. Naylor's where wee part in a cheerfull pott of Ale. I come about 9 to Wigan see Mr. Peake and Mr. Cumberbach at Betty Finches, come to my lodging after 10.

6 It threatens but rains not. I receive my Suzy's Letter with an hectoring Letter in it from Ed. Harris. About 10 wee go, Mr. Peake for Winstanley, Mr. Cumberbach and I to Ayrfeild. Hee walks round from the House to the Grove of yong Okes, thence to the Meadows and the ridded Ground, sees my Situacion, plantacion &c, talks very well of planting gives generall directions particular about pruneing the Trees. After some refreshment wee go to Holland where at Thomas Naylors a couple of Chickens are ready rosted, tollerably don. About 4 wee set hence, call at Winstanley, stay about 2 hours, set thence about 6, call at Newton pretty late, near Warrington meet some of the Clergy comeing from the Clergy Lecture, reach Warrington about 9, after a Bottle of port to bed about 11.

7 A dull morning and full market. I pay Mr. Haile for Mr. Vaudry on Account 25^{li} & receive 25 probats [21] from him. See the News and part with Mr. Peake and Mr. Cumberbach. I dine Mr. Sedgwic with mee, stay till 2 of Mr. Blackburn in expectacion to examine him, hee comes not. I sett out in fair weather and halting at Frodsham a little reach Chester safe (D. O. M. G.) about 6.

8 A fair day repose, apply to busienes, pay the Chancellor on Account 62^{li} :5^{s}, to Mr. Callys 40^{li}.

9 The weather alters to rain, wait on the Bishop on account of Licences to serve the Cure of Whitegate & Denton at the request (not directly) of Mr. Cholmley and Sir John Egerton but do not succeed. My 55th Year enterd upon Det D. O. M. vitam F. F. F.

10 A very rainy day at home in Books, busienes and Accounts, write to Mr. Price mencion his horse.

11 Trinity Sunday, Archdeacon Entwisle preaches, 9 preists and 7 Deacons are ordain'd. I see the News dull and ill in Portugal.

12 The rainy weather continues apply to the processes for the Iure patronatus of Eccleston.

13 Wait on my Lord with the Chancellor about a Commission de Iure patronatus of Wycliffe to which Mr. Smales by the University of Cambridge, Mr. Gilpin by Mr. Hodgson is presented, apply with diligence to the Commission and processes in both rectorys and to a Commission to swear and take the subscripcion of Luke Coates, Clerk to the Vicarage of East Cowton.[23] In the Evening at the Fountain with severall particularly Mrs. Egerton, H. B. and Mr. Meredith.

14 Finish all the Commissions and processes to the satisfaction of the Bishop, dispatch the process for Eccleston by Mr. Chapman and Mr. Meredith write to Dr. Pope and inclose a Bill of 40^{li}, write to Mr. Minshall about my shell and to T. Gorst. In the Evening at the Fountain with Sir Henry Bunbury and my brother Partington.

15 Still rainy, a Court day the 1st in the Term, moderate Busienes admits repose. In the Evening at Mr. Holland's with Mr. Hodgson.

16 Draw a Declaracion for Samuel Leadbeater in reparacion of Mrs Peake's reputacion. wait on my Lord Bishop with Mr. Eaton, Bayliff of Leverpool. After dinner with him and Mr. Woodward a descendant from Woodward of Shevington, at the Fountain cheerfully for wee bring the matter up to 17 pints of Claret.

17 Extremely indispos'd from the Claret, tho Good repose most of the day, in the Evening venture out to Mr. Pickmere's where with Mr. Tho. Cowper and Stringer & Hodgson 3 Tall Boys.

18 Still indispos'd but helpt by Elixir, stay at Home, read Hospinian and Durantus de Consecracione.

21 In Chester diocese the rural deans or their surrogates had power to prove wills under £40.

23 L.D.A.,CD/PP/4, East Cowton Parish Papers.

19 I draw a Confession and peticion for Mr. Robert and Mrs Alice Kenyon inclose it in a Letter to Mr. Walmesley of Wigan. The Bishop comes to mee about Leverpool, Eccleston and Melsonby, complains of the burdens of his Affairs, and too sensibly under 'em says, Hee is in a mind to resign the Bishoprick.

After Noon the Bishop hears the case of Woodchurch the Chancellor, Dean Archdeacon are present, the Recorder and Mr. Gamul for Burches, Mr. Kenrick for Coppock. The matter decently argu'd and defended, but no point setled is dismist. I begin the sentence of the Consecracion of the Church.[24]

20 I take a usefull walk on roody. The News brings the 3 Generals P. Eugene, P. Lewis of Baden and D. Marlborough to a conference near E. of Bavaria and promises great Events. I proceed in the Sentence finish that for the Church.

21 Finish that for the Church Yard shew both to the Bishop, hee reads and approves draw the Form of the Address to bee offerd the Bishop on the place. In the Evening take a walk with Mr. Boyer on roody after with him and Mr. Egerton at the Fountain, wee make it out Bottles a peece and cheerfully.

22 Write to Mr. Styth inclose the Form on the place, and to Mr. Vaudrey for 29 Licences. Court day, Examine 4 Wittnesses ex parte Harrison, Take leave with my Lord designing to Morrow for Wigan, see Mr. Minshall just return'd from London. At the Fountain with Mr Boyer, 1 pint.

23 Early prayers.[25] Dispose Matters for Eccleston & Leverpoole, pay the Chancellor $37^{li}:15^{s}$ which makes what I paid him since the Visitacion 100^{li} on Account, pay the wash woman 30^{s}. write to Mr. Price, see the News, Susa in Savoy, by the French. Porto Legro in Portugal taken by the Spaniards. In the Evening with Alderman Allen, wee drink 3 pints of his rich Lisbon white wine.

24 Fair day brings ordinary busienes, indispos'd from the Lisbon wine, write to Mr. Atherton, Gorst and John Cross, examine Mr. Blackburn against Cash, make an extract of the presentacion to Eccleston. In the Evening take a Bottle with my cozn Peake at the Fountain, pay Mr. Eaton his Note of $16^{s}:5^{d}$.

25 A moist day. Mr. Bland, Archdeacon of Limrick has a polite discourse on 'Lay not up Your Treasures on Earth'&c. The News carrys the Spanish Arms successfully in Portugal. Afternoon I wait on Lord Kilmorey on the matter of an Administracion of Mr. Charles Middleton.[26] At prayers, after which the Chancellor lastly with Lord Kilmorey. Egerton, Offley, Warburton Done, a full company, at Sir H. Bunbury's till 10 a clock.

26 The Chancellor, Dean, Recorder, Mr. Egerton, Capt. Birch, myself and son Jack set out from the Coffee house past 9, come in good weather to Warrington about l, dine there, sett out about 5, halt at Newton, come to Wigan about 8, wee wait on my Lord, find him and his domesticks mellow together. All

24 The documents necessary for the consecration of a church were:- 1) the petition; 2) sentence of consecration; 3) consecration of the churchyard.

25 The Cathedral had two morning services daily; Morning Prayers at 6.00 am, and Mattins at 10.00am.

26 Prescott, as deputy registrar, issued letters of administration after probate.

things pass here very civilly, betwixt the Chancellor and Mr. Taylor. I go to my Quarters at my cozn Holt's. About 8 Mr. & Mrs. Kenyon appear, confess their incestuous marriage are admonisht give bond and a Decree passed.

27 About 9 in a moist morning, set out for Eccleston, where a great confluence of Gentry, Clergy, vulgar spectators. About 11 wee go to the church, the Chancellor, Dean and Sir Christopher Graenfeild are Commissioners, the Jury is extraordinary for Quality 16 in number. The Recorder alone on Lathom's side opens the Cause, the main Iugulum of which is the credit of a copy of a Deed of Settlement made by Lathom. Mr. Starkie, Walmesley, Ashurst, Vaudrey all for Crispe oppose the admission and reading of it. Mr. Starky with vehemency and obstinacy, Sir Christopher answers and obviates his Law and reports, the Chancellor apprehends the Equity with ardor, the matter grows warm, the Jury approve the Coppy, a record of Comon Law reciting the Deed is at last producd, this confirms the Jury, they give their verdict for Lathom against Crispe about 3. A brisk shower falls, wee go to the little house and dine promiscuously. I see among others the Governor of the Island Mr. Mawdesley returnd lately. I return hence with Mr. Egerton about 6 a severe shower on the way. Wee come about 8 to Wigan shew my Lord the verdict, hee orders institucion to bee made against morning.

28 A very rainy day, wee sett hence about 12, are accompany'd by several, wee call at Prescott where the Chancellor, indispos'd stayes. The Bishop is mett by the Corporacion a mile. Mr. Egerton and myself pursuing near come while the Bishop is viewing the new Church, wee light, go in, return with the Bishop to the Town, wait on him. I have severall offer'd but chuse the lodging at Mr. Houghton's tho a rainy and discouraging day, yet many crowd thither on all sides.

29 A fine and dry morning, rise early, wee wait on the Bishop at Mr. Cleavelands the Mayors, about 9, a great concourse of the Clergy, thither about 10 to the Solemnity adjusted proceeds hence. The Clergy 42 in number, two halberteers makeing way go first, myself next alone, next the Dean and the preacher Mr. Styth, next the Mayor and the Bishop preceeded by the sword and their Several Maces next, the Chancellor, then Gentry and others. Wee pass easily near to the south door, upon the Bishop's approach to it, great crowding. The Bishop enters the church putts on his habit and returns, the Mayor presents the common peticion, after the Oblacion, both are read by my self. The Bishop enters the Church alone takes possession and in a few minuits returns. That door and the rest are open'd and people like a torrent flow in with irresistible force at every door;many complain, cry out, and loose parts of their habits, but a good and great providence prevents mischeif. The Church fills with a great murmur, a mighty swarm;when full, the murmur ceases. The office begins by the Bishop with a prayer of Consecracion, hee sits in a Throne near the pulpit, next the 1st chaplain Mr. Taylor begins the service of the day, the Bishop intermixes proper prayers, an anthem, 89 psalm is sung by Holcomb, after the Nicene Creed the sentence of Consecracion read by the Bishop. Mr. Styth has a very sound discourse on 3 verses of those of Solomon at the Consecracion of his Temple,

justifies our Consecracion and service takes occasion to rebuke the papist and dissenter;Commends in generall the piety of the Town in raising a structure so magnificent among Warrs losses, taxes in 4 Years, and enumerates particular Benefactors. After Benedicion by the Bishop, the people flock out, the Bishop follows in the Churchyard surrounds it by procession, on an Area of boards convenient uses proper prayers and reads the sentence of Consecracion of it. After Benediction and his habit put off, proceeds to the Talbot but not in the same order;here a good dinner ready sett, all the Tables fill'd. After dinner I get the sentence attested. The Bishop and Corporacion go to Evening prayer, returning I am invited by Mr. Peters, Mr. Travers and I drink a Bottle with him. After at the Talbot late with Mr. Woodward and Eaton, thence to bed.
30 A warm morning tempts to walk out, then drink severall morning draughts vidt. with Mr. Smalwood, Sit Richmond Coffee house, Mr. Egerton with his Lady treat the Chancellor and his with a good company at the Talbot. After dinner a free glass moves round. About three, they take Boat. After I with Mr. Travers, Jack with mee, see Mr. Swerbreck, here wee have a full and free Bottle thence to Mr. Houghton's, where I meet with Mr. John Blackburn, wee continue the Claret in Winwick discourse, and Jeremy Bates humor is much our subject and end the day or rather begin another.

JULY 1 Under the effects of yesterday. After prayers at the Chapel I make my Bill low as I can, amounting to 5^{li}:14^{s} in Mr. Styth's presence, hee brings it to the Mayor who orders Mr. Eaton to pay mee the sum. I dine at Mr. Houghton's after I wait on the Mayor, Mr. Styth with mee. About 3 take Boat with Capt. Clayton, Mr. Langton of Preston and his wife, wee have a fine calm passage to the Rock, about 4, and thence a fine journy where I come safe D. G. about 7.
2 After Elixir keep home, a soreness of throat increases on mee.
3 The pain aggravates in my throat. I have 8 ounces of blood drawn. I write to Mr. Stratford and inclose Mr. Liddell's Letter and to Tho. Waterhouse about Mr. Price's health, repose and read the rest. Mr. Hurleston dy'd about three a clock this morning.
4 Yong Mr. Branker from Leverpool calls on mee. I give him my little Emerald to cutt my Crest upon. I pay Mr. Foulks 30^{li}. Mrs Grear a Guinea, lend Mr. Savage 1^{li}. The News brings an Account of the defeat of 9000 Spaniards by the Marquis Das Minas, a Portugeze General, digest Letters Acquittances &c;still more indispos'd from my throat. Mr. Morrey in the Evening, sitts with mee, wee drink a Glass of Claret.
5 The pain of my throat still confines mee. I write to Mr. Watkins about my shell, to Mr. Oates I inclose a copy of Tovie's Will. I receive a Writt from Chancery against Mr Dod, myself & one Kilshaw at the Suit of James Wainwright. I desire Mr. Cottingham to imploy his brother to appear for mee, draw a short Account of the 7 first Earls of Chester for Mr. Byrom of Manchester. Mr Hurleston's Funeral proceeds hence to Plemstall about ½ hour after 10 at night.

6 A cool morning, my pain not lessen'd still confines mee so that I go not to Court, write to Mr. Byrom. After dinner it rains much. I am easy after repose in the Evening the pain returns.

7 The good news comes confirm'd of the Victory of the Allies over the Bavarians & French at Schellenburg, and of the Portuguese over the Spaniards in Castile. A dull day and so spent, till in the Evening Mr. Egerton, Birkenhead, Mercer see mee, order 4 Bottles of good Claret hither which are cheerfully and freely empty'd.

8 Weather continues wett and cool. Suzanna mea Lucinam ut in proverbio invocat;adest Domina Anderton praetoris uxor obstetrix, domi recessa, revocata, dolores frequentius incessunt, dies in expectacione sumpta, nox partum accelerare videtur.

9 Circiter horam sextam matutinam D. O. M. G. salva matre natus mihi filius. Domi e morbo me contineo. DDae Anderton et Partington ad me prandent, publica Nuntia victoria in Bavaricos abentas fidem dant ulteriorem. DDi Bouchier et Boyer me vesperi visunt.

10 Ex epoto Elixir invalesco. Episcopo Cestriensis, Archidiacono Richmond Johnanni Cross et Do. Samueli Prescott scribo. Dno Partington de racionibus solvo 10^{li}. Vesperi primum e morbo evolo. Ad Fontis cum DDi Peake et Bouchier vinis rubri mediocriter. Domino Episcopo Kildare scribo.

11 In Roody cum Do. Minshall caelum serenum experior, bene satis cedit. Nuntia publica parca satis;post praeces vespertinas Dm. Egerton Clericum in Sponsorem Filioli mei nondum baptisati rogo, promittit libere. Dominum Cowper vesperi visimus, ille et Ego, cerevisia parum [parumper] generosa accipit.

12 De Cerevisia mediocriter. Calor me domi continet. Dno. Gorst scribo insignia Gentilitia Moreton de Moreton mitto. Praecibus celebratis D. Boyer, Minshall et Ego ad Fontis conferimus;nos vinum tempusque liberi et hilariter nisi quod de Filio Ranulpho Ds. Minshall retulit sumpsimus.

13 Iuridicus non sine strepitu. Do. Gulielmo Holland Q. B. E. de Filio suo apud Me collocando primum scribo, rem vero obtectam habeo meipsum supprimendo. Testu 4 ex parte Harrison examino.

14 Parum in Caelo calido in roody deambulatum. Nuntia publica e Danubio desiderantur. A Lusitania Chiliadem steward in Castle David collatum et obstinate propugnans(propugnatem)in summum discrimen adductum tradunt. Mr. Cowper tells of his brothers contumely, desires my mediacion.[27]

15 A walk for an hour in the Feilds, refresht & easy. In the Even, Mr. Smith senior of University with him and Mr. B.

16 Mr. Fogg preaches in the Quire. The news scarce. In the Even with Mr. S. at Mr. B's. Write to the Bishop & Mr. Close.

17 Apply to Duaren' de Sacris Ecclesiae Ministeriis. 24 years since my 1st marriage.

27 See Appendix for a translation of these passages.

18 Busienes and Letters, the Forenoon. The news yet good beyond the Danube. At night at the Fountain with the Chancellor etc.
19 Wee begin to purge the office of useless & corrupt records. In the Even at the Fountain with Dr. Griffith etc.
20 Write to my Lord, inclose a Bill of 500^{li}. Last Court day, moderat Busienes, my throat sore anew. Examine 3 Wittnesses.
21 After a walk the News. In the Evening write to Mr. Walmsley inclosing Testimonial.
22 A walk in the Feilds, write a congratulacion to Mr. Price, examine 3 Witnesses Cook.
23 At the Quire when Mr. Fogg preaches, the News yet good on the Danube.
24 A walk in the morn, my Appeal about the office succeeds. In the Evening walk to the Barrel Well with Mrs Fox, Seddon, Morrey, with them at the Fountain. Write to John Crosse.
25 St. James' Day. Pay Mr. Haill 21^{li} 18^{s}. Write to my cozn Parr by Mr. Fox.
26 Rainy, write to Mr. Cotton about my shell, read.
27 My son Xtened by the name of William.
28 Up early in Books and the office, write to Mr. Peake.
29 After a walk, Busienes and Books.
30 At church, Mr. Newton has a rambling sermon. In the Evening at Little St. John's.
31 Write to John Cross, Mrs Trotter and Close. In the Evening Dr. Griffith brings Mr. Elwood a Fellow of Dubline College LL. B. and Mr. Howard a scholar painter to mee. I entertain them, after wee walk to the Bowling Green.

AUGUST 1 A fine calm morning, at early prayers. After take a walk on roody thence to the Coffee house where the matter of Savoy desperate. Pay Mr. Eaton 1^{li};19^{s}.
2 After prayers write to Mr. Edgley, walk, intent on the office. Q. B. E. write to T. Gorst.
3 After prayers a walk, my Hay harvest, the rain after dinner breaks the work.
4 After prayers and a walk on roody, returning meet with a Trajan out of the rubbish, finish hay harvest 9 Loads. Meet the Bishop returned from Wigan.
5 Write to the Commissary of Richmond, read. After prayers at the Fountain with Sir H. B. , Chancellor, ArchDeacon of Limrick &c very freely.
6 After a brisk walk, to the Church where ArchDeacon Booth preaches on the Sacrament. The news defective for want of Mails. In the Even at the Chancellors.
7 A walk in the Feilds, indispos'd. Gratias de salvo puerperio [28]&c. In the Evening with Mr. Boyes at the Ship.
8 The News very thin. I receive from Mr. Jebbe for 12 Licences. After prayers

28 Trans: 'Thanks for a safe labour.'

with Mr. Mills a Fellow and Mr. Estoft a Gentleman of Balliol College, Oxon, at their Inn the Golden Talbot.
9 Intent on the Office. Receive Institution from the Bishop to that of Woodchurch.
10 I see the Chimney under the office made up. In the Evening receive my Shell finisht.
11 Our 17th wedding day, intent still on my work in the office.
12 Write to Mr. Watkins and Mr. Houghton of Leverpool, intent at the office, pay off the Mason.
13 Mr. Lancaster preaches a good sermon. On 'abhor that which is evill'. The good News of the great victory of the Allies over the French and Bavarians fill the Town with Joy and demonstracions of it. Read Ciprian de Gratia Dei et Idolorum vanitati.
14 After early prayers ready for V. Royal but prevented by Mr. Smith's busienes with my Lord Bishop. Write to Mr. Rider, pay Alderman Ince upon Account 30^{li}, Mr. Minshal for the Register Book a Guinea. In the Evening at the Fountain with Mrs. Smith of University College, Oxon and Bowyer; Antiquity and learning the discourse.
15 Early up yet the rain prevents my journey to V. R, apply to the office write to Mr. Chetle. In the Evening visit the Chancellor, my S. and I the Bishop, after late at Sir H. Bunbury's.
16 Write to my cozn. Parr, about 9 sett out in a fair day come to Vale Royal about 12, dine with Lady Soames and Mr. Okes. After with Mr. Fr. Ch. in his chamber, conclude to write to Mr. Chamberlain about the Minshall Breif.[29] After Mr. Okes and I take a fine walk. After supper wee, Sir Peter Soames and myself especially, set to a Bottle of Claret, drink liberally, part late.
17 Rise late and indispos'd, design for Chester, dine with Lady Soames and Mr. Okes. After with Mr Okes go to the Green, fall in the Sellar, in company with Sir Peter, Mr. Bruen, Mr. Cowper, Allen, Stanley, the Glass go's full and fast about. I drink incautiously hence to Mr. Francis in the dineing room while the Games go on. I am unluckily diverted, and at last by Sir Peter and Mr. Elcock, to a degree, to bee remember'd detested, repented;by the help of my Man as well as my mare, gett difficultly & stupidly to Vale R. The Figure I made I forgot, and have therefore great reason to abhor Det. D. vitam paenitere ante acta(hodierna praesertim) reliquam probe, sobrie et caute agere.[30]
18 Rise about 10 not without severe sense and reflection on my yesterday misfortune. The News of the great Victory at Hockstead on the Danube comes confirm'd with particular Letters and circumstances which make it the comple-

29 Briefs were national appeals for funds to rebuild a decayed church, or one destroyed by fire, as well as houses.
30 Trans: 'May God grant that [I] repent of [my] previous actions (especially yesterday's) and that [I] conduct the rest of [my] life rightly, soberly and carefully.'

atest of many Ages. I stay to read it, then mount before 12, call on Wm. Dod, return in a cool Air sensible sentiments about two.
19 Indispos'd of the journy and the consequences of it. Write to Mr. Bouchier and to Mr. Chamberlain about the Minshall Breif. Mr. Chapman gives mee Slynehead's Book.[31]
20 After Elixir stay at home, entertain'd in domestic reading.
21 Yet indispos'd to apply to Busienes. I read Slynehead's Book over. My Lord is earnest about the Entry of the Institucions.[32] I buy about 23 Yards of old Wainscoat of Robt. Ryder, am with Mrs. Jebbe and Rhodes at the Fountain.
22 My Lord dines at Rocksavage. I apply to the Institucions.
23 Proceed in a short Entry of the Institucions.
24 My Lord is concern'd at the delay of the bookes for Thanksgiving for the victory of Blenheim.
25 I acquaint my Lord of my progress in the Entrys, and hee is well pleased.
26 Finish the Entrys breifly and put the presentacions in Order, lend Mr. Whalley 4^{li}.
27 Dr. Entwisle preaches, tho very infirm. Wee visit my son William ill of the Gripes.
28 A fair day, the Joyner enters on setting up the old Wainscoat in the office, the Books come by the Carrier. I write on Mr. Chamberlains Letter to Mr. Cholmly.
29 Wee dispatch away the Books, I acquaint and surprise my Lord who is well pleasd with it.
30 The Joyner proceeds slow tho I am intent upon the work.
31 Intent on beginning 3 books, one for Episcopal Instruments & the 2d for Institucions, 3rd for Wills.

SEPTEMBER 1 On Busienes, the Books and the office, pay Mr. Foulks 20^{li}.
2 A rainy day, at home in Books and Busienes, till Evening, when at ArchDeacon Booths with Sir Henry Bunbury, Mr. Brook, Mr. Egerton, after at the Fountain with Mr. Bowyer.
3 A moist day. Mr. Fogg preaches. Wee agen visit the Child, in the Even at Sir Hen. Bunburys.
4 Sir Henry setts out with his Lady and sister, Dr. Entwisle, tho infirm, accompanies them, I still attend the Lazy Joyner.
5 After busienes & books, in the Even Mr. Minshall and I mount and meet ArchDeacon Stratford from London on Halton Heath, return in a shower, stay an hour or 2 with my Lord and his welcome son. Rainy weather, the man has not yet finisht the wainscoat. In the Evening at Mr. Harpers with Mrs. Colly and Bowyer before whom Jack rehearses his speech.

31 Peter Slynehead or Slainehead's pamphlet was a vicious attack on the Church and its officers.
32 The Institution Act Book 1688–1752 is lost. The only means of identifying incumbents is by reference to the parish papers and the visitation Call Books.

7 The day of thanksgiving, calm and fair, the Bells and joy begin early, wee are at early prayers after that in the parish church. The Dean preaches after which before a vast number Jack speaks his oration plainly decently.[33] I dine at my Lords with a great company, thence to prayers, after to the Pentice where a liberal Entertainment, universall joy and illuminations fill and beautify the town. I end the day with ArchDeacon Stratford in his chamber.
8 Indispos'd, repose and recover. The Chancellor comes from Crewood, who the Archdeacon and myself go late to good Claret at the Falcon, dispatch 5 bottles, sitt freely and freindly till 2.
9 Relaps severely, repose, complain, repent.
10 Sunday 13 after Trinity, ArchDeacon Stratford reads the prayers morning & Evening & preaches. In the Evening I am with him and the Chancellor, liberally entertaind by Mr. Egerton at the Barn, wee come home about 11.
11 I take a walk on roody 4 Turns. After that with the ArchDeacon to the Chancellors where wee drink a dish of Coffee and part with him for Crewood; write to Mr. Shaw, Mr. Asheton, John Cross. The sheriff (Baskervile) and Judges come in. A hare is given mee by Madam Wainwright which is made a good supper to the ArchDeacon, wee have a Glass of Claret with it.
12 Indifferent from the free supper. The News does not yet gratify with further Successes. Mr. Cowper has a sermon before the Judges, of Oaths, against perjury &c. In the Even after prayers go with the ArchDeacon to Mr. Harper stay at his Ale till 8.
13 After a tedious night a more lucid morning. I turn Berty Geographiam, apply to enter the presentments, dispatch 5 Deanaries, recollect this Diary for the last month vidt. since Aug. 15th.
14 At early prayers proceed in the Deaneries, pay Hen. Maddock on Mr. Vaudreys order 15^{li}. In the Evening at the Falcon with ArchDeacons Booth and Stratford, Mrs. Cowper, Wells &c very cheerfully.
15 After a walk the news which affords yet expectacion only. In the Evening return to the Falcon with most of the same company.
16 Indispos'd, walk and recover, write to Sir Henry Bunbury allegorically about the state of the Town, to Mr. Shaw and John Cross. In the Evening at Mr. Woods with Mr. Egerton and Bowyer.
17 After a walk on roody, refresht. Archdeacon Stratford preaches on, 'They love Darknes rather than light &c'. a very good discourse. I dine with him at the palace. After prayers, go with him, Dr. Thane and Capt. Hulton to the Castle where the Engagment betwixt Sir Geo. Rook and the French much the subject, the Governor treats liberally with good wine, wee stay past 10.
18 After a good walk refresht, indifferent busienes. In the Even after prayers, the ArchDeacon and I take one Turn on roody, thence to Alderman Bennets

33 Jack was selected from the boys of the King's School to give the Latin oration on the victory at Blenheim.

where wee meet with Dr. Thane, Mr. Colly, Callys, Alderman Allen are liberally entertain'd with good wine.

19 After 4 Turns on roody, read the news reciteing the Engagment. In the Evening with the same company Capt. Breholt added, entertain'd at Alderman Allens with excellent Claret.

20 Indispos'd from the practice of Entertainments, write to Mr. Crofton and Topping:invited, I go and dine with Mr. Egerton, his busienes is Advice about the Abjuracion, on that subject till 4, then adjourn to Archdeacon Stratfords chambers where the discourse is reviv'd and warmly pursu'd. In the Even at Archdeacon Entwisles in his absence with ArchDeacon Stratford the treat is supper and wine, wee stay till 11.

21 St. Matthews day at early prayers, then to busienes, the Bishop of Mann and his Lady call on and sitt with us. I go with him to Mr. Harpers, after I am at the Chancellors at his entertainment of the ArchDeacons, where Mr. Egerton, Dr. Thane, Mr. Boucher;wee stay freely and late.

22 After Coffee at Mr. Bouchers and a brisk walk exceedingly refresht. The Chancellor speaks to the Archdeacon on my busienes and is answer'd freindly. The Bishop of Mann and his Lady sitt with us till noon. I dine with the Archdeacon at Mr. Egertons where his brother Philip, Dr. Thane &c. after dinner to good wine till 4.

23 After Elixir some releife, some Busienes and Books. I write to Mr. Wilkinson on Mr. Harpers account. After at the Falcon with the Archdeacon Mr. Henchman, Mr. Hughes of Wem each a Bottle, 1 over.

24 Indispos'd from the Quantity, take a brisk walk, turn the Canon Lawes about Mrs. Oldfeilds case write fully to Dr. Bullen of it. After prayers at Alderman Allens with Archdeacon and Mr. Hulton where good wine.

25 Praepare for a journy tho the day very tempestuous. Archdeacon Stratford and I sett out about 11, with great difficulty sitt our horses over Saltney, come to Northop about one, refresh very freely & freindly, about 3 mount, scour (the storm abated) over the mountains, have a calme road in the valley come safe to Llanenny about 6, are kindly receivd by her Ladyship in her chamber;they fall into discourse of their Archbishop Williams and Dolben. Wee 2 sup in the parlor, the Fire and 4 Bottles of white wine warm the conversacion, the matter of the Registry fully mencion'd hee generously considers my circumstances, assures mee of his own interest and my Lords good purpose and value for mee, and perswades to ease and security, as to their Favor Unde D. O. M. G.

26 In a fine calm morning I rise about 7, take a walk thoro the Feilds near 2 miles to Denbigh see the ruinous Castle. At the post office read the News and repeat it to the ArchDeacon (yet in bed) about 10, wee walk in the Garden till dinner, after which about 2, mount in hazy weather come by Penbid to Mold about 6 where the Archdeacon meets his singular Freind Dr. Robert Morgan. I leave them at the Inn and tir'd retreat to my brother Jones, shee at Wrexham.

27 After Coffee wee part with the Dr. and mount about 11, come safe home D. O. M. G. about 1. I repose, in the Evening wait on the Archdeacon at the palace.

28 First Court this Term. The ArchDeacon setts out hence for Namptwich about 11. I examine 8 wittnesses for Harrison and Nixon.[34] Step into the town, and at the Fountain find the wine bad.
29 The Fair day crowded. I take tho' a walk on roody. Mr. Ollerhead presents us with Fowl, and dines with us. In the Evening at the Rose and Crown, Mr. Callys and Mr. Watkinson wee take our Bottles at least.
30 After a walk in Busienes, write to John Crosse. After prayers and the Town, Mr. Egerton Clerk invites mee and Mr. Brampton to his chamber, treats us liberally with his Ale, but it succeeds not.

OCTOBER 1 Indispos'd with Mr Egertons Ale scarce get to the Quire to hear Dr. Graham the Dean of Bath & Wells preach, hee has a good plain sermon on peace. The News brings Sir Geo. Rook well received at Court. After prayers read 2 Homilies of the right use of the Church, 1 of Idolatry.
2 A delicate Morning. Mr. Boucher and the rest go to Malpas. I take 5 turns on roody, write to Mr. Vaudrey for Blanks [35]; am with the Bishop on Ned Roberts account, hee promises his Favor. Hee delivers the Address drawn by himself to bee fair writ. I draw a requisicion to swear Mrs. Price of the Castle of Dublin his Administratrix, inclose it to Mr. Wilkinson. My cozn Holts come to see us.
3 A delicate day, at early prayers. After in Busienes. The Bishop, Dean and Chapter sign an Address to the Queen for the late Victories. After prayers with Mrs. Dod and Bowyer at the Falcon after at the Golden Talbot neither place good Claret.
4 Another fine day, A Court kept for the Deanaries of Chester and Wirrall easy dispatch. In the Evening at Mrs. Allens with the Chancellor, Capt. Breholt, Mr. Fogg and Mr. Bouchier at a Bowl of punch on Mr. Elingtons Account.
5 Indispos'd from the punch, an easy Court, our Wigan Freinds dine with us, repose after the late dinner, walk the roody late.
6 My cozn Holt leaves us. The news brings nothing but expectacion of better from Landaw. Wee sett out past 9 come to Frodsham before 12 in a delicate day, busienes easily dispatcht. Wee return in a sweet Evening before 6.
7 After early prayers and a walk on roody,write to Mrs. Nixon, Pilkington and Holland of Wigan. After Evening prayers and a walk,at the Fountain with Mr. Hindley the candidate for Aughton[36] and Mr. Tyrer of Ormskirk.
8 After early prayers 4 Turns on roody. After Evening prayers with the Bishop about the Commission of Wistatson, thence with the Chancellor thence with the Dean. Because of my journey to morrow, write to Archdeacon Stratford, Mr. Crofton, Mr. Morrey, John Cross, Hugh Charnock.
9 Write to my cozn Parre, make ready and mount at the Coffee house about 10 in a delicate day, come to Oulton before one. Mr. Egerton receives mee kindly,I

34 C.R.O., EDC.5(1704) No.11, Knutsford.
35 These were printed forms with blank spaces for inserting the names of the parties concerned.
36 For the clergy of Aughton and Ormskirk, the only sources are the Call Books.

walk about with him, after dinner with him and his Lady (Mr. Crane absent). After dinner come thoro' Wetenall Lanes now passible, come to Namptwich before 6, meet then the Chancellor & Dean, examine 2 wittnesses unsworn for Pemberton. Poor Sam Prescott, my oldest & truest Freind, dies about 12 at night in the Isle of Man, suddenly of one Imposthume.

10 Tuesday,a wel and delicate morning. The Chancellor, Dean & myself walk (2 miles) to Wistaston – a confluence fills the small church, betwixt 11 and 12, the Court sitts, the Commission is read in poenam &c, the process gos on, the Jury(16) impannell'd, sworn. Mr. Hunt and Price Councel on Sir Tho. Delvers part (hee not in possession) begin. Mrs. Masterson, Hawkins and Wetnall, on Mr. Walthals side, answer and defend the possession Deeds, Records and Wittnesses produc'd, read, sworn on both sides, after the Councell in possession first, then the other Mr Price, the last harangue the Jury. Recorder Comberback one of the Commissioners Sums the Arguments and evidences, on both sides, and leaves the Event to the Jury. Tis now about 4, the Jury only continue in the church about 2 hours, then not concurring in a verdict,the Commissioners returning adjourn the further Execucion, and admonish the Jury to bring in their verdict in the church of Namptwich betwixt 10 and 12 tomorrow. The company dissolves the Jury and Gentlemen hast to the Lamb at Namptwich where they dine about 8 a clock. After company dispos'd into their Quarters,Mr. Jones of Bangor and ArchDeacon Shore stay and wee drink our Bottles in my chamber.

11 Indispos'd from the supper and wine, ly till 9, hast to the church, call the Court, prayers intervene. After these, the Jury assemble, I draw their verdict specially wherein 10 are of opinion the presentacion belongs to Mr. Walthal, six to Sir Thomas Delves. It appears as a party concern, like Men separating, the Commission dissolves. After dinner receipt of the Fees. I about 3 sett out,and in a delicate evening and way come safe (D.O.M.G) to my Corner about 6.

12 Court day small busienes. Mr. Fogg surrogate. The Train'd Band up, marches thoro all streets to Show no great signs of opposicion in the Election tomorrow.

13 Apply to Busienes, the train'd Band repeats appearing. The Election of Mayor, proceeds quietly, my brother Partington is unanimously chosen. Mr. Peck and Mr. Tho. Houghton are sheriffs. I with Mr. Smith see Mr. Harper, from thence I see the new Mayor, thence to the Ship with Mrs. Leftwich, Oldfeld, Mrs. Cowper, Bowyer, Yates &c very cheerfully and late at the Ship.

14 Indispos'd, warm, restles, I meet with Mrs. Cowper, Hodgson and Stringer, wee drink our morning Draught of white wine at the Rose and Crown, thence I dine with Cowper, Lownds, Oldfeld &c at the Golden Talbot, wee drink a glass of Claret, after I recede home.

15 Difficultly rise to wait on the Mayor to the Quire where a Confluence on that occasion. After prayers, agen at the Mayors, pretty late. Mr. Boucher and Ned Roberts go to Namptwich.

16 Write Letters and dispatch the Administracion with the Will of Mr. Price to Mr. Wilkinson. In the Evening at the Fountain with Alderman Allen and the

Recorder, Mr. Smith with mee. Make and send a Citacion against Mr. Proddy of Cartmel returnable the 19 November.

17 In a delicate Morning, the Chancellor and I sett about 9, wee come to Midlewich before one. Small Busienes, easy of dispatch. In the Evening Mr. Cowper treats us liberally with Ale & tollerable Claret.

18 The Fair begins here. The Morning Frosty we walk to Hulms Chapell where to good stomachs a very good Dinner. Mr. Cowper with us. About 3 Mr. Boucher and myself set forward and in a fine evening come to Macclesfield before 6.

19 Apply to the Aristum Tolosannum contract it. The rest of the company come in a frosty morning about 10, the Busienes is Small. The Chancellor after dinner go's forward to Stockport. In the Evening, Mr. Chamberlain and I sitt 2 hours with Mrs. Hulme and Denham. Mrs Patten the Grandmother and Mrs. Stanley the Aunt are here placeing Sir Thomas Stanley's 2 sons with Mr. Denham.

20 A sweet and calme morning. After Coffee Mr. Boucher and I set out for Stockport, come about 12, the Busienes, tho not much is bustling. The fine weather alters to rain, about 4 in a small shower wee sett out hence and come to Manchester before 6.

21 After Coffee solace, apply to Busienes the number 17. The weather discourages, I am apprehensive of a sore throat but keep warm and use Figgs these prevent it. In the Evening, the Chancellor after other company liberally promotes a Glass of Claret, the practice of the Delegates in the matter of Slynhead and Noseworthy much the discourse.

22 Not so rainy as yesterday.Mr. Ashton has a good discourse on 'What shall a Man prophet if hee gain the whole World' &c. Mr. Molineux a candidate at Preston and his Lady dine with us. Hee shews dexterity in Affairs of parliament but is really on the wrong side. Mr. Ashton procedes on the same Text after noon. After the Chancellor and I had visited the Warden, wee appoint to meet Mr. Pigot and Mr. Ashton at the Crown. I step to Mr. Pigot find him at prayers with his Family. Hee comes with mee to the Crown, where the Chancellor, Mr. Ashton and wee stay till ten.

23 The weather seems recoverd, tis calme, fine and frosty. About 9 sett hence, come to Bolton about 12, the Dinner not ready the Chancellor and Mr. Boucher proceed in a pett. I stay with the Warden &c. See Mr. Haddon, his family in a sick Circumstance. Sett hence about 3 come to Blackburn about 6, receivd as usually by Mr. Price, who yet seems abated in health and vigour. I write to my Suzy.

24 After Elixir coolness and ease. Apply to Busienes.

25 The rest to Chorley, the Chancellor and I for Croston where about 2 wee dine with Mr. Pilkington, I first meet here with Account of Sam. Prescott's death and Jo. Eaton's recess. Mr. Egerton meets us from Eccleston wee see the ruinous Chancell belonging to Mr. Hesketh,drink a Glass of good wine, come to Ormskirk about 7 by the Moon. I lodg at Mrs. Dod's, shee gives mee an Account of her London Expedicion.

26 A fine morning, the weather resumes its former good Quality is fair and calme. I have some moments as well as great reason to reflect on the sudden death of my true contemporary Friend Sam. Prescott. The Busienes all along is easy here. I see John Walmesley (Q.B.E.) my new Tenant, am with Roger Walthew and his dissenting Friends of Rainford. After Busienes, Coll. Ashton and Mr. Kippax,difficultly dismist. The Chancellor, myself, Mrs. Boucher and Hulton, step to W. Barton, hee treats us generously with a Boul of Punch.
27 After conference with Mrs. Dod, hast to the Wheat Sheaf all ready to mount. Before 9 wee set out in a delicate morning. After a short stay at Holland, come to Wigan about 11. Busienes dispatcht, the Chancellor hastens for Warrington, I write to my Suzy. Mr. Boucher, Hulton and I drink a Glass of Wine, come about 8 to my cozn. Holts. Yong Waldons Concern for his Uncle, moves mee sensibly, I give him 10^{s}.
28 Cool after Elixir and easy. About 10 set out. I call on Jane Hulme thence walk the rest, see the work don this summer. John Cross accounts to mee about the Ashes sold. Hugh Charnock pay mee 10^{li}. I pay Geo.Molineux &c 3^{li}; 8^{s}; 6^{d}. Returning am treated by Jane Hulm and Wm. Whaley's wife. I sett Whitley Hall, call on my cozn. Prescott and give him directions about the Miller, come to Wigan by the Moon. Sitt with our Friends of both Families.
29 Rise early to the News. After that to the Church where Mr. Taylor preaches. After Dinner I repose. In the Evening with Sir Roger Bradshaigh the Corporacion and the three Lawyers. After this with Mr. Holland at the Eagle and Child where, at large the matter of his sons comeing to mee is discours'd. Hee seems well pleasd, wee drink (which hee pays for) 4 pints of Claret. About 11 to cozn. Holts.
30 Indispos'd enough. After Tea and Brandy about 10 sett from hence, the weather and way inviteing tho I intended only Beausey, resolve for Chester, call and stay an hour at Warrington; sett thence about 3, the evening grows hazy and dark, the moon riseing recovers and I come by its Light safe to my Corner D.O.M.G. about 7.
31 After Busienes and Letters read, I wait on the Mayor. The Town is filld with persons & expectacion of the Duke of Ormond from Cholmley, hee comes not. I wait on the Bishop and give him a short report of our Journy. Hee speaks to mee about Mr. Massies pew. In the Even I see poor Jo.Eaton.

NOVEMBER 1 At early prayers with my Suzy. Step into the Town, buy Spelman de non temerandis Ecclesiae and the poor Widows plea. The Duke comes to Mr. Andertons about noon and presently proceeds to Sir John Conways. Mr. Smith after about 2 months, parts tenderly with us. In the Evening Mr. Boucher & I drink Mr. Smith of University College, his token a Bottle of Claret.
2 Court day, the Busienes small, the day rainy. I examine 1 Wittness for Davenson, 2 for Tipping, pay Mr. Foulks in mony and stamps return'd 57^{li}, read Spelmans Epistle to the reader.
3 After a rainy Night a cool moist morning. The News brings the Imperialists

on the Counterscarp of Landaw. I recollect this Ephemeris from the 9th of October. I pay the Chancellor on Account 40^{li} in silver and 20 Guineas. Apply to Busienes. At Night Mr. Colly, Bowyer and myself drink our Bottles of good Viana at the Fountain.

4 A dull moist day indispos'd, write to Mrs. Milward, Hutchins, John Cross, pay John on Account 10^{s}, pay Mr. Colly for the Bishop 40^{li}. Write larg to Mr. Chetle on the matter of presentments. In the Evening at the Mayors, with my brother Puleston of Havod-y-Wern &c.

5 The day celebrated in City Formalities. Dr. Thane preaches on 'Love your Enemies'&c. The News yet incertain, silent about Landaw. After Evening prayers My Brother Puleston and Ned P. visit mee. Jack reads Speeds Account of the Popish Plott and part of the History of Cataline. Remember with sharp Concern my Loss of my Lord Derby this day 2 Years since.

6 After prayers and a walk of 4 Turns, write to Sir Hen. Bunbury, Dr. Pope with a Bill of 30^{li} and to Mr. Empsoul. Receive from Dr. Prevarus a Quarter of a years rent due at Midsummer last 1^{li}:10^{s}. After prayers wait on the Chancellor, to the Bishop, on Mrs Eddows Account, the matter of the Clerk of Wigan, Mr. Porter and Proddy menciond. After this to ArchDeacon Booths where Mr. Egerton, Brook, the Mayor are treated with honest discourse and Claret. After I read Sir H. Spelman de non temerandis Ecclesiae.

7 The Forenoon idly spent over Coffee and Tea. Wee dine at the Mayors in a great Company. After dinner the Men recede to Claret, the women have musick and danceing, I stay till 11.

8 A cool moist day yet hott and indispos'd. After prayers Apply to Salusts Catalinarium Bellum finish it and his Oracion against Tully and his Epistle de Rep ordinanda to Caesar. At the Fountain an hour this Evening,with Dr. Nicols.

9 A dull moist day. Court day,I examine 5 Wittnesses on Taylors Will.In the Evening Mr. Boucher & I send for and drink a Bottle of Claret.

10 A Rainy day, little of News, none of Landaw, I draw a Certificate or recomendacion on Ned Roberts Account. After prayers Mr. Proddy appears before my Lord, the Chancellor &c in the palace, in obstinate, denys rather than confess. After at the Fountain with Mr. Bowyer lastly at the Mayors.[37]

11 Indispos'd. But after 4 Turns on Roody recreated, write to Mr. Wettenhall of Wistaston. Mr. Proddy comes in a better disposicion to mee, before noon. Wee discourse his Affairs And after Dinner, I apply to the drawing his Answer to Articles extrajudicially given, it takes mee up till 6 at night. John Cross the Joyner after 15 months absence in Scotland, returns to his Mother.

12 A moist dull day. Eucharistiam sanctissimam recipio Det Deus O.M. vitam meliorem.[38] Dr. Entwisle preaches. The News dull. After prayers my Lord calls

37 C.R.O., EDC.5(1704) No. 4, and (1706) No. 6, for the case against Proddy, vicar of Cartmel. Thos. Proddy,M.A. (deacon at Carlisle 11 March 1687, priest by John Ebor., York 3 June 1694) was collated to Cartmel 19 Dec. 1698 at £80 p.a. L.R.O., Richmond Call Book ARR 1701.

38 Trans: 'I receive the most Holy Eucharist. May God the best and greatest grant [me] a better life.'

mee to his Study about Mr. Proddy. After this at Mr. Mayors where I meet with Mrs. Anderson and lament the ill fortune and Circumstance of her husband the Alderman.

13 A very sharp storm most of the Night and till noon with rain. Mr. Proddy dines with mee. I write to my cozn. Parr. About 2 Mr. Proddy appears before the Bishop & gives his answer and confession to the Articles and submitts, the matter warmly discust betwixt the Chancellor and the Dean – the Bishop adjourns till betwixt 9 and 10 to morrow. In the Evening I treat Mr. Proddy with a glass of wine and his Neighbor John Barber. Hee is cheerfull & diverts, with Jack in Horace.

14 A fair brisk day the wind N. yet very little News. My Lord receives from the Lord Keeper a summons to Parliament the 23 current.Mr. Proddy appears at the Time before the Bishop & Chancellor, the Dean and ArchDeacon Entwisle present. Hee very solemnly admonishes Mr. P.to an holy sober and exemplary Life for the future, adding his benediccion, but dos not dismiss him till he hears from the Denunciators. Mr. Proddy pays the Fees 1^{li};6^{s};0. I dine with my Lord, Alderman Morrey and Sheriff Peck. After prayers apply to Busienes.

15 At early prayers, after to Busienes. Send the little Mare to John Bentley's Feild at 10^{d} the week, pay Mr. Vernon the City Duty as for 8 Tonns of Coal 8^{s}, write larg to Mr Rowel and about the matter of Institucion &c. In the Evening at Lady Otways where I am wittnes to her sealing a Deed of Sale of the Advowson of Windermere to Dr. Fenton for which the consideracion seems to bee to her 130^{li}. Sir Christopher Phillipson joining in the same Deed.[39] After this Mr. Lambert and I go to the Fountain where for 3 hours freely over a Glass of Claret.

16 A dull day. My Lord Bishop comes into the Court and by a very solemn and grave Harangue against the vice articulate, admonishes Mr. Porter of them, forbids him the conversacion of the 2 women Thurstan and Foster, inhibits him from the Execucion of his Deacon's Office in this diocese and condemns him in Expenses[40]. I write to Mr. Trotter. After Evening prayer invited, go to Mr. Egertons, where Archdeacon Booth, Mr. Brook and Mr. Philip Egerton. Wee are liberally entertain'd with good wine. I return with the Archdeacon about 11.

17 Indispos'd from the wine last night. Mr. Philip Egerton reads his resignacion of Barthomley before mee, after, presents it to the Bishop, who accepts it.

18 I go about 10 with Ned Roberts to my Lord. Hee grants him his Admission to a proctors place and administers the Oaths of Allegiance and Supremacy to him. In the Evening I am at the Talbot, Mr. Pickmore's who tells mee his Case of the Organ.

19 Mr. Lancaster preaches in the Quire. The News yet slack. After prayers at

39 Advowsons, or the rights to present incumbents to benefices, were bought and sold as real property until 1933, when this practice was abolished.

40 C.R.O., EDC.5 (1704) No. 10, and EDC.5 (1703) No. 15, Bunbury.

the Chancellors, I this Evening first observe a Familiarity extra-ordinary betwixt N.R. and M.B.

20 I apply to reading and Busienes, wait on the Bishop who tells mee he will take no less than 85^{li} per Annum for the Deaneries, I having yet this year paid only 80 but promise him the other 5^{li}. I write in the Evening to Mr. Wilkinson about institucions &c.

21 The News enlarges bring Landau and Traarback very near Attack or Surrender. In Books and busienes. In the Evening with Mrs. Colly and Bowyer at the White Talbot. After at the Mayors where with Mr. Bowyer a Bottle of Claret freely.

22 From last night severely indispos'd, draw up however the Bishop's Decree against Porter, the rest of the day in Books.

23 After Elixir easier. Last Court Day of this Term. Ned Roberts is admitted to his place as proctor on Iudicis Sinistra.[41] I dine with the Chancellor, Mrs. Brooks, Bruen &c at the Bishops. I examine 6 witnesses against Holt, 1 against Hunt.

24 A bright windy day. My cosens Fleetwood and Leech are here about Administracion of my cosen Hulmes goods. The Chancellor and myself wait on my Lord, on Mr. Proddy and Turners Cases. I write to Mr. Peake and Denham. In the Evening at the Fountain, hear and pitty Mr. Eatons Case.

25 After a windy night a dull day. Go down to Mr. Cartwright on Mr. Whaley and Hutchins Busienes. Write to James Close of Furnivals Inn. Apply to Cicero de Oratore. In the Evening at the Mayors where with Alderman P. Partington & Mr. Proby, a Bottle of good Claret.

26 Yet another dull day. Mr. Lancaster preaches in the Quire. The News do's not determin Landau. After prayers with my Lord Bishop, many taking Leave of him. After at the Mayors to get a pass for one Burton upon Sir Wm. Parsons Letter but it do's not succeed. I stay here till 9 and with Alderman P. Partington & Mr. Hulton, dispatch 2 other Bottles of good Claret.

27 A brisker day. I wait with others on my Lord Bishop. Hee takes Stage Coach for London about 11 a clock. I write to Mr. Holland about his son. At dinner at the Mayors where all Clergy but the Chancellor and myself. A Gentile and plentifull Entertainment. In the Evening Archdeacons Booth & Entwisle, Mr. Clopton and myself retreat with the Mayor into lesser room. Here variety of talk, animated with 4 Bottles of French Claret.

28 A fair calm morning, recover the Feast by a brisk walk on roody. After wee repair to Mr. Bouchers, drink Coffee, talk of and Rate the matter of my Bond to him now from 300li to 150li. I promise to pay 50li and give a new bond for the 100li. After dinner and repose proceed in Tully de Oratore.

29 A fair mild day. Apply to Busienes. After prayers Mr. Hayhurst and 2 Mr.

41 Trans: 'on the left hand of the judge'.

Leavers are dispatcht about taking out the original will of their Grandfather. After which our Bottles at the Fountain.
30 St. Andrew, a dark and dusky day. I repeat my domestic celebration of Lady Charlott Cornwallis her birthday, this is the 26th of her Age. After prayers at the Golden Talbot with Drs. Entwisle and Thane, 2 Cowper Bros. Mr. Bowyer and myself. Wee have Church of England discourse, the Archdeacon comes about to that side. I writt to Mr. Proddy, Mr. Shaw and John Crosse.

DECEMBER 1 A sharp not frosty morning. The News confirms Landaw surrender'd, Gibraltar reliev'd by Sir Lake, Traarbach obstinate, Verrue turnd to a Blockade. Indispos'd all day, at Night turn Tully de Oratore.
2 A cold not frosty day. I pay Mr. Foulks 10li write to Mr. Price. After Dinner the Chancellor calls on mee, wee go to Mr. Bouchers. Thither I order a Bottle of Mancks Ale where wee and Mr. Maurice drink it, thence Mr. Maurice and I with Mr. Chancellor to Alderman Allens where hee treats us with 3 Bottles of Claret, 1 light French. Write to Dr. Jones of Llanhychon, draw a Certificate for Ned Roberts in order to his being a Notary.
3 A rainy dull day. News dull. I am in the Forenoon at St Peter's Church where Dr. Thane preaches sermonem [? fictihsum] usurpando ac flebilem. After Evening prayer in Books. Mr. Boucher comes over, hee intending to begin his journy for Oxford tomorrow, wee join in a bottle.
4 A clear day. The Chancellor, Mr. Boucher and I subscribe the Certificate. I inclose it in a Letter to my cozen Parre. Mr. Boucher cancells my old Bond of 300li. I enter a new one of 100. I trust my Shell with him to Poyner hee sett out about 11. In the Evening Mrs. Wylrant formerly Mrs. Stephen Borrell sees us from my Lady Stephens. Shee gives us an account of Dublin, the Government, our Friends &c.
5 The News yet on expectacion about Traarbach. I apply most of the day to the Chancellors Accounts. After Evening Prayer at the Falcon with Archdeacon Booth, Dr. Thane and Mr. Callys.
6 A brisk yet calm day, take 5 Turns on Roody. After dinner repose. After prayers at the Fountain am with Dr. Thane, Mr. Bowes, young Will. Allen, write to Mr. Lingard about one Booth, presented.
7 A very sharp frost begun. About ten a great company go down to Mr. Bunburys at Boughton, attend his Herse, here I meet with Mr. Crane. I accompany the Herse to Backford with Mr. Crane to dinner about 4 a clock. About 6 I go down with him to the Barrs, Mr. Egertons, where with Mr. Wilbraham of Deerfold, Mr. Brooks and Mr. Crane wee are entertained generously with a good Claret, till 11 a clock.
8 The Frost very sharp. Indispos'd from last Night. The News diverts not much. In the Evening at the Fountain with Mr. Swarbrech and Mr. Bowyer till 10.
9 Frost still severe. Apply to Busienes, write to Mr. Close of Furnivals Inn & to my coz. Parre. At home all the cold day. In the Evening in Tully with Verrem.
10 The Frost still severe. Archdeacon Entwisle preaches in the Choir. The

News brings Gibraltar back into danger. After prayers at home in Books sparsim.

11 The weather blackens and the Frost seems to relent. I give the 3 oaths to Ned Roberts, return the Commission and write to my cozen Parre and Mr. Holland to both on the subject of a Clerk into my office. Mr. Bowyer and I after Evening prayer visit, sending 2 Bottles of wine before us, Alderman Anderton who talks fancifully of his own defences but has no compassion for his fellow sufferers Winstanley and Eaton.

12 After a good walk on Roody, at the Coach and Horses with Mr Crane, Peter Eden, widow Sherlock, after dine at the Mayors in a great Company, retreat to the next room to company and a Glass of wine. Thence to the Chancellors to a Bowl of Punch with Mrs. Egerton, Brook, Down too freely.

13 Indispos'd from punch and variety. After Dinner call'd to the Mayors where my Brother Jones executes a Deed for the secureing of a Jointure to his wife and delivers them to mee as Trustee. After this, Hee, Mr. Wynne the performing Atturny and myself go to the Fountain, drink 2 Bottles cheerfully.

14 The Indisposicion (not withstanding Elixir) continues, the weather tho very mild yet frosty. My Brother Jones executes a Bond of 600^{li} penalty for the further security of 18^{li} p.Annum (out of his personal Estate) to his wife. After, the day bestowd on repose & reading variously.

15 A delicate mild morning. After a walk on Roody at the Mayors where I hear the Case of the two or 3 Men imprest. In the Evening my Brother & sister Jones, sister Pontney and Mrs. Beale visit us. They sup and stay late.

16 Pay Mr. Chapman 3 Guineas which with 3^{li} formerly amounts to 6^{li} 4s 6d. Write to Miles Gerard and return the Subpoena against Mr. T. Partington. Write to Mr. Crofton. A.M. an Assistant to Richard Clark a Sailer of Lancaster to gett him clear of an Impressing, makeing the Recorder, who was readily so, his Friend. In the Evening at the Plume of Feathers with Mr. Warrington and Mr. Minshull where the 1st lays the later a Bottle of Sack that the Conformity Bill will pass this Session. R. Clark comes to me civilly and gratefully bestows a Bottle of Claret for the office I did him.

17 Am affected with my old distemper, a sore throat, keep warm at home. Hear the Lesson &c read and turn some of the Scriptures.

18 The Frost begins afresh very briskly, after a walk into the Fields refresht write to Sir Henry Bunbury, Mr. Hutchins, John Crosse. After Evening prayer at the Ship with Mr. Chancellor, Archdeacon Entwisle, Dr. Thane, Liberally each a Bottle.

19 The frost continues. I take a brisk walk on roody, yet indispos'd. The News brings the Conformity Bill rejected in the House of Lords by 21 voices. Traarbach surrendred. After prayers agen at the Ship with Mr. Chancellor, Dr. Thane, Mr. Bowyer more moderatly.

20 After Elixir cooler. The Frost relented, write to Dr. Pope and Mr. Archdeacon Stratford about the Cheeses sent to them and to Mrs. Muddinson. Pay Mr. Boucher the arrears of his interest, to the 4th of this month, 1 Guinea & ½ Guinea, finish the Chancellor's Accounts.

21 St. Thomas Day mild. After some turns on Roody in books variously.
22 After a walk see the News very lean and giving only Expectacion. After Dinner repose. In the Evening at Mr. Willoughbys strong Ale, cheerfully with Mr. Cowper and Mr. Allen, Mr. Cowper bestows on mee a stone, a rarity the Bed or matrix of the Entroclae.
23 Severely indispos'd from last Nights ale. Elixir helps something. A very sharp day thoro the market with my Suzy. In the Evening meet accidentally with Mr. Whaley, hee tells mee of his expectacions and his Brother promises to retrieve his Estate.
24 Sunday-a sharp day. Mr. Shawe preaches in the Quire. The News still slow. In the Evening read and hear read.
25 A mild cool day. The Dean preaches. Sanctissimam impertimus coenam. Det D.O.M. vitam puriorem. After prayers apply to reading and hearing read. Write to Dr. Jones.
26 St. Stephens day mild. At early prayers. After take a brisk walk on roody. See the News yet scanty. In the Evening I entertain the 3 Rope makers with Ale and Beefe.
27 After early prayers and a walk to Books. In the Evening at the Fountain very moderately. Mr. Warmingham the Chirurgion an honest and usefull Man bury'd toNight.
28 A fine brisk day. After early prayers and a brisk walk to Bookes and Busienes. In the Evening wee visit Mrs. Mary Oldfield at her mothers, the rest of the Evening in Books.
29 A very brisk morning. After early prayers and a brisk walk on roody wherein Jack reads part of the Life of Boetius, I seek the News where Gibraltar is furiously attackt and resolutely defended. After dinner Dr. Thane and Mr. Menes Minister of Little Budworth drink a Glass of my Ale pretty freely. In the Evening my Suzy and I visit some Friends, at the last stay at the Mayors.
30 A cool moist day. I pay Ellen the maid due about a week hence 40s. I dine with Mr. Chancellor and Archdeacon Booth at Mr. Egertons, the dinner elegant, the Entertainment after, very gentile and liberal. Wee stay till 10 and dispatch above a dozen Bottles of good Claret.
31 After so much good wine tolerably well. Hear Mr. Newton at Little St. Johns in the morning – the news proceeds not. After prayers at the Coffee House where Mr. Holland comes to mee. I adjourn that matter of Moment to the next Morning. Hence Dr. Thane and I to the Fountain where over a moderate Glass of Wine wee (as he phrases it) part with the Old Year.[42]

1704/5

JANUARY 1 Q.B.E. at early prayers. Mr. Holland comes about 8. Wee treat on the busienes of his son, hee seems mostly to suspect his health but declines

42 The custom of dating the year from 1st January was slowly spreading, though officially 25 March was regarded as New Year's Day until 1752.

not my condicions. Hee staies & dines with us. After Evening prayers wee go to the Fountain. Renew the discourse and mix the Affairs of our Country, draw on the time past ten. A mild day and Night.

2 Indispos'd tho after Elixir, solace till Noon. Hear the news giveing hopes of Gibraltar, apply to Bookes.

3 A fine calm day, draw 10 ounces of Blood to help a scorbutic humer off. Apply to Mackenzies precendency.

4 A mild day, take with Jack 4 Turns on roody, write to John Cross. I dine at the Mayors with Mr. Subdean Wright, the Recorder, Sheriff Peck, Mr. Wettenhall, their Ladies, a great company. After a free Glass with the Mayor, thence about 6 home. Write to the Bishop of Kildare, turn Livy &c.

5 Take in a brisk Frost a walk of 4 turns. The News makes most of the Succors to Gibraltar intercepted or diverted by the French from Cadiz. I apply to Busienes and Accounts. In the Evening at the Fountain with Mr. Winstanley and Eaton, their difficult Circumstance about Security to the Queen, is much of our discourse.

6 The Frost agen relents, my son Ken comes into danger of Life from the Chinecough. I write a Letter (in his name) for Mr. Winstanley to Mr. Shakerley and to my coz. Parr. After Prayers at Little St. Johns, before dinner, a shorter walk on roody. In the Evening to Busienes and write to Mr. Wilkinson.

7 A brisk air, not very frosty. I take a walk on roody. After to the Church, Sanctissimam impertio Eucharisticam D.O.M. det vitam vera Xtianam.[43] The ArchBishop of Dublin (King) is a Communicant. Mr. Fogg preaches. In the Afternoon, Bingley near 80 dies suddenly in the parish Church. After prayers at the Coffee House where slender papers. In the Evening Mrs. Mayoress is with us. The Child gives us some melancholy thoughts.

8 After early prayers in the Office with John Cross on design of the Clerks seat, prepare for my journy to Wrexham, write to Sir Henry Bunbury on behalf of Mr. Winstanley and Easton. Set hence after 2, come to Wrexham, Jack with mee about 5, meet with Dr. Jones at the Red Lyon with other his Company. Wee lodge at my Uncle Eytons, Bryn-a-funan.

9 After prayers the Commission for examining wittnessess on Sir Paul Pindars Will from the praerogative[44] is open'd in the Church. Dr. Wynn the Chancellor of St. Asaph, Mr. Price, Vicar of Wrexham, Mr. Lloyd, Warden of Ruthin, and Mr. Jones, sit as Commissioners. Dr. Jones a party sine revocacione procuris presents it & produces Mr. Peter Ellice, Mr. Peter Davies and Richard Jones, Barber, wittnesses and desires the further execucion to bee adjourned to Stephen Jones house, the Ship, where Mr. Dawes, a Commissioner on Madam Dorothy Pindars part comes, assumes the Execucion with the rest. Mr. Andrew

43 Trans: 'I share in the most Holy Eucharist. May God the best and greatest grant [me] a true Christian life.'

44 'Praerogative' refers to the praerogative court for proving wills of persons holding property in other dioceses.

Swift an Atturney of Shrewsbury appears as substitute and administers Interrogations; the Commission consent to leave the Execucion to mee privately. I examine Mr. Ellis & Mr. Davies and at Repeticion read over the Articles, Interrogacions and deposicions alternatium. I end about 9 after which I go with Mr. Davies to Richard Jones where hee treats mee with bottles of Claret. Wee are free and cheerful and part about 11.

10 About 9 a fine morning, I return to the Ship, begin the Certificates but intermit and examine Richard Jones. Hee is examind about 12. Wee dine at the Red Lyon after which I finish the Certificates which the Commissioners sign and the Commission is clos'd and directed. Mr. Swift gives mee 1^{li}; 5s for examinacion on the Interrogacions. Dr. Jones 3 Guineas for the rest. After this I see my brother Puleston at Mr. Hughs lodging. After wee go to R. Jones where hee treats mee with a bottle of wine. Hee appears heavy & dormitabund. After I go to Bryn-a-funam where after divercion of the place and a bottle of good wine, to bed about 11.

11 A fair mild day. I visit the Gentlemen and Ladys at the Mount, see the improvements, drink Coffee here, dine at Bryn-a-funam. Here my uncle Eyton sharply reprehends his son Jacks ill and obstinat manners. Hee treats and parts cheerfully with us. My coz. Kendrick and Jack Eyton bring mee to the Red Lyon where over a glass of wine I take occasion to advise Jack Eyton to admonish of the danger of a maritime loose life, bringing a near & sensible example. My own son (D.G.) takes good notice of this admonicion and recollects it in the way. Wee come safe home about 5 when beyond my hopes I find my son Ken recovering out of danger.

12 After the News dine & repose. In the Evening see and deliver messages to Mr. Egerton and Done at the Coffee house. After I see the Chancellor comeing thence, meet with Mr. Foulks, wee go to the Ship, stay there till 12.

13 Indispos'd severely, in Books variously and soe while away the Day.

14 A very hard Frost. Mr. Hulme of Macclesfield has a good Sermon. The News seems full of Success to the Emperor. Ragotzy defeated, a French Envoy taken and expos'd. A great success in a sally by the Duke of Savoy on the Beseigers of Verue. In the Evening Mr. Hulme comes and sitts 2 or 3 hours with us.

15 The Frost relented. I take a walk on roody. I draw a Certificate to attest the burial of Anne Hopkins of Esckusham widow 17 Dec. 1698 as appears by the Register Book of Wrexham. I write to my coz. Parr & Mr. Okes. In the Evening Mr. Hulme and I drink a Bottle at the Fountain after I had bin Bearer at the Funeral of Mrs. Hughs late of Dysart (at St. Maries Chr.)

16 After a brisk walk on roody well refresht. The Chancellor sees mee I pay him for repeticions for the last year $1^{li};16^{s};8$. Wee go to the Coffee house where a printed paper of Sir John Lakes success against the French Fleet meets with little credit.

After dinner Archdeacon Booth visits mee, I treat him with my Antiquitys and the last Bottle of my Mancks Ale. Hee seems pleas'd with both. After this I go to the Fountain where with the unfortunate Debtors, Winstanley and Eaton, a cheerfull Bottle.

17 A mild day, cooler after Elixir. Pay Mr. Boucher for the last years Caveats[45] 4^{li}, send Copies of the proceedings against Noseworthy to the Bishop. Contract the Deposicions against Huxley, at 4 meet Mr. Aubry and Mr. Hulton & discourse on that subject. At night read Archdeacon Booths Articles of Enquiry.

18 Q.B.E. the first Court of Hilary Term, a mild day the Busienes so. I examine 1 Witnes for Alderman Ince against Hurleston. The Evening in Rosinus.

19 A cold day yet take the purging spirit. Examine another witnes for Alderman Ince. Write to Mr. Price and Mr. Rider. Draw a Declaracion for Huxley. Visit Alderman Allen, who treats mee with a Bottle of excellent, a pint of indifferent, wine, he is sending his son Thomas in a laudable post to China, of the Mayors removal High Cross stone and his offence at it.

20 At early prayers, the morning severely cold. I repeat the Spirit, walk all the Rowes, write to S. Prescott about my rents. After Dinner repose, after in Books.

21 A severe frosty morning. Mr. Subdean Wright preaches. After I see the News, yet cold as the weather. After Evening prayer at the Chancellors after that at home in Books.

22 A most delicate morning. At early prayers. After, uneasy to take Horse till I spoke to the Mayor to return the old Cross Stone. Hee says people will laugh at the sudden alteracion &c but hopes of gratifying mee. Anima absoluta. I take horse at the Coffee house past 9, in a fine day pass the Forest and meet Mr. Okes in the same minuit at Sandy way. Hee tells mee his Busienes, vid, his Offence at teaching children to write in the Chancel of Namptwich Church, ita etiam absolvit Animam. Wee dine on Hen and Bacon, are cheerfull. Mr. Charles Booth comes to us. Wee part about 4, I come most by the Moon, over the Forest to Olton. Mr. Egerton, his bro. Philip with him entertains mee freely.

23 The Frost holds. After dinner I in his Sheas come with him, hee call at his stable see his running horses, halt at Tarvin where Sir Thomas Billots troop is muster'd, a raw and unskilfull appearance. After an hour proceed, come to Chester safe about 6. I stay at a good Bottle with him till past 8. Hee all along us'd mee with a generous Civility. Safe at my Corner D.G. about 9. Alderman Matthew Anderton son of my late good old Freinds affected with Gout, Dropsy and Adversity dies about 8 at Night.

24 After Letters, Busienes and repose. In the Evening at the Fountain with the Chancellor, Aldermen Allen & Bennett, Dr. Thane, Mr. Peake, Mr. Jas. Egerton, wee all agree to bee cheerfull, drink our full Bottle each. I and the 2 last stay late. Mr. Whaley calls and pays mee the 4^{li} lent him last August.

25 St. Pauls, a foggy day, unable to celebrate it as I ought. At Mr. Boucher with Mr. Peake thence to dinner and repose. After Evening prayer and some

45 A caveat was a legal document to prohibit any person other than the lawful patron from presenting an incumbent to a vacant benefice; C.R.O., Caveat Books 1600–1791.

busienes at the Fountain. I pay Mr. Eaton for 2 Gallons of good port and 17 pint Bottles 17s.

26 After a brisk walk on roody and the Coffee house to Busienes. The Assembly meets and choose my brother Ned Puleston Alderman in Mr. Andertons place. I am wittness with Mr. Collys and Mr. Cowper to my Lady Otways execucion of 3 Deeds concerning the sale of some Lands in the parish of Hawkshead. After at Mr. Andertons house and thence attend his Funeral at St. Johns, here on melancholy reflections. Thence half an hour at Mr. Cowpers thence for relief at the Fountain.

27 The day foggy, dispatch Busienes and Letters to Mrs. Styth, Markland, Bert, Entwisle. After Dinner attend the Mayor to the Hall where Ned Puleston is sworn Alderman. Mr. Birkenhead of Backford, Freeman. Thence with Dr. Thane to the Fountain, the Mayor, Sherrif Peck, Alderman Puleston follow us. Wee stay treated too freely till 12.

28 Severely indispos'd, stay at home in Caves Historia Literaria. After prayers, I Jack with mee take a walk to Blacon point. Call on the Cross stone at the Startstone, the rest in Books & reading.

29 About 10 I attend Mr. Hopes Herse out of the Town to the limits of the County of Flint. After dinner and busienes Mr. Williamson the Yeoman of the Pentice calls on mee. Wee confer about bringing back the stone, wee go to it, see it workt square, hee is grevously affected with the unwary removal of it, promises his assistance. Wee go to the Fountain where Alderman Puleston & the 2 Mr. Birkenheads find us. Wee are treated by the Alderman and Freeman.

30 King Charles 1st his Martyrdom. The 56 year celebrated paenas publicas meritissimas avertat Deus summe misericors.[46] Mr. Elison of Pulford preaches a sound discourse of Obedience to those set over us. After at the Coffee house where little News of devotion. Apply to the History of that glorious Martyr read by Jack. After prayers, a walk to Blacon, see the stone ready workt. After meat, Archdeacon Booth sends for mee. Wee over a Bottle of wine draw out the Evening in discourse on the Day, the discipline of our Church agreeable to Councils, Canons Fathers &c.

31 The stone is return'd in the Night, the Town surpris'd, various and comical conjectures past at the place. Mr. Bouchers company, my Suzy and I dine at the Mayors. The stone mencioned. After prayers I am with the Chancellor, Dr. Thane & Mr. Done at a cheerfull Bottle at the Fountain. Dr. Thane tells us of an indever with the Bishop to make Dr. Entwisle Register for the use of his Daughters.

FEBRUARY 1 Q.B.E. a moist morning, indispos'd after a bad and watchfull Night. Court day, the Busienes evenly carryd on. I examine 2 Wittnesses

46 Trans: 'May most merciful God avert the most deserved public penalties'. Prescott observed this day with solemnity.

Rymmer contra Hunt. In the Evening Dr. Thane and I recreate in our pints at the Fountain.

2 The weather rainy. Candlemas day. Mr. Fogg has a good discourse on, 'lay not up Treasure on Earth &c'. After this to the Coffee house where expectacion of good News from Gibraltar. After dinner in sorting (especially stamp) Accounts. After prayers and Books to the Fountain where Aldermen Allen & Bennett. David Parry intrudes and disturbs the company.

3 My Suzys 38 Birth day. Dat. D.O.M. dies candidiores.[47] I write to my Lord include an English proces for his Visitacion to Mr. Walthall, Vaudrey and John Cross. After Evening prayers recollect for a fortnight this Ephemeris, the rest in Books.

4 After a better Night an easier morning. Dr. Thane has a good discourse on Ps. 37 v.1. Sanctissimam caenam impertio, det D.O.M. vitam congruam.[48] After Evening prayers turn Dr. Goodmans Winter Evening Conference.

5 After a tedious night repeat the golden Drops (80). I write to Sir Henry Bunbury. After Busienes and Evening prayers with Mr. Swarbrecke at the Fountain.

6 The Queens Birth day the 40th. Q.F.F.F.Q.S. I repeat the drops, walk in a delicate frosty morning, see the News yet of no great Moment. The Day is publicly celebrated, the Common Hall illuminated. The Mayor treats the Gentlemen (I counted 54) with Claret, the Queens health first begun on the Knee, follow'd by 6 others all ended with Huzzas. After the solemnity at the Hall, Dr. Thane and I go to the Fountain, where wee end the day cheerfully in 3 pints. After dinner, I waited on Archdeacon Booth to see the Chancellor.

7 A sharp day, indispos'd from the other, apply to Busienes. In the Evening at the Fountain cheerfully with Mr. Pemberton late Steward to the late Mr. Fleetwood of Penwortham a discrete, decent and cheerfull person. Wee pass the Evening in Lancashire discourse. Q.B.E. the Earl of Derby marry'd to a daughter of Sir Wm. Morley of Sussex, Knight of the Bath.

8 A Court day, indispos'd, the Busienes easy. I draw Alice Robinson her supplecatory Oath, the rest in Books.

9 About 11 a clock, the Chancellor and myself go out for the Lach. Diverted in the way by setting, tho no partridge taken. Wee dine there. Hee swears, I examine Mr. Manley. Wee are civilly entertain'd and return home as all went on Foot about five a clock. Mr. Valentine, Atturny and Mr. Shawe, Steward come to mee from Mr. Atherton about two Aministracions with Wills annext, to him and his 4 sisters.

10 After the golden drops repeated and early prayers, I take a walk in the Rowes; it being a cold and moist day. I examine 2 more (the last of) Alderman Inces Wittnessess, write to Mr. Okes and Mr. Crane.

11 After a walk of 4 Turns, to the Church where in the Quire, Mr. Bowyer has

47 Trans: 'May God the best and greatest grant brighter days.'

48 Trans: 'I share in the most Holy Supper, may God the best and greatest grant [me] a fitting life.'

a good sermon. The News run dull. After prayers I go with Mr. Egerton to the Chancellor. Hee shews us the 2 Mr. Offleys Letters about the decicion and his full and sharp answer to them. After a Bottle here amongst us I go to my S. at Ned Pulestons where hee treats mee with a pint of better wine.

12 A hazy morning yet take 4 Turns. I promise Mr. Allen to speak to the Bishop of Man about a debt of 50^{li} due to Bishop Bridgman. After dinner Busienes. I write to my Cozen Parr and John Cross; I pay Mr. Callys more on account of the Deaneries viz. 5^{li} to Mr. Fogge my rent 3^{li} 10s. In the Evening with him & Mr. Allen at the Fountain, after with the Chancellor, Dr. Thane, the Mayor, Mrs. Wells and Bowyer, the matter of the seat in St. Peter's Church warmly mencioned. The Chancellor, Chagrin, ingages mee to stay the next day to discourse on the matter at the Ship and take Care of the Ordinarys right and jurisdicion. Wee stay late drink above our Bottles cheerfully.

13 After a hot night a fevorish day. After dinner agen to the Fountain, where the Mayor, Mr. Wells, Mr. John Lea, Mr. Bowyer, Mr. Mayor and I only, go to the Ship. Wee discourse on the controverted seat. The Mayor proposes to Mrs. Bailey one near it, new built. I interpose on the Chancellors behalf. Shee at first warm but when calmer sticks to her expectacion of the controverted seat. I advise her to comply for peace and the Chancellors ease but add no discouragement. Wee relate of Negociocions at the Fountain. The Chancellor comes to us, wee repeat the success to him. Hee is satisfied his right is not violated, tho ignorantly invaded.[49] The wine and time pass on as the last night. Mr. Wells and Mr. Lea pay 20s.

14 After wine and Elixir feavorish, with remorse, indulge with torment, no Busienes or ease. In the Evening I receive a Cheese a token from my cozen Sale.

15 After repeated Elixir, still disorder, confusion, with difficulty dispatch the Busienes at Court. Take in a causa pendoris, Watkinsons answer and Matthew Lithgoes informacion. After this venture to the Fountain, where I find the Chancellor, Subdean Wright, Dr. Thane, Mr. Bennett and Mr. Garner. I come late to the meeting and venture not in a Bottle.

16 After less quantity of Elixir take 4 turns on roody, see the News. At 4 meet Mrs. Selby and Mrs. Adams. I pay her 50^{li} and 3^{li} (1 years interest). After that, go there to Dr. Thane where wee stay pints, the heat is kept up by continual, tho little Fuel.

17 Proceed in Fevor, Elixir remorse, complaint of Constitucion, take a walk of 4 Turns, pretend after to Busienes. After prayers in the Evening go (Jack with mee) to see young Mr. Bunbury at Boughton. After buy & read a Hymn to Neptune in praise of Sir George Rook.

18 Recovering, go to Church where Mr. Shawe a petty Canon, has a good sermon on Job.5 v. 17. The News is considerable. After Dinner begin Tortura Torti. After prayers with my 2 elder sons, take the air to Blacon, return to Tortura.

49 C.R.O., EDC.5(1704) No.2, Chester St. Peter: EDP1/78.

19 In a delicate morning, at early prayers. After on roody 4 turns. Write to Mrs. Markland, Asheton, Ward, John Cross, recover'd my weeks misfortune. After dinner call'd by the Mayor and Chancellor to the Fountain, thence see the controverted seat in St. Peter's, thence with them and Mr. Cowper at Mr. Hollands, thence return to Dr. Thane, Mr. Shawe petty Canon and Mr. Hodgson at the Fountain where wee part in pints.

20 A thick and palpable Fogg in the morning. After early prayers I take a walk of 4 Turns, Jack with mee, am extremely refresht. See the News dull suspending. After dinner at 2 races on roody, one for the Bell, the other for a Cup of 4^{li};13;4d. This Mr. Callys horse getts easily. After at the Hall where drink in it. After this – home where apply to Busienes. Mr. Massies 2 daughters Ann and Margaret see us first today.

21 Ash Wednesday severely cold. At early prayers, thence after a walk of 4 Turns in Busienes turn Carranza and Richerius Conciliorum. After Evening prayers and Dinner with Mrs. Vaudrey, Cowper and Murrey at the Fountain too cheerfully for the night and till 10.

22 I wait on the vice Chamberlain, hee shews mee a Copy of a Grant from K. James 1st exempting Marton Grange from Tith. Hee sees the Chancellor, setts out, I quickly after vid. about 11, come to Warrington about 3 dine on Sparlings. After wait on the Bishop of Man at Sankey Hall, a dull place, see his Lady very weak. Stay an hour with him together with Mr. Legh, the Minister & patron, hence to Beausey about 6. Mr. Atherton comes an hour after, discourse on Elections for parliament keep us up past 12.

23 I hear, (here) first of the Delegates sentence on Lady Grosvenors side. See the House improv'd still in ornaments. After Tea about 11 sett for Holland, at Ayrfield about 2 walk about with J. Cross and the new Tenants. Design more ridding. I receive 20^{li} 10s part of the last years rent. Mr. Molyneux's 5 Guineas and 8s 4d. Ian Hulms ½ years rent from John Cross. Dine there pleasantly on a Tost, in a left Bottle of white wine & cheese. Sett out about 6 come to Wigan & my coz. Holt about 7.

24 St. Matthias day. After dinner I go to Holland, my coz. Holt with mee. The Account of the Milners are stated and the matter fully and greatly manag'd by my Solicitor Sam Prescott. My coz. Holt much more taken with his magniloquence, than John Cross. Jules Milner pays 5^{li} the rest in Distress. Wee stay till 6 and at Tootells Coffee house end in a Taster of good Brandy.

25 What I suspected, my throat infirmity aggravates upon mee to a melancholy degree, confin'd to the House, I betake mee to Tully, De Officio. After dinner I see James Winstanley of Haigh, a joyner but quite an undertaker in Architecture. Wee have some discourse on a Design at Ayrfield. I write my coz. Walmesley and in the Evening my coz. Carter, my she coz. Holt with me. Mr. Holland sees mee here civilly. The pain of my throat aggravates.

26 After a dreadful Night the morning relieves. Tho a sharp day I venture on the journy, set hence before 9, reach Sankey about 11, stay with the Bishop of Man an hour, move him for his interest which hee promises on Mr. Allens behalf in the Case of 50^{li} due from the Island. Hence to Warrington refresht sett out about 2. Mr. Johnson the noted Atturny with mee. Hee is civil on the road, wee come safe D.O.M.G. about 6.

27 After Turns on roody, the slender News. After dinner my brother Jones comes. Wee in the Evening go to the Fountain where over our pints his ambicion to be Chaplain to the Earl of Derby and my History of the late Lord are subjects of the discourse. Mr. Done & I jointly venture a Guinea with Mr. Braithwaite that Gibraltar is not this day in the hands of the Spanish and French.

28 At early prayers. After them repeat my Turns on roody. After that write to Sir Henry Bunbury on Mr. Eatons behalf. To my Bro. Jones sermon in the Choir, a very mean & artfull discourse, moving Concern in his Freinds, contempt in others. Shee is here today. After dinner the Mayor, gentlemen, Clergy and Citizens mount to meet my Lord Bishop, the day is favourable. Hee is mett and regularly attended to his palace by 210 Horse & ten Coaches. At entring his Gates they give three Huzzas, a full and affectionate regard. In the Evening at the Coffee house, thence with my brother Jones to the Fountain. Mr. James Egerton comes to us. Wee transgress our pints. I with Alderman Ince, Mr. Ball & Ned Roberts are wittnesses in my office to Mr. Whitmore of Thurstington his signing and sealing his Will in Duplicates.

MARCH 1 Q.B.E. Court day, the Busienes agreeable to my indisposicion which is relieved by repose. After prayers and the Town at Home not the Fountain.

2 After early prayers 4 Turns on roody. The Chancellor with mee about the seat in St. Peters. I send pipes to Mr. Okes and write to him. After prayers with the Bishop thence among the Jockeys at the Coffee house. End the Evening at the Fountain with Mr. Eaton.

3 At early prayers, thence 4 Turns on roody. I meet here with Mr. Hutton, the seat in St. Peters and Roger Matthew the discourse. I write to my coz. Parre, include a Bill of 25^{li} vid. 15 my own and 10^{li} Ned Roberts. After Books and prayers at Mr. Minshalls shop, then to Ale and Home.

4 A cold and rainy day. Mr. Fogg has an Ordination sermon, 2 priests, 4 Deacons admitted, thence to barren News. After prayers at the Coffee house with Mr. Egerton, thence to my corner and small parcell of Wine.

5 A dry but cool day. I take 4 Turns on roody. Returning Mr. Winstanley gives mee a Tast of Mr. Colleys white port, shews mee Mr. Shakerleys Letter wherein Bradley Name omitted. Recourse to Farndon race where Mr. Egertons Mare getts the smal plate. After Busienes and prayers a walk, Jack with mee, on roody. I tell him of my design to take him with mee on the visitacion. In the Evening Mr. James Egerton and I take our pints at the Fountain.

6 A cool morning. I write to Dr. Bullen and Mr. Gandy. After Dinner equip for Farndon stopt by Crowds at Eaton Boat, hasten thence after 2, Jack with mee. Come before the race begins, see the company and competitor Horses, vid. Rock, Lord Manners, Camel, Lord Mollineux's rid by Mr. Massey & Godolphin, Mr. Egertons, they make 3 fine close Heates. Camel the 1st, Godolphin the 2nd, Rock getts the 3rd Heat. After the race, almost a race home about 6 a clock. In the Evening meet according to appointment on the Field at the Golden Talbot. Sir Peter Soames, Mr. Ch. Cholmley, Mr. Cowper, Yate &c. Wee are cheerfull and free in our flattering sophisticated wine.

7 Severely ill and apprehend mischief, even poyson, from the wine. After dinner the 2 Cowpers, Yates, Aldersey come and divert the melancholy drink my domestic. Wee freely after this adjourn to the Fountain where the Mayor joins us. Wee are cheerful to Bottles each and part about ten.

8 Inauguracion Anniversary 3rd celebrated. The Fevor continues, yet I write to Mr. Powel Schoolmaster of Preston and Mr. Woods of Rainford.[50] Examine 3 Wittnesses on Ashe's Will. Gentlemen invited meet the Mayor &c. in the Hall where a Ring consisting of 100 or near the number. The Queens Health is drunk on the Knee, 6 others standing. I apply at Night to Elixir.

9 After a walk of 4 Turns refresht. See the News which secures Gibraltar to the 27th of the last month. Indisposition and repose take up the Time. After prayers in the Town. End at the Fountain in a pint of Claret.

10 A cool calm day. Write to Dr. Pope and inclose a Bill of 30^{li}, to Mr. Travers and Mr. Shawe of Preston. See Mr. Egerton instituted to Astbury. Richard Sherlock, Butler of Queens College Oxon calls on mee. I lend Mr. Chapman on Account 10^{li}. See the Warden of Manchester at Mr. Pickmore. Hee remembers his former promise to mee, to bee a remembrance to the Bishop on my part in case of the Registry. In Accounts with Mr. Boucher I write full to Mr. Moulding in a Case of parish Clerks depending at St. Asaph.

11 A brisk morning. I take 4 Turns on roody. Mr. Philip Egerton has a sermon in the Quire on Joel 2 v. 13, indifferent oratory, worse elocucion a great auditory. The news affords nothing but expectacion. After Evening prayers and Books, I am invited near 8 to Mr. Egertons, where after a delicate cold supper, a Bottle of Wine, Himself, his Brother and Mr. Done made up the Conversacion to 12 at Night.

12 Down to roody, exercise, 4 Turns. I acknowledge my Answer as Executor to Mr. Dod, to Wainwright's Bill upon oath, before Mr. Hulton and Mr. Houghton. Write to Mr. Kippax, Sam Prescott and John Cross. In the Evening at the Fountain with Dr. Thane & Mr. Bowyer. Wee are cheerful above our pints and part at 9.

13 A severe cold day and high wind. John Cross begins on the Clerk's seat in the office. After Busienes, to the Coffee house where Gibraltar agen brought into danger and the Lords and Commons continuing and multiplying their unhappy Quarrells. Mr. Royston of Cheadle calls on mee on the matter of Election of those wardens. After prayers I go to the White Talbot and at his request sit with the Warden of Manchester above 2 hours at Ale.

14 A very surprising deep snow faln 4 or 5 inches. At early prayers I write to Mr.Styth. Mr. Legh of Lym has an elegant and rhetorical discourse on 'Bee ye sober and vigilant &c'. After Dinner with the Chancellor to Dr. Thanes, intent

50 *Ibid.*, EDC.5(1704) No.6, Rainford.

on the work at the Office. The snow wholly dissolvd before Night. In the Evening at the Fountain with a fully company, the Chancellor, ArchDeacons Booth & Entwisle, Dr. Thane, Mr. Legh the preacher, Mr. Royston and Callis. The discourse on Elecions, & House of Commons free and honest.
15 A cold and rainy day. Dip in an anonymous Book stil'd An Abstract of Canons &c. heretofore unknown and unpractic'd with a learned and severe Answer. Court day, I examine 4 wittnesses on Robinsons Will. In the Evening return to the Abstractor.
16 A cold morning. After prayers take 4 Turns on roody, see the spoyls the late high Tides have made. After news and Books in the Evening at the Fountain with Mr. Swarbreck. Hee treats mee with his fortunate circumstance and a Bottle.
17 A rainy day. I go with the Chancellor to Lord Bulkley on Mr. Roystons account, with Mr.Minshall to Mr. Egerton on his own Account, both seem to succeed mediocriter. After about 12, Mr. Minshall and I call at Mr. Bell's take a morning draught of Wormwood Ale. Sir H. Bunbury, his Lady and Bro. return from London. My S. and I visit and stay with till 9.
18 A cold moist day. Mr. Fogg has a good sermon on (Watch & pray &c). The News has the parliament dissmist by her Majestie in a speech Wednesday last and prorogued to May 1st. The Fort of Verue taken, hopes of Gibraltar. After Evening prayer, I visit Alderman Allen. After home and proceed in Sulpitius Severus.
19 Write to Mrs. Ward of Legh, Styth, Hoghton. Mr. Patten comes about Mr. Levers Will perplexes. About 1 set out for Eaton Boat, come about 2. I dine meanly on Fish, wee drink public healths pretty freely. The company beside the Chancellor and fraternity, Dr. Thane, Mr. Fogg, Capt. Spark, Mr. Mather who gives here Mr. Russells anniversary treat. At home safe D.G. about 7.
20 A fair day. I take 4 Turns on roody. See the News, Verue desperat, Gibraltar uncertain. A confluence to the race, 3 horses the 1st, 2 the 2nd Heat. Mr. Egertons Godolphin getts both & the plate, A Tankard about 27^{li} value. In the Evening at Sir H. Bunburys with Mr. Legh of Lym till 2, the discourse run on parliament, elecion speeches.
21 Extremely indispos'd, hot, unhappy. Young Mr. Poole and Mr. Bootle of Liverpool call on mee. Mr. Booth makes choice of Mr. Houghton and an uncle of his, his Tutors before the Chancellor. After the yong men and I take a morning draught (4 pints of white wine) at the Fountain over this, acquaintance and relacion contracted. Elecion at Leverpool, Brazen Nose and Mr. Shippen a Fellow there particularly mencioned. After dinner and repose Books. Mrs. Anderton sees us at Night. I fly to Elixir.
22 After an unhappy morning, better and cooler. A court day and the last of the Terme. Mr. Massie shows his deed wherein the Seat or Seats in St. Oswald is generally mencioned and Mr. Jones the Churchwarden, produces 3 schemes (wherein the seat is mencioned) to the Bishop who seems easie & acquiesing. After noon a brisk race of 4 Hunters wherein Mr. Colley is victor. I am with Mr. Bruen, Mr. Cowper, Sir H. Bunbury after at the Hall, drink sack in the plate.

Examine 2 Wittnesses against Ottiwell, write to the Bishop of Kildare, prepare for my journy tomorrow.

23 After Letters to Dr. Bullen and Mr. Gawdy, expectacion of the Bishop of Man and Dinner, I set out for Lancashire, storms accompany all the way. I come to Warrington about 5, proceed not, discourag'd by the weather. Mr. Page here shews mee his peticion and Warrant for a rehearsing. Mr. Bunbury of Boughton interr'd today at Stoak.

24 I go from Warrington about 7. An unusual Fall of Snow happens betwixt Ashton and Wigan, a Cloud slic'd larg. I come steep'd to Wigan before 10 stay and dine with my coz. Holt. About 2 mount again. My coz. Holt brings mee in a clear afternoon to Chorley. Wee stay an hour there in politicks, hee seems apprehensive of Fanatick designs. I go home past 5 reach Preston about 8. Am at the Mitre, see Mr. Powel the schoolmaster, hee delivers mee my coz. Fleetwoods Book of 16 Discourses of Relative Duties from the Author.

1705

MARCH 25 Annunciacion a brisk frost. After News and Coffee mount about 9 come to Garstang by 11, the Inn full of indifferent company among whom young Barth. Fleetwood. I hasten to the Church Town. Mr. Richmond absent I dine with his 4 children and curat Latus. Thence about 2 for Lancaster, come thither by way of Cockerham, about 5 to the Sun. Thence find out Mr. Vaudrey, Mr. Blackburn &c. I am with all his Lawyers and after an indifferent Bottle such a Lodging.

26 I attend at the Court the Forenoon, meet young Jeffrey Prescott after at Coffee with him. Thence visit Dr. Fenton, hee treats i.e. dines mee with Cockles. I stay at his house in Swinburn & Godolphin till 1. Thence to Mr. Winckley and Langton, thence to the Court. The great Cause comes on, Blencoe Judg, Mr. Blackburn shows concern. The Cause open'd and evidence produced on both sides. My part is to give the form of the oath of an Executor which gave an ill aspect to the Codicil the Executor had writt and cancell'd. The Judg sees the perplexities proposes heads for reference which are agreed to and past into a rule. The controverted Estate to bee distributed into 3 parts, one to Lever 2 to Blackburn.[1] A most severe cold day. I loose my 10s sword in Court. In the Evening at a Bottle at the Sun with Mr. Vaudrey & Richmond, rudely disturbed all night.

27 A rainy and stormy morning. Young Hebbletwaite, Mr. Trotter's clerk offers his services to mee, I appoint him on tryal. About 10 sett hence the same way I came to the vicarage of Garstang. Mrs Blackburn, Ashurst, Vaudrey, Richmond, follow. I dine slenderly here. Mr Blackburn owns my kindnes to serve him, gives me for Viatici 3 Guineas. About 4 set hence come in good

1 Lancashire Record Office (L.R.O.), Lancashire wills; *ibid.*, Quarter Sessions Orders QSO 1700–1706, for Lever v. Blackburn.

company before 7. At the Mitre see the High Sheriff Spencer deep in wine, hee is civill to mee, tells mee he is above the world & has 15000[li] at command. Mr. Ashurst and Mr. Vaudrey drink a Bottle in my Chamber wee part about 11.
28 A fair calm day To the Coffee House where a Law Confluence. Thence to Dr. Holbrook entring into a Rheumatism. Here Mr. Peploe comes and tells me the passages betwixt him & Mr. Whitehead, living unprofess'd, and since of the resentment of his widow & daughter at some general expressions of his in the pulpit. After this I meet with Mr. Pemberton of Penwortham, drink wormwood, at the Dog with him, call on Mr. Vaudrey at Mrs. Pattens with the 2 sisters Stanley. We mount about 11 come by Eccleston call at Mr. Hoskins, Heskin Hall, whence Mr. Egerton gon to Chester. Wee part near, I thoro Mawdsley and Bishpam, come into Lathom, call on my coz. Hill at Blith Hall, hee receives mee civilly an hour or 2. Thence to Ormskirk about 6, meet here with Mr. Wm. Holland, Mr. Tuck &c drink my Bottle and to bed at Mr. Dods.
29 A very rainy day. After Mrs. Dod talkt her Busienes and reminded mee of Accounts, Mr. Kippax and I about 11 mount, come to Rainford about 12, go to the Chapell open the Commission, dine dully, examine before 9, six Wittnesses.[2]
30 Proceed in Examinacion. See the neglected school, dine as before, examine 6 witnesses more. It rains and snows exceedingly,all Streams grow to rivers and the road is fill'd. Yet about 6 Mr. Stratford, W. Plumb and I mount, near Rainford and near Bold, pass the swelling waters with some difficulty. Suspect but find Sankey cause of the ebb Tyde very passable. Wee come (D.G.) safe about 9 to Warrington, rejoice at our success.
31 A fair morning, the Fresh swells at the Cawsey, the Tide returning draws it into the Common store. Wee set hence about 8 and come D.O.M.G. safe home about 12. Afternoon in repose, Busienes, Friends. With Sir Henry Bunbury in the Evening.

APRIL 1 A cold blowing day. The Bishop preaches on Phil. 2 v 5. The News not yet express on Gibraltar. Read the Sermon of my coz. Fleetwood on the 5th Commandment. After prayers &c Coffee House. Mr. Egerton and I see, sit with, scarce drink with, Mr. Chancellor, the time taken up with melancholy conjectures on the great and most public Altercacions suppos'd to be made this Night by the Queen in Council.
2 At early prayers intent after on the work in the Clerks office and busienes. Write to my coz. Parr, Mr. Wm. Taylor and the Bishop of Kildare. After prayers with Archdeacon Booth wait on Sir Henry Bunbury, where in company and parliament discourse we draw out 3 hours and a Bottle.
3 A fine springing day. After 4 Turns on roody and Busienes at the Coffee house the News secures Gibraltar and makes Lord Cholmley of the Privy Council. After Noon the Chancellor calls on me, I go with him to Toms of the Rose & Crown where over 3 pints of wine hee imparts to mee the revival of Dr.

2 C.R.O.,EDC.5(1704)No 6, and (1705) No 8, for the case against the master of Rainford School.

Norris his Applicacion to Mrs. A.G. and the reconciliacion of his late silence to it. This with other private matters fully instrusted Mr. Shaw from Beausey with mee on Busienes.

4 A warm day. The National Fast celebrated. I write to Mr. Rider, Mr. Fogg has an excellent Discourse on Exodus 33 v.15. In Books variously till Evening prayer. After Meat in the Evening 3 or 4 Turns on roody.

5 At early prayers, a brisk morning. Write to my coz. Holt and John Cross. To Busienes and Books the rest.

6 A sharp day Good Friday. Dr. Entwisle has a curious discourse on 1 Ep. Peter c. 2, 21. The News is not so full of Changes as was expected. Wee still expect and fear. To Books variously till Night. Richard Woods pays Fees on Account of the late Commission 5^{li}.

7 After early prayers a walk of 4 Turns, Jack with mee on roody, with my Lord who speaks of and expects against some particulars in the Dean Rurals account vid. those for and to the seal keeper. He fixes on the 2 Daies for his Visitacion of the 5 adjacent Deanaries.[3] Paid Mrs. Oulton for Beer since Feb. 1703. 7^{li}.19, to Peggy Birchall 3^{li}.

8 Easter Day calme but sharp. My Lord Bishop has an excellent discourse on 1 Cor. 15 v. 20.Sanctissimam coenam participamus. Det D.O.M. vitam condignam.[4] Mr. Archdeacon Booth's little son the youngest bury'd to night. At the Funeral a conference betwixt Sir Henry Bunbury and Mr. Kendrick the lawyer. After the Funeral wee are late past 12 with Sir Henry Bunbury. The News makes Sir John Lake victor over the French.

9 A sharp day. Mr. Thompson of Lymm has a good discourse on Romans 8 v. 34. To Books till prayers. After them to the Chancellor with Mr. Collier, once a Fellow of All Souls, now a parson in Kent. Mr. Colly, Dr. Nichols discourse academical fresh, loyal, diverting, wee dispatch 3 or 4 Bottles of Port part about 9.

10 A calmer day. I wait on the Bishop who speaks to mee of Alderman Ince his behaviour to his eldest son, and of Mr. Fitzherbert his seducing proselytes. I wait on Sir Roger Mostyn at Sir Henry Bunbury. At part of Mr. Walkers sermon on Lev. 6 v. 4 before the Judg & Sheriff. After dinner fall in with Mr. Walker, Minshall, Gibson at the Baggs. Wee drink our Tall Boys thence home.

11 After a rainy night fair. I write to Mr. Swainson and in his to Mr. Rowel ex obliquo. To my coz. Holt about a Horse he lately bought. Pay Mr. Worger on Account 30 sh. the later half of years Tax for the office 2^{li}. In Books, Jewel and Busbequius. In the Evening in the Town not in company.

12 A springing rain at early prayers. At the Hall as formal Tenant to the precipe in the Bishop of Kildare's Estate, Moreton and Demandent in Mrs. Anne Gerards Estate, Crewood. See a poor woman Ellen Bury try'd and found

3 The deaneries were Chester, Wirral, Bangor, Middlewich and Frodsham.

4 Trans: 'We partake of the most Holy Supper. May God the best and greatest grant [me] a worthy life.'

guilty of the murther of her Bastard Child. I write to Mr. Asheton and send 6 Licences. In Busbequius. In the Evening at the Fountain with Mr. Powel, my coz. Fleetwood's Nephew and young Mr. Ja. Rothwell of Newton.
13 At early prayers. Good News by way of France that Admiral Lake has sunk 2 taken 3 ships of Pontis Squadron before Gibraltar. We expect it better. Mr. Powel dines with us and staies a Glass after. Yong Rothwell being ingaged in the Town, I proceed in Busbequius. In the Evening Mr. Peters calls on mee, wee go to the Fountain, talk on the Elecion Controversy at Leverpool. Hee treats mee here with 3 pints of Viana.
14 A cool but springing day. Prorata Account with Mr. Boucher. Pay him on them 3 Guineas, write to Mrs. Styth, Houghton, Vaudrey and John Crosse. In Busbequius and som busienes pay John Cross l^{li};19^{s}. In the Evening call'd to the Fountain where the Chancellor, Archdeacon Entwisle, Dr. Norris, Mr. Lupton, this day instituted to Richmond, and I drink 5^{s}, a token from Mr. Pemberton of Bedale, with Addition. Part at 9, I write too to Mr. Gandy.
15 I take early in a fine morning, 4 Turns on roody. Mr. Colliere has a very ingenious discourse on 2 Cor. 2 v. 11. The success of Sir John Lake is confirmd still from France only. Mr. Lupton in the afternoon has a good & grave discourse on St. Luke. I proceed in Jeuell near the end. About 9 go to Mr. Lupton at the Falcon, wee fall into the affairs of Church and learning and carry on the discourse over 3 pints till 2 in the morn.
16 A wett cold day very indispos'd, with my Lord who gives mee Notes printed to disperse to the Rectors and Vicars, to discover the Sequestracions and Hardships of the Parliament Times. I while away the day in the Athenae Ox and end Jewell. Sir Henry Bunbury, Mr. Booth, Mr. Adams & myself are about 9 a clock forenoon at Mr. Hurlestons House, desir'd wittnesses, to see him, his son Charles & Brother sign and seal Articles of marriage betwixt John his eldest son & Mary daughter of Sir Jo. Williams of the County of Hereford.
17 A springing small rain. I apply to and read Busbequius his 4 Epistle Legationis Turcia. Write to Mr. Massie about his vote at Leverpool. No Express yet from Admiral Lake but his success otherwise confirmd. With my Lord after prayers. Hee insists on the residue of the Account of the Deanaries, scruples at the viaticas expensas determins only the latter part of the visitacion. After this to the Fountain where Mr. Chancellor, Dr. Norris, Dr. Thane, Mr. Bouchier, Dr. Nicols, Mr. Ogle. The discourse is Dr. Norris, Indian Expedicion, Lady Calveleys Age and Infirmity.
18 A soft rain. At early prayers. Thence to Busienes and Busbequius. Finish his 4 pleasant Epistles Legationis Turciae. After Dinner Mr. Chancellor calls on mee, wee go to my Lord who receives our visit kindly. Wee are on severall matters particularly on the Visitacion. Hence the Chancellor and I go to the Fountain, hee communicates to mee the Beginning and progress of Dr. Norris, his applicacion to Mrs. Ann Gerard. Hence to Mr. Minshals shop. Hee and I visit Alderman Parnel sick, thence to the Feathers where wee part in a pint of Ale.

19 A brisk kindly morning. After early prayers to busienes. I write to Mr. Vaudrey about his being chosen Churchwarden of Bowden. Pay the Chancellor for 22 Institucions $14^{li}:13^{s}:4^{d}$. Court begins with clamor of Mr. B. and H.[5] the Chancellor too much mov'd, admonishes them to decency and regular peticions. I examine 5 Wittnesses on 3 several Matters. After that about 8 to the Fountain where with Mr. Pickman and Eaton relax over 3 pints.
20 After early prayers examine 2 more Wittnesses against Harrison. At the Coffee house, see the News. 5 Men of Warr repeated lost of Pontis Squadron, Confusion at Constantinople the Grand Seignor fled to Asia, the Visier depos'd. In the Evening vid. about 5 at the Funerall of Mr. Jonathon Bruen bury'd at St. Maries. Thence at Mr. Swarbrecks with the Chancellor, Mr. Wright, Dr. Thane, Mr. Boucher and Mr. Robert Warburton treated by Dr. Norris. Here Mr. Wright has sharp reflecions on his being appointed to preach the visitacion sermon. Thence Dr. Thane, Mr. Boucher & I in 2 pints at the Fountain.
21 Indispos'd down to roody 4 turns, write to Mr. Stratford Archdeacon about Sir William Ellis Bond and my son Jack to John Crosse. After noon with Mr. Minshall at the Plume of Feathers thence at the Fountain end in a pint thence home.
22 Mr. Subdean Wright has a good discourse on [?] The News in expectacion. After prayers the Evening spent in a Walk and Books.
23 St. George's Day. Her Majesties coronacion 4th Time celebrated. After a walk Letters. People crowd in to the races, the Great City plate easily got by Mr. Egerton, the Horse scarce escapes the resentment of the Mob. Another ridiculous and false race betwixt Mr. Minshals Mare & pony diverts the Feild. After the race, The Queens health &c drunk in the Pentice, many Gentlemen treated. After with the Chancellor, Sir Wm. Meredith, Mr. Callys and Boucher, drink 5s a token from Archdeacon Stratford to whom I write this (not Satur)day.
24 Indispos'd, confin'd at Home 2 other Books than Busienes. After dinner Mr. Bennet of Knowsley and Mr. Murrey of the Island see mee. Wee freely remember the House of Derby. After a Turn to Mr. Minshalls where Mr. Murrey buys a Bible for $1^{li}:2^{s}:6^{d}$. Wee go, Mr. Denton with us, to the Fountain where wee carry on the discourse in singular pints.
25 St. Mark's, reliev'd something by Elixir. I wait on Major Walthall to my Lord with 2 Requests, unwilling 1st, to deliver up his Bond for security against the Quare impedit; 2^{d} to give in the presentacion in order to have it entr'd. After noon with them, the Mayor, Mrs. Wever, Minshall, Hulton freely at the Fountain, the rest gon Mr. Hulton and I add our pints in Court discourse.
26 Severely enough dispos'd for Busienes. Examine Wittnesses in Heardsley, Holts, Harrisons Busienes. Recover but falsly with a pint at Night.
27 Continue fevorish. The Chancellor and I wait on the Bishop, hee tells us his despair of performing the Journy and inclines to put off the visitacion, to

5 B – Bouchier or Boucher; H – Harrison.

September. The Chancellor shews usual resentment. The Bishop at last deliberates till to morrow. In the Evening novi Fluctus.[6] Mr. Egerton of Eccleston and I dispose of 2 pints at the Ship over which an Account of Mr. Heskins domestic temper surprises mee much.

28 Under uneasy Apprehension at the weeks divercion. Divert in Books and difficult repose. My Lord determines Q.F.F.E.F.S. to visit this summer. After prayers the Chancellor sends for Dr. Thane and myself to the Fountain where I stil with the heat of 4 pints among us advances the Fevor and at Night repeat, but mildly Elixir. Give a Bill of 15^{li} to my sister Partington.

29 Sad reflections torment. After 8 down to roody amplify the exercise which occasions my stay from church. Supply it with Jack's reading and Books. After prayers and Tertullian a Turn (Jack with mee) on Blacon marsh. Recreate with a mixt Tankard of Claret and Ale.

30 At early prayers. After good effects of last Night Elixir, much more cooler, easy, happy (D.G.) I write to Mr. Price about a Family at Bodvary pretending to be related to him. After Dinner apply to Busienes particularly presentments enter the 5 home Deaneries. In the Evening at the Coffee house full of Lord Kilmorey and other Gamesters. Sir Henry Bunbury and Mrs Ann Eyton sit with us in the Evening.

MAY 1 A soft rain auspitious to the summer. At early prayers. After apply to Busienes and particularly the Entry of 8 presentacions till Noon, then to a dinner elegant with Sir Henry Bunbury a delicate Rhombe prandii caput.[7] After with Sir H. to see Sir Roger Mostyn at the Golden Talbot where they part in a Bottle. After prayers call'd to Mr. Cottinghams when Alderman Ince, Wilson, Mr. Hulton and Churchwardens tell mee they have chosen a seat in St. Oswalds for my wife. Wee talk on parish affairs wherein Mr. Hulton magnifice ubicunque se effert,[8] Cosens & Tenants violently drawn in. After his noise I sit with the rest an hour, part freindly.

2 A calme sweet day. Apply to Busienes, take 4 Turns on roody. Pay Mr. Jones the sadler, for my new Sadle &c $1^{li}:11^{s}$, write to T. Gorst, include to him a Letter from the Bishop of Kildare. In the Evening return to Books and end that in the domestic proporcion of Claret.

3 A blowing morning not stormy. I write to Mr. Trotter, my Coz. Holt, John Crosse. I examine this Court day 3 wittnesses on Mrs. Harveys nuncupative Will and as many against Barns Dennis.

4 After early prayers at the Coffee house. The News gives an ominous defeat of the French on the Moselle, the Emperor dead or dying, the K of France ill of the Gout, that of Spain phrantic of a Feavor, the Seige of Gibraltar rais'd or turnd to Blockade. The Canary Islands shook, broke and almost depopulated by

6 Trans: 'new disturbances'.
7 Trans: 'turbot the main dish for lunch.'
8 Trans: 'bears himself everywhere with magnificence.'

a terrible Earthquake and new Etnas form'd. Lady Calveleys Funeral solemnly celebrated, attended by many Gent and coaches. I attend to Christleton. I draw a Nominacion of Mr. Robert Wright A.B. to Winwick school. Mr. Legh signs and seals it, in my presence. My Lord admitts and Licences him. At 5 I attend on Mr. Fitzherbert to the Bishop who receives him candidly and admonishes him fully and freindly about admitting many more than his own Family to Mass and openly to the Affront of the Laws and religion established humanitate summa cum gravitatis iunctanius[9]. Mr. Fitzherbert promises caution & observance of the Monicion with thanks and after a friendly pipe recedes.[10] About 6 Mr. Colly, schoolmaster Wright and I go to the Fountain where wee join Dr. Thane and Mr. Fogge. After our civil pints wee part about 9.

5 After early prayers a usefull walk on roody 4 Turns. A soft genuine rain falls in it a visible and sensible plenty D.O.M. I write to Mr. Topping & Empson, pay John on Account of his wages 1^{li}. In Busienes afternoon. After prayers at the Fountain with the Chancellor Mr. Horton and Mrs. Hulton, indifferent conversacion for an hour & a pint.

6 Sanctissimae Eucharistiae participes sumus.[11] Dr. Thane has a good sermon on [?]. The News recovers the Emperor, and makes the K. of France almost desperately ill. In the Evening Mr. Boucher treats Dr. Thane and Myself with one Bottle French wine.

7 A fine morning draws mee to roody 4 Turns refresh. The News makes another Turn in Constantinople favorable to the peace of Carlowitz. Apply to Busienes till the Evening then at the Fountain with Mr. Chancellor, Dr. Thane, Dr. Norris, Mr. Horton, Mr. Colly pretty liberally. After receive Mr. Marsdens Latin Letter.

8 After early prayers 4 Turns on roody refresh. Mr. Crane calls on mee, at his request I write to Mr. John Worsley husband to Mr. Byroms widow about $23^{li}:10^{s}:8$ receiv'd by Mr. Byrom of Dr. Sherlock estate. The residue of which is to day, distributed amongst the Legatees. A Mountebanck of a numerous Grex fill the street and houses with speculacion. In the Evening to the Fountain with Mr. Crane, Peter and Robert Eden, here freely our Bottles a peece.

9 Indispos'd examine a tedious wittness against Dennis.[12] After Noon and repose busienes & Books. In the Evening my S. and I late enough with Mr. & Mrs. Peck at my Lady Bunburys.

10 I take a walk to the Navigacion Work. The last Court this Term, small Busienes, no Wittnesses. In the Evening at the Chancellor and Dr. Thane here Mr. Marsdens Latin Letter read. Part in 4 pints.

11 A brisk cool morning. At early prayers. After 4 Turns on roody write to Mr. Cholmley of Holdford, send him in a Box Dr. Hicks 2 Vol. in a paper, Dodwell

9 Trans: 'with the utmost humanity [?combined with seriousness.]

10 See J. Bossy, *English Catholic Community 1570–1850* (London, 1975), pp 175–6, for details of the Fitzherbert family.

11 Trans: 'we are partakers of the most Holy Eucharist.'

12 C.R.O., EDC.5 (1705), No. 3, Dodleston.

and Allens Letters. Examine 1 wittness against Dennis. In the Evening at the Fountain freely with Dr. Thane, Mr. Murrey and Hodgson.
12 Indispos'd in my Head. After a small walk draw from the right Arm about 9 ounces of Blood, am very sick and fainty. Write 2 Letters to Mr. Massie about going to Leverpool; read & repose the rest.
13 Not fully recover'd yet resolve on a journy to day. Dr. Entwisle preaches on Rom. 8 v. 34. Dyer makes the French King dead of an Apoplexy. After Dinner Dr. Entwisle, Mr. Massie and I call at Sir Henry Bunburys drink a Bottle of Claret with him. Set hence in a fine afternoon past 3, go easily, the way fair and dry, come to Warrington past 7, refresh and to Bed about 11.
14 Rise about 5 in a delicate morning. Indispos'd from early hurry of the Coach and Carts. About 6 wee set out, call at Beausey, where the Family being in Bed, wee stay not, proceed the lower way by Penketh, Croston and Roby, a tedious long way, come tir'd to Leverpool about 11. Find the Exchange crowded and the Elecion begun. Call at the Talbot, thence to the crowd, meet with some Friends of both sorts. Wee 3 join Mr. Marsden and others, go to the Coffee house, consult, about 1 wee are brought to the Railes near the Bench and give our votes (about 8 of us)singly for Mr. Clayton. The Elecion, Noise and hurry proceed in great variety, the windows & Balconys filld with Female spectators. Mr. Massie & I dine at our Inn, thence I draw him to Mr. Swarbrecks where I treat him with a Bottle, thence to the Theatre of Action. Wee attend till near 6 when the Election finisht. Norris has 393, Clayton 453, Johnson abov 500 votes, a good Event. I return to Mr. Swarbrecks and with my young kinsman Ralph Prescott and Mr. Peters continue past 9. Thence to my Inn and after some time in Dr. Entwisles room, to my chamber.
15 About 7 rise not without indisposicion. Visit (Mr. Styth with mee) both the elected Members. Mr. Clayton receives mee freely, friendly the other civilly. From the latter to Mr. Hoghton, thence to my coz. Prescott. The News here brings the death of the Emperor. I apply to the Execucion of 2 Commissions for swearing the Executors of Preeson & Daniel Wills. This brings the day near 12 and the Rock Boatmen are importunate. Alderman Cleveland, Mr. Styth & Peters brings us to the Boat. Dr. Entwisle and myself (Mr. Massie return'd last night to Warrington) have a delicate & speedy passage. Wee call on Mr. Pool at Bebington where place and persons sordidus et sordidati.[13] Wee stay about 2 hours entertaind by him with Brandy, Ale, Rusticity, the discourse Election and Neutrality. Wee come safe to our Focos (D.G.) about 6.
16 Indispos'd repose and recover. Apply to some Busienes write to Mr. Topham to give the Clergy Notice of the Election here. In the Evening the Chancellor sends for mee to the Fountain, where over 2 pints, I acquaint him with our Leverpool expedicion, and particularly how the best Quality were on Clayton, the meaner & Fanatics on Norris's part.
17 After a brisk walk on roody refresht. To the Church where Dr. Entwisle

13 Trans: '[place] filthy and [persons] dirty.'

continues a discourse on Rom. 8.34. I dine with my Lord Bishop where among others Mr. Wright and his sons Ned & Jack, lately Batchelors from Cambridge. After dinner with Mr. Wright at the Chancellors. Mr. Harper, Dr. Entwisle and Mr. Boucher, a tedious attendance. In the Evening at the Fountain with Dr. Thane & Mr. Shawe over 2 pints. This is twentieth anniversary day since my Lidia dy'd. D.O.M. det mihi vitam faeliciorem.[14]

18 After early prayers in a brisk morning 4 Turns on roody, fresh to Busienes. I receive from my Lord the Archiepiscopal Mandate for Elecion to Convocacion. The News Letters give little of foreign, account of many elections in which many new. The Town is instant on meeting Mr. Shakerley, all who have horses mount them. I go in Lady Otways Coach with Dr. Thane. Wee with many of the Horse hover at Christleton. Hee comes there about 6; the company not dispos'd in good order bring him in about 7. The Horse join the Foot at Boughton both together computed to 500. Dr. Thane I & go into Sir H.B. drink a Bottle there. After I go to the Raven where Sir Tho. Billot, Sir Roger Mostyn, Sir H. Bunbury, Mr. Egerton, Mr. Shakerley, Mr. Bruen & 20 men, minor Gent. The near Elecion confusdly talkt on; 9 Bottles drunk, the company dissolv'd.

19 Refresht, tho later, with a walk on roody. To busienes and Chronology. In the Evening the Chancellor calls on mee, wee at the Fountain revive the matter of Dr. Norris. Hee shews mee a Letter from the Dr. where in a hansom assercion or confession of his sincerity and Devocion for the Church of England. Wee dispatch 2 pints and ½. After at the Coffee house see the News, the forran yet in suspencion. Poll ends at Lancaster to day Stanley 1760, Shuttleworth 1758, Bradshaw 1162, Farrington 798 Shuttleworth left 500 unpoll'd.

20 I fly to my relief, 4 walks on Roodee thence to the Church where Mr. Fogg preaches. At the Coffee house when Sir. H.B. and Mr. Shakerley consider the new Elecions not to despair. After prayers, I go with Sir H.B. Mr. Shakerley, Mr. Egerton &c to the Shire Hall, where they order the manner of the seats and 5 Tables where the votes are to be taken. After Mr. Shakerley invites the company to his late Lodging in the upper Ward. Here good wine liberally given the conversacion is of Elections parliamentary practice, attempts to Aristocracy &c & holds till 12.

21 The wine hurt only by Quantity. I apply to Busienes of Visitacion, write and inclose a Commission for calling the Clergy of the Archdeaconry to elect a member of Convocation to the Commissary. Write to Mr. Robert Hebblethwaite to come to mee the 7th June. I wait on My Lord with a Catalogue of the Clergy of all the Deaneries in this County. After Busienes &c 8 a clock Go to Dr. Thane, Mr. Callis, J. Cowper his Father in Law Sherwin & Mr. Adams at the Fountain. Wee are on the public subject and part about 10. Mr. Bancks Atturney writes to mee that Mr. Taylor dy'd about 5 a clock in the morning Yesterday.

22 After a Walk on roodee extremely refresht. My Busienes Q.E.B. begins in

14 Trans: 'May God the best & greatest give me a more fortunate life.'

Exhibicions. I wait on my Lord. They go to Church ½ hour after 9. Mr. Wright Subdean has a grave and affectionate discourse on Tim. 1 c. 3 v. 15. Near 12 the Court of Visitacion sitts, the Clergy call'd, my Lord harangues them on these Heads, 1 vita inculpata, 2 Directio Familiarum, 3 Catchisandum Iuniorum 4 Visitacio Infirmorum 5 verbi aeterni studium 6 preces ad Deum pro auxilio divino in munere fungindo assiduae et ardentes, haec agenda consideranda in proxime conventum retulit.[15] I in the Afternoon dispatch Exhibicions. My son Jack (Q.E.B.) is my Clerk in that Busienes. After go into the Town, the Candidates for parliament come in with great numbers, Sir Geo. Warburton and Sir Roger Mostyn are judgd to have the superior numbers.

23 A fine day & favorable to the public work. Crowds of Freeholders flock into the City. The Court begins about 11, they poll at 5 Tables, Archdeacon Booth at one of them, first for his nephew Langham Booth only, hee is noted and deprecated for it. The Favor of the Court rejects the votes for the old Candidates. The Dean in the Evening heads about 60 of the Clergy, they vote in a body, the oaths without distinction are put, an indignity much censur'd. The poll continues till 7, the greater number much on the yong candidates side. Out of the throng of the Gentlemen at the Golden Talbot, Mr. Cholmley of Holdford, Sir Peter Soames, Mr. Thomas Legh & myself, convey ourselves to the Fountain where in 2 hours, wee are followed by Mr. Legh of Lyme, Cholmley of Vale Royal, Downes of Shrigley, Swetenam of Swetenham, Swetenham of Haviley, the Mayor & Mr. Johnson of Macclesfield and several others. Wee are free & cheerfull, the company contracts about 12 and Mr. Cholmley of Holdford, Sir Peter Soames and myself extend the Time in a warmer Bottle till 3 in the morning.

24 With sharp apprehensions and an aching head rise about 9. The necessity overcomes the indisposicion, apply to busienes by Force. To the Church and hear an excellent & close discourse of Archdeacon Shore on the Dignity and Duty of the Ambassadors of Christ on Cor. 5 v. 20. The Bishop varies his discourse on these heads, Lectio sincera precum publicarum, Direccione populi in precibus domesticiis. Hic proponit, An Earncst Exhortacion to Housekeepers, Catechismus inculcatus Inde Bishop Beveridge his Exposicions. In Confirmacionem, Iuniorum praeparacio, Infirmorum visitacio, privata exhortacio popula habenda Studium verbi sacri praesertim T.N. preces continuae. Animarum curae eorum commissarum, cura summa. Dignitatis mundis commissi conservacio fides diligentia. Testimonia de moribus, ordinibus sacris indignorum, Ecclesiarum et mansorum, Ecclesiasticorum sartorum tectorum conservacio Scholarum in Institucionem pauperendo Findacio. Conventus inter Clerum continguum et confabulacio frequens sed non tabernis habenda. Dissentientium tractatio blandior papistarum in parochiis detectio et iudicium,

15 [Summary of Bishop Stratford's charge to his clergy] Trans: 1 a blameless life, 2 direction of families, 3 catechising the young, 4 visiting the sick, 5 study of the eternal word, 6 ceaseless and ardent prayers to God for divine assistance in discharging their office. This agenda was to be considered at the next assembly.'

vita inculpatior qua Clerici sunt. Votum denique pro se de suo mundo defungindo in quo Cleri competitiones invocat[16]. My Brother and sister Jones with us. After dinner apply to Exhibicions till 6, thence to the Hall with the Dean leading about 12 of the Clergy, the mayor about 40 Citizens. The Affair takes a good aspect and by common consent the majority seems to reside on the old ones sides, they seeming to pole 10 for 1 at some boothes several hours together. About 7 the Court adjourns and the 2 old Candidates are carry'd to the Golden Talbot in a vast and from quality, laudable Corona of exulting Freinds. Indispos'd and conscious I extricate mee from all company & sculk home. Here alarm'd with unexpected ill News that the young Candidates are 400 superior in Votes. This strikes a damp on that side and all indevors are used to draw in the Night more votes out of the country.

25 Surprise and Fear on the old, Confidence and triumph on the new ones part, fill the Town. I decline, much as I can, the sight. Mr. Cholmley and others hasten out of Town. The poll goes dully on and equally till 12. Col. Stanley (D.Bt.) is here on the young ones side. Exhibicions detain mee home. Mr. Henchman dines with us. After prayers Mr. Bowyer, Colly, White the new Organist, and I go to the White Talbot for 2 hours at Ale. The poll ends in these Numbers, Offley 3165, Booth 3088, Warburton 2878, Mostyn 2665. The Minority of Booth, hee not being of age till 8th June next is here. The Corrupcion of voteing men, the makeing of 1000 fraudulent Freehold Leases, and double trebles and more voteing of many will in parliament bee objected. A Ball is made by the fortunate Offley, many decline to bee there. In the night the windows of the Cathedral and St. Marys are especially batter'd, concluded to bee done by the party which cry'd all the Week, Down with the Church.[17] My Brother and sister Jones go home about 9, Harry with them.

26 Indispos'd write to my coz. Parr and Mr. Rider about the late Elecions & Exhibicions of the Clergy Instruments. The Town dull on the insuccess of the Elecion. In the Evening I have recourse to my walk, it flatters, not much refreshes.

27 A brisk wind and threatn'd rain. Take a walk early in the Town. See little News save Elecions, at the Coffee house, where Dyers gives Stanley & Bradshaw sett up by the papists and presbyterians. Mr. Fogg preaches. After prayers in Scott's Christian Life. After that Jack with mee, a brisk walk on Blacon Marsh.

28 After a melancholy Night a better day. At Church where Archdeacon Entwisle preaches on Mark 16 v. 20. In the Evening in Dr.Scott, Xtn Life. After

16 A development of the charge in fn.15; a literal translation has not been attempted. The bishop's exhortations touch upon such subjects as public and private prayer, preparation of confirmation candidates, visiting the sick, the study of the Scriptures, the upkeep of ecclesiastical buildings, the provision of education, meetings for discussions among the clergy, the treatment of dissenters and papists, and the general maintenance of spiritual standards.

17 G Holmes, *British Politics in the Reign of Anne*(London, 1967).

this at Sir Hen. Bunburys. After that end at the Ship with the Chancellor and coz. Kendrick in 4 pints of Claret.

29 After a walk fitter for Church where Mr. Kippax of Ormskirk preaches on Prov. 2.14 The sermon is Historicall out of Lord Clarendon, plain, honest but rustick. Wee dine with Sir H. Bunbury, Mr. Shakerley a full company, at the Mayors. After prayers over, I go with Mr. Ward & Mercer the younger to choose coins. At Mr. Collys Cellars for Mr. Lownds, wee tast deep, generously treated.

30 Indispos'd beyond the help of a Walk yet try it. Wee dine on bacon at Mr. Bouchers dogmatically and freely treated. The Mountebank and Funambulo possess the Afternoon. Dr. Entwisle and Mr. Kippax are here spectators. After the Crowd dissolv'd, I refresh mee a little with a walk.

31 After Elixir Cool and easy. William Taylor brings to us Mrs. Betty Sandford to board some time with us. I write to Mr. Vaudrey and Mr. Asheton. I pay Mr. Foulks on Account 30^{li}. In Busienes & Books till Evening, with Mr. Chancellor, Mr. Kendrick and myself in pints at the Fountain.

JUNE 1 At early prayers after a walk of 4 Turns on Roodee. Apply to Books of Visitacion most of the day, which after a short walk at night, concludes in a domestic pint.

2 A fair warm day at the early prayers. Write to John Crosse and Alderman Banks, proceed with the Visitacion Books and end the Catalogue of the Clergy. At Evening Mr. Hicklington a Candidate Deacon for Nun Mounton [Monkton] calls on mee, wee in a Bottle at the Ship remember Mr. Empson.[18]

3 Fine Weather without desir'd rain. Archdeacon Entwisle has a good sermon on 1 Thes. 5 v. 14. I am present at the Ordinacion of 10 Deacons 4 preists. After sanctissimae Coenae particeps Vitam det D.O.M. puriorem.[18a] A crowd of Strangers at Evening prayer among that Lord Cults bound for Ireland makes a Figure. After something read I walk the estuary (Jack along) to Blacon point a fair carpet. After finish the day in domestic quantity.

4 After early prayers write to Mr. Crosly including a Catalogue of the Deans of Chester and to Mr. Empson. Hear my Lord give his grave Charge to the fresh ordain'd dismissing them to their Cures. Pay Mr. Boucher for the Dr. 5 Guineas for the Bishop of Kildare, write to the Dr. and include the Bishops Book and MS containing the State of the Case. Finish a Catalogue of the Clergy for my Lord, Read a Tryal of Witches before Judg Hales.

5 Refresh by 4 shorter Turns on Roodee. Return to Businės, see the News yet imperfect. Apply to the Bishop's Catalogue of the Clergy. Hee returns in the Evening from the Clergy meeting at Warrington. I attend the solemnity of Mrs.

18 L.D.A., CD/PB/7, Nun Monkton; L.R.O., Exhibit Book Dch. 1709. John Hicklington (M.A. Glasgow, deacon York 21 Sept. 1690, priest York 3 June 1694), licenced to the Cure of Nun Monkton, 4 June 1705.

18a Trans: 'I partake of the most Holy Supper. May God the best and greatest grant [me] a purer life.'

Walley's Funeral, just out of Town. After examine 2 Wittnessess against Harrison. My coz. Molyneux bury'd today at Warrington, dead at London and marryd there for (as tis said) 2 months before to Mr. Borran.

6 I examine 2 Wittnesses more against Harrison. Mr. Lambert bound for Worcester, London, Epsom, tells mee of Mr. Trotter's illness, his confidence of success with Dr. Pope. In the Evening at the Fountain with Mrs. Wood, Colly, Bowyer.

7 After 4 Turns on roodee fresh for Court where a moderate Busienes. I examine 2 more Wittnesses against Harrison. After noon about 4 visit Lord Cholmley in his new province the Castle where a good company. The Glass passes an hour, the Mayor and Alderman follow their present of wine. The Chancellor, Capt. Spark, Mr. Warburton, Mrs. Done and I go to the Rose & Crown stay near our Bottles. After return'd home call'd over to Sir H. Bunbury, I stay over good Claret with him and Mr. Thos. Legh till past 2. Robert Hebblethwaite comes to assist us in the Visitacion.

8 Severely indisposd, attend the Bishop. After prayers hee sitts in the Consistory, the Clergy of the Archdeaconry are calld, few appear to choose their proctor for Convocacion. My Lord in Latin explicates the occasion, admonishes them to elect a person fitt and able to serve tempore procelloco Ecclesiam minitante, electio latini inceptam, haesitanter et difficillime procedit. Dr. Marsden consentientibus tandem suffragis in procturem Clerici electus est, procurio consignate conventus dimissus.[19] Some of the Clergy among whom Mr. Poole, take a cold dinner in the palace. I hasten hot to domestic Mackeril. After call'd by Mr. Heath & Iwam Brooks, Brother to Mr. Cottingham, detain'd there by them and Mr. Daniell till 5.

9 After Elixir and a walk refres't D.O.M.G. Natalitia 55 nostris aris & focis celebratur.[20] I write to Mr. Archdeacon, Dr. Stratford and Mr. Parre, to John Crosse. Finish the Bishops Catalogue and deliver it after prayers. I write to the Bishop of Kildare, dispatch a pint with Mr. Eaton at the Fountain and another apud penate.[21]

10 A hott day. Mr. Newton has a long, inconcludant, ambulatory, uncertain discourse. After at the Coffee house where the last Clause of Dyers Letter tells a Battle has hapnd twixt Marlborough and M. Villars, the victory on our side. After Evening prayers to the Coffee house agen where a mixt room of protestants and papists among them Lord Frederic Howard, brother to the late uncle, to the present Duke of Norfolk. Hence to see the Chancellor. After a walk of 4 Turns on Roodee Jack & Heblethwaite part of it with mee thence safe from company home.

11 St. Barnabas day. At early prayers. After in preparacion for our Journy.

19 Trans: ' . . . the Church when a stormy time threatens, the election [? begins in Latin and] proceeds hesitantly and with great difficulty. At length Dr. Marsden is elected proctor of the clergy by harmonious votes, and after this is recorded, the assembly is dismissed.'

20 Trans: '[My] 55th birthday is celebrated at our home and hearth.'

21 Trans: 'at home.'

Lend Mr. Savage on his Note 20li Q.B.E. My Lord Bishop, the Chancellor, Mr. Callys and all the company set out from the palace about ½ hour after 2. Wee ride down the Town with the Coach. The Chancellor and I call'd on light at Mr. Egertons out of the Barrs, wee stay an hour and a Bottle with him. Archdeacon Booth's resentment of my circular Letter part of the discourse. Mr. Egerton write to Mr. Legh intimates the seasonableness of his invitacion of the Bishop to Lyme. Wee proceed past 4 and following the Coach easily come near ½ hour short of it to Derford, a venerable seat where the Bishop is generously receivd. Mr. Edgley reads the prayers for the Evening ab in quine tonam,[22] odly ingrate sound, yet better as to order than expected. My Lord takes Notice of the hast in beginning and also after the end of the preceeding prayer not leaving time for the peoples concurrence in Amen. Hee concurrs in condemning the haste a Fault, but owns not himself guilty. So mild the Animadverter, so bold the Criminal. Here is a numerous appearance of a third Generacion. I walk hence past 8 to Namptwich, come to Mr. Churches a Butcher at my Lord Cholmleys Arms, they provide a private lodging at Mr. Woods next door.

12 Prepare early for Busienes. The Clergy find mee here at new Quarters. Mr. Egerton has a polite, orthodox and learned discourse on 5 Matt. 16. My Lord after entertains the Clergy with a speech of the contents of those at Chester, with some variations. For some time after that ended, I am at the Lamb, thence to dinner and Busienes at Churches. My son Jack is my exhibiting Clerk and performs well. Great applause is given to Mr. Egerton for his Sermon. I am with him, Mr. Wilbraham of Rode and a good company, an hour, after with Archdeacon Vaughan, Mr. Callys &c at a Glass at the Lamb. The Busienes competent.

13 The Chancellor & Mr. Hulton go by Hulmes Chapell. About 10 the Bishop comes from Derford. Wee attend him, the day hott and dusty. Hee sends his compliments by Stapleton into Crewe. Wee have a hott and tedious journy, stop and drink a Bottle of Sam. Ratcliffs Ale at Astbury, come to Congleton after 2. The Mayor an honest gentile firm young man, his Fraternity of 7 Aldermen and others meet the Coach at the end of the Town. The Bishop lights, walks with them, a crowd attending to the Inn, the Georg. Here the Bishop & his company is civilly treated at the charg of the Corporacion. I meet with Mr. Starkie formerly of Stretton among the Aldermen and T. Gorst. Wee set hence near 6 and in a fine evening passing by Gawsworth a showing but low Square House of Human and Horse Lodgings mixt and compos'd, wee come about eight to Macclesfield. Here the Mayor, Mr. Hawkins an Atturney with a more considerable Fraternity meet the Bishop at the end of the Town. Hee alights, walks with the Magistracy thro a Crowd to the Mayors. Here hee is very affectionatly & generously receiv'd. Wee go to our Quarters at the Sun.

14 A messenger is early at Lyme with Mr. Egertons Letter and brings one to mee from Mr. Legh desireing mee to make his Invitacion to the Bishop. I wait

22 The fifth tone in plainsong.

on my Lord with success and write answer accordingly. The Busienes begins. Mr. Royston has an excellent discourse on 1 Cor. 3 v. 3. His subject is Charity but a steady and austere constancy to the Church and its discipline maintain'd, the phrase high & severe, the pronunciacion grave and authoritative, the doctrine sound & majestic, very unusuall in the pulpit, yet forcd by the insincerity of the Age. My Lord proceeds with variacion yet rather of words than matter. Our Busienes is competent here and pretty silently done. The Chancellor gos to Lyme. After busienes with Sr. Wm. Meredith cheerfull at parting.

15 About 9 wee set from this generous Corporacion, come by Adlington to Lyme about 12. The Cascade is shewn in its variety to the Bishop and company. The House to those who had curiosity. About 2 wee sitt to a plentifull Dinner, the Family (Ladies particularly) not yet return'd from Haydock. Mr. Legh is civil and ample in everything. The Bishop and company return with Applause of the House and Master. Mr. Chancellor (such is his inclinacion) and I stop at Mr. Arderns in Stockport wee do some busienes there. The Bishop possesst by his Manchester Friends hastens forward, wee come an hour after. Step to the Wardens, they at supper, the Chancellor warm and chagrin difficultly defends the Delay. After a pipe here return to our Inn and rest.

16 The Busienes begins, my Book defective from the Apparitors negligence.[23] The Warden has a grave and substantial discourse on 1 Tim. 4.16. Hee comments fully on the Ordinacion Vows. My Lord in his Charg recomends the Sermon, more than once to the Clergy. The Busienes here proceeds tollerably and is considerable. Mr. Ashton accounts for 33 Licences. After this I go with Mr. Ashton, Mr. Ashe the Chaplain unluckily follows to the Crown. We are join'd by Mr. Daniel of Daresbury, Capt. Leigh of Westhaughton and another Gentleman. The wine good, warms a difference between Ashe and Capt. Leigh concerning the Elecion at Lancaster. Hee gives the Capt. language very provokeing, the Capt. in a heat, answers it with a slap on the Face with the back of his hand. This hightens the matter almost to Fury, in Ashe to vows, threats, challeng, the company interpose Advice and indevor reconciliacion which is made but imperfectly. About 1, Mr. Asheton and I leaving Ashe, not the Capt., part with the uneasy place. Come home and preparing for bed, Mr. Egerton of Shaw and Mr. Geo. Kenion come to my Chamber, the conversacion easy and acceptable keeps up past 3 in the morning.

17 Severely indispos'd and feverish yet equip and wait on the Bishop who preaches to a great auditory. Wee all dine at the Wardens, an elegant dinner but disordr'd Appetite. I repose after and am easier, visit in the Evening, Jack with me, Mr. Pigot where kindly receiv'd we stay till nine. Return'd to the Inn, take a pint with the Chancellor, so to Bed.

18 The weather continues as all along hitherto hott, glowing. The warden agen invites all the company to dinner. My Lord takes notice of mee of my absence

23 Apparitors were the court summoners responsible for delivering citations to those required to appear in court.

from the Church afternoon yesterday, the Chancellor excuses it from the unseasonable disturbance of the Inn the night before. After the dinner over, I (Jack with me) step to the Library, see it particularly the Volumes of Gravius, those of Grecian Antiquity by Gronovius, Returning to the Inn before 3, wee meet the Bishop unexpected and a company of the Town conducting. The excessive heat makes us resolve to stay an hour, wee are most of that at the Crown. Thence proceed slowly, we reach not the Coach, nor is met by any from Wigan. A strange mark of the rudenes & ingratitude of the place. Wee come past 8 lament in vain our delay. After some discourse with Mr. Marsden to whom I deliver the proxy for Convocacion, I go down to my coz. Holt where I find the smal pox begun on the eldest son.

19 John Cross and Mr. S. Prescott see mee on my Holland affairs. John pays & accounts for 28^{li}. I pay him 5^{li}. for 2 years and 9^{li}.9s. to Margaret Hulme alias Worthington. The Busienes proceeds. Mr. Markland has a good Sermon. Hee proves and reprehends the schism of the Dissenters by apt arguments and examples. My Lord entertains the Clergy with the substance of the same discourse. Wm. Taylor sees mee on Mr. Stratfords Account. Hee acquaints with the demands of the 2 Ladies Henrietta & Elizabeth Stanley. I impart to him my design on Edens House and Mr. Hill. Hee promises his Freindship. The Busienes is considerable and fills our hands. No compliments, no Civility from the Town to my Lord.

20 After Tea, Coffee and preparacion, Dinner, the day scorching. I examine Ed. Rainford against Walthew [24]. About 2 wee go towards the parsonage, meet the Coach, attend it. The Town husht, negative and averse to Civility to the Bishop, shutting their doors & spying thoro windows. At Standish the Chancellor and I deviate from the Coach, fly to the parsonage for cool releif, meet (in Mr. Haydocks absence at Mrs. Birchall of Holland my kinswomans Funeral) with excellent smaler Ale and Bottle of French wine. Mrs. Haydock treats freely. In the cool Hall wee solace an hour or more. The youngest son of Sir Ed. Chisnal and Mr. Rigby son of Alexander are there. Pursuing slowly, tho' in a nearer road, wee reach not the Coach, come a quarter of an hour short, wait on the Bishop, he animadverts it. The Chancellor imperfectly excuses, from the Heat, dust and supposicion that his Lordship did not expect a nearer Attendance. The Ayr of the suspicion morose. I stay supper, venture on a little hott Fish and Capon. Countenances return'd after supper, wee retreat to Quarters at Mr. Fieldings.

21 The Heat continues, I am releived by Elixir. Busienes begins, the Bishop attended. Mr. Armetriding has an earnest affectionate and excellent discourse on 1 Phil. 27. The Clergy with humility, the laity with gravity fully instructed. This seems to have the preference of the other and to bee omnibus [?numis parfecta]. The Bishop remembers it with great applause in his Charge, and Coram Clero desires him to print it. The Busienes here not tumultuous. After 4

24 C.R.O., EDC.5 (1705) No. 8, Rainford schoolmaster.

the Chancellor and Mr. Hulton return for Warrington. Mr. Fisk a Yorkshire Gentleman, haveing Busienes about an original Will staies with us, proposes a paieing pad and acts the Jockey. I write to Mr. Trotter and at parting give 2 Guineas for his pains to Mr. Hebblethwaite.
22 Account with Mr. Price, wait on the Bishop. Mr. Price urges to stay dinner for venison sent on purpose must be eaten. Mr. Boucher reluctant but considers and stays too. Mr. Price is kind to Jack presents him with half a Guinea and brings him to the Bishop's Table. About 2 in the extremity of the heat, wee sett out. Mr. Price and his Neighbors attend the Bishop to Mould in Water. After frequent calls to wash down the Dust, wee come, meeting market people only, to Wigan, about 8. See Sir Roger, with his company at Bayliff Masons, looking on the coach passing. Wee attend it to the parsonage, wait on the Bishop there, congratulate the successful dispatch of the Visitacion. I (with Jack) stay supper and after are dismist with Favor and Benedicion. I call at the Inn on Mr. Boucher. Hence to my coz. Holt where warm, I mention the singular unkindness & rudenes of the Town to the Bishop.
23 Up at 5 prepare the Carriage. Yet part not from hence till past 7. The morning pretty favorable and cool. Wee come to Warrington before 11 when the Sun began to prevail. Here wee dine, shelter and solace till past 4. I see Shaw, Mr. Atherton's Steward, and reprove him for 2 bad Guineas, offered in payment to Ned Roberts. Wee change them. We call on Mrs. Callis, Boucher &c. At an easy rate and under a more favorable sky come safe D.O.M.G. half an hour after Eight. I receive Dr. Bouchers Letter with the M.S.
24 Sunday. The Dean preaches but is difficultly heard. The News brings misunderstanding betwixt Prince Lewis of Baden & Marlborough. After prayers I see the Chancellor, after that take 3 Turns with Jack on Roodee.
25 The Fair fills the Town I write to Dr. Boucher and Mr. Parre apply to Busienes till noon. Invited dine at Mr. Pickmores with Mr. Vaudrey, Lord Gerard's Steward of the Court of the Ministrels, the dinner and wine in the indifferent, In the Evening I return to Busienes and end the crowded day in a sole domestic pint. Pay the Chancellor 100^{li}. I hear from Tom Taylor a melancholy Account of Mr. Robys circumstance and am affected by it.
26 At early prayers, after to Busienes. Send Mr. Hulme a Box of pipes at 2. The news scarse moves. About 4 the Duke of Ormond arrives here at the Falcon. About 5 (after prayers) I wait on him surrounded with Gentlemen in attendance. Hee promptly takes notice of, applys, and asks mee of the company in Town. Mr. Egerton, Sir Thos. Hanmer &c. I stay an hour when hee takes Coach for Cholmley. In the Evening, Mr. Towns of Dublin sees us. Wee sup late with him, his son and Yong Mr. Manley at the Mayors, come home in a soft shower about 11 a Clock.
27 Instead of roodee, I take a Turn in the Fair. Pay Mr. Bennet for Mr. Vaudrey 40^{li} and Mr. Foulks 70^{li} on Account. Ned Humphreys comes from the Bishop of Kildare. Mr. Lancaster and his wife visit us. Hee has much of his peice on the Anvil in Defence of the Clergy against the Imposicion of Taxes towards

the Highways &c. After Busienes, into the Town to Mr. Minshall whence manu invitati[25] Hee and I go over to Alderman Starkey. Hee recieves mee with particular civility, treats us with 2 Decanters of October Ale and wee part in the same Terms about 9.

28 Indispos'd from the Sharpness of the Aldermans old Ale. Cool and a Court day. No Busienes but silent continuances. I congratulate the ease. Write to the Bishop of Kildare and send him copies of Dr. Bouchers letter. I meet with Mr. Egerton of Eccleston, wee conclude the Evening in three pints at the Fountain. Paid today to my brother Partington 8^{li};12s;4d.

29 St. Peter's Day. At early prayers, am taken on roodee with a fine shower, come off but return and make up above 4 Turns. The News yet dull on the Moselle but the Lisbon Fleet of 300 in number arrivd. I procure a Bill of 40^{li} from Alderman Allen, pay Mr. Boucher 40^{li}, twenty of which part of the 100^{li} I owe him. After prayers ArchDeacon Booth greets me as formerly, talks on Books and saies hee has a List of the Members return'd. Enquires after Hammond L'estrang his Alliances of Divine Offices &c. In the Evening at the Fountain with Dr. Thane & Alderman Allen. Wee draw on the Evening in easy conversacion and 4 pints.

30 I recover ease by a walk of 4 Turns, write to Dr. Pope and inclose the 40^{li} Bill. Desire his Thoughts (Q.D.A.) in case of Mr. Trotter's death. Send ArchDeacon Booth my Hammond L'estranges Alliances, pay John upon Account 1^{li};10s. After Accounts of presentments inspected a Turn on roodee, thence home and in domestic pint conclude the day.

JULY 1 Q.F.F.F.Q.S. A fine and cool morning. Mr. Newton in the Quire has a loose incoherent discourse on Joh.4 v.7. Sanctissimae Eucharistiae particeps sum. Det Deus vitam deni congruam.[26] The news yet suspending. After Evening prayers apply to Stearne de Obstinacione. After 1 Turn on roodee to my claret modicum & rest.

2 After some showers in the night a cooler morning, at early prayers. Proceed in Guthrys Memoirs, write to Mr. Parre about Dr. Pope and the registry. After Evening prayers & Busienes, Dr. Thane and I draw out 3 pints & the Evening at the Fountain, return home about 9.

3 A bright morning. After early prayers to roodee where in a cooler Breeze refresht by 4 Turns. I examine 2 Wittnesses in Lady Calveleys Will. Mr. J. Cowper tells mee of Archdeacon Stratford made Canon of Christ Church, and kindly suggests his capacity as such to help my son John into the Foundacion of that House Q.B.E. I pay Alderman (Allen) which I had by Bill on Friday 40^{li} & 12s 6d extra. Pay Mrs. Morgan 20^{li} and give her a fresh Bond for 10^{li} payable 2nd of July, next pay to the Collector my Tax to the poor 7s & to the Ornaments of the Church 3s 6d. I receive of the Bishop of Kildare 5 Guineas from T. Gorst and

25 Trans: 'invited by hand'.
26 Trans: I partake of the most Holy Eucharist. May God grant [me] a fitting life at last'.

write to him and Mrs. Jebbe. After prayers and some Busienes About an hour at the Rose and Crown with Dr. Thane, the 2 Cowpers, Mrs. Fogg, Callys, Hulse, good company but prickt wine.

4 A cooler morning. After early prayers at the office slightly consider'd, take 4 Turns on roodee refreshing. Apply to the Entry of the presentments. Mr. Stratford comes from Wigan, tells mee my Lord expects mee there Saturday or Munday next. Examine Mr. Adams on Lady Calveleys Will.

5 Court day. Apply to Busienes, draw Watkinsons Declaracion and Slaters Suppletory Oath. After Court with Mr. Parkinson at the Fountain before dinner. In the Evening proceeding in the presentments, At Night with Dr. Thane dispatch 2 pints at the Fountain.

6 After 4 quick Turns in a thin coat on roodee refresht. Apply to the presentments enter more than 6 Deanaries. In the Evening Mr. John Hurleston mett by 100 Horse, brings home his young Lady. I venture on a supper. After that to the Fountain where I fall into the company of Mrs. Clopton, Cowper, Lloyd then Mr. Bruen and S. Taylor the glass gos about to 1s 6d shott and near 12.

7 Indispos'd finish the presentments, venture tho after Elixir on 4 Turns near Noon, am refresht. Apply to Busienes, finish the presentments and prepare for my journy on Munday. Take a Turn in the Evening and my domestick wine.

8 At the Quire where Mr. Shaw preaches on 'Let Love be without Dissimulacion.' A fine confluence magnifi'd by Mr. Hurleston and his Bride. The News yet in suspense. After prayers I step to the Chancellor where, Q.B.E. Dr. Norris seals the Licence, Bond and forces a Guinea on mee for the Licence. After a Turn on Roodee & returnd home, calld over by ArchDeacon Booth. I go to him. Hee treats mee with his old Freedom & orthodox discourse. Another Bottle call'd in. I use the advantage it gives mee. I introduce the matter of the late Elecion and his censure of my Letter with my wager on his vote. Take upon mee to reprehend his derersion and defend myself but with all decency. Hee is civil and denys his Censuring of mee. Wee part in good Freindship about 12.

9 Indispos'd from the last nights quantity of good wine. Set hence past 10 in a cool Breeze, reach Warrington past 2. Mr. Page tells mee hee has a Black pad, by his description I judg'd him fit for Mr. Archdeacon Stratford. I come to Wigan about 8 wait on my Lord and thence to my cosen Holts, the house full I lodg in the chamber, my Lydia dyd in the first time since.[27]

10 After prayers my Lord considers Mr. Rigby of Aspul (son of Alex.) his Claim to the seats under the next Arch on the North adjoining to the Chancel, hee produces a private scrol under the hand of Alex. Rigby an Ancestor of his Family, setting forth a reference betwixt the then Heir and Bishop Bridgman in 1622 to Sir Geo. Booth and Sir Piers Legh wherein the 2 Knights adjudg'd it on the Rigbys side, but advises him to give the Bishop leave to sit &c, likewise an

27 Henry's first wife Lydia died on 18th May 1685. Henry never entered the room in which she died for twenty years.

acknowledgement under a Churchwardens hand That hee and his partner sate in the 1st seat by permission of Mr. Rigby in 1634. And it appearing that Mr. Rigby has a Tomb or vault under and has had quiet possession since the restoracion. My Lord said hee would not now further dispute nor oppose his Title tho the papers hee produc'd were private, and tho the manner of choral seats in that part of the Church shewd that was formerly the Chancel, and tho Bishop Bridgman had set his Letters I.B. on the opposite seat which Letters were alter'd by a small knife into I.R. signifying Joseph Rigby, but said if hee mett with further Evidence on behalf of the Rector's Right hee would still claim the seats as such. Mr. Rigby seemed satisfy'd and both acquiescd. After dinner my Lord imparted the Informacion hee had against Mr. Hall, Fellow and Mr. Ashe, Chaplain of Manchester. After this Mrs. Haydock, Markland, Colly, Johnson and I are at Tootells, thence in the Evening invited to my cozen Holts where their daughter esteem'd in danger and is christen'd privately, call'd Dorothy, the company among whom Colly and Johnson stay freely entertain'd; about 10 the company dispers'd, I to bed.

11 I wait on my Lord about 9. Hee after Tea takes a Turn in the Demean, I attend him, thence to Church. After a short Dinner hee takes Coach for Croston, I attend along, wee come thither about 4, see the Church and Mr. Hesketh's (Becconsal) Chancel decreed to bee taken down. My Lord seems to doubt of the lawfulness of it as being (tho a crazy one) member of the Church.[28] After a prick'd bottle of good wine and a tankard of Ale wee part with Mr. Pilkington, come at a good rate thorough dusty Lanes to Eccleston. Here my Lord sees the Dilapidacions of the parsonage. Mr. Egerton the Rector now at Chester. The Tenant a woman, in suspense offers the Sellar Door, wee meet with good Ale and Beer in Bottles, make bold with them. I by stricter search discover some wine, bring out 2 pints, find it right French, but touch'd a little. Refresht with this variety wee return and come to Wigan about 8, stay at the parsonage till 10. My Lord well pleas'd with the Expedicion.

12 The weather continues excessive hott, the small pox very common and unusual mortality of 30 a week makes many apprehensive. After 9 begin a walk indispos'd thoro the demean towards Standish encourag'd by the Breeze &c: tempted by the prospect, stretch my walk to the high Feilds, on the side of Standish Hall. Here over against Ayrfeild see and consider the prospect, in my return hott almost to intollerable, before refresht of the walk near 12. I find an agreeable company with my Lord, Mrs. Newcome, Cowper, yong Newcome, Mercer &c. At dinner, I to Mr. Cowpers fillero haust[?um] in salutem Dmni Norris et Dmni Gerard hodierna. Uxor eius poculum haurio Genialem.[29] After dinner wee adjourn to Mrs. Smiths where neither good wine or Ale yet cheerfulnes. About 4 I set for Ayrfeild take a walk down to the Bridge thorough

28 C.R.O., Bishop's Register EDA2/4 f.28, Becconsall Chapel, Croston.

29 Prescott drinks to the health of Messrs Norris and Gerard; the exact meaning of the Latin is not clear.

the meadows where observe breaches, by Edens, thoro the Grove of Okes home it is a pleasant walk. The Tenants appear orderly and have made the House so. I consider on takeing down the Kitchen part, and wish for a better Circumstance to make mee here a summer recepcion. Return hence about 8, call at the old Clerks who shews mee a sign of an Owl in an Ivy Bush, intended to bee hung up; return to Wigan about 10.

13 About 8 I go to my Lord, hee shews mee Archdeacon Stratfords expected Letter telling him hee was install'd Canon of Christ Church the 6th, admitted to the Degree of Dr. of Divinity the 7th and chosen Treasurer of the College the 9th current. I congratulated with his Lordship, part with him 11 stay and dine at Mr. Walmesleys, after Tea with Mrs. Holt, comeing to horse am hindered by Rymmer, a Witnes of Mr. Boucher who I examine upon Interogacions. I saw James Winstanley of Haigh an Architect and discourse him on my design rather phantasm at the Ayrfield, hee promises to see the place and send mee a Draught, near 7 I sett hence come in a cool Evening to Warrington about 9.

14 About 8 proceed hence bring and ride a black pad of Mr. Pages in prospect of Archdeacon Stratford, call before 11 at the vicarage of Frodsham. Mr. Davies urges mee to dine with him, the day and time of it excessive hott I comply. Hee acquaints mee of an unhappy misunderstanding betwixt him and his wife from the Affair betwixt him and Mrs. Ogle her kinsman. The dinner homely yet shee cheerful at it. Dr. Norris and his Lady remember'd, my Lydia kindly mencioned by her. After Dinner, Cyder gos freely about. Mr. Dun his Curate A.M. of Scotland a forward and unexperienc'd Clergyman is with us. At 5 I come hence and D.G. safe home before 8.

15 I had to quench thirst last night, recourse to Elixir e lassitudine and that stay at home. After Evening prayers I attend on Dr. Norris and his Lady (marry'd Thursday last). After this wait on Sir Tho. Hanmer at Sir H. B's where the Duchess of Grafton, my Suzy and I sup with and stay late entertain'd.

16 I repeat 4 Turns on Roodee, am recreated, write a full Letter to Dr. Stratford, in the Evening in the Town, a small shower today refreshes but secures not.

17 I still repeat the walk, the day excessive hott, indifferent to Busienes or Books, Letters and prints bring the good News of English and Dutch Armies under the command of the Duke of Marlboro having forc'd the French lines, broke 24 Squadrons of Bavarian Horse, taken 2 Leift. Generals, 1 Major General, 80 Officers, 10 Guns, 1400 prisoners &c, and advanc'd near to Lovain. Again wee are at Sir H. B's at supper, take my share in Claret only.

18 After refreshing 4 Turns, apply to Busienes, examine three wittnesses against Dennis, write to T. Gorst, Mr. Styth and Mr. Markland, after a short walk conclude the Day in a domestic pint.

19 At early prayers. Pickering the Joyner, views the unboarded space in the office, measures it, so dos J. Cross the space for the presses. The Court passes tollerably the busienes competent. I examine 2 wittnesses against Harrison, 3 on Rigbys Will. After this I visit the Chancellor wee drink in cool Bottles of French wine in his Garden, hee tells mee his design for London and to remove to a less

house. Dr. Norris and his Lady come to us. After this I visit the Mayor hee treats us with a good but worse Bottle of Claret. I pay Mr. Stratford for 193 Books of Articles.[30]
20 I recover by repeated 4 Turns. The Bells very early tell the confirmacion of the good News from Flanders. I see it so at the Coffee House. Sir Tho. Hanmer sees my Coins. Dr. Norris, his Lady and company visit us. In the Evening at the Fountain with Mr. Maul a ClergyMan of Ireland, Mr. Bowyer and Mr. Rhode, wee have much of Books and variety of Learning, till near 12.
21 Indispos'd from the heat of the day and the wine of the Night, I write to Dr. Stratford (inclose Mr. Davies Account of the Tiths of Frodsham Parish) to Mr. Stratford at Wigan and John Cross. Borrow of Mr. Maul and read some of the Memorial of the Church of England. In a walk to the Waterworks &c Thunder and short showers. Mrs. Dod in her return from London calls on, and lodges with us.
22 Vicesimus quartus a Matrimonio cum Lydia mea charitas initio hac incipit die, det D.O.M. Feliciora.[31] Mr. Maul has in the Quire an elegant sound and ingenious discourse on Jer.10.17. The News from near Louvaine increases. Mr. Entwisle, Bunbury and Dod dine with us. After prayers and the Coffee House, I go with Mr. Egerton, Brooks, Done to the Chancellors to wait on Dr. Norris, wee are liberally treated in the out Green square with Claret, the undertakeing the office of Justice is much the subject besides the present successes abroad, wee part about 9. The Ladies keep here their conversacion amd mee up past 11.
23 I state Accounts with Mrs. Dod, pay her 5 Guineas remains 7^{li}.2d to Ballance. I write earnestly to Wm. Harrison about my Bond to Mr. Holt, to Mr. Crosby about Mr. Trotter, and to my cozen Parre. Mrs. Dod go's about 11. A fine shower falls, the Carpenter begins the Summ.peceis for the Floor in the void space in the office. I finish the Memorial. The shower lasts the longest for 3 or 4 months, till 5. In the Evening Dr. Thane calls, I go to the Raven with him for choice wine, but it proves doubtfull. Mr. Callys, Maul and Shawe come to us. Wee stay past 10 and call at the Coffee house where for want of a Mayl, little news by the way.
24 Indispos'd have recourse to above 4 Turns on roodee, tis cool and I refresht. I send back to ArchDeacon Booth sive rituale Graecorum illustratum opera. R.P.F. Jacobi Goanparisini Ordinis F.F. praedicatorum S. Theologiae Lectoris nuper in Orientem. Missi Apostoloci parisiis 1647. And to Mr. Maul, the Memorial of the Church of England borrow'd of them. Sir John Werden gives us a visit. After one Turn on Roodee, home to my domestic Quota.
25 St. James Day. Wee are at early prayers. The weather after the full Moon last Night appears alter'd to a disposicion to rain. Write to my cosen Parr fully

30 Books of Articles consisted of 43 questions concerning the parish, to be answered by the churchwardens prior to visitation.
31 Trans: 'Today is the 24th anniversary of my marriage to my dear Lydia: May God the best and greatest grant [me] a more fortunate life'.

my thoughts about Dr. Pope. About 10 sett out in a cool breeze come to Cornish before 1, dine on good Bacon & Beans, am kindly received. Mr. Adams candidate for Holt is there, so is Mr. Homerston and Taylor, these 3 are favourable to him, and that busienes takes much of the Time. I return at 5 call on Tom Davy in Farn, thence over the Boat visit Alderman Allen in his reesne, hee treats us with a Bottle of good Claret. I return well D.G. about 8.

26 Last Court day, the Chancellor and Mr. Hulton and Stratford absent. I write by Mr. Clutton to Mr. Peck, to Mr. Wareing and Hebblethwait, examine 6 Wittnesses. After at the Fountain with Mr. Green of Prescott, lately come from Hanaker, My Lord Derby's in Sussex, that Family and something of practice of Courts, dispatch 2 Bottles and carry the conference to 12.

27 I examine a 2nd Wittness for Wright against Ackers, after take 4 Turns on roodee, see the News in expectacion The work of the office go's on. Attend Sir. Tho. Hanmer at Sir Hen. Bunburys, they last night return'd from Chatsworth and Lyme, take a Turn, Jack with mee, then meet Dr. Thane at the Fountain, 2 pints and 9 a clock sends us home.

28 I take a full walk on roody attend the busienes at the office. After prayers attend ArchDeacon Booth in his visit of Sir Henry B. many things past in the usual Language and some not without reflection on the Honorable ArchDeacon. After I Turn on Roodee late home.

29 Indispos'd yet to Church. Dr. Thane preaches on 4 Phil. v.6 lapses into his impotent Tone almost ad infantiam. I see Mr. Ludlow at the Quire, hee tells mee first that my good Lady Stephens dyd last Tuesday. After prayers Mr. Ludlow and his Lady visit us an hour, much of Lady Stephens and our Acquaintance. After a Turn on Roody to Bed.

30 After 4 Brisk Turns refresht. Mrs. Hulton of old Acquaintance dyd abt. 4 this Morning, I write to Mr. Stratford to excuse my coming to Lord till Thursday noon. See the work of the office. After 7 at night Dr. Thane and my self invited by him to celebrate Mr. Bouchers birth day hee entering on the 67 Year in 2 Bottles of good Claret.

31 After the office and a visit to Mr. Hulton, I take 4 Turns on Roodee, read part of the Memorial with Remarks. See the work and contrive more. After a dusky Turn on Roodee domestic Claret.

AUGUST 1 Q.B.E. A bright warm day, apply to Busienes prepare for my journy tomorrow, attend the work in the office, recommend the little Designs concluded on, to Pickering the Carpenter. The Funeral of Mrs. Hulton, this Evening solemnly perform'd. Sir Hen. Bunbury, Mr. Shakerley, Capt. Spark, Mr. Callys, Mr. Boucher and my self Bearers, the company consists of women only invited. Mr. Fogg has a sermon on Lord let now thy servant depart in peace,near the End gives the Deed a good and full Character. After the Solemnity an hour at Sir Hen. B's with Mr. Shakerley, Capt. Spark, Mr. Wm. Bunbury. I write to Mr. Gorst and Mr. Topping.

2 In a cool morning, sett hence about 6 come to Warrington about 10 relax half an hour, proceed and reach Wigan about 1, find my Lord and Company set to dinner. Room is made for mee & Jack with mee. After dinner the Busienes mencion'd. First a mutuall complaint betwixt Mr. Clegge and the Schoolmaster, they and some of the parishioners are affected, appear, the accusacion and defence perplex and difficult, it is at last referred to Mr. Marsden present. The matters appear trivial against Mr. Taylor the Schoolmaster, but those if promoted, of consequence against Mr. Clegg who in his defence is malepart to the Chancellor and reprehended for it by Mr. Marsden. Next enters Mrs. Pilkington who claims a right to sit in the Seat belonging to the house sold to Mr. Herle, hee allows that hee gave her leave till she disturb'd his servants good as she is, shee in a passion returns, vilifies the servants, scorns to sit with 'em my Lord rebukes her pride and passion. As Mr. Walmesley & my cozen Holt interpose, shee indevors to represse 'em, the most malitious words and reflecions are us'd, Mr. Herle saies her Father used to call her Brandy Whore, and adds hee knew her to sell potts of Ale. Shee replies shee never sold pins Incle &c tells him of a whore hee had and mencions him as of the brood of the rebellion. Mr. Walmesley shee calls of yesterday and reminds him of being Clerk to Hen. Rowe &c. It appearing shee has no right but by Mr. Herls permission my Lord gives her liberty to sit in his seat meaning his servants, which shee is made by the Chancellor to understand so. Other matters particularly those against Mr. Hall of Eccles and Mr. Sherdley are mencion'd. About six wee leave the Bishop, go to Smith the Inn where the Hous is seiz'd by Execucions and severall setts of Bayliffs, a miserable confusion. The Chancellor gos to Prescott towards Speake. After a pint of Claret in the porch, and the vault made by Mr. Herle seen, I go to cozen Holts, Mr. Walmesley comes and talks conceited and unseasonably about seats in Churches and prescription to them. I am movd and differ in my sentiments. My cozen Holt his wife with child is ill of the Jaundice. Dr. Holbrook with her.

3 Rise early, see the silent News, to the parsonage where I meet with Mr. Johnson, wee begin a walk together which carries us to Mr. Standishes Coppice near the Hall, return about 10. After prayers to my cozen Holts where at dinner my cozen Walmesley's Case appears on the sudden desperate. My cozen Holt shows tender and passionate affection. I go up, find the House in tears and confusion, the Drs. Grundy and Holbrook, in silent astonishment. Mr. Colly happily calling on mee is desir'd up and reads to which shee answers the last prayers. This danger is attributed to the Jaundice suddainly struck to her Stomach which rejects everthing. Mr. Colly & I in some hopes, go to see Mr. Haydock, hee receives us liberally with good Ale and 2 Bottles of good wine on the decay. Wee return before 7 find the happy soul surrender'd about 6. I heartily condole the amazeing loss, go to prayers at the parsonage, stay after with my Lord, return and write to my Suzy.

4 I hesitate about my return and resolve to pay my last office at the Funeral of the excellent person, stay within for the much greater part with the afflicted sister. In the Evening start out Jack with mee, wee follow the river to Haigh wood, ascend this, see it lessen'd by a Fall of fine Oaks, proceed up to the House, here taken with a shower (one of the first this summer), wee see the

Gardens and Canals, show'd by the Gardiner, return thirsty and in rain about 8. I at prayers desire my Lord's leave to bury my cozen Walmesley in the Chancel, hee not without scruple but for her sake grants it.

5 A fair day return. Mr. Colly preaches before Mr. James Bankes, after Noon. In the Evening Mr. Bankes and I are treated by Mr. Entwisle with 2 Bottles of Claret, after this see my Lord, thence to my Quarters.

6 About Nine, I Jack with mee, go to Ayrfeild, walk about, see the wrecking, call at Holland, where for his services I give cozen Sam Prescott half a Guinea, wee talk about the exchang of our Shops. I hasten hence to Winstanley, come soon enough to dinner. After which videlicet about 2 sett for Wigan. Mrs. Ashurst in our company has a fall from her horse. Shee is frightened but releiv'd by my Bottle, return to my cozen Holts about 3 the company invited thickens, Mr. Cecil Booth, Mr. Hoghton, son of Sir Charles, Mr. Mort, Mr. Banks, Mr. Kenyon and young Charles Herle are Bearers. I am among the relacions distinguisht by a Hatt Band and Gloves. The Funeral proceeds solemnly about 5, a great and fashionable company attends. Mr. Jackson has a good discourse and gives the good deceased person a hansom and just Character. After the Funeral I wait on my Lord and take leave, thence return to my Quarters.

7 After Tea and preparacion take horse about 10, reach Warrington about 12 send to Mr. Vaudrey, hee comes wee account I pay him 36^{li} there leaving a Ballance. At first seems to rain in earnest and the long Drought to be extinct. Set hence after 5 in a steeping showr, this continues to Stretton, call at Budworth whence Mr. Henchman is absent, proceed to Holford, come well wett about 8, wee are generously and kindly received and supplyd. After securitys from the Wett. Mr. Cholmley, Mr. Walley & myself sit up in the Hall till 2.

8 Indispos'd till 11. After dinner a visit to Sir Geo. Warburton is propos'd, hindered by showrs, till 4 then mount, reach Arley by 5. This is an ancient noble woodhouse built high about a Quadrangle, a Moat almost compassing it. Here wee find with Sir Geo. Lane, Coll. Ashton a young officer, Mr. Hall and his son. The wine on decay is hasten'd round and full. About 8 wee remount, reach Holford about 9, solace till 1.

9 The indisposicion eas'd by Elixir, Mr. Cholmley from cold gott very indispos'd. Mr. Clopton dines here and talks and solaces the Afternoon. I bear the diversion. We agree on an early Hour to Bed to recover the malady.

10 Refresht, prepare for return, at parting Mr. Cholmly gives Jack a Guinea, wee come with him and his Lady (they in my Chariot) to Northwich. I turn to Davenham where by Mr. Marburys assistance, I apply to Mr. Richard Holford for an Account or Rental of the Thiths of Budworth and Frodsham, hee promises to send it, set hence about 2, call at Tarvin with Sir Hen. Bunbury, Mr. Bruen &c at the Green. I return D.G. safe about 7.

11 After a stormy Night, a rainy morning. I see how the work is advanct at the office, attend it, write to Dr. Stratford. Wee celebrate our Marriage day with domestic Joy. D.O.M.G. the rain continues and the Waters advance.

12 The weather cold and dropping. Mr. Lancaster has a long sermon in the Quire, the news yet denying. After prayers I visit the Chancellor and his brother

Mr. Geo. Jackson come today from Speake. After wee visit our poor Child Will and part with him as in a desperat condicion.

13 Indisposd to busienes, take a walk of 4 Turns on roody, see the work at the office. Mr. Whaley calls on mee proposes to take up 80^{li} more and to renew the Security. I remind him of my services and his severe usage in the bargain hee made mee. In the Evening I am at Sir Hen. B's where treated with a Bottle.

14 After a walk not much inform'd by the News. Dine at the Mayors invited with the Chancellor's Family. After dinner liberal Fellowship in wine & strong Beer. In the Evening however invited at a Glass of wine at ArchDeacon Booths with Sir Hen. B. Mr. Brooks Govenor and Mr. Bowyer, the conversacion dull and more reserv'd tho the ArchDeacon uses his old free phrase. All receded save myself, the ArchDeacon acquaints mee with the suddain and to bee condol'd death of my good old Freind, Mr. Rowell of Durham. I heartily lament it.

15 Indispos'd, hott, conscious. Yet after Dinner Mr. Jones of Bangor calling, I go with him to the Falcon. Wee agree here D.V. to see Chatsworth and the other wonders next Year. Dr. Thane and Mr. Fogge come to us. Mr. Jones gos home, the wine good, wee lengthen the shott and the Evening. Mr. Fogg pays mee here the Wardens Bill $13^{li}.6^{s}.8^{d}$

16 Extreme indisposicion and deep reflection. I write to my Lord and inclose the proceedings at Holt about their Elecion of a Minister, rest and repose create no Ease.[32]

17 After Elixir, some abatement of the indisposicion. The News is fill'd with Accounts of the losses at Sea from the late Storm. I attend but in pain the busienes of the Office.

18 A very rainy day, not yet recover'd, recreate in Books, attend the work, write to Dr. Stratford & inclose Mr. Richard Holfords Rental of Great Budworth & Frodsham.

19 Mr. Peter Foulks one of the proctors this year of Oxford, has in the Quire a sound and excellent discourse on the last clause of 28v of the 40 Chapter of Isaiah. The Letters bring nothing but new Relacions of Losses at Sea. In the Evening at the Chancellors. Hee, Mr. Jackson and Sheriff Peck come home with mee, wee quietly diminish my little Stock of wine.

20 The weather dispos'd to rain. I visit Mr. Peter Foulks in the morning, am all along under the unhappy effects of the last weeks Life, uneasy, hott, irregular. About 4 Mr. Minshall and I go out to meet my Lord Bishop returning from Wigan, wee do so at Hoole, hee comes here about 3. About 6 hasten to the Fountain where Mr. Peter Foulks, his brother & Dr. Thane, wee make it out one Bottle a peece and draw the conversacion to 11.

21 Attend on the Bishop on several matters, hee mencions Holt and Woodchurch. I write to Mr. Peck on the former. Again in the Evening at the Fountain with the 2 Brothers Foulks till 10.

32 C.R.O., Call Books for Holt chapel.

22 Attend my Lord in the morning about the matter i.e. suggested Symony of Woodchurch, write to Dr. Stratford. About 2 The Holt Candidates attend my Lord. Mr. Adams with Mr. Peck the Mayor and about 80 others on his, Mr. Clutten and about 7 on his part. My Lord is offended at the number and reprehends it. The matter is discust with confusion my Lord blames the popular Election and is prepossest against the major side. At last the controversy resolvd into these 3 proposals. To refer the choice to another meeting of the parishioners to bee apointed by my Lord. To allow of the Election of the Mayor and Corporacion. Or use his own power in admitting a Minister. My Lord dismisses the company and takes some daies to deliberate. I am with Mr. Peck &c an hour at the Coach and Horses, observe their humor, variety of passion and dejection. I write to Mr. Green of Poulton to bring wittnesses on his brothers behalf to prove the Allegacions of Symony against Mr. Janny of Woodchurch. In the Evening I wait on Bishop Lindsey of Killaloe at the Pyde Bull. Stay 2 hours treated with 2 Bottles of Dublin Claret.

23 A fair what has rarely happened since the 7th Morning, take 4 Turns on roodee Jack with mee. See Mr. Peake and Adams. A Thanksgiving for the success in breaking the French Lines solemnisd. Mr. Lancaster has in the parish church a sermon on Ps. 115 v. 1 mixt with English History. I dine at the Mayors where the Magistracy at Dinner all Venison very good, vary'd and well got, the wine flows about and the company grows warm. In the Evening at the Chancellor's with the Bishop of Killaloe where the busienes of the day cooly menciond. Hence to the Mayors. The Town is illuminated few dark houses. I step at last to Will. Willoughby's where the Mayor of Holt, Mrs. Homerston and Adams in Expectacion of the Event of their Busienes.

24 A rainy morning. I am under last Nights hot effects. The Mayor of Holt &c see us before noon. I step to the Coffee House where the success of Prince Eugene against the Duke of Vendome is a welcome paragraph, thence to the Chancellor, desire him to apply to the Bishop on the behalf of the Mayor of Holt &c. Hee promises, performs, comes to tell mee his Success. I draw an Instrument to be signd by the Bishop whereby from the reasons of the divisions about the Election of their Minister hee assumes the Nominacion. I attend his Lordship with it and hee approves it. I stay with his Lordship an hour, thence to the Mayor's where Sir John Williams, Capt. Hurleston, his sons, the Mayor of Holt &c at a Boul of punch. Sir John appears as a person of good parts and breeding. Capt. Hurleston rude yet with signs of honesty receives him here the 1st time. The punch gos swiftly round, the Capt. immers't sleeps, the rest lowd and warm & thus wee leave em.

25 The weather still showry. I am still hott. Mr. Stodard from Mr. Empson directed brings mee a Letter from Mr. Gelibrond, about the Nominacion of himself to Kirk Hammerton by Mr. Walmsley. I go with him to my Lord, who takes his subscripcions &c de hene esse. I write to Mr. Gelibrond, My Lord influenced by Mr. Stratford raises new scruples and insists upon the Mayor of Holt and Mr. Homerston subscribeing their consent to his Nominacion. I procure it, and upon this hee grants his Licence to Mr. Adams to serve the Cure at Holt. The Mayor of Holt &c rejoice, after dinner go to the palace to return thanks to my Lord, but hee recedes, they see his Secretary. I go with them to the Fountain, where wee part well pleasd with the delayd Event in a Bottle of Wine. They go about 4, I write to Mr. Gandy.

26 Constant rain the Forenoon. Mr. Brett a most inform Orator entertains, mortifies and diverts the Quire with his discourse on 2 Chron. c.v. half of it is Tussis Screatus and unseemly gesture. The News makes the dispute betwixt P. Eugene & the D. of Vendome on the Adda doubtfull. In the Evening after 4 short Turns, Wee visit Mr. Wm. Bunbury where wee find Dr. Thane, Mr. Ward, Member for Newton & Mr. Hugh Foulks.

27 A moist morning yet walk on the Walls round to the East Gate with Mr. Mayor, hee tells mee of his takeing Cotton of Lord Abingdon for 21 years. I sell the Bishop of Kildares horse for 7^{li} to Mr. Blackburn of Trevallyn, see the Chancellor, wait on the Bishop about Mr. Green of Poulton. The Judg (Jekell) comes in attended by the Sheriff (Legh of Adlington). My Lord Derby's Goods are publishd and sold. Wee go down to the melancholy places. I see the disrepair and lament it. Wee buy not tho desire some particular of them.

28 At early prayers. The weather wet and showry. Yet venture on 4 Turns on roodee, am refresht, see the Letter but no News. Am present at the Beginning of Appraizment of Mr. Brocks Goods. Mr. Walker preaches the Assize Sermon but I hear it not. A slender appearance of the whiggish Gentry. In the Evening at the Fountain, 3 pints and hours with Mr. T. Cooper.

29 Tho a wetting morning, take 4 Turns. See the Chancellor, afterwards the Bishop on the Busienes of Woodchurch which is put off till Saturday. Divert in Sir James Turner his pallas armata. And in the Evening invited by Mr. Tyrer, take a Bottle with him at the Fountain.

30 A fine and cheerfull morning injoy it in 4 Turns on roodee. This is (D.O.M.G.) my son Jacks birthday, hee entering on the 16th year, wee have a domestic celebracion. Mr. Whaley calls after dinner, Wee go down to Mr. Cartwright. Hee comes to the Fountain promises to procure 80^{li} in a Fortnight. Mr. Whaley and I stay our Bottles over which hee was all gratefull, acknowledgment, protestacion &c. I remind him of my hard Bargain in the Haldrous &c. hee promises a better and of the most contiguous Land if wee proceed in this to a Bargain. I write to John Cross about Holt Bridge.

31 Not so fair a morning indispos'd, try 2 turns on roody, return defatigate. In the Evening dispatch the 1st Book (of the Grecian Arms) of pallas armata.

SEPTEMBER 1 A fair morning Q.B.E. After Elixir easy, take 4 Turns on roodee, call at the Chancellors where they conclude to begin their journy to Oxford Tuesday next. I write to Mr. Boucher and to Mr. Mallory, proceed in Pallas Armata. In the Evening at the Fountain with Mr. Chancellor, Dr. Norris, Dr. Thane, Mr. Jackson till 9. This day about 2 Mr. Green brings 2 Wittnesses, Mr. Wm. Robinson the schoolmaster and Wm. Bennet of the parish of Woodchurch, I examine them before the Bishop and Chancellor upon the Allegacions of Mr. Greens peticion concerninge a Simoniacall contract betwixt

Geo. Burches the patron and Robert Janney the new Rector there, the Informacion tho without oath, seems to amount to a vehement suspicion of Symony.

2 Indispos'd mov'd by a fair morning, I take 4 Turns on roodee, happily refresht go to Church where Mr. Lancaster has a sermon on part of the 1st v of Psalm 22. Sanctissima inde Cenae, Ego et S.mea participes. Det [?dein] D.O.M. vitam agere pie sobrie casti[33]. After prayers at the Chancellors thence to the Mayors, where Mr. Mayor treats with a Bottle.

3 At early prayers after which the Bishop, who makes return, on the back of Mr. Greens peticion, That he is of Opinion that the Informacions are sufficient Grounds for her Majesties Royal presentacion. Afternoon see Tho. Gough do some odd finishing work at the office. The Chancellor calls on mee about 6. Hee treats at the Ship, Dr. Thane, Mr. Fogge and myself the wine not gratefull, these 2 and myself try the Falcon where 3 pints of better wine draw us till 11.

4 The weather yet holds fair, Severely indispos'd, take only 3 Turns on Roodee, part of Coll. Rooks Regiment exercising upon it. At the Coffee House scarcity of News. After dinner Mr. Whaley calls on mee is meek, precarious, promising Q.B.E. I go down to Mr. Cartwrights with him, enter Bond for 80^{li} to Anne Dannald widow. I leave his Deeds of Security with Mr. Cartwright to be alter'd, returning call on Mr. Minshall, hee invites to Mr. Brocks Ale in the Sellar, under part of a Quarter adds to my indisposicion. I go home proceed in Pallas & to Bed.

5 Reliev'd by Elixir, rainy weather return'd. I write to Wm. Borrett Esq. of the Inner Temple about the Storm Breifs. Mr. Bouchier returns from Oxford &c. but without my shell. In the Evening Mr. Morrey and I draw out 2 pints and three hours at the Fountain. Mr. Trotter, my good old Acquaintance and Brother in office, dies about 7 this morning.

6 Still hopefull weather, after early prayers 4 Turns on roodee, with my Lord about Mr. Proddys Admonicion 14 Nov. last. I write to Mr. Hebblethwaite. In the Evening return to the Fountain where with Mr. Egerton of Eccleston, Mrs. Colly and Mercer exceed our pints. Mr. Egerton tells an ungrateful story of Mr. Stanley.

7 A delicate Morning, after early prayers, draws mee down to roodee where 4 Turns. The News lands 10000 in Catalonia and joins them with 4000 Malecontents, divert in Books and in the Evening at the Fountain.

8 A duller day and windy. Yet take 4 Turns on roodee. Dr. Stern the Dean of St. Patrick's sees mee, mortifys mee with the account of Dr. Maddens Collecion worth intrinsic value 30^{li} sold for 60^{li}. Mr. Whaley calls and at Mr. Cartwrights executes a new Deed of Security to mee, pays the interests of the 20^{li} to the 11th of this month, wee drink a glass of wine at the Fountain. After they are gon Dr. Thane calls and staies mee a pint longer. I write to Mr. Ward of Leigh & inclose

33 Trans: 'My Suzy and I are then partakers of the most Holy Supper. May God the best and greatest grant that [?henceforth I] live piously, soberly and chastely.'

Watkinsons Declaracion. I write to my Brother Puleston, the History of a Coin of the 2nd year of Vespasian, the reverse hee standing, Rome kneeling, a 3rd Figure, Rome resurges.
9 A dull yet not rainy day. Mr. Newton preaches after his desultory way in the Quire. The News adds little but expectacion. After prayers (the weather well) I step into the Feilds. After that I am with Dean Sterne at his Quarters the Golden Talbot, where over 3 pints wee have discourse on Books and our Collegiate acquaintances past 10.
10 After early prayers to my refreshment of 4 Turns tho the wind blustring. Thence to Coffee at Brother Partingtons shop. After dinner to the Office where the Great press gos up. After prayers to the Fountain with Dr. Thane, wee send for Dean Stern, and Sir Henry Bunbury and Capt. Phillips find us. Wee fall on the matter of parliament the manner of Elecion by the commonalty &c. return about 11.
12 Roodee and 4 Turns, recover against a greater Evening draught. The Bishop sends about an order to the Churchwardens of Eccleston to provide a Surplice for the Curate of Duglas. After dinner to the office where the press almost finisht and another design'd. Mr. Lambert is here, tells of Mr. Trotters death and his succeeding him. After prayers hee and I go to the Fountain, wee meet here Dr. Thane Mr. Gerard the Grocer & Mr. Denton the Draper, have a mixt discourse advance the shott to Bottles apece & 10 a clock.
13 Descend in a cool Morning to my recovery, perform 4 Turns. Mr. Dean Stern and Lambert call on mee. I write to Mr. Marsden about Rigbys Will & Mr. Glests Goods. Dine at the Bishops where Sir Christopher Wandesford Sir Henry Bunbury, Dean Stern, Mr. Colier, Mr. Swetenham &c to the number 12. Scotland and Holland most of the subject. Mr. Lambert shews mee his Deputacion upon Mr. Trotters death dated 8 May last. Hee presents mee with a Gold Coin of Ed. 3rd worth a Guinea. After prayers Dean Stern calls on mee wee go to Roodee take 2 Turns. Hee tells mee his design of writeing on the Nature of Virtues and Vices and of Cases of Conscience wherein the Clergy are concernd in the execucion of their Function, this to be in Latin. Wee come from the Green to the Fountain, where over 2 pints the discourse of Books reviv'd & continu'd till 10. Mr. Jones, Atturney an old Neighbour, dies this Evening.
14 After early prayers A walk of 4 Turns. The News yet suspending, moderate in Books and Busienes. In the Evening a dull moist one at the Fountain with Dr. Thane 2 pints.
15 After prayers repeat the Turns. The News of the lewdnes of the Chancellors servants Richard & Mary surprise & divert the Town. I write to the Chancellor (to day at London) and John Cross. Mr. Jones is interr'd this Evening near 9 after a tedious expectacion of the invited. Mr. Fogg had an excellent discourse on 'So teach us O Lord to number our daies that wee may apply our Hearts unto Wisdom'. I follow my Lord up into the palace and congratulate his access this day to the 17th year of his Session here. Hee is pleas'd with the Duty and wee celebrate in 1 Bottle of Claret.
16 A fair morning and indisposicion tempts mee to 3 Turns. Mr. Henchman

has a good sermon on Hosea 6. v. 6, 7, 8. The News still unactive. After prayers in a calm Evening I go Jack with mee over the Estuary to Blacon point.

17 After 4 Turns agree with Mr. T. Brock on cheif points. After Busienes and Dinner sit with Mr. Mayor, his brother Puleston, Partington and Jo. Savage at my Neighbour Cottinghams till 5. Thence Mr. Bowyer and Colly call on mee to the Fountain, where 2 pints. Thence remove to the Hope and Anchor where Mr. Collier, yong Mercer, Ward, Taylor, Dr. Nichols, where supper, wine, songs and diversion detain till 11.

18 Indispos'd labor for a stomach about 4 Turns, read to please and flatter. In the Evening my Lord Bishop comes over to mee, smokes a pipe and accepts a reserv'd pint of Claret. After that I find yong Mr. Allen at the Fountain where each pint keeps us past 9.

19 A calme and pleasant morning. After early prayers invited to more than 4 Turns on roodee. In Books and Busienes variously. Rooks Regiment (Columbine Lt. Col.) march to Neston.

20 After prayers tempted by the fine calme morning to 4 Turns. At the Office about the Locks & Keys. After Books and easy Busienes a domestic dose of Claret.

21 St. Matthew's a delicate morning. After prayers I go (Jack with mee) round Sutton Heath. I reckon this walk equal to 4 Turns on Roodee. Mrs. Betty Stanford fetcht home by her Brother. The News yet very dull, Accompted with Mr. Foulkes & by my Note own myself indebted to her Majesty, for stamps from him $167^{li}.4^{s}.9d$, draw up an Agreement betwixt Mr. Boucher, my self and Thomas Brock which is executed at Mr. Bouchers chambers. Wee drink 2 Bottles on the occasion. After (about 10 at night) invited go to Sir H. Bunburys where Lord Cholmley, Mrs. Egerton, Brook, Bruen, Recorder. I am admitted with a full Glasse, the lesser go briskly round for an hour, then part and disperse.

22 Indispos'd, with difficulty write to the Chancellor, complain, repose. In the Evening after a walk and Books retreat to rest and Elixir.

23 A bright morning draws mee (Jack with mee) to roodee where 4 shorter turns, recover. Ordinacion had 5 Preists, 9 Deacons. Mr. Shaw has a good sermon to them on 1 Tim. cap. 4 v. last. The news sounds well from Catalonia only. After prayers with Mr. Egerton at the Coffee house, designing to morrow for Oulton, if the weather prove favorable.

24 A wett morning, at early prayers. I resolve not to go to Olton, write to Mr. Lambert, Farmer, Mr. Okes and my cozen Parre, treated by Mrs. Roberts with Coffee. Mrs. Mayor, Mrs. Cumberbach and my Suzy are turn'd over near the milk stoop in Lady Bradshaighs coach but by great providence D.G. without much harm. Dr. Thane and I have 2 pints at the Fountain.

25 After prayers 4 shorter Turns on roodee wet with an high Tide, pay Mr. Hodgson his note $1^{li}.13^{s}$. See the News yet tardy and suspending. After Books and dinner Dr. Thane and Mr. Bowyer with mee sees a stack of hay in Handbridge for which 9^{li} demanded. Wee continue a walk of an hour, thence to the Fountain where wee refresh in 3 pints.

26 After early prayers and busienes wait on the Bishop. Mrs. Proddy, Clegge and Lambert are the subjects, and I write presently to Mr. Chancellor of them. After dinner with Mr. Cartwright about Mr. Brocks busienes, hee advises to take advice before the Articles drawn. I meet with Mr. Henchman & his wife, Mrs. Risley. After prayers Dr. Thane, Mrs. Henchman, Colly, Egerton, Mercer, Bowyer, Shaw and my self at the Fountain, dispatch an high shott in all above Bottles a peece.

27 I draw an order and sequestracion for the supplying the Cure at Cartmell to the Churchwardens by reason of Mr. Proddys, irregularity and incapacity. Write to Mr. Vaudrey and include our state of Accounts by which Aug. the 6th, I am in arrears 108^{li}. This is the first Court this Term moderate Busienes. I dine with the Bishop, Richard Wood of Rainford the only Guest besides at a full Table. I examine 5 Wittnesses recreate in Domestic Allowance at Night.

28 After prayers in a fine morning recreate in 4 Turns. The public papers yet suspend Expectacion. After Noon Mr. Gooden brings mee my Fine shell snuff box in a case made by Poyner which comes to a Guinea. I pay it to Mr. Boucher which with the purchase ½ a Guinea $2^{li}.10^{s}$ in Gold and for fixing it on the Shell, paid Mr. Watchking 2 Guineas makes the whole a costly Curiosity and I hope the last of that kind amounting to $6^{li}.5^{s}.3$. In the Evening at the Fountain with Mr. Gooden, his country companion, Mr. Cartwright and Mr. Bouchier wee dispatch our Bottles.

29 Indispos'd about 9, see the Cattle Fair meet with Mr. Page, hee promises to change the Horse and to take Care of his Busienes before the Delegates perform a chase to Blacon point &c of about 5 Miles. I receive a parcell of 27^{li}.13s from Mr. Vaudrey.The Fair brings not busienes. Reading and domestic Claret end the day. J. Houghton, Mr. Dodds servant tells mee the ingrateful News of my Lord Derby ordering his Goods at Lathom to bee sent out of the Country.

30 Not well, have recourse to Roodee and 4 Turns, mistaken return too late for the Church. The News gives the prince of Hesse Darmstat kill'd before Barcelona, yet hopes too, it is not so. After prayers retreat to domestic Catechisme, reading & repose.

OCTOBER 1 Q.F.F.F.Q.S.[34] precibus celebratis. 4 spatiis in roodee paractis. Ad Camdens Annalium Jacobi Apparatum, me confero. Episcopum adeo. Nundina procedunt. Dominus Jones de Mold et Uxor ad nos sunt. Dom. Cancello scribo. Pransus cum Dom. Jones in Forum descendo equinum, ubi parca varietas; post Vespertinas Archidiaconus Booth ad Fontis allicit. DD. Thane et Bowyer rogati adsunt, singulas sumimus ampullas post ad Dmn Bunbury cum DD. Jones dies modo in Nox clausa.

2 Evino male satis, me roodee coniicio v paractis spatiis refectus. Nil publico in Gemellos. Dno. Stephano Fox A. LXXX agentis 27 Septembris natos. 2 Testes ex parti Hurleston examinati post prandium socordia occupat. T. Gorst scribo, domi haero sparsim in libris, semo carnatus et Elixir potus cubitum eo.

3 Nocte pluisset, dies clarescit, evanescit dolor. 2 Testes alteri Hurleston

34 For the translation of the next twelve entries, see the appendix.

examen subeunt D. Jones et Uxor redeunt. Vesperi delitescens. Dno. Praton, Ed. Puleston et Pigots Fratribus obvius sum forte Ad Fontem. Nos conferimus, singulas haurimus ampullas.

4 De hesterno dolor. Et recipio Epistolam D. Lambert et responsa do Episcopo prius consulto. Dies juridicus resparca, fuanus et requie refectus. Joanne Mecum in roodee descensum Subtus Muri propaguaculum ibi, ossa quae humani restarent corporis versus septentrionem et Austrum despoitas . . . reperta in Ossuarium proxime, deponere spondet, quater de ambulatem. D. Thane me reditum. Arcessit Ad Fontem itum tres Rubris horasque consumimus.

5 Nondum bellae satis. Caelo sereno et clementi, me conjicio. 5 spatia conficio. Literae pubeam de Gestis silent militaribus, parum Tabulato, do precibus finitis ceterum diei Cornelio Nepoti Sex Imperatorum vitas lege.

6 Precibus habitii, die domi sum. DDs Cancelor et Pope et Vaudrey scribo. Libris attentior ceterum diei his sumo.

7 Mane lecto surrectus preces celebro matutinas. Literas recipie Dominus Parre in quibus et Cancelor modo Londini et Dr. Pope memorati. Ds.Egerton in choro brevem nervosam vero Concionem, habet super 1 Cor. c. 11. v. 20. in sacra Synaxi participes sumus, vitam det D.O.M. piam, justam, sobriam precibus finitis vespertinis, Ds. Bunbury accesscens, Ad. Falconis Dominum Ludlowe Dublinensem, visum comitor, adest Phillips Centurio, et Cena et vino nos libere recepit. Ds. Ludlow, vir munificus cui Fortuna longo et largo afflaverit cursu.

8 E Nocte et vino intempestis aegre est. Ad preces mane me confero, dein ad Episcopum, Literas Ds. Pope ad se monstrat. DD. Bouchier, Hulton et Roberts. Malpas eunt, pluviuscula a Roodee non detinet. 4 conficio spatia, pransus requie, refectus. Vesperi Ad D. Bunbury regatus traevo D Ludlow, Allen, Morgan et Ego caena etiam et rultre hilariter satis exceptis Status regni Convivii Argumentum.

9 Elixius parum petus convalesco. Vocatus Do. Episcopo officium par prante res detacta et delata responsa. D. Pope. Editum parochialis Wigan pro Negotie in libris inde plerumque Dies Littera publica principe, Henrie Darmstadiensem ad Barcelonam oppugnatam dant selopo casum vitas et Imperatorum Nepotis lego.

10 Dies oritus lucidior preces celebrate. Dies Decantibus Cestris et Wirral dictus. Obseqium Episcopo. Cancellarium Officci nimis neglecti accusat absentem. Huic rem scribo et describo Episcopus sedet judiciater gravem mitam et diligentem repraestat. Delaciones inspicit omnia rite satis. Post vespertinas ad Peckii Commentaria et Nepotis vitas me confero.

11 Matutinas celebro Caelum lucidum et suave me, roodee trahit, ubi 5 spatia perficio. Pransus ad Nepetem re [?] Tremestre Tributum X[s] pro officio solvo impositum. 2 Testes Hurst extra Iudicium jurati examen subeunt. Vesperi Ds. Thane, Allen, crassus et Ego singulas herminas ad Fontem ebibimus.

12 Post preces in campum meum roodee descendo, 4 spatia conficio. Civitas tota praetori eligendo intenta Ed. Puleston 410, Gul. Starkey 457. Ds. Williams 310. The Bench by a majority 15 to 5 vote for P. out of the House. Hee names J.

Stringer his Sherif, the commonalty chuse Mr. Hulmes the other. I present the Mayoress with 2 Guineas. The Mayor is attended home, I along. After this at the Fountain with Sir H.B., Sir Tho. Billot, Mr. Shakerley, Bruen &c. Wee drink above our Bottles.
13 Indispos'd. Write to Mr. Chancellor, Parre, Page. After repose to the Fountain with Dr. Thane and Mr. Berrisford, above our pints at the Fountain. After this go in the dark to the Mayors, mistaken, pass and fall down the stairs leading to the back of the Plume of Feathers, fall backward, am hurt and amaz'd but have reason to thank God, for the preservacion. After stay an hour with the Mayor, a brisk shower falls.
14 My pain increasing, I draw 8 ounces of Blood, stay at home till prayers. After these wait on my Lord on the Chancellor's account and for his commands in the Visitacion, hee is in good temper and more equal. After this visit yong Mr. Warren, who had bin a fortnight here sick of Rheumatism, prepare matters for my Journey tomorrow.
15 I write to the Commissary of Richmond fully about his cause with Mr. Lambert and inclose it to Mr. Lambert. Sett hence about 10, reach Namptwich about 2, find the Busienes easy, write hence to the Chancellor. My Lord Bishop's present sentiments Take in Company near a Bottle, lodg in a private House.
16 Wee go hence, about 9 the shorter, tho troublesom road, come to Midlewich past 11, here little Busienes and after that treated at Mr. Cowpers. The rest Ale, I drink my Bottle of Claret. Mr. Hulton in this Conversacion has a long and fulsom Account of his power-makeing it sole, of the Choice of the Mayor of Chester.
17 In a calme fine morning before 9 sett for and come to Macclesfield about 11, the Busienes dull. In the Evening Mr. Hulton and I invited, go to Mr. Hulmes house, called the parsons, are well reciv'd by his gentile wife and her Father Mr. Higinbotham. After Mr. Hulme brings us to an Ale House under the Hill, where good Ale, wee return about 9 to our Quarters.
18 St. Luke. The company divides, Mr. Boucher and Ned Roberts to Henley, Mr. Hutton & Stratford to Mr. Davenport of Midford, I to Lyme, I come there about 12. Mr. Legh absent at Manchester. His Lady, Mrs. Sarah Banks &c. at Dinner. After Mr. Richard Legh, Mr. Ogle & Mrs. Legh shews her alteracion of Rooms and her closet. Condoles sensibly the death of a little Dog, their pett. I walk about entertain'd with the furious roaring and Amours of the Staggs near the House. After supper about 12, Mr. Legh returns, wee continue Conversacion till three.
19 Rise indispos'd about 10, take a walk about the Cascade with Mr. Legh, after in the Buttry, Mumm and bread and Cheese. Stay there till 1. Thence quiet to Stockport come at the End of the small Busienes, thence about 4 for Manchester, reach about 6. Mr. Thornley comes to Mr. Boucher and myself, deep in drink and attacks us with rude language which provokes twixt him and mee some sharp Altercacion.
20 After Elixir easier, Not one appearance at Church, a considerable Number

afterwards. Our Busienes of Wills &c. (even here) at a Low Ebbe. After that over, Dr. Holbrook, Mr. Asheton, and our company (most of it) to the Angel where, in tollerable wine wee pass some Hours. Here Mr. Hulton on occasion of mencion of him, vehemently uses the Richmond Commissary.

21 The weather continues fair and brisk. Mr. Ashe the Chaplain preaches Fore and After Noon on [?] sound and short. After Evening prayers Mr. Stratford and I invited, drink a Glass of Claret with Mr. Pigot. After this, I visit the Warden, repeat Claret there, return about 9.

22 A brisker morning. Wee sett hence about 9, come to Bolton before 12, tempted tho against designe. Stay dinners here, do some Correction Busienes, start about 2, come to Blackburn about 5, venture to sup on Mrs. Prices good Mutton and Capon and after Ale to Bed.

23 A very blustring morning, clear Ease after Elixir. Slender Busienes at the Church & office. At dinner the Busienes of the Whiggs manag'd twixt Mr. Boucher and Hammond. I examine 3 wittnesses on Brandwoods Will. After a private Hour in the vicarage & formal supper call'd out to Coll. Nowell of Read and Receiver Thornton, hear his the Coll. loyall, orthodox and obliging profession, the story of Tallard his interposing in the Elecion at Nottingham, on the Whiggs side. Mr. Thornton asleep, wee drink liberally for the Time, part at 10.

24 A sweet morning. I make an Epitaph for Mr. Oddys Grave, after a dish of Coffee set out after 9, come by Brindle to Chorley at 12, meet small Busienes, good Company, Mr. Haydock & Pilkington. Set hence about 4 come to Wigan and Finches before 6. I ly at my Cozen Holts.

25 Set about 8, pass Holland not without melancholy reflections, the way frosty & slippery, reach Ormskirk about 11. The Busienes here proporcionable to the rest. Mr. Marsden is here on Glesk Case, the 2 sisters Sandford choose Mr. Kippax their Tutor. Mr. Hesketh makes a confus'd complaint against his Lady, charges her with Consorting with papists and refuseing his Bed, hee shows irregular multiform passion to Mr. Marsden, Kippax and myself, detains us till 10, then I to Mr. Dods.

26 After a good rest, cool and easy. The rest started early for Warrington. I stay, finish my particular Account and Debt with Mrs. Dod paying her $7^{li}.5^{s}$ I go with Mrs. Marsden and Kippax visit the afflicted Family (Chisnalls) at Grippy Hill. 3 daughters appear affected with astonishment, not disturb'd to Action, the son (about 14) seems under the power of Distemper & Charm. Stareing first, falls backward then into convulsivi and frantic Accions, is sometime distorted, blind, deaf, runs thoro a vicissitude of Disorder, for half an hour, and returns to the Circumstance of his sister. Wee went to prayers well adapted at the beginning of the Fitt. My old acquaintance Mr. Cropper (once Cook at Knowsley) is here & Grand father to the disorder'd person. Mr. Marsden interposes grave sayings, and gos hence to Mr. Stanley. I sett hence about 11 and lessning the long way, com to Warrington about 3, find the Busienes agreeable, dine on a Woodcock. In the Evening relax with Mr. Shaw, Mrs. Golborn & Darbishire his Ward and Edmund Taylor who unlearn'd gives great proofs of cheerfull, mannerly & sagacious parts and Sagacity, commended by good principles.

27 A calm and pleasant morning, not happily free of the last nights wine. Sett hence about 9 and at Frodsham before 12. At the Church usuall Busienes. Mr. Davies, Surrogate thence to small Busienes and dinner. Mr. Boucher suppresses not peevish and petulant Temper, wee quit hence before 4 and return safe ad Lares D.O.M.G. about 6.

28 Under the help of Elixir, confin'd at home. My Lord has a private ordinacion of 2. Wee are startl'd with the ingrateful News of the event of the meeting of parliament. Smith who had 248 chosen Speaker. Bromley haveing 204 of the senior side. I dispatch 6 Capitula of Tertullians Apology, to Bed and Dream of a new world.

29 After early prayers, attend my Lord, hee communicates Letters and Busienes, I report. Hence to roodee and recourse of 4 Turns, whilst writeing to the Chancellor am call'd to the palace where Grange Warburton, a pure Fanatic teazes impertinently the Bishop about his Chapelry for which hees presented and Rails about the Altar. In the Evening I return to my Lord with a cautelary Letter from Mr. Wright & not to admitt Mr. Johnson to the Curacy of Farnworth, promising a more worthy Candidate recomended by the Families of Bold and Beausey. After a Letter to Mr. Wright, to the Fountain with Mr. Hitchcock and Crosby. After there with Dr. Thane, yong Lawyer Foulks & Mather.

30 Mediocriter me habens me in aestuarium roodee amicum conjicio caelo rigescente, sex spatia conficio inde convalesco. Do. Chamberlain scribo. Litterae publices nil afferunt bonis, Suffragia Bromley dantes 15 officiorum damno multator. Negotii parum Do. Bankes de Wigan post meridiem me visit re tribulares narrat.[35]

31 Frosty 4 Turns, write and inclose a Copy of the presentacion to Kirklington, to Archdeacon Shore.[36] Invited dine elegantly at the Mayors with Mr. & Mrs. Peck, Partington &c. In the Evening visit Lady Bunbury pay Mr. Foulks to day 53^{li} write to Mr. Wright of Cronton.

NOVEMBER 1 A very hard Frost, I Jack with mee take a turn on Sutton Heath, call at the candidate Nurse. After dinner Anthony Close calls on mee, discourses on the Commissary and Mr. Lambert. After prayer and some Busienes, at the Fountain with Dr. Thane, Egerton, Colly, Mercus freely.

2 Indispos'd from the Quantity recurr to 4 Turns on roody and recover in a delicate frost. After dinner pay Pickering his Note, repose an hour Mrs. Egerton and Brook come to mee. I wait on Mr. Egerton to my Lord. Hee imparts his

35 Trans: 'In indifferent health, I hasten to the friendly tidal waters of the Roodee, the weather freezing, I complete six turns and then feel better. I write to Mr Chamberlain. . . .'

36 L.D.A., CD/PP/5, Kirklington Parish Papers; L.R.O., Call Book EDV2/6. Robert Ashton, M.A. (deacon Chester 1672, priest Chester 1673), instituted on presentation by the Crown due to lapse.

design of 2 schools, it pleases. After in the Evening Dr. Thane and Mr. Boucher drink a Token Bottle at my Fireside.

3 The frost continues I take 4 Turns on roodee. After write and inclose a Bill of 30^{li} to Dr. Pope, write to Mr. Lambert and Mr. Wright of Cronton. In the Evening to the Bishop of Meath, read Plautus pseudotus.

4 The weather relents. Dr. Thane preaches on Prov. 9 v. 12. The News brings Losses at Sea, the Earl of Galloways arm taken off by a Canon Bullet before Badajos, not then taken. After Evening prayers proceed to the xvith Chapter of Tertullian Apologia, visit after Lady Bunbury.

5 Frost returns, I take 3 Turns on roodee. Anniversary centenary of powder Treason. Dr. Entwisle preaches on St. Luke 9 v. 55.56. The Bishop sends for mee and gives order for a Citacion against Mr. Hall of Eccles. After Evening prayers and Salust, At the Fountain Dr. Thane, Mr. Bennet & I, 3 pints and hours.

6 The Frost gently receded. I perform 4 Turns on roodee, pay Alderman Allen the 30^{li} return'd to Dr. Pope. After some Applicacion, Mr. Wright of Cronton calls on mee, desires my assistance with my Lord about the Curacy of Farnworth, I leave his papers with my Lord. After Mr. Wright, Mr. Ainscough their Candidates, 6 Contributes and myself are liberally genialiter at the Fountain till 1.

7 A brisk cool morning receives mee indispos'd. About 9 Mr. Wright, Mr. Ainscough & company come to mee. I attend 'em to my Lord. The Testimonials on both sides produc'd and the matter particularly discust. Mr. Wright answering readily and well, objections made by my Lord. Dr. Entwisle is an ambiguous Advocate. My Lord grants a Licence to Mr. Ainscough. Mr. Wright and hee come home with mee and express their thanks. The Chancellor and his Lady return about 4, I wait on them. After go with Dr. Thane to the Fountain where freely 3 pints.

8 A mild morning. Court Day, calme Busienes, examine 3 Wittnesses on Butlers Will. In the Evening the Chancellor calls on mee, tells mee his and Mr. Parrs result wants mee to go up to London in the matter. Dr. Thane & H.B. come, wee are at the Fountain.

9 A calme morning. I perform 3 Turns on roodee, after meet the Chancellor, wait on him to the Bishop who produces all the present complaints on his hands to us. After Dinner and prayers recreate in Plautus.

10 A moist Ayr, yet perform 4 Turns on roodee. Apply to Busienes, pay Mr. Chancellor 40^{li} on Account of the Visitacion, proceed in Plautus, a dull rainy Evening detains mee at home.

11 After a walk of 4 Turns, in a stormy morning, too late for the Church. After Evening prayer, with the Mayor, Alderman Partington and the 2 Sheriffs at Ale with Mr. Willoughbies, proceed today in Tertulians Apology.

12 After Elixir Ease. Write to Mr. Wareing and apply to Busienes, in the Evening after Plautus at the Fountain with the Chancellor Dr. Thane, Mrs. Kendrick and Hulton.

13 I repeat 4 Turns. Apply to Busienes, dine with the Bishop where

Archdeacon Entwisle, Mr. Chancellor, Bunbury, Green &c. Return to Plautus, after with Mr. Birchal of Holland and his kinsman at the Fountain above pints, wee stay till 12, Write to Mr. Peake about Knutsford schoole.

14 A calmer morning draws to roodee where above 4 Turns. I apply to Articles against Mr. Hall. Mrs. Betty Sandford sees and parts with us, pays for her Table 4 months 4^{li}. After repose, recreate in Trinummus.

15 A sharp Frost, attend my Lord in the morning. A court day competent Busienes. I examine 4 Wittnesses on Gaskells Will. After divert in Plautus.

16 About 8 begin to examine Walthews Witnesses. I apply to 'em all day and about 9 at night end with 14.

17 About 9 set on the rest, dispatch the other 4 about 12. Affected with severe Head Ach repose an hour, the Chancellor then calls. I make an order for Richard Bebington. After wee go to the Fountain dispatch 3 pints over Familiarity and Busienes.

18 After Elixir easier stay at home till noon. Dine with the Mayor where a good dinner good company, Sir Richard Vernon, Dr. Thane, Mr. Cowper &c. After prayers return to Tertullion, Indispos'd still repeat Elixir.

19 About 10 call'd to my Lord where before him and the Chancellor, 3 of the parishioners of Cockerham represent their Case. The vicar Mr. Winter in prison, the Cure neglected, dilapidation of the vicarial Buildings, desire, which my Lord grants, a Sequestracion to the Wardens of Cockerham & Ellell. I draw it full and specially, it takes up the short day. In the Evening a good company the Chancellor, Drs. Entwisle & Thane, Mr. Cowper, Bowyer and myself cheerfully pass some hours at the Fountain.

20 After a rainy night a cool morning, I endevor at ease from 4 Turns on roodee, but am disappointed. The News has nothing gratefull but the surrender of Barcelona 14 Oct. confirm'd. After Noon, Mr. Seddon for the Isle of Man Calls on mee, wee recount the Affairs of the Derby Family some hours. Hee teaches mee to direct to Mr. Lewis Monniere at the Earl of Derbies in New Queens Square, Wesminster.

21 Helpt again by Elixir, head and stomach recover, a stormy day succeeds a Stormy Night. I write to Mr. Monnier apply to Busienes. After prayers I meet Dr. Thane at the Fountain, the Chancellor comes, staies an hour with and leaves us. Wee stay past 9. I take occasion my design to the Dean and Chapter about my Lease, hee hears mee not with the Generosity I might expect from the services I have don him. Mr. Stapleton, the Bishops Gentleman, here with mee this day 7 night, died of a Fevor about 10 at Night.

22 After an uneasy Night, calme and compos'd in a calme and temporal morning (D.G.) Court Day, competent Busienes. I examine 2 Wittnesses for Harrison twixt 4 & 5 inter examiandum, a very vehement storm rises, shakes windows dos not overthrow but lasts not an hour. I examine at night 2 Wittnesses against Holford schoolMaster of Goostry.[37]

37 C.R.O., EDC.5 (1705) No. 5, Goostrey.

23 I examine 3 more Wittnesses against Holford. The News brings the manner of Barcelona surrender and Lord Havershams speech. Before prayer wee attend at the palace on Mr. Stapletons Funerall, a decent company the procedure solemn and affecting. After that and prayers invited, the Chancellor, Dr. Thane, and myself, treated by Mr. Boucher, chamber, with 3 Bottles Irish wine.
24 A calmer morning invites to 4 Turns on roodee, I draw a special Declaracion of penance for Richard Bebington. Write to Mr. Hurst about going to examine his Wittnesses at Tarbock. After Noon the Chancellor and I attend the Bishop, the matter of Mr. Ellis succeeding Mr. Stapleton is mencion'd with Favor. The Bishop dos not determin. After prayers Mr. Chancellor & I to the Fountain, turn Mr. Kendrick in the way. Dr. Thane and Mr. Hugh Foulks follow us wee stay past 9.
25 Indisposicion tempts to roodee where I take 4 short Turns in a stupendious scheme of Sun, thicker Ayr and the plain, return too late for church, apply to Tertullians Apology. After prayers in the Evening, finish it, and enter on the Life. Richard Bebington perform'd his order in a great Congregacion today at St. Michaels solemnly when Mr. Leftwich had prorenatu a Sermon on Marriage is honourable &c.
26 I recurr for help to roodee, perform 4 full Turns. Apply to Busienes and Books. After prayers, at the Fountain with the Chancellor, Sub-Dean Wright and Dr. Thane, they go at 8, wee stay till past 9. I renew my request about my Leases, hee promises his Assistances.
27 Tho in a moist morning, repeat 4 Turns am refresht. I attend the Chancellor to the Bishop with a peticion from Mr. Downs and others of the Chapelry of Pott about the deplorable condicion of the Chapell. I dine at the Mayors, with a good company 20 Ladies 15 gent, some stay together there till 8. I here take the Opportunity to speak to Mr. Sub Dean Wright and Mr. Foulks, they promise their Assistance about my Lease.
28 After a stormy Night such a day. I write for my Lord to Mr. Winter & a relaxacion of the Sequestracion of Cockerham, to Thursday the 10th of January, his Lordship is pleas'd with them. I tenderly move my design about a Lease for Lives and try whether hee would give his consent. Hee kindly answers, hee would do what hee can, not contradicting his own injuncions. That hee can't move the Dean and Chapter in it, but will not contradict if they grant it. I attend the Chapter, they refuse to grant for Lives, but for 21 years, they agree to contract the 2 Leases into one, I paying double seal mony only this time, they do it with Civility and favor. I am gratefull to my Lord and content (D.G.) with what they do. After prayers Dr. Entwisle, Thane and myself go to the Fountain are cheerfull in our pints and at home before 10.
29 A dull moist morning, I write to T. Gorst. After attendance on the Bishop, Wee go to Court where Busienes competent. My Cozen Edward Hulme dines with us. I examine 2 Wittnesses on Harrisons part, 4 against Holford. At 7 invited, go down to the Chancellor where Dr. Thane, Mr. Boucher & I treated with 4 Bottles good wine and a wild duck supper, wee part about 12.

30 Indispos'd from Supper and late wine. I proceed on the Wittnesses against Holford, dispatch the remaining 3. After Noon attend the Chapter receive and approve my Lease concluding both Tenements. The Dean, Q.B.E. seals & delivers it to mee, with a solemn and kind Benediction. Pay double seal money $6^{li}.13^{s}4d$, half of which reckon'd for the Fine, a Guinea to Mr. Foulks for the Lease and Counterpart 5s to the 2 Virgers and here too $3^{li}.10s$ the last years rent ending at Michaelmas to Mr. Fogge Receiver. After Adjournment Dr. Thane and I meet at the Fountain where 3 hours and pints privately hee treats with 2 & ½. Moist dropping weather, concludes the day and month. I remember with my domestic company Lady Charlott Cornwallis her 27th Birthday.

DECEMBER 1 Q.F.F.F.Q.E. A calm but moist day. I meet the Warden of Manchester on Busienes at the Coffee House. To Books and Busienes. After prayers with the Warden at Mr. Pickmores where wee settle Accounts. I pay Mr. Pickmore the Bishop of Meaths Bill $1^{li}.13^{s}$ stay here with the Warden till 9.
2 A dull continu'd rainy Season. I keep at Home turn Tertullian. After Evening prayer the News with the King of Spain and other Letters from Catalonia to the Queen divert us.
3 Still moist and heavy, I take leave of the Warden. Thence to Busienes and Books write to Mr. Styth, Travers and Wm. Harrison. After Noon wee visit Lady Salisbury and Mrs. Oldfield and her family. In the Evening at the Fountain sent for by the Chancellor and Dr. Thane stay till 8, after write and indorse T. Gorsts Letter to the Bishop of Meath.
4 After a tedious night reliev'd about 4 in the morning by Elixir. A dull moist day, apply to Books some busienes. John Cross & his man begin to wainscot the new room. I write to Mr. Okes on John Billingtons account.
5 The weather rainy and blustring. Apply to Busienes and Books. After prayers with the Chancellor attend on the Bishop where severall matters depending are mencion'd. Wee after go to the Fountain, Dr. Thane follows wee pass 3 hours and 4 pints.
6 A constant rain and near Noon a very violent and loud Storm, a remarkable high Tide and Floods abroad. The storm continues till Night vehement. The last Court Day of this Term, the Busienes competent. The Bishop in Court expects Mr. Hall, hinder'd by Gout and Storm, pains cease, my Suzy her Friends call'd about her, I go to Alderman Allen, hee entertains mee near 4 hours with 2 Bottles good Claret and under concern for Ships at Park Gate, grave discourse.
7 The Storm ceas'd, rain and hail succeed. I write to Mr. Cholmley of Holford and send him an Oxford Almanack. My Suzy D.G. is safely deliver'd about a quarter past 9 of a Son. At the Coffee House where little News save the presents & Honors to the Fortunate Duke of Marlborough at Vienna.
8 The stormy weather over, I take 4 Turns in Roodee, the walk not much defac'd. I write to my Cozen Holt, her and to Mrs. Ryder. After prayers the Chancellor, Dr. Thane & I at the Fountain three hours over 4 pints. Mr. Legh sends mee a shoulder of an Hind.

9 A mild day I receive a Letter unexpected from the Earl of Derby kind. I stay at home and go on in Tertullian Ad Gentes well pleas'd. After prayers I write to Mr. Legh, Mrs. Holt agen, Mr. Page and John Crosse.
10 A fine mild day, 4 short turns on roodeë, dispatch John into Lancashire with the Letters writ last Night and send to Mr. Legh, Mr. Dodwills and Mr. Allens Letters recommending them to his reading, write to my Lord Derby and promise my service to procure the Library at Knowsley. I fall into Salusts Bellum Iugurthinum ingaga read it over.
11 A mild but frosty morning, invited by it take 4 full Turns on roodee. The News brings That the Lords by a great Majority on Saturday night voted. The Church in no Danger. I turn Florus. After Noon dull snow and sleet.
12 Rainy, the Rivers up travail interrupted. John returns with Letters and 10^{li} from the Tenant at Ayrfeild. In the Evening at the Fountain with Dr. Thane & Mr. Kendrick. Mr. Poole the yonger of Leverpool detains us with long and great Stories.
13 Still moist and rainy, strang weather at this Time. I at the Warehouse meet Sir H. Bunbury's present am surpris'd as much at the safe Urn as the broken Box. I attend the Chancellor on Mr. Pages Account hee receives mee and the Busienes with uneasy chagrin and morosity. I admire, resent and resolve. The day in thinking and reading spent, reliev'd by him in better temper. Dr. Thane and Mr. Kendrick at the Fountain with the addicion of 5 pints. I writt yesterday to my uncle Eyton to lend his daughter Ann tomorrow.
14 Indispos'd and heated by the wine. The Chancellor calls on mee, wee attend my Lord, Proddy, Winter, Scholfeild are subjects yet depending and troublesome. After an hour here I recurr for ease to roodee, find it in 4 Turns. About 2 our invited company come, about 3 The Child is baptized by Mr. Fogge in St. Oswalds church. Edward Puleston, Mayor, Edward Partington Alderman and Mrs. Mary Oldfield for my cozen Holt his Sponsors, his name Edward. After the company vizt Chancellor, Dr. Thane Mr. Fogge, Bowyer, Colly and Kendrick beside the Godfathers draw to close order approve of the Ale and wine and are cheerfull till 9. I attend Lady Bunbury over, find Mr. R. Booth with her sister, hee gos, I stay an hour & Bottle.
15 Hot and uneasy tho helpt by Elixir. I write to Sir Hen Bunbury my cozen Holt and Mr. Okes. Turn Roman Antiquity de Urnis sepulchralibus. Receive Mr. Eytons Letter and resent it.
16 A tollerable tho moist morning, reliev'd by 4 (2 long 2 short) Turns on roodee, receive my Lord Derbys second Letter, apply to Tertullian Ad Gentes, finish that and after prayers Testimonium Animae & Ad Scapulam. A brisk rain at and after prayers.
17 A clear and more hopefull morning and painfull head and stomack draw mee to 4 Turns on roodee. I attend the Bishop who tells mee hee writ to the Archbishop of York in Pages case. I write this to Mr. Godfrey Lee his proctor and to Mr. Bennet about the Earl of Derbys Library. After prayers with the Bishop. Hee desires mee undertake the reduceing the Liveings in the

Archdeaconry of Richmond into a scheme,[38] reminds mee of a Book lent mee Jacobi Philipps Thomasini de Donariis ac Tabellis Votivis Utini 1639 f4°f. Apply to Busienes some Accounts.

18 A rainy night succeeded by a wett morning and Day. With my Lord about the small Liveings. The News afford no Good. In Busienes write to Mr. Hulme about the Liveings of the Deanery. The Mayor of Macclesfield, in Busienes, his name Clayton, invites mee to his Inn the Golden Talbot treats liberally with Claret and honest Conversacion till 12 at Night.

19 It continues rainy, extremely indispos'd yet attend the Bishop before and after Dinner till night. Wee finish Deanery Amounderness. Hee is pleas'd discourses, freely & freindly & treats mee with good wine. Sir Francis Leicester assumes his office of High Sheriff. I am witness to a Leas to the Earl of Abingdon the Bishop's ruling.

20 A Clear calm Day. I attend the Bishop wholy, wee dispatch Lonsdale and Furnes Deaneries. After prayers Mr. Bowyer and I take 3 Hours and 2 pints at the Fountain. Roman Antiquity our discourse.

21 Rain and snow mixt. The News brings an Address to the Queen and resolve from both Houses on the 14 December, That the Church is in a secure and flourishing Condicion under her Majestys Government &c. Apply to Accounts, write to Mr. Cholmley of Holford about his leaveing Holford. After prayers Dr. Thane calls and sitts with mee till 9, Books our discourse.

22 I receive Mr. Bennets answer write to my Lord Derby and inclose copies of mine to Mr. Bennet and his to mee, write to my Cozen Parre, Pay Mr. Vaudrey 14^{li} on the Stamp Account, to Mr. Chapman his last years Salary $5^{li}.10^{s}$. To Mr. Lawrence the Taylor 18s. I write to Mr. Bennet, proceed in Accounts.

23 A cold and frosty morning. I hasten to roodee perform 2 short and 2 long Turns. An Ordinacion 4 Deacons. The News proceeds dully, I read de Oratione et ad Martyros of Tertullian.

24 A moist dull day. I write to Peter Walkden schoolmaster of Standish and to Mr. Okes, attend my Lord about the Account of the small Liveings under 80^{li}. I hear of yong Mr. Pulfords death. Mr. Wm. Massie dines with mee. I look on this occasion on the Ephemeris of my London journey in December 1685. After prayers I communicate to Lady Bunbury, Mr. R. Booths design on a Licence for her sister. I receive quasi virgula divina suppeditatas 25^{li}.11.4d for 26 Licences, write to him and inclose 2 Licences.

25 Christmas Day cold and moist, not rainy. Sanctissimam Caenam Dominicam in coetu frequenti inpertio. Antiphona de Christi Natalitiis e propheta Isaia et Luca Evengelista composita ad preces vespertinas expectacionem frequenti decantata est succedit mediocriter, post preces ad Tertullianum me confero L de poenitentia lego et de Carnis Resurrecione dimiatum.

26 Dies nebulis obductus, me ad raciones supputandas confero, aliquantulum procedo, Caeterum diei Libris Dominus Hobson cerevisia domestica excipio per

38 L.D.A., RD/B1/1, Return of Poor Livings, now transferred to L.R.O.

eum. Literas Domini Jebbe et Gorst mitto.
27 Musicae antiquae Authores, et Wettenhall de Musica Cathedralis verto Caelum nubilum est.[39]
[*No entries until 8 January 1705/6*]

1705/6

JANUARY 8 A calm fair day. After preparacion for my journey set out about 1, come to Warrington before 6, relax there with Mr. Page and Deane, to bed about 11.
9 A brisk Frost. Mr. Hurst comes hither early. I draw a Letter for Mr. Page to Mr. Godfrey Lee. Write and inclose a scheme of Enquirys after his Chapells to the Dean of York,[40] set hence about 9, call at Widnes at Mr. Wrights, a Tanner, on Mr. Aynscough, the Curat of Farnworth. Wee dine there on a roasted Goose. After treated with Mr. Aynscoughs Strong Ale proceed 2 Miles to Edward Williamsons of Tarbock. Hee and [*blank*] Woods the other Witnes are sworn before Mr. Bere, Surrogate and examined. About 4 set hence to Prescot and there Lodg at the Pyde Bull widow Houghtons. I sent to Mr. Bennet of Knowsley but hee comes not.
10 I see Mr. Lyme, Hee tells mee the story of his dangers in his Bagnio and wee take up the rest of the time, on my Late Lord Derby. About 10 a Letter comes from Mr. Bennet. After mount for Winwick come readily in a sharp and frosty day by St. Ellen thoro Burtonwood, to Winwick, about 1 to dinner, am engag'd and entertain'd with a variety of learning. Mr. Edward Finch carrys it with a torrent of Fancy, the Dean with Gravity, the Treatment tho trying, valuable. After 10 prayers thence imediatly to my old room, Lord Derbys chamber.
11 The Frost continues, I walk to Warrington. At the Coffee house where Mr. Patten shews mee the designs and plan of an Oratory. Mr. Vaudrey sees mee at Mr. Pages, wee dispatch 2 pints of White wine. I set hence after 12 come safe home D.G. about 5, wait on my Lord Bishop.
12 Repose after lassitude, the Frost continues. I write to my Lord Derby my late correspondence with Mr. Bennet, read Letters in my Absence. In the Evening at the Fountain with Dr. Thane.
13 The weather continues frosty. Mr. Shaw preaches in the Quire, well yet

39 Trans: 'I share the most Holy Lord's Supper in a crowded congregation. An Antiphon on Christ's Nativity composed from the prophet Isaiah and Luke the Evangelist, is to be sung at evening prayer, a large concourse is expected, it turns out to be mediocre. After prayers I turn to Tertullian. I read L. De Poenitentia and the Resurrection of the Flesh.
26 A cloudy day. I apply myself to reckoning accounts, I achieve very little. The rest of the day in books. I take domestic ale with Mr. Hobson. I write letters to Messrs. Jebbe and Gorst.
27 I turn authors of ancient music and Wettenhall on Cathedral Music. The sky is cloudy.

40 Borthwick Institute of Historical Research, Bishopthorpe papers R.Bp.68/6, for details of Kirby Ireleth parish. (Temporary reference.)

long on [?]. The News brings revolt in Spain, to Charles 3. After prayers with Mr. Boucher and Capt. Vesey nephew to the Archbishop of Tuam, an ingenious Gentleman intent on his Advancement. Wee dispatch 5 pints and stay an Evening too late.

14 The weather still freezing. I am with my Lord about the small Liveings of the Archdeaconry of Chester most of this day vid. till 8 at night, dispatch the greater part. At night Mr. Adams Curat and Mr. Davies of Holt call on mee at the palace, wee go to the Fountain are cheerfull over 6 pints till past 2 in the morning.

15 After prayers return to the Bishop. Wee proceed, I dine with him ArchDeacon Booth and Mr. Kendrick &c., indifferent company there. Wee dispatch all the Deaneries as far as the returns serve.

16 The weather holds cold and dry. Reliev'd by Elixir not recover'd. After some Busienes and a Letter to Mr. Bruen now at London on J. Massies Account, to my Brother Partington, where at a good Dinner, Mr. Booth and his new Lady, Lady Bunbury, Mr. Chancellor, Dr. Thane and their Ladys &c to number 12. After dinner at White wine, strong with ingenuine spirits. Hence to the Fountain with Mrs. Cooper, Wells, Sherwin. The Chancellor is prevail'd to stay till 2, the discourse torrent on Books, learning Lives.

17 Still seasonable brisk and dry weather. I hot and indispos'd. The first day this Term, Mr. Hall appears in Iudicio. My Lord reproves his Crimes gravely admonishes earnestly, supports tenderly. The Dean and most of the Canons present. A favorable day, no Wittnes. My cozen Holme brings mee 10^{li} from John Cross. I write to him back. My Lord Bishop comes over to mee, stays an hour, drinks a pint of good Claret among other things Mr. Hesketh is our discourse and seems a fresh provocacion to his journy to parliament.

18 A fair yet windy day. I go to roodee, recreate in 4 Turns. After with Mrs. Vaudrey, Patten and Golborn with my Lord. They lay the design and plan of the Oratory before him, hee receives them freindly, approves the piety contributes 5 as I do 1 Guinea.[41] After Letter to Mr.Okes repose and prayers. Dr. Thane calls on mee, wee pass 2 pints and 2 hours at the Fountain. Severall Sellars are set up in Watergate Street and wine in Emulacion, rash sold and drunk by all the Town at 1s 3d the Quart.

19 Fair and calm yet dull. I recurr to roodee perform 4 Turns, write to Dr. Pope, inclose a Bill of 30^{li}. write to my cozen Holt about the 100^{li} lent to Sam Prescott and to the Bishop of Kildare about the Legacy of 100^{li}, the rest relax at home.

20 A calm morning, some small rain. I go to roodee take 4 Turns return to Church. Mr. Subdean Wright preaches on Eccles 2.5. The News dull. After prayers wait on Dr. Norris his Lady &c. return'd I write to my cozen Parr and to Mr. Styth about Tom Birchall.

21 A fair calm day. I set out about 9, about a Quarter before 12 see as this day

41 Possibly the proposed church of Holy Trinity, Warrington.

12 month, Mr. Okes entring on the Forest from the demesne, meet him in the same place and moment of time an accident unusual. Hee entertains mee with the melancholy Account of 2 Friends, Mr. Daniel of Daresbury and Mr. Holford of Moulton, dead, the former on Saturday, the latter this morning, both in Mr. Holfords home. Mr. Charles Booth comes to us, and wee dine at Sandyway, chiefly on Hen and Bacon. After are cheerfull and freindly over a glass of small new & bitter Ale. Mr. Okes treats, it costs him 2s 6d. About 3 go hence to Vale Royal when 1st Lady Soames, after Mr. Francis Cholmley treat mee with civility and welcome. The Cause of Fenwick and Lady Grosvenor take up much of the Evening. Mr.Cholmley promises to print the Case and expose the Fraud and Confidence of the papists in it. Hee treats mee with a Bottle of Claret and sees me about 10 in my chamber.

22 The weather fair and very cold. The morning spent in walking about. About 10 to Mr. Francis Cholmley, sett out for Shavington. I stay and dine with Mr. Peter Soames, his Lady & Mr. Okes. After dinner Sir Peter treats liberally with good Ale and wine, presses my stay. I make way thoro near 2 Bottles of Claret, set from Vale Royal about 4, the way good and the horses willing, come safe (D.G.) in an hour and a half to my Corner.

23 A cool frosty day. Indispos'd more from lassitude than wine. The 2 Brothers Jack & Will Massie see mee. Wee talk the Busienes of Tottenham High Cross. Jack produces a Copy of Mrs. Pulford's Will which from several reasons, I suspect. They dine with us. I write to Mr. Parker about his design'd Burial place in Chelford Chapel Yard. Dr. Thane calls in the Evening, draws mee to the Fountain where wee dispatch 3 pints of Claret new at 10d the pint are cheerful & easy.

24 A brisk Frost. Court Day moderate Busienes. After prayers in Seneca's morals & Busienes. I write to Mr. Hulme about the Commission to examine Mr. Higginbothom's Wittnesses, a Snow falls before 9 to Night about 2 inches deep. Mrs. Ince, our good old Neighber & Lanlady dies about 12 tonight.

25 St Paul's day. I am at early prayers. Apply to the Return of small Benefices, write to Mr. Topping, return the Coins hee sent and inclose 2 Guineas with directions to buy particular Coins 13 in Number. Wee dine at Mr. Bouchers on elegancies, Harslet and Wild Duck, the Ale small and disagreeable. After prayers, return to Busienes. Mr. Page calls on mee. End the Day in Seneca de Ira.

26 A mild Thaw. I wait on my Lord on Account of the returns and Mr. Page write to my cozen Parr for an Abstract of Mr. Pulfords Will and to Mr. Godfrey, about Mr. Page's Busienes, in Seneca de Ira. After prayers the Chancellor, Dr. Thane and I to the Fountain. Alderman Allen comes to us, wee stay warm'd above pints and after 9.

27 Very much indispos'd to Devotion, Stay at home and read variously. The snow & Thaw about Daventry retarded the paquet by the loss of a Boy, therefore it comes not here till after noon and then brought no News. After prayers at my brother Partingtons, thence with him to the Club where Mr.

Warbuton, Lea, Walley . I send for a pint of Claret drink it in the round. I stay past 10.

28 A cold and rainy day. After Busienes and Dinner. The Apparatus of Mr. Inces Funeral begins. After prayers the Compy great and solemn proceed to the Church, about 6. Mr. Shaw has a good sermon on ps. 73 v. 6. The Funeral ends about 8.

29 Finish and examine the Accounts of small Liveings. The Chancellor, ArchDeacon Booth and a great company dine with my Lord. After prayers the Chancellor, Dr. Thane and myself are treated by Alderman Allen at his home, each a Bottle and 2 redundant, the wine otherwise intended proves but indifferent.

30 Martyrdom of King Charles 1, very much indispos'd by the wine overnight. I write to Mr. Bruen the 2nd Time about Tottenham Estate. Mr. Fogg has a grave discourse on . . . Jack reads Nelson's Introduction to the King's Tryall. I draw a Scheme for my Lords visitacions, since Bishop, bring it, which pleases. Wee have over a pint of Claret, some discourse of the Country.

31 A fair day. Wee take leave with my Lord and his Coach about 10. Moderate Busienes at Court. Mr. Hultons confidence meets with a Check, for attempting (usual only in him) to take a Will introduc't upon a Citacion into Court and to Copy it for the probat. In the Evening take 4 short Turns on roodee. After at 5 at the Golden Talbot where with Mr. Charles Booth and Mr. Whaley 4 pints of good white wine before 9.

FEBRUARY 1 A moist dull morning and rainy day. Mr. Elcock calls on and putts many Questions at Mr. Pulfords former and later Wills, even to a taedium. After prayers and Coffee, Home (where little news) to the Fountain with the Chancellor, Drs. Norris and Thane. The Chancellor reminds mee of a Book long ago lent Bronchursts Centuriae with reflections on Borrowing Books and not returning them. We stay till 4 hours and 5 pints consum'd. After this at my Lady Bunbury's, where among other Ladys she [?me de] somno pomeridiano corripit.[42] Here stay late past 11. I sent a pott of Charrs and Letter today to Mr. Francis Cholmley.

2 Another moist and dull day. I write to Mrs. Lambert, Page and Parker, to the last about a Dormitory in Chelford Chapel and inclose a Form of Certificate. Write to Mr. Eyton at his request, the Formalities of Wills and Codicil, deviseing Land. In the Evening after prayers read the Articles and settlement on Mr. Hanmers marriage with Mrs. Booth. After wait on Lady Bunbury.

3 A dull, moist & rainy day. Dr. Thane has a good and grave sermon on Rom. 2 v. My Suzys Birth day (39th) kept in domestick Celebracion. In the Evening write to Mr. Parr, Mr. Aynscough, Mr. Fishwick.

4 A Fair day, take Horse about 9, come to Vale Royal about 12. Mr. Francis

42 Trans: 'reproaches me for sleeping in the afternoon'.

Cholmley & Mr. Okes gone to dine at Holford. I Dine with Sir Peter and Lady Soames. After dinner take this Opportunity and step in a fine afternoon and Way to Oulton 3 Miles to see Mr. Crane, hee receives mee gladly and treats mee freindly in his Chamber. I send a direct compliment to my Lady Egerton who is too indispos'd to be seen. She returns civil Thanks with a pint Bottle of good Claret, our treat improv'd, wee are cheerfull, free and recollect old passages. Among these warmths, I tell him of my Suzys desire to know his Arcanum how to stop Blood. He seem'd a little shy and surpris'd but after a few scruples, tells mee as a particular Friend and the 2nd (Peter Eden the other) to whom hee has communicated the Secret. That these are the solemn words in the Name of the Father, of the Son and of the Holy Ghost, Blood stand thou in A.B. nameing the person, to be thrice repeated with Reverence, not authority, as in invocateing the divine Help, not commanding the disorder. He added that it was very effectual but ought to be very cautiously used, and communicated to very few. I part with him about 5, return to Vale R. before Mr. Francis C., after supper cheerful and free the Conversacion. He is oblig'd by my pott of Charrs. Hee treats mee with a Bottle of Claret. Hee, Sir Peter and myself stay togeather till 10.

5 Shrove Tuesday, a stormy and rainy day. I read Lady Braidshaigh and her Maid Morrice their Answers to Lord Kilmoreys Bill and the sentence of Dismission by the Delegates on my Lady Grosvenors part. After with Mr. Cholmley in his study, some discourse on them. Hee directs kindly a Guinea to my son Harry. After Coffee with Lady Soames, and mention of the Countess of Huntington her most imprudent marriage of a French prisoner at Lichfeild. To prayers and after them a good Dinner. That over a Bottle of Claret, my share, this and the good conversacion of Mr. Cholmley, Sir Peter Soames and Mr. Okes keep mee past 3, tho it rain briskly all the way and especially on the Forest I come safe (D.G.) to my corner before 6.

6 Ash Wednesday fair, very different to the preceding. Go to Choir where Mr. Fogg has an instructive discourse on Joel V.11,12. Hee tells the Nature and reasons of Lent and the Customs of this day. I apprehend Cold gott from the Wett yesterday am stiff and full of pains advis'd by Dr. Norris take Venice Treacle. Harry reads Nelson on Ashwednesday. This is the 41st Anniversary of the Queens Birth, but from the Fast day scarce celebrated.

7 Indispos'd from my cold and Cure, tho Court day stay at home, the Busienes very small. I write to Mr. Page and at night to the Bishop of Meath to him on Mr. Cholmleys request. End Seneca's 3rd Book de Ira, begin that De Brevitate Vitae.

8 Yet under the Effects and Cure of my Cold, stay close at home, write the 2nd Time to Mr. Styth about T. Birchall. Finish Seneca de Brevitate Vitae, dip in Marianas History of Spain. Receive a prohibicion from the Exchequer in the Busienes of Wright contra Archer.[43]

43 C.R.O., EDC.5(1705) No. 10, Croston.

9 A clear day. I write a long Letter to Mr. Okes, inclose Harry's to Mr. Cholmley, To Mr. Monnien. After some Busienes and prayers with the Chancellor, Drs. Thane and Norris at the Fountain, wee part after 5 pints and 8.
10 A cool fair morning. Rise to early prayers. After take 4 Turns on roodee. Apply to Tertullian de Poenitentia. See the scanty News. After prayers proceed in Tertullian de Resurrecione Carnis. Mr. Atherton one of the Rectors of Liverpool dies this day.
11 A very brisk Frost. Rise to early prayers. After perform 4 Turns on roodee. I write to my Lord Bishop now at London, congratulate his safe access thither, and send him only 3 particulars to add to the return of the small Liveings, receive and answer a Letter to Mr. Okes, receive a Letter from Mr. Gandy inclose the inclos'd and write to Mr. Hall of Norley.
12 A fine milder morning, dispatch Busienes in Ned Roberts absence at St. Asaph, write to Mr. Bera of Preston and inclose a Decree to swear Heyes an Administrix, Mr. Murray a Curate to Mr. Gipps calls on mee about Mr. Greenhalgh of Brandlesome. Mr. Hawkins and Mr. Cartwright call on mee. Mr. Lancaster prevails with mee to write to Mr. Legh of Lyme on Mr. Walker's account.
13 A fine morning, at early prayers. I transcribe the Accounts of the Deaneries of Frodsham and Midlewich, write and inclose them to my Lord Bishop. Wee are extremely surpris'd with the shocking News of my Brother Jones of Mold his death which happen'd about 11 last Night. My Suzy go's hereupon to assist my sister. In the Evening the Chancellor, Dr. Thane, Alderman Allen, Mr. Callis and myself meet Capt. Breholt at the Ship, who brought a token of ½ Guinea to us to be drank, from the Bishop of Derry, the wine proves bad and ingrateful, finisht here about 10. Mr. Allen invites us to his home, Dr. Thane the Capt. and myself, treats us intempestive with Brandy and Isquebagh. I am on a suddain much disorder'd and indispos'd by it.
14 Fair weather. Still extremely indispos'd go to Court where moderate Busienes. After dinner and repose examine four Wittnesses of Cowband against Tyley, recurr to possit and Elixir.[44]
15 A brisker day, a storm of Hale after Noon prepare but go not to Mold am hindr'd by the examinacion of 2 tedious Wittnesses of Blundel against Ryley. Tom Birchall gos back to Formby. I give him 5s, write in his behalf to Mr. Styth and inclose 4 Licences and Bonds to him. A severe storm of Hale afternoon. My Cozen Holt surprises us with her kind visit from Wigan. At the Fountain with Mr. Chancellor, Alderman Allen and Dr. Thane till past 9.
16 A wett cool day. I write to Mr. Legh now at Haydock on Mr. Walkers behalf. Little Applicacion to either Books or Busienes, pay Mr. Foulks on account 20^{li}.
17 Quick vicissitudes of Stormy and Fair moments, with my Coz. Holt the Forenoon but return with compunction to Tertullian de resurrectione Carnis.

44 *Ibid.*, No. 7, Preston.

After dinner expect a fair interval, with a design for Mold but the weather more stormy and rainy prevents mee. I send John & write to my Suzy. At Evening prayers at Litle St. John's. In the Evening, my Lady Bunbury comes over carry'd my coz. Holt and mee to her supper. I venture on good cold Beef and Sellery, her Ladyship adds a Bottle of Claret to the Entertainment.

18 A sharp yet clear Forenoon. Too great and to bee condol'd Aberration from Busienes and virtue. I write to Mr. Fra. Cholmley an Account of the Bishop of Meath's answer and to my coz. Parre. My Suzy returns from Mold, a sharp Storm arises about 6 & continues.

19 Still stormy, receive Letters from the Bishop that his Metropolitan has prevail'd with him not to visit the other Archdeaconry, the next summer, dull News from Spain and Hungary and from Poland that the Swede has totally defeated 12000 Poles and Muscovites. In the Evening after prayers at the Fountain with Mr. Chancellor, Drs. Norris and Thane.

20 A calme fair day. I perform 4 Turns on roodee. After in my return am treated with a morning Draught of Whitewine. After Dinner short repose. In the Evening Dr. Thane comes to mee, wee send for a Bottle of Claret.

21 Good weather. Court day, moderate Busienes. I examine 1 Wittness on the part of Basnet against Cumberbach. At Mrs. Mayors with my S. and Coz. Holt treated with fatt Oysters (fulsom and difficult to digest) before dinner. In the Evening, Sister Partington and her company with us stay late at Cards.

22 A calm fair day. Ned Roberts gos to Mold on Sister Jones' Account, attend on Busienes, write to Mr. Colly and to Mr. Johnston about the Brief for Iniskillen.

23 Prepare for my journy, mount about 11, come in a calm day about 2 to Vale Royal, dine on Fish recover'd from Dinner. Stay 2 hours freindly entertain'd by Mr. Fr. Cholmley & Mr. Okes. Go hence past 4 and reach Holford about 6, find Mr. Cholmley parting with his Tenants, hee receives mee as alwaies, freindly. After supper and short diversion to bed before 11.

24 I rise about 8 and in a fair calm morning, repeat all the solitary and solemn Walks about the House, and without, reflexions on the Time of my Acquaintance with this Family, the Vicissitudes in that and my own private state. A Breakfast is provided about 10, wee sitt down but are too full of the present scene of parting, to eat the partridg &c. About 11 Mr. and Mrs. Cholmley make the Effort, pass thoro a Lane of condoling and praying Tenants and Neighbors, a melancholy sight. About 1 wee come to Vale Royal where a noble Dinner and good company. Mr. Fr. Cholmley all along shewing his affection and Esteem to Mr. Cholmley of Holford. Set hence about 5 come to Olton past 6. Lady Egerton receives them kindly. After wee sit down to a good Supper. Mr. Philip Egerton is here and entertains, for my Lady. After Supper a glass of Claret. I see Mr. Crane ill on the Gout in his chamber, to bed about 11.

25 A fair calm morning, I see Mr. Crane, hee freindly communicates his purpose to leave the substance of his Estate, to a Charitable Use. Robert Eden, Executor and myself S.D.P., in some Trust. After Breakfast and a plentifull Glass of Claret, wee part hence about 10, come to Cholmondely about 2. Wee see the Greenhouses, Gardens, Fountains, Grottos, Aviaries, Canals a vast and redundant variety of delight & pleasure. Wee walk to the End of the long Walk, come hence about 4, reach Whitchurch and the Red Lyon about 6. Mr. Dod meets us here, After Supper a plentifull Glass of Wine, late to bed vidt. about 1.

26 Disturbed before 5. Mr. Cholmley, his Lady, Mrs. Croxton, Lord Chief Justice Pyne of Ireland and Mr. Robert Booth take coach about 6. Mr. Dod and I come in Mr. Cholmleys coach now sold to Mr. Clopton to Hampton post, hee turns to Malpas, I proceed in it to the Plume of Feathers, relax with Mr. Dutton the fatt Lanlord. About 1 take Horse, observe the Coach road difficult and almost impassable, come safe (D.G.) about 3 to my corner. After in the Evening at the Fountain with the Chancellor and Dr. Thane, till 9, this keeps up a heat & ferment in my Blood.

27 Extremely indispos'd and unhappy, repose and repent all day. In the Evening, Dr. Thane draws me to the Fountain, wee drink our pints, I chuse the white wine which succeeds.

28 A fair (Court) Day. Mr. Cooper dies this morning about 6. The Busienes small. I examine a Witnes on part Blundel. In the Evening with Dr. Thane at the Fountain.

MARCH 1 Q.F.F.F.Q.S. A fair day. I perform 4 Turns on Roodee, see the News suspending. In Busienes and Books. In the Evening with Mr. Cartwright at Mr. Bouchers chamber where entertain'd with a Bottle of Claret, but no Busienes as intended.

2 A brisker day. In Busienes and Books. At Night, our company invited to Mr. Bouchers where treated with another Bottle of Claret.

3 Yet fair but windy. At home sparsim in Books. The News yet suspending. In the Evening drink my pint of Claret in the Ale Club. Mr. Done return'd from London gives Account of our common Friends.

4 A rainy brisk day. At home in Books and Busienes. In the Evening wee finish the Articles and Bonds with Mr. Thomas Brock as bearing date 21 September last. Hee does his part with an indecent sullenes. Wee are treated with another Bottle of Claret. My coz. R. Holt comes to us.

5 A fair day. The News of Lancaster petitions against the papists and the zeal of both Houses of parliament in bringing and promoting Bills against them most mencion'd. About 2 my Coz. Holt and I mount for Farndon races, come hither before they begin. 4 run the 1st Heat a fine one, Minshalls a black Horse gets it. Lord Mollineuxs Horse hurt against a pole, runs no more, the black gets the 2nd Heat upon which the success is yielded. I see Mr. Legh of Lyme here, Sir Peter Soames &c. wee return about 6. After at the Fountain with Mr. Chancellor, Dr. Thane, P. Partington and Coz. Holt, thence Dr. Thane & I wait on the Bishop of Ossory, Hairstongue, at the Pyde Bull. Hee entertains us with Freedom and a Bottle of Claret.

6 After rain a fair day. Mr. Barnston of Churton is buried today. Ned Roberts & Jack for mee attend the Funeral, a chargeable scarce solémn one. In the Evening at the Fountain with Mr. Morrey. Over 2 pints Mr. Lancasters Case mencion'd.

7 A clear yet windy day. My Coz. Holts return. I write to John Cross, a Court of small Busienes and very speedy dispatch. After an easy repose in the Evening my Suzy and I visit Mr. Cooper & Mr. Callys after that Mrs. Worger.
8 A cloudy not rainy day, the 5th Anniversary of her Majesties Inauguracion. I go to the Church St. Oswalds. Mr. Lancaster has a sermon on Titus 3v.1, indifferent oratory. The News surprises that the warm Bills against the Growth of popery drop in both Houses. After prayers at the Pentice where in about 7 Glasses, the day is celebrated. Mr. Thomas from Dr. Stearn is with mee in the Pentice. After wee part in our pints at the Fountain.
9 A brisk morning. I take 4 Turns on roodee, pay Alderman Ince 30^{li}, to Ellen the Maid 2^{li}. Sir H. Bunbury returns from London, from Whitchurch on my Black Nag sent yesterday, I wait on him. After evening prayers at the Fountain with Mr. Hulton and Mr. Cartwright, read the princess Sophias's Letter to the Archbishop of Canterbury, that of Sir Rowland Gwynne to the Earl of Stamford, and a Letter to the Author of the Memorial of the State of England. My son Harry is hurt by a fall and carry'd home, surprises that D.G. no great harm appear'd.
10 A mild day. Subdean Wright preaches in the Choir a good and seasonable discourse . . . Mr. Thomas in St. Oswalds another such on psalm 19, 13. No News but the Collacion by Gentlemen of $250,000^{li}$ to the Assistance of Prince Eugene, secur'd by the Emperor out of his province Silesia. I draw a Form of presentacion to Leverpool. In the Evening wee visit Mr. Mayor ill of a cold. I write to Mr. Colly.
11 A brisk wind. Wee prepare but go not to Mold. I write to Mr. Styth and inclose the Form and to Mr. Topping. In Busienes and Books mediocriter. In the Evening visit the Mayor where I find Sir Richard Vernon a well qualify'd Gent. well acquainted with Horace.
12 A rainy day, in Busienes and Books. After prayers meet Mr. Hulton at the Fountain on Matters depending in Court. Hee uses his ordinary stile in affairs Ecclesiasticall and military. Hee calls St. Werberg's My Lane, and promises upon his Honor. Hee has a Message from Mr. Hutchinson and I a Letter from Tom Gorst on the Dilapidacions of the Chancel at Astbury. After 2 pints wee part. I go to Sir Henry Bunbury find there Dr. Entwisle, the Recorder, Dr. Chetwood with him, they sup. Hee entertains with good Claret liberally I stay till 11.
13 A windy morning, indispos'd from the quantity and Tune of the wine. Write an Answer to Tom Gorsts Letter refuseing the ½ Guinea from Mr. Hutchinson. In the Evening the Chancellor calls, wee go to the Fountain where Dr. Thane and Mr. Bowyer come to us, our pints cheerfully.
14 A rainy day, last Court this Term, the Busienes short. I receive an answer from Mr. Styth and reply fully. Apply to the Deaneries, write to the Bishop of Meath and to Mr. Hulme of Macclesfield.
15 Still rainy. The News has an address from both Houses to the Queen against Sir Rowland Gwynes Letter and the Loan of $250,000^{li}$ to the Emperor is almost full. I proceed in the Deaneries, dispatch all save Frodsham. In the Even at the

Falcon Sir Henry Bunbury, Chancellor, 2 Archdeacons, Drs. Norris & Thane, Mrs. Kinaston & Callis are here, they have a pretty supper but intollerable wine.

16 Fair but brisk. I finish the Entry of the presentments write to my Lord Derby and Mr. Hutchinson. I draw the final Decree against Daniel Harrison. About 4 in a cold blustering Evening wee (My Suzy and Jack) set out for Mold, come save D.G. to my sister Jones about 7.

17 This day more stormy. Wee go to Church where Mr. Penant the Curate reads the prayers and has a good plain Sermon on 1 Cor. 11 v 28, 29, exhortory to the Sacrament in both Languages English & Welsh. And the prayers and Catechism so afternoon. Wee see the Church its regular architecture & Monuments.

18 A calmer yet cold day. Mr. Wynn of Farm and Mr. Wynn old Atturney are here in Advice and Conference. Jack takes a Catalogue of my Br. Jones Library.

19 A calmer day. Wee look over the pamphlets. I fix on Bishop Pearson Vindicilles Ep. Ignatii, my Suzy on 2 others, Luca's Happiness and Parker's Eusebius. Wee pay my sister for them. After Dinner wee equip. To fulfill an inconsiderate vow, I go to visit Mr. Wynne of the Tour, my sister with us. Hee is not at home. Wee set hence about 5 and come safe D.G. in a dusky Evening about 8. I meet here an unwelcom Advice from Tho. Waterhouse that my worthy old kind rever'd Friend, Mr. Price of Blackburn died the 14th current about 6 at night of an Apoplexy, and a kind Letter from Dr. Pope.

20 A Fast observ'd. Dr. Entwisle has a very good discourse on Deut. 5 v. 29. I go to the Coffee house, the News has vast preparacions by France in all parts the Numbers amount to 235,000. I write to Mr. Jebbe and inclose 6 Licences. After Evening prayers and Dinner, Dr. Thane and Mr. Callys call on mee, wee go the Fountain where Discussion. Dr. Thanes clerk comes to him, wee dispatch 4 pints. About ½ hour after 8 at night a vapor or radius observ'd by some persons, long and streaming in the Sky. I return home perceive, in the North some parts of it.[45]

21 Prepare for Vale Royall, soon after 8 Dr. Thane, his clerk, myself and Jack set out. I part with the Dr. at Sandyway and come to V. Royal past 11. I notify to Mr. Francis my present brought of a Rea Fish. After prayers, full dinner part of the Rea, part of which . . . After that the Busienes in Ireland recommended to the Bishop of Meath mencion'd. I deliver to him 3 Letters writ to mee by the Lady Bradshaigh about her Maids 100^{li} lent Mr. John Grosvenor. Mr. Cholmley kindly shews mee his room retreat wherein favorite pictures but especially 2 lately sent to him from France. Hee comends the Features of that, hee suggested of the young . . . which indeed are fine and promising good and generous inclinacion, hee finds exprest the Features of the Family and adds a character of early and great Qualificacions. Mr. Okes is kind to Jack talks on Books with him, shews him the Furnace &c. Mr. Cholmley gives him 5^{li}. Wee part hence after 5 and haveing a fine Evening and no stops come D.G. safe home before 8.

45 A reference to the Aurora Borealis, seen as far south as Chester on occasions.

22 A mild cool day, Goodfriday. Mr. Fogge has a good Sermon on Luke 23 v 28. After at Coffee house where News of the parliament prorogu'd to May 21. A good prospect in Spain on the part of King Charles. Alicant surrendr'd to him. After prayers and Supper, I sit with Sir Hen. Bunbury 2 hours in his Closet, where over a Bottle and ½ of good, account of proceeding & speeches in the House.
23 My Suzy (sent to) gos to Wrexham to my sister Jones. I take 4 Turns on Roodee. Apply after to Busienes and Books. After prayers I visit the Mayor where Mr. Chancellor, my Susy returns.
24 A fine cool morning, at early prayers. After 4 short turns on roodee a thick Fogg falls, is nauseous yet the walk helps and recreates. At the Quire where the Dean preaches almost unheard on Luke 24 v. 26. Sanctissimam participor caenam. Det D.O.M. vitam puriorem.[46] After Evening prayers at the Coffee house where Sir Hen. Bunbury and Dr. Norris enter on an Argument about the Government. After in the Evening with Sir Hen Bunbury, hee receives with good wine.

1706

MARCH 25 At early prayers, a double Holy Day, a glorious sunshine, take 3 Turns on roodee. I write to Mr. Parr and inclose a coppy of Taylors Will. After Busienes and prayers wait on Mr. Chancellor end the day in a domestic pint. Pay Mr. Williams 3^{li} a years interest due 19 last month.
26 Still fine weather, at the Quire where Mr. Fogg has a good sermon on Acts 26 v. 8, after at the Coffee house where scarcity of News. The town fills with Spectators of the race, it proves very dissappointing, a black Horse of one Mr. Minshall easily getts 2 heats of an unequal Gallope. Bruce the old Horse pacer is thrown at the height of his Gallop, astonisht, but D.G. recovers. After the race, Mr. Chancellor, Callis, J. Cowper, Bowyer, Boucher & myself take our pints at the Fountain.
27 The weather still pleasant, apply to Busienes and prepare for the journy tomorrow. Make Sequestracions for Leverpool, Grapenhal, Blackburn. In the Evening, sent for, go to the Mayor at the Fountain, with whom Alderman Page and Mr. Newton, Dr. Thane comes to us, wee stay about pints part past 9.
28 A dull tho fair and calm morning, equip for the Journy, write to Mr. Wilkinson & inclose the Blackburn sequestracion. Mr. Boucher and I set out past 9 reach Warrington past 2. Refresh here, See the Oratory begun the Foundacion round up to the Floor, wee give our 1s each to the workmen, call on the Warden of Manchester at the Coffee house, proceed home after 4.[1] I send John with Mr. Boucher from Wiswawl to Holland. Jack and I come to Wigan past 7, I Lodg at my Coz. Holts.

46 Trans: 'I share in the most Holy Supper. May God the best and greatest grant [me] a purer life.'

1 See F.R. Raines, *Rectors of Manchester and Wardens of the Collegiate Church,* Chetham Society, N.S. vols. 5 & 6 for information on the Wardens.

29 Set hence and come to Holland before 9. Wee open the Commission and I examine a Wittnes before noon, after examine 5 more. In the Evening visit my coz. Fleetwood shee appears old & dissagreeable. After return to George Lyons where R. Walthew with his humor is uneasy.

30 In a delicate morning and prospect Jack with mee take a walk to Rough park, in less than an hour, this refreshes; to the Busienes, dispatch about 7, 7 more wittnesses, finish, receive the Charges which Mr. Gill pays cheerfully with a generous Gift of ½ Guinea to Jack. Wee drink a Bottle of the 4 of Claret brought from Chester and part about 11.

31 A sweet and cheerfull morning. I rise before 7, Mr. Boucher returns. I (with Jack) take a long walk up to the Milne, thence to the furthest shaw park down to Rough park Wood, to the House, visit my natalem That amum.[2] (John Byron the Tenant) hence, return to Holland in about an Hour, refresht to Church, Mr. Birchall has a good plain discourse. Hee and John Cross dine with mee at George Lyons. Hee repeats & continues the discourse in the Afternoon to a great Congregacion, adorn'd by the Families of Ashurst and Banks. Mr. Owens late purchaser of the Abby is here with a Train of his Ladies relacions, among which my coz. Carter and his. After sermon all these Ornaments at George Lyons where a plain distinction appears betwixt the principles of Mr. Banks and Ashurst on occasion of menconing Mr. Lesley and his Adversrys. After this I see my coz. S. Prescott and his wife, Mr. Birchall with mee thence wee adjourn to the old Clerks, here severe reflecions on Mr. Owen, his sordid and fanatical humors. Wee stay friendly and liberally at strong Ale till 1 a clock.

APRIL 1 A blowing morning threatening alteracion of weather. I ly later indispos'd. About 12 set to Ayrfeild, it holds fair, I with Jack walk round the Estate, see the Husbandry, ditching &c. from Whitley Hall call on Jane Hulme, old, 86 at least, in bed yet apprehensive. I bespeake here 200wt Cheese, order the tumbling Kiln to be taken down. Receive from John Walmesley 10^{li} which makes 30^{li} from Wm. Naylor a Years Rent ending at Lady Day 1^{li}. Wee dine on Eggs and Collops. I have a Bottle of Claret and 2 Bottles of Ale, hence returning visit Mr. Roby in his Adversity but mention it not, about 6 come to Holland, stay a while at George Lyons but proceed and come to Wigan about 8 where too kindly receiv'd.

2 Too kindly in the morning too. My she Coz. goes with mee to visit Mrs. Banks. Wee dine here. About 2 set hence away. I never went thoro Ince Golbern, Lawton to Winwick. I am well pleas'd with the way, call and see St. Oswald's Well, thence call on Edmund Taylor and come about 6 to Beausee am receiv'd kindly, Sir Peter Soames and Dr. Yarborough here. Wee continue freely and liberally past 12.

3 A brisk but fair day. Wee visit the stables and Oxhouses both greatly built

2 Prescott was born at Rough Park.

and well furnish'd. After dinner I present Mr. Atherton with Walker's Book of Medals, some Saxon and some Roman coins and promise if I live to instruct the Young Heir of his Family in them. I attempt to go about 5 but am drawn and invited back, the yong Heir adding his affections, and Force. Wee resume the matter of Conversacion liberally and continue it near 12.

4 Still brisk and blowing. Equipt about 8 Geo. Bate comes, wee celebrate this the 6th marriage day of the good Mr. and Lady of this House. I stop at Warrington indispos'd, rest till 2 and come (D.G.) safe to my Corner before 6. Dr. Thane invites mee out to the Falcon. Tom Gorst and Mr. Hodgson of Leighton in Lancashire follow, 2 Bottles of Claret keep up and increase my indisposicion.

5 A brisk day, severely indispos'd. Tom Gorst and Mr. Hodgson call on mee. I keep house, condole my Folly and misfortune. Mr. Green prevails today in an Action of Simony against Mr. Janny, Rector of Woodchurch.

6 My Indisposicion continues and confines mee. In the Evening I read 30 pages of Mr. Lancasters Querela Cleri Anglicani.[3]

7 Yet indispos'd and confin'd, read Tertullian de Jejuniis. After prayers I with my Suzy visit the Chancellor, ill under an Ague, here Dr. Norris tells mee the Queen has interpos'd and assum'd the Controversy betwixt my Lord Derby and his Neece. After I end the Day in a domestic pint of Claret.

8 I take 4 Turns on roodee tho windy. Write to Mr. Lambert about the Case of Caton Chapelry undecided betwixt him & Mr. Close. Apply to Busienes. In the Evening with Dr. Thane at the Fountain.

9 Repeat my walk on roodee thence to the Coffee House where News is considerable. I dine with the Chancellor. After dinner Mr. Markland calls and ends an Account of 48 Licences. In the Evening DD. Thane & Norris and Mr. Markland and myself take a liberal Glass at the Fountain, this keeps up and agravates my Distemper.

10 Very fevorish and indispos'd. A Court for the Deaneries of Chester and Wirrall. I with difficulty undergo it. After noon a small Company meets the Bishop about Christleton. After that Ceremony, Mr. Subdean, his son, Wetenhall, Dr. Thane & I end the Evening at the Fountain.

11 The last Court Day of this Term, the Busienes competent. I indispos'd from the 2 daies before.

12 The Chancellor and I waite on the Bishop several matters in order to the visitacion as others mencion'd.

13 Prepare matters in prospect of the Journy, write Letters to my coz. Parre &c. in the Evening recreate.

14 At the Quire, Mr. Shaw preaches. The News yet in the clouds, in the Evening at Bro. Partingtons.

15 It rains, Mr. Boucher, Hulton and Roberts set for Malpas. I wait on the Bishop and Chancellor.

3 'Pleas of Anglican Clergy'.

16 Answer an important Letter of Mr. Lancaster about his Querela. After dinner in a cool day set out for Namptwich, come there before 4. After Busienes wait on Madam Church, Mr. Wetenhall, Mrs. Bullen relict of my late ingenious and valuable Friend Dr. Bullen.
17 About 8 set hence come the next way not thoroly good to Midlewich. The Chancellor not come. Mr. Egerton and Vernon dine with us after which Busienes and Tom Gorst, Mr. Hulton and I go to Mr. Egerton at Mr. Vernons where elegantly and liberally treated with very good Claret. Wee stay past 9.
18 About 8, a fine morning set for Macclesfield call only and last at Hulmes Chapel, come easily to Macclesfield about 11. After dinner busienes competent, in the Evening with the Mayor Clayton, Alderman Johnson, Mr. Hulme and Mr. Denham very civilly entertain'd. My Friend, Mr. Gery, is under the misfortune of the Charge of Incontinency, applys to mee. The said company condemns him.
19 A sweet day set hence about 9 call at Havilah where civilly and plentifully entertain'd (the rest going on) by Mrs. Margaret and afterwards her Father, Mr. Swetenham, in the Garden here. I walk after to the Town where tho not dinner busienes is much over. After which I visit Mr. Shalcross who receives gentileey. Mr. Bolton brings mee down to Newton, where an excessive rainfall fills the ditches, brooks and lanes, accompanies us perpetually to Manchester where very wett, wee refresh. Dr. Holbrook comes. Here is Sir Thomas Bellott on his applicacion to Mr. Gilliam with company attendence, musick.
20 Refresht by Elixir, Mr. Hoghton of Leverpool is sworn by Commission from the praerogative before the Warden. The Busienes is considerable. After it to the Angel. Yong Mr. Greenfeild comes to mee as recommended to my Friendship, by his late Father Sir Christopher Greenfeild my good Friend of whose death (about 2 weeks ago) I first hear in this place. A company is gott and stays too long together. Dr. Holbrook treats them with Lobsters.
21 Good weather. At the Church where Mr. Clayton preaches well before, Mr. Ash indifferently afternoon. I see Mr. Pigott and Dr. Yarborough and am very civilly treated by both.
22 After some Busienes set hence about ½ hour past 9, reach Bolton past 12 dine, set out about 3 and reach Blackburn about 6. Wee are invited by Mrs. Wilkinson sister to Mrs. Price to the Vicarage, all to Supper. I only lodg there, shee shews mee a Catalogue of Mr. Price's Books (wherein his personal estate mostly consists) valu'd at 102^{li}. I think it is very high. Shee freely communicates the Circumstances hee dy'd in.
23 I account and settle with Mrs. Wilkinson all matters betwixt Mrs. Price, the Chancellor and myself. After dinner and all Busienes among which that betwixt Wilkinson and Dewhurst, wee go agen to supp at the Vicarage. Here is discourse twixt her Friends and mee about Mr. Prices bay and black Geldings which is adjourn'd till tomorrow.
24 A fair morning, wee with some difficulty and some odd expressions on her side, proceed to a bargain. I give her 14^{li}10s for the Geldings before 10 sett hence come to Chorley about 12. After Busienes about 4 sett out in a showr which

improving and continuing raises the waters to a formidable height. Mr. Hulton leading passes the most deep rapid & dangerous stream, gos on unsociably and unfriendly, without staying or giving notice to the Followers, is censur'd with common voice for it. Wee come safe (D.G.) in a vehement rain to Wigan where at my Coz. Holts I gladly meet with my Suzy.

25 St. Mark's Day, much wett falls, here. I repose and stay. The rest after dinner go to Ormskirk.

26 The News too uncertain brings the beating the French Fleet and raising the seige of Barcelona. I giving credit to it, set the Bells at Holland on ringing leaving a shilling to drink. John Cross meets mee here and gos with mee to Ormskirk where I bestow my old Mare on him, enjoyning him to bee a tender Master to her. The Busienes here is very considerable. I examine too, 3 Wittnesses on Mrs. Wilson of Tunley her Will, after a tedious day and a Glass with the company I lodge at Mrs. Dods shee being at Chester.

27 The rest before, I set hence about 10 reach Warrington quickly after 1. I find my Horse press too much and suspect him. Leaving here Mr. Boucher & Roberts set hence about 5 in a fair Evening, come the Golborn (now the worse way) to Wigan about 8 a clock, my Horse confirms my suspicion to discouragement.

28 At the Church before noon where Mr. Jackson preaches mediocriter. The News of Barcelona lies in conjecture. After dinner solace too softyly. In the Evening take a walk with my coz. Holt and particularly in the present Mayor, Adam Banks, Tenement, Sir R. Bradshaigh's Land wherein out of malice Mr. Sumner has caus'd Cole mines to bee sunk and great devastacion to bee made.[4] Wee after visit the Mayor and at a private Ale house drink with him.

29 A fair day. After noon, the women ride, I walk to see Mr. Brown at his comely and comodious seat at Ince. Hee receives us with good respect and welcome. Wee walk about the Gardens, orchards &c. observe a good situacion, return about 8.

30 The weather continuing fair, wee go to Ayrfeild, my coz. Holt with us, come there about 1. My Suzy, coz. Holt and myself walk almost round the old Estate, the day and season (Q.B.E.) afford a great variety of walk and prospect, return'd, wee are decently entertain'd with cold Lamb &c and the Bottle of wine. I left ten crowns, the Feast over, return about 6 and calling at the Owl in the Ivy bush reach home about 8.

MAY 1 The weather turns rainy. A Fair begins here but is slender in Cattle. In the Afternoon the Lady Philippa Standish, Lady Gerard, Mrs. Banks, Mrs. Poole &c meet at a play or Farce acted in the Hall call'd Bateman, the musick is comended. Mr. Banks, Mr. Mayor, my coz. Holt and I are at Tootells at Ale past 8. It rains severely.

2 Holy Thursday it seems the proper Fair day, great and unusual scarcity of

4 For information on early coal mining, see *V.C.H. Lancashire*, vol. 3.

Horses. In the Evening, wee visit Mr. Walmesley who treats indiscreetly with sweet meats made by his late good Lady, matters of meditacion to the company and 2 Bottles of good Wine.

3 The rain over, invited wee (Cosen Holt with us) go to Winstanley, are entertain'd at a good Dinner. After the Men see the fancied pleasure of killing Rooks by a Stone Bow, my coz. Holt kills twenty. Wee part about 6 and come home about 7. Jack meets us here from Chester with Accounts and Letters.

4 The weather dull and discouraging, wee stay at Home save in the Evening dispatch visits to Mrs. Latham, Mrs. Entwisle &c.

5 The weather clearer and hotter. At church twice, Mr. Johnson preacht. Mr. Banks & his Lady dine with us. John Cross sent for I admonish about his kindnes to the old Man and leave Hugh Charnock's Bond with him. After Evening service and Ale with Mr. Banks and the Major, I, Jack with mee, step to the parsonage of Standish. Mr. Haydock treats us liberally with good cold meat and French wine which with the Heat of the walk, made some false steps in the way home.

6 Very much indispos'd from the Evening, work the Forenoon and repose too softly in the Afternoon. In the Evening late about 9.

7 In preparacion for our Journy and visits. My coz. James Holt, expected comes from London. A Bottle of wine and some hours spent on his recepcion.

8 A fair morning, not yet recover'd to return, take leave about 9 come to Beausie about 12 are generously receiv'd at Dinner and after till past 4 then remount call at Mr. Page's on horseback, proceed at a good rate, call at Hoole on the Child Ned, before Sunsett and return safe to our Corner (D.O.M.G.) before 9.

9 Refresht wait on my Lord Bishop pay him 2 Mortuaries, the one 6 Guineas for Blackburn, the other 5^{li} for Liverpool, [5] then follow (on Horseback) the Chancellor &c. to Eaton Boate, here our Anniversary Chad on this day celebrated, Mr. Mather there Dr. Norris, P. Partington, Mr. Proby, the Chancellor, Guests. I see Alderman Allens house and return about 6. I send to Dr. Thane, wee end the day (adding Mr. Williams his vocal musick) in wine at the Fountain.

10 Solace see the News, read and write Letters.

11 Apply to Busienes and write Letters to Mr. Parr and Will. Massie. Fall in with the Chancellor and Dr. Norris at the Fountain. After the Coffee house, thence to Sir Hen Bunbury who gives Mr. Walley and I a plentifull Glass of good Wine which keeps us too late.

12 Whitsunday, extremely indispos'd, confin'd till prayers. After which the Bishop of Killala, from Ireland, calls on us. I attend him to our Bishop when Dr.

5 Although mortuary dues were abolished in 1535, they continued to be collected in Chester diocese, since a proportion of them were part of the bishop's stipend. In 1755 it was agreed that these should cease on the next voidance of Waverton rectory. This did not occur until 1767.

Smalridge's speech in presenting Dr. Grabe, much our discourse. After to Alderman Allens where treated till 10. Lastly to the Bridghouse where kindly over a pint of bad wine, much of our common Busienes as Legatees to Mrs. Stephens.

13 I procure a Bill of 40^{li} from Alderman Allen and send it to Dr. Pope, write to Mr. Okes. The Bishop of Killala, Alderman Allen, Dr. Thane, I and my Susy dine with Sir H. B., an elegant dinner, good wine, and enough of it. Yet after at the Fountain, most of the Company to worse wine.

14 Kept up in a Fevor, dine with the Bishop of Killala, Sir Hen Bunbury &c. at the palace, a noble Chine of Beef the Head Dish. One Mr. More from London, a pretender to Court and acquaintance with Dukes &c, ordinary yet in dress and Figure, diverts the company. After Dinner the Bishop of Killala and Dr. Thane to my house, I entertain with Hulmes Chapell. After this to Alderman Allens where with dull port, wee pass the Evening and before 10 part with the Bishop of Killala at the Cross.

15 Reliev'd some little by Elixir, yet in pain, unfit for Busienes. The Bishop of Killala took Coach this morning for London, leaving his Mare with mee. After dinner and repose I am call'd on another service to celebrate. Sir Hen. Bunburys and my Ladys seaventh marriage day. Sir Geo. Parker an honest Gent. of Sussex, Dr. Thane, my brother Partington & I the Men invited. A supper and musick adorn, wine fills and finishes the Feast.

16 Notwithstanding Elixir, Fevor pain repentance, a cool and moist day, at home in some Busienes till call'd at night by the Chancellor, Sir Henry, Dr. Thane to the Rose & Crown where Sir Geo. Parker and Capt. Breholt also, indifferent wine, Scolops and Oysters, wee stay till the post brings from France, Accounts a great probability of relief of Barcelona, part about 11.

17 Uneasy the Elixir continu'd. At the Coffee house, hear the News repeated with confidence. After Evening prayers relaps agen into the company of the Chancellor, Dr. Norris, Thane, Egerton, Richmond, Shawe, at the Fountain, the wine dull and heavy dissolves us about 10.

18 The pains attend the Infirmity. Mr. Hen Richmond calls on mee this morning, instituted to the Mediety of Leverpool. I take a small walk am something refrest, repose after Dinner does it more. All the people upon expectacion of Barcelona, they fill the Coffee house & are surprised with a victory obtained Whitsunday last by the Army commanded by the Duke of Marlborough in Flanders near Louvain over the French, their best Troops cut off.[6] I reced & rejoice in a domestic pint. I write the Bishop of Kildare and Mrs. Wilkinson about Mrs. Stephens Legacy.

19 Brisk and cool. Ordinacion Sunday. Mr. Lancaster has a Sermon on the occasion. From the Church, see the News of the victory confirm'd. Barcelona remains in conjecture. After Evening prayers Jack and Harry with mee, I go to

6 The Battle of Ramillies, 1706.

the Feilds see the Horses, after the Child Will, at Upton, refresh there. 15 Guns are fir'd from the Castle and the Bells express joy.
20 Cooler yet not recover'd. Apply to Busienes. Send a paper of the News of the victory to Mr. Dod of Malpas and Mr. Wright. After noon apply to the neglected Ephemeris, recollect one month. Expect but in vain to night further News. My Suzy and I very freindly entertain'd with 2 Bottles Good wine by Sir Hen Bunbury and my Lady, the kindness stays us till 12.
21 D.O.M.G. recover'd to ease and coolness, recollect the rest of this Diary, to this day. To the Coffee House where the victory in Flanders confirm'd. Barcelona suspended. I visit Sir Peter Soames (comes with his Lady to Mrs. Otleys last night) I pay Alderman Allen for his Bill & return 40^{li};10;0 as lately, on Account to Mr. Vaudrey 40^{li}, to the Chancellor 50^{li}. to the Bishop 45^{li}, to Mr. Foulks 70^{li};3;4d. After Evening prayer with the Chancellor and Dr. Thane, the first time at Mr. Winstanleys (the Bacchus), here talk of News by way of Exeter that Barcelona is releiv'd, the Spanish & French beseigers cutt to pieces.
22 Indifferent, draw 10 Ounces of Blood, write to Mr. Parr and Mr. Wm. Massie Draw a Certificate for Mr. Parker, and after Dinner write to him and Tom Gorst. After prayers invited, go with Dr. Thane, Mr. Colly and Mr. Bowyer to Mr. Egertons at the Barrs. After a Turn in the Garden hee treats us with 3 Bottles of excellent Claret. The fearful progress of the cheif Ministry and Archdeacon Booths's inconstancy, matters of discourse. Wee return before 9.
23 I attend my Lord (with Mr. Chancellor) particularly on Mr. Proddys Busienes. I write to my coz. Holt about Sam. Prescotts Bond. First Court this Term. Judicial matters easy, yet not admitted so. I dine with my Lord, where Mr. Leigh of Aldford and Mr. Rutter. After, they treat mee kindly at the Fountain. I make a step to see my Horses at their Grasse, then seeing the Child Will, at Upton return before 9.
24 At early prayers. Our great expectacion is gratifid from Account of Spanish Brabant, declareing for and submitting to K. Charles 3rd, the French army cutt and diminisht to 23000 and fled nearer France, and better confirmacion of the Releif of Barcelona, hence the Bells and Joy. After prayers attend Lady Soames in her enquiry after lodgings, after in Mr. Collys Chamber, thence to Mr. Bouchers, with Dr. Thane, where a Bottle, thence Home.
25 Delicate season not hott, continues. I consult Heraldry in answer to Mr. Le Neve Norroy, who offers mee a Deputacion and the Books about Leasing the Vicarage and Glebe of Bowden. I write to John Cross about a dozen Bottles of wine from Mr. Egerton of Eccleston. I pay Mr. Holland for 5 Ounces of Hair 7s. 6d and makeing my Wigg 6s, to Sheriff Stringer for a Hatt 10s. After prayers with them at Mr. Hollands. After 7 take a walk to my Horses, thence to Upton, Jack with mee, return about 9, then refresh in a Glass of Claret bestowd by Lady Bunbury. A bailiff's wife Kills her husband & is sent late to prison.
26 Prayers, sermon and Sacrament in the parish Church where Mr. Shaw preaches on 'Bee yee sober, bee vigilant.' Sanctissimae Eucharistiae mihi

participi, sobrie et caste vitam agere det D.O.M.[7] After prayers see the news confirm'd and improving in the Netherlands. I write to Mr. Le Neve Norroy. Call on Sir Henry Bunbury late, part in a Glass of wine near 11.
27 A rainy morning hinders my setting out. I write to Mr. Whitehead Curate of Rachdale, to my coz. Parr and Holt, the rain constant, hinders till 4 when I and Mr. Stratford mount, come to Middlewich after 7, stay entertain'd by Mr. Thomason in his porch till 8, come to Hulmes Chapell before 9.
28 The Morning rainy, wee set hence about 8, come to Congleton, the Black Lyon, Mr. Shaws, before 10, open the Commission in the Chapell at 11, 9 Wittnesses, ending with Mrs. Leving at her house about 8. I lodg at Mr. Markland, Apothecary a decent and quiet retreat.
29 I proceed with wittnesses till 10, when to the Chapell where prayers and a good loyal Sermon by Mr. Malbon the Curate, this Anniversary is celebrated here in an extraordinary manner, each house loyal especially having Oken boughs set up before it, in some places Flowers added, as well the Kings preservacion in the Royal Oak as his Birth and return being remembered. I examine 8 more Wittnesses and finishing about 6 walk up to Astbury with Mr. Jebbe. I see Mr. Egertons design in a new Mansion, hee entertains in the old with good wine. Mr. Hulme comes to us about 8. Some plainly unkind words happen twixt the great Rector and Mr. Jebbe. Wee part about 11 and return to Congleton about 12.
30 I draw the Bill of the Commission charg which is generously paid by Mr. Hulme. I come hence and to Hulmes Chapell (observe Sommerford and Swettenham on the way) before 2, dine here and examine 1 Witness on the part of Holford, School Master, of Goostry, come to Middlewich reach Kinderton Street before 6. Here Mr. Parker and Cowper stay mee. Mr. Tatton, Dr. Foley, Mr. Hulse are of the company. The phisitian warm and loose in discourse, takes affront at my preference of his valuable Brother late Bishop of Kilmore's learning to his, hee parts in a huff, Mr. Tatton civilly. I go to Mr. Cowpers where drinking with Mr. Parker & Hulse continu'd late and to bed about 2.
31 Extremely indispos'd. Wee take a Walk to Ravenscroft a sweet situacion. After dinner wee are entertain'd by T. Yates at a free Glass, after many Healths, the 2 Pigotts of Eaton and I mount about 4, come in good weather to Tarvin Green, stay there above ½ hour. I leaving them come safe (D.O.M.) to my corner about 7.

JUNE 1 Indispos'd, elixir'd, keep home, save to the Coffee House where still acceptable, Confirmacions. The weather hott too, contracted indisposicion continues. After busienes perfunctory Dr. Thane in the Evening calls on mee, we go and recreate in 3 pints good wine at the Raven. Stay till the News arrives

7 Trans: 'I partake of the most Holy Eucharist. May God the best and greatest grant that [I] may live soberly and chastely.'

which more authenticly confirms the Seig of Barcelona raisd on 1st May O.S. the day of the Suns Eclips.

2 The weather turn'd to fair. Mr. Fogg has a good Sermon on ps . . . v.6. After prayers I attend Mr. Egerton in his visit of the Bishop, who receiv'd both civilly but with Oporto. After to the Coffee where I meet Capt. Boswell who about 12 years ago did great and generous service to Mr. Legh &c in discouraging and discussing a new prosecucion upon Irish Evidence. I return him thanks here. After treat him at the Golden Talbot with 3 Bottles good but dear Claret, my brother Partington comes and adds another.

3 Very hott weather and occasion confines to House and some Busienes. The Bishop, Dean, Dr. Thane go after dinner to Warrington. In the Evening past 6, step (Jack with mee) to Upton, where wee meet with Mr. Thomason in his recreacion of laying Netts for Fish, return about 9.

4 Tollerably recover'd tho the weather extreme hott. See the News rather confirming than adding. In the Evening I take a Turn on roody. After with Lady Bunbury and my Susy, see the Child Ned, like not but suspect his blewish colour. After a walk, home on the Walls to Lady Bunburys where part in a pint of Claret. The Bishop &c return from Warrington.

5 After 10 a clock prayers, wee visit Lady Soames, shee treats with Tea and Coffee. After Dinner desir'd, I attend Mrs. Proddy at the Coach and Horses in Bed indispos'd, shee gives mee the very melancholy History of her Husband.[8] After prayers I go to see a curious peece of perspective representing the Church of Harlem. I here to pick our severall (20) prints and buy a Sett of the 12 Ceasars for 4s. After am at the Fountain with Mrs. Colly, Partington, 3 sheriffs &c drinking, effects of wagers, wee part about 10.

6 Apply to Busienes, a Court Day, competent Busienes, incompetent noise. I examine Mrs. Proddy and Kilner, am call'd to the Raven, to the Chancellor and Dr. Thane, I stay till 9.

7 Severe hott weather. The News confirms and adds some places in Flanders. I write to Mr. Gorst. I pay my Brother Partington 15^{li}.1s. in part of $24^{li}.7^{s}.9\frac{1}{2}$d. After prayers with the Man who shewd the perspective of the Church of Harlem. I pick out 22 prints. The room fills with Madam Egerton and other Ladies. After this, to the Fountain where with the Mayor, Recorder, Dr. Thane, Mr. Hulme the sheriff, Hulton, Adams, I stay till 10.

8 A glowing day, yet indispos'd, venture on a Walk to Blacon Point, a breeze near the river cools the way. I am tird yet refresht. I write to Mr. Williams about the Forms of Thanksgiving, to Mr. Page of Warrington and my coz. Holt. After Evening prayers at the Fountain with the Chancellor and Dr. Thane till 9.

9 Q.B.E. dies natalitius mihi lvi. Det. D.O.M. vitam reliquam sobrie caste et inculpate agere[9]. Dr. Thane has a good and grave sermon on . . . Many from

8 C.R.O., EDC.5 (1706) No. 6, Cartmel.

9 Trans: 'My 56th birthday. May God the best and greatest grant the rest of [my] life to be sober, chaste and blameless.'

Ireland at the Choir, the present Bishop of Kildare, Dr. Ellis, the day anniversary remembered ad Lares meos.[10] After Evening prayers, Jack with mee, I step to the Feilds and Upton. After return'd to Mr. Bouchiers but end the day in conjugall domestic pint of good Claret.

10 At early prayers. After in a Breeze on roody, recreate in 4 Turns, write to Mr. Parr & Mouniere, with Sheriff Hulme consulted about a Certificate on his part to Norroy. After Evening prayers call'd up by my Lord Bishop on Mr. Proddys Busienes and others. John Cross begins afternoon to return to the Office. At the Fountain in the Evening with Dr. Thane, Capt. Vesey, Mr. Boucher, Here the Commission in order to a Will of my late daughter Lidia is executed. I write and enclose it by Capt. Vesey to Mr. Wilkinson.

11 St Barnabas, a fine calme day. I rise early and see the News. Mr. Hulton comes and about 7 wee mount, come to the Rock, hour before 10, meet a Boat of the Custom house, go in it about 11 and in a fine calm passage come to the Talbot about 12. After dinner examine Mrs. Kent on Mr. Higginbothams behalf. Shee is in bed as very ill, yet peevish and testy. I dispatch in ½ an hour. Thence wee adjourn to Mr. Swarbrecs, Mr. Stith, Houghton, Peters, Travers with us, wee stay till 6, come back in the same Boat. Wee have an equal fine passage, drinking 2 Bottles of Mr. Peter's punch by the way, return in a sweet Evening about 10. Step to Sir Hen. Bunbury and commemorate Mr. Robert Cholmlys birthday with him.

12 Repose longer. After some Busienes. In the Evening at Tom Hatfields with Sir Hen. Bunbury, Mr. Chancellor, Dr. Thane till 10.

13 Court day, moderate Busienes convenient to my indisposicion. In the Evening Dr. Thane and I wait on Mr. Chancellor hee treats us with 2 Bottles of good Claret.

14 I see the News very little increasd. About 11 in a cool day go to Upton, where a Dinner at the Appointment of Mr. Thomason, Willoughby & Bateman. Mr. Hulton, Alderman E. Partington, Page, Burroughs and Crosby invited too. After dinner Fellowship, that by Mr. Hultons long storys, interrupted. After him gone, revivd an hour or 2. My Bro. Partington and I return over the Heath, call at Newton where the young Capt. Hurleston entertains us civilly with a Bottle of Ormond Claret.

15 The weather alters to rain. Indispos'd at Home in Books. After a walk conclude the Evening in Domestic Claret.

16 It rains almost perpetually today. At the Choir where Dr. Entwisle has a good sermon on Hebrews . . . See the News not yet increas'd, Ostend beseigd. After Dinner at a Glass of Claret, Mr. John Shakerley with him. I return to my Corner and after repose read Hooker &c.

17 After an uneasy Night a better morning. Agree with Robinson the painter to undertake the retreat room at 4½d the yeard, pay 1s in Earnest, with my Lord Bishop and write to Mr. Bunbury of Holcroft about the Chapel of Newchurch.

10 Trans: 'at my hearth.'

After dinner in the Office sorting papers till 6. In the Evening with Mr. Cartwright at the Fountain, hee repays mee 10 Guineas borrowd, with wine & thanks. I receivd at noon, a Letter from the Bishop of Meath, send it with 2 Lines to Mr. Morrey.

18 A moist season yet. The News advances not, with my Lord in search of a verdict in Iure patronatus Wycliffe about 2 years ago but do not (since not deliver'd into the Registry) find it.[11] I receive Mr. Le Neve Norroys civil answer. After dinner calld over by Sir H.B., drink a Glass or 2 of Claret with him, Sir Peter Soames, Dr. Chetwood. After at the Office in Dust, continue till 8. The Forms of Thanksgiving come, End in domestic wine.

19 The wett weather continues. Sir Hen. Bunbury and my Lady to go Lyme. I turn Canon Laws about the punishment of Drunkenes in Clergy men and Schoolmasters. At the office some part, pay Mr. Vernon for 30 loads of Coal, the Duty 18s, with my Lord after prayers, among other things the sentence against Walthew discourd. From the office, home, where a domestic pint.

20 At early prayers. At Busienes and Books, till Court, where competent Busienes. The Bishop is there proceeding to final Decree, but is with difficulty prevail'd with to deferr it against Roger Walthew, till Wednesday next. I examine 3 Wittnesses on Tristrams Will, write to Mr. Ludlowe on Enquiry after Mr. Barrys Estate. After at the Fountain with the Chancellor, Dr. Thane, Norris & Mr. Callys, here the Chancellor signs & seals his Arbitracion twixt Mr. Egerton and Mr. Lawton, wee part under Bottles before 9.

21 At early prayers, after which a walk to Upton refreshes. The News and Army at a stand. I draw Monicion against building a school in the Chapell Yard of Lower Peover. After prayers and Busienes at the Golden Talbot, where I see Thrasonic vanity in Sir Wm. Read, a Chirurgion, once Mountebank, his Gold punch Bowl, a plate, Tumbler and 6 dishes all massie Gold before him, hee lookt bigg, fine but yet rustic and ignorant-bursting with Epicurisme and success. Mr. Frith and Capt. Boswell introduceing mee. I drink 2 gold dishes full of punch over the gold plate held by them. After I recede with Mr. Hodgson and wee drink 1 Bottle French Claret.

22 Wee are alarm'd early with an Account of the Bishop of Meaths arrival at Park Gate. After my Lord and myself had searcht near 3 daies I find the Commission and Verdict in Iure Patronatus Wycliffe. The Bishop of Meath and his Lady come to my Corner about 12. I write to Mr. Okes and Tom Gorst. After prayers I wait on the Bishop of Meath. Hee sees the Chancellor who gives us a Bottle of good Claret.

23 A cool day, Mr. Newton in a full Quire has a cursory sermon, the Bishop of Meath, his Lady, Mr. Close, my self and my S. dine with the Bishop of Chester who makes Apologies for his Dinner. After prayers I attend my Lord of Meath and Lord DonyLeare to the Bishop, hee treats with port. After and visits over,

11 L.D.A., CD/PP/9, Wycliffe Parish Papers, for a copy of the iure patronatus.

the Bishop, Dr. Thane and I take 2 Bottles of the Bishops good Claret at my Corner.

24 Fair day. I write to Mr. Le Neve and Mr. Parre. The Bishop of Meath his Lady, Mrs. Close, Tom Gorst dine with us. After Busienes and prayers, wee go to Dr. Thanes where the Chancellor meets with us, after 3 Bottles wee adjourn home where Supper and 2 Bottles more. John Cross brings mee the remainder of John Walmesleys rent. I offer 2^{li};10s, hee takes 2 Guineas for his pains.

25 Bustle and preparacion for the Bishops going, fill the House. The Bishop gives Tom Gorst a general release. Hee repeats his generous proposal to take Jack to Ireland with him. The News yet dull. After dinner the Bishop &c take coach for Whitchurch. I invited go to Mr. Hockental at Mr. Cottinghams, hee desires Advice about a Commission to uniform Shotwick Church.[12] After I go to the Fountain to the Chancellor, Dr. Thane, Mr. Bennet thence to Mr. Minshalls auction.

26 Indispos'd severely. After prayers about 11, Mr. Walthew according to Adjournment appears before my Lord in the palace, my Lord renumerates and admonishes him of his Crimes and exhorts reformacion sub paena for the future, injoyns a Declaraction and condemns him in Expenses. After dinner and repose I, Jack along, about 6 set for Shotwick, I see the Church, Mr. Hockenhall and Mr. Harvey meet mee here, I am civilly entertain'd at the Clerks, return after 9.

27 The day appointed for Thanksgiving, tis something rain fore noon. Dr. Thane has a very good discourse on Deut . . . in the crowded parish church, a common Joy & Noise, fill the Town. After prayers At the Fountain whith Mr. Hoghton, Heir to Sir Charles, Mrs. Charles Bunbury, Minshall, Hoghton, the Glass passes full and freely even to distinction of humors, the yong Heir seems to inherit the opinions of his Family. After this my Suzy &c walk thoro the streets illuminated, to the Chancellors and the Mayors and after 12, home.

28 A very rainy day, under it and indisposicion unhappy, keep home. Some busienes and in the Evening a pint with Dr. Thane at the Fountain.

29 St Peters day, at home and in Bookes, the weather yet wett, in the Fair with my Suzy.

30 The Dean has a good grave and full sermon on Romans 12. Owe nothing to any Man, but to love one another, hee is difficultly heard in a great Congregacion. The news stands. At Church after noon Mr. Cradock, Chaplain to Lord Gower has a very ingenious discourse on Psalm 1.v.1. In a full Quire many from Ireland. Anthem 14th part of 119 psalm. The Chancellor & I attend the Bishop after prayers, the Chancellor desires on Mr. Bennets request a partial relaxacion of young Porter of Bunbury. After, I, Jack with mee to Upton, back about 9.

JULY 1 At early prayers. After about 9 wee sett for and come to Wrexham about 11, dine with my mother Puleston. Madam Ann Davies sees mee here,

12 C.R.O., EDA2/4 f.34, for Shotwick pews.

relates all the passages of Mr. Barrys address to Madam Catharin. Wee wait on them at the Mount, thence to my uncle Eyton's, Bryn y funan, here Mr. Price comes to us, wee stay till 7 & tho it has rained much in the way, wee come dry home about 9.

2 The weather still rainy. At the office and in some Bookes and Busienes. Indispos'd in my stomack, pay Mr. Burches 1^{li}.4s, to Jane part of wages 5s. After repose, into the Town. I meet with Mr. Wells, wee go to the Golden Talbot where Mr.J. Cooper and Mr. Hulse come to us, wee drink our Bottles cheerfully and part about 12.

3 After a tedious morning dull and melancholy, it raines to occasion, the prayer against rain. I take one turn on roody. After Prayers and an hour in the Auction, I return to home and Busienes. Draw the Case of the Parish Clerk of Wigan.

4 I give the Case to my Lord, hee seems pleasd, shows mee a Case drawn long by himself. Court day, moderate Busienes. After dinner at the office. After prayers attend my Lord on Mr. Porter of Bunbury, his behalf, hee excepts against the Testimonials and refuses to grant a General Relaxacion upon it. I draw it into better Form and deliver it to Mr. Bennet. I write an answer to Mr. Ludlow about Mr. Barry. About 7 go to the Golden Talbot where Dr. Entwisle and Thane, Mr. J. Cooper and Mr. Callys, one Dr. Tyler of the Diocese of Hereford comes with Mr. T. Cooper to us, wee pass the Time cheerfully and finish our Bottles and Conversacion about 11.

5 The Bishop gos early (about ½ hour after 5) for Wigan. At the office over the painter. The News brings Lord Galway within 50 Miles of Madrid. I write to T. Gorst about Hodsons Administracion. Dr. Thane dines with us draws Hodsons Administracon of Gooden specially. After prayers, in the Evening go to Upton, the 2 Boyes with mee, refresh in a domestic pint at Night; paid Mr. Foulks 5^{li} on account.

6 At the office, pay the painter (Robinson) $2^{li}.1^{s}$. Dr. Thane fails, Mr. Cooper (John) my Suzy and I dine with the Mayor. After dinner sitt freely past 4. Thence Mr. Cooper my brother Partington and I adjourn to the Golden Talbot, Sheriff Stringer joins us wee drink cheerfully our Bottles.

7 Tho Mr. Cooper preaches, I am too indispos'd to go to the Quire. After dinner sent for, go to the Talbot to Mr. Hulme the new vicar of Blackburn. I stay with him past 6, hee seems an honest Gentleman having a veneracion for Mr. Price's memory and solicitous to imitate him. Mr. Wilde of the Excise a civil person is with us. Mr. Hulme treats with freedom and Claret, returning calld in by Lady Soames, sup at Mrs. Oldfields. Here yong J. Allen appears in his infirmity, tho not very troublesome.

8 Attend Mr. Hulme to the Chancellor, who approves of him, as Surrogate. After with my Suzy attend on Lady Soames at Tea. In the Evening shee, Sir Peter and Sir Hen. Bunbury, see in a drink, a Glass of wine and Hulmes Chappel Ale.

9 After a Walk the News which gives an uncertain account of Prince Eugene, his success and passing the Adage. In the Evening invited to with Dr. Thane to a

Bowl of punch, Sir H.B., the Chancellor and Mr. Done here, wee conquer a great Quantity and this us, part about 12.

10 Severely indispos'd, in Fevor and repent all day. Freindly Elixir at Night.

11 I draw a Sentence of relaxacion for Porter. At Court where small and short Busienes, Mr. Hulton and Mr. Stratford absent. In the Evening Dr. Thane and I drink pints with Mr. Bouchier.

12 After a walk and the News demurring, to some Busienes and reading. Give 8d for the Coats of the ancient Nobility painted. After prayers with Dr. Thane, Mr. Percival, student of Christ Church, Mr. Egerton and Callys, at the Golden Talbot and good Claret until 11, the matter of Mr. Dodwills late Book much that of discourse.

13 A rainy day. I write to my Lord Bishop, Mr. Vaudrey and Parre. After noon in dullness and constant rain, repose, pay Mr. Foulks another 20^{li} upon Account. In the Evening to the Talbot with Mr. Percival, Egerton, and Callys where 3 Bottles and the conversacon.

14 After an unhappy Night severely indispos'd. Mr. Cooper has a smarter vindicacion of his sermon this day 7 night at St. Peter's and censurd by disaffected persons. After noon at St. Oswald's where Mr. Percivall has an excellent discourse on Matt. 5. v. 3. After prayers I (with Harry) step to Upton, return before 8, sent for by Dr. Norris, go to the Fountain where I find with him Sir Richard of Lincolnshire and Mr. Worsley of . . . a Member of Parliament, these travelling, enquire after Antiquities and Curiosities they had seen my Altar. I give them account of that and the Antiquity of Chester. After the Drs. receded, they pressing wee stay, fall into a warm dispute of the nature of Government, they admire not the method of Nature in primogeniture nor Hereditary succession or Monarchy. I suspect them of the deprav'd humor of the Age as to Religion and the Church of England. Wee part civilly about 12.

15 The weather fairer. The Travelling Gentlemen call on mee about 9, see my Coins &c, see oblig'd. I write to my Lord Bishop about the Letter from her Majesties Council, about the papists and to Mr. Bradshaw about Sir John Crews reflection on Surrogates. Mr. Percival returning for Ireland calls on mee, takes a Stirrup Cup of Hulmes Chappell which with the weather socordiam inducit.[13] After prayers and Books, I go down to the Chancellors, they are just return'd from Malpas. After some turns cogitabundum, see the Letters arriv'd but no news, refresh in a domestic pint.

16 I intend but, from constant rain, go not to Wrexham, apply to the search of a Confirmation granted to Mr. Ball of Ormskirk, find it decreed 19 July 1694[14]. Give 1s. 6d for an Oval Table for my greater room in the office, there afternoon searching the Consistory Books for 1637 about Mr. Wm. Johnson then parish Clerk of Wigan, after recreate in a domestic pint.

17 After a rainy night, a constant rain makeing Floods to great damage of Hay

13 Trans: 'induces apathy.'

14 C.R.O., EDC.5 (1694) No. 14, Ormskirk.

&c. I write to my coz. Parr about a Confirmacion granted to Mr. Ball of Ormskirk, the Letter to bee seen by my Lord Derby, to Mr. Rider and Anthony Close, to all about the Inspecion of our Offices by Commissioners from the Stamp Office. After dinner renew a search about Wm. Johnson. After prayers at 6, Mr. Chancellor, Drs. Thane and Norris and Mr. Boucher come to Mee, to end the Bishop of Meaths Beneficence of Claret. Wee send to the Bishop of Killaloe (Lindsey) who comes and shares in the wine and conversacion, wee dispatch 5 (the last) Bottles. I write to my Lord Bishop (at Wigan) about the search and about Mr. Winter of Cockerham, his relaxacion.
18 Continu'd rain makes formidable Floods carrying hay and bridges before them. A Court and by consent, the last of this Term, moderate in busienes. After dinner I walk towards Blacon, to observe the river. After prayers and some busienes, I am with Mr. Chancellor, Drs. Thane and Norris and Mr. Hulton at the Apollo, Mr. Winstanleys, wee stay our pints till nine.
19 The rain ceas'd, sun returns. I take a Turn on Roodee, see the news no addicions to the last, after dinner repose. My sister Jones comes to us. I, Jack with mee step to Upton. After in Sohowarts Observacions.
20 After an unhappy night a dull morning, releive by a Turn or 2 on roodee. I write to Mr. Winter of Cockerham. My sister Jones lends mee 50^{li}. I give her a Note at present and promise her such Bond and security as shee shall direct. Prepare for my Journy to Lancashire. In the Evening Dr. Thane comes to us, wee send for and drink a Bottle of Claret & part past 9.
21 At Church in the Morning, see the little News and take leave with the Chancellor before dinner. After prepare for my journy. After 3 Mr. Boucher and I set out, come easily to Warrington before 8. Here wee meet with Mr. Barlowe an Atturney, hee keeps us up with Claret and Goodens case (wherein hee is Sollicitor) till 1.
22 A good cool and fair day, sett hence past 9, Mr.Boucher go's to Rainford, I to Farnworth. See the Chapell, a good pile one well situated. In it I observe the seat in controversy betwixt Hurst and Blundel on the back of which the Letters W.C. & E.C. and Figures 1602 relateing only to the seat.[15] I see the Oratory belonging to the Family of Bold. Several ancient Figures in it. Hence the School a very mean Fabric, built by Bishop Smith of Lincoln born in this Chapelry.[16] I refresh some hours in the Inn, the Griffin, with Mr. Ainscough the Curate and old James Plumpton. Hence to Prescott where I see Mr. Lyme in his delightfull Garden. Hee entertains mee and Mr. Bennet with made Wine. Mr. Bennet after treats mee, the vicar absent at the vicarage, with Venison pasty & good Ale. After this hee brings mee to Knowsley, the neglect and desolacion of the place with recollection of the order and hospitality I have seen, are too hard for mee. Hee treats mee in my chamber with a pint of the old Claret, and bestows on mee a pair of my late Lord's Gloves, the sun is too deep in the West, about 10 I reach

15 *Ibid.*, EDC.5 (1705) No 1, and (1706) No 4, Farnworth.
16 See W. K.Jordan, *Charities of Rural England* (London, 1961).

Ormskirk, ly at Mrs. Dods, pay to Mr. Fearnhead, Mr. Oundreys Man, this morning upon the Stamp Act 110^{li}.

23 The sessions are begun here, the place throng'd. About 11 wee go to church the Commission twixt Rigby and Gill is open'd, Mr.Kippax surrogate, the further examinacion adjour'd to Mr.Mawsdley, where after dinner I examine 7 wittnesses. Mr. Boucher and I walk to the cold Bath, a fine spring well accomodated. After part in pints at the Wheat Sheaf.

24 Apply and examine the rest produc'd here. Mr. Rigby pays the Charges after which wee drink a Bottle at the Wheatsheaf. It is confirm'd by all especially the Domestics that a marriage is agreed on betwixt Mr. Jonathon Case and Mrs. Dod.

25 St. James a fair day. I visit my old Acquaintance, Mrs. Stanford, Mr. Boucher with mee. She plays on the Virginals. After Coffee here, wee mount for Holland come there about 12. After dinner Mrs. Gill is produc'd before Mr. Birchall. I examine her in 2 hours. Mr. Boucher gos for Warrington, Mr. Hulton and I liberally entertain'd by Mr. Birchal and Sam Prescott, stay late come to Wigan after 9. I come to my cozen Holt near 12.

26 About 10 wait on my Lord, hee imparts some of his busienes, I dine with my cozen Holts. After prayers wait on my Lord, stay supper and till 9. Mr. Holland and I hence agree to drink a Glass of wine at Tootells, here wee sitt recollecting earlier Affairs till 3 in the morning.

27 In bed till 11, rise indispos'd; pass with my cozen Holt an unhappy hott day. At prayers meet with Mr. Ashton of Prestwich. Hee Mr. Colly, Johnson and Stratford draw mee into the late snare Tootells, Mr. Ashton obliges, I stay this Night till 12.

28 A fine day. Mr. Ashton has an excellent Sermon. My cozen and I dine with the Bishop who receives cheerfully. Hee shews mee an Address he had drawn. Mr. Horrobin of Billing, Mr. Boltons imitator, preaches afternoon. My cozen Holt and I attend Mr. Ashton to his Inn, Tootells, wee part in white wine. After with both my cozen Holts visit Mrs. Banks, return home about 9 and end the day in 2 pints of Claret.

29 Extreme hott, affected and fevorish. I with difficulty draw an answer for my Lord to Mr. James Lowther of the Inner Temple, wait on him with it, hee likes it, mencions other busienes, return to my cozen Holts indevor (but in vain) to repose. After a short dinner my cozen Holt and I calling on Mr. Birchall go to Ayrfield, wee walk to the work at Holts Bridg then thoro the meadows (a fine walk) home. I entertain them with 2 Bottles of Scotch Claret, it proves good, tho on the Frett, wee are cheerfull, they well pleas'd. Wee call at Mr. Birchalls, have a free Bottle of Ale and come late to Wigan (about 10). I hear today of and lament Mr. Robies difficulties increasing upon him, his Cattle being seizd to day by Mr. Wiswall.

30 Better from the journy & wine. I attend my Lord receive his Letters and commands, set hence after 10 in a fine cool day come to Frodsham about 2, rest at the Inn 2 hours with Mr. Davie, come home safe (D.G.) about 6, wait on Mr. Dean with my Lord's Letters and give the Address to bee writt over.

31 Write and dispatch Notes to the adjacent Clergy to come and signe the Address. After dinner repose. After that in the Town, end the day in a domestic pint.

AUGUST 1 Q.B.E. I write to Mr. Colly about Ribchester &c and inclose an Act of Mr. Dicconson's Administracion. About 11 The Clergy about 30 meet in the Court. The Dean makes a short Harrangue about the Address, that tho ready drawn, it is not impos'd but offer'd by the Bishop, it is read and unanimously subscrib'd. I write to my Lord and return the Address by Mr. Chapman. Dr. Thane dines with us. In the Evening at the Bacchus with Sir Peter Soames and Dr. Thane where cheerfull over 3 Bottles strong port.
2 Some indisposicion from the port. I take a short walk on roodee. See the News, Prince Eugene over the Po. At the office search for but find not the Correcion Book for 1637. End the day in a domestic pint.
3 Receive my Lord's Letter and Thanks about the Address, dispatch 2 Administracions infra. I am at the Fountain in the morning with Dr. Fisher of Dublin, Mr. Swerbreck &c, wee dispatch 4 pints, it affects mee. After dinner and repose, Books and after a walk on roodee, a domestic pint.
4 Dr. Thane has a good discourse on . . . I see the news not much improvd. Menin invested. In the afternoon Mr. Fogg has a good sermon in the parish church. My Suzy and I visit Miss Dod. After I go to the Mayor's, where Mr. Cradock, a person of good parts and learning, desires my Acquaintance and shows an inclination to Antiquity. Mr. Lea is with him wee drink some Glasses of port wine and part about 9.
5 Applyd to Elixir last night, something easy. I write to my cozen Parr I take in 9 loads, good ones, of the Alderman's Hay, the weather altering, prevents the 10th, this diverts mee. At night at the White Talbot where Dr. Thane, Mr. Hulton, Mr. Pickmore and myself empty 4 Bottles good Irish wine. Mr. Hulton continues his usual phrase.
6 I take in the 10th load, the charge of Housing amounts to 3^{li}. I, ill of my Stomack step to Upton am refresht. Step to the news, scarce a step further. After dinner in Books particularly Schowarks Historical Observacions in which The House of France, End in a domestic pint.
7 After a tedious morning from my stomack, a tollerable day. I write to T. Gorst & John Crosse. I am informd my coz. Hulme of Ormskirk widow died yesterday and is to be buried at Holland to morrow. In the Evening Dr. Thane, Mr. Collys and I try agen Mr. Pickmers wine, find it port, try the white Lisbon, after call at Sir Hen. B's where end in a Bottle of excellent wine.
8 Indisposd, take a walk of 4 Turns on Roodee. Mr. Cartwright shares in 3 of 'em. After dinner Mr. Cooper, my brother Partington and Mr. Cradock call on mee. I show the last my Coins & hee is well pleasd. I treat them with my Midlewich Ale. After about 7 wee adjourn to the Fountain where Mr. Shaw joins us, wee advance near one Bottle.
9 After an unhappy night a fevorish day. At My Lady Otways request write to

Mr. Yates of Whitehaven to come and bee Witnes for her at Lancaster Assizes Thursday next. Repose but not recover. In the Evening meet with Mr. Cowper in the same circumstance, wee sitt a while at my brother Partingtons where Mr. Bowyer finds mee. We adjourn to the Fountain, hee is today come from Wigan, imparts his resolucion to accept the offer'd Curacy, wee stay 2 pints.

10 Still uneasy, speak to the Dean about going to Lancaster, wee conclude to set out on Tuesday. I write to Mr. Colly. I search the Books but in vain to find the Entry of Licences of parish Clerks. In the Evening receive a welcome supersideas of my design'd Journy to Lancaster. At a Bottle with Sir Hen Bunbury and his Brother, wee part thence about 10.

11 Delicate weather continued. Dr. Entwisle has a sermon on "pray for them that despitefully use you and persecute you". Wee see the News promising success in Italy and Spain. This (D.O.M.G.) is our nineteenth marriage day, wee have a domestic Celebracion. After prayers in the Broad Isle, Robin Forest (Mr. Banks man) tells Dr. Entwisle and myself That Mrs. Dod was marry'd Thursday last at Walton. I see her daughter here at Mr. Hughs, but do not acquaint her with the News. After, Jack and Harry with mee, I walk to Blacon Point And end this day in a domestic pint of good Claret.

12 My stomach still affected, seek relief from 4 Turns on roodee and find it. Apply to Lassells Journy into Italy. After noon, in the office, turn Books of Entry in vain to find Licences granted to parish Clerks. After prayers with Dr. Thane and Mr. Bowyer at the Fountain, we relax in 4 pints. After I write to my cozen Holt.

13 Rise to early prayers. After see Mr. Cholmley of Vale Royal at Sir Hen Bunburys. Thence to Roodee where I perform 4 Turns. After see the News, which gives the Fleet of the descent sail'd from St Hellens, proceed in Lassells. About 5 in the Evening, the Bishop of Killala returns from London, I attend him at the Pyd Bull. Wee send to Dr. Thane, the wine is very good and very dear, wee cheerfully empty 5 Bottles at the Bishop's charge.

14 Uneasy from the Quantity, releiv with a walk, after Dinner, Dr. Newton and Mr. Lownds call on mee, they propose the Drs. trying practice in this Town. I do not discourage. Wee drink freely of my strong Ale. In the Evening, the Dr. and I attend the Bishop at the Bull. Alderman Allen joins us, wee dispatch with the same cheer 4 Bottles.

15 Disturbd, hasten to 4 Turns on roody, the Bishop is here, wee proceed to the Mayors where a noble Entertainment of Venison, wee sit with the Alderman and Council, take a free Glass after, yet return to the Pyd Bull, send for Dr. Thane drink, cheerfully, each a Bottle.

16 Refresht by a walk see little News. The Bishop, my S. and I dine at Sir Henry Bunburys elegantly. After are entertain'd with elegant wine, the weather turns rainy. In the Evening invited, the Bishop, his Brother and myself go to Alderman Allens, hee treats us and Dr. Thane (sent for) with 4 Bottles of the same wine.

17 The malady continuing I recurr to my cure on roodee, the Bishop after dinner gos for Wrexham. Dr. Griffith lately come recommends and introduces mee to the Bishop of Kilmore and Ardagh, (Dr. Wettenhal) at the Plume of Feathers. Hee inquires after old praxes in our way and is pleasd with Maranta, hee mencions Dr. Pope as an old Friend to him, I as a generous Master to my self. Take a Turn on roodee, thence to a domestic pittance of Claret.

18 Tollerably recoverd, at the Church, Mr. Fogg has a very good sermon against Atheism. The news not yet entertaining. After noon the Bishop of Kilmore preaches in the parish church but I hear him not. But agen wait on him and sup with him at the Feathers, thence to the Chancellor where wait on his Lady, Mrs. Norris &c in the Chancellors absence, thence to my Brother Partingtons & home.

19 I wait on the Bishop of Kilmore and take leave of him. Hee gives a sermon of his own titul'd, Invisibilia. After to roodee and 4 Turns. Mr. Boucher begins his journy for Oxford. Turn on in Lassells, in the Evening Dr. Thane and I relax in our pints at the Fountain.

20 Still repeat my course at Roodee, see the news yet suspending, read variously, see the Bishop of Killala, his son at the Pyde Bull, the Bishop not return'd, return to my domestic pint.

21 From prayers at 10, see the Chancellor return'd from Oxford. Apply all day to various reading, the Bishop of Killala returns from Wrexham. My Suzy, Jack and I are late with him cheerfully in his chamber and dispatch 3 Bottles.

22 I perform 4 Turns on roodee, the Bishop is here till Noon, after dinner takes horse for Leverpool. Go on variously in Books and end the day in a quiet domestic pint.

23 After a walk the News and Dinner, at the Pyde Bull with Dr. Newton, Mr. Lowndes and Mr. Richard Ward. Go slowly on in variety.

24 Refrest on roodee, write to Mr. Stratford, Mr. Boucher and John Cross. The Bishop of Killala returns from Leverpool. Dr. Thane and I wait on and stay 4 Bottles with him & late.

25 To the Quire where Mr. Newton has a sermon without nerves or method, the News keeps all in suspense especially in Italy and Spain, a wett discouraging day. After prayers the Bishop, my Lady Bunbury and I, in her coach, wait on Lady Shackerly, she receives and, for an hour, treats us all very courteously. After this visit The Bishop, Sir Henry Bunbury, his brother, Dr. Thane, Mr. Pooley and my self late at the Bishops, cost 4 or 5 Bottles very cheerfull & in poetry.

26 Indisposed, attend the Bishop all morning, sign and deliver to him, my Letter of Atturney made to Mr. Ludlowe. Go with him to the Dolphin, dine with him there, my S. follows, wee part with him about ½ past 1, hee design'd for Holywell. I am to direct Letters for Him to Mr. Thomas Kirkwood, Merchant in Danmark Street, Dublin. In the Evening at the Fountain with Mr. Chancellor, Dr. Thane, Mr. Jackson, wee dispatch our pints, Dr. Thane & I staying a pint after the rest. The Judges, Jekell and Lovell come in attended by Mr. Holford the Vice Sheriff & some Gentlemen.

27 A rainy day. The News brings Menin surrender & on Honourable Terms. After Dinner invited, go with Dr. Thane to the Chancellor where hee is entertaining Dr. Gardiner, Warden of All Souls, Mr. Glynn son & Heir of Sir William Glynn, Mr. Smith, liberally and elegantly. The good Claret circulates, and it rains fast, the Warden &c go off at 5, wee stay longer. After this I step to see with my S., Lady Soames in her new Lodgings, Mrs. Mercers.

28 After a tedious morning, venture on the Golden Scurvy Spirit, take a walk of 2 Turns. After Dinner to some busienes. After prayers with Dr. Minshall, prevail that his son Randle go to morrow to Knowsley, to see the Library &c, give him directions about that affair. Trafford the Quaker is releasd by the Judges upon an Error they find in the Signature vid. the Term of the Diocese wanting. About 9 sent to, step over to Sir Hen Bunbury where hee entertains Dr. Thane, Mr. T. Birkenhead and myself with good wine and Beer till 11. I pay Mr. Thomason for Wills Quarters at Upton so many weeks 13s, To Peggy Birchall 2^{li}, formerly 1^{li}.

29 I repeat, after a painfull morning, the Golden Spirit, take only, therefore 2 Turns in a fair morning. Write to Mr. Mawd of York, my Lord Bishop of Chester, Mr. Gerard of Tarvin. I go to the Castle in Expectacion of Mr. Lancaster's Cause, tis put off till tomorrow. Randle Minshall gos to Knowsley to see the Library, on my Account. In the Evening at the Fountain, with Mr. Lancaster, Davie, Aldersey, his Cause and 2 Bottles take up the time and discourse.

30 I go about 9 to the Hall. Mr. Lancaster's cause is heard. Error and irregularity found in the Warrants and authority of it to levy the Assessment. His Council, Serjeants Parker and Cheshire, Queens Atturny Mr. Winnington, Recorder Cumberbach and Mr. Ward, seem to manage the cause with skill and Decency. On the other part Serjeant Hooks, Mr. Hunter and Masterson with difficulty and less oratory. The Cheif Judge is prudent and fair. Sir Salathiel manifestly partial, hee acts the Advocate and Satyr, reflects on Mr. Lancaster as a quarelsom person. The matter by his means ends in a special Verdict, the merits included. I dine with Mr. Holford of Newbrook the representative High Sheriff, a noble Dinner yet mixt company, the number about 30. After the Sheriff gon to the Hall, Mr. Henchman, Chaplain, Mr. Peake, Vaudrey, Booth of Macclesfield and I drink a Bottle till six. Mr. Vaudrey here an Affecionate man in behalf of the Church in opposicion to Sir Salathiels management, but an indifferent Orator. Jack 16 this day.

31 A very rainy day almost perpetual. I step into the Town, the streets for an Hour are washt with a rapid Current. Randle Minshal returns with an Account of the Library of my Lord Derby, represents it great and noble, of most of the Fathers entire. History especially French, constituted of Folios above the proporcion of the other volumes, he reckons the whole 2900. My Suzy and I this Evening remember the last to bee Jacks birthday.

SEPTEMBER 1 I Jack with mee take 2 early but short Turns on roodee. The News still holds the Fate of Spain and Savoy in sharp suspense. Mr. Lancaster preaches in the Quire on Romans 7. My Suzy and I invited, dine at the

Chancellors, here the Norrises and Jacksons at a polite dinner, part a Hanch roasted. After prayers Mr. Dod of Broxon sees us and wee wait on Sir James Eyton and his Lady and daughter at my Brother Partingtons. After this I am with Sir Hen Bunbury and his Brother at his House till 10.

2 Releivd by last nights Elixir and 1 Turn this morning, write to my Lord Derby an Account of Randle Minshalls expedicion to Knowsley and to Mr. Stratford at Wigan about Mr. Lancaster's Causes. In the Evening at Sir Hen Bunbury's with my uncle Eyton, Sir James Eyton, my cozen Kendrick the ladys have a supper. Wee are liberally treated till 11.

3 I begin to remove (Q.B.E.) Records from the House to the Office, repeat the Golden Drops. Take 2 short Turns on roodee, Jack with mee. The News brings Prince Eugene near Turin, hold Spain in suspense. I apply to reading. End the day in a domestic Quota of white wine.

4 A rainy morning after severall rainy daies. Yet I repeat my Drops and short Turns. I pay Mr. Townsend for ½ a Tun of old Hay 1s 9d per contra 17s 5d. Sir James Eyton in the Morning, Lady Kilmory, Mrs. Cholmley of Vale Royal, Lady Eyton &c in the Evening visit us, the rains continue. After various reading I conclude in a domestic pint of white.

5 The weather still rainy and uncertain. Yet in a lucid interval perform 4 short Turns, write to Mrs. Case and John Cross, pay to the Collector of the Land Tax one half Years payment for the Office 2^{li}. Apply to Books till 9 then invited over to Sir Hen Bunbury's where Sir James Eyton, his Lady, daughter &c a full company. After a few Glasses part before 11. I take my Horses in from the Feild.

6 A cool morning, at early prayers, after in brisk Ayr take 4 Turns on roodee. See the Letters but no News, it continues rainy to deprecacion and danger. In the Evening, the Chancellor, Dr. Thane and I try the Rose and Crown part after 9 and 4 pints.

7 I repeat 4 short Walks. The ordering the Scrinia in the office gos on. The weather windy with rain. I repeat the golden drops. In the Evening call'd thither go to the Rose and Crown where Sir Peter Soames, Sir Henry Bunbury, Mr. Bruen, the Chancellor, Dr. Thane and Mr. Langford. The Chancellor and Dr. Thane go about 9, the rest stay and that cheerfully till 1.

8 A dull and melancholy day and what is worse, spent at home. Mrs. Fitzherbert, our good & gentile neighbor, dies about 2. Mr. Whaley applies for what I give my Letter to Mr. Vernon on his part. I write too, to Mr. Seaman by him. After 7 call'd over to Sir Henry B's where Sir James Eyton & his company sup, wee after drink a Glass of Claret and part after 10.

9 I repeat my drops and 4 short Turns, Jack with mee, the weather yet rainy and the Fresh high. I pay Samuel Garret for Grass for my Horses and the Bishops Mare 4^{li}. Finish Lassells. Capt. Hurleston, another considerate old Neighbor, after a sicknes of about 6 weeks begun by a frolick[17] at Holywell, dies

17 A frolic was an eighteenth-century energetic country dance.

betwixt 7 & 8 this Evening. Dr. Thane and I take our pints at the Fountain and part before 10.

10 After the Drops repeated, 4 short Turns on roodee. At the News which only affords Expectacion, Wee take leave with Sir James Eyton and his Lady and daughter, going for Wrexham. Mrs. Compton dines with us. After prayers I am inform'd my Lord Derbys Library is sold to a Bookseller (Johnson) of Lichfeild. I am with Mr. Minshall an hour at the Plume of Feathers, thence, it raining exceedingly, wee go to Mr. Inces, near Eastgate, stay 2 hours, thence to Sir Henry B's where after a glass of French Claret, past 10 home.

11 After an unhappy morning, recur (Jack with mee) to a short and long Turn on roodee, the weather scarce permitting, write and send 6 Licences to Mr. Styth, appoint S.D.P. the next Visitacion. In the Evening, invited, at Archdeacon Booth's, Sir Hen Bunbury, Archdeacon Entwisle, Mr. Mayor and myself make up the Company, wee are treated with about so many Bottles of Claret, wee have a great deal on parliamentary Affairs and part near 11.

12 Warmer from the plain scurbutic drops, go down (Jack with mee) to roodee take 4 Turns in variety of Storms and sun shine, write to Mr. Ashton and Mr. Thornley. About 2 attend with the Mayor, Sir Rowland Stanley brother Partington &c the Corps of Mrs. Fitzherbert, on horseback to the end of Hanbridg only. In the Evening, at the Fountain with Mr. Chancellor & Dr. Thane, wee part after 4 pints about 9.

13 A calmer day, I with Jack take 4 Turns in fair weather. I recive my Lord Derbys answer which quitts mee of the Library and pleases mee. The public Letters give relacions and fair hopes of great victories and success on our part in Italy and Spain. Mr. Charles Booth desires propose to rejoice too at the Fountain, wee do so in 5 pints of Claret and part before 9.

18 A fair and brisk morning. I after early prayers and golden drops, take 4 short Turns on roodee. Fill Citacions for the Deanaries of Chester, Wirrall, Frodsham.[18]. After Evening prayer attend (with the Chancellor), my Lord in the Case of Mr. Winter vicar of Cockerham his violacion of the Sequestracion and about the vacancy of the rectory of Halton. I make a Form of Citacion against Mr. Winter, read 2 or 3 chapters of Hickerings scandalous Essays, end in domestic Quota.

19 Another brisk and cold morning, the wind at N. After early prayers a walk to Beach pool, to see how the Waters fall and after that, 2 Turns on roodee, am refresht. I dine with my Lord where Mr. Bridgman eldest Son of Sir John, Mr. Aldersey, the Dean and ArchDeacon of Chester. After prayers apply to Busienes. My sister Jones comes and makes us determine on a Journy tomorrow. At Sir H. B. with her at Night.

20 Prepare for a Journy, tho weather not clear, tis 4 before we (my Susy, sister Jones, Jack & myself) set out and past 6 before wee reach Wrexham and my

18 Citations were orders for clergy, churchwardens and schoolmasters to appear at the visitation and exhibit their licences. New churchwardens had to swear their oaths of office.

mother Pulestons, there wee lodg, wee end the Evening in a pint of Whitewine.
21 St. Matthew's, an hazy day. About 8 I go to Bryn y Funan, desire Sir James out into the Garden, introduce a proposal from Mr. Cholmley of Vale Royal to his daughter, hee receives mee with civil respect &c, mentions his Esteem of the Family and owns the proposal a great temptacion and Honor, desires tho time till Munday to consult yonder woman, his Lady. Wee go to prayers. I dine at my mother Pulestons. In the Evening to Bryn y Funan, thence Sir James invites the company and treats with Claret at Mr. Jones's the Barbers.
22 A blustering day with misty rain. Wee go to the Church and fill my brother Pulestons pew, the Curate of Gresford preaches both fore noon and after, wee scarce hear the Sermons. A full company of relacions dine at Bryn a Funan, go to wait on my Lady at the Mount. Here Dr. Edisbury, also Mr. Peter Davis with good Ale, receives the company liberally.
23 At 8 I attend Sir James for his answer. Tis civil but negative, rather his Ladys than his own. I take a sharp walk in a sharp shower to Erthiggwell, it recreates. Wee go to Havodywern and dine there civilly receivd. After Noon walk about and see the improvements, particularly of the Wood, return about 5 go and take leave with Sir James, his Lady and daughter. At Bryn a Funan end in a domestic pint. I writt this morning to Charles Booth a full Account of my Negotiations and insuccess with Sir James.
24 After the sight of Turin News confirm'd. Sir James and his Coach for Whitchurch. My Bro. Puleston, sister Jones, Jack and myself, for Wales set out past 8, wee come to Oswaldstry about 12, call at 2 Inns, dine at the Queens head. After 2 proceed slowly in bad way, wee have 5 miles to Llanamonach, thence in exceeding bad way, 3 miles bring us about 6 to Mr. John Davies, where the Family full, wee are civilly receiv'd, to bed about 10.
25 A dull morning, wee directed over mountains, come 2 miles off into the public road and to Myvod 5 and thence to Mr. Jones's, Llanlothian 3 long miles, the nearer approach to his house steep and frightfull by the river side, wee reach about 1 not without inconvenient, wett from the roads. After dinner and a walk into the Feilds the good Ale gos round in civil Entertainment till 11.
26 About 11 Mr. Jones riseing late, Wee enter on Busienes. Mr. Jones hears and answers civilly, desires a full discovery of the personal Estate of his brother, which wee promise. As to the addicional Bond hee desires to consult, is satisfy'd with the Settlement, a messenger is sent 9 miles to the Tenant and brings back that the old woman who had 10^{li} p.A. from the estate, is lately dead, scarce bury'd. Jack gos (5 miles hence) to see Pool and Powys Castle. After late dinner and supper the Ale circulates, Jack returns with a good Account of his Excursion. Mr. Jones vicar of (Llanvain) the place, joins our company, wee have much of Books and learning and no little Ale continuing till 11.
27 Wee part in good Freindship about 9 come a nearer way to Myvod and thence to LlansanFrayd about 1. Refresh at a Jolly Milners house, in his Ale and the provision Tongue. Wee brought hence in a good hard road 5 miles to Oswaldstry. Wee arrive there about 5, Jack and I light & see the Church, some Monuments particularly that of Mr. Lloyd of Aston, (Lord by the Heiress of

Alabanie) of Whittington. Wee lodg at the Queens head a decent Inn.

28 I with Jack rise early walk near a mile to a Hill round or ovall cloath'd on the sides with woods, on the Top an Area of about 20 Acres a delicate place, the sides round girt & fortify'd with 2 some higher places, ditches and ramparts. This Hill has great and most probable marks of a Roman Encampment, and Castrametacon, a way down to a rivulet to the West an advanc'd agger toward the East of the Area, where probably the praetorium was. Wee return to the Inn seeing the ruins of an old castle by the way, before 9. The Town is wall'd, above a mile in Circumference it is calld in Welsh, Croic Oswald, perhaps from the place of King Oswalds suffering, tho that on Winwick Church is said to be in prato Marcelde vocato.[19] Here is a good school, Mr. Pool Master, a fine rich Country, adorn'd with the Houses and Estates of a considerable Gentry surrounds it. Wee sett hence about 10, come to Cherk where wee pass out of Shropshire into Denbighshire about 4 Miles from Oswaldstry, here wee light see the Church and several Monuments of the Midletons, Lords of the Castle and the Territory adjacent and one of Dr. Belcanquay who was at the Synod of Dort. Hence over the Newbridge and thoro Ruabon, wee return safe before 3, dine, rest and in the Evening recreat in a pint of White wine. Sir Thomas Powell of Horsley bury'd about 10 this night, at Gresford.

29 St. Michael, doubtfull morning yet proves clear near morning service ended, we take Horse come to Cornish before 12, dine and are kindly received here, remount about 3 and come safe to our corner by Borras and Marford after 5. I wait (sent for) on the Bishop, hee tells his design of seeing Alderman Ince tomorrow. After wee visit Sir Henry Bunbury, end the Journy and Evening in Claret.

30 The Fair has fill'd the Town, John Cross and John Walmesleys daughter come to it and sees us. I wait on my Lord on Busienes, see the Chancellor, take a walk of 4 short Turns, discourse John Cross about Mr. Whaley and the Bank and my engagement with him. In the Evening at 6 Charles Booth calls on mee, wee go to the Fountain where my Negociacion is told at larg by him, the Affair of Vale Royal fully as they ly betwixt the young Heir, his mother and Mr. Francis Cholmley. This takes about 3 hours and 2 Bottles and a half.

OCTOBER 1 Indispos'd from the wine. After News dinner repose and prayers. I am calld to Sir Henry and punch, Mr.Jo. Bunbury and Mr. Moreton with him. Sir Henry return'd from the Christening of Mr. Hurleston's yong Heir. Joseph Bunbury had drunk too deep on that occasion and falls. Mr. Moreton movd with the Liquor shows much of Conceit and peevish temper. Wee part before, as usuall, it improves to ill language and Quarrell about 10.

2 I take a walk of 4 Turns the weather inviteing. Apply to Busienes, attend with Mr. Chancellor, the Bishop about presentacions lately made to the rectory of Halton, draw a Citacion against Mr. Bordley to show cause (Canonice nil

19 Trans: 'In the meadow called Marcelde'.

obstante) why the other presentee Clerk Mr. Rishton may not bee admitted & Mr. Langton is here importunat on Mr. Rishtons Account.[20] After prayers I go to Mr. Reynolds, to see Capt. Richard Atkey a proctor of Exeter, here is a great company well advanc't in Wine, it lessens in a short Time to the Capt., Mr. Quash, Mr. Reynolds and myself. Mr. Quash in discourse is kind and warm in Friendship to Mr. Gandy but very obstreperous, arbitrary & quarrelsom to Mr. Atkey, who tho hee commends Mr. Hawker (my old Acquaintance) mentions Mr. Gandy with great and decent respect. This pleases not the little Tyrant who would violently extort a better opinion of Gandy. The Capt. treat mee civilly, desires my correspondence and promises to write. The Glass passes fast and the Time with equal haste till 10.

3 Court day, attend in the morning, my Lord with Mr. Chancellor, Mr. Winter is there and his contumacy objected. Hee appears, after judicially confesses submits, my Lord (quoad hoc Negocium) continues it to his palace betwixt the hours of 2 & 4 when Mr. Winter, the Sequestrators, Wardens & some other parishioners appear, the Accounts of the Sequestracion are stated, the costs tax'd to $6^{li}.19^{s}.7d$. the sum redundant expended by the Sequestrators ($4^{li}.6s.8d$) is recomended to bee all ow'd by the parishioners in their Assessments. After this my Lord proceeds on a more private Denunciacion of Crimes against Mr. Winter, insimulates Him with paternall concern, relates the particular Crime of his breaking a Bottle of wine devoted for the Sacrament with an imprecacion and Curse of it, and the parishioners rashly pronouncd with religious fervor, passion, Tears, exhorts him to repentance of this sin especially, and gives him a most grave and pathetical admonicion to live soberly piously and peaceably for the future and takes to deliberate, on his contempt, in violating the Sequestracion in proxime. I examine 2 Wittnesses ex parte Gipps. And at 6 go to the Fountain and there to Mr. Winter and 7 of his parishioners. Mr. Colly and Stratford invited, 3 hours are past in easy and freindly conversacion, promises on future peace and Affecion on both sides. 7s spent, paid by Mr. Preston out of the common purse, wee part in full reconciliacion and great hopes before 10.

4 A calme morning invites mee down, Jack with mee, to 4 Turns on Roodee. After some busienes to the Coffee house, where the News putts Casal & Milan itself into the possession of Prince Eugene. After dinner with Sir Hen Bunbury who invites mee but gos alone to Vale Royal. After prayers, at the Bacchus with the Chancellor, Drs. Thane and Norris, wee have 5 pints in easy conversacion about the present successes. After this I go to my sister Partingtons where my Suzy, Mrs. Lloyd (once Barbara Ellis) and her fair daughter. Wee return home before 10.

5 After melancholy Fitts in sleep, a more easy morning. I recurr to 4 Turns on roodee, I pay Mr. Cartwright 3^{li} interest for Mr. Whaley to Mr. Dod, 13s 4d to Briscoe the Smith. Apply to Busienes. At prayers the Dean speaks warmly to mee about the Dean and Chapter's right to all the seats in St. Oswald's

20 L.R.O., DRCh.37, Halton Parish Papers.

(excluding the Ordinary) in the Evening Sir H. Bunbury returns from Vale Royal wee sitt 2 Hours and Hee treats with a Bottle of Claret.

6 After early prayers in a calm morning, three turns on roodee. At the Choir where Archdeacon Booth delivers a long sermon mixt all humanity fast, his Text is . . . The success vastly improves in Italy, the surrender of Milan, surprizal of Casal, desercion of Pignorel &c confirm'd. A defeat by D. of Marlborough, of Vendome's Army credibly hinted, from Expresses. After prayers and Mr. Boucher visited, my Suzy and I with four of our eldest Children go down to Lady Shakerley, shee treats us with great civility and Freindship, kindly remembers old acquaintances, revives with Venison pasty, good Ale, Fruit and Thanks. Wee come in Moon shine home past 10.

7 A calm morning, some mention of the Deans pretence to the seats in St. Oswald's betwixt the Bishop and Chancellor. I write to my cozen Parr, Mr. Case, Mr. Hockenhal, Mr. Jones of Bangor. After Noon to Busienes. End the Evening in a domestic Quota of Claret. Mr. George Townsend a young Gentleman of Warwickshire, eminent for piety and devocion here for several Years, dies this morning twixt 6 & 7.

8 After a rainy night, a fair morning, the Letters discover the rumor of the defeat of Vendomes Army to bee false, but tells the Grand Fleet for discent sail'd the 1st current. The Chancellor and I take Horse before 11 come to Shotwick Hall about 12 are liberally entertained by Mr. Hockenhall with a good dinner and good Claret, wee see the Church and the Necessity of Uniformity of Seates.[21] After a Dram of Brandy at Madocks, mount after 5 return after 6.

9 Indispos'd from the Brandy at Shotwick, a delicate day, a Court held for the Deaneries of Chester and Wirrall, easy of dispatch, with Mr. Hockenhall at Will. Wiloughbie's, draw his and the other Wardens presentments there. In the Evening past 5 meet Sir Rowland Stanley and Mr. Pool of Bebington at the Bacchus. Mr. Bennet comes to us, wee continue (after Sir Rowland gone) past 9.

10 Indisposicion continu'd, a Court day, the busienes easy. Mr. Boucher and Stratford absent. After repose, recover'd to Bookes, end the day in retreat and domestic Quota. Mr. Ed. Wright of Stretton my old valu'd Friend & Acquaintance dies about 4, After noon. Det Deus vivere, ut moriar subente.

11 A most delicate morning, the Chancellor and I after 10 from the Coffee house set out for Frodsham, come to Church there past 12, the busienes easy and short. Dr. Norris comes to us at the Lyons Paw. Mr. Davies dines with us Mr. Cheshyre comes after, wee stay here past 4 and in fine Moonshine return about 7. Alderman Puleston, Partington is chosen Mayor without Opposicion, Mr. Davies a Woodmonger and Mr. Sayer a Leadmonger or plumber, sheriffs.

12 The weather holds fair apply to Busienes. The Busienes of presentacion to Halton judicially and summarily heard before the Bishop and Chancellor. Institucion decreed to Mr. Rishton, hee giving Bond to save the Bishop

21 C.R.O., EDA2/4 f.34, for Shotwick pews.

harmless.[22] In the Evening at the Fountain with Mr. Rishton and Jeffry Prescott his solicitor. After at Sir Hen. Bunbury's where Mr. Cholmley of Vale Royal till past 10.

13 The weather still fair yet indisposd. The News yet good from Italy but retracts Casal. Mr. Shaw has a metaphisical discourse on St. John 4 v. 24. The Quire crowded from the new Mayor's access. After prayers wee visit the late Mayor, hee mistakes the behaviour of the Choir Officers to the Aldermens' wives, is too full and warm on the subject. After I am at Sir Hen. Bunbury where Mr. Cholmley still, wee are cheerfull till 11.

14 Apply to Busienes, attend Mr. Chancellor to the Dean with whome wee have discourse about the Dean and Chapter Rights to dispose the seats in St. Oswald's Church, the conference ends freindly.[23] I write to John Crosse, prepare for a journy tomorrow. Waite on my Lord for his Commands. Mr. Hultons son Wm (about to go to London to bee a Clerk in the Common Law) takes leave of us. I gave him 5s. Mr. Whaley calls on mee in the common difficulty, desires still my assistance and freindly offices to Mr. Vernon in his behalf. I prepare for my journy tomorrow.

15 About ½ hour past 9 the weather fair, Mr. Chancellor, Mr. Stratford and I sett from the Coffee house. Wee proceed slow make a halt at Tarporley, eat cheese with Gusto, reach Namptwich about 2 where small Busienes. Mr. Chancellor as in all succeeding stages, urges and inculcates the recommendacion of the Scotch Clergy. Hee and I sit an hour with Mr. Bradshaw, I after see Mrs. Church at my cozen Parrs request. After wait on Mr. Wetenhall and Family, from thence, return to the Lamb, where after a pint to bed about 10. Mr. Wright is bury'd this day at Tilston.

17 Wee set hence past 8, the Chancellor calls at Crewe, I proceed. About 12 reach Midlewich where a good dinner, little Busienes. About 6 wee go to Mr. Cowpers, divert with him past 10. After an hour, as last night, in Tullys offices, to bed past 11.

17 A fair morning, I see Mr. Vernon, hee receives mee civilly, I speak to him on Mr. Whaley's Account, hee promises kindly, I follow the company, call on the Chancellor at Hulms Chapell. Wee proceed and come to Macclesfield about 12. After Busienes in the Church and Dinner, the Mayor and Alderman Clayton see us. Mr. Gery the Clerks busienes discoursed. After an hour in Tully to bed before 11.

18 St. Luke, a delicate frosty morning, wee proceed about 9, reach Stockport before 12, the Busienes holds us till 4. Wee come to Manchester in the dark about 6. Dr. Holbrook sees us. After an hour in Tully to bed about 11. Mr. Pigot was acceptable Company to Night.

19 The day favorable, the Busienes competent. The Chancellor and Warden

22 See fn. 20.

23 C.R.O., Dean & Chapter Act Books.

have some warm discourse on Commutacions within the Deanery. After all Busienes over The Chancellor & I go to Dr. Holbrook's where wee and Mr. Pigot are kindly entertain'd with Nutts & Ale.

20 At Church Forenoon, Mr. Asheton has a good sound discourse. After dinner Mr. Charles Hilton, the Lawyer comes and detains us. In the Evening, wee visit the Warden to day indispos'd. After Mr. Tho. Kenyon and his Lady, her brother Richard Norris there, wee have a capon to Supper awkward carving and 2 Flasks of good Wine.

21 A fair morning, wee after Coffee and Brandy, set hence about 9, come to Bolton about 12, here some Busienes and Dinner stays us past 2. Going very slow in the dark, 2 miles short of Blackburn, a Lanthorn welcome, meets the Chancellor & I on the Hill descending towards the Town. Mr. Hulm, Hull and Nixon see us, wee after Larks at supper and Ale recede to Mr. Fieldings after 9.

22 The Busienes here competent, repairs of the Church and a new Lich Gate into the Yard, discust betwixt the Vicar, Churchwardens and Mr. Livesey. Edmund Greenhalgh shews a hopefull yong Chestnut Gelding. I write down directions about Licences, Wills and Adminstracions to Mr. Hulme, who omnibus numeris seems a good Successor to our good old Freind Mr. Price. His sister behaves with great disobligacion to all and to her good Brother's memory. After some Ale and a Bottle of good Claret at Mr. Feildings to bed about 11.

23 Before wee go I speak to Mrs. Wilkinson to do justice to her Brother's memory and make a good Monument on Mr. Price's Grave, shee answers sordidly. Mr. Chancellor speaks to her to send the Books Mr. Price entered the Wills and Administracions hee prov'd and granted into the Registry, shee answered with hesitiacion and peevishness.[24] Wee set hence about 10, go by Brindle, it proves rainy and blowing. Wee come to Chorley about 12 where some Busienes, wee set hence before 4 reach Wigan before 6. My coz. Holt dangerously ill on pains of her stomach. I am in bed there about 10.

24 See my cozen Holt in the morning hear her and descripcion of her distemper. Go hence after sworn Mr. Thornton as Executor to Sir Christoper Greenfeilds Will; past 9, reach Ormskirk about 12. Here is competent Busienes, it rains excessively, I examine Mr. Marsden on Mr. Rigbies part against Gill, hee is tedious in Examinacion. After a Glass of wine to my lodgings now Mrs. Case's past 10.

25 In a rainy morning about 9, wee sett out, the rain holds past Holt and I come to Wigan about 12, here is competent Busienes. Wm. Green, a Walker of Cloath, swears and curses offensively. Mr. Chancellor provok'd, informs the Justice, Adam Banks, upon oath, the Justice deep in drink takes little regard, sends not for the Criminal.[25] About 10 having writt to my Suzy, take leave of the company & to my cozen Holts.

24 Mr. Price, as vicar of Blackburn, was surrogate of the rural dean, and proved and recorded wills in the probate books retained in the vicarage.

25 The Correction Courts also dealt with common swearers.

26 A fair morning the company gon, I write to Mr. Haydock and Hudson sending Licences. After dinner sitt with my Coz Holt, visit Mr. Herle late ill of the Gout. Dr. Francis Worthington, Oliver Leatherbarrow, my coz. Holt and myself have a Glass of his Ale in the Evening. Oliver is full of and comical in his discourse and performances in Coursing Hares.
27 A fair morning take a walk in the Demean, see the scene of my Nativity and Youth. At church where Mr. Ward vicar of Leigh preaches, and very well, before and after Noon. Lady Bradshaigh visits my coz. Holt. After Hee and I join in a Bottle of good Claret, sit late.
28 St. Simon and Judes Day, fair. Mr. Entwisle and I set for Ormskirk about 9. I stay at Holland see the scaffold in the Church, the roof teer'd and as I am inform'd securely. Three Graves are new open for 3 Neighbors, old Margaret Gaskel (my mothers God daughter) is one of them. After discourse with Mr. Birchal and one of the Wardens about boarding the roof of the Church, I proceed come to Ormskirk and to Mrs. Case about 12, see the security of Mrs. Ann Dod as shall come to his hand wherein Richard and Bertie Entwisle Esquires and John Houghton Yeoman are Trustees. After Dinner proceed in the Matters of stateing the personal estate wherein Mrs. Case is reluctant and evasive, so little done to Night which ends in white wine and a small Bowl of Punch.
29 About 10 Mr. Vaudrey and I begin a method of Account and tho shee is averse, wee proceed & after dinner finish it, the Charg being 2182^{li};3;3¾d discharge 1620^{li};7;0d remains on Account and to bee divided twixt Mrs. Case and her daughter 561^{li};16;0d, hee promises to secure the half (all being in Bonds) when recoverd. Gives a Note pursuant to the Will to pay the value of the Household Goods as in a schedule taken to Mrs. Ann Dod at her mothers death. Things at last turn to great satisfaction and the day ends in strong Ale and a large Bowl of punch.
30 Some odd matters are concerted today and the meeting determines about 11 to common satisfaction. Wee are treated with a full morning draught and with a Guinea a peece, make way thoro sack and Orange water, mount about 11 come by Holland and Haydock (Mr. Leigh not there) accompany'd with rain most of the way, wee reach Warrington about 3. Mr. Shaw and his Churchwarden come here to mee in my retreat, wee pass some hours in white wine and they leave about 9.
31 A fair day, I mount about 8 and return D.O.M.G. safe to my Corner about 12, dine and gladly repose, in the Evening wait on my Lord Bishop, hee desires my attendance to morrow. After a domestic pint of Claret to bed about 10.

NOVEMBER 1 All Saints a cool and Frosty day. I (Jack along) take 4 Turns on roodee. After to the Church where Mr. Dod has a good discourse proving the Angels to be ministring Spirits. After at the Coffee house where scarcity of News. After Dinner, at the palace where a publique meeting about the Charity School, my Lord subscribes 100^{li}, Nine others 20^{li} a peece by which benefacion their annual payments end, but they their heirs and Assigns, to be Trustees, and to have their Election of Boys in their Turns for ever.[26] After prayers meet Mr. Davies in the broad Isle, hee gives mee a Coin, a Trajan, to consider I retire home, recreate in Antesignen's Terentio, and in domestic quota.

2 Not so sharp as the preceding day, write fully to Mr. Haydock on Mr. Theophilus Garenciers part and to my cozen Parr. I attend my Lord on Mr. Winter's new complaint of his parishioners and fresh peticion for relaxacion. The rest and after prayers in Busienes and recollection of my late Journy.

3 A rainy dull day, Dr. Thane has a good pressing discourse on psalm 34 v.1. Sanctissimo Eucharistiae hodie particeps sum. Det dein D.O.M. vitam puriorem.[27] After prayers I visit Mr. Minshall ill of Gripes, hee tells mee of a Duel appointed at 4 a clock to day on roodee, betwixt Mr. Hulton and Mr. Mather carefully intimated and prevented by the Mayor and recorder. After invited at Sir Hen. Bunbury's where Sir Roger Bradshaigh, Archdeacons Booth and Entwisle. Dr. Thane, Archdeacon Booth and I chuse Claret, the rest punch, the conversacion free and general but too much time & on this day too much liquid spent.

4 Indisposd thoro mind and body from last nights Freedom, write to Mr. Winter, see little News at the Coffee house, in the Evening Mr. Hodgson and I agree to each a pint at the Fountain. Mr. Chancellor comes to us and makes them 4, I pay Mr. Foulks 70^{li}, the Chancellor 50^{li} and Mr. Callys 45^{li} on Account of the visitacion past.

5 A cooler brisk day, Mr. Jones of Bangor calls on mee, wee go to the Coffee house where little more News, thence to the parish church, where the Mayor and companys with Ensigns resort. Mr. Fogge has a sermon on psalm 107 v 1 and 2, represents the Atrocity of the intended Massacre of the day and takes temporizing on occasion to bring the magnify'd deliverance by the Prince of Orange in 1688, into Balance with the other.[28] I meet in the broad Isle the Bishop of Ossory. After prayers I go to the Bacchus where for 2 hours gratefull conversacion with Masters Craddock Mercer and Shaw, thence invited to the Bishop of Ossory where with him Dr. Thane and one Mr. Cross oriundus of Lancashire, and Mr. Martin a laudable Clergyman, the Bishops brother in law, wee converse and the Glass gos freely round, past 12.

6 Indisposicion increas'd, am invited yet to dine with Mr. Egerton, The Chancellor, Mr. Cecil Warburton makes up the number. After dinner 2 Bottles thence call'd on, wee go to my Lord about his busienes, mostly about Mr. Winter, hence to the Ship where Dr. Thane comes to us. Wee have 4 pints, and after the Chancellor gon another.

26 C.R.O., Articles Preparatory to Visitation 1778, EDV7/1, Chester, for details about the Charity School.

27 Trans: 'Today I partake of the most Holy Eucharist. May God the best and greatest grant [me] henceforth a purer life.'

28 5 November was observed as a State holyday, when a statutory office was to be recited as printed in the Book of Common Prayer.

7 The Disease aggravated the night as well as daies to be lamented. To Court where Mr. Cheney call'd for irregular Christening makes a canting defence. The Bishop very gravely harangues on the sacrament, and the ancient and modern Administracion of it. Tis hop'd Cheney is convinc'd. The Chancellor showd passion to be condol'd. After dinner and repose, refresht, take Mr. Gill's answer. About 6 follow Dr. Thane and Mr. Jones to the Ship where the Club advances to a Bottle and brings mee to bed about 12.

8 Very weary of the Claret life and Nights. At home all day in repentance and reflection. Yet call'd at Night, return to the Chancellor, Dr. Thane and Mr. Hugh Foulks, at the Ship, where more than a pint go's easily down but the effects vehement and unhappy.

9 A dull day, I am with my Lord, deliver the rest of the returns of the papists, write to Mr. David Lloyd, a proctor of St. Asaph about a disturbance which hapn'd betwixt 2 Gentlemen in the Church of Northope. Mr. Whaley is still tedious and importunate. I repose but not recover fatigu'd by a constant tho small Current of Wine and its effects.

10 At the Choir, where Mr. Shaw has a good Sermon on St. John 8 v. 51, the Church full of Officers military, soldiers new raisd and Attendants. The News brings the Grand descending Fleet to Lisbon. After prayers, I wait on Mr. Egerton in his visit to the Bishop, wee stay an hour civilly receiv'd. After Mr. Boucher and Mr. Crompton see us. The 2 first sermons of Industry by Dr. Barrow are read, and, I hope, not without effect.

11 After an indifferent night a fair morning which temts mee to Roodee, very wett, yet perform 4 Turns (2 of which shorter) which refresh to busienes. Write to Mr. Wareing and send him 4 Licences and to the Bishop of Meath, now at London. After Noon with my Lord about the return of the papists. I undertake at last, to propose a Method and finish Chester Deanery by way of specimen. My sisters Partington and Puleston see us this Evening. Mr. Greenfeild comes in elegantly drest, I venture on Ale tost & cheese to supper, am forc'd in the night to take releif in Elixir.

12 A very rainy close Forenoon, with my Lord about the return of the papists. The victory of the Saxons over the Swedes confirm'd. Opposicion in Scotland, to the Bill of Union. After prayers with the Chancellor and Dr. Thane, at the Ship, here Mr. Greenfeild and Colly come to us, where the Lancaster Gentlemen in healths, go round. From hence with the 2 later to the Pyd Bull. Mr. Bowyer comes to us, white wine and Tobacco in the Nose discompose mee, to sickness and patter, wee part abruptly about 10.

14 A dull day especially from the Night, easy therefore welcome busienes at Court. After dinner refresht by repose, proceed in the returns. At 6 to Dr. Thane's where Mr. Egerton, Mr. Chancellor, Mr. Cecil Warburton, Sir Henry Bunbury and my self are the Guests, wee pass the Time liberally in noble Healths, are treated with 9 Bottles of good wine and an elegant supper, and part after 10. I pay Mr. Egerton for his wine sent to Ayrfeild 19s.6d.

15 A dull day, fresh pain and complaints, after News dull too, dinner and repose. I go to the Rose and Crown where to the Master, Tom Hatfeild, Mr.

Whaley, I with him enters into Bond for 80^{li} at six months. Mr. Cartwright procurd it, hee is with us, a dish of Woodcocks gott and wine detain us till 10. I writt to Roger Walthew about John Mee. My Lord read the 2 sentences for vacancy of Eccleston and Taxal.[29]

16 Another dull day succeeds. I draw a Certificate of the Execucion of Coker's Commission. My Lord comes over with further supplies of returns, is sollicitous for dispatch. I draw a Commission for Uniforming the Church of Shotwick, and free from other, end the day in an innocent domestic Quota about 9.

17 A cold morning, not early ready stay at home, read St. Cyprian on the Lords Prayer. Afternoon at the parish church where Mr. Fogg has a good Catecheticall discourse on Eccles 5 v 4,5,6. In the Evening write to Mr. Lownds, 2 other sermons of Industry (Dr. Barrow) read, call'd over past 8 wee go to Sir Hen Bunbury's where Dr. Thane, wee stay past 10.

18 After no easy night, a dull morning. Apply till noon to Busienes. Wee dine and elegantly at my brother Partington's, where Mrs. Mary Lloyd, solace in good Ale till 5, then invited to the Barn (Mr. Egerton) where Archdeacon Booth, Mr. Brooks Governor, Mr. Lancaster and myself are liberally receivd, the wine, Church of England History, discourse, healths go on till 11 when the Archdeacon and I (the last men) return in a cold and rugged temper of the night.

19 After such a night a tedious morning. Apply to Busienes write to Harry Topping. After some Busienes in the Evening Upon a praedesign'd Assignacion to the Falcon, where Sir H. Bunbury, Mr. Chancellor, Dr. Thane, Dr. Norris and myself entertain our wives with a Hash of Chicken & Shoulder of Mutton al a reign, the conversacion free and diverting, the wine scarse indifferent the Bill calculated for the Company amounts 1^{li}.8s, the men make it 6s a peece and wee part about 11.

20 Indispos'd unhappy and useless in Busienes or Books. After dinner and repose refresht, calld to Mr. Boucher where the Chancellor, Dr. Thane, Capt. Breholt, Mr. Allen and myself are entertain'd with 4 Bottles, 2 of which strong Irish French wines, wee part in good Time at 8.

21 Court day fair and competent Busienes. I examine 5 Wittnessess, recreate in domestic Quota at Night.

22 After a dull night a more cheerfull morning. I go to and perform 2 long and 2 short Turns upon Roodee. See the News, the Duke of Marlborough return'd Monday last, after Dinner am call'd over to Sir Hen Bunbury's where Mr. Davies who excuses my not seeing him at his House since hee came to Town, here is Capt. Breholt and Mr. Townsend, the Glass go's round briskly and wee are cheerfull. About 6 I return to my Account of the papists and to bed about 10. I lend Mr. Davies Calvisiuss Chronicles.

23 The weather dull not rainy, I recurr to roodee and finish 2 long and 2 shorter Turns, write to Mr. Markland, apply to the return of the papists till 6, then to the Bacchus with Dr. Thane, where Mr. Mercer instituted this day to Eccleston, Mr.

29 L.R.O., DRCh.37, Eccleston Parish Papers; C.R.O., EDP1/266, Taxal.

Colly, Shaw, Stratford, Berkenhead. Wee are free and cheerful the wine runs round briskly till 9.

24 A dull day, Mr. Archdeacon Booth preaches in the Quire his delivery negligent and tone subrustic, tho the matter good. The News carries an Article or 2, Scotland tho the country remonstrate against 'em. After prayers I apply to the return of the papists, read the 5th Sermon on Industry, am calld over sitt an hour with Lady Bunbury, my Suzy and my Coz. Kendrick, part past 11.

25 Dull, dark, rainy. I proceed in my tedious return, wait on my Lord about them, write to my coz. Parre. After noon go to visit Mr. Davies find him with Mr. Cally at Mr. Cally's home, sitt an hour over Wine and Beer. Mr. Mainwaring is here also, return to my returns, write to Mr. Lowe of Huyton for his return.

26 After a stormy, rainy night, a dull and doubtfull day. Apply to the returns 2 hours, dine at the Mayor's (Puleston Partingtons) in a full company, thence with Sir Hen. Bunbury, Mrs. Bruen, Cowper, Gamul, Foulks, Fogge to Hadfeild, the Rose and Crown, are cheerfull there, drink our Bottles part past 9.

27 Take a walk of 4 Turns on Roodee, returning Lady Shakerley meets, draws mee, to her House, treats me with free Freindship and Sherry. After noon and repose apply to the returns till 9.

28 Court day, dull easy of Busienes, I take another walk of 2 Turns. After dinner, Mr. Davies calls on mee. I go with him home, wee find my Lord Bishop visiting Mr. Mainwaring here, hee pays too his visit to Mr. Davies and Alderman Johnson. I stay a Bottle with Mr. Davies, thence to the Coffee house. After this Dr. Thane calls on mee, wee stay 3 pints at the Fountain return at 10.

29 A wild day, the News only Scotch the 3rd Article read and approv'd, the Mobb insult the Lord Commissioner.[30] After dinner repose and progress in returns, invited go about 6 to Sir Henry Bunbury's. Mr. Bruen, Drs. Entwisle and Thane, Mrs. Davies junior, Booth, Longford, Foulks, Kendrick & my self are entertain'd with supper, punch and claret, wee celebrate Sir Henry's birth day now the 30th are cheerfull and stay past 11.

30 Indisposd from continu'd freedom. After dinner go with Dr. Thane to Mr. Davies, after an hour there return to my returns. I remember Lady Charlotte Cornwallis in a domestic Celebracion of her birth day this the 28th.

DECEMBER 1 Sunday a calme morning. I take 2 Turns on roodee, am too late for Church, apply to St. Cyprian. After prayers in the Evening have Dr. Scott read on the Ministers of the spiritual Kingdom of Christ yet make some progress in the returns, am calld over, part in a glass at Sir H.B.

2 Take 2 Turns on roodee, write to my coz Parr to forbear yet his mony, carry on the returns.

3 After 2 Turns and the Coffee house proceed on the returns. After Evening prayers go with Archdeacon Booth and the Warden of Manchester to Mr.

30 There was strong opposition in certain quarters to the Union with Scotland.

Calys's, hee treats with good Claret liberally.

4 Apply to the returns, in the Evening, at the Fountain with Mr. Davies and Dr. Thane, wee charg the Bishop of Worcester with the common objections to his conduct in church and State Affairs. Hee alleages his integrity, applicacion to study and imputes all to neglect or remissness in Affairs.

5 I rise early to the returns, tho invited go not to dine with my Lord; about 3 afternoon finish this Archdeaconry. Mr. Davies and Dr. Foulks of Llanbeder call on mee. I go to the Fountain with them, wee are free and cheerfull, and the Glass runs briskly round in Bottle High, the Dr. shews an honest, orthodox and bold disposicion, hee promises to lend mee Dr. Browns Discourse of Death, a short one.

6 Indispos'd refresht by a walk of 2 Turns, see the News. The Scotch parliament advances on the Articles with steady resolucion, tho the people murmur, rise and rage in several parts. I relax today and wait not on my Lord, having sent the returns of this Archdeaconry to him.

7 In Busienes. After prayers wait on the Bishop hee is pleasd with the returns, communicates Busienes and delivers the returns of the other Archdeaconry to mee. And lastly treats mee with wine. After sent to, go to Mr. Davies and Dr. Thane at the Fountain, wee exceed our pints.

8 The sharpest Frost of this winter. I rise early and by the full Moon go on roodee, a fine schene of the pailing Moon and rising day entertains mee, refresht return to the Church where Archdeacon Entwisle has a good discourse on Luke 2 v. 9 & 10. At the Coffee house where the Articles are carryd on in the Scotch parliament. In the Evening see Sir Hen. Bunbury under complaints of his Stomach. Mrs. Booth, Bruen and Cooper come in, the misfortunes of Mr. Braithwaite his Goods being seized for his Debts much of the discourse, wee treated with Claret part after 10.

9 A cold frosty morning, I recurr to roodee 2 Turns performd, call on Lady Shakerley shee receives mee liberally with a Breakfast and discourses, ingages mee (which I promise) to call. After Dinner I begin on the returns of the Archdeaconry of Richmond. I go with Mr. Wm. Massie to wait on Lady Salisbury, wee find her in State, shee sends for her coz. Williams and refers the Contract, to him, mention is made of the rate of the House, but it is not concluded, shee designs to see the House before. After this to the Raven where Capt. Hulton, designing to begin his journy, to morrow for London had invited the Mayor, Aldermen Partington and Puleston, Mr. Chancellor, Dr. Thane, Mr. Hugh Foulks, Mr. Hitchcock, Sam. Filkin & myself, the wine go's round, Hunting most of the discourse & Filkins rustic complements of his Landlord, the shot rises near 15s, the Capt. pays 5s for himself and Filkin, the rest tho invited, the rest.

10 Storm and Snow the morning, wine and repentance disturb and confound my head. I advance little beside complaint, till refrest by sleep return and promove a few sheets. About 8 Lady Bunbury is deliver'd of another daughter. About 9 sent for, go over and congratulate with Sir Henry, stay till 12.

11 The weather cold and snowy, relapsd into Fevorish pains and complaints.

The Warden of Manchester sees us and shews mee Mr. Ogden's Collecion of Medals. I offer 10^{li}, hee takes 'em back, refresht by repose return to my returns, promove to some degree free from all but domestic Quotas.

12 The weather continues too severe for roodee. I proceed in the returns but at Night invited go to Dr. Norris his Lares the 1st time where the Chancellor, Dr. Thane, Coz. Kendrick and my self are treated with an elegant Supper and Italian wine liberally, wee part about 10.

13 After helps and complaints return to busienes, the News continues the Scotch progress, a rhetoricall Speech of the Lord Keeper to the Duke of Marlborough and his apt answer. I proceed till 7 then to my brother Partington's, where Mr. Davies and his son, Sir Hen. Bunbury, Dr. Thane, Mr. Bruen, Mr. Cowper's Coz. and my self are liberally treated with a full and elegant Table, and excellent Irish wine with a large Bowl of Punch, the discourse diverting stories. Mr. Cowper, Kendrick and my [self] stay a redundant Bottle, part past 1.

14 A severe rain with melting snow incomodes, the Market yet a great one. After Dinner and repose refresht to Busienes, calld yet to the Fountain about 5 to Mr. Davies and Dr. Thane. Mr. D. gos at 8, wee taking the 4th pint stay till 9. I return to my papers and finish Kendale (the 5th) Deanry.

15 A mild morning and recess of pain, invites to roodee about 8, where I take 4 short turns. To church where Mr. Fogge has a very good discourse on Lam. 3 v. 39, 40. At the Coffee house where none but industrious News. The Convocacion Address and the Queen's Answer, both of better phrase & contents. After prayers Mr. Davies takes a dish of Tea with mee, wee discourse matters of Mammetrectus and Catholicon. I after apply to the neglected Ephemeris for the preceeding part of this month & refresh in domestic pint.

16 A dull and rainy morning, I write to Mr. Cholmley now at Tivitnam, and to Mr. Parr junr. After that apply industriously to the Deanry of Richmond which I finish about 6, am then sent for to the Fountain to Dr. Thane and coz. Kendrick, sit three hours and pints out with them, return to the Oar and sit past 12 on Catheric Deanry.

17 Another dull day. Apply to the remaining part, at 2 interrupted by Attendance on Lady Salisbury in her view of Mr. Massie's house. Mr. Williams and his Lady are with her, they seem well to approve yet make some objections, at 4 I return to Boroughbridge Deanry and finish the whole Transcripcion. (D.O.M.G.) about 7, write to the Bishop of Meath and my Coz. Parr, recreate in domestic quota.

18 A dull yet fair morning. About 11 to roodee for a stomach, perform 4 full turns. After Dinner and prayers wait on my Lord, acquaint him with the tedious returns finisht, hee is pleasd, shews mee the ArchBishop of York his Letters and expectacion of him this session. After that, sent for to go to the Fountain to Mr. Davies, Mr. Chancellor, Dr. Thane, wee stay 3 pints only. After this the Dr. and I call on Sir Hen. Bunbury who treats us, Mrs. Booth, Whitley, Kendrick, Foulks (Hugh) with very noble port till 11.

19 A mild but heavy day. In the Town chuse mee Frize and plush for Coat and Breeches. Down to Mr. Holmes, where I stay till he has found and certifyd Holway's Coat and descent for Mr. Thornley's Freind, for which I pay 6s. 6d. After dinner write to Mr. Whitehead and Thorneley. In the Evening draw out the Names and places of the popish preists in the diocese, read Chronicon pretiosum, dip in Spotiswood and solace about 10 in domestic Quota. Paid today Mr. Ilsley the Smith for locks &c in the office 4^{li}1s.
20 Another such day recurr to roodee, perform only 2 Turns, call on Lady Shakerley who treats mee with Apples and Civility, I apprehend a sore Throat, stay in on that Account, proceed in Spotiswood about the reformacion and the Union proposed by James I in 1604. Sir Hen. Bunbury's 4th daughter christened, namd Frances. About 8 Dr. Thane comes over to mee, wee clubb for a Bottle of Claret here, he go's about 10.
21 A fine bright morning, I apply to Alderman Allen who gives mee a Bill of 40^{li} to Dr. Pope, write and inclose this to Dr. Pope and on this St. Thomas day, write to John Crosse to pay 5^{li} to the Church wardens of UpHolland for the use and repair of the roof of the Chapel, paid John, on Account of wages 1^{li}.5s.0d. In the Evening Dr. Thane and I to the Fountain where 3 pints and return about 9.
22 A dull day yet dry. At the Choir where the Dean has the Ordinacion Sermon on 'For ye are Ambassadors of Christ'. The news represents the King of Sweden writeing to and marching with a great Force 40 [or] 50000 to restore the Elector of Bavaria to his Country. Address of the Lords to the Queen, to continue the Honours and Estate of the Duke of Marlborough in his daughters or female posterity. After prayers I receive a Letter and his Father's Will from my Coz. Holt, write to him and Mr. Bowyer, turn still Spotiswood and end in domestic quota.
23 From the nights indisposicion, rise past 9, a brisk and bright morning, down to roodee and perform 4 Turns.
[No entries between 23 December and 23 January]

1706/7

JANUARY 24 Rise about 9 indisposd, Mr. Egerton full of busienes, Mr. Sayer and I after a breakfast gett out about 11, come easily in a fair but brisk and windy day, home about 3. I repose till 5 when I venture on a supper and eat heartily, to bed about 10.
25 St. Paul's day, perpetual rain, at the Church where Mr. Fogg has a sermon. After Evening prayers, Mr. Davies, Kendrick and I to the Fountain where 4 pints before 9.
26 A dull day. Mr. Fogg agen preaches on 12 Rom. 19. In the Evening, wee visit Alderman Puleston are liberally receivd with Supper, wine and Ale.
27 A blustring morning. I take a Turn on the Walls, after visit Lady Shakerley, shee entertains mee an hour. In the Evening at the Bacchus with Mr.

Chancellor, Dr. Norris his brother, R. Norris and Squire, Mr. Squire of Dublin College, Mr. Kendrick and my self, wee drink a token 6s from Mrs. Richmond and Styth, cheerfully Mr. Kendrick advances & pays the Shott, wee stay till 11, call at brother Partington's, reach home about 1.
28 Indispos'd rise at 11. After dinner repose and recover'd invited go to the Raven about 6, where with Mr. Bennet, Mr. Bridge and young tall Jeffry Prescott over 7 pints a great deal of Preston News, wee stay till 10.
29 About 11 after an uneasy morning, I take 4 Turns 2 long 2 shorter on roodee. After dinner Mr. Davies calls on, and stays with mee, in my Study till 4. At six, go down to wait on Mr. Vice Chamberlain, find him at Mr. Lloyds over against Mr. Bennett's, Mr. Tindal and Newcomon there, the V. Ch. gos, Mr. Benet and I stay an hour, then follow him to the Raven, where Mr. Houghton of Park Hall and Mr. Foulks with him, wee have mixt healths, popish especially, drink good Claret freely till 12.
30 Extremely fevorish and unhappy ly till Noon. Apply to sort, for my sister Jones, papers belonging to the parish of Mold. At Evening prayer The Martyr's day kept and most naturally, by constant rain.
31 Still indispos'd, take a walk round the Walls see the News. The Queen's speech to the House recommending the Union. ArchBishop of Canterbury has leave to bring in a Bill for the Security of the Ch. of E. read Bishop of Sarum's Sermon before the Queen on the Thanksgiving day. After Evening prayer, at Mr. Bouchers with Mr. Chancellor, Alderman Allen, Capt. Breholt, wee drink 4 Bottles of remaining Irish Claret, strong dull sweet part hence about 7. After the Chancellor and I go with Alderman Allen recover our palates with 2 Bottles of much better wine, part hence about 10.

FEBRUARY 1 A moist and windy day, indisposd, write to Mr. Birchall of Holland. After dinner Mr. Davies comes to my study, staies till prayers. After these to Books till domestic Quota & bed.
2 Purification, a moist morning and windy day. Mr. Newton preaches on Luke 2.22, a strang and desultory discourse. I see the News, the king of Sweden yet suspected and fear'd. After prayers and Mr. Bouchers chamber, home. Lady Bunbury visits us. After a Quota and poppy an uneasy Night.
3 After 4 Turns on roodee in a calm morning, I see Lady Shakerley shee treats mee with Nancy. My Suzy's 40th anniversary birth day, tis celebrated inter domesticos. After prayers to some Busienes. In the Evening solace in a domestic anniversary pint.
4 In a delicate clear morning, see Mr. Taylor's Engine and further works, perform 4 shorter Turns on roodee. The News makes the Swedish King more formidable and tells That the ArchBishop of Canterbury brought in a Bill, Saturday last for the Security of the Church of England, as by Law establish'd and that it was then read the 1st Time. Apply the afternoon to Accounts. After prayers, To the Bacchus, call'd by the Chancellor, Dr. Norris, Mr. Kendrick are there also, wee drink near our Bottles, wee part about 9. I find Lady Bunbury, Mrs. Thane &c at cards having supt there, to bed about 12.

5 Indispos'd from the wine and late season, write to my coz. Parr, take a walk of 4 Shorter Turns. After prayers return to the Bacchus, here on Capt. Hulton's assignacion, Alderman Puleston and Mr. John Cooper with his brother and Mr. Lowe of Midlewich follow, the company mixt the discourse dull and ingratefull, wee part about 9.

6 A fair and cool day. The Queen's Birth day celebrated very fully here. Her Majestie compleats the 42nd year of her Age. I compleat 2 longer and 2 shorter Turns, see Lady Sh. shee treats with Nancy and civility. After Dinner repose. After prayers Mr. Davies and I to the Fountain, Alderman Puleston comes from the Pentice, draws us thither, where in a Bottle of indifferent Claret, the public healths go round. Will Plumb behaves him here, with remarkable confidence. After the Formality here, Mr. Davies and I return to the Fountain. The Recorder comes to us, wee stay in a variety of discourse, our pints and part about 10.

7 A mild day. The Account of the debates in the House of Lords upon the 2nd reading of the Bill on Munday takes up and astonishes the thoughts of many. The Generosity and zeal of Lord Nottingham and 5 other Temporal Lords much applauded, the silence and degeneracy of the Bishops condemnd, the confederacy of the opposite Lords for its certainly effects and adversity to the Church admir'd and fear'd. Wee dine with Lady Bunbury Mrs. Thane, Mr. and Mrs. Cowper at Alderman Puleston's. A fire begins very formidably but is by applicacion of Engine and industry well extinguishd. Mr. Cowper and I stay with the Alderman at Claret till 5, then remove to Tho. Holland's, Mr. Bruen, T. Cowper, Mrs. Partington, Stringer &c come to us, the Debates and the Church Advocates are much the Subjects of our discourse which ends in one Bottle of Claret about 11.

8 Extremely indispos'd and fevorish. After dinner repose, a very stormy day and indisposicion confine mee till Evening prayers. After them in Books, to my domestic Quota about 10.

9 The morning calme invites to 4 shorter Turns before Church on roodee. ArchDeacon Entwisle preaches on Gen. 7 v[?] Tis a good discourse mixt with his ambiguity. The News promises a 2nd reading of the Bill in the house of Commons the 7th past, makes the Czar's designs in Poland great. After prayers turn a manuscript of the additional Lives of Bishops to Godwin's Catalogue. About 8 Sir Peter Soames sends, I go and find Mr. Cholmley of Vale Royal with him, wee dispatch 2 Bottles of sweeter wine and part about 10. A very high storm this night.

10 The storm continues, yet, after some busienes, venture on roodee 1 Turn about it, call on Lady Shakerley who entertains mee with Mum and civility. To Busienes, After prayers and Coffee house, Mr. Davies and I to the Bacchus, where over 3 pints Freindly about his son and family, learn'd about Authors particularly about Dr. John Rainolds whose learning hee admires and magnifys part about 10.

11 A calme and delicate morning, write to Mr. Okes and include Jack's verses on the last Thanksgiving day, perform 4 Turns on roodee. Dr. Prevarus pays

mee 3^{li} half a Years rent due at Midsummer last. I proceed in Accounts, write to Capt. Atkey of Exeter, read the Epistle preface of Hakewells Apology, solace about 9 in domestic Quota.
12 A brisk morning, I write to the Bishop of Meath proceed in Accounts. Take 2 shorter Turns on roodee, See Lady Shakerley, who obliges with Mum and civility. After dinner Busienes, pay the Dean and Chapter's rent for my House till Michaelmas last 3^{li}.10s. I proceed to Sect. 3 in Hakewell. Write to John Crosse and (my coz. Beale with us) end in domestic pint about 11.
13 Cool and dry, I write to my coz. R. Holt. Court and little Busienes, apply to the Chancellors Account for April Visitacion, advance pretty near the end. I write to Mr. Pigot of Manchester and Mr. Bolton. About 6 to the Bacchus, where the Chancellor, Mrs. Davies, Foulks, Hulton and myself stay above pints, the discourse wherein Mr. Davies primas agit, is miscellaneous. After the rest Mr. Foulks and I stay and end the Conversacion with the House of Derby about 10.
14 At early prayers in a fine brisk morning. Wee are surpriz'd with the sad News of my Lord Bishop being seizd 8 a clock last Sunday in the Evening with an Apoplexy and palsy. I recurr to my solitude roodee, take 4 melancholy Turns. Call on Lady Sh. and refresh with Mumm. After dinner I go to the White Talbot to Mr. Bowyer, who with Mr. Shaw stay till 4. Mr. Davies and (later) Lady Soames, see us this Evening. The impressions of melancholy News makes an uneasy night.
15 A brisk and bright day, Mr. Murrey calls on mee, hee writes by special Express, the ill news to Mr. Philip Egerton, I by post to the Dean of York, proceed in Hakewell. Mr. Davies comes to my study this Afternoon. After prayers in the Evening, find Mr. Chancellor at Mr. Holland's. Thence Hee, the Mayor, Capt. Spark, Mr. Foulks and myself remove to the Bacchus, where Mr. Proby joins us, mixt discourse particularly the Bishop's doubtfull case, wee stay our pints and part about 9.
16 A delicate brisk morning, to early prayers. I receive Letters from the Dr. and Mr. Stratford giving the sad Account that my Lord dy'd about Noon on Wednesday. The great Bell tells the unwelcome News to the City. I see the other News not material. But the Act for the Security of the Church had past the Royal consent, I hope very material Q.B.E. I take 4 shorter but very melancholy returns on roodee, returnd stay at home, wait at Noon on Mr. Chancellor. After dinner write to Mr. Empson, the Warden of Manchester, send Mr. Empson a Crown to drink. Write to Mr. Pennant and send him a Book, Common places of the Bible, for his Lessiur. Give Mr. Chapman 40s for his Viaticum. See the Chancellor about, hee gives Mr. Chapman his Letter to the Chancellor of York, returnd, & refresht in domestic Quota. But impressions are deeper and admitt of little sleep.
17 Another such morning. Go to early prayers, write to the Bishop of Meath and to Mr. Rider, after on the Walls, but not roodee, wait on Lady Sh. shee gives mee Glass of Mum. The Loss of my Lord mencion'd. I show Mrs. Owen my shell snuff box, read Dr. Moss, his excellent Sermon on the 30 of January.

After Dinner apply to Accounts. After prayers and Books, about 7 receive from Madam Egerton an invitacion to the Barrs, to come and keep her brother Philip Egerton company. I readily go, sup there too. Wee 2 alone talk on the subject of Succession, in the See as farr as modesty admitted, hee appears pleas'd with my inclinations, to his success, tells mee his interest and the freindly measures they take. That tomorrow hee intends to apply to Mr. Bridgman, now near Oswestry, about the Affair of Wigan, wee handle the subject freely and freindly over 2 or 3 Bottles of excellent Claret & part about 12.

18 A misty morning, I see the News, but scanty Yet, receive the Bishop of Meath and my Coz. Parr's Letters condoling my Loss, and hazard to my Circumstances by my good Lord Bishop's death. The day becomes bright and inviteing, I go to roodee take 6 Turns, the day humors the Meditation. After Dinner thoughtfull still, the day delightfull still, take a walk to Blacon point and semicircle the Marsh complete about 3 miles, return about 4. Dip in Wicami vita. The Chancellor calls mee about 6, wee go to the Bacchus, send to Mr. Davies who comes to us, in the Variety, Canon Law is part of the Discourse, the great Loss of the excellent Bishop and my great share in it an affectionate part. Mr. Davies tells that News of the Fr. Kings death is arriv'd today by the Exeter post, wee have only 3 pints and part about 9.

19 A brisker day. After 4 Turns on roodee write to my coz. Parre. Apply to Hakewell. Wee yet enter not upon Busienes in the Office. Mr. Davies is here in my study after Noon. After prayers wee step down to the Coffee house, thence to the Fountain, here Mr. J. Cowper and after Mr. Wells comes to us. Wee after Mr. Davies gon, have free discourse make up our Bottles and part about 11.

20 Indispos'd from the Bottle. Go down to Mr. Egertons, they inform mee That presentacion to Wigan is given to Mr. Ed. Finch,[31] this adds hopes and refreshes. After dinner Mr. Cowper and I meet at the Golden Talbot, refresh, and mount about 2 at a brisker rate and in a brisk day, reach Whitchurch after 5. Wee find Dr. Stratford alone. Hee tells us the Circumstances of my Lord's death. Wee see Mr. Colly and Stratford in another room, condole with them and return to the Dr., wee sit late over indifferent wine and I the later, part with him about 12.

21 The Herse, Coach and Undertakers sett hence about 6. Mr. Cowper and I stay and refresh in Mull'd sack. Mr. Fletcher comes and has some reflections on Mr. Egerton's competicion. Wee follow after 7 and overtake the Herse &c near the Plume of Feathers. Wee are readily admitted thoro Mr. Dawson's Ground, Mr. Cowper and I call on him, hee gives us excellent Ale. Wee come to the Glass house about 1. Send a Messenger to the City, upon which Coaches and Company come to a great Number. Gloves are dealt to all and Hatbands to particulars, scarfs to very few, myself of this number, past 3 put into order, wee

31 Edward Finch was rector of Wigan and Canon of York. His brother Henry Finch was dean and second rector of Wigan. See G.T.O. Bridgeman, *History of the Church and Manor of Wigan*, Part 3 (Chetham Society N.S., vol.17.)

proceed to the Barrs, here the Corporacion and Clergy serv'd with Gloves &c are ready. I dismount and walk on the side of the Clergy. The Herse and Funeral proceeds, the day very clear and calm, in good order. At the Hall, the Corps are taken out of the Herse, the Coffin remarkably grave and rich cover'd with velvet and gilt plates. 6 Bearers, 3 of which noble Clergymen attend, it proceeds to the Quire thoro the broad Isle and a vast concourse. Mr. Subdean Wright reads the prayers, Mr. Lancaster the Lessons. The Dean has a Sermon, too little heard on Dan. 12. v. 3 The Quire hung in great solemnity and crowded with great affection, about 6 the Office is over the singing was not comended. Severall of the Clergy attend Dr. Stratford to the palace, Mr. Finches, Mr. Chancellor, ArchDeacon Booth, Mr. Richmond and myself stay and sup with him. After Mr. Finches and some others receeded, I stay with him, deliver the Keyes of my Lord's Chamber and Study to him and come home about 11.

22 A very brisk and cold day. I dine with the Chancellor, Dr. Entwisle, Mrs. Colly, Boucher &c invited by the Doctor at the palace with him. Hee produces my Lords Will, tis read and matters consequent discours'd. Sir Wm. Meredith, Mr. Foulks and Ned Massie comeing in, give interupcion to the designd privacy, all others rejected. Wee stay till 5. At 7, I return with my brother Partington. The Dr. mencions busienes to Him and in discourse promises mee Lord Clarendon's History, wee drink our Bottles and part about 11.

23 In a thin cold Air step down and perform 4 Turns, not without thought on roodee. After, not yet well, stay at home, read. ArchDeacon Booth's Letter informs That the Bishoprick is dispos'd, the person not namd in it. After prayers at the Coffee House, where Mr. Egerton adds that none of the candidates of this diocese is the Man, this aggravates thinking. About 6 to the palace where the Chancellor and ArchDeacon Entwisle with the Doctor many Conjectures on the person, free and blunt Language to the Chancellor, wee drink Bottles & part at 10.

24 At early prayers, after these, 2 short but heavy, Turns on roodee. Thence to Mr. Bouchers Chamber where wee meet Dr. Stratford, hee privately gives mee hopes of a Successor, not yet mencion'd in whom he has great Interest. I write to Dr. Thane. After Noon, Dr. Stratford calls on mee. Hee, my Brother Partington and I call, and chuse a parcell of Claret, at the Bacchus. In the Evening Mr. Chancellor, Mr. King and my self drink our Bottles with the Dr. at the palace. They use a Freedom and railery to the Chancellor of which his tender and passionate constitucion is very impatient, wee part about 12.

25 To early prayers, indisposd, after expect the news of a Successor, not without suspicion and dread. Hee is not yet nam'd in the Letters, which administers some hopes of happier deliberacion of the Court. I go down and ruminate on't, 6 full Turns on roodee. After call on Lady Sh. shee recreates mee with a glass of Mum and some hopes of Mr. Egertons success. I dine at the Chancellors with Drs. Stratford and Entwisle and Mr. King. After dinner and a glass the rest receded to Tea. The Chancellor and I express our hopes and Fears of a Successor, I leave them here, step to the Barrs, but find not Mr. Egerton there but at the Coffee house, hee gives mee no hopes. I come home about 6 stay there and to bed about 9.

26 Ash Wednesday a moist morning threatning rain but clears up to Sunshine, before noon I write to Dr. Pope and my coz. Parre. To the Quire where Mr. Fogg has a good discourse on Joel 2 v 12, 13. After prayers invited, dine with Dr. Stratford and Mr. King in the palace. After Dinner, the Chancellor comes, the usuall Banter and Chagrin receiv'd. 3 Bottles of Claret empty'd, wee part at 9.

27 Court day. The Archiepiscopal Stile us'd,[32] many dependencys, slender Busienes. I dine at Dr. Entwisles with Dr. Stratford, the Chancellor, Mr. King, Mrs. Bold and Mrs. Mary Atherton are there invited too. After dinner and 3 a clock return and draw Tho. Whittakers answer. After that stay at home and refresh in domestic quota.

28 At early prayers. After not without Fear expect the News of a Successor, but no Letter mencions him. I ruminate over 4 shorter dull Turns on roodee. Wee dine with Dr. Stratford, Mr. Chancellor and Mr.King at my brother Partingtons where they are elegantly treated. At 6 invited, the same company gos to Alderman Allens, hee receives us with excellent wine and plenty of it, the discourse is still freindly controversy, the Chancellor uneasy yet sociable. Yong Mr. Dolben late from E. India comes to Us occasions a Bottle more. The Dr. kindly promises to take his Godson Will. The good wine extinguishes not dull Thoughts wee stay till 12.

MARCH 1 A brisk morning ease in it my good wine indisposicion, by 2 long and 2 shorter Turns, call on Lady Shakerley to acquaint her with the Arrival of her kinsman Dolben which shee had heard. After prayers to the palace, thence with the Dr., Mr. King and ArchDeacon Entwisle to ArchDeacon Booth's. Hee treats kindly, but with part, 4 Bottles which with the various discourse brings the time to 10.

2 After early prayers and as Canis ad Nilum,[33] to the News, take 2 long and 2 shorter Turns on roodee, some Letters have it that Archdeacon Booth is Bishop and hee is complimented by the Dean & myself. Hee seems not to have had any notice of it, or believe it. The Quire full at Even prayer, Mr. Dolben & Mr. Aphleck and part of their Families from E. India, several Gentlemen among Mr. Fleetwood now of Penwortham from Lancashire, in order to the race tomorrow at Farndon. After prayers at the Coffee house, where, as every where, every person but one cheerfull. D.O.M. det meliora. End in domestic Quota.

3 A dull morning after a melancholy night. Apply and writ Mr. Commissary, Mr. Empson, Mr. Parr, Mr. Markland, Mr. Heyes. The Bishop of Man calls on us at Noon. I wait on him to the Deanery where Dr. Stratford and Mr. King After to Alderman Morrays and to the Golden Talbot where with his company,

32 Upon the voidance of the see of Chester, the spiritualities lapsed to the archbishop of York, John Sharp.

33 Trans; 'A dog to the Nile'.

at 4 hee takes Horse for Warrington. After prayers, I write to the Bishop of Killala. At 7 invited go to the palace, sit with the Dr. till 10. 3 pints, free & freindly discourse.

4 A fair brisk morning. The News yet leaves us in suspense about the Bishop. Hope, suspicion and Fear exercis'd. A great resort hence, as yesterday, to the race at Farndon. Under the melancholy effects of the Vacancy and a cold confin'd at home till night. Then to the palace where Dr. Entwisle, my Bro. Partington, Mr. Cowper and my self stay near our Bottles and 11 a clock with the Dr.

5 A delicate calm morning, Mr. Lambert who in a fortnight, saw Dr. Pope by a good Account of his health, refreshes. I take one more cheerfull Turn upon it, on roodee. Call on my Lady Sh. who (the Mum spent) gives mee a Glass of sack, toast and civility. About 5 Mr. Chancellor calls, wee to to the Bacchus, where my Bro. Partington and Mr. J. Cooper find us, wee stay past 7 all (except the Chancellor) adjourn to the palace where (Mr. Thos Cooper added) wee stay cheerfull past 10.

6 A clear frosty day, a hard Ice. Court day, the Busienes soon over. I take 4 short Turns on roodee in a brisk and bright Air, am extremely refresht. Stay at home till prayers. At 6 down to Mr. Egertons, where follow Dr. Stratford and the Chancellor. Mr. Egerton receives fully with a decent repast and excellent Claret, the Dr. is much on secret and uncommon passages in the Government. The true French tempts our stay, I compute no less than 2 Bottles each, wee return under a bright Moon about 12, the streets quiet.

7 Indispos'd from the Quantity and season of the night, repose till noon. After that refresht. The news favours ArchDeacon Booth. At the Coffee house in the Evening, meet with the Warden of Manchester, go with him to the White Talbot, where over my pint wee have full discourse on the Candidates to the Bishoprick, part at 9, returnd home, receive a surprizing Letter and in it a severe Charg and reprehension, from His Grace of Canterbury and other Trustees for Iniskilling Breif together with the unwelcome News of the dangerous state of my uncle Peck's health to bed about 11.

8 The Bells early notify the day of her Majesties inauguracion, shee comenceing the 6th year of her reign. I write to Mr. Blackburn of Orford, inclose Col. Ashton's Administration to my coz. Heyes, write fully to Mr. Johnston in answer to the ArchBishop's Letter and Charg. In the Evening Mr. Chancellor visits mee on occasion of the ArchBishop's Letter. Wee to to Dr. Straford and, after a Turn on the Walls, to the Pentice where day is celebrated, drink here almost a Bottle each, hence the recorder and Bro. Partington with us, to the Bacchus where over 3 Quarts of Claret the freindly controversy betwixt the Chancellor and Dr. Stratford is renew'd, too infirmly maintain'd on the Chancellors part. My bro. Partington takes the Dr. and myself to his house, where wee end the day in a Bottle of Irish Claret about 12.

9 Severely indisposd, confin'd till Evening prayer. From then visit the Dr. indispos'd. After at Lady Bunbury's where wee stay till 10.

10 A rainy morning. I draw an answer to the ArchBishop's Letter, write to Dr.

Thane and send the Answer to his Grace, writ over by Jack Q.B.E. It continues a steeping rain till Night. I keep in doors, save at Evening prayers. After which in Godolphin till 9, then recreate in my Quota.

11 A frosty morning at early prayers, Send Jack to see my uncle Peck about a month ill of pleuritic indisposicion, look over a Box full of my late Lord's papers, sent mee by the Doctor. Today ArchDeacon Booth gives out that his Interest is not sufficient to procure his succession, But that the Bishoprick is promis'd and Mr. Callys hints to Dr. Freeman, these give fresh uneasiness and Concern, Lament and refresh in domestic Quota. I paid 3^{li} interest for 56^{li} to Mr. Williams, due the 19th of last month.

12 A brisk and cool Ayr. I write to the Bishop of Meath and Mr. Davies (now as I hope with the Bishop of Worcester) inclose the whole Case and desire their Favour and Assistance. Mr. Livesay calls on and leaves with mee 5^{li};18;6d collect'd at Blackburn for the Scotch Episcopal Clergy. I write to Mr.Hulme and Hamond. At 8 calld over to the palace, where with Dr. Stratford is Dr. Morgan, Mr. Bowyer, Colly and myself. Here that Dr. Freeman is mention'd as generally concluded on to be our Bishop. He is said to ly under a worse Character than any of his Coat.[34] This gives deep & fresh impressions. Det D.O.M. et bene vivere mala pati,[35] other discourse intermixt, wee stay together till 11.

13 After too sensible and anxious Cares and reflections early pressing on mee, rise about 7 in a bright, but brisk morning, the roodee wet, take a dull walk round the Walls. After to Court where short busienes, the Chancellor absent under an Ague, examine 3 Wittnesses on Pate's will, dine invited with DDrs. Stratford and Morgan at the palace, a Lent Dinner. After examine a tedious wittness against the Accounts of the Churchwardens of Burnley,[36] retreat to dulness, at last recreate in a Quota of white wine and to bed about 10.

14 A delicate morning, after a Night of Torture. The News not yet more positive about the Bishop. Silence itself has some solace. With DDrs. Stratford and Morgan at Mr. Bouchers, they take horse there at 10 for Penbedow. I take a longer and short Turn on roodee, Call on Lady Sh. but drink not cause of a draught of Mum before my walk. Indispos'd of my cold. In the Evening at the Coffee house, where Mrs, upon the Authority of Lady Crewe's Letter to her sister Norris, confirms the choice of Dr. Freeman to the Bishoprick. D.O.M. avertat, this still magnifies our Fears. I visit the Chancellor about 7 and find him under the same impressions. At home dilute and diminish my Cares by domestic Quota & Conversacion.

15 Something reliev'd by Elixir, a dull calm day, dip in Hick's Letters and Godolphin, pay John on Account of his Wages 10s. Mrs. Alice Harpur is bury'd this Evening. After that 2 turns on roodee, quota and Bed.

34 Dr. Samuel Freeman, dean of Peterborough, rector of St. Paul, Covent Garden, prebend of Canterbury.

35 Trans: 'May God the best and greatest grant [me] to live well and to endure evil.'

36 C.R.O., EDC.5 (1706) No. 2, Burnley; L.R.O., DRCh.37, Burnley Parish Papers.

16 Such another day, expect definitive News but wee are respited and recreated by silence and probability, that the Successor will not bee declar'd till parliament ended. I draw about 10 ounces of Blood, read forenoon the Book of Job, after Evening prayer proceed till 9 in Hakewell. Apply to Quota and repose past 10.

17 Dull yet dry, consider and propose 2 schemes for the intended visitacion to Mr. Chancellor. I take 2 longer Turns on roodee, call on Lady Shakerley, shee tells mee the story of widow Hurleston's marriage to Mr. Wilson of the Custom house. After prayers Mr. Aldersey and Mr. Colly call on mee, the first promises mee some Coins found in a Lordship belonging to Mr. Bridgman near Oswestry. I apply to Haķewell & about 9 to my Quota.

18 A cool sharp morning. The News yet keeps us in uneasy suspense, And wee dread its declaration. I go to the Coffee house where the Letters, save the confusion about Poland and Saxony, are silent. Afternoon Mr. Chancellor, Dr. Norris, Mr. Boucher and myself take horse for Eaton Boat. Here Mr. Hulton, Mr. Mather and with him, Mr. Robert Booth and Mr. Tindale meet us, the adventitious company is ungratefull to the Chancellor, but hee resolves on keeping Temper. Our Chad Anniversary is here celebrated. A good dish, Fish and Flesh prepar'd, Conversacion is civil and easy. Dr. Norris diverts with his East India expedicion, wee drink some Bottles after dinner of Claret, carrying a mixt discourse, mostly on Travail. Wee return to Chester about 7 and at 8 I go to the Dr. and Mr. King return'd, to the palace. The Dr. receives with 2 Bottles of good Claret and free conversacion. I return to my Corner about 10, a stormy night.

19 A fair morning but sharp wind. Apply to Books rather than Busienes, write to Dr. Thane. I & Ned Roberts are witnesses to Mr. Holme, his signing and perfecting Articles and a Bond of performance betwixt Mr. Le Neve Norroy and himself. In the Evening after some progress in Hakewell I go to the palace where with the Dr. and Mr. King, the Chancellor and Archdeacon Entwisle mixt discourse and good wine keep us till 11.

20 A fair brisk morning, Dr. Stratford pays mee my Lords Legacy to mee 40[li]. Indispos'd I (while the company is at Mr. Bouchers chamber) step to roodee, go round it and return refresht, find the Chancellor at Mr.Bouchers, wee go to Court, quickly dispatch there. I examine another Wittness against the Churchwardens of Burnley. After 4 wait on Mr. Townley of Townley at the Golden Talbot. Mr. Adams of Cholmley and Mr. Boucher there with him, wee stay in philosophy and Mathematicks here 2 hours. Hence Mr. Townley, Mr. Boucher and I return to the Bacchus, here Busienes and mixt discourse. Mr. Townley appears a well foreign bred and ingenious Gentleman. Our Civility to him is indevour to palliate and reconcile the Chancellor's morosity, which hee like a Gentleman indevor'd only to justify himself from a subtile reflection form'd by Whittaker his adversary. Wee proceed in pints (I think 6) & part not till 2 in the morning.

21 Severe indisposicion keep mee late in Bed and useless all day. The News affords only expectacion. I receive a Letter with all alleviacion and comfort in respect to Dr. Freeman, from Dr. Pope and an answer from Mr. Davies, in which demonstracion of his freindly Applicacion to the Bishop of Worcester, on my part who promises to speak to the Arch Bishop of York. I avoid company today and refresh in my Quota at night.

22 A fair mild day, recover'd to care. I write to Mr. Davies,meet Dr. Stratford and Mr. King at Mr. Bouchers. Invited go with them at 1 to Mr. Egertons, where the Chancellor comes, wee have an elegant dinner of Flesh and Fish, that just over, Sir Roger Mostyn, passing by post, is calld in tir'd and harrassd, refreshes, tells us the present affairs, sharply and satirically. Gives us Bernard (the Queens Chirurgion) his Character of Dr. Freeman, hee stays 2 hours till 6 wee another at least. Yet after 8 I go to the palace where Mrs. Callys, Hulton, Colly, the good wine circulates with the Talk, wee stay after 10.

23 Too much indisposed for Church or a Book. receive a Letter from the Bishop of Meath. Go and Stay till 11 with Mr. Boucher. After Evening prayers Dr. Stratford and Mr. King call on us. After these gon to the Chancellor I apply to Hakewell and about 10 to my domestic Quota.

24 A very sharp morning. Wee take leave of Dr. Stratford and Mr. King at Mr. Bouchers. They design to night by Cholmondeley to Namptwich. I write to the Bishop of Meath. After take against a strong Gale, 2 short Turns on roodee call on Lady Shakerley, am detaind above an hour by her Civility. After a late dinner repose, then return to Hakewell & my Quota.

1707

MARCH 25 Q.F.F.E.F.S. A cool day and brisk wind, prevent (what I intended), a step to Vale Royal or Cornish. I go to the Quire where Mr. Gibson preaches the Anniversary, his Text Hebrews 11.v.6. After the sermon to the News, which seems full of a peace proposed by France to Germany. After dinner, the Chancellor calls, Hee, my Brother Partington and I try a Quart of Ale at Mrs. N. Inces thence try a pint of red, at the Raven, neither good in its kind. Over these our discourse is much of Dr. Stratford, his too high humor, too mean frugality and industrious evasion to serve his Friends. About 7 I take 2 shorter Turns on roodee, call on Lady Shakerley stay near an hour, refresh in my Quota.

26 A cool but calmer morning. The Goods of the palace exposed to sale, wee step thither, see the malancholy scene in that House. I write to Dr. Thane. After take 2 longer & 2 shorter Turns on roodee. Write to the Warden of Manchester on the subject of the visitacion on his Deanery dureing the Vacancy, then return to Hakewell. My sister Jones comes to us to night, refresht in a pint and to bed after 10. Ned Roberts writes today to Mr. Borrett for his advice about the Orenge Breif.

27 A cool bright day, I write to John Crosse. At Court the Busienes is easy of dispatch. After Dinner to Busienes and after prayers return to Hakewell, till my Quota over and 10 a clock.

28 A delicate day. Letters, but no good News as to the Succession. I take 2

longer and 2 shorter turns on roodee, call on Lady Sh. but stay not. After Dinner apply to my sister Jones Busienes. At the palace about 5 and buy 3 good chairs, 6 ordinary ones, and other odd things. In the Evening a little in Hakewell, the rest, in expectacion of a call from Sir Peter Soame and Mr. Banks & my Quota.
29 Another delicate day. My sister Jones agrees with Mr. Whitehead the Lapidary for a Monument on my Brother Jones and a short inscripcion on the Gravestone for 10^{li} paying in Earnest 5^{li}. I write a full Answer to Mr. Johnston's Letter which I received last post, draw heads of Articles betwixt my mother Puleston and sister Jones, by which my mother is to assign her jointure and Arrears of it, and my sister is to maintain her laudably but these condicions to my surprise, displease my sharp sister. Shee takes them yet with her.
29 After prayers I take two Turns on Roodee, thence return to Hakewell and end in a Quota of white wine, paid 2^{sh}, today to the Collector for the last ½ Year's Tax on the Office.
30 A small rain in the morning. At the Quire, where the Dean preaches on 'Our Conversacion is in Heaven,' hee is scarce heard. The News has offers of peace, but uncertain. The evacuating Italy by the French certain. After prayers Mr. Colly comes in with mee, confirms the report of Dr. Freeman, hee having bin Lord Sunderland's Tutor. After (Jack with mee) take 4 shorter Turns on roodee, return to Hakewell and refresh in a Quota of white wine. My Suzy and Jack entertain mee with an ungratefull Account of Peggy Birchall, her ingratefull and sullen behavior to us and the Children.
31 A delicate bright and brisk morning. I write to the Bishop of Meath and inclose copies of Mr. Johnstons last Letter and my Answer. I write too fully on the Breif subject, to my coz. Parre. Mr. Stratford comes busling and too officiously in with particular confirmacions (from his Friend) of Dr. Freemans Succession. I take 2 short but thoughtfull Turns on roodee, in my way thither calld on Lady Shakerley who entertaind mee freely with Accounts of the very ill state of her Health &c, her designs for Shrewsbury and if Dr. Hollins advise so, the Bath. In the Evening recurr to Hakewell, and after about 8 of the other colour revive my Claret Quota. Pay to the Collector 6s for the last ½ Years tax on my house in Abby Court.

APRIL 1 After a dull repose, get up to early prayers. The public News as well as our Episcopall still suspending, write to Mr. Vaudrey for Stamps. I write to the Commissary of Richmond and Capt. Atkey of Exeter, pay Mr. Foulks on Account 20^{li}. After dinner about 3, wee take Horse for Cornish by way of Huntington, call on and drink a Glass of good Ale with Mr. Massie, at Farndon, come to Cornish in fine dry wether and ways about 6, are very freindly received and after a dramm go to bed about 11.
2 I rise before 8 take a Turn in the Estate, where I observe large Feilds and in good order. After dinner young Mr. Homerston, for his Father, civilly comes to see mee, wee drink a Glass (I sack) after dinner. My Uncle Peck well recoverd has an History of himself, his strength and performances sometimes bordering on Lewdnes in gratefull; past 3 wee sett out, my sister Jones and young

Homerton with us by Borrass, to Gresford, wee see the Church and particularly 2 Monuments erected by Mr. Robinson. After a Glass of good Ale at the Clerks house, wee mount about 6 come readily home & safe (D.G.) ½ hour after 7. After short supper and Quota to bed before 11.

3 A delicate day, Tom Birchall and his sister go on my horses, to Wrexham I search the Accounts about Ayrfeild concerning the office of Overseer of the Poor. I receive Mr. Ph. Egertons Letter about an Address to her Majesty on the Union, and shortly answer it. The last Court day of this Term, the Busieness competent. I examine 3 tedious Wittnesses on Websters Will. At Night relax in Quota and to bed.

4 Another delicate day, I receive a kind Letter from the Bishop of Meath, the public Letter now names Dr. Freeman our Bishop and yet other Intimacions support us. I see Lady Sh. and after, take 2 longer Turns on Roodee, the weather pleasant and yet too warm. Mr. Whaley is with mee gives mee some Account how my Lord Derbys cause was diverted from Tryal at Lancaster, hee tells mee of his own progress with his brothers, makes tedious circumlocucions, and promises to give Mr. Cartwright Notice of his payment of 100^{li} next month. After prayers in Busienes. After 7 to Mr. Boucher's chamber where I find Mr. Chancellor and Mr. Allen. Over 3 bottles of dull sweet French wine, free discourse. Mr. Allen gives Account how the country about Manchester, magnify Mr. H's Authority in the Court, at which the Chancellor grows Chagrin to silence part about 10.

5 Not easy after last Night's Claret. I take in a bright and warm day 2 long Turns am refresht. After dinner and 2 a clock, to the Chancellor who is indisposd and on bed, on an Ague. I say something to him on Mr. Phil. Egertons Letter, thence to the Barr; where about 3 Mr. Egerton also indisposd and repos'd. Mr. Brooks the Governor comes and after some Turns in the Garden, Mr. Egerton comes to us. Hee and I have some mencion on his Brothers Letter, I tell him of the difficulty and hazard in proposing an Address to the Clergy, hee takes it right. Wee go in, the Governor and I drink a Bottle, Mr. Egertons Cold confines him to his private cup. Hee writes to his brother wee part about 6. I proceed in Hakewell and end the Evening in white Quota.

6 In a fine morning I take 4 shorter Turns, stay at home in Hakewell. The News still suspending in a vicissitude of Fear and Hopes. The public News is silent. After prayers Mr. Stratford confirms his Covent Garden News from a Letter from a Lawyer, who had from a Clergyman son in Law to Dr. Freeman. I divert it in Hakewell and white Quota.

7 After scurvy Drops, I take a Turn out of the Northgate, recreate in Coffee at Lady Bunbury's, write to Dr. Thane. After prayers Mr. Chancellor draws Mr. Colly, Shaw and myself to the Bacchus, here, Conjectures, suspicions, desires, about the Successor, wee drink 5 pints indifferent wine and part about 8.

8 A fine soft rain falls. After 10 a clock prayers, to the Coffee House. Mails are wanting but not Letters to confirm Covent Garden success, from my coz. Parr and others. In the Evening, after prayers My Suzy and I call on Mr. Boucher. Hee takes occasion, I take it abruptly, to speak of the Accounts betwixt us, is dogmatical and directing in Advice to mee about the Accounts of my Office, I receive this with deep resentment but I hope with just manners. I step down near 8 to see Lady Shakerley, find her, in her mixt company, but in her usual Civility, return to my Corner refuge and Quota.

9 A cool, not rainy morning and day. I write to my sister Jones Account to Mr. Jones of Llanlothian. The Fast is had today. The Dean preaches in the Quire on 2 Chron. 7 v. 14. After Church, I write & inclose Licences to 9 Surrogates. After prayers and Dinner, Lady Bunbury and old Mrs. Lloyd come over to us. Mr. Crowe of Dublin, comes to them, and to treat 'em sends for a Bottle of his own rich French Irish wine, they stay till 9.

10 After Elixir easier, a warm Sun Shine. I pay Peggy Birchall 1^{li} which with 40^{s} paid lately by Ned Roberts makes 3^{li}. Shee gos with her Brother on my Horses to Leverpool. I write to Mr. P. Egerton wait (on his Account) on the Chancellor at the Coffee house. Hee concludes to speak to the Dean about the matter of an Address, dos so at 4 a clock prayers. After which Hee, Dr. Norris and myself go to the Bacchus, in variety of discourse, drink each his pint, I white wine, wee part hence about 8.

11 Good Friday, the day calm and sunny. I take after 7, 4 Turns on roodee unequall but ordinary. The Dean has a sermon in the Quire on Matt. 26.v.39. The News affords not much beside the D. of Marlboro landed Friday last, at Flushing. I receive Dr. Stratfords Letter which gives Ground to believe Dr. Freeman, will not bee the person. From the Commissary that hee had seen Dr. Freeman, that hee is a ready, brisk, ingenious, merry Man about 60 haveing 3 sons, as many daughters, has 600^{li} p.A. of his own Acquisicion, tho hee owns it not positively, will be declard Bishop of Chester, Sunday next. I write to Mr. Egerton and wait on his brother at the Barrs about 3, return to prayers, after these and a light Dinner, I go to Mr. Whitehead, the Lapidary, discourse with him on the Monument on my brother Jones, take a Turn in the Feilds, return about 8 thence to my Corner, Hakewell and Quota.

12 A fine but cooler day, write to Dr. Stratford inclose copys of Mr. Johnstons last Letter and my answer. To Mr. Waite the whole Narrative, and desire his Assistance, Mr. Pinfold, of the Commons, about a Copy of a Will. After prayers take 4 shorter Turns on roodee. It prepares for Quota and repose.

13 Easter, and indeed a glorious day. The Dean has a sermon in the Quire on Acts 2 v. 32. Cenae sanctissimae particeps sum Det D.O.M. vitam agere Christianam.[1] After prayers my son Ken first time so, go's with mee to roodee in a delicate Evening. The Horses and Company afford him divercion. Wee take a Turn about Jack and Hee, call on Lady Shakerley, shee is kind as usuall, to them. I call on Mr. Boucher to wish him a good journy to Little Worley which hee is to begin tomorrow. After return to Hakewell. Mr. Boucher comes over to mee and wee end the Evening in our several Quotas. No Letter mencions a

1 Trans: 'I partake of the most Holy Supper. May God the best and greatest grant [me] to lead a Christian life.'

Successor this Day. God direct her Majestie in that important Choice.

14 A delicate warm day. To the Quire where Mr. Shaw has a sermon on Col. 3 v. 2. After dinner I go with design to meet the High Sheriff, Mr. Swettenham, to Boughton, hear hee is past, thence the back way, to the Bridg and over Hough Green where I perceive hee and his company went thro the Water gate street to the Ford where the Judg had found them. I return and meeting the company below the Custom house, accompany it to Castle Lane. After about 6 to the Hope and Anchor, where ArchDeacons Booth and Entwisle, the Chancellor, Mr. Shawes, the uncle and Nephew, wee have much not very gratefull discourse on the Succession. We have an elegant Shoulder of Mutton a la Rein, and good wine, part at 10. Mr. Shaw paid mee opportunely for 12 Licences.

15 After Elixir reliev'd. Another Summer day. Mr. Cowper lame of the Gout and carryd into the pulpit, preaches before the Judge &c, his subject Humility. Dr. Thanes Letter this post, turns the News to Dr. Willis. I receive a suspitious Letter from the Commissary of his prejudicial offices, to his supposd successor Dr. Freeman, am extremely movd. After Dinner and repose, about 5, I mount and meet my Lord Derby nere the Gate on this side Dunham on the Hill, hee receives mee civilly, so his Brother. I wait on him to his Lodgings, Mr. Swarbrecks, where with about 20 horse, hee comes about 7, stay an hour with him, return to my Corner & Quota past 8.

16 A delicate day.Tom Gorst calls on mee, this morning. I begin an answer to the Commissary but, not likeing the subject, quit it, invited dine with Lord Derby, Mr. Stanley, Mrs. Starkie, Hornby and the Sealkeeper, do so, the Claret and discourse pass freely round. After about 4, wee wait on my Lord to the Walls, over Roodee, here wee see a race, not much sport, betwixt 8 sadle Horses. Mr. Eaton of Leeswood is victor. After this I fall in company of Mr. Philip Egerton, Mrs. Wells, Lancaster, Evans, Rector of Stockton (near Bridgnorth) Cradock, Aubrey, Aldersey, Jebb, Mr. Hurleston at the Bacchus. I propose the matter of Address, Mr. Egerton seconds it and succeeds tollerably. Mr. Lancaster entertains with his Case. After our Bottles here, wee part part 10. I bring Mr. Lancaster, Evans and Aldersey to Mr. Lancasters, here discourse renewd. And before the rest Mr. Aldersey makes a spontaneous promise, That if the impropriated Tiths of Bunbury, ever come to him and his power, hee will restore them to the Church. And in case hee can't, hee will indevor to influence his Son to restore them, and desires us to bear witness of this his promise. I stay uneasy past 12.

17 Repose too long indisposd, desired by Mr. Cowper I make his Apology for not attending, to my Lord Derby, hee being very severely handled by the Gout, my Lord receives the excuse, with great Civility. After Dinner and repose, At our next neighbours Mr. Cottinghams with Mr. Egerton, Dr. Hutchinson, Mrs. Fogg, Murrey &c an hour not tasting the Ale. After this company dissolvd Mr. Murrey and I only to the Bacchus, here wee have the Affairs of the Succession and Address fully, over 3 pints, part 12.

18 Our Letters exercise us with the same incertainty. Agen invited, I dine with Lord Derby to his brother vice-Chamberlain, Mrs. Hornby, Peters, Chadwick,

Coll. Daniel and Capt. Warburton are added, the Coll. talks bold and subrude about the Law charges in the County Palatine, yet my Lord receives and hears him with too much hansom, Civility. After dinner and 3 Glasses I take leave of my Lord, see Mr. Cowper yet ill of his Gout. The Address after evening prayers discoursed in the Chapter house, the Dean produceing a long ingratefull at first, but now reduc'd to inoffensive. The Chancellor, Mrs. Egerton, Murrey and I recurr to the Bacchus, send to Mr. Jackson, hee comes and transcribes it fair in the room, which stays us till 11.

19 Tho indisposd, I write fully to the Commissary, and shortly to my cozn Parr. The Address is signd by the Dean, Mr. Lancaster and Fogge, after dinner I go to the Chancellors where Mr. P. Egerton with the Address. I go to the Dean & presently bring back his circular Letter to the Clergy. To prayers and after them with Mr. Cradock and Mr. Shaw, to see Mr. Cowper, thence to the Bacchus, here Mr. Chancellor finds us, hee shows mee his Letter to the Dean of York, wee stay freely our pints. After I see little Master and Lady Bunbury, where after 2 or 3 Glasses of Claret, I come late with my Suzy home.

20 A blowing rainy morning. Dr. Stratford and Mr. Waites Letters different still refresh and torment us. I stay at home indisposd. The public Letters speak of the D. of Marlboroughs speedy expedicion to the K. of Sweden, now at Leipsick. After prayers and Mr. and Mrs. Boucher visited, I return to my corner, Hakewell and Quota.

21 Too much wine, but too little rain. Ned Roberts and Mr. Stratford sett for Malpas early. I write to Mr. Empson fully, to DDrs. Stratford and Thane. After prayers Sir Hen. Bunbury returns home from the Bath. I about 6 go down to Lady Sh. shee tells mee of her design for the Bath & returnd I visit Sir H. B., wee leave him about 9. I turn in Hakewell and make up an ordinary Quota.

22 I receive Mr. Johnstons Letter answering my last. I see Mr. Boucher who mounts after 7 for Namptwich in a fine soft rain. This post is silent in our doubtfull case, God grant an happy Declaracion. I agen visit Lady Sh. and take leave of her, as going to the Bath. I call on Sir Peter and Lady Soames, shee pays mee $3^{li}.3^{s}$, I laid out at the Coach mans Funeral. I send for & receive the Iniskilling Breifs loose and confusd from Mr. Madock. About 5 invited go to Mr. Davies where Sir John Conway and the Chancellor with him, some of the discourse is high and low Church. I from hence about 7 home, write to Mr. Johnston & Alderman Houghton of Leverpool. I paid Bro. Partington to day 16^{li}.2.6d.

23 Equip early, in a doubtfull morning. After 9 The Chancellor and I sett for Midlewich, in the way twixt Over and Winsford Bridg, a severe storm falls on us, wee come to Midlewich after 1, find not much of Busienes. Mr. Phil. Egerton is here, with whom about 4 wee go to Mr. Vernon, indispos'd yet in splendid & full Circumstance hee treats us with Claret and what hee calls Parnassus, a rich and pleasant wine, wee return from him about 9.

24 A fine morning, I pay Mr. Seaman for a Barrel of Ale for Sir Hen. Bunbury $1^{li}.8^{s}$. Wee sett hence about 8 call at Hulms Chapell and the Chancellor rideing slow, reach not Macclesfield before 12. After Dinner & Busienes over I (Jack with mee) walk about 2 miles up the mountain, return very thirsty. After some pause, Mr. Chancellor Mr. Hulme and I go to Ale near the bottom of the Town where I quench my thirst.

25 In a delicate morning proceed to Stopford come there about 12. After Busienes, Mr. Bolton and I visit Mr. Shalcrosse frightened with an Ague. The Chancellor, Mrs. Beresford, Ardern, Swetenham, Bolton go down to Newtons, where wee have a bad Claret, hence mount, Mr. Bolton, in the way, entertains mee with Mr. Shalcrosse his subtile dealings with him, about the rectory of Taxal, wee come to Manchester about 8 recreate and to bed about 11.

26 A very welcom and constant rain falls. After prayers I apply to receiving presentments and swearing the Churchwardens, the Warden satisfy'd with our Commission, sitts Surrogate and is not diminisht in his province. Hee makes a mean proposal to divide the Fees of the presentments. After the competent Busienes over, invited, the Chancellor and I and the Wardens too go to Dr. Holbrooks, where Mr. Pigot joins us, here wee are liberally entertaind with good Ale and Neats Tongues, part 10.

27 A cool, not yet rainy morning. Mr. Sedgwick has a very good Sermon on . . . After dinner I, Jack with mee, the weather fair and very warm, set on Foot to Prestwich church, miss our way, yet come at the Beginning. Dr. Holbrook rideing follows, Mr. Scholes in Mr. Ashtons absence has a plain dull Sermon. After which wee go to the Deanry, are civilly entertaind by Mr. Ashtons sister, wee stay till 6 but hee returns not from Oldham. Wee come in a fine Evening and direct walk, to Manchester past 7, call on Mr. Pigott, and sitt with him and his brother in law Mr. Linley till 10. The Chancellor went this morning to Winwick, to propose the Address to the 2 Honorable Rectors.

28 Past 9 wee sett in a fair day for Bolton, come there before 1, dine cursorily, sett thence before 4 and reach Blackburn about 7, here the Chancellor meets us, as to the Address, re infecta I ventum here on a supper, Chickens sent by Mr. Hulme, recur to Elixir and my bed at Mr. Feildings about 11. I write hence to my Suzy.

29 Reliev'd by Elixir. After Busienes about 4 invited by Mr. Lievesey, The Chancellor, Mrs. Hulme, Hulton, Jack and myself, go to his House. Here hee entertains us, very agreeably with the sight of two fine Horses and an Ox of the first magnitude. After, in his House, with excellent Ale, Hamborough Tongues dryd and other Edibles very decently producd and all along a generous welcome, the Temptacion keeps us near 10. Mr. Hulme in the way, turns to his wifes Fathers house. The Chancellor buys of our Landlord Greenhalgh a Chestnutt pad, for 10 Guineas and a half, is to exaltacion pleas'd with the Bargain.

30 A Cattle Fair begins here, wee sett hence about 9, some small rain falls, wee come to Chorley before 12. After dinner and the small Busienes, set on for Wigan, where wee come about 7. I go to my Lodging, my cozn. Holts about 10 where I find Mr. Bowyer, lately returnd with them from Winstanley. I remember with concern the expireing and venerable Term of old England.

MAY 1 Q.F.F.F.Q.S. The Union of England and Scotland commences.[2] Wee go to the Church where Mr. Bowyer has a good Sermon on ps. 123 v. 1. I dine with my cozn. Holts. About 3 with my cozn. Holt, Ned Roberts and Jack, go to Holland where I visit Mr. Birchal lately marryd to Mrs. Mary Taylor, see the midle roof of the Chapel, after wee proceed to Ayrfeild, take a walk, pleasant from the prospect, wood and water: returnd wee solace in 3 Bottles of excellent wine and a Shoulder of Mutton decently prepard, the most gratefull repast in the journy. I receive from John Walmsley [?], from Wm. Naylor his rent 1^{li} from Jane Hulme 8s:4d from the Tenant at Whitley Hall the rest of his rent. This stays us late, yet I call on the old Clerk, reducd by Mr. Sefton to Difficulty, return to Wigan about 10.

2 A rainy day the Busienes compitent. I speak to Raph Whaley concerning Scotch Claret,[3] write to Mr. Waite and inclose a Copy of the ArchBishop of York's Letter to mee, in order to bee printed. Visit Mr. Bowyer at the parsonage, see the dilapidacion of the Barn with the Chancellor. After wee step, next way to my coz. Holt's where wee drink a Bottle of my wine, from Ayrfeild, and to bed about 11.

3 A scene of dark intervals of Hail and rain, stormy. Wee set out in one, past 9, stay not in Holland, come to Ormskirk about 12 where the Busienes holds considerable. In the Evening Mr. Tyrer invites & treats the Chancellor, Mr. John Wright and myself with a Bowl of punch. Will Barton comes to us, talks briskly and sensibly wee relax till 10 then to the Inn.

4 A fair day, a head indisposd. Wee go in the morning to the Church where the Curate (Hull) in a desultory and immusical Cant, is scandalous and almost intollerable in the prayers, the Vicar mean & perfunctory in his Sermon. After dinner about 2 the Chancellor and the rest take horse for Warrington. I after repose about 4 take Horse to Lathom. My Lord Derby just rid out, I meet with Mr. Sudel, hee leads mee and Jack about some part of the House, treats with a bottle of Manks Beer, discourse about pronunciacon occasiond by that mistaken one of the Curate of Ormskirk, and of the late Earls treatment of his mother and Brother. About 7 my Lord returns, receives mee civilly, invites mee to stay, but at my desire dismisses mee before 8. I return to Ormskirk about 9.

5 In a fair cool morning I set out before 9, come to Beausee about 12. Wee are here civilly receivd. Mr. Atherton is infirm and languid, impatient of the Coach, takes the Air on Horseback rideing double pedententium. After 4 sett hence, make a halt, on horseback at Mr. Pages, proceed and come safe home (D.O.M.G.) about 9.

6 A hotter day. I see the News am still as in the Journy too entertaind with the Commissarys Letters and confidence about Dr. Freemans Succession. In the

2 The Act of Union was not a popular measure, and was bitterly opposed and criticised during its passage through Parliament.

3 Scotch claret was a cheap red Bordeaux wine.

Evening with Mr. Chancellor & Dr. Thane at the Bacchus, solace over our pints, and at home about 10.

7 Indisposd, yet attend the Busienes of Visitacion of Chester and Wirrall Deaneries. My Suzy and I dine with Sir Henry Bunbury, a fine Carp, caput prandii. After Claret here, calld to Mr. Cottingham's by Mr. Hockenhull the Minister and Curat of Shotwick, sitt freely at Ale with them past 8.

8 A very warm day. A Court but moderate busienes. After dinner and repose, in the Evening meet with Dr. Thane and Mr. Clopton, wee go to the Ship. Mr. Foulks comes to us, wee stay here involvd in Mr. Cloptons Geneology and more than our pints, till 10.

9 The weather very dry. The News of a total defeat in Spain of the Confederate army, shocking this Mr. Waite saies, hinderd the Declaracion of our Bishop, Sunday last. In the Evening, calld, go to the Bacchus, where the Chancellor, Dr. Thane and Mr. J. Cowper, wee are cheerfull on grave Affairs, stay above our pints till 10. I took a walk of 4 short Turns on roodee, twixt 10 & 11 in the morning.

10 Hott weather added to indisposicion, sparsim in Busienes and Books. In the Evening, wee see my sister Partington, returnd this night from London, shee treats mee with a Bottle of Claret, stay there till 10. I writ this morning to Dr. Stratford and Mr. Waite.

11 A cooler morning, a dew not rain. Deep silence today as to the Successor, till an Officer (one Spencer) late come from London, reports with confidence That Dr. Willis, is the person fixt on and to bee declar'd in Council, Tuesday next. At the Quire where Dr. Thane has a good discourse on . . . The Spanish ill News something diminisht. I in the Evening, apply to Lipsius de Constantia and go thoro the 1st Book, End in domestic Quota.

12 The weather, hot to scorching. I write to my cozn Parr, proceed in Lipsius with pleasure. In the Evening, at the Bacchus with Dr. Thane, Mr. Cowper, Jack Stringer, wee are above pints & till 10.

13 In a warm morning, I rise to early prayers. Mr. Waites Letter silent as to his Candidate. I take 4 full Turns on roodee, recollect my Concern here, on that subject, & congratulate that silence. After dinner Dr. Thane and the Chancellor drink a Glass of my Ale, with mee. About 7 wee and my Bro. Partington, meet at the Bacchus, wee drink our pints, the conversacion not very proper, part before 10.

14 The morning seems to promise but gives not rain. I write to the Commissary about the ArchBishops Option of Bowden and my own Gratitude to his Grace. I finish Lipsius de Constantia and compose an Epitaph to bee cutt on my Bro. Jones Gravestone at Mold, in the Evening see the stone. After at Sir Hen. Bunbury, where hee treats Dr. Thane, Mr. Wally and my self with 3 Bottles of excellent wine, wee part after 11.

15 Not without some indisposicion, I rise to the Court, the last of the Term. The Busienes small, I examine 1 Witnes on Websters Will, the day very hot. After dinner a short repose. In the Evening Dr. Thane calls, wee go to the Bacchus, where over 2 pints of white Wine free discourse which ends about 9.

16 A cool gray morning invites to 4 short Turns on roodee. Mr. Waites Letter concludes his confidence in Dr. Freemans success, Dr. Stratford's gives hopes of a good Man, but names him not. The Battle of Almanza variously magnifi'd and diminisht. Dr. Thane comes, and sitts an hour, after Dinner. After prayers Sir Peter Soame, Mr. Chancellor, Drs. Norris and Thane, Mr. Bowyer, Mr. Jolly and myself meet at the Bacchus, wee bring the Shott to 10s in Claret, pass the Time easily, part about 10. I paid on Account to Mr. Foulks 55^{li}.

17 A bright day yet some Ayr cools it. Jack applys this the 2 days to drawing exemple Characters on my brother Jones Gravestone. I write to Dr. Pope, my coz. Parr, & Mr. David Poole now in Lancaster Castle. I pay on Account to Mr. Chancellor 50 Guineas. Turn Lipsius his works. In the Evening after 5 month (or circ) interval, go to the Fountain with Mr. Thomas Cowper, wee drink our freindly pints. Mr. Cradock went with mee to the Gravestone, wee saw the Characters well finisht.

18 A bright day, rain desir'd in the prayers. Mr. Lancaster has a Sermon on Isaiah 50.v.10, stilo et elocucione mediocri subduro.[4] The Spanish insuccess still lessen'd. Inclinacions to a commocion in France still more probable. I finish Dr. Hakewells excellent Book Q.B.E., solace in a domestic pint.

19 The morning cloudy promising rain, but the wind W too high. I take therefore only one short Turn on roodee, divert in Lipsius, volumes, admire his knowledge of the old, and Ignorance of the modern, Rome, Begin the visitacion Accounts. In the Evening, I meet with Morrey, wee at the Fountain, choose the Bishop, rejecting many of the Candidates, thus wee empty our minds and our pints and part near 11.

20 It offers fairly to rain. I go to early prayers. After these and Mrs. Worgers News (which reports Valentia and most of the Kingdom submitted to the French) I take, in a soft shower 1 short Turn on roodee, where I have some demonstracion of the vicious Temper of the Bull there, return to Lipsius. After Dinner, Dr. Thane sitts an hour with us. At 4 I take Horse, and in cooler even, ride beyond Helsby where I meet my cozn. Holt, wee come home about 8 refresh and to bed past 11.

21 A warm morning, the Clouds vanisht. I read Mr. Wilkinsons Bill and Deposicions upon it, about a way thoro Stanny Demesn to his (Hoom) House. After Dinner and a Glass, I go (my coz. Holt with mee) to see the Inscripcion on the Grave Stone, after this Dr. Thane, my coz. Holt and I go to the Fountain, stay our pints and return home about 10.

22 Holy Thursday, a cool morning I (Jack with mee) take 4 short Turns on roodee. After at the Quire where Mr. Woods, has a good sound sermon on the Ascention. After Dinner divert in Lipsius. In the Evening at the Rose and Crown with Mr. Chancellor, Dr. Thane, Mr. Wells and Cradock, here wee wish for choice & (by the post) expect a Bishop. I receive my Letter but no Account, wee part unsatisfy'd (save the diversion) about 11.

4 Trans: 'style and elocution somewhat hard and mediocre'.

23 Indispos'd from the Quantity and late season. In bed receive the News that Sir Wm. Dawes is nam'd our Bishop this comes from a Letter to Dr. Thane and presently spreads over the Town. I take, in small rain, a short Turn on roodee, thence to the Coffee house, where little chance of news but from that Letter, Tho' it thwart the desir'd success of Mr. Egerton, yet in respect of other Competitors it pleases, return to turn Lipsius. In the Evening sit an hour at Dr. Thanes, observe the Frugality there, Thence to my Corner and Quota.

24 A warm morning. Two of the parishioners of Cockerham apply for advice and Assistance against their obstinate Vicar Mr. Winter, I write to Mr. Hebblethwaite, recurr for recreacion to Lipsius. Sir Hen. Bunbury pays mee for Midlewich Ale $1^{li}.8^{s}$. For Hopcare Cheese $1^{li}.10^{s}$. In the Evening disappointed of company stay at Home. Lady Bunbury comes over to us, wee expect, in my Corner, Confirmacion of our late good news but, in vain, till 11.

25 A fine dropping day, wee enter on it in earnest expectacion of the success of Sir Wm. Dawes, all Letters are silent in that matter, save one to Mr. Mather from Mr. Nath. Booth of Mottram, this reduces us to our former Fears. Mr. Lancaster has a good sermon in the Quire on St. John 15 v. 26. Mr. Shaw, in the Afternoon, persists to further offence on the Text 'Wives obey your Husbands, as is fit in the Lord'. In the Evening I take 2 Turns on roodee, Jack with mee. The Bull here approaches Wickstead, and hee (ignorant of his Temper) provokes him, but without harm. Lady Bunbury agen sees us this Evening, which concludes after 10, in domestic Quota.

26 In a doubtfull morning as to rain, step down to roodee, where tho' disturbd by the Bulls angry approach, take 2 Turns, after which visit Lady Shakerley who return'd Friday last, shee entertains mee with civility and a particular Account of her expedicion to Shrewsbury, near 2 Hours. Invites mee to put my Horses in her Orchard. After Dinner Lipsius and the Gravestone seen finisht. I go to the Rose and Crown to the Chancellor & Dr. Thane, wee stay 2 hours and 2 Bottles in votes for Sir. Wm. Dawes or his rich Competitor.[5] It rains vehemently, part & sharply all the Time. After this at Sir Hen Bunburys with my Suzy & Cozn. Holt, good wine here, wee part about 11.

27 Indisposd, receive a short Hint from my Cozn. Parr that hee hopes Sir Wm. Dawes will bee the Man with a good & short Character, other Letters in Town mencion him and Dr. Freeman seems to vanish in a very ill savor. Affairs in Germany take an ill aspect, new Kingdoms invaded in Spain, some loss at Malines. I meet with Mr. Daniel Chadwick of Preston who was present at the barberous Execucion of the Earl of Derby, hee remembers the History of the Time and the Officers in and aginst Lathom House.[6] In the Evening about 6 the Chancellor, Warden of Manchester, Dr. Thane and I go to the Rose & Crown.

5 The rich competitor was Dr. Freeman.

6 G. Ormerod, *Civil War Tracts (Military) for Lancashire*, Chetham Society, O.S. Vol. 2. This volume contains details of the execution of the earl of Derby.

Mr. Boucher comes, wee stay our pints and till 9. I sent my Horses to Lady Sh. this morning 'twas showery all day.

28 Reliev'd by Elixir and a cool showry morning. I write to my cozn. Parr and reprove his Incertainty. I read the 2 sermons of Mr. Shaw which had occasion'd so much reflection from the Women, think 'em sound but severe. I begin after upon the Accounts conclude in domestic Quota, still showry.

29 The Birth and return of King Charles 2nd celebrated. Mr. Fogg has a good Sermon on Psal. 96 v. 10. I proceed in Accounts. In the Evening at the Fountain with Dr. Thane, Mr. Callis, 2 Cowpers, Mr. Bletchington, wee drink above our Bottles of port, the expected Letters come not tho' wee stay near 11.

30 Indispos'd to Busienes. See the News, which gives Expectacion of a Battle in Flanders. No private Letters mencion our Candidates. That public one at the Exchange, Dr. Willis. A vehement showr falls at prayers. After which I (Jack along) in a sweet Evening walk to Upton, see the Grass to which I intend to send my Horses. Thence back and to Lady Shakerley's where I see the Horses and am civilly treated with a Bottle of Sage Ale. After that a Quota.

31 Disturb'd sleep from the Ale &c. I write to Mr. Parker my thoughts about his designed Burial place in Chelford Chapel, proceed in the Visitacion Accounts, return to Lipsius. In the Evening after 8 take 2 Turns on roodee, the weather calm and the Sun not sett, refresh in domestic Quota.

JUNE 1 Q.F.F.Q.S. No private Letters about the Bishop. Dyers mentions Sir Wm. Dawes as concluded on to bee our Bishop. Mr. Fogge has an excellent Sermon on . . . .Sanctissimae Eucharistiae particeps sumus, Det D.O.M. vitam pie, iuste, sobrie et caste instituere.[7] Sir Humphrey Mackworth at Church & Sacrament. After prayers I look over the printed pretended Catalogue of my late Lord Derby's Books. Lady Bunbury comes over & sups with us. Bell [Arabella] falls ill of Gripes or pleurisy. I have some discourse with my cozn. Holt, wee sitt up till 1.

2 A disturb'd uneasy morning. The weather still rainy. I write to Mr. Johnston an Account of my receipt of the ArchBishops printed Letters. At the church where Mr. Fogge has another good sermon on St. John 10 v. 37,38. After prayers Sir Hen Bunbury, Sir Peter Soames, the Chancellor, Drs. Norris and Thane and myself at the Ship. Sir Peter and myself stay after the rest. Mr. Langford at last finds us, wee stay till 12. I receive here my cozn Parrs Letter saying the Odds are on Sir Wm. Dawes side. I find my poor child Bell in miserable pain.

3 Hott and indispos'd am aggravated from the extreme pain and danger of the Child now under the pangs and shocking Appearance of Death, shee aged 8 years, 12 March last, departs this unhappy Age about rather before 11. The Family falls into sorrow & disorder from the suddain loss of an excellent Child.

7 Trans: 'We partake of the most Holy Eucharist. May God the best and greatest grant [me] to build a pious, just, sober and chaste life.'

Mrs. Worgess news gives Dr. Blackhall to us, Sir W. to Exon, Our Friends and relacions visit us after noon. I receive Lady Jones parcells of Goods by Wagon, it continues rainy.

4 Something (Elixir helping) recovered from my indisposicion, I pay the Wagoner $3^{li}.6^{s}.6^{d}$ Write to my cozn Parr, Sir Henry and my Lady Bunbury take leave of us for Bettisfeild. All Accounts represent Lady Shakerley very very dangerously ill since Saturday last, her pains fixing in and affecting her Head. I apply to Tullys consolatory Epistles and find refreshment. The Manner of the Funeral consider'd. After their supper and my Quota to bed about 11.

5 The weather still rainy, I return to Tullys Epistles particularly V lib iv and xiii, xiv, xv, xvi, lib V &c continue in them most of the Day. About 7 at Evening a decent company about 40 meet here to attend the Funeral which proceeds quickly after, and Mr. Shaw doing the Office, and my Arabella is bury'd (in the Grave of 5 of her Brothers and sisters within the railes on the North side of the Altar) before 8. I return to my Thoughts, God grant Success and effect to resolutions of a better Life, thus sensibly admonisht of the incertainty of a Life to bee really repented of. After supper and a small Quota to bed before 11.

6 The weather cool and windy. Dr. Stratford's Letter to my brother Partington certainly determines on Sir Wm. Dawes and Dr. Blackhall to Exon and Chester, but adds tis not yet certain, whether is designed to whether See, so wee remain uncertain yet in the Successor. The Affairs of Spain desperate & so of the Upper Rhine. The Bishop of Ely Dr. Patrick above 80 years of age is reported dead. The Bishop of Exon declar'd Sunday last, in Council, Winton. After prayers the 2 Archdeacons Booth & Entwisle take a Turn in the Broad Isle, the affairs at Court, the defeat in Spain, and the nameing of the Bishops, talkt of. The former gives hopes (come fresh from his Waiting) that the Ministry is inbarrasd and comeing over to the Church, That Canterbury has no Interest at Court, That Dawes and Blackhall are opposite to his Temper, That the Latter has Kist her Majesties hand for Exon, therefore the other to come to Chester. I return to Tully and Lipsius, and After domestic Quota to bed past 11.

7 I take 2 Turns on roodee, after write to Lady Jones and Mr. Hebblethwaite. In the Evening go Lady Shakerleys, hear the Account of her distemper. Mr. Shakerley is civil to my Enquirys. I return to my Corner and Quota. I finish Accounts of the presentments & deliver all to Mr. Boucher to consider.

8 The Dean preaches (being Trinity Sunday) on Rev. 4 v. 6 a sound and usefull sermon. The Letters bestow Winchester and Ely, are silent in the rest, and give no good prospect of public affairs. After Evening prayers and a hott day, I (Jack along) step to Upton, see my horses at Grass, refresh, return'd and to bed.

9 Dies [? natalitia] ab Anno 1649 computando mihi LVIII Annu aetatis. Lipsii alligindis de quo dolendum pro eis Quot magnos Doctos Bonos actat superari Det D.O.M. vitam meliorem sanctiorem castam.[8] I take 2 Turns, cool from the

8 Trans: My birthday, 58 years of age reckoned from 1649 . . . May God the best and greatest grant [me] a better, holier and chaste life'.

river, the day scorching, I write to Mr. Lambert. My Aunt Peck and sister Jones come to see us they dine here. After prayers my cozn. Holt and I see Dr. Thane indispos'd. At supper a small domestic Commemoration, it keeps us up till 1.
10 To wear off the indisposicion, I take 4 Turns, call at Lady Shakerley where I am told Death is at the Door. The Letters bring nothing from Flanders nothing Good. I pay Sarah the Maid her wages 2^{li}. The Visit of Freinds takes up some hours. In the Evening in the Town with cozn Holt, pass the later part as the rest, in supper and Quota.
11 St. Barnabas, cool with some rain and wind. I pay Mr. Whitehead for his work on the Stone in part $3^{li}.10^{s}$. After dinner about 4 ride out (shee designing for Warrington) with my cozn. Holt to Trafford where, wee meet with her Husband on this accident, shee returns with him to my Corner. I, Jack with mee, go to Saighten to Sir Hen Bunbury's children where I find Miss Suzy feverish, impatient and under the like complaint with my Bell, wee return the shorter way by Huntington about 9, after supper to bed about 11.
12 Court day moderat Busienes. Mr. Ph. Egerton agen menciond to day with some probability. A severe sultry heat affects mee. Sir Hen. Bunbury comes about 5 with good news from Saighton. About 7 my cozn. Holt and I go to Pickings to Sir Peter Soame and Sir Hen. the 2nd Barronet and my self under take a Bowl of punch of 3 Quarts, my cozn Holt a bottle of Claret, wee pass the time cheerfully past 10.
13 Cool from a breeze. Lady Shakerley dies about 7 this morning much lamented. My cozn. Holts return for Warrington about 11. I deliver 50 Guineas to him to deliver for mee to Mr. Vaudrey. I go to Mr. Holmes the Herald to see his Books concerning Mr. Leftwichs Family. After dines with Sir Hen Bunbury & Mr. Robert Booth at Sir Peter Soames Lodging. After dinner plenty of good wine has great effect upon my indisposicion from punch. I reckon on 2 Bottles on my share, return full about 5, fall sick and to bed about 8.
14 Indisposd to all Busienes. Mr. Leftwich is with mee with domestic Muniments of his Family. After Dinner, about two the Earl of Pembrook (with no grand retinue) enters the City, is receivd by the Corporacion in a speech by the Recorder. Lights at the Hope and Anchor where (after his Dinner) the Dean (accompanyd with the Clergy) harrangues him also. He confirms, by his belief, the News of Sir Wm. Dawes and saies Dr. Freeman was ill of a Fevor, when he left London. After repose I step to the Post Office in hope of definitive Letters meet none at all, Mr. Shawe & Hodgson are here with mee till 9.
15 Reliev'd by Elixir. In a hott day the Quire crowded more with Spectators than Auditors. Lord Pembrook exemplarily and his company present, Dr. Thane has a good sermon on Ps. 25 v. 5. The Public Letters bring nothing but small velitations from the Armys, no Letter mencions our Successor. The Earl is at prayers and after these with his company go's on Foot to Pentice. I run in the Stream of Spectators. The Table is loaden with a splendid Copia of Sweetmeats, to which wine is added, the room full, the Treat is dispersd in Tollerable Order, some divercion is made by throwing out some of the Sweetmeats into the Street, where the Mobb after scrambling take the sweetmeat deep out of the dirt. The

Earl returns from this Entertainment before 7. After which I (Jack with mee) step to Upton and see my horses and return in a delicate Evening about 9.
16 My Lord Pembrook with a small retinue, gos before 5, by coach, towards Holyhead, the rest by Sea. Jack and Ned Roberts go to see the divercion of races at Wrexham. I draw a Monicion to the Churchwardens of Manchester to quiet the Warden in his seat, lately granted to him. I write to my Lady Jones & Cozn. Parre. In the Evening at the Ship with the Chancellor, Dr. Thane and Mr. Callis where in pints of dull claret, wee stay till 9, expect after, the post at the Coffee house ½ hr in vain. I draw a Testimonial on Mr. Leftwich's pedigree.
17 A close morning, not rainy, apply to dispatch of some busienes. The Letters barren of everything, but expectations,no mention of the indispos'd Bishopricks. After dinner and prayers, I turn Lipsius his X Centuries of Epistles, reading some obiter. About 7 I visit Mr. George Shackerley in the House of Mourning. Take my domestic Quota about 10.
18 A windy morning out, warm within doors. I apply further to Accounts and come to particular designacions of the residue. After a brisk walk, the wind favoring to my horses, beyond Upton Hall am refresht by it. After prayers, invited go with the Chancellor, ArchDeacons, Booth and Entwisle and Dr. Thane to the Falcon, here 5s. sent by the Dean of Wells (Graham) to bee drank with the Chancellor and Dr. Thane, is melted & cover'd. Discourse & conjectures on the Succession but resolve all into incertainty. Here I am told of Mr. Leftwich is remarkable Frugality in saving, and charity in giving 20^{li} to the Charity School. I paid 30^{li} to Mr. Foulks.
19 After an unhappy and uneasy night, a better day, small Busienes in the Court. I write to Mr. Vaudrey and Thornley, examine 2 Wittnesses on Mrs. Lightbowns nuncupative Will, after about 5, My Suzy and I take Horse to Saighton to see Sir Hen Bunbury's 3 children, infirm and slowly recovering, wee return in a sweet Evening about 9. I conclude the day in domestic Quota.
20 I rise early and prepare for Attendance at Lady Shakerley's Funeral, go down to the House before 7. Not without sensible reflections on a Life of 58 years, observe and contemplate on the melancholy solemnity, I meet with Alderman P. Bennet and Mr. Sam Taylor in the Company, compare and find our ages concurr within or near a Year. At 9 the Herse moves attended thoro the Town by about 100 horse. At Tarvin the Number reduced to a very few beside the Mourners, a cool Gale make the journy tollerable and (saveing the occasion) pleasent. About a mile short of Midlewich, refresh on venison pasty and cold meat prepard. Here the Body taken into a room hung with Black and lightn'd with wax candles, this pensive solemnity lasts not 3 hours; before 5 wee proceed come to Lower Peover Chapell about 6. The service begun by Mr. Yates, The Curat of Gresford has a sermon (Let mee dy the death of the righteous and let my last end bee like his). Hee gives a plain substancial Character of the good Lady thoro the several stages of her Life, Youth, marriage, widowhood, which indeed did not exceed or reach her merit. Since I had the Honor to know her in all the stages, I was extremely affected with an esteem of her memory, other thoughts naturally ariseing from the loss of a valuable person & the

consideracion of my own Mortality. I see many Gentlemen of my Acquaintance. The solemnity over about 7, Mr. Egerton lays kind commands on mee and diverts mee from my intended retreat to Hulmes Chapell. Wee call at Mr. Yates in expectacion of good (but meet with dull) wine, proceed in the cool Evening and come to Olton about 10. Thirsty and harrassd from the heat & Fatigue, wee are to a wonder, recreated, by a Bottle of excellent Claret. I go to my Chamber about 11.
21 Extremely refresht by a good lodging and sound sleep, I rise about 7 see the ruins of the old and progress of the new work, am especially pleas'd with the Gallery leading to 6 vaults or Sellars. I step to the Church & see his Chancell alterd and adorn'd. Mr. Thelwal and Mr. White call about 10. Mr. Egerton and they take horse for Cholmley, I go to Massies in the Forest, sitt with Mr. Crane 2 hours, hee sees not to write or read and scarce gos without a guide and help, having the addicion of a Gout. Hee appears pleasd and refresht with my visit, entertains mee with a bottle of small Ale and at parting with good Brandy. I sett hence (the weather hott) about 2, reach Chester and (D.G.) my corner about 5. In the Evening, Mr. Boucher surprizes mee with an Account of the Chancellor's apprehencions and Fears from some Infirmity long since known (but not till now discover'd) by him, inexpressible uneasiness & suspicion make them resolve on a journy to Dr. Fowke. After supper under the security of Elixir, to bed about 10.
22 I receive my cozn. Parrs Letter telling the news stands for Sir Wm. Dawes without contradicion or doubt. Dr. Entwisle has a good casuisticall discourse on Acts 3 v. 19. The public Letters have no Action. After prayers I am engagd to Pickings where Sir Peter Soame, Mrs. Bruen, R. Davies, White, Langford, Walley, Cowper meet and trifle away the Evening. Sir Peter and I drink 2 Bottles of good Claret but fretty, the rest punch, wee part about 9. Mr. Fogg trys mee about an irregular Licence betwixt Capt. Conningsby and Mrs. Carr now passing to Ireland. I am unwilling to comply since no good aspect appears.
23 A cooler morning apply to some busienes, write to my Cozn. Parr. After prayers calld to the Ship, when Mr. Chancellor DDrs. Thane and Norris and Mr. Callis, wee stay above pints, part about 9. Mr. Fogg tells mee of other sentiments hee now has of the indevord Marriage, and that for 1000^{li} hee would not have marryd the unadvis'd Couple. After in the Town, fell into the company of Mr. Bruen and Cowper, wee go to the Rose & Crown & finish with our pints.
24 After a feverish tedious night, pain and remorse, I receive Mr. Vaudreys Bill, am surprizd and affected at the sum. No Letter mencions any Candidate to the See. I step and see The Fair, unfrequent from the common want of mony. After repose, return to Lipsius. I meet with Mr. Seddon of the Isle of Man, who tells mee That my Lord Derby was sent for by Express from the Queen on complaint of Irregular practice in his Chancery made by my Lord Anglesey and went hastily from Lathom the 16th current with pain, I expect the Event.
25 After an unhappy night and complicacion of pains, an indispos'd morning. Mr. Baddiley, a Clergyman of Hampshire, sees us from my brother Ken Puleston, wee have some mencion of his (Kens) wife's unreasonable expectacion

about the Bond my brother Puleston and myself are ingagd in for her husband. I recurr to Lipsius. In the Evening, Mr. Seddon of the Ile of Man, calls on mee. Wee go to the Bacchus where wee (over 2 pints of white and ½ pint of sack) have an History of the House of Derby and the Island, with the Healths concurrent, past 10. I was witness this day to my uncle Eytons signing and perfecion of his Will and cancelling a former in my Office.
26 Indisposicion succeeds an uneasy Night. The Court affords small busienes. In the Fair, I meet with Mr. John Blackburn and Mr. Glass, wee take 2 pints of white wine before dinner. About 3, the Chancellor & Mr. Boucher set for Dr. Fowks, they ride my 2 horses, recreate still in Lipsius. About 6 my Suzy and I go visit Mrs. Owen and Mrs. Carter. Mr. Geo. Shakerley comes in and entertains with Claret, apply to my Quota.
27 A cool morning out of doors. This post affords mee no Letters and the public Letters no News. I take 2 long and 2 shorter Turns on roodee, am extremely refresht, return to Lipsius and Seneca sparsim. About 6 Dr. Thane calls, wee go to the Fountain after so long deviacion from it, find the Claret good, wee talk & drink 3 pints.
28 After an uneasy night, I try Soughtons drops in spring water. At 10 of Clock prayers, write to Mr. Cholmley at Twitnam. After Evening prayers to the Bishop of Killala and to Capt. Atkey of Exeter. End in my Quota.
29 Rise about 6, take a walk about the walls, the weather hott but windy. No Letter or News about a Successor; public Affairs still held in suspense. The Dean has a sermon in the Quire on Acts 10.v.24. After prayers I (Jack with mee) walk to Blacon point and back by the river. After returnd about 7. Dr. Thane comes and acquaints mee, That hee is told by a good hand, That Mrs. Egerton told shee had it lately from a good hand, That Sir Wm. Dawes is certain to succeed. After this wee are at my brother Partingtons in a mixt company, I drink near a pint of white wine, part there about 10.
30 After a tedious night, some remains of indisposicion. I write and inclose to Mr. Smith of BrasenNose a Testimonial on Mr. Phil Egertons part who is about to take his degree in Divinity, to my cozn. Holt about 50^{li} and to John Crosse, I dip in Livy about Funeral Orations. After prayers read his amazeing descripcion of Annibals March over the Alps into Italy. In the Evening send to Pickings and solace with a pint of Excellent French Claret.

JULY 1 I rise to early prayers. Tho I intended, resolve not for Wrexham today, the morning stormy. My cozn Parrs Letter that some say Sir Wm. Dawes has refusd the Bishoprick, except hee keep his Deanary of Bocking in Essex near which his paternal Estate. The public Letters have little beside Polish confusion, I read agen, with Jack, Annibals Alpine Expedicion. After prayers Dr. Thane calls, wee join and send for a Bottle of Pickings Irish Claret, tis good but fretting, hee parts with mee about 9.
2 At early prayers, after write and inclose a double requisicion to Mr. Peter Barret, prepare for my journy. I set out on Mr. John Inces young horse past 9,

come to Wrexham before 12. After dinner at my mother Pulestons and prayers Mr. Jones, Mr. Jack Jones and Davies come to see my sister Jones, after Greetings & impertinence Busienes menciond, my brother Puleston and I go with them to their Inn, the Red Lyon. Mr. Jones produces the Deeds of the Lands hee proposes to give in security for the 200^{li}, a method by Lease, release and Bonds for performance is agreed upon.[9] Here is a variety of Liquors none good. I go to see Mr. Price,my coz. Kendric comes wee sit cheerfully past 12.
3 Tho indisposd rise early at Brin y Funan, go to the Lyon, see the rough draught, make some scruples at the form of mortgage from 3 years to 3 years, come back and acquaint my uncle Eyton, hee gos, sees the draught, disapproves it as new in that particular, they defend it and produce a precedent in the same Estate, my brother Puleston after makes like objections, but the draught proceeds, wee go to prayers, after to dinner wee crowd the little parlor. After dinner I compute the interest due, it amounts to 27^{li}, pays 12 and gives a note for 15^{li}. After scruples magnif'd, the Form which in this joint case, I thought tollerable stands. Wee are all at the Lyon where Mr. Jones executes the Deeds, 3 of us are witnesses. After some glasses of white wine, wee part. My Coz. Kendric, sister Jones and I to Brin y Funan, after calling on the Vicar, to Dick Jones, where over 3 pints mean Claret, wee resume cheerfull discourse and part about 10. I go to my mother Pulestons where I end the day in ½ pint of white with my sister Jones.
4 Rise in a fine morning about 6. See Madam Ann Davies on her knees industriously trimming the Camomel Figures of the little Garden. Step to the Vicar to enquire after the News of this post, tis small even in expectacion. This the first Anniversary day of my Cozn. Eytons marriage to Mrs. Moreton; her brother Gerard and I celebrate it with condolency. My sister Jones expresses great acknowledgement of my pains in her Affair and sends 20^{s} to Jack for 1 Quarters danceing. I mount before, return D G safe to my corner about 12. After dinner and repose, a walk into the town, to find a Claret companion, missing one return to my Quota.
5 A cool morning, rise to early prayers. I (Jack along) step to Upton and see my horses after their journey to Dr. Fowks. I write to Jeffrey Prescott and inclose to Mr. Wall with desire to receive from him, for a copy of Sir Christopher Greenfeilds Will 15^{s} and from Mr. Thornton $1^{li};3^{s};4^{d}$. At dinner my Uncle Herle surprises us from Wigan, hee brings a kind answer from my cozn. Holt about the 50^{li}, another Certificate for Mr. Ph Egerton at 5 I bring it to his Brother at the Chancellors, inclose it in my Letter to Mr. Ph., Mr. Egerton, Dr. Thane and I stay and drink 2 Bottles with the Chancellor return home before 9.
6 Mr. Fogg has a good discourse on Lam. 3 v. 39, 40. Sanctissimae Eucharis-

9 To avoid the limitations of the Statutes of Uses in creating trusts, it became the practice to lease the property for one year at a rent of five shillings and the following day after the lease to issue a release to the parties. A bond and obligation were usually entered into under a penalty of twice the sum agreed for sale to fulfil the terms of the release.

tiae particeps sum. Det D.O.M. sancta vivere faeliciter mori.[10] The News still suspending. After prayers about 7 go, Jack with mee, take 2 longer and 2 shorter Turns on roodee. After recreate in a pint from Pickings.

7 An excessive hott day, indisposd to every thing but Livy. I pay Mr. Whitehead 20^{s}, the remains of 5^{li} for his work about the Gravestone, my sister Jones being present. My Suzy, shee and I dine invited with Lady Salisbury with whom Mrs. Mary Davies. The old Lady is in her great & fickle humor, but receives us gratiously. The post comes early, but brings yet only expectacion of D.[of] Savoys descent into Provence. My Sister Jones brings and leaves, her papers with mee, discourses on her affairs with the parish of Mold. Cornelius Nepos and a pint of Pickings conclude the day.

8 Another such hott day. My Sister Jones comes about 9. I take directions about her Mold papers, and pay her the Interest of 50^{li} shee lent mee 20 July last, by discounting for the Grave stone $2^{li}.10^{s}$, paid to the Recorder 10^{s}. Shee leaves in my hands 70^{li} to bee put out for her, dines here and gos back to Wrexham. Dr. Thane sitts here till 4, excessive heat forces mee to retreat. After 6 the Dr. returns, wee join and send for a Bottle of Pickings Claret, it proves excellent, yet has little influence on the Dr. affected this Evening with a remarkable torpor in Conversacion, hee gos about 10. I read the 1st Book of Boetius de Cons.

9 A cooler morning. I write to the Commissary of Richmond and fully, especially about Mr. Winters Cause. I finish the Account of the last Visitacion with Mr. Boucher, the sum of which to the Chancellor comes to $90^{li}.17.0$. I pay $3^{li}.4.5$ redundant to Mr. Boucher to bee allowed by him in other Accounts. I proceed in Boetius, close the Evening with my Quota.

10 Court day, the Busienes short and moderate, ends before the Morning prayers. I take 2 Turns on roodee before dinner. Dr. Thane and the Chancellor call after prayers, wee shelter in my brother Partingtons hall from the Heat, and here dispatch 4 Bottles sent from Pickings. But this later part about the wine I recollect belongs rather to the last Evening and that wine to this.

11 In a cool morning the wind making it so, I (Jack with mee) go to Upton to see my Horses where in the farther grounds, observe their pasture bare and scanty. Dr. Thane signifies his mind to go to Bettisfeild, I decline it. The News brings yet little but amusement. In the Even Dr. Thane comes and wee first pay a visit to the E. of Cholmley then go to the Bacchus where Dr. Chetwood & Ch. Fletcher come and advance us.

12 Indisposd and unhappy, ly till 7. Dr. Thane comes, I write to John Crosse to pay all rents to my Lord Derby, upon the death of Mr. Wright of Trinity[11] yesterday, Mr. Adams desires my interest to the E. of Derby for Mr. Swinton, I prefer Mr. Oliver to him. After 9 the Dr. and I take Horse in a day of hott and cool Gleames, by Turns, wee leave Farndon on the right, go over Crew Green,

10 Trans: 'I partake of the most Holy Eucharist. May God the best and greatest grant [me] to live holily and to die happily.'

11 C.R.O., EDP1/70, Chester Holy Trinity.

by Calecot thoro Shocklach, over Threap-wood to Hanmer-hall, that on the right, proceed and reach Bettisfeild about 2. Wee find Sir Thomas and the Duchess at Dinner, are kindly received and fully refresh'd with a good dinner and fine wine. Mr. Betton is here, after solace in wine. Sir Thomas shews the Dr. and mee his Gardens and walks, among which the close one of a furlong in length. From hence into the park where hee leads us to 5 several seats in different prospects, all very pleasant. After supper a Bottle of excellent Claret, to bed about 11.

13 About 9 wee on horseback attend the Dutchess's Coach to Church. Dr. Thane has a good and affectionate discourse on St. John 15 v 5. Wee return, Mr. Lloyd of Halghton added to us, to Bettisfeild about 2, sit down to a fine and plentiful dinner. Mr. Lloyd is cheerful and stays till 4. After 6 the Coach (wherein the Duchess, Lady Bunbury and Dr. Thane) Sir (Tho) and myself on Horseback, go Hanmer Hall, walk thoro the fine Gardens, which afford a great and pleasant variety, are treated with excellent Cherries, See some of the rooms, great and stately, but unfurnisht. Sir Thomas tells us his Designs of building a Front to the South. Wee return to Bettisfeild after 8. After supper and a Bottle to bed about 11.

14 The Dr. and I rise about 6 divert till 9 when Mr. Hanmer of Fenns (now High Sheriff of Flintshire) calling, Sir Thomas, the Dr. and I mount, wee go thoro Hanmer, by Emerald park, Halghton &c and come to Bangor before 11. Mr. Jones treats with good Ale and sage Tea, here the Company increases, Mr. Jones of it. Wee pass the 5 Fords near Abenbury, over Rose Nesney to Gresford. Here Sir Henry Bunbury, Mr. Harvey meet us, a company of about 20 Gentlemen in all, among Mr. Yale a fortunate Gentleman remarkable. After dinner (wherewith Sir Tho treats the Dr, & myself) the Gentlemen make matches, variously, the rest concern'd in wagers, the Dr. and I only are peripatetic spectators in the cool Breezes. About 7 Sir Tho., Mr. Hanmer, the Dr. and I mount, come at a good rate to Chester before 9. Sir Hen and Mr. Harvey follow in the Coach, wee sitt down to an elegant and (from a haunch of venison) noble supper about 10. After which good Claret and female Toasts go merrily round till 2, then full to my Corner.

15 About 11 indisposd yet wait on the company, and they return my visit and are here a while. I miss the Bishop of Man who was last night here and left mee his book stil'd, the principles and Duties of Christianity, compos'd for the Island. In the Evening, take 4 Turns on roodee, adventure not to goe into the great Company, but after my domestic Quota to bed before 11.

16 Still under the effects of a liberal Life and uneasy, I write to Mr. Peirson, my sister Jones & Mr. Pennant of Mold. After dinner, go over with the Chancellor and Dr. Thane to Sir Henry's where the Glass circles freely in a Company of 20 Gentlemen, amongst whom Dr. Entwisle appears a very melancholy spectacle, till about 4, when Sir Tho & Mrs. Hanmer mount for Mostyn. Sir Henry & Mr. Harvey, take Coach for Holywell. After a short recess, I (Mr. Seddon of the Isle of Man with mee) follow the Chancellor and Dr. Thane to the Bacchus, here is too Mr. Crow of Ireland, filling the

Conversacion, wee clubb (save Mr. Seddon) above our pints, return about 9.
17 Indisposd from the wine and unhappy Constitucion, rise not till 9. At Mr. Bouchers chamber an uncomely controversy about the matter of practice in the Manchester causes, begins and advances to a pitch to bee lamented, betwixt the Chancellor and Mr. Boucher which is afterwards renew'd more publicly in Court, little els of moment mov'd there. I with Mr. Hulton share in 2 pints of white wine, with Mr. Faulkner, Apothecary of Manchester, before dinner. At which Mr. Shaw and Mr. Banner Churchwardens comeing on the Iniskilling Breif, sitt down with us and are liberally receivd. I write & inclose 6 Licences to Mr. Asheton. In the Evening I Take 2 short Turns on roodee, after at the Coffee house see the lean News. After home and my Quota.
18 A cool morning and rainy. I read the 4 and 5 Books of Boetius. I receive Mr. Empsons Letter about Mr. Winters Case and Absolucion at York, and Mr. Cholmleys from Twitnam wherein hee suspects Lord Wharton & his party provokd by the Bishop of Winchester's behavior with indeavor to fill the vacant Sees with Men of their Turn. I write (after prayers) to Mr. Empson, Mr. Penant, my cozn. Holt, shew that to Mr. Empson to the Chancellor return about 9 and end in domestic Quota.
19 Rise and in a rainy morning go to early prayers, write full to Dr. Stratford and inclose an authentic Copy of the late Bishops Will in it. After the rain over, mount about 10, Go (the road wett and tedious) to Burton, the Bishop of Man not there, go to his Brother Samuel Wilson in Little Neston (Mr. Seddon of the Island along with mee), here we are receiv'd kindly by the Bishop and at a cleanly Country Dinner, the drink sharp bottle Beer, Syder and Brandy, wee mix the 2 later, wee stay about 3 hours. Mr. Seddon setts out for Leverpool, I for Chester about 4, I come home before 6. Dr. Thane (sent to) comes over about 7, wee send for a Bottle of Pickings and part (after dull 2 hours) about 9.
20 A fair morning and day. Mr. Newton has a chast discourse on 1 Tim. 6 v. 9, many attend strictly, few understand, the sermon. The News gives hope of Thoulon invested the next post. I speak to the recorder about Mr. Oliver, hee agrees with mee and promises to write to Mr. Oliver. After prayers I (Jack with mee) take two long Turns on roodee. After I call on Alderman Allen communicate my design to serve Mr. Oliver, hee approves and encourages, tho hee signd with others of the parish an Address to my Lord Derby in behalf of Mr. Kirkes. Wee drink a Bottle of Dublin wine dully, so prevailes his temper, and part about 9. I give Jack for his Viaticum to Manchester 13^s4^d.
21 After a morning of pain and unhappines, rise before 8. Save a Breeze from the N.W. the day very hot, I take 2 long and 2 short Turns on roodee. See there a Man and a small Boy about 12 years old do, as I guess run the Course, they strive, run fast, but the Boy easily is Victor. I divert in Claverius, Q.B.E. Harry gos today to Mr. Golborn to school,[12] hee is paid 5^s for his Entrance. After prayers and Claverius, I seek Dr. Thane, meet not him, but Mr. Morrey, hee

12 R.V.H. Burne, *Chester Cathedral* (London, 1958), *passim* for King's School.

comes here & sends for a Bottle of Picking, wee drink it in Busienes and too much Noise, from whence I find him further affected with drink, fore hee came, than I desir'd. Hee urges on his Sentiments on the Fathers till 10. I receive Mr. Waits long Letter wherein hee revives the Expectations of Dr. Freeman as certifid in those parts by Lord Wharton.

22 After an uneasy Night, rise more early. See the News extremely barren. Q.B.E., draw about 7 ounces of Blood, communicate Mr. Commissarys Letter to the Chancellor. After prayers, begin a Letter to my Lord Derby. Dr. Thane comes about 7 and interupts mee, wee send for a Bottle of Pickings Claret, are duller from the Commissary's hint of Dr. Freeman, wee part before 10. I return dull to my Letter.

23 After the easiest Night in near 6 months, I rise to early prayers – after them, return to my Letter to Lord Derby and finish it. I write too, to my cozn. Parre, Mr. Croxton (who was here about 8 a clock last Night on my Lady Dunmores busienes) dy'd suddainly, this morning in his Bed, a Morte subitanea, libera Nos Domine.[13] The rain is perpetual this day and easily disswades the Chancellor and my self, from viewing Stoak Church Yard, extremely affected with the sultry heat of the day, indispos'd to Busienes and Books. I receive a seasonable supply of the mony for 20 Licences from Mr. Styth and Mr. Richmond. After 6 Dr. Thane comes, wee send for a Bottle of Pickings and dully enough pass the time over it till 9.

24 After uneasy sleep return'd, rise about 7, the morning dispos'd to wett only not raining. I write to John Cross on Account of my purchase from Sir Ed Chisenhale, to bee deliver'd to the Jury and to my cozn. Holt. The 18 Manchester Causes, most of the Busienes of the Court, answers personally given in them all. It rains for 3 or 4 hours. After prayers the Chancellor, Dr. Thane and I go to Tom Hollands, Send for a Bottle of Pickings wine which proves dull, and another from the Ship, which proves prick't port wine.

25 A fair sun shine. I see Mrs. Worgers empty News. I send for my sister Jones, she comes about 3. Mr. Wm. Bunbury dines. At Church this morning, Mr. Gibson has a mean Sermon on Matt 4 v. 21, 22. It rains almost constantly in the After noon. My sister Jones and I confer, on her Mold Affairs. In the Evening I try a pint of my purchas'd wine from Wm. Higgenson and suspect it prickt. Jack returns from Manchester.

26 A doubtfull morning, threatening only not raining. I prepare and mount for Mold before 9 come hither before 11, find Mr. Benet of Knowsley here, send for Mr. Pennant who tells mee the Vestry was not to meet till 2 and by accident of a Funeral, will bee deferrd further to day. Wee 3 dine on Mutton, and in Ale, remember and reconcile the House of Derby. About 2 Mr. Pennant & I walk to the Church & his House. About 3 Mr. Wynn of Tour and the Vicar come to the Church. I meet 'em, and in the porch acquaint 'em with my busienes, go with 'em to the Vicarage, where I discourse the Vicar alone. A number not appearing

13 Trans: 'From a sudden death, deliver us O Lord.'

to make a Vestry, wee saunter, go to Ardow Powells, where Mr. Mostyn of Kilkin & 5 or 6 more. The Funeral is past 6, after which the Vicar, 3 Churchwardens, Mr. Wynn, Mr. Lloyd, Mr. Pennant & some more compose the Vestry, the Busienes propos'd and apposd, the Gentlemen are scrupulous, evasive, unkind. Mr. Wynn refuses and Mr. Lloyd with difficulty (after hee had subscribd) suffers his name to bee to the Discharge from the writeings 18 in Number, the Vicar promotes the subscripcion. Mr. Wynn remains obstinate. About 8, the evening dark, the matter is finisht, I deliver the writeings, Mr. Pennant and Roberts a Churchwarden, my Lanlord at the Goat, go to my Chamber with mee, wee drink 3 potts and part past 10.
27 A misty morning, a numerous and comicall company pass for Halliwell [Holywell]. I set hence about 8 and reach home (D G) about 10, wee dine at my brother Partingtons. I meet great News, Naples surrendr'd, Prince Eugene past the Var, Sweden reconcild to the Emperor and from the Bishop of Man, that Sir Wm. Dawes will be our Bishop. After prayers I take (Jack along) 2 Turns on roodee. After which a Quota of Pickings & to bed about 11.
[*No further entries until 18 August*]

AUGUST 18 A fair but blowing day. I write to the Commissary of Richmond and Mr. Matthews of Whaley. Sir Hen Bunbury and My Lady B., Mr. Chancellor, his Lady and 2 sons dine with us. Sir Hen Bunbury, his indisposicion in his stomach, makes the shorter stay afterwards. After 5 I take 2 Turns on roodee, the wind high. I see the conjectural News which makes the matter of Thoulon very doubtfull. I solace in domestic Quota and to rest about 10.
19 The weather still blowing, I take 4 Turns on roodee, which mightily recreate. At the Coffee house where all uncertain, save D. of Devonshire dangerously ill. My Suzys pains increase, Obstetrix non Lucina invocata.[14] After prayers, The Dean and I discourse on our journy to Lancaster. About 6 my Cozen Holts come unexpected. The pains aggravate et partus appropinquare videtur.[15] My Cozen Holt (shee) and I go over to Sir Henrys where at Supper, about 3 Quarters after 8 News brought mee that a daughter is borne a few minuits before D.O.M.G. sospita Matre.[16] Wee return home and have some Entertainment on the Occasion.
20 My Cozn Holts proceed hence towards Bath, about 8 setting out. Shee leaves her ring with mee. I write to and send John for my sister Jones. Draw a Monicion to Geo. Richardson to deposit in the Registry 19^{li};3;3½ for the use of the Church of Manchester. Turn Plautus and Terence. About 9 recreate in a pint domestic.
21 After a deep dew, a mild and fair morning I (Jack with mee) take 4 Turns on

14 Trans: 'The midwife not called for the birth'. Lucina was the Roman goddess of child bearing.
15 Trans: 'the birth seems to approach'.
16 Trans: 'With the mother safe, thanks be to God the best and greatest.'

roodee. I write to Mr. Tatlock, divert in Books, Plautus and Caesars Commentarys. After prayers about 6 Mr. Pool of Bebington calls on mee, draws mee from Caesar to the Hope and Anchor, where over 2 Bottles at his Charg hee mostly entertains mee with a fond Account of his happy Circumstance videlicet, a good wife, hopefull children, and a plentifull estate.

22 Sensible of the wine last night and a mild and sweet morning tempting, I take 2 Turns on roodee. Want of 2 Mailes makes all the news conjectural save that the D. of Devonshire dy'd on Munday. I turn Titles De Aedituis. After prayers I take 2 Turns on roodee which makes a domestic Quota more gratefull about 9. I paid the plumber for that work on the Consistory $6^{li}.14^{s}$ 0.

23 A delicate morning, I finish and read the 2nd Book of Caesar's Commentarys. See the work don over and in the Court, write to Mr. Chamberlain, in petty France, Westminster, to Mr. Empson and John Crosse, pay the Masons Note of work about the Consistory $2^{li}.14^{s}$ and the Carpenter $6^{li}.5^{s}$. I read the 2d and 3d Book of the Commentarys and take my domestic Quota.

24 I rise to early prayers, a delicate morning draws mee to two Turns on roodee. The News makes the matter hott, but uncertain at Thoulon. I stay at home and prepare for my journy. After prayers At Sir Hen. Bunburys where Mr. Owen of Cundar, Mr. Booth and Tyndal. After Mr. Peppard, Town Clerk of Dublin (who brought a token of $2^{s}6^{d}$ from Sir Wm. Parsons) calls mee over. Hee, his son and I dispatch 2 Bottles, good wine from Pickings, and part about 10.

25 A delicate morning, I pay Mr. Williams 20^{li} of his bond and $1^{li}.10^{s}$ interest due to the 19th instant. I write to the Bishop of Killala. After 9 The Dean and I mount, Mr. Peppard and his son, overtake us. Wee have a warm day, call and drink at Preston on the Hill, come to Warrington about 2, dine on Salmon and indifferent Claret, see the new Chapell. The Dean and I proceed about 4, reach Wigan before 8, Mr. Bowyer and Mr. Tatlock come to us, wee refresh and to repose about 10.

26 An excessive hott day, John Cross meets mee here and pays mee 5^{li} residue of the Ayrfeild rents. I send by him an Acquittance for 53^{li} to John Walmsley and give John 2^{li} for his pains. Mr. Bowyer and I see Mr. Scott and call at my Cozn. Holts. Wee see the news with great aspects on Thoulon, dine and solace till 4, Mr. Bowyer then setts out as Mr. Tatlock with us, wee halt at Euxton and come to Preston about 8. Mr. Vaudrey comes to us at the Mitre, wee have here better wine and drink a Bottle and to bed about 11.

27 Lord Derby who came last night, gos forward about 8 with a number (but few Gentlemen) attending, about 8, wee sett out about 10 come to Garstang before 1, here wee meet with Mr. Owen and do not easily put him off. After an indifferent Viaticum, wee take horse, about 3, several overtake or fall in with us, among the rest Mr. Garsden, Atturney of Stockport who (about Ellell) communicates to mee his design of marriage with Mrs. Tricket, of a Fortune of $7{,}000^{li}$. Wee come to Lancaster about 6, the Town is very full of people and expectacion. The Dean of York and the Rector his brother see us, wee are

directed to the Talbot. Wee wait on the Dean and the Rector at their near Quarters. I stay, drink a Glass of Claret, part with them about 10.
28 After Elixir, ease, I wait on my Lord Derby at the Mermaid. Hee discourses mee with civility about the Busienes of his rectory of Trinity. Wee go to Church where Mr. Fleetwood nephew to Mr. Fleetwood of Rossal has a good and ingenious discourse on the 9th Comandment. Wee dine with the 2 Brothers at the Queens Arms. After, wee are told the Cause will not come on today. Mr. Bowyer, Wells and I go down to the Salt Ayr and Bouling Green, wee meet with Mr. Lambers & Mr. Barton, adjourn to Mr. Foxcrofts where wee take near our Bottles in tolerable wine and part about 8. After with Mr. Sudel and Mr. Hulme past 10.
29 The delicate weather continues. At the Coffee house with the Brothers most of the Forenoon. The Dean, Mr. Bowyer and I dine at our Quarters where among other good dishes, wee have a venison pasty. The News here runs adverse, That the seige is raisd at Thoulon. Wee are sumond to Court about 4. I write to my Suzy, attend at Court, Bury of the Exchequer is Judg, other Causes come on and especially that betwixt the Town of Lancaster and Mr. Thornton about the Wharf where 20 Wittnesses are sworn, on both sides, the Judg takes their evidence in writeing and repeats it to the Jury, who presently give Verdict for Mr. Thornton, which verdict did not agree with my Sentiments since I took the evidence to bee more firm on the other side. Twas past 9 when the Court rose, Mrs. Bowyer, Lambert, Wells, Holland &c and I go down and refresh at the Sun, wee are cheerfull, drink our Bottles and part about 12.
30 I rise about 5, the morning delicate. The 2 Brothers, the Dean, Mr. Bowyer &c and I are in Court before 7. The Cause is brought on by the defendant Finch, by proviso, a Jury impannelld whereof Matt. Page, Foreman, the plaintiffs Councell makes a weake monicion on pretence of material Escripts wanting, upon which the Cause is non suited. I stay some other short Causes, one particularly by Lady Bindlos for rent, wherein Sir Tho Parker artificially examining, makes a poor woman publish her Fault, by asking her whether such a Bargain hapnd before her 1st Child and after, whether before her marriage – to both which she answerd No. Mr. Bentley treats the forenoon, the Dean and I with good wine. Our Affadavits that wee came on this Cause only are drawn, which wee sign at the Inn and acknowledg in Court to the Crier. Lord Derbys cause is begun, Mr. Butler, Foreman of the Jury, Sir Tho Parker &c my Lord, Serjeant Cheshire, Mr. Ward &c my Ladys Councel, this cause is concluded. Bury and Pilkington part of her dowry. Wee set hence about 12, come to Garstang before 3, stay and repose past 5 come to Preston by the Moon about 8, recreate in Claret past 10.[17]
31 The weather threatens alteracion, so dos the News from Thoulon. Wee go to Church, Mr. Peploe has a good discourse on Matt 7. v.[?]. Mr. Burton a Gentleman of a great Estate in the South, is here on his Travels in the North of

17 For cases heard at Lancaster, see P.R.O., Lists and Indexes XLV.

England, hee and his brother dine with us on a noble Fish calld Brett &c. After dinner Mr. Bowyer and I visit Mrs. Franks. Shee entertains with good old Beer, wine, Cinnamon waters, Nutts &c. In the afternoon Mr. Bowyer follows Mr. Peploe to the Vestry and thence advances the pulpit, has a good sermon on the same Chapter of St. Matt v [?]. After Sermon invited by Alderman Sudell wee are civilly receivd by him. Mr. Bowyer and I wait on Mr. Rawsthorn and his pregnant Lady. Return to and recreat a while with the Dean, hee receded, wee sitt an hour with Mr. Rich, Norris and Mr. Squire, with whom I concurr in honourable Character of my Lord Derby.

SEPTEMBER 1 Q.B.E. Wee set hence about 8, the weather is rainy and, near Standish, a great showr falls, rideing (as all along) briskly, wee come to Wigan about 11, here wee dine, see the News. Mr. Scott, Cozn. Holt here, I receive a bag seald of 20[li], wee call on Mr. Herle who designs to morrow for Bath. Wee dine solace, mount about 4 and the weather all along showry reach Warrington about 7. The Bishop of Man and Mr. Shaw see us at the Inn, after Mr. Page (now private) sees me. After half a pint of Sack, to Bed about 11.

2 Wee equip take leave of the Bishop of Man, and mount about 8, find the roads deep, frequent Showers. Wee come safely home D.O.M.G. about 12. After dinner repose. Dr. Thane in the Evening calls, wee send for a Bottle of Pickings, it proves mere port, wee dispatch it about 10.

3 Recreated by Elixir apply to Letters and Busienes. In the Evening at the Rose and Crown with the Chancellor, Dr. Thane, Mr. Callys and Allen. Wee drink over our pints, part about 9.

4 The weather tollerable, I take a walk of 4 Turns. After dinner go over to Sir Henry B's where Sir Thomas Hanmer come from the Assizes at Holywell, stay and drink good wine till near 5, when returnd, the invited Friends come in. About 6 wee go to Church. Mr. Shaw christens my daughter by the name of Susanna. Mr. Foulks, Godfather, my sister Jones and Mrs. Crompton Godmothers, return'd, more Friends come to us, and about 8 Sir Thomas Hanmer and Sir Henry Bunbury and Mr. James Cotton, wee are cheerful and the company receded about 10.

5 I wait about 8 on the Bishop of Man at the Golden Talbot, hee tells mee, with circumstances, the insuccess of my Lord Derby, direct verdicts against him in the Cause of Dowry, and that relateing to Holland, Skelmersdale &c and that a special verdict past in the 3rd relateing to Lathom. This gives mee deep impressions. His Lordship intending quickly for the Island calls on my Suzy, parts about 10. I (Jack with mee) take 2 shorter and 2 longer Turns. After repose and prayers, I meet with Dr. Thane and the Chancellor at the Coffee house, wee adjourn to the Rose and Crown, where Sir Henry Bunbury and Mr. Cotton come to us, the Dr., Mr. Cotton and I stay longer make up our Bottles and 10 a clock.

6 Indisposicion and fair weather tempt mee to 4 Turns. Recreated, I write to Dr. Stratford, Mr. Parre and Peirson. Mr. Whaley (as since my return) grieves mee with his difficulties. I promise all possible assistance. I recreate in Books, particularly Caesar. In the Evening take my domestic Quota.

7 The morning fair, I go to early prayers and after the dull news, take Jack along, 4 shorter Turns on roodee. Stay at home with my Suzy. After prayers visit Mr. Boucher. Thence to my Corner and my Quota.

8 After early prayers, apply to Busienes. I write to Mr. Chamberlayn of Petty France and fully to the Commissary, the Chancellor having read my Letter, Mr. Whaley brings his Friends, Dod and Knot, they give mee Bond for 20^{li} for 6 months. The weather turns very rainy, the Sheriff (Swetenham) comes in about 2, the Judges (Jeckell and Partington (this the 1st time) about 4. Mr. Whaley intreats and about 6 I go down with him to Mr. Vernons chambers, hee not there wee go to the Hall where some monicions are made. After the Court wee return to Mr. Vernons chambers, hee gives little encouragement to my intercession expecting all the mony (100^{li} already paid) the remainder 17^{li} without forbearance. Mr. Kent is civil & more humane. I return with him affected with his difficulty. I recurr to Caesar and Quota.

9 At early prayers, thence the silent News. Mr. Whaley tells mee he tryd Mr. Vernon further who instead of Abatement or Forbearance, adds interest to the mony remaining on Ballance which for a year has bin due (the sum 67^{li}). Hee in this extremity, resolves to go into Lancashire and try his brother for 10^{li} more, I go to Church where Mr. Cowper, before the Judges, has a sermon on Judges 2 v 19–21. Hee, takes in too florid phrases, to magnify her Majesties Admiracion and particularly in the distribucion of Justice by Judges whose lives and examples were the best exposition of the Laws &c perfectly temporising, in him surprising. After prayers apply to Books to consider where the right of conferring Dignities in the vacancy resides; this occasiond from the extreme danger Dr. Entwisle is reduced to.[18] Dr. Thane putting the Question. To bed about 11.

10 After Elixir cool and easy. Read in the morning the 7th Book of Caesars Commentaries. After noon the 8 I writ to Dr. Stratford, Lady Bunburys Account of Dr. Entwisle. It rains almost perpetually. I stay at home, end the day in my Quota of white wine.

11 At early prayers, I write to Mr. Bowyer and John Cross, pay Mr. Dod on Mr. Whaleys Bond 3^{li} for a Years interest of 50^{li}. Give to Mr. Anderton a Jacobus, pay Wm. Higginson for 16 Gallons and ½ of wine 4^{li};2^{s};6^{d}. After prayers at Tom Hatfeilds with the Chancellor, Drs. Egerton, Thane, Norris, Mr. Offley brother in Law to Dr. Egerton and Mr. Peter Foulks, wee dispatch above pints each and part about 9.

12 After early prayers a delicate brisk morning tempts mee to 2 shorter Turns on roodee. Mr. Egerton has a Cause about an Highway with the D. [duke] of Shrewsbury and has a verdict on his side. After dinner I go down to the recorders, after to Dr. Norris to speak with Mr. Wetenhal, here I meet with him

18 The questions were: could the vacant prebend be filled during a voidance of the see of Chester if Dr. Entwistle died; and could a new archdeacon of Chester be appointed?

and tell him of my Applicacions to Lord Derby on Mr. Olivers part, and the Event. In the Evening, Dr. Thane comes, Dr. Egerton interrupts with the Account of his Cause about the Glebe, recedes, wee send for and dispatch a Bottle of Pickings and part about 10.

13 Another bright morning tempts to 2 shorter Turns. Mr. Whaley calls and tells mee of his dispatch with Mr. Vernon and shews mee his discharge of the ballance of the Account upon the back of it. I proceed in Caesar, read the 1st Book of the Civil Warr. The report about Dr. Entwisle uncertain, only otherwise in this, That his Case is desperate. I end the day in turning Justin and a domestic pint of white wine.

14 The weather altered to rainy and stormy. The News very barren. The great Army still defeated in attempts, to fight, by Vendosme's evasive Conduct. Archdeacon Booth has a good discourse (except to mee the Quotacion of Juvenals 13th Satire) on Ps. 119 v. 1. After prayers I read Cyprian de Gracia Dei, Ad Donatum. I am calld over to Sir Hen B's where Hee, his brother Mr. Cotton & I dispatch 2 Bottles.

15 After a rainy night, a wett morning. At early prayers after at Mr. Bouchers who shews mee Dr. Bouchers sharp reflections on the Manchester Articles. The News from Wrexham comes that Dr. Entwisle dyd there about 8 a clock this morning. I write to Dr. Stratford and Mr. Bowyer. After Noon Mr. Sudell calls on mee. After prayers He is inducted by Mr. Fogge into the Church of Trinity,[19] I go to him and his company at the Ship who after remove near his Church, to the Yacht. Here Jack Shakerley comes in, shews some his humor, a medal of the Coronacion of King Charles 2nd and a purse of Gold. I leave the company here. I write to old Mr. Entwisle by Mr. Sudel, return to Caesar past 10.

16 After a stormy and rainy night it continues rainy. After prayers I see Mr. Sudel, setting out, find Mr. Berty Entwisle at his lodgings in bed at the Old White Lyon. The news still dull and inactive. The 2 Entwisles (Brothers) call on mee, I go in to the Town with them the elder, buys a suit for mourning. After prayers they call agen, after a Turn on the Walls, wee invited go to Sir Henry Bunburys. Hee with excellent wine and very honest parliamentary discourse entertains us, till 10 a clock.

17 At early prayers. After call on Mr. Entwisles thence tempted by the fair morning, take 4 Turns on roodee. I write to Dr. Stratford and my cozn. Parre. Ad praeces vespertinas S. mea propter puerperii pariculum evasam D.O.M. gratias reddit.[20] About 6, I call on the Entwisles, wee go to the Bacchus, are free and freindly over 5 pints and part about 10. Coulson begins to whiten the Court.

18 I take 4 Turns in another delicate morning. I apply to rather divert in Caesar. After prayers Dr. Thane calls, wee go and tast the new Scotch Wine at the Bacchus, take 3 pints, part about 9.

19 C.R.O., EDP1/70, Chester Holy Trinity.

20 Trans: 'At evening prayers my Suzy gives thanks to God the best and greatest for having survived the peril of childbirth.'

19 The weather agen alters to rainy. I see Coulson going idely on, am dull and indisposd, the News still suspending. Company equip to meet the Funeral, under a showr it comes to church about 4. Mr. Lancaster has a sermon on Isaiah 57.v.1–2, the Character hee gave are differently consider'd. After the solemnity ended Dr. Thane, Mr. Jones of Bangor, Aldermen Partington and Puleston my brother Puleston of Hawodywern and I stay above our pints and part about 10.
20 A dull morning, and indisposicion along. My bro. Puleston advises to send Jack to the University, intimates, but does not exhibit. I pay the parish Clerk the Church dues for Churching 3s and to the Collector of the Window Tax 6s. About 6 I go to Dr. Thane, the 2 bros. Foulks and Mr. Callys at the Rose and Crown, wee drink 3 bottles of the Scotch Claret. The Bishop of Meath his Lady &c come to us about 6 (I at the Tavern). After supper and a Bottle, to bed about 11.
21 The night was very rainy, and the morning more than disposd. Wee (the Bishop and myself) go to Church. Dr. Thane has a good sermon on 14 Luke 11. The News still empty and suspending, wee stay in till prayers. After which and visits over Dr. Thane comes to the Bishop, wee dispatch one Bottle of my wine. After supper and prayers to Bed past 10.
22 Refresht by Elixir, I see the work in the Consistory. Search for and find Mr. Wilsons orders amongst the late Bishops loose papers. In the Evening, my S. and I pay a formal visit to Mr. Peter Foulks and his Lady, his Father treats with a Bottle of good Viana. After, I go to the Bacchus, where Mr. Chancellor, Dr. Thane and Mr. Collys, wee dispatch above pints before 9. Mr. Callys pays mee 5^{li} from Dr. Stratford. At home supper and more come, upon which Elixir repeated.
23 A fine calm morning, I attend the work. See the News still suspending. Mrs. Lucy Bunbury sends and acquaints mee of her sisters dissatisfacion about the Drs. grave and her desire to have the Body of his first Lady removd to it. In the Evening, I acquaint the Dean with her request; hee is willing to gratify it, if Dr. Stratford gives his consent, I accquaint Mrs. Bunbury, shee ingages mee to write to the Dr. Tom Gorst came at Noon, Mr Moreton at night. Tom and I slip from the Bishop and step for an hour & ½ to Mr Moreton at the Pyd Bull, wee consult how to introduce him to his Father in the morning. Wee return and sitt with the Bishop till 10.
24 Indisposd even after Elixir. I write to Mr. Peirson and return the Commissions with my objecions to him. I write to Dr. Stratford, Mr. Moreton waits on the Bishop who, at first receives him cooly. In a little time I indeavoring to serve both, some discourse is movd. Mr. Moreton promises with diligence to apply to the study of Divinity and qualify himself for holy Orders, the Bishop gives ear & incouragement & recommends Tho Aquinas his Summa (2d 2d) and Suarez de Legibus to him, hee is more facile and kind the longer the Dialogue lasts, and the yong man recedes with great satisfacion, about 11 a clock. After dinner and Attendance, the Bishop, I with him visit the Chancellor, thence to prayers, after which to Mr. Partington (not at home) and Alderman Allen who treats with a Bottle of Irish Claret; hence to my Corner where indisposd under Attendance and an idle habit. It rains fast, Till to bed about 11.

25 The morning fair yet threatening. I go to early prayers, see the Court almost finisht. Mr. Parker calls on mee on Dr. Edisburys busienes. The first Court day affords little Busienes, save the Manchester Causes, some Altercacion.[21] After Dinner, Attendance and prayers, calld I go to the Chancellor, Dr. Thane, Mr. Foulks and his clergy son to the Rose and Crown, wee drink about pints. The Chancellor is Chagrin about the wine, I return to my Attendance and from thence to bed about 11.

26 At early prayers in a fair morning. Wee are put into fresh and sharp expectacion of the declaracion of a new Bishop before her Majesty went to Newmarket yesterday, but not a sillable of it in the Letters. I wait on the Chancellor about the inconcludency of the Manchester Articles. About 10 the Bishop of Meath and I take his Chariot, come to Eaton ½ hour past 11. Wee are receivd by Mr. Cholmley and Mr. Okes. Dr. Edisbury, Mr. Price &c are here. I go with them to the Boat House & leave the Bishop here, the Dr. and I discourse on the matter of the Commission. Our Chancellor comes, wee dine here, they return and I go to the Bishop, wee come home about 5. I find my cozn Holts return'd from the Bath; they stay an hour and go hence to the Raven. Dr. Thane comes in a sharpn'd humor, wee divert the time till 11.

27 About 7 in a fair morning go down and take leave with my cozn. Holts and uncle Herle, thence to roodee, where I take 4 shorter Turns. I write to Dr. Stratford. After prayers Sir Hen Bunbury, Mr. Legh &c come over to visit the Bishop, hee is well pleas'd with it; they drink a bottle of my wine and another of Sir Henrys. After this Attendance, Supper and another Bottle till 11.

28 The weather very cool. The Dean preaches but is scarce heard on . . . The News still very low abroad and silent at home. After dinner, some repose. After prayers a visit to Lady Bellots house, thence back to Dr. Thane's where a Bottle of strong port. Thence home where the Bishop repeats, who hee had with earnestness often menciond his proposals & desire to take Harry over with him and at his own charg to educate him, at Kilkenny school & I rather incline to mencion the Charterhouse to him Q.B.E., hee approves and promises to write to the Duke of Ormond &c. After some discourse on this, supper and a Bottle to bed before 11.

29 St. Michael, A fair brisk morning, after early prayers I take 2 longer Turns on roodee, write to Mr. Jebbe with 6 Licences, pay Mr. Chapman on Account l^{li}. I receive from Mr. Richmond, Fees for 7 Licences and send him 4 Licences & Bonds. Dr. Thane today, as Mr. Mosse of Manchester yesterday, acquaints mee with the very ungratefull News of the death of Dr. Watkinson the very good and learned Chancellor of York, my great & worthy Friend who Mr. Moss represented to dy suddenly, the last week. The weather alters to rain. In the Evening the Bishop, Dr. Thane and I go to Alderman Allens, hee treats us with three Bottles, while here a vehement storm arises. In the discourse the

21 C.R.O., EDC.5 (1707) Nos 1 & 2. Also Consistory Court Book EDC1/102 n.f. 1706–1708.

Alderman mencions Dr. Egerton, as reported with great certainty, to bee our Bishop. Dr. Thane is movd at this, grows peevish and untreatable. Wee go hence to Dr. Thanes, where his humor and the storm continue, wee return home about 10.

30 Indisposd from the wine. I see the News which is very little improvd, the weather continues rainy and windy. I pay Mr. Boucher $2^{li}:6^{s}$ part of the 5^{li} returnd by Dr. Stratford. Mr. Wells pays mee for 10 Licences. In the Evening I meet Mr. Mosse at the Bacchus, wee have the Circumstances of the Manchester Causes and stay over these and 2 Quarts till 10.

OCTOBER 1 Indisposicion advanc'd, scarce releivd by Elixir, unfitted for Busienes or Books. In the Evening, The Bishop and I go over to Sir Hen Bunbury, hee treats and diverts with wine, punch and imitacion of the Bishop of Kilmore. After our return, to my Corner, the Ladys Bunbury, Legh &c come to us. Mrs. Legh confirms from Lord Cholmley the news of Dr. Egertons succession. After attendance and a Glass to bed about 10.

2 A cold and rainy weather, the waters riseing about. A Court day of small Busienes save the Manchester altercacion. After dinner and repose recover a cooler temper. Wee are in the most wistly expectacion, tonight of a new Bishop. Dr. Thane recovers of his Fear conceivd of Dr. Egerton by enquiring further, in the Town. His hopes of the Archdeaconry make him impatient of what hee thinks adverse and careless of his Friends. I write to Dr. Edisbury, stay at home in Attendance. After a moderate glass & late expectacion of News to bed after 11.

3 After a stormy night, a very cold and brisk morning. To early prayers after which a concourse to the Coffee houses, where little besides dissappointment, and the K. of Sweden his advance into Poland, proceed and end Caesars Commentarys. After prayers Supper and late attendance and to bed about 11.

4 After early prayers, a fine calme morning, inviting, take 4 shorter Turns. The Fresh is very high & by its Force has broken down the Cawsey near the Bridg. The good Bishop of Meath writes favorably in behalf of mee and my son Harry, in order to have him admitted to the school of the Charterhouse. Directs to Sir Wm. Robinson at his house in Albermarle Street near Piccaddilly and incloses a Letter to the Duke of Ormond, in it. I write to Dr. Stratford my cozn. Parr and Mr. Chamberlain & Dr. Edisbury. After prayers I attend the Bishop to Mr. Egerton and Lady Bellot. After at the Bacchus, where Dr. Thane Mr. Peter Foulks and I drink parting pints with the Chancellor. After this the Bishop and I go over to Sir Hen and Mr. Legh but finding the place, warm'd by Glasses, retreat in less than an hour and part about 11.

5 A cool and haizy morning. The News affords little besides Savoy takeing the City not yet the Castle of Susa and the Swedes progress in Poland. The Bishop has a summons from Capt. Brecholt of his design to sail tomorrow. Mr. Fogg has an excellent sermon on psalm 26 v. 6. Great preparacion made for the Voyage tomorrow. Many come to us to take leave of the Bishop, among the rest, the Chancellor who being to begin his journy for London tomorrow, and too much affected with the Apprehension of danger from the Infirmity hee labors under, takes mee apart, in the same room with impotent and kind passion indevors to express his Danger from his case and his Friendship to mee, in passionate and lowder Terms calls mee Dear Freind, Dear Mr. P. kissing mee, conjures my kindness to his Family. I promise as one justly oblig'd my many Favors. Wee return to the Company vid. The Bishop, Dr. Thane, Mr. Legh, Mr. Moor, Alderman Allen who seemd not to take Notice of this passage. After the company, supper, a Glasse and discourse, to bed about 11.

6 A milder morning, the weather and wind, fair. I go to early prayers, the Bishop and company intent on their voyage, the Captain impornatra. Lady Jones generously gratifies my Family for the Trouble they gave it. The Bishop, Chancellor and Mr. Legh take several Coaches and horse, at the same time i.e. about 10. About 11 the 2 Commissions of Edisbury are open'd in Court before Dr. Thane, upon Mr. Bouchers Allegacion, the Execucion is prorogud to Namptwich the 16th current. I write to John Crosse. After prayers, my Suzy, Mrs. Crompton and I see the Coffin of the former Mrs. Entwisle buryd Nov. 1697, taken up firm and whole in order to be removd to the Drs. Grave, this night. After divert at home in Hirtii Bello Alexandrina and domestic pint past 10.

7 The morning fair tho frosty, after early prayers invites to roodee and 4 shorter Turns. The Letters afford little news, but rumor of a peace betwixt the Swede and Muscovite. I divert in the Fair where Mapps, pictures &c are sold. I write to Mr. Parker on the Edisbury Commission and a Letter summons to Sir Thomas Delves. End the Alexandrine and enter on the African War, recreate in a pint till 10.

8 A calm and warm morning, the wind still favorable for Ireland. After early prayers perform 4 full Turns on roodee end the African warr, write to Dr. Stratford. Solace at home in a moderate Quota.

9 A delicate morning invites to early prayers and 4 shorter Turns. A Court day of moderate busienes and little Noise. Dr. Thane Surrogate. After prayers I go on with and finish the Spanish Warr and end the day in a domestic pint.

10 After early prayers and the litle News I take 4 Turns on roodee. After Dinner the Election of the Mayor grows warm and doubtfull, about 3 it Turns in favor of Starkey and Page; Williams has 312, Page 383, Starkey above 400, these are housd, the bench vote 15 for Page, 3 for Starkey (manifest partiality) Williams of the Bear and Mr. Hodgson are Sheriffs proposd, and without voting, chosen, Mr. Hodgson enters the Honor with dejection and reluctancy. I go among the rest to attend the Mayor home, thence Mr. T Cowper & I call at Sheriff Hodgsons where an empty house and resolucion not to enter at in, presents rejected &c, hence Mr Cowper and I go to Tom Hatfeild, his brother Mrs. Blechington, Oldfeld, Mr. S. Taylor, Aldermen Ed. Partington and Puleston come, wee are cheerfull the Glass circles freely about till 10, the Symbola amounting to $2^{s}6^{d}$ a peece.

11 Extremely fevorish whether from the Quality or Quantity of the wine last Night, indevor to repose and recover. And in the Evening invited by Sir Hen

Bunbury go down to Pickings where Mr. Bruen, Cowper, yong Ravenscroft, Ned Puleston at a Bowl of punch. I venture on this liquor rather than Claret, but it succeeds not, wee part about 10. My Suzy writ and inclosd as a present today half a Guinea to Sheriff Williams.

12 My indisposicion aggravated to an unhappy degree, confind to bed past 10, with difficulty make ready to go down to Sheriff Williams with my Suzy and I do in Sir H. Bunbury coach about 12. Wee find a great company, a great cold and confusd entertainment, wee return about 3. I am still in torment and at night recur to Elixir.

13 The pains something alleviated yet tormenting even by reflexion. I take 4 shorter Turns on roodee, dine too freely which keeps up indisposicion, apply to the Deanaries easily run thoro six, after Evening prayers, repeat 4 shorter Turns to help my stomach, return to busienes & Books.

14 A mild morning not yet recoverd I go about 9 with Mr. Wilkinson to Stanny, wee call on Mr. Charles Bunbury, hee detains near an hour with the sight of his Collection of Mortiers Cutts, hee has them (about 60) pasted a length and rolld up which I design to imitate. Wee ride thoro the Demesn, Moor rake to Hoom House, consider of a way to the solitary mansion. Mr. Wilkinson and I return thoro Stoak, call on company and go a Coursing, wee see 4 and kill 2 hares, return after I had bin 9 hours on horseback, refresht about 6. Dr. Thane comes, I eat a boyld chicken, and wee clubb for a bottle of Pickings,[22] part about 9.

15 I find the exercise yesterday serviceable to my health from the ease this morning. I prepare for a journy. I write to Mr. Bowyer and Mr. Lambert. After dinner Dr. Thane, Mr. Boucher and I set for Namptwich about 2 come there about ½ hour after 5, refresh in tollerable Claret & to bed about 10.

16 The weather fair and mild. To Celsus in the morning. About 11 to the Church where 3 Wittnesses, Wolf, Walker, Wooley are producd. I examine Wolf with some difficulty before I (not the rest) dine, the others before 9. Wee after meet at a Glass in sharp expectacion of the post and Bishop. The post comes about 10 brings mee from my cozn. Parr, That the Queen was expected that day viz. Tuesday and that Dr. Freeman, the early competitor dy'd that morning. To bed about 11.

17 The weather still mild and fair. To the Church about 11, there adjourn to Mr. John Bromhall where Sir Tho Delves is and expects us, hee is producd and examind before dinner, earnestly invited by Mr. Bromhall, I stay and dine there with Sir Tho Delves and his Lady. Sir Tho is obliging & invites mee (while in these parts) to his house at Doddington. After dinner Dr. Thane and Mr. Boucher come. Mr. Bromhall putts his strong Beer freely about till 4, thence wee (I paying my coz Parre visit to Mr. Church) go to Mr. Wetenhalls where wee meet with strong Beer, but not so much. Wee part hence about 9 return to the

22 Pickings and Manks (see above, 16 Jan. 1704/5) were local brews of ale.

Lamb and fancy wee moderate the old Beer in a Gill of Brandy, and so to bed about 11.

18 The weather still favorable. I am affected with the Beer yesterday, write to Dr. Edisbury, Mr. Peirson, my coz. Parr, Tom Stringer, before 10, Wee sett hence, I, Jack and my Man, part with the Dr. Mr. Boucher and Mr. Chapman and call at Pool where I pay Mr. Elcock a visit long due. I am receivd civilly by both, in an old house and pleasant situacion. Hee orders a small pond to bee drawn and takes 2 couple of Carp for mee. Wee dine here and after dinner Mr. Elcock urges the Glass to the healths of many honest Gentlemen, stays mee till 4 or near it. Wee mount and seeing the night & darkness approach wee spur on in fair ways, suceed and come (D.G.) safe to my Corner before 7.

19 Extremely indisposd, confind to my bed and House. The News of little moment, in the Evening Dr. Thane sees mee. I treat him with a pint. I recurr to Elixir prepare the Certificate.

20 After early prayers, apply to the return of one Commission against Josua Edisbury Esq., write to Mr. Peirson. I dine on Carp and Harslett too elegantly, it upbraids in spite of Brandy. After prayers, I take in defence 2 shorter Turns on roody, after Dr. Thane and I venture on a Bottle of Pickings. An express passes from Ireland with the ill News of the Lisbon Fleet.

21 The weather Turns very rainy and continues so all day. The News as dull. I proceed in Celsus. In the Evening, At the Rose and Crown with Dr. Thane and Mr. Allen of Abby Court, wee dispose of 4 pints, after wee call att my Brother Partingtons and add to the Clubb.

22 I send the other Commission against Elizabeth Glegg and write to Mr. Peirson, indisposicion is above all Busienes, yet in the Evening, Dr. Thane and I share a Bottle of Pickings.

23 At early prayers. A Court day of little Busienes and Noise. Wee are now in the utmost expectacion of a new Bishop by the next post. After prayers Dr. Thane and I go to the Rose and Crown, wee advance the Discourse on the Bishop, the inconveniences and dissapointment, wee share 3 pints, the last cheerfully, and part at 9.

24 After early prayers, apply to the post office in the most importune expectacion, meet with dissapointment, still. Here the ill news of the outward bound Lisbon Fleet consisting of 130 transports in which besides men, Ammunicion &c 1,000 Horse, convoyd by 4 men of warr, one of which, the Royal Oak escapd, but shatterd. I take 4 Turns on roodee. My sister Jones comes to us shee receives her 70^{li} deposited with mee and borrows 10^{li} of mee. I write by her to Mr. Price. About 7 invited go over to Sir Henry B's where Dr. Thane, Mr. Amos Meredith, the 2 Foulks Brothers and myself are entertain'd with an elegant supper with a shoulder of Venison and excellent Claret.

25 A dull day, from indisposicion worse, I divert most of it in Caesar. In the Evening send my Letter writt, last night to Mr. Chetle, at the Rose and Crown with Mr. Davies, Drs. Thane & Norris wee part about 8. I after read Caesars Life before Edmonds Observacions.

26 A mild bright day. The News that the Brittish parliament met on the 23rd, that her Majesty by the Chancellor directs the Commons to choose a Speaker upon which returnd Mr. Smith, the last Speaker was unanimously chosen by them. A miserable inundancion of the Loire betwixt Orleans & Blois expectations of a bloody dispute on passing the Vistula by the Swede, the Czar opposing it. Mr. Gibson has in the Quire a good discourse (some similes omitted) on Heb. 13 later part of v.5. After prayers I apply to read some of the psalms and prophets. Dr. Thane comes with joy and tells mee his hopes of success in the Archdeaconry. Wee pray God may direct her Majesty about that hour to the choice of a good Successor, hee stays not, I send for my pint and to bed before 11.

27 A brisk wind, the weather yet fair. After early prayers and 4 Turns on roodee, read the different Opinions in the Manchester papers. After Evening prayers calld go with aversion to the Rose and Crown, here Mr. Davies, Dr. Thane, my bro. Partington and I dispatch briskly 5 pints. My shee cozn. Molineux of Hawkley calld on us and laid out the suspected fraud of Mr. Barron pretending a marriage with the late Mrs. Molineux and to a right, to all her estate. I read the 8 Book of Caesars Commentarys.

28 A fair but brisk morning. At early prayers, about 10 I Jack along set out for Eaton Boat thoro the medows, come thither about 11, step to the Hall where I wait on Mr. Cholmley hee is full of severe Questions as well concerning my private Circumstances as the Affairs of the State. The Chancellor returns (from London) over the Boat unexpected, dines with Dr. Thane and myself. After dinner wee step over to Alderman Allen, hee treats us with the 2 last Bottles of Claret in his Sellar. Mr. Okes comes here to Us. The Chancellor and Dr. Thane mount here about 4. I stay an hour with Mrs. Okes, Ives, Massie, Dennis at the Boat, after all but Mr. Massie, come in an hour to the Bear, where parting in 2 pints, wee come (D.G.) safe home about 7.

29 After a stormy night the morning so, wee go to early prayers. I after turn Manlius. I enter Warrington Deanary, write to Dr. Stratford and Mr. Kippax. After prayers at the Rose & Crown with the Chancellor, Drs. Thane and Norris, wee stay our dull pints, part about 8. I turn Durantus de Libellis.

30 The wind high and the weather rainy, at early prayers. I enter Frodsham Deanary, write to Mr. Vaudrey. A Court mild in busienes. Apply to Gail de Libellis, write to Mr. Mosse of Manchester about the Gold Otho. Dr. Thane with concern, tells mee his insuccess about the Archdeaconry. I return to Caesar and solace in my private Quota.

[No further entries have survived between this date and May 1708]

1708

MAY 3 Munday. Visitacion at Malpas. Mr. Boucher, Stratford & Roberts go.

4 Visitacion at Namptwich. The Chancellor and I sett hence about 10, come hither about [?]. After Busienes I see Mrs. Church give her Account of Mr. Lovick's Family, Mrs. Degg is with her. I go with Mr. Bradshaw to the parsonage, sit an hour, thence home.

5 After Coffee at Mr. Wetnal's, wee mount about 9, the weather fair, come about 12 to Midlewich – here good company not much busienes. After which wee are treated by Mr. Cowper with good Ale, indifferent wine.
6 About 9 set hence and in cool rideing come to Macclesfield before 12; the Busienes considerable. That over Alderman Johnson and Mr. Hulme take us down the Hill to indifferent Ale; returning the Alderman treats us with a Dram and good White wine.
7 In a fine morning, proceed to Stockport, the Busienes ended, Wee with Mr. Shalcross, Swetnam, Arden &c. go to the Bowling green hence, the wine and Ale indifferent. Here at the door a Rustic very rudely reflects on our Company.
8 At the Church, 1 person only appears on Correction, The Busienes rises to 20. In the Evening Dr. Holbrook entertains us with very good Ale, edibles and welcome a mighty Lobster and collection of Cheeses part of it.
9 Sunday; Thanksgiving for the dissapointment of the late Invasion, rememb-br'd in a prayer compos'd. The Warden has a good sermon touching the occasion. In the Evening, I see Dr. Yarborough's considerable Collecion. After at the Warden's, thence Home.
10 The Chancellor and I write, and hee to the Chancellor of York sends 80^{li}, I,92^{li} to Mr. Empson. Mr. Shrigley undertakes to convey the purse of Gold. Wee call and dine at Bolton, come thence in a perpetual showr about 6 to Blackburn. I write my Lord & my Suzy.
11 It continues rainy, the Busienes smal save Mr. Kippax. I chuse out some of Mr. Price's Library to the value of 2 Guineas and give direction to write to the present Owner about them. The Chancellor and I see Mrs. Hulme.
12 The weather still moist, wee sett out about 9 come by Brindle to Chorley about 12; here Mr. Farrington and Haydock are of Company, proceed not without rain and come about 7 to Wigan.
13 Holy Thursday; After prayers, The Chancellor and myself dine at the parsonage with the Honourable Brothers.[1] The approaching Elecion furnishes Discourse. After this I go (but about) to see my coz. Finche's new House and desire his Friendship in Mr. Roby's Milne.
14 The visitacion, Fair and Market fill the Town. Sir Roger Bradshaigh in behalf of the Corporacion appears in Court and protests against the admission of Mr. Holland, to bee Warden as namd by the Rector, but no other in his place, being return'd, hee is admitted. The Rector presents Sir R's. ruinous Oratory, busienes competent. The Town fills with Voters. The Chancellor gos to Ormskirk.
15 The day of Elecion, confluence of Voters, I go to Tootells where both his Brothers attack Mr. Callis. I meet the Commissary come to give his vote right, about 10 my coz. Holt and I set for Ormskirk, reach it calling at Holland about 12, the busienes here full, a severe showr falls about 4. The Chancellor intended for Speake, but go's not in the rain. I see Will Barton.

1 Dr. Edward Finch was rector of Wigan and his brother Henry, dean of York.

16 Early up; The Chancellor, Mr. Boucher, myself and Mr. Roberts before 7 mount, by melancholy Knowsley to Huyton betwixt which and Childwall a brisk showr, come into the Church wett about 10. Mr. Markland has a preparatory discourse on the Sacrament. Here is Dr. Norris and his Family. After Sermon, wee go to Speake, after dinner walk thoro fair pastures to Garston.
17 Walk about the ancient house which is not without Grandieur. After Tea, Mr. Boucher, Mr. Roberts and I come over against Runcorn boat, 3 Horses and ourselves, save Mr. Boucher – the wind blowing fresh, the Boat men attempt, but can't work over the Boat. Wee disembark go to Warrington dine and recreate and thence in a fine Evening come safe home (D.G.) about 8. [*blank to 21*]
21 After News, Coffee and Dinner, Mr. Callys, myself and Jack, sett out in a fine day, come to Whitchurch about 6; quickly after my Lord and his company in 2 coaches, pass by to the Red Lyon.[2] Wee follow in ½ hour are kindly receiv'd by him, wee stay, sup and drink liberally, and about 11 return to the George.
22 About 11 the Coaches sett forward, the weather tho threatening rain, very good, wee accompany it, come to refresh and stay an hour at Hanley. Wee with difficulty retard the coaches, company increases, and coaches about the Glass House there seem about 250 Horse of the better sort. I am Nomenclator, Hee is conducted by a full room into the palace before 6. My Suzy and I stay and sup.
23 Sunday. Mr. Lancaster preaches, the Quire is full. My Lord administers (which I also receive from him) the Sacrament. Mr. Fogg preaches after Noon where the Bishop appears in his seat without the Episcopal Habit. I introduce severall to him. [*24 blank*]
25 After News, invited, go dine with Mr. Egerton where Mr. Finch and Bridgman Candidates for Wigan. Sir Hen Bunbury, Mr. Chancellor afternoon drink freely. Sir Hen & myself about 5 return to the palace where the Mayor & Aldermen &c. are visiting the Bishop; the Glass here moderatly. After I go with Sir Henry; Mr. Bridgman, Done, Thane to the Ship & extremely overcome.
26 The bad wine rather than the Quantity, affects mee exceedingly with pain and fevorish heat. I am confind to bed till 6 at Night. Mr. Couchée comes to mee about the Presentacion and Institucion of Mr. Wood to Bowden.[3]
27 I had promisd but not able to ride to Mold, send Mr. Roberts and Jack thither on my sister Jones, her Account; the vestry there proves insuccessfull to her. I wait on the Bishop and present Mr. Powel Candidate for Deacons Orders.
28 Several of the Candidates for Orders are recomended to mee, and I endeavor to serve them.
28 My Coz. Powel dines with us. In the Evening at the Bacchus with most of the Candidates together.
30 Mr. Shaw preaches gravely and fully upon the Ordinacion, 18 Deacons and

2 Sir William Dawes was enthroned as bishop in February 1708. The section of the diary dealing with this is lost.
3 C.R.O.,EDP1/44, Bowden Parish Papers.

8 preists therabouts are ordain'd. The Bishop performs this office with a Solemnity, Ease and Gravity to Admiracion. After dinner I go to the palace, thence to the parish Church where yong Mr. Leche delivers well a good discourse against Hypocrisy, walk after to Upton. [*31 blank*]

JUNE 1 Tuesday. The Anniversary Charity Sermon, my Lord could not attend at Warrington. Hee dines today in a good company at Sir Hen. Bunbury's, sitts there to, and returns after prayers. I am invited over about 5. Mr. Egerton, Chancellor, Bruen & Hare there, My Lord is provokt to full Discourse on the Prince of Wales is clear in an Imposture.[4] Wee drink excellent Pontac till 9.
2 In a cool yet mild morning about 10, Sir Henry Bunbury and my Suzy in the Coach, I along set out and come safe over Runcorn about 2, thence in Dr. Norris' Coach, wee come to Speake about 6.
3 I take a Walk into the Wood where noble Timber is in falling, Thence near the Seaside, thoro Oke and Firr Groves back to the House. Tea, Dinner and after this Angling, the Arts to pass the Time. I take another Walk by the sea side thoro the Demesne to Garston, admire the greatnes of the Closes, wood, water, situacion and all the blessings of nature in this place.
4 After Tea the Company take Coach for Leverpool, I home for Chester come over safe to Runcorn about 1, to Chester about 4. [*No entry 5th.*]
6 Sunday. My Lord has the first Time, an excellent sermon in the Quire, upon the subject of Confirmacion before a frequent Auditory. After prayers Mr. Lambert calls on mee. Hee, Mr. Cowper and I go to Pickings; wee sent to Mr. Callis, hee comes to us. Wee dispatch 2 Bottles good, but low, Claret.
7 I go with Mr. Lambert to my Lord where the peticion of the Clergy of his 4 Deanarys for keeping a Consistory Court at Kendale is exhibited to his Lordship, hee approves of it.[5] In the Evening at the Bacchus with Mr. Lambert.
8 Visitacion for the Deanary of Chester. The Bishop has a full Company at Dinner, and after prayers and a grave Exhortacion from his Throne, to the Candidates, hee confirms (Miss Grosvenor the 1st) about 500 persons.[6]
9 This day to a blush and almost confusion, I reckon 58 if not 59 Years not being able to recollect many, but very few Actions of my own that afford mee true satisfaction, which I easily can, almost infinite underservd mercies from God.
10 Court day of small Busienes. The Bishop has a great Company at Dinner amongst the rest Sir John Crew and Mr. Lee of Darnall. Sir John discourses mee on the Affairs of the Deputy Herald of these parts.
11 Upon a Letter of Notice of the Death of Mr. Butler, Tuesday last, received about a quarter before 7, my Lord is ready accinct and in the stage coach about

4 This was the future Young Pretender.
5 This Consistory Court at Kendal had a short existence, from 1708 to 1719. The Act Books of the Court are in Lancashire R.O. In 1719 the Kendal Court was absorbed into the Archdeaconry Court based at Lancaster from 1719–1748. The Act Books are in the Lancs. R.O.
6 Prescott records the numbers confirmed by Bishop Dawes and details of the sermons preached.

½ hour after 8, I waiting on him, Wee remember this as the 14th birthday of Mr. R. Cholmley; very rainy till Afternoon.
12 The Town is surprizd, event Concern, at the suddain Expedicion of my Lord. I treat Mr. Stringer, Bingley & Haslam at Hatfeild, with a morning draught, to my Lord's Health. I write to Mr. Morrey.
13 Sunday. Dr. Thane has a good sermon in the Quire.
14 I write to Mr. Le Neve, the conference with Sir John Crew, and particularly, his inclinacion to buy Mr. Hulmes' Collection.
[*15 blank*]
16 About 9 Mr. Chancellor, Dr. Thane, Clutterbuck, Maryon, my self &c, sett out come (excurring by Burton & Denhall) to Neston about 11; the Busienes is presently dispatch't in the Church. Wee are all after entertaind at the vicarage, with a noble dinner and excellent wine. Wolstenholme the younger, before wee mount, treats us with 2 Bottles; wee return about 9.
17 Court day.
18 About 9 Mr. Chancellor, myself &c sett out, come to Frodsham Church past 11, dispatch there and to the Town, the Busienes slender. I write to Mr. Edmonds of Bowden about the old vessell I expected here. In our return at Trafford bridg, wee watring our horses, run some hazard in the Quicksands. Mr. Chancellor's horse most ingagd & hee tumbles into the Water.
19 After dinner the old Vessell comes, sent by Mr. Edmonds. I send him with my Letter a Guinea and pay the special Messenger 4^s with intimacion that if hee approve not of the Guinea, the vessell shall be returnd. It was found this day 3 weeks by a Man digging 2 yds perpendicular in a Moss a mile from the Church of Bowden.
20 Sunday. This morning about 2 my youngest Child Suzy, after a great weakness with Convulsions for near 3 weeks togeather, leaves this troublesom candidate, I hope to a happy Life.
21 At Home in Bookes and Busienes till 9 at Night when the Child is privatly interrd; a few freinds and relations accompanying the small Solemnity.
22 The day pre fixt for the choice of a proctor in Convocacion, a few (8 in number) appear. Mr. Finch of Wigan is propos'd by the Dean, the rest are unanimous in the choice of him. I am extreme ill of a pain in my Stomach.
23 I write to Mr. Finch now at York, of his Eleccion and include the proxy to him. Elixir taken last Night has the Contrary effect, discharges and gives ease (D.G.) to my stomach.
24 The Fair day, I take in the morning, 4 Turns on roodee.
25 Richard Southworth speaks to mee on Aspinwall's behalf, about the Green House. I write to John Crosse and include to him a Letter to Mr. Hill about the value of the Bank.
26 Variety of Busienes and Letters upon it.
27 Sunday. Mr. Fogg has an excellent Sermon in the Quire, on the happy and pleasant condicion and state of a religious Life. I read 2 Chapters in the Whole Duty of Man.
28 After early prayers a usuall Tour on roodee, some Busienes determind I go

about 5 to visit Alderman Allen and Mr. Okes at Eaton, the Alderman a shocking spectacle. Alderman Morrey & Mainwaring there also.

29 I still venture to lend 25^{li} to Mr. Whaley hee giveing mee a Warrant to confess Judgment. My sister Jones gives hopes of her help in this difficulty, returns today to Wrexham.

30 After early prayers an accustomd Walk and Busienes. In the Evening I intend (Dr. Thane with mee) to wait on Lord Cholmley in the Castle. Wee are there diverted from our purpose. Upon this Mr. Chancellor, the Dr. & myself go to the Bacchus, take our Freindly pints. After this, part of my pint at the palace.

JULY 1 After an unhappy Night, rise about 8. I write to my Coz. Holt about their journy to Buxton and another 50^{li}. After dinner Dr. Thane and Jack go to Eaton to visit Alderman Allen. Mr. Cholmley in the Crisis returns in a Coach and 6, from London. About 8, I go over to the palace, stay till 10.

2 After disturb'd imperfect sleep, rise to early prayers, about 8 begin, and about 9, finish 4 full Turns on roodee; apply to Busienes till 4. Mrs. Pierpont visits us in the Evening, staies 2 hours, wee bring her back to the palace, Mr. Maryon just return'd from the Peake gives us an Account of the Wonders.

3 After early prayers I write and inclose a process to Winder of Preston. Write and inclose an Account of the storm Breif to Mr. Borrett of the Inner Temple, write to my Lord Bishop with design my Letter will meet him at Coventry.Mr. Egerton's desire, that hee will call on him on Tuesday at Broxon. I receive hopes from my sister Jones of her Assistance, more gratefull still, since Mr. Foulks, today, prest mee earnestly for mony. I go down to Mr. Egerton, after Dinner hee and his Lady conclude to invite Mrs. Pierrepont on Tuesday to Broxon. I write to the Bishop of Meath and acquaint him That Alderman Allen dyd this day about one at Eaton of an Asthma. I do, as I have great cause, condole the loss of an usefull, religious and good Man, an old & generous Friend. I draw 8 Ounces of Blood about 11. At 8 my Suzy and I, as frequently since my Lord went, sup and stay at the palace till 10.

4 A delicate mild day. Dr. Thane has a good discourse on (And I will give thee rest) sanctissimae Eucharistiae particeps sum Det D.O.M. bene et caste vivere.[7] After prayers Mr. Hughs (presented to Frodsham) calls on mee, wee drink a Bottle of my Wine, over it, much of Christ Church. I read a passage in Hooker of Fasts.

5 After Busienes and Dinner in a fine cool day I sett out after 3 and come to Broxon about 6. Mr. Egerton being gon to Edge, I follow him thither. Mr. Dod receives mee with good old Beer and a Gamon, wee stay freely 2 hours, return to Broxon about 9, after drink near our Bottles of Claret, to bed after 1.

6 Indisposd by the wine, do not so happily tast the sweet situaçion Gardens prospect. About 9 I sett hence in Mr. Egerton's Coach with 6, come to the

7 Trans: 'I am a partaker of the most Holy Eucharist. May God the best and greatest grant [me] to live well and chastely.'

George in Whitchurch before 11 find my Lord preparing for Broxon, wee take the Coach after 11 and return to Broxon, at 1 where my Lord's Coach, Mrs. Pierepont, my Suzy, Mr. Clutterbrook in it, and out Horseback, Mr. Chancellor, Callis, Dr. Thane, Mr. Marion meet us. All see and admire the prospect. The company is entertaind with great elegancy as with great plenty, the liquid all coold with ice. About 6 well pleasd, wee take Coach and Horse and come, in a Carreer in an hour and half, to Chester. After I leave the palace, Mr. Hughes comes, wee go to the Fountain, after to the Talbot, drink our Bottles, part about 12.

7 Indisposd from the wine and journy, yet attend Mr. Hughs to the palace where, in the Chapell, my Lord very solemnly institutes him to Frodsham.[8] Mr. Hughes acknowledges my Friendship with great Gratitude. I write to Dr. Stratford, wee invited, dine with my Lord. Thence to prayers, after these Mr. Clutterbrook, Maryon and myself consent to drink Mr. Egerton's health at the Bacchus whence, after our pints, home before 8.

8 My distemper aggravated, I indulge in bed, till about 9. Mr. Clutterbrook kindly alarms mee with a probable report from the Bath of a great victory obtaind by the Allies over the French, in Flanders. I find the report spread and credited in the Town, to an impatient expectacion of the post. The Funeral of good Alderman Allen is solemnly attended by the Maior and Aldermen, Bishop, Clergy, Gentry. Mr. Fogg preaches the sermon, a good one with deserv'd mention of the Dead. After this the Dean of Bristol, Archdeacon Thane, my brother Partington and I expect the post at the Rose and Crown, it comes before 10, and presently the good report is confirmd and express't by Bells and Bonfires; returning I call at the palace & there congratulate.[9]

9 About 9 in a fine cool morning, take a Turn round the Walls to ease my malady from the Wine. The prints and Letters are full in confirming the Victory, leaving it tho' great, imperfect, and everybody in expectacion of still greater success. I read the Memoirs of the Earl of Leicester, Dudley, and about 9 recreate in my domestic pint.

10 A cool day the wind blowing brisk N.W. I take 4 shorter Turns on roodee, write to Mr. Ed. Finch, Rector of Wigan, about Hindley Chapel, to my coz. Parre about my design'd purchase and 50^{li} to Mr. Borrett about the storm Breif and to Mr. Morrey about my Lord Confirming at Neston July 17. No other express because of contrary wind but oblique Letters confirm news of the victory.

11 The weather still cool. Mr. Henchman in the morning has a good discourse on Matt. 5;3 in St. Oswald's it being there, a sacrament day. My Lord preaches after noon at St. Peter's on Psal. 21 v7 wherein the character of a good prince and the happines of his people, by reason of his goodness and piety, hee very much magnifyd, plainly intimating the exemplary vertu and piety of the present

8 At this period institutions to benefices were performed in the Bishop's Chapel.
9 The Battle of Oudenarde.

Queen and the Successes of her reign. I almost end the 1st admirable Book of Hooker's Ecclesiastical Polity. After recreate in a domestic pint.
12 After early prayers write to Mr. Pierson, inclose Hartleys Citacion with the requisicion, charges whereof $16^{s};8^{d}$. To Mr. Vaudrey, about stamp money, and to my sister Jones. After 10 a clock prayers, my Lord, Mr. Chancellor, Mr. Clutterbrook and myself, take his coach, reach easily Utkinton about 1. Here at a fine House, in a noble situacion and prospect, my Lord and his company are very fully and generously receivd at a good dinner, in a fine room & afterwards Mr. Clutterbrook and I go up to the Summerhouse, not into it, here the prospect pleasantly great, wee set hence about a quarter after 5 and come home so much after 7. My Suzy there wee stay at the palace past 9.
13 The papers confirm, not yet increase, the News. Mrs. Dod, Greene, Bruen, Cooper &c dine at the palace. I introduce and escape. In the Evening, Mr. Gregory calls on mee with a Letter from the Bishop of St. Asaph. I upon it see Mr. Bingley, who with Mr. Holland, coz. Kendrick, myself, go to the Ship where wee join Mr. Cowper, where wee are cheerfull, drink our Bottles and part about 12.
14 Mr. Gregory calls, I go into Town with him, hee trys Mr. Kirks about going to St. Asaph, who with rudeness putts him off. Mrs. Gregory, Bingley and myself go to the Bacchus, send to Mr. Croxton who readily promises to go to St. Asaph with us 3 weeks hence. In the Evening saunterring, I meet with Mr. Allen in Abby Court, Alderman Morrey, Mr. Walley, Fellow of Trinity College, Dublin and Virginia. Mr. Lloyd invited, come to his House where [we] are entertaind with a large Bowl of punch and a Bottle of good Claret, wee part about 12.
15 After an odd night a sick morning, unable to go to the Court, yet after dinner examine Jane Fogge, a suspected Witnes on Josua Swifts Will. I finish her deposicion after 7. Am indispos'd all Night.
16 Some Flandrian papers give further Accounts of the 2 Armies, the French incampt on the Dike betwixt Ghent and Bruges, the 2 Allies haveing broken the French Lines and designing to besiege Lisle. I examine with sick difficulty 2 other Wittnesses, on Swifts Will. In the Evening about 6, The Chancellor and I introduce Mr. Boucher to the Bishop, who receives all civilly, wee stay a Bottle or 2 of wine, and part about 8, write Mr. Vaudrey and my coz. Holt.
17 After almost a sleepless Night, I rise about 5, am with my Lord before 6, wee breakfast in Tea, sett out in a cool morning before 7 and come to the vicarage of Neston before 9. My Lord gos to Church about 10, the Candidates, of 9 parishes, to Confirmacion flock in. After prayers hee begins with those of Neston parish, confirms all, vid. above 400. About 12 My Lord and his company vid. the Chancellor, Archdeacon, Mr. Clutterbrook, Maryon and myself are entertaind by Mrs. Murrey with a plentifull dinner, Caput cujus a Carp of extra size, and good, tho not so good as his former, wine. Wee sit past 4, mount, call at Park Yate, where after 2 Bottles good Claret, remount, ride by the sea side to Burton, return in a cool sweet Evening about [?] harass'd with rideing and indisposicion early to Bed.

18 I see the News which seems rather to inlarge the Busienes, than the conquest. Mr. Walley, Fellow of Trinity College, Dublin, preaches in the morning in the Quire and my Lord afternoon in St. Oswalds on the same Text vid. 1 Cor. 10 v 12; they manage it with different not contrary sentiments both with great applause. Mr. Walley comended for decency and nice Oratory, the Bishop for strong divinity, Affection in Delivery and facility of it without help of Notes. Mr. Egerton draws mee to dine with him and his Bro. the Doctor and at his request, I write to Hen. Bunbury (now at Wrexham) to prevail with him to ingage Sir Richard Midleton, to meet my Lord at Wrexham, on Wednesday. In the Evening, I read Heylin's introduction to the Life of Archbishop Laud and with my coz. Kendrick, recreate in my domestic pint.

19 Up at 6,and after prayers and finishing the 1st admirable Book of Hookers polity, take 4 full Turns on roodee. My Lord, Mr. Egerton, Chancellor & Archdeacon go about 9 in the same (my Lords) Coach to Cholmley. Apply to Busienes, and Speeds Edward 3. My Lord returns about 8, wee wait on him till 9.

20 The Letters still rather inlarg our expectacion than knoledge. I go to Mr. Egerton, am excusd from dineing with him. But hee, Mr. Legh of Lime &c to 20 dine with my Lord, myself invited on the occasion of Mr. Legh; wee sitt after till prayers. After these ended, My Lord, Mr. Egerton, Mr. Legh, his lam'd bro. Francis and myself are invited to the Chancellor's where good Claret of several sorts gos freely round. Mr. Fr. Legh tells how very barborous the French were to him with their prisons, and the whole sharp action wherein hee lost his right Leg in the Ruby; variety of discourse well manag'd by my Lord. Mr. Langford intrudes unseasonably, My Lord and the Archdeacon go about 9. I take the Hint and go then, the rest stay freely till 11.

21 About 10 wee sett out for Wrexham (my Lord, Mr. Egerton, Mrs. Pierpoint and my Suzy) in my Lords Coach, wee come thither in cool weather about 12. Wee step before dinner to see my mother Puleston and sister Jones, thence to Sir Harrys where wee dine, Mr. Jones of Bangor and Mr. John Davies added to the dinner. Wee sit but free with good wine till prayers, after with the company improv'd by my brother Puleston and Mr. Price, the Glass revives about, I step to see my Uncle Eyton and Coz. Moreton. My sister Jones lends mee 50^{li} opportunely to Mr. Foulks Account. The Coach and company sett home about 7 and return (D.G.) about 9. I stay a Bottle or 2 with Mr. Egerton at the palace.

22 Indispos'd but to Court, where competent Busienes and the day by consent, the last of the Term. After repose, refresht, I write and inclose 20 printed Direccions for my Lord's Confirmacions to him. After 1 Bottle at Mr. Bouchers, with the Chancellor, about 6, I examine 3 old Wittnesses ex parte Pool contra Wetenhal and end past 10.

23 After a windy Night such a morning. I see the papers still promising more Action. I sett off my intended journy for Lancashire to day and apply to busienes, write to Mr. Ayde, and for my sister Jones, a Letter to her bro. Jones, which I inclose togeather with an acknowledgment for the 50^{li} to her. My Suzy and I wait on the Bishop, about 7 hee treats with freedom and a Bottle of Pontac till 9.

24 About 9 in a cool and calm day sett out, come to Warrington, call on Mr. Shaw at the school past 12. Hee refreshes mee by saying hee has and can pay mony for 22 Licences. Hence with courage, call on Mr. Vaudrey, thence to Beausee where I dine, after which the weather alters to vehement rain, is constant to Night. Mrs. Banks of Wigan adventures, I stay persuaded by the Ladies, Mrs. Atherton and Lady Soames. Sir Richard Vernon and his sister come soakt in the rain.
25 St. James's and Sunday. About 9 set hence go the more private Golborn way, come to Wigan near 12, dine with my coz. Holts. Afternoon to Church, where Alderman Baldwin's son has a sermon on, 'Let mee dy the Death of the Righteous and let my later end bee like his'. After Church at Mrs. Banks. After my coz. Holt and I to the Eagle and Child where after 2 pints, wee come home. Mr. Bowyer with us, hee treats with a Bottle of good wine, which is drunk in Banter and perpetual mention of his Mistress Marjery Letherbarrow.
26 It rains afresh, this keeps mee within. Mr. Herle and Bowyer dine with [us]; after 4 Mr. Bowyer, coz. Holt and I set out come to Ayrfeild about 5 stay 2 hours, drink 2 Bottles cheerfully. Here the woman Tenant tells mee of a noise of Knocking thrice heard in the House, upon alteracion or death in my Family, as upon the late deaths of my 2 daughters Arabella and Susanna. Wee return to Wigan about 8. I execute a Bond for 50^{li} to my coz. James Holt for 6 months, receiving the mony I pay interest 3^{li} for the other 50^{li} due August 1st. Mr. Bowyer sends another Bottle down, follows it, and wee end it cheerfully about 11.
27 The rain abates, but Douglas is high in the meadows, prejudicial to Hay. Set hence about 9, call at Mr. Rothwells in Newton about 11 where with Mr. Alanson, a bottle of strong Beer; hence to Winwick. I find Mr. Crane at a small dinner, eat some coarse Mutton with him. Hence to Warrington about 1, pay Mr. Vaudrey on account 70^{li}. Mr. Shaw sent for to swear and Ex . . . We fall on the Busienes of the new Chapell (which holds) till 6, when Mr. Winstanley and Bolland of Chester, mount, wee ride fast, and I come (D.G.) safe about 9.
28 Early up, My Lord setts out about 8, rides fast to Holt where wee come about 9, are entertaind by Mr. Adams with wine. Here are about 300 confirmd. His Lordship, Sir Henry Bunbury &c. come to Cornish about 1 where the Entertainment is full and decent. About 5 the company parts, my Lord proceeds to Malpas, I return gladly to Chester. I paid here my sister Jones 3^{li} for interest of the former 50^{li} due 22 current. I find my Suzy at the palace, where with Mrs. Pierrepont wee end the Evening.
29 I indulge to rest and repose and am not guilty of busienes. In the Evening, Mr. Egerton, ArchDeacon Thane send for mee to the Bear, where Sir Peter Soame. Mr. Warburton and Done are added, the wine is good, wee drink above our Bottles, pay 2^{s};6^{d} a peece, I come home past 10; about 400 confirmd at Malpas.
30 About 9 in a fair morning, sett out, come thoro the 5 Fords, to Bangor about 12. The Confirmacion of about 300 ends about 1. A great company Clergy and Gentry dine with Mr. Jones at a full and good Dinner. After 2 hours in Wine

&c, My Lord setts out conducted past 4 of the Fords by Mr. Geo Shakerley, wee come by Borras and safe home about 8. I stay with his Lordship at the palace past 9.
31 The Weather grows warm, apply to Busienes and Books. Mr. Whaley comes to mee after inspection of Mr. Hills Letter in which hee concludes the Estate to be worth 960^{li} and adds 40^{li} for its conveniency, this computacion displeases Mr. Whaley who uses peevish reflections upon it. I acquiesce in the Judgment of the Letter, hee recedes as dissatisfy'd.

AUGUST 1 A very warm day. My Lord preaches in a full auditory in the Choir. The News still holds us in Suspense. After Evening prayers, I discourse Mr. Egerton on the Busienes of Warrington Chapel. Apply to proper reading and finish the day in a privat domestic pint.
2 Rise at 5, at the palace before 6, my Lord mounts after Tea, before 7, wee come to Frodsham Church about 9, light and are received with wine at the School. Here I produce Mr. Marsden's Latin Letter to my Lord. About 10 his Lordship gos into Church, confirms at the least 400. The day grows excessive hott, his Lordship fatigud recedes into the school about 1, refresht, walks down to Mr. Speeds, where a nor hott nor cold dinner on the Table. Mr. Hughs is very uneasy at the ignorance. Mr. Cheshyre and other Clergy dine with my Lord, who setts hence about 4 and returns to the palace about 6. Hee has a dinner ready, is glad to relax. I stay, dine, refresh in Claret and come home about 9.
3 The day hott to an excessive degree (wee fancy to that of Spain). I am with Mr. Egerton about his company at Night. Hee concludes on my Lord, the ArchDeacon and myself only. About 4 I am with Sir Rowland Stanley and Mr. Pools Trustees, no conclusion amongst them. About 5 I go down to Mr. Egertons where wee are the company designd. Mr. Athertons and Mr. Shawes Letters are introduc'd to my Lord, the matter of the Chapel is discoursd. His Lordship resolves to deliberate And desires in the interim, for his Assistance & Direction, the Case may be drawn up by consent, and the opinions of 3 Civil and 3 Common Lawyers procurd. Mr. Clopton comes uninvited about 7 but in an hour recedes. My Lord gos at 9, the ArchDeacon and I about ½ hour past 10.
4 Very hott weather added to the heat of Yesterday. My Lord go's at 4 early to Namptwich. I about 11 meet with Mr. Cowper, Bro. Partington, Mr. Bletchington and myself, share with him in morning Rhenish. The day glowes on, I repose, in the Evening, am treated with Jack Wright at Sheriff Hodgson's with old Beer and Claret. After I go to the palace where wee stay with Mrs. P. till 10. Mr. John Massie of Coddington, after a short alarm, dies also as hee deservd, much lamented about the same hour 10.
5 I finish the draught of Mr. Pigots Confirmacion. The workmen who began yesterday, proceed to the repair of my House in the Abby Court. Mr. Whaley on a necessary occasion, prevails with mee to lend him 1^{li}. About 4 the weather grows cooler, and an hour after, great Thunder and unusuall spread & languid Lightning. I am affected with difficulty of hearing. About 7, Mr. Egerton sees and stays a Bottle with mee, about 8, my Lord returns wett thoro by Thundery

showers, go's immediatly to bed. I am an hour after in his Chamber where wee drink burnt Claret.
6 The News is of 14 [ships], 1 taken, a Spanish man of Warr very richly laden, sunk, 1 Galleon rich, taken, another burnt, Apply to busienes. After prayers my Lord and Mrs. Pierrepont go in the coach to Newton, takeing mee and my Suzy along; all civilly received, return in a pleasant Evening about 8 and stay at the palace, past nine.
7 At early prayers, thence to Busienes. I write Mr. Shaw an answer to Mrs. Atherton, and his Letters. I see Mr. Egerton about Mr. Crew of Utkinton, his Will prov'd as hee saies in May 1668. Mr. Whaley borrows another sum for which and others, hee gives a Warrant for Judgment of 30^{li}. I the first Time (Q.B.E.) this morning cheifly by Mr. Egerton's advice, putt off my 20 years companion Flannel and take the Callico. In the Evening, prayers ended, my Lord and Mrs. Pierrepont, give us a visit. I am fortunate in good wine, they stay cheerfully and easily till 9.
8 The News grows, Duke of Savoy descends into Savoy, wee bombard Bolloign near Calais. Mr. Lancaster preaches in the Quire on [?] I write to Mr. Massie on the Affairs of Bebington. My Lord preaches at St. Maries after noon. After prayers I write to my Coz. Hill, coz. Holt & Mr. Ludlow. About 8 wee step to the palace, stay ½ an hour and return to a domestic pint.
9 My Lord, Mr. Clutterbrook, Mr. Couchee, Servants and my self, mount about a Quarter after 4 in a fine warm morning, the heat and the day grow to geather, the Forest cool & pleasant, wee come to Midlewich ½ hour after 8. Refresht my Lord go's to Church about 10 confirms about 500. Wee sit to an elegant dinner at Mr. Cowpers where venison & fowl & Fish in variety. Mr. Egerton, Cholmley, Shakerley, Cotton after dinner wait on my Lord, turns in the Garden, fellowship in the Arbor, last till night. Wee part the company I lodge at Mr. Thomason's where to bed before 11.
10 After attendance on my Lord, I go to Mr. Pa̎rkers where Mr. Lownds &c, here Tea, it rains 3 hours briskly. My Lord confirms about 300. About 1 wee go to Colton, where Mr. Colton and his Lady receive the company pretty larg with a full and hansom dinner and good Claret, before 5 sett hence, wee have a fine Evening and some signs of rain; come to Macclesfield a Quarter after 7. The Mayor, Aldermen and indeed the Town meet his Lordship at the entrance into the Town. Hee alights and walks in the throng sollemnity to the Mayor (Mr. Rowe Dean's) house, there I do the office of Nomenclator, a small supper is brought, after indifferent wine, but hansom civility lasts near 10.
11 A very warm day and straight chapell make the Confirmacion of about 500 troublesome. Sir Wm. Meredith, Mr. Legh, Downs &c pay their regards, a throng dinner not very elegant, presses the Table, the Aldermen dine apart. About 5 my Lord setts for Stockport, Mr. Nicols meets him with about 60 horse, wee come to the parsonage before 8, a supper is prepar'd. Mr. Arden, Warren, the Brothers Swetenham &c stay with my Lord. After this Mr. Nicols begins with the Evening but to surprise falls into a private (Dn. patria) prayer. Mr. Nicols forces mee and my Horses to bee his Guests.

12 Walk about and see the neglected and ruinous State of the ample and noble rectory. Mr. Nicols rather teases than diverts my Lord with his poetry, stild Liturgici.[10] In his Creed, he introduces in a few verses the 2 sacraments. My Lord notes and dissuades that, corrects in some words. To Church after 10 where about 200 confirmd. I take notice of the very mean matter and work of the new Galleries.[11] A great number of the Clergy and Gentry adjacent to the number 20 making 2 Tables, dine with the Bishop, amongst these Mr. Cecil Booth, betwixt my Lord and whom a very warm controversy about non conformity, my Lord affirming hee never knew any dissenter that differ'd from [him] upon a principle, but upon humor, pride, prejudice or the like. His Lordship to those present seemd to do Justice to his own character and to the Church, to their great satisfaction. Mr. Haddon was present, interpos'd and remembers. The conference and day continud hott till 6, when my Lord walks down to the Bridg, accompanid with Gentlemen. Here hee is receivd by the Warden and the Gentlemen of Manchester who by the way increase to near 200 horse and thoro crowded streets my Lord comes to the Wardens house about 7. Hee over takes near Manchester, Dr. Linford, Mr. Yong and another Cambridg Friend. Mr. Ashton of Prestwich and I recede to the Bulls Head. Thence I go his Guest with Dr. Holbrook home.
13 I call on Mr. Pigott acquaint him of the Confirmacion of his seat in Prestbury Church & leave it with him, hee is well pleasd. My Lord is at the Church before 10, confirms about 500, returns about 1 to the wardens, where a plentifull and elegant dinner fills a larg company. In the Evening, Drs. Holbrook and Yarborough, Mr. Haddon, Shrigley and myself go to the Angel. Jack comes from Chester to mee. Wee stay till 10 and at home the Dr. and I till 12.
13 Attend on his Lordship at the Wardens, thence to Church, hee confirms about the same number 500. Two Tables fill'd at the Wardens with Clergy and Gentry; after dinner and a Glass to prayers. After them my Lord, the Warden, Mr. Clutterbrook, Copley &c and myself go to Hulme, Sir John Blands, where the Lady and her fine daughter perform excellently on the Harpischord in Consort. Sir John invites down and treats in a larg vault, towards the river, with variety of good wines, after this the Lady, in the parlor with a fine cold supper. Wee part hence about 9 stay a Bottle at the Wardens, I come home about 11.
15 My Lord preaches in the morning to a most frequent Congregacion esteemd to be about 5000 on 1st St. James v 22. A full and splendid dinner agen at the Wardens. Mr. Bolton preaches afternoon. After prayers the 2 Drs. Holbrook and Yarborough, Churchwardens, Mr. Shrigley and Mosse at the Angel; after at the Wardens, wee stay till 10, the Dr. and I make it 12 at home. 700 confirmd after Evening prayers.
16 My Lord and his company with the Warden and Mr. Copley sett out about 10, 2 miles short of Lime, Mr. Legh, Egerton and Cholmley with other

10 C.R.O., EDP1/254, Stockport Parish Papers.
11 *Ibid.*, EDC1/103, n.f.; EDP1/181, Macclesfield Parish Papers.

Gentlemen meet my Lord. Mrs. Legh calls me up to desire mee make Apology for the small and late Dinner, it makes about 3 a great one for itself. After Dinner and a Turn on the bowling Green, wee are calld to see the rarity proper to this place, about 100 staggs driven by the keepers to the Gate, tamely as Cattle, tho sometimes riseing and insulting each other. My Lord and Mr. Cholmley are complimented by giving their sir Names to 2 Staggs. The Hospitality receives about 40 Gentlemen and Clergymen besides servants. After Bowls and retreat to Wine supper succeeds. My Lord, Mr. Egerton and Mr. Legh retire on the subject of complying with the Government and Abjuracion. I go to my roome about 10.

17 I take a walk: About 10 the company alarmd to the Hunting of a stagg one of the herd at the Gate yesterday, about 3 couple of Hounds sett on 2 brace, but at last single out the sacred Beast. Mr. Legh, the 2 Bros Cholmley and a few more pursue on horseback, my Lord & his company ply upon the Cage, and betwixt it and the Gate of the House, the adventitious Crowd of Spectators almost fill the space, the noble Sport is seen as in a Theatre, almost every passage, the pursud Stagg, after a wide ring comes to the pool, recovers, ascends the park, trys in vain several Avenues now shutt upon him, returns to the pool, thence makes an effort toward the Stables, presst recurrs to the pool, is seizd & overturnd in it but recovers, forces again thro the Crowd pursu'd to the Wall of the Garden behind the stables, where hee panting stands a fair innocent Mark. Mr. Cholmley at the 2nd shot with a Bullet entring near the Ear brings him dead down the precipice. I am averse to the Catastrophe, abhorring cruelty. The noble sacrifice makes part of the magnificent Entertainment at dinner at which about 40. After that and a showr to the Bowls. Safe in the numbers, I ply at Ease. In the Evening the conference betwixt my Lord and Mr. Legh is renewd, the number gos to supper, I to bed agen about 10.

18 After Tea &c about 9, My Lord, Mr. Egerton, Legh, Dr. Egerton &c sett out for Buxton, thoro the park to Waley Bridg 3[m], thence to Shalcross 1, thence over Buxton Moor & in it by Whitehall 5 miles, all in a wild and uneven road to Buxton. About 12 a clock, Mr. Egerton, the Doctor, Mrs. Legh, Shalcross, Downes, Jodrel, myself and Jack go into the warm bath, swim and divert ½ an hour. After Mr. Couchée and Mr. Clutterbrook bring mee and Jack, near a mile to Pools Hool. Wee 2 only with Guides and candles enter the horrid Antrum, pass over the higherway with great difficulty to the Queen of Scotts pillars, are told and admire the Figures in the way, return thoro the lower passage, step up and see pools fancyd Cubicle, and are restord about 40 minuits from our Entrance to the Day. Wee hasten to Buxton, take remains of the Dinner, over, Mr. Statham an Atturny and Trustee for yong Mr. Pierrpont, treats all my Lord's company. Mrs. Egerton comes hither in all 42. A brisk showr falls, wee mount about in it and it is about constant over the Moors 8 miles to Bakewell where wee come steepd about 7 to the Red Lyon, common applicacion is made to avoid danger from the rain.[12] My Lord, Mr. Egerton, Mr.

12 The application in this instance was a large measure of brandy.

Legh are interrupted by Mr. Bromhall's confidence. By artifice, I remove him out of their company, I and Jack lodg at a private & decent House.

19 About 10 wee go to Church, the congregacion is great in expectacion of my Lord's sermon on the solemn Thanksgiving, hee from Fatigue is excusd. The Curate has a very unstable discourse on [?]. I see the ruinous Monuments of the Rutland Family. Mr. Bagshaw sees & compliments (with a present of course wine) the company. About 2 my Lord, Mr. Egerton, Dr. Egerton and my self in Mrs. Statham's Coach sett for Chatsworth, the rest on horseback. (Mr. Legh being return'd home) Mrs. Egerton and Mrs. Billot in the Chariot and six. Wee in an hour, come to the magnificent palace, are conducted thoro the noble Apartments admire, with them, the costly Furniture even to lassitude and stupidity. The Gardens, Groves, Fountains, Statutes [*sic*], Cascade &c are another Toyl as well as pleasure. The Duke was in the House but not seen, cause hee understood the busienes was Curiosity. A decent repast of Wine and Tea was sett to refresh the Company. Wee return'd to Bakewell about 7 and after recollection in the Inn to bed about 10.

20 All equipt about 7, Mr. Egerton treats all (horses excepted); hee and his company return to Astbury by Leek. My Lord, Mr. Clutterbrook, Couchee myself, Jack and 2 servants pass over again to Chatsworth, rise up by the stand, thoro the park to Eastmore, cross it, fall into Scaresdale, ride thoro Chesterfeild thence to Mr. Nevil's, near Oldcoats, (in all about 11 miles) about 12 a clock, wee walk down to Oldcoats, observe the great but inconvenient model and contrivance, dine, after, with Mr. Nevil, the dinner substantiall, the Beer good and old, the wine decay'd. Invited my Lord walks half a mile, to the Earl of Scarsdale's Sutton (the Earl of Nottingham). Wee are well received by the Genteel Cook, with 2 sorts of wine. I make bold for a Bottle of that after my Lord gon to bed, distinguisht by a long Cork, and am banterd for it. To bed about 11.

21 Indispos'd from the strong Beer at Mr. Nevils, wee walk about the Gardens and House, expecting dinner, till 3 when the Earl returns, Sir John Waters and 2 coaches of Ladys (8) with him. Wee sitt down to an elegant dinner of the modern mode. After it the wine of the long Cork go's (in the highest healths wee can invent) round till after 9.

22 Indisposicion continues till releivd by a Nap at Church where my Lord in the Forenoon preaches the same Sermon as at Manchester. After another exquisit dinner, prayers in the Church after, wee return to the long Corks. I desire, but fail of seeing Hardwick 3 miles, Jack sees Bolesover Castle a mile hence. Wee part early with the Earl and to our Chambers about 10.

23 About ½ hour after 6 mounted, wee ride by Welbeck and thoro a Wood the noblest Timber I ever saw, this the Duke of Newcastle's, enter on the Forest of Sherwood, pass presently, Worksop, a fair House of the Duke of Norfolk, and the Town of that name, thence 2 miles to Ryeton, an hunting seat of the late Mr.Pierrepont of Oldcoates (11 miles). The House lately burnt, the walls of the Gardens full of Fruit, wee look about ½ an hour, 700 acres (most barren) belonging to this Estate. Wee remount, ride in a most delightfull road thoro the

Forest, pass Thoresby belonging to the Marques of Dorchester, come to Rufford a noble seat belonging to Sir Geo Savile. At an ill kept Alehouse near after 7 long but fine miles, wee light, find only cold beef eatable, wee trust not the fatt and greezy Lanlady to cook up a breast of Venison shee offerd. Sir Geo. Savil sends 2 bottles prickt wine as many of hard small beer, about 4 on horsback ride in the like fine way and ayr 10 miles to Nottingham where wee come safe about 6. Wee loose no Time in running about, see the late Mr. Pierrepont's House and Gardens, the Market place and the Castle, a noble pile, Mortimers Hole &c; returnd to my Lord, drink with him and 2 Friends of his, Gregory and Farwell, above my pint of bad wine, and to bed about 11.

24 About 7 on Horsback, wee pass Wollerton a mile from Nottingham, a noble and fine situated Stone house of Sir Thomas Willoughby, the park surrounded with a new brick wall, wee pass the river Earwash (dividing the Counties) at Stapleford, come to Derby, leaving a place calld Little Chester a mile on the right hand, to Derwent, over which a good Bridg into the Town 12 miles, before 11 to the sign of the Buck Couchant. Wee go to All Hallows, (a fair Church with a remarkable high steeple) to prayers (the day of St. Bartholemew). Wee observe here the Monuments of the Devonshire family well preservd in a Chapell on the south side of the Chancel. Din'd about 2, wee mount, come (10 miles) to Ashborne about 5. My Lord fatigud, go's to bed about 6. The Curat comes to the Inn, knows little of our way forward. I leave him with Mr. Clutterbrook and to bed about 10.

25 My Lord rises and calls, about 3 wee are ready and mount about 4 in Moonshine, presently cross the River Dove, rise the mountains into the Morelands of Staffordshire, fall into difficult roads in a barren and wild country, the road falls down a steep rocky way to a dry Channel of rude and horrid aspect, after half a mile wee meet the stream, falling at once out of sight under its bed or chanell, proceed over wild Mores, a rude road, uneven precipices; after 4 hours at a good rate for the way come to Leek 8 miles in their Account. Here at the Cock wee stay about 2 hours, trimmed and refresht wee cross the Charnet at the Town, enter into almost equall unpleasant roads, ride by Horton, leave Mole on the left, Biddulph on the right hand, ascend the Summit limitts of the Countys, descend about 2 miles and come (8 such miles) to Astbury about 1. The Family just din'd another dinner is prepard. The Dr. and his Lady entertain freely, the House previous one all side, filld with workmen and Noise of Axes and Hammers. About 5 sett hence in a fine cheerfull way. The Dr. brings my Lord to Hulms chapell where the Ale falls short of its Character. Wee come to Midlewich about 7, to the Queens Arms. Mr. Cowper comes and stays an hour. To bed about 10.

26 About 7 (the weather and way fair) sett hence, at Kelsall a dusting showr drives us under the Shelter of Trees. I borrow at Tarvin, Mr. Gerrards Coat for my Lord. Wee come (D.O.M.G) safe to the palace about 11. Wee presently drink Tea and after my Suzy and I dine there. After some repose to Letters and Busienes.

27 The weather turns rainy. At 8 Mr. Chancellor and I wait on my Lord about

Admission of a Curate to Hindley Chapell. After morning prayers Mr. Hindley, Mr. Worthington & John Prescott and others on Mr. Lever's part chosen by the Inhabitants, and Mr. Alanson and Mr. Smith on his part chosen by Mr. Finch. Those prove the Eleccion by the people for 6 or 7 successions not interrupted save in Bishop Pearsons time, by Mr. Samuel Shaw and they produce a Copy of a Decree in Chancery of the Dutchy, to confirm that custome. These mainly plead the original Right of the Rector which is eccepted too in the Sentence of Consecracion says the Custom was broken in Mr. Shaws time, is not directly, but by precarious interpretacion, intended to bee confirmd by the Decree and that the remissnes of the Rectors, ought not to hinder the present successor. The Chancellor and my self appear averse to popular Elections. My Lord blames the remissnes of his predecessors, who were also Rectors of Wigan, especially the last in complying with the Election of Mr. Jackson by the Inhabitants. Hee seems rather to incline to the precedents, but takes time, a fortnight, to deliberate and to write to Mr. Finch, now at York. I dine after 18 days absence with my own Flock. In the Evening at the Coach and Horses with Mr. Hall, Seignor Vagany gos thence with mee to Sir Hen. Bunburys where wee cheerfully drink our Bottles and part not till 12.

28 Indisposd take a walk of 4 Turns, write to my Coz. Parre. After dinner and repose, I wait on my Lord at the palace. Sir Tho. Parker and Mr. Nathaniel Lea are with him. I sitt down for two hours, the Glass and discourse proceed freely; after those gon I stay the domestic supper – Bottles, wee part past 9. I lend Mrs. Whaley upon her Note 2^{li}.

29 The News brings both the great armys in sight of Lisle and each other and all people to the expectacion of the Event. Mr. Lancaster preaches in the Quire on psal. 139 v.7. My Lord sends to mee to dine with him and last Nights company. In the Even, after prayers, I (Jack with mee) take 4 Turns on roodee. After recreate and conclude in my domestic pint.

30 This day (Q.B.E.) my son Jack finishes the 18 year of his Age, tis domesticly remembered. Apply to Busienes and Books. The Judges, Jeckell and Pocklington come to Town attended slenderly by the Highsheriff Daniel and his company. Wee earnestly expect News but are adjournd to the next post. Mr. Clutterbrook, Mr. Maryon ill flusterd and I drink a Bottle of my wine. I writt agen to my coz. Parre to receive mony for Peggy Birchall.

31 Mr. Whaley after the last experiment with Mr. Marsh tells mee hee and his wife wholy rely on my favor and compassion, my Inclinacion is greater than my Circumstance. I make no promise nor dos the Bargain seem to allow of it. Mr. Gregory, from St. Asaph calls, wee conclude on this day sevenight to bee there. It rains almost continually, Sir Hen Bunbury, Sir Geo. Warburton, Mr. Cholmley &c dine with my Lord. In the Even, Dr. Thane & I take our pints at the Bacchus, after hee comes home with mee, wee find Mr. and Mrs. Couchee, sister Partington &c, finish another Bottle about 10.

SEPTEMBER 1 After a rainy night the morning so. I lend 6^{li} more to Mr. Whaley on his Note, hee is importunate for 20^{li}. Apply to Busienes and Books, to my Lord to speak to the Judg on Alderman Johnsons Account. Lord Rivers, the 2 Judges, 2 County Members, Sir Tho. Manwaring and Sir Tho. Aston &c dine this day with my Lord. In the Evening, at the Blew Posts with Mr. Chancellor, Archdeacon, Mr. Elcock and Proby, wee drink our pints and part about 8.

2 A fair cool morning giving hopes of the future weather. After early prayers, my Suzy & I are at Tea with my Lord who, with the Archdeacon takes his coach for Oulton, about 9, the Chancellor follows about 10. My Suzy & I dine with Mrs. Pierrepont, a roasted haunch caput prandii. Wee sitt till 4. After prayers, I take 4 shorter Turns on roodee. I write to Mr.Ludlow about Mrs. Stephens Legacy and after a domestic pint to bed after 10.

3 After early prayers see the News, which says the Allyes took on the 5th the Counterscarp before Lisle in sight of the French Army, which not attempting to releive the Town retir'd towards Tournay. I go down to the Hall where Alderman Johnsons cause is heard. The evidence about the words confusd, and on the other hand, his complyance with the Government and Settlement of the Crown, in the House of Hanover well attested, the Judg is severe in direccion of the Jury, who after half an hour recess, bring him in Guilty. Mr. Morrey dines with mee, after wee at my Ale, sitt till 4. I draw a Form of peticion for the parishioners of Hool, about 2 Galleries. At 8 invited by Mr. Pierrpont at the palace, where treated with venison, wine and Fruit, wee stay till 10.

4 At early prayers: About 8 Mr. Whaley comes, repeats his hard Circumstance which alwaies affects mee. I lend him to serve his present necessity and to avoid Arrests 4^{li}. About 9, I go down to the Hall to see Mr. Johnson, the Judges come, and his Cause calld. The Chief Justice, in a long prefatory Harangue, setts forth the revolucion Settlement on the House of Hanover, and the Union, aggravates Dissaffection to and especially scandal and reflection, comends the Gentlemen for the prosecucion of this Crime, and after some pause on the value of Mr. Johnsons Estate, real and personal as in 3 Affadavits before the Court, Hee tells him The Court thinks fitt to fine him in 40 marks (26^{li}:13:4d) that hee stand comitted till it bee paid, and give Surety for good behavior for 3 years. Hee pays the Sheriff by Note the mony, gives Bond for good behavior presently and is dischargd by proclamacion. Hee treats with Tea at the Coffee house in Castle Lane and I part with him about 11. After Dinner Mr. Hebblethwait brings Mr. Lambert's Letter, a Decree (ready ingrosst) to settle a Court at Kendale. I read the Translacion of Cicero of Freindship. Solace in my domestic pint at night. A constant rain from noon to Night.

5 The News confirm the lodgment on the Counterscarp but not till the 7th of theirs, the 27th of August of our stile. Mr. Fogg preaches in the Quire on psalm 51, v.3. Wee dine with Mrs. Pierrpont on roast Beef and venison. It rains most of the day. I (after prayers) answer Mr. Lambert's Letter. After at 8 to the palace where after one domestic Bottle had among 4 wee return about 9.

6 Mr. Whaley in his usual importunate way comes to mee for advice how to procure an Employment, detains mee till Mr. Foulks succeeds importunatly for mony. I hence take 4 shorter Turns on roodee. In the Evening Mr. Howard a painter and scholar sees my Coins. I present him with 3 smal English coins. Mr. Edwards the Stamp Inspector sends for mee to the Bacchus where Mr. Foulks and Adams with him, wee drink on freely, send for the News which brings Lisle to Capitulacion. Wee stay till 1. Mr. Foulks treating.

7 Severely indisposd; Mr. Whaley comes early. I write to Mr. Styth and Swerbreck to assist him in enquiry after an office in the Custom House. About 10 I take horse, come to Vale Royal before 1. Here is a full and good Company. I find my Lord and Mr. Egerton expected mee sooner to Oulton. Here is a plentifull dinner and good wine, this detains us past 5. Wee come to Oulton before 7, prayers, then supper ended, wine and Decanters succeed, keep my Lord, Mr. Egerton, Drs. Thane and Egerton and myself till 11.

8 About 9, the morning not rainy wee sett hence by Petty Pool, Northwich &c to Arley, come before 12. Here is another full and laudable company, 20 in number, an agreeable Dinner, excellent Ale & Beer and indifferent wine which Sir Geo. promotes, after dinner. Sir Fran Leicester, Sir Hen Bunbury, Sir Peter Soames, Mr. Egerton, Cholmley of Vale Royal, Drs. Egerton and Thane, Mr. Legh of Whitchurch, his brother Egerton, Mr. James Banks &c. are of the company. Mr. Lord, Mr. Egerton and the 2 Doctors sett hence about 5. Mr. Maryon and I stay another Flask, setts out near 6 in a great showr which continues to Northwich, the darkness follows, wee with difficulty find the way, missing it twice, but come, cum Deo, safe to Oulton in prayers before 9, return to good Wine till 12.

9 A fair morning rises, wee walk to St. Peter's Well, see the new Apartments and their fine Furniture. The Coach (wherein Mrs. Pierrpont and my Suzy) comes after prayers and 12. Lord Kilmory with the Vale Royal Family come, Mr. Wells and Mr. Cowper from that Quarter, a good Company to a plentifull Table generous and full recepcion. Tho Mr. Egerton had from the first been signally gentile and engageing to my Lord, had pursud it here in a whole weeks plentifull and splendid recepcion of his and his Company, yet today hee seemd to give to his Friendship greater improvement and perfecion by subscripcion of 100^{li} to the repair and beautifying of the Quire.[13] 2 Coaches and the rest on horsback sett out about 5, wee come from Stanford Bridge in the dark and reach Chester (D.G.) safe before 8. The company (as invited) the Chancellor added meet at the palace about 8 Sir Hen. Bs railery trys several of us and the Chancellor till hee grew chagrin. Wee are treated with pontac and part about 11.

10 The public papers are uncertain about the Affairs in Flanders; the weather continues dull and rainy. After diversion in Books, I go over to Sir Hen. Bunburys where my Lord Bishop, Sir Peter Soames, Mr. Egerton, Mr. Chancellor, Dr. Thane, Mrs. Clutterbrook, Maryon, Kendrick and myself are generously and fully treated with good wine; railery and liberty are revivd, to a great degree, the Glass runs freely and the Time till 12.

13 Of the Cathedral.

11 Extremely indispos'd yet, calld, step over to Mr. Egerton about 10. After dinner, several and the last William Holland formerly of Lathom, calls on mee. I entertain 'em freely, with my own Ale, this proves tedious to myself. In the Evening step to the palace, where wee end the day in the usual quota of pontac.

12 My indisposicion extremely aggravated, notwithstanding Elixir, confines mee home. My Lord preaches and confirms (about 40) at Christleton, Mr. Clutterbrook (it seems) first trys his Talent there, at preaching. After prayers and about 7, in the rain, wee go to the palace. I here keep up an unhappy degree of heat, by a pint of pontac to my share and part about 10, this the day my Lord Bishop enterd on the 38th year of his Age, wee celebrate the Birth day, at home and in the palace.

13 Repeated Elixir scarce helps my unhappy malady. My Lord gos to Sir John Crews, the Forenoon bright and pleasant, the after rainy. I apply much to Books and some Busienes. I receive a Letter from the Bishop of St. Asaph with his sermon on the 19th August, by the Carrier. Sent for at 8, my Suzy and I go to the Chancellor where I find my Lord, Drs. Thane & Norris, with him. I deliver a sermon from the Bishop of St. Asaph directed, to my Lord, it is partly read & comended; the wine is good and the quantity moderate, wee part at 10.

14 The indisposicion is still continud with its unhappy effects. The News holds the world yet in suspense about the storming of Lisle and attacking the French Army. I take 4 Turns on roodee and am recreated. After dinner, solace, returning to Books & Busienes. Mr. Whaley comes, tells mee his success at Leverpool, desires mee to speak to my Lord for his Letter to Mr. Andrews of the Customs, I do so and gives mee some incouragement. I show my Lord the Commissary's draught of an Instrument to constitute a Court at Kendal, hee orders some Correction and omission of some Clauses. I go with his Lordship and Mr. Clutterbrook to Archdeacon Thanes, the Chancellor and Warden of Manchester come to us, wee drink 2 small Flasks and 1 Bottle and part before 10.

15 After a rainy and melancholy Night a rainy day, till night constantly. Apply to Busienes, write to the Bishop of St. Asaph, include a special Form of Commission to his Chancellor, in his absence, this winter. Correct the Draught from the Commissary. Mr. Whaley brings mee a Letter from Mr. John Gillibrand threatening Foreclosure by Bill and tells mee of another Donn for 4^{li} and upwards, here in the City. I write a Note directed to himself promising him to supply him with 6^{li} by Michaelmas and draw a Testimonial of him to the Bishop in order to his Letter to Mr. Andrews. In the Evening I meet Mr. Cowper of Midlewich, at the Bacchus, wee have a single Bottle of good wine over which hee tells mee surprizeing Things of Mr. Lownds, of his having 2 or 3 Children by several women, and suspected of conversacion with Mrs. Walley. Wee dip in and commend the Bishop of St. Asaph's sermon and part about 9.

16 The morning fair, my S. and self at early prayers, thence with Mr. and Mrs. Dennis, to my House in Abby Court. Wee conclude on his having it at 6^{li} per Annum, hee paying Tax for the windows and rent for the Water, and to enter at

Michaelmas, hee pays mee a Double Luidore (1^{li};14s) in hand. Returning home (Deus bene) Mr. Whaley meets mee, tells mee his craving town Creditors requires 40s to day. I give him (Q.B.E.) the Luid'or, have all along dreadfull apprehensions on the general Bargain. I wait on my Lord before 9. Hee discourses on the Table of Fees, promises to consult other Bishops especially on the particulars of Letters of Orders. About 10 a clock Mr. Whaley comes sweating for the other 6s to pay Harper his Creditor, I lend it. I write to John Cross. After dinner I attend Mr. Legh of Lyme at Sir Hen. Bunburys, hee comes on. I shew him Jacks poems on his Staggs. After I go with him to the palace, hee stays an hour with my Lord. Jack gives him a fair Copy of his poems, hee is exceedingly pleas'd with them. I go with him to the Castle, thence to the Bear, where after a Bottle of good wine, hee setts about 5 to Eaton. Dr. Thane desires and I meet him at the Bacchus, at 6 My coz. Kendric is there with him. They enter upon a discourse of their mony, the former 50^{li} the other 1500^{li} to Mrs. Kingston, the Drs. personal the other real security. The Dr. shews peevishnes and despair, the other inward repose, in his great security. This scene is ungratefull and tormentous to mee, conscious of my own obligacions, from which God in his good time deliver mee. The rest of the time is dully & insipidly spent. Uneasy I urg to part which wee do, at the end of one Bottle about 8. I take refuge at the palace where my Lord &c, I and my S. stay while more generous wine and discourse, go off till near 10. A small rain keeps up the rivers about, of the consequence of which general complaints and fearful Apprehension. Mr. Whaley showd mee his answer to Mr. Gillibrand.

17 After an uneasy Night, rise about 8 in a rainy day. The News carrys the famous Seige heavily on and the Swede beyond the Nieper, Sardinia surrender'd and Fenestrells taken by Savoy. Mr. Legh sends Jack a Guinea. I draw a Letter from my Lord to Mr. Andrews, after morning prayer. I bring it to him, hee likes it and signs it. I presently meet Mr. Whaley who takes a Copy of it. After dinner Mr. Swerbreck calls on mee and after prayers Mr. Lambert. I go with him to my Lord, who tells him the reason of his Alteracion of his Grant, and presently dispatches the correct one. Wee go down to the Bear where the Chancellor, ArchDeacon, Mr. Kendric and Maryon at good wine, wee drink our Bottles and part at 9.

18 The quantity tho not much occasions unhappy and uneasy Reflections. I deliver the Grant to Mr. Lambert. Hee gives to Mr. Couchée and my self, each a Guinea, to Mr. Roberts half a one. Mr. Whaley calls for my Letter wherein I affectionatly represent his Case to Mr. Styth, I lend him 20^{li} on this expedicion to Leverpool. I affected with his & my own difficultys recurr to roodee in a fair interval, take 6 Turns in deep meditacion, (2 of these long ones), am releiv'd (D.G.) by them. After noon rain, after prayers and a Letter to Mr. Bowyer. I go to the Candidates for Ordinacion at the Bacchus where 8 of the 12. The discourse resolves in whether of the Universities is more ancient and whether a right and left Hand in Nature, very indifferently managd. It ends about 9.

19 A fair cool morning. The Letters bring in a Hornwork before Lisle at the expense of 2000 killd & wounded. Mr. Lancaster has a sermon on the occasion.[14] After prayers, Dr. Griffith and Mr. Denham, see mee. After my Suzy and I wait on my Lord till 9. Thence to Sir H. B. where 2 Bottles stay mee till 12.

20 The morning fair, I send John to Capenhurst for 6 Bottles of Dr. Griffiths good wine. I write to my coz. Barton of Rufforth a Letter consolatory about my coz. his good wifes dangerous illness. I deliver to my Lord (takeing Coach for Aston) Jacks Lyme verses. I write to Mr. Vaudrey and Parre; the day dull with some rain. After prayers and Books to the Coffee house where the News about 7 is only repeated in the Letters. My Lord, the Chancellor and Dr. Norris with him returns past 8. Wee stay with Him, at the palace, till 9. I am surpris'd by my coz. Parrs Letter telling mee, hee shall quickly use the 200^{li}.

21 Mr. Whaley comes, tells mee of his insuccess at Leverpool, desires my further applicacion to my Lord; a Mist, scarce rain, driven by the south wind. This being the Feast of St. Matthew, Mr. Aldersey preaches in the Quire. My Lord rebukes the rude behavior of one of the blew Boys. A company of 20 in number dine with my Lord, sitt till prayers. I go with Mr. Egerton to his Horse at the Barrs, I tell him of Mr. Whaleys extreme difficulty, hee lays it on their expensive Liveing and shews no Bowells. After prayers I attend on my Lord to Dr. Norris, here his Lordship, the Chancellor, Drs. Norris, Thane & myself in liberal discourse, take our Bottles of good wine, return to the palace about 9, thence home before 10.

22 After a Night of tormenting thoughts on Mr. Whaleys and my own difficulties, rise to early prayers. After these fly to 4 Turns (2 long) on roodee. Mr. Whaley comes, I tell him as the Bishop promisd hee will speak to Mr. Andrews and join with him in what is proper, on Mr. W's behalf. I apply to and enter 5 Deanaries. I receive Mr. Egerton's Letter about his meeting my Lord at Broxon tomorrow, and answer it. I write agen to Mr. Styth, still solicit his Favor and tell him what my Lord has promis'd in joining with Mr. Andrews on Mr. W's account. At 5 I wait on my Lord, where the Dean and Prebendarys are takeing leave of him. After their recess my S. and I stay on, a free and cheerfull Bottle of pontac part at 10. Mr. Clutterbrook & Maryon follow us home and wee empty one of Dr. Griffiths bottles and to bed about 10.

23 A fair and hopefull morning & (Q.B.E.), the beginning of this Term. I go to early prayers. After equip for Whitchurch, my S. in the stage. My Lords coach setts out a ½ hour after 9, wee come in a fair morning to Broxon about 1. Mr. Egerton receives the company with good wines, ale, Ham and Tong; shows my Lord all the rooms and conveniences of the House, generously offers it to him for a summer retreat and advises him to take the Tiths of the Township for the accomodacion of his stable, especially my Lord and Mr. Peirrepont, are well pleas'd with the House &c. The Coach gos about 4, Mr. Clutterbrook, Couchée and myself stay some bottles after, till past 5, then cheerfull and warm reach Whitchurch in an hour & Quarter. I go to the Georg to Mr. Bunbury, who

14 Marlborough captured Lille and proceeded to dismantle the fortifications.

comes to the Red Lyon and sitts with my Lord. Wee part about 10, my S. and I dispos'd, to a private lodging.

24 My Lord proceeds about 8. My S. and I after seeing Mr. Leigh, Mr. Jenks and Burges, go hence about 11 in a fine road, till wee come to the Finger which directs to Bangor, wee come thither about 2 find Mr. & Mrs. Jones at home. Wee walk about and in the Church (I hope an auspicious and happy place to us both) for a stomach; return to the rectory to our dinner about 4. Mr. Archdeacon Shore (sent to) kindly comes, wee are cheerfull together past 8 with the Archdeacon, return by the Moon.

25 The morning dusky not rainy, wee part with our kind Friends about 11, come to Wrexham at 12. Wee dine with my mother Puleston and sister Jones, My uncle Eyton and his 2 daughters come to us after, wee sett hence after 4 and reach Chester (D.G.) safe past 6. The company from the palace comes to see, and take leave with us; stay freely past 10. In this time, Mr. Whaley's brother Henry and his Solicitor Mr. Nayler come to mee, tell mee a series of Mr. Whaleys practice in drawing about 150^{li} from him, on his single bond, they desire my Assistance, I promise my Freindship. After Elixir to bed about 11.

26 The weather holds fair. I see the News now speaking great and hopefull successes about Lisle vid. a body of 18000 defeated by Cadogan indevoring to intercept stores and provisions in 700 wagons and 3000 of Monsieur Le Motts said Army killd, the Garison in want of powder and a supply prevented. Mr. Whaley comes under great Apprehensions of his brothers designing an Accion against his body and Goods. After phisic, I stay at home till Even prayer. After these Mr. Cartwright comes and draws a Judgment from Mr. Whaley to mee of 62^{li}. Hee with utmost suspicion consults how to avoid Arrest. I extremely share in his confusion. After releif from a domestic pint to bed before 11. The Chancellor and Mr. Maryon sett out about 2 for Whitchurch.

27 The night not without unhappy reflexions, is something reliev'd by a fair morning. Wee go to the palace and see my Lord's Children, take leave of them, they takeing Coach about 9. I give to Harry for his Quarterage to Mr. Henchman 10s. I write the first Time (Q.B.E.) to Mr. Gellibrand about my purpose to undertake Mr. W's estate. In the Evening, Mrs. Whaley comes to mee, tells her melancholy story, wherein much of her Husbands unaccountable Falsities in concealing and colouring his debts to her, shee begs my expedicion in the purchase, and is ready & desirous to join in the sale. Mr. Foulks is obstinate in delivering Blanks to mee, and plainly refuses, so that my Busienes is ad incitas redactum. The Account is stated and I give him an acknowledgment of 103^{li} in Arrear, upon this hee pleasd to send more blanks, this added to Mr. Whaley's affairs impresses deep. In the Evening, Mr. Egerton sends for mee. Hee the Archdeacon and I go down to the Bear, recreate in 3 Bottles of good wine and return about 9.

28 Difficulties return in a bright morning. Upon his earnest Letter I lend Mrs. Whaley 4^{li} and rather this morning than last day give my Acknowledgment to Mr. Foulks upon which the Stamps succeed. I apply to roodee and by 4 full Turns am recreated. About 11 Dr. Thane, myself and Jack mount for Farndon,

come to Ince about 12 where Mr. Egerton is surrounded by his Friends, wee dine and the horses are drawn to the Feild at 3. About ½ hour after, Hee & Mr. Minshall slips a pole and darts directly on him and his Horse, bruises him on the thigh and shocks him and his horse severely. Mr. Egerton looses a stirrup and betwixt recovery of that and himself the Horse trips and falls. Mr. Egerton amazd falls of and is not able to stand from the stroak. His horse recoverd back and further than the place of the Fall, hee remounts, gallops in, is weighd but disturbd. The Gentlemen exclaim at the unfair & barbarous action of Minshal and adjudge the wager (50 Guineas) to Mr. Egerton. Minshal confesses (from shooting the pole) hee had lost. Yet after on pretence Mr. E. did not remount where hee fell rideing the Course again. Wee return home about 6 and the Archdeacon and myself over 1 Bottle recount the misfortune at the Bacchus and return about 9, returning from Farndon I see Mr. Vaudreys man who tells mee That Stamps are orderd for mee thence, which is welcome recreacion to mee.
29 I go to early prayers, the weather turns rainy. From a fearfull Letter last night from him, I go to Mr. Whaleys house, hee in bed. I indevor to lessen their fear of his Arrest, thence to Mr. Cartwright on that affair, thence to Mr. Egerton who, from his Blow, was in bed. Mr. Wilbraham is there writeing the transacion to Lord Cholmley. Mr. Edwards, Inspector of the Stamps after his view of the office, parts civilly & satisfy'd. Mrs. Whaley (by her daughter) sends mee word, her son is accusd by a woman from Manchester for selling half a Guinea for 8s and that upon tryal of it provd only a Farthing, shee threatens further prosecucion and pillory. Shee begs 12s to prevent this. I lend it her imediatly. Mr. Molding dines with us. After prayers Dr. Thane, Mrs. J. Wright, Walsh, Molding and myself take our bottles at the Bacchus, wee are alarmd by the Fire Bell, upon occasion of the Hostler by a candle putting an old barn and stable behind the Green Dragon into a Flame, this comes near and threatens Capt. Hultons house. I go thither, find consternacion and disorder yet great industry in the Citizens to prevent the progress of the Fire which (D.L.) it does about 11.
30 Discompos'd I take 4 full pensive Turns on roodee. Upon another urgent Letter Mr. Whaley receives from mee 3^{li};14s. I write to Sam. Prescott and John Crosse. After prayers and some busienes, I go down to see Mr. Egerton. After Mr. Wilbraham, Done, Egerton of Shaw and Peak gon, I stay a Bottle with Dr. Egerton, expect, but in vain, the post till 11.

OCTOBER 1 Q.F.F.E.F.S. I begin this month with early prayers. After see the papers of News which for want of Mayles repeat in other Terms. In a delicate day I take 4 full Turns on roodee. Hen. Whaley comes here, insists, importunes and threatens, sometimes submits his case to mee and is particularly concerned for 50^{li} for which hee is Surety. Hee and his sister meet here, fall into passion, accusation, recriminacion, it seems shee has bin perfidiously treated by the Whaleys. Shee is all confusion almost to desperacion, I heartily condole her misfortune. I apply to processes for the visitacion. In the Evening, Mrs. Whaley comes, I show her a short prospect of the whole Charg, melancholy to both. I relax in a domestic pint and with imprest ideas, to bed after 10.

2 After a morning of tormenting reflection rise to early prayers. I write to my Lord (inclosing a Letter) an Account of Mr. Egerton's accident at Farndon, apply to Busienes. Mrs. Whaley sends her daughter to crave 50^{s} an instant debt to one Dean a Baliff, I send it with reluctancy. After prayers at 6 Dr. Thane and I go down to Mr. Egerton, the Dr. his brother only with him. Wee are desird to stay, drink 1 Bottle, return before 10.

3 Rise something less indispos'd, go to early prayers. After see the News takeing the Raveling & Tenaills in the Ditch. Mr. Fogg has an excellent discourse in the Quire on Phil. 3;20. I receive the Holy Sacrament and D.G. cum hac insolitam Animi alacritatem.[15] In the Even, Mr. Torvin son of that of Warwick sees us with my coz. Prescott's comendacions. After him wee go over to part with Sir Hen. B. designing to sett towards London tomorrow. Wee indevor to persuade him to stay till my Lady go. Hee (as usual) entertains freely with a Bottle and with difficulty, wee part near 12.

4 Not rainy, nor bright, at early prayers. I apply to entering the Lancashire Deanaries. After dinner Mrs. Whaley sends her poor sensible daughter with a Letter from Mr. W. almost a week absconded, in the country, and desires mee to send, which I do, 10s. The adversity of this Family strikes deep, falling in with the difficulties it has now involv'd mee. I go over to take leave with Sir H. Bunbury going but digressing to London. My Lady shews more than ordinary Concern at his going so soon without her. After prayers I finish the entry of the Deanaries & indevor to recreate in a pint of Scotch about 9.

5 In a rainy morning, at early prayers. The papers, tho no Mail, give hopes of takeing Lisle. I fill the processes of the Lancashire Deanaries. Mr. Chancellor inter agribudines meas sends mee a Letter with my Bond, dated 1 Jan. 1700 for 30^{li} inclos'd, having indors'd the payment of 10^{li}, this is a sharp extremity. I return the Bond beg yet his patience and inclose 4 Guineas. His man gon, Briscoe the Smith desires his mony (1^{li}.3s) for work in the Abby Court. I desire too his forebearance. Mr. Pemberton, Vicar of Hanmer[16] desires my advice about Tith-hay and gives mee for it quasi virgula divina donum 5s.[17] After prayers I go to Mr. Egerton, where the Chancellor and Mr. Foulks haud faciles Creditores, yet this accident is an alleviacion. Wee with other company are free, the Glass gos round till ½ hour after 8.

6 Indisposicion detains mee from early prayers. I recurr to roodee where I take 4 full Turns, consider what is proper for Alderman Allens Monument, reduce it rudely into writeing. After dinner and Busienes Mr. Speed, Grocer, Creditor to Mr. Whaley of 8^{li}.13s calls on mee, is earnest for my promise, which I refuse. Hee threatens fore hee returns home to enter his Accion against Mr. W. After prayers Dr. Thane, I go down to Mr. Egerton, find Mr. Done and Mr. James Egerton with him. A discourse of Apparicions is started, the Glass moves freely

15 Trans: 'with it, thanks be to God, unaccustomed joy of mind.'
16 C.R.O., EDV2/14.
17 Trans: 'as if by a divining rod a gift of 5s.'

(Mr. Egerton excepted) round till 9. I writ to Anthony Close and inclosd a Copy of the Grant for a Consistory at Kendale.

7 At early prayers, the morning frosty invites mee my indisposicion to 4 full Turns. A Court today makes them brisk and releiving. Peter Slaynhead appears in Court, inter Causus, rudely applys him to the Chancellor, asks him (with indecent laughter) whether hee had answerd the Questions on paper hee gave him, and tells him hee is ready to pay him for his answers 5 Guineas, and makes ostentacion to produce them, and tells That hee had a paper in his hand, which if hee will answer, hee will give him four score Guineas, or to this effect. The Chancellor blames this behavior admonishes and gives him caution to bee silent and civil, yet hee continues rude & loud very indecent in his words, slighting Excommunicacion, saying hee had bin excommunicated, knew the charge of it and how to come off and to that purpose continuing his noise and rudeness. The Chancellor admonishes him 1°, 2° et 3° solemnly and hee not ceasing his rude behavior and contempt, the Chancellor decrees him contumacem ac in poenam excommunicandum esse.[18] I examine 2 Wittnesses on Chadocks, 3 on Houghtons behalf, finish about 8 recreate about 9.

8 After an extreme cold Night a sharp frost, at early prayers. The News tells the French Army retreated under the Canon of Bruges, the seige of Lisle succeeding, of 1300 [*sic*] reduced to 5000 in the Towne and that tis accounted as lost, by the French. I examine 2 more Wittnesses on Houghtons part. I receive Mr. Gillibrand's answer, kind and full, and Sam. Prescotts opinion of the purchase: these are to mee providential and refreshing. After dinner I correct my Epitaph on Alderman Allen nearer satisfacion. After prayers (Jack along) take 2 full Turns on roodee. Mrs. Whaley comes, repeats her melancholy History, in variety of passions and keeps us in this sad diversion past 10.

9 A milder yet frosty morning I go to early prayers and after in a pleasant Ayr take 4 full Turns. I write to my coz. Prescott to offer the Bank and my small meadow to my coz. Holt for 1200^{li}, the meadow I value at 150^{li}. To Mr. Gillibrand that I gratefully comply with the Favors in his Letter, if this offer to my coz. Holt succeeds not, and that at the visitacion at Blackburn the 26th current I shall bee positive and to John Cross about Ja. Aspinwall, and of what I had writt to my coz. Prescott. Mrs. Whaley sends her daughter for and has 5s. After prayers Mr. Chancellor Coll. Proby, Mr. Allen and I go to the Bacchus, The Coll. is a well bred man easy, not vain, talks and sings well. Wee stay 3 Bottles and part before 9 the Evening very cold.

10 A very bright morning. The News not without Clouds. Maj. Gen. Webb come over as feard with ill boding News that the promisd General Attack on Lisle was on Thursday last, the Beseigers having recoverd to the Ditch. Mr. Newton at his cursory rate, preaches in the Quire on Prov. 14 v. 14. After prayers expecting him, I draw out Mr. Whaley's Charg now 965^{li};16;8. After to Reading, thence to Recreacion in a domestic pint, till 10.

18 *Ibid.*, EDC1/103 n.f. Trans: 'contumacious and in pain of excommunication.'

11 The morning releives the severe Torments of the Night. At early prayers Ned Roberts gos to Malpas, Jack to Wrexham to fetch my sister Jones. The weather milder and the occasion perswades to roodee where I perform 4 Turns. I inclose a petition from Blowick to my Lord, write to Mr. Vaudrey and my Coz. Parre. Mrs. Whaley, about 3, comes and tells mee shee has sent to her Husband, her son Henry, to come home and wonders hee came not on Sunday night and if hee come not (for shee suspects H. to bee false like his Father), Shee will send Thomas tomorrow. After prayers I begin the last Visitacion account. My Sister Jones comes about 7 and, with reasons, declares shee has wholly rejected Mr. Ridley. I recreate in a domestic pint, to bed about 11.

12 A brisk morning the wind (as several daies past) at East. I go to early prayers after these to the News which reduces all the outworks to the Ditch and takes port Mohun in Minorca I go down to Roodee, revolve and begin to suspect Mr. W. in some false practice. At my return, I meet Mr. Vaudreys Letter which is reasonably instant for mony. This read the Collectors come in for 2^{li} half year tax for the office. I pay it under these aggravacions. I by chance hear my daughter Peggy read the 6, 7 & 8 ver. of psalm 62 which (with comfort) balance the other contrary accidents. I receive a Letter from my Lord, kind and cheerful. After dinner step to Mrs. Whaley where I see a miserable scheme of relative duties, shee inveighing against her husband, her son H. just come in from Daniels Ash, gives her suspicion, contradicions. Hee promises to try to find his father by going to Mr. Whitealls, coachman of Broughton. Mr. Foulks sends mee a Bond to read, it adds to the rest, I consider. After prayers I meet Tho. the younger son. Hee tells mee his brother is gon for his Father, this alleviates suspicion. I call on my S. and sister Jones at my bro. Partingtons shop. Hence wee go to my brother Ned Puleston to wait on Mr. R. Mostyns 2 daughters and bring 'em over to my bro Partingtons. Wee come home before 8. I indevor to obliterate my sadd impressions of the day but find 'em almost insuperable in the night.

13 After a severe Night refresh at early prayers. By their effect I write to Mr. Cotton and Mr. Staples of Inner Temple Lane, preparing for Court of Visitacion of the Deanries of Chester and Wirral. Mr. Wm. Massie comes gives mee a Bag of mony in consideracion of my pains and Charges to London on his Account. I did not expect it, but esteem it in this difficult Crisis as a prompt and most seasonable assistance of the Almighty providence of God and desire to bee thankfull. I after count the mony and it amounted to 19^{li};3s. I reverence and rejoice at this great if not miraculous dispensacion. The matter of the Court is easy. After, I see Mr. Whaley recount to him and rebuke his Falsities, his wife dos so with too much passion. Mr. Cartwright by our consent, is to draw Articles or Contract in order to the Bargain. After dinner write to Mr. Egerton about his health, to Mr. Morrey about wine. After prayers step to Mr. Whaley find him in his papers; hee tells mee the interest I paid to Hatfeild and Dannald is included in a Judgment. I have reason to suspect him false here; hee gives mee a Note of near 100^{li} in debts in the Town, a new amazement. While I stay, a Dunn comes for horsehire 10s. I lend it, go dissatisfied, recreat about 8 in a domestic pint

which yet cures not the new impressions.
14 After a stormy and uneasy night to early prayers. After these I apply to Mr. W's Letters, put them into order and find his assertion about the Interest mistake or imposicion. A Court of small busienes. I examine 1 Wittnes a parte Gilbert. Mr. Cartwright sends mee a rough draught of the Articles twixt Mr. Whaley and I. I write to Mr. Shaw with regard to Mr. Atherton. I send the Articles to Mr. W., hee writes for mony. After prayer Mr. Powel calls on mee, who with Mr. Chancellor and myself go to the Bacchus wee drink 4 pints freely. I return about nine. Mr. Powel with some reasons assurd us that the young Heir to Dunkenhall, is sent to bee educated at Winchester School which wee congratulate.
15 After a severe Night, morning remains. I go to early prayers. See and take leave with Mr. Powel. The News gives great hope of the surrender of Lisle by Capitulacion. I send by Jack 10^{li} to Mr. Whaley. I go to Roodee perform 4 long, 2 short Turns, in deep meditacion on my great undertaking. Wee are invited by my sister Partington, to dine there with my Lady Bunbury. Whilst here the Eleccion of Mayor proceeds without opposicion. Alderman Manwaring is chosen. Mr. Cumberbach the 1st Sheriff, Mr. Denton the 2nd, about which Eleccion a controversy at larg, but Denton carries it by 100 votes. I go Jack along to Mr. W. convince him about the Interest. They shew here a most melancholy scheme, shee being passionate and full of Criminacion almost to Fury. Wee stay an hour with pain, return home about 7, Ned Roberts &c went to Frodsham; Spirits a little recoverd, recreate (after consideracion of Mr. & my sister Jones Busienes) in a domestic pint of good wine, and to bed about 11.
16 Better success last night, in a sharp morning to early prayers. After write to my Lord, Mr. Egerton, Mr. Feilding. I except against Mr. Foulks propos'd Condicions and hee writes as offended. I answer it. After prayers some Busienes. I expect Mr. Cartwright till past 8 to bring the Articles and see 'em executed, but hee comeing too late, tis deferrd to Munday. I receive a civill Letter from Robert Holt, offering to lend mee 200^{li}.
17 A very sharp morning. The new Mayor comes to the Choir and is signalisd by an Anthem. The Letters putt us yet back to expectacion, not despair of Lisle. Lady Bunbury is so kind as to dine & sup with us. Mrs. Thane dos the later too and stay past 10.
18 The wind alter'd rain succeeds. About 9 Mr. Cartwright, Roberts, Jack and myself go to Mr. Whaley with the Writeings, hee examines and is satisfyd with the Charg. I pay 10^{li} chargd us on Saturday last. They execute the writeings and tho Mrs. Whaley out of apprehension of her difficulty and her husbands fatal monagery dos it with passionate reflections on him, yet with honest and decent applicacion to mee. I inclose a Copy of the Articles to Vice Chamberlain Starkie, write to Robert Holt with the phrase his Letter requires and presently depend on 100^{li} and to John Crosse to sett the Bank. Afternoon, the weather returns to fair. Ned Roberts go's to Nantwich. After prayers I apply to a special Administracion of Sir John Mainwaring's Term in Cotton Hool. I send at his request to Mr. Foulks an acknowledgment of 164^{li} on Account, while busy Mr.

Rhodes comes, tells that many Letters in Town with great confidence and Credit certify that an Express came Thursday night. That Lisle[19] was surrenderd. After Busienes,Mr. Rhodes, Leftwich, 2 others on busienes and myself go to the Falcon, wee (as Bells & Bonfires do) congratulate the acceptable News in 3 Bottles at 3s a Bottle. Wee stay till 10. I find Lady Bunbury at home. Wee pass an hour part at 11.

19 The wind and weather returnd to Frost. At early prayers, after prepare for a journy. See the Chancellor, after that Mr. and Mrs. Whaley, they importune my care and kindness, as depending on mee. I am sensible of their difficulty and misfortune to forgetfulness, almost of my own. I write to Mr. Fearnhead for a Quarter of Licence Bonds. The Chancellor and I dine at our homes. About 2 wee sett out and come in a sharp Evening about 5 to Oulton. Here are Mr. Ambrose Thelwall, his Lady, Dr. Egerton, Mr. Alex Walthall and Mr. Bird. Wee drink good Claret liberally till 11, then to bed and tho I am directed to a good one, am extreme cold and scarce sleep one hour.

20 Past 9 sett hence, come to Midlewich about 11. The busienes is slender. After dinner with Mr. Cowper, visit Mr. Thos. Yates, after Mr. Vernon who treats with magniloquence and a Bottle. Indispos'd yet go with Mr. Chancellor & T. Yates to Mr. Cowpers where wee are free and cheerfull till 10.

21 Refresht by sound sleep, rise to a milder day. The Chancellor is at a difficulty about his sick horse and hires a very tall awkward one of a Quaker. Hee and I follow the rest and come to Macclesfield about one. When dinner and busienes over, hee, Mr. Hulme and I seek out Alderman Johnson, find him at tollerable Ale with 2 honest Aldermen. Wee stay 2 hours freely, hee is too full of his late unjust persecucion and boasts of the indifferent success. Wee call at his house, returning take Drams of Brandy and to bed about 11.

22 The weather very mild and pleasant. Wee proceed to Stockport about 12. I examine here 2 Wittnesses on a nuncupative Will. Am extremely offended at the rude behaviour of Etchels, one of the Chapelwardens of Disley. Busienes is hastn'd, wee sett hence, Dr. Holbrook with us, about 4, come to Manchester before 6. We try the Angel, where 2 pints of base wine, return to our Quarters and to bed about 10.

23 The weather yet fair. I read the 1st Book of Tullys Offici. Step to Mr. Pigot who signs his peticion, The Chancellor signs his Confirmacion. The Busienes here is less than usuall. The Conversacion is ingrosst by the subject of the pious subscripcion of near 2000^{li} to the erection of a new Church.[20] In the Evening Dr. Holbrook treats us with strong Ale and a smal hansom repast wild Duck part of it, wee part about 10.

24 Made easy by Elixir, at the Church, the Warden preaches in the morning, Mr. Ash afternoon. In the Evening wee visit the Warden (where good wine) thence Mr. Mosse (where good ale, welcom and bad wine) thence Mr. Pigot,

19 Lille.
20 St. Anne's Church, Manchester.

where a hansom Entertainment and supper, more tollerable, yet not good wine. Wee stay here till 10. I am forcd to recurr to Elixir.

25 The weather still favorable. The Chancellor willing to relax putts off Blackburn and Chorley, gos to pay a visit to Mr. Hopwood. Wee (the rest) set hence before 10 come to Bolton about 12. Here my coz. Kenyon tells me my coz. Holt was deliver'd on Friday of a daughter, din'd about 2 sett hence and reach Blackburn in tollerable light. I write to my S. here. We are treated with an elegant supper at the vicarage where Mr. Hulme with great Civility putts me in possession of my old lodging.

26 The weather threatend, it hurts not. My Coz. Jeffrey Prescott, from Mr. Starkie, brings the deeds of the Bank ready drawn and by Mr. Rishton I receive a Satisfactory Letter from Mr. Gillibrand. My Kinsman tells mee of a Chancery suit intended by Hen. Whaley, leaves the Deeds with mee. Mr. Rigby Lawyer of Lancaster and Mr. Livesey stay with mee till 8. After Mr. Hulme and I retire to the Vicarage where after 1 last pint of good Claret wee part about 11.

27 I take the Accounts of Mr. Hulme and Kippax, leave the Choice of an Apparitor to Mr. Hulme, the weather fair and calme, I go by the way of Brindle, come to Chorley about 12. I meet with Robin Holt, hee is very solicitous and troublesome about an Investry and Account of one Whaley, who owd him 3^{li}. Hee is evasive in his offer of 200^{li} saying hee would rather I took the whole than 100^{li}, hee having a good security to place it upon, but saies, rather than fail hee will prevail with my coz. Holt of Wigan, to accomodate mee or hee will yet do it. I look on the Favor very incertain. Jeffrey Prescott calls and gives me good satisfaction about Mr. Gillibrand, hee being now at Preston with the Trustees of Dunkenhall. After small busienes here wee start at 4 come to Wigan before 6 where wee meet with Mr. Chancellor, Hulton, Hitchcock. Wee try indifferent wine and part about 10. I go to my coz. Holt.

28 St. Simon and Jude Festival. The weather alters to rain and storm, diverts the Chancellor from Winstanly, myself from Holland. After dinner and a visit to my coz. Holt, in her straw, our Company invited, go to Mr. Bowyer, wee find him in a new great and well furnisht house. His wife of mean appearance, no conversacion. Good Ale, indifferent wine, a dish of woodcocks, cold pigg, Nutts and Tabbs, the Entertainment scarce gratefull to mee. The rain continues a while, yet wee go to our Lodgings before 11.

29 The weather dull not rainy. After the busienes of the Church and dinner a throng of my private Affairs, attack mee. John Cross brings John Walmesley and his son about abatement of the present arrears and the future rent. I abate $4^{li}.10^{s}$ now due, and promise to sett it for the next year at 50^{li} and to abate as occasion shall fall. James Aspinwall and Kindsley come Candidates to the Green House. I appoint 'em to meet mee at Holland on Monday. Hen. Whaley and Mr. Naylor his Solicitor bring Mr. Morts Letter to mee on his behalf. I pay respect to the Letter & promise to do what I can to prevail for a consideracion of Him, and to do something on my own Account. Then in the Throng comes a servant from (as he calld him) the Lord of Standish, gives mee his Masters service with assurance That hee had bought Whaleys Estate, upon a good consideracion and value, without any reserve or collusion. This surprizes, but does not shock mee, tho I at first, take it to relate to the Bank, but afterwards understand it relates to that Whaley in whose personal estate Robin Holt (who was here too) is so importunatly concern'd. To these succeed Correcion busienes. At length all vanish into ease, because only amuzement. I receivd a good Letter today from my son Jack on the subject of our late Bishop and my Affair with Mr. Whaley. I write to my Suzy And in the Evening, wee agree to solace, in 2 Bottles of wine and part about 10.

30 The Chancellor go's hence to Chester. My coz. Holt promises mee to help mee with 100^{li} of his brothers. Past 9 I sett hence and come to Ormskirk past 12. Mr. Marsden is here and shows Dr. Baynards fond Letters upon his marriage 26 April last. Mr. Tho. Legh sees mee on a Disturbance given him and his Lady by one Aspinwal in Bostocks seat in the Church of Aughton.[21] The busienes which is not yet over, Mr. Stratford and I, go to see Mr. Sudell. Hee entertains with good Ale and grave discourse on the Affair of the Church & its Friends. About 9 wee return to the Inn where wee conclude the day and visitacion in a Bottle of white wine with Mr. Hitchcock and to bed past 11.

31 Wee rise early in a calme fair morning, dispatch and disperse. The rest to Leverpool, Myself, Mrs. Stratford, and Roberts, to Holland. Mr. Birchall ingages us to dinner, from Church wee go to him. Hee receives with good Ale, mutton Cutlets, and roasted Hare. They go for Warrington after dinner, I to the Church, Mr. Birchall, Prescott, his son Hulme &c come with mee to Geo Lyons where the Ale is good and keeps us together freely past 10.

NOVEMBER 1 (Q B E) I rise early on All Saints, a delicate frosty morning. I walk (calling on John Crosse) to the Bank, see the House particularly tis sadly out of repair as the Barn &c. Like well the site of them, walk down to Douglas, see the wrecking, thence to Ayrfeild, thence back to Holland about 10. In the way overtake Mr. Whaley of the Green, move him about an exchange with his higher Hay and Croft, for my 2 Feilds at Whitley Hall. Hee saies hee is not in power but promises his consent if his son (of which John Crosse gave mee hopes) will exchange. I go to prayers. After these and dinner, Mrs. Birchal, Prescott, Holt, Roby &c come to mee. Among these Kindsley, a subtile country man. Wee treat on the Terms of the Green house. I ask 240^{li} Fine & 30^{s} a Year rent, hee bids 230^{li} and 20^{s} a Year, wee do not conclude, nor am I willing because of my hopes to exchang Whitley Hall. They drink and stay. I use an artifice to gett off by going to Mr. Birchalls, Mr. Roby gos with mee, wee stay an hour Freely, and I return to Geo Lyons and to bed about 10.

2 Early up in a fine morning, come to Wigan about 9. My coz. Holt in his brother James (of London) his Name lends mee on Bond of this day 100^{li} payable the 2d of May. I dine here with him, set hence about 2 and come to Beausee before 5. Mrs. Atherton indispos'd and weak, keeps her Chamber and

21 C.R.O.,EDC.5(1708) No 4, Aughton.

Bed, therefore I see her not. She sends down her excuse with desire to mee to call on Mr. Shaw, on the affair of the Chapell tomorrow. Mrs. Vernon and Mrs. Banks are here, wee sup together. After which Mr. Eckersol, Mr. Emmott a painter and myself, empty a larg peggd Tankard and to bed about 11.

3 The wind is brisk and cold. I pay Mr. Fearnhead (who sent for came thither) for Mr. Vaudrey 70^{li}. About 10 sett hence, call on Mr. Shaw at the school, hear his cases and discourse on the matter. I commend to him Dr. Boucher and Sir Ed. Northey for Civilian and Common Lawyers, part after 11, sett forward and at an easy rate come (D.O.M.G.) safe to my corner before 4, dine or sup freely, after to the Bacchus where with the Chancellor, ArchDeacon, Dr. Norris, Mr. Callis, I take a full pint and return about 9.

4 The weather dull and rainy. I step to Mr. Cartwright with the Bank Deeds, write to Jeffrey Prescott by his advice for a Dedimus, to acknowledge a Fine. A Court day of small busienes, no wittnesses, repose after Dinner. After prayers to the Bacchus, where the Chancellor, Archdeacon, Dr. Norris, Coll. Proby and Will. Proby, wee stay entertaind by accounts of Dr. Norris and the Colls Travails, drink above pints, good wine and part before 10.

5 This day is celebrated in the City with the usuall solemnities. Mr. Lancaster has a sermon in St. Oswald's on psalm 124 v. 5th. The News proceeds with the attack of the Citadell, the Government boasts to defend it as long as hee did, the Town which was invested the 14 of August and surrenderd 28 Oct. All passes betwixt Ostend and betwixt Brussells and Lisle, are yet seizd by the French Army, provision scarce in ours, tho' tis said near Ipres this has seizd a store of 20 days. The Moscovites have cut off 10000 Swedes. After Dinner repose and after prayers vid. at 6 meet Dr. Griffiths and Mr. Cottingham at the Bacchus, wee dispatch 2 Bottles and part about 10.

6 Mrs. Whaley comes with her Complaints too just, and I tell her the Neighbor-History of her Husband too true. She borrows 40^{li} of mee and promises to send for him (now in Wales) to come and execute the Deeds. I recollect this Ephemeris from the 19th of October. Paid Mr. T. Dod 3^{li} interest due for 50^{li} the 10th of September last. In the Evening, after a domestic pint wee visit Lady Bunbury where I add near another.

7 After early prayers see the News which gives further hopes of the Citadel, and enlarges the Country to our Army. Dr. Thane has a sermon in the Quire on Rom.2 v. 3 Sanctissimam Eucharistiam recipio Det D O M pie caste, recte vivere.[22] After prayers in Books till 10. I receive from Mr. W. his brothers release.

8 I go about 8, Jack with mee, to Mr. Whaley, all circumstances are menciond, a tedious & ungratefull Conversacion for about 3 hours. I receive the Rector of Wigan, his Letter with the Agreement about the Nominacion of the Curat of Hindley to bee registr'd.[23]. I after prayers, sent for, go agen to Mr. Whaley, hee

22 Trans: 'I receive the most Holy Eucharist. May God the best and greatest grant [me] to live piously, chastely and rightly.'

23 C.R.O.,EDV2/14.

delivers to mee 5 more releases from his brothers and sisters. I stay with him, other 3 hours, importunatly detaind and heartily pitty the occasion. Hee desires amongst other things, my advice whether hee should adventure to London or Dublin, I (as hee indeed) rather advise to the former. After a domestic pint to bed before 11.

9 I write to Mr. Finch Rector of Wigan, about entry of the Hindley Agreement, The News takes a good view and enlarges by Dixmyde &c a larger province to our Army. In a fair calme morning, I take 2 long and 2 short Turns. I go to Sir Wm. Meredith who imparts to mee his danger of being made High Sheriff, desires my interest to my Lord. After prayers, I go with Mr. Chancellor, into the Chapter House, where Mr. Dean shews mee my Lords Letter of the 6th about Hanley, and a plan of the Floor of the Quire. After this the Chancellor, ArchDeacon and I go to the Bacchus, take 2 Bottles and a pint of tollerable port and part before 9. I receive Mr. Whaleys long Letter to serve and advise him and particularly whether to remove now to Mrs. Ellis a periwig maker, I am in this for the Affirmative,

10 A fair calm day. I write a long letter to my Lord and inclose Sir Wm. Merediths in it. I write to my Cozen Parre, direct Mr. Roberts to pay the Chancellor on Account of the late Visitacion 50^{li} D.O.M.G.E.L. About 5 I go (Jack with mee), to Mr. Cartwright's to forward the Execucion of the Deed, find him in his office, thence I go to Mr. Cottinghams find him not, send his man into the Forest Street (Mr. Oltons) to seek him. Wee return to Mr. Cartwright. Hee reads over, fills the Blanks, indorses Attestacions, putts too wax and prepares the 2 Deeds and Bonds. About 6 Mr. Cottingham comes to Mr. Cartwrights I go presently with him & Mr. Whaley who acknowledges and subscribes an Affadavit (drawn by his directions) before Mr. Cottingham as Mr in Chancery. I return to Mr. Cartwright stay near an hour and returning by the Horse and Baggs, perceive 3 or 4 Horsemen ride by; hope tis the Vice Chamberlain and company. I call Mr. Prescott, and as wisht, Jeffrey Prescott hears, stops and rides up to mee. I tell him wee are going on the Execucion of the Deeds, desire his company and that hee will call on Mr. Cartwright and myself at the Bacchus, which hee promises & performs about ½ an hour after. In the interim, I send Jack with the Deeds to Mr. Whaley, who reads 'em over. Before 8, wee to to Him. Hee and his wife readily execute the Deed and upon Delivery of it to mee, shee adds a blessing and affectionate good wishes, the Lease bears date 20, the Deed the 21 of October last. After this they acknowledg a Fine, by vertue of the Dedimus which Jeffrey Prescott puts up. I take the Deeds, come home before 9 and with D.G. recollect the dispatch on a private pint.

11 The weather turns rainy. I write to Mr. Marsden and to John Crosse. It is a Court day of easy dispatch. I see Mrs. Whaley before dinner, shee tells mee of her husbands escape in her cloaths last night, for fear of his brother Henry now in Town, to Mrs. Ellis, the manner was comical, and shee tells it cheerfully. After Dinner in a dull and rainy Hour, Mr. Cartwright calling I go with him to Castle Lane, Mr. Bennets. The Vice Chamberlain is busy & detaind by Mrs. Ellice, Meredith, Mr. Kenyon, Vice Chancellor of the Duchy of Lancaster speaks to mee on Hen. Whaleys account, after about 3 hours attendance, the Vice Chamberlain signs and seals the Deed in the presence of the same Wittnesses vid. Mr. Cartwright, Jeffrey Prescott and Edward Dod. Hee and Mr. Kenyon lay out Mr. Whaleys fraud to his brother, press mee to pay what is yet in my hands to him. I tell him why I can't and the Circumstances of my involuntary purchase and Show Mr. Vice Chamberlain, Hen. Whaleys Release of 50^{li} his porcion upon Articles. Hee seems satisfyd of its validity. I returning in the rain call at the Bacchus where Mr. Chancellor & Mr. Hulton, this accounts for Decrees past today; the Chancellor is paid 5^{li} Hurst Comutacion towards his expenses against Noseworthy and allows mee 5^{li},[24] Claytons Comutacion towards the repair of the Consistory. Hee expresses himself kindly & tenderly to mee, on that occasion. Wee pass the Time and 4 pints and part about 9.

12 A cold morning. I see the News advancing slowly to the Citadel but inlarging the Ditionem[25] for provisions. Dean Booth and his brother in Law, Hales a Clergyman call and see my Coins &c. Hen. Whaley about 12 comes to mee, drunk, claims a share of the Bank saying it is betwixt us. Threatens that hee ventures His Life and soul with mee in the recovery of the 250^{li} his brother has cheated him of, binds it with a dreadfull Curse, and further adds that if hee do not recover it, hee will be hangd on a Gallows before my door. I rebuke his behavior upon which hee becomes humble as before, furious & phrenetic. After dinner Vice-Chamberlain Starkie calls on horseback upon the sequestracion of Grapenhale void yesterday, by Mr. Earls death. I tell him of Whaleys behavior, Hee advises mee, to take no Notice of him. About an hour after Mr. Alanson the Candidate Rector of Grapenhal calls on mee, desires a search of the last and a new Form of Sequestracion,[26] hee gives Ned Roberts 5s. After prayers about 6, Hee and I go to the Bacchus, the busienes of Hindley and, most public Affairs become subjects of our discourse, And the best of the Clergy and Gentry, of our Healths. Wee draw out almost 4 hours with 4 pints. I send to Mrs. Whaley 5 Guineas & 12s.

13 Indispos'd I betake mee to roodee in a sharp morning, 4 Turns relieve mee. I write to Mr. Crosby on Mr. Whaley's account and to Mr. Fearnhead. After prayers at 6 I go to Mr. Whaley at Charles Banners, hee designd to begin his journy to morrow but defers it. Hee gives a discharge for the sum of 13;13;4, the remaining one by the Articles, at the foot of the Copy of them, and a receipt of 10^{li} which hee paid formerly to Mrs. Gillibrand shee comes inter haec, and all matters are recounted & as much as in us lies, setled. I return at 9 find Lady Bunbury kindly at supper here, shee stays past 11. I sent Mr. and Mrs. Whaley 3 Guineas and 10s.

14 A dull rainy day. The News improves on the Citadel and enlarges the provision-province. Mr. Lancaster has a good discourse on Matt 26 v 'Not my

24 *Ibid.*, EDC.5(1702) No 10, Preston.
25 Ditionem – authority.
26 C.R.O., EDV2/14.

Will but thine &c'. After prayers in Caves Historia Literaria till 9. After step over to Lady B's where my S., wee dispatch a pint of Claret, back at 11.

15 A dull morning and indisposicion keeps mee in bed too long. Jack and Ned Roberts go to Wrexham. A long answer to Mr. Mort and a short Letter to my Lord, with one to mee, from Sir Wm.Meredith inclos'd, takes up the Time till 12 a Clock. Dr. Thane pays mee 1^{li};5^{s};6 which has bin 9 months unpaid for his Dionisius & barely thanks. I admire his Forgetfullness or inconsideracion, of my pains at London, for him. After prayers Mr. Chancellor, Dr. Thane, Coll and Mr. Proby and myself go to the Bacchus, drink each his Bottle of good Claret cheerfully and at home before 9. I write a Letter recommendatory on Mr. Whaleys Account to Mr. Ashurst now in the Temple, his daughter takes it about 10 from mee and 5^{li} part of Mr. Gillibrand's 10^{li}.

16 A brisk morning turns heazy. I indispos'd recreate by 4 Turns on roodee. Apply to Busienes, write to Mr. Styth. After prayers see Mrs. Crosby at her sister Whaleys. Here I stay above 2 hours detaind on a dull subject. Shee promises to bee Trustee to my Donarium, to Mrs. Whaley, provided shee incurr no danger, shee is cautious, easy in a good Circumstance and is full of Advice to her sister. Shee trys and after, by her Letter, urges mee to tell the summ I intend to give her sister. I promise to satisfy her in the morning. After domestic pint to bed about 11.

17 Another heazy morning. About 9 I go to Mrs. Whaley and understand her sister went back before 6. I acquaint her of my design to present her with 40 Guineas, shee is not satisfy'd expecting as shee tells mee 100^{li}, advances the Bargain and her own Concurrence with it. I in short promise her 50^{li} which I take to bee equal to both and above my Circumstance. Shee importunes for another 50^{li}, if a year hence, argueing her way, which rather (considering my former purchase &c this, with the constant trouble and Care, my compassion for her family, had created in mee for 10 years last), moves mee rather to Anger & resolucion, than pitty. I procure a Bill of 40^{li} from Alderman Allen and inclose it to Dr. Pope, proceed in Busienes. After prayers my uncle Eyton comes to us this Evening, wee divert the Time over a Bottle of my wine, hee lodges here. After 2 Acts in Heauton Timorumenon, I go to Bed about 11.

18 A fair morning. Lady Bunbury takes Coach for London. I write to Mr. Gilibrand and inclose a Sequestracion of Grapenhale to Mr. Bordman,[27] the Curate there; a Court of slender Busienes. My uncle Eyton stays and dines with us. I examine three Wittnesses on Davenports Will. After the other Acts of Heauton timorumenon, I go to Mr. Whaley, find him yet incertain where to go. Hee now with his wife inclines to Dublin, desires my Advice, I am unwilling to determine for them, for fear of insuccess. Shee comes and rather ruffles than reconciles. I advise him to sincerity for the future in his Busienes, and conversacion. Hee desires my Favor still to his wife and Family, as they shall

27 L.R.O., Exhibit Book DCh.1 1691. John Boardman was patron of Grappenhall when he presented Henry Walmisley to the benefice.

deserve, which I promise him, take leave about 9; return to my Corner and domestic pint and to bed about 11. Mr. Mercer our olde Neighbor is bury'd this Evening.

19 A dull yet cold morning. The News makes slow approaches to the Citadell of Lisle, says Sir Richard Onslow was chosen (unanimously) Speaker on Tuesday, that Lord Wharton, for the Leiftenancy of Ireland, and Lord Sommers, for the presidency of the Council, have kist the Queen's hand. I with Mr. Bowyer at Mr. Bouchers. Litle Busienes intervenes. I proceed to the third Act of the Adelphi. After prayers meet Alderman & Mr. Allen at the Bacchus. I pay the Alderman here the 40^{li}, hee gave mee his Bill for and 10s Exchange. Wee remember good healths in 3 pints od decayd French and part at 8. I end the Adelphi. Mr. Whaley went at 4 this morning for Leverpool.

20 A brisk cool morning. I send Mrs. Whaley by her daughter $5^{li};14^{s};4^{d}$ viz. 14s;4d the last remaining sum of the Articles and 5^{li} the remaining Sum of Mr. Gilibrands 10^{li}. I examine 3 Wittnesses on Walkers Will and Interrogacions, read out Hecyra, write to the Bishop of Meath and Mr. Ludlowe. Solace in domestic pint, and to bed after 10.

21 After a stormy Night a brisk and cloudy day. Audenard, Brussells and Antwerp threatend by the French Army, whose mocions are more formidable, the Army of the Allies vigilant and resolute, whence a Battle expected. Mr. Fogg has a good discourse on Philipp.3 v 8. After prayers at 6, Dean Booth and his brother Hale come to mee, hee signs 2 proxies for Convocacion to Mr. Whitfeild and Dr. Aldrich, they stay and are free with mee over 2 Bottles of good Claret till 9.

22 A cold day, frost and snow. My right Arm exceeding painfull admitts not writeing on my desk. I yet with difficulty write to Mr. Feilding. I divert in Books. In the Evening about 4 the Chancellor sends, I go down to him, thence to Dr. Norris's where Mr. Egerton and wee three empty 5 Bottles of good Claret in good Healths. The News comes to Mr. Egerton, it gives instant hopes of the Citadel, end expectacion of a Battle, to prevent the retakeing of Audenard and Brussells by the French. Wee stay till 10. Ned Roberts pays Mr. Callys for the Deaneries 40^{li}.

23 A very sharp day, the wind full North. Indisposd, I am relievd by 4 full Turns. Divert in the Beginning of Clarendons History and after repose read out Phorinio where I meet an opportune moral Rule well exprest. At non quotidiana Cura haec angeret Animum.[28] Solace therefore in a domestic pint, to bed about 11.

24 A very sharp Frost. I write to my Lord & acquaint him with the Caveat entr'd about Grapenhale. Mrs. Whaley sends mee her Husbands Letter writ at Leverpool, hee begs her pardon for concealing his Circumstances from her, and desires my consideracion of her, as deserving. I pay Mr. Lancaster rent for my House 3^{li};10s. I draw a Monicion against Aspinwall in the Cause of a Seat in

28 Trans: 'But this daily care should not distress the mind.'

Aughton Church.[29]. After prayers Dr. Thane (come about 4 from Cherk) calls on mee, we go to the Bacchus, drink a dull Bottle part before 9.

25 The cold and Frost continue. I write and repeat my Busienes to John Cross. A Court of small Busienes. After Dinner solace. After prayers I draw a Commission for the parish of St. Johns,[30] read over Andria and after solace in a domestic pint, to bed about 11.

26 The Frost still sharp tho the wind at S.E. The good News of the French defeated on the Scheld & the seige of Brussells raisd, fills the Town with Joy and Noise. I take 5 Turns on roodee, receive John Crosse's answer to mine of the 11th. I am confirmd about the good News by Dyers and private Letters. I begin Eunnelius. After prayers I correct the draught of the Commission for St. John's, go to the Chancellor, Dr. Norris and Coll Proby at the Bacchus, wee congratulate the great News in 3 Bottles and part about 8. I finish Eunnelius save the last Act.

27 The weather excessively cold. Apply to Books, read the last Act of Eunnelius. Send Mrs. Whaley by her daughter 15s. After that 2 Guineas. After prayers sent to, go to the Recorder, where Mr. Egerton, Recorder, Dr. Thane, Mr. Walker and I drink 5 Bottles of the Recorder's strong wine and 1 Flask of Florence sent thither by Mr. Egerton. Wee carry the conversacion, even and cheerfull part about 10.

28 So indispos'd from my wine, I stay in complaints at home, till Evening prayers, the weather still very cold, tho the wind at S. The late good News only confirm'd (2 mails wanting). After prayers my S. and I go to see Mrs. Mercer and her Son, now, there. Thence to Mrs. Worger, thence home: after domestic pint to bed.

29 The Frost continues severe. I examine Mr. Bridges on Mr. Heath's Will and write to John Crosse. After prayers the weather turning to rain, my Suzy and I go to see Mrs. Whaley, shee tells her design to sell Lace, reflects on her husbands managry intemperatly. Wee return about 7, I write to Mr. Bell of Hawkshead[31] to Mr. Bolton and my sister Jones. Begin Heauton timorumenos. Solace in a domestic pint, to bed about 10.

30 After rain, frost returnd. I see the News which represent to Action on the Scheld less bloody since the French made no Opposicion, the Citadel of Lisle surrendr'd and Ghent sends a Deputacion to the D. of Marlborough. After reading for the day (St. Andrews) proceed in Heant. After wee visit Mrs. Hopwood at Dr. Norris's. After prayers finish Heant begin and end Adelphi, the Lady Cornwallis her birthday (now the 30th) is remembred in a domestic celebracion of it, after a pint to bed about 11.

DECEMBER 1 Q.B.E.P.E. A cold not freezing day. Examine 2 Wittnesses on

29 C.R.O., EDC.5(1708) No 4, Aughton.
30 C.R.O., EDP1/73, St John's Chester Parish Papers.
31 L.R.O.,Exhibit Book DCh.1 1691,f.32, Hawkshead. Thomas Bell, M.A. (priest Chester 1668), curate of Hawkshead 12 August 1680.

Mr. Heaths Will, pay Mr. Hatfeild, a Years Interest for 80^{li}, due the 15th November 4^{li};16s I read Hecyra & Phormio. After domestic pint to bed before 11.

2 A cold day, the weather frosty. This the last Court day; it concludes the Term in moderate Busienes. I examine 3 Wittnesses on the part of Pimlow against Warmingham. Dr. Thane comes over to mee, wee clubb for a Bottle of Picking's wine, it proves well, wee despatch it about 10.

3 There is small remains of Frost, wind at S. The News repeats the shamefull retreat of the French Army, the success at Brussells, but makes Ghent defend itself against a Siege. I turn some Bookes. In the Evening about 6 I go down to Mr. Egerton, where I meet Mr. Chancellor Drs. Norris and Thane, Coll. and Mrs. Proby, all invited. Mr. Egerton entertains liberally with three sorts of good wine, an elegant short supper, the Top of it a Shoulder of winter venison don to temptacion of mee. The rest go at 10, I stay an hour longer.

4 Extremely indispos'd from the generous Entertainment last Night, confind to Bed till noon, after, but in vain endevor to repose. After prayers I see Mrs. Whaley. After that divert the indisposicion, by the preface to Plautus, take a pint of burn'd Claret and to bed past 10.

5 The Frost wholy gone, melted into rain. The News brings the Consternacion of the French retreated Armys preparacions at Ghent to abide a Seige, the Pope submitting to the Demands of the Emperor, the uncertain Fortune of the Swede in Muscovy, the Citadel yet not surrender'd. Mr. Henchman has good discourse on Galatians 6 v,7,8. After prayers Mrs. Whaley comes to tell mee, that her brother Henry W. is in Town. I go down to Mr. Bennet, upon my Lords Letter about Mr. Bunnels exhibicion to Pembroke Hall, Cambridge. I read Hooker's 2d Book of Ecclesiastical policys and after a domestic pint to bed about 11.

6 A dull morning. Hen Whaley comes to mee in the most submissive Form delivers Mr. Morts civil Letter. Hee desires mee to free him from 50^{li} for which hee is bound with his brother. I tell him of his former behavior in the Town and my own house, towards mee. Hee confesses, whines, submits. I promise Nothing. Hee desires mee to consider of his case, and promises to bring his sister Whaley to mee. I write to my Lord and inclose Mr. Bennetts answer to him. After Dinner Mrs. Middleton,Lady Shakerleys cousin German sees us. After prayers Dr. Thane calls, I go to the Bear with him where over 2 Bottles of good wine, I tell him the story of my Bank purchase, wee return about 10. I write to Mr. Styth.

7 A dull but mild and fair day. About 10 Mr. Boucher in his peevish way, tells me of my too much rescrudnes to Ned Roberts and that therefore hee had desird him to acquaint mee of his intended Marriage, directs mee to take occasion proper, to discourse him on the subject. Mr. Foulks breaks into this discourse and Mr. Boucher receded. Hee renews his demand of a Bond, wee differ about the Clauses and are tenacious of our several Sentiments, adjourn the debate to Friday or such time. About 11 my Suzy and I mount and come to Eyton after 12, the dresser beating for dinner. Wee are civilly receivd by my Lady and Mr. Cholmley (Sir Richard at Vale Royal). I pass the afternoon with Mr. Cholmley and Mr. Okes freely in Claret &c. Eyebright; about 4 wee remount and come D.G. safe about 5. I recreate in Plautus and domestic pint till 11. Alderman Hand, was buryd at Trinity Church, this Evening, Jack representing mee at the Funerall.

8 A dull day with some rain. Mrs. Ursula Lloyds Corps well attended by Coaches move out for Overton. I send Jack as my representative, and write (by him) to my sister Jones. I inclose John Crosse's draught of Mrs. Pierrepont's Chamber and Dressing room to my Lord and add something on Mr. Allansons Account. I dip in Books and read wholy Amphitruo and Asinaria of Plautus, these and domestic pint make it 11.

9 A dull and heavy morning, yet I venture (and am reliev'd by 4 Turns) on roodee. I write to John Cross, about the new rooms at the Bank. Mrs. Whaley acquaints my Suzy with the unreasonable Expectacion of her mother Sefton and sister Crosby this Evening while Dr. Thane and I are treated by Alderman Allen, at his house, with 3 Bottles good Claret and Oysters wee part thence about 10.

10 The morning wett discourages a walk. The News comes confirmd with 21 Articles of the surrender of the Citadel of Lisle on the 29th Nov. O.S. and the investing of Ghent, by the Allies. I expect but hear not, from Mrs. Whaley or her sister. I read Auluraria. After prayers ArchDeacon and I go to the Pyde Bull as a new Fountain, wee dispose of 3 pints good Claret and part before 9. Read after 2 Acts of Captivi.

11 A fair morning and mild. Mrs. Whaley comes to mee, I discourse her fully on her Affair with her sister Crosby and on the reflecions shee (her sister) made on my purchase, shee gives mee some satisfacion. I promise to tender her 50^{li} which Mrs. Crosby is to tender to her as paid to her on Munday. I write to Mr. Bradshaw, about Mr. Stringer of Namptwich. After prayers, Mr. Chancellor, Archdeacon Thane, Coll. Proby, Major Lloyd, Mr. Proby and I meet at Tom Hatfeilds, wee have Claret upon the Turn & easy Conversacion, drink 4 Bottles and part about 8. I read out Captivi of which I think its own Character (by the Grex) very just. Huiusmodi paucas poeta reperiunt Comaedias, Ut boni meliores fiant.[32]

12 A calm day. The Italian part of the News surpriseing, the Pope submitting to with Condicions, the Emperor proposes, and turning from Enemy to Ally. Dr. Thane preaches in the Quire on Matt. 23 v. 6. After prayers I finish the 2d and proceed in the 3d Book of Hooker's Ecclesiastical Polity. Refresh in a pint, till past 10.

13 After rain in the Night, a fair calm, nay warm, day. I go down to Mr. Cartwright & discourse him on the Busienes of Setling securely the 50^{li} I give to Mrs. Whaley, this takes the Time up, hee promises, but fails, to bring the writeings at noon when Mrs. Whaley and her sister Crosby, dine with us, they after stay till prayers. After which, and something in Books, Dr. Thane calls wee

32 Trans: 'Poets devise a few comedies of this kind, in order that the good may become better.'

go to the Bear where wee meet with excellent wine. Jack Wright (from Mr. Townsend's over the way) where Sir Richard and Lady Grosvenor comes to us, wee drink 3 Bottles & part before 10.
14 The weather calmer. I recreate by 4 Turns on roodee. The News for want of Mail, continues in the same posture, save that it says the King of Sweden with 30000 had totally defeated 60000 Moscovites. After dinner, my Suzy and I discourse Ned Roberts on his intended marriage, in the Circumstances of this, hee makes a great complaint of Mr. Hultons insolent and unjust behavior in his practice, and the incouragement indulgd him, by Mr. Chancellor and myself, seeming too deeply affected with Mr. Bouchers Sentiments. My Suzy and I about 3 go down to Mr. Davies I am with him near an hour. After prayers I go again to the Bear where Mr. Egerton, Mr. Davies, Dr. Thane and my Coz. Kendric and I drink each our Bottle and part about 9.
15 After a tedious night, I rise before 8 walk away my indisposicion in 4 Turns on roodee. About 10 I go down to Mrs. Whaley, subscribe a Note stampt dated of yesterday testifying my depositing 50^{li} in Mrs. Crosbys hands, to the use of Mrs. Whaley and her children. I tender the mony (46 Guineas & 11s). Shee counts, receives and under her hand on the same paper acknoledges the receit of it to the said Use. Tho Mrs. Whaley owns the sum given without any the least condicion on hers, or promise on my part &c yet shee forgets to thank mee for it. My S. tells mee of her further discourse with Ned Roberts wherein hee setts his services more immodestly than expected, at least on the same square, if not above my rewards and Favor. Mrs. Whaley and her sister, after dinner come, they return mee the 50^{li} I tender'd, I pay her 20^{li} besides the 5^{li};8s shee had in part of the 50^{li} and acknowledges the receit of it. They both continue importunate to mee to add the 5^{li};8s, forgetting (not thanking mee for) the beneficence in the 50^{li}. After prayers a while in Hooker and Synopsis Canonum, read Epidicus, refresh in a pint, to bed about 11.
16 A calme day. I take 4 Turns on roodee, am extremely recreated, I write to Mr. Jebbe and Mr. Fearnhead. After prayers, I read Pseudolus and Trinummus, refresh in domestic pint, and to bed about 11.
17 Yet calm weather. The papers rather suspend than bring News. I receive a Letter from Mr. Whaley now at Dublin with one inclosd to his wife, whose cause twixt Burnet and her son is heard today insuccessfully to her. After dinner Dr. Thane and my coz. Kendrick call on us, prevent my repose. In the Evening I read Rudens, in qua Fabula vicissitudinis rerum elegam adumbraeo as the Dauphin Editor. T. Naylor of Holland sees mee in the Evening, gives mee a melancholy Account of the Circumstance and Disposicion of my Tribules there, I condole it. Wee remember the better part in Ale & Wine, I write to John Crosse by him, hee leaves mee before 8, I to bed before 11.
18 A calm and pleasant morning draws mee inclind, to roodee and 4 Turns which refresh mee. I write to Mr. Bradshaw of Namptwich and Mr. Le Neve and on Harts busienes to Mr. Banks, now Mayor of Wigan. After prayers Mr. Chancellor, Mr. Davies, Coll Proby, Mr. Langford, Mr. Proby and my Self meet

at T. Hatfeild's, wee make up each a Bottle and part before 9. I read 1 Act of Truculentus.

19 A dull day inclind to rainy. The News continues great preparacions to attack Ghent. Mr. Fogg has a good Sermon on St. Matt 5 v. 44. After prayers I see Mr. Boucher and Mrs. Whaley. I write to Mr. Mercer of Eccleston, about Wine and Gloves. After a domestic pint to bed about 11.

20 From disorder in the Night, ly after 9. I write fully to Mr. Mort and to Mr. Lambert, proceed in Truculentus. I write in the Evening to Mr. Whaley, and to Ned Humphreys on his Account. Inclose both to Caleb Emerson in Essex Gate near the Good-woman, a Glass shop, At 6 I go to Dr. Thanes, where I find with him Mr. Egerton and Mr. Chancellor, wee dispatch 8 Bottles of his good Claret & part about 10.

21 Extremely indisposd and fevorish from the Quantity of good wine, keep in bed till 11. In pain all day. Yet after prayers the Dr. desires mee to go to the Bear, by the Fountain, to recover his Spirits sunk low under the care and beneficence of exerting 20^{li} to his brother Hide, now bound for Carolina, 1 Bottle helps, and the 2nd dissipates the Chagrin. Wee return before 9. I end Truculentus.

22 My indisposicion diminisht by Elixir yet troublesome. I write to Mr.Bradshaw. In the Evening Mr. Stringer calls on mee too late to see Mr. Chancellor. About 6 Mr. Aldersey and his Brother draw mee to the White Bull and Mermaid. Dr. Wigley and Mr. Stratford come to us. Wee dispatch 6 Bottles of Claret in Campaign Conversacion and part about 10.

23 A dull rainy morning, my indisposicion continues. Mr. Stringer comes after 10. I go with him to Mr. Chancellor, the scene is troubl'd, confus'd, Commutacion is menciond but the one dos not ask, nor is the other prepar'd to offer a sum. At length 10^{li} is menciond hee proposes to pay down 5^{li} and give his Note for the other 5^{li}. Hee asserts that Mr. Hulton incouragd him not to appear, saying if hee forbore 2 Visitacions, the matter would be connivd at. I write to Mr. Bradshaw to forbear Denunciacion of the Excommunicacion till hee hear further from mee.[33] After 11, I (Jack along) sett for Eaton. My bro. Ned Puleston follows & overtakes us. Wee come after 12 and before dinner. I am freely receivd by Sir Richard and Mr. Cholmley, sitt at Claret till 4. Mr. Cholmley takes mee into his Chamber, gives mee an amazeing and melancholy Account of the Mr. and Mrs. and regimen of this Family. Hee delivers the Case, Bill and answer in the Cause twixt him and his Nephew Cholmley, to mee to read at Leasure and to use his words, desires to do him the Favor to accept a Guinea then offer'd more. I sett hence about 6, come in the dark (but D.G. safe) home about 7, to bed about 10.

24 Not clear of my continud complaint – a dull moist day aggravates it. I read out Stichus. After prayers Mr. Crosby calls and (designing for Lancashire

33 C.R.O.,EDC1/103 n.f.

tomorrow) takes leave of us. I stay at home till prayers. After read, to bed after 10.

25 After a stormy Night a rainy Christmas day. Dr. Thane has a good discourse on 4 Gal.v.4. After Evening prayers I proceed in the 3 and 4th Books of Hooker, having ended the solemn Day and refresht in a gratefull domestic pint to bed about 10.

26 St. Stephen, a cold day the wind N. The papers bring the gratefull News of the Surrender of Ghent on Munday last. Dean Booth preaches in the Quire on 1 Ep. St. John v. 9. After prayers I finish the 4th Book of Hooker besides 2 of his sermon. And to bed well about 10.

27 A brisk Frost today. I write to Mr. Rider and Mr. Sedgwick and recreate in 4 Turns on Roodee. In the Evening invited to share in a token from Mr. Walley of Dublin College, a Luisdore, in Irish wine at Mr. Allens in Abby Court. Capt. Breholt, Recorder &c to the number 9. Wee drink every Man his Bottle and 2 in common. I part thence before 10. John Cross comes.

28 Snow falls in the morning. John Cross pays mee 20^{li} from John Walmesley 6^{li} from widow Corles & 3^{li} from Molyneux the Tenant of Whitley Hall. I continue at home all day. After prayers the Chancellor, Drs. Norris and Thane, Capt. Breholt, Coll. Proby and my self drink our Bottles at the Bacchus, they treat us with a small pasty of Derby Venison which succeeds very well. At 10 wee part.

29 It freezes and hailes. Not indisposd nor easy, stay at home. After dinner entertain Will. Willoughby and John Cross. After prayers Mr. Egerton and ArchDeacon Thane sending I meet them & Mr. Callys at the Bear, the wine is on the Turn, yet wee cheerfully empty 5 Bottles before 10.

30 A sharp freezing day. I take John Cross and Jack along, wee perform my ordinary 4 Turns and beside the walls of the City. John Cross talks his Busienes in my Affair. I pay him for the 2 last years 4^{li} and 9^{s} for Letters and charges laid out. I write by him to Mr. Alanson, Mr. Boardman and Mr. Molyneux and send new Ox Almanacks to Mr. Birchall and Sam. Prescott.

31 A Severe Frost. I read over Mr Fr. Cholmleys Bill, the Answer to it and Letters. My Brothers Partington and Puleston and their Company dine with us, the company stays all day and till 10 at night. I read Aschams 1st Epistle to Sturmius and other parts. My most dear and honoured Friend Mrs. Atherton of Beausee dies about 9 this day in Lester Feilds, Westminster.

1708/9

JANUARY 1 Q.B.E. The weather still very severe, I write to Mr. Feilding, Parre, Le Neve, Anthony Close. At home in Books and papers till Evening prayers. After which wee visit Lady Soame, who gives us a melancholy Account of good Mr. Athertons desperate Health and of the tenderness of the Heir, wee stay about 2 hours. After a domestic pint to bed about 10. Jack is taken with a delirium, falls and hurts his head near his left Eye that safe by good providence.

2 More snow with continud Frost. Mr. Henchman has a good discourse on

Matt 26 v. 26,27,28. After prayers at home, Mr. Crompton visitts us. I dip in Hooker, after private pint to bed about 11. The post expected last night from the difficulty of the road comes not in till 12 to Night.

3 I see the papers wherein Bruges and the neighboring passes are evacuated. The French make ostentacion of numerous Troops drawn down to Flanders. Mr. Boucher discourses us in Ned Roberts affair. Wee dine at my brother Ned Puleston where wee meet my brother Partingtons Family, wee are receivd with an elegant dinner and good liquors. I stay till 5 thence wait on Lady Soame who concludes on Mrs. Atherton's death, tho the Letter left her alive. After this, sent to, go to the Chancellor's where Mr. Mayor, Mr. Egerton, Dr. Norris, Mr. Sudell.[34] The wine passes frankly round, till a Tryal at Tables twixt the Chancellor and Mr. Egerton proposd, this takes up 2 Hours.

4 The Frost continues, and I at home till prayers. Mr. Alanson comes after dinner for Institucion to Grapenhale.[35] The Instruments are prepard today. After noon my Suzy and I go to Newton to visit the Mr. and Mrs. of that Family, shee being in the straw.[36] Wee stay above 2 Hours and Mrs. Upton and Mrs. Fogg return with us about 6. After which Mr. Alanson comes to mee, wee in good healths dispose of a Bottle of my wine and part at 9.

5 Mr. Alanson by special Commission is instituted by Mr. Chancellor to Grapenhale. About 10 my Brother Partington, Mr. J. Stringer and my self set out on foot, come to Eaton before 12. I am kindly receivd by Mr. Cholmley, wee discourse his Busienes in Chancery. Hee sends ½ Guinea a Xenium to Jack.[37] After dinner, Ale, wine and Smoak with free conversacion is promoted, wee stay till 5 and return about 6. I refresh in a domestic pint and to bed about 10.

6 The weather still severe. At the Quire where Mr. Lancaster has a sermon on the Epiphany. Wee dine at my brother Partingtons. After dinner my brother and Alderman Puleston, Partington, Capt. Briscoe and my self sit warm, and empty 5 or 6 Decanters of his Good Ale and part after 9.

7 I try 4 Turns on the rood-Ey, now coverd with snow and am recreated. In the Evening Mr. Green of Prescott calls and wee drink a Glass of my Claret.

8 Wee suspect from some Notes, Ned Roberts is marryd this morning. My Suzy and I commemorate this day of which our own was designed 22 years ago. Wee dine at Sir Wm. Merediths with our Neighbors and acquaintance invited, are civilly treated, stay till 4. In the Evening, wee visit Mr. Mercer and his wife, and after Lady Soame, where the melancholy subject of Mrs. Atherton's death is handl'd till 9. The Frost relents all day but mildly.

9 The Frost is return'd with severity. Mr. Fogg has in the morning a good discourse on psalm 26. 6. The News and pacquet boats stoppt by the Frost. After prayers I receive a Note to attend Mrs. Atherton's Corps at Warrington on

34 Christopher Sudell, M.A., was rector of Holy Trinity Chester from 1707. He held the living of Leyland in plurality from 1720–1733, and then the vicarage of North Meols from 1733–1735.

35 C.R.O., EDV2/14.

36 i.e. in childbed.

37 Xenium – a gift.

Tuesday at 11 a clock. I wait on Lady Soame.

10 About 8 I set out on Foot, Jack accompanys mee to Frodsham and pleases mee in the way. Wee come thither at 11, dine well, at 1. I set forward, Jack returns, the wind hight at S.W. Harry Whaley, who had bin at Chester, to try agen my consideracion of him, finds mee here, gos along and entertains mee with his Case. Hee promises to deliver the Counterpart but cunningly as hee thinks, forbears till hee sees my inclinacion. I come easily to Warrington about 4. I visit Mr. Patten, after retire to the Eagle & Child to bed about 10.

11 About 10 I step to Beausee, see presently Mr. Cholmley and Mr. Okes. Here is Sir Richard Vernon and Mr. Banks. Wee are in expectacion of a Messenger, return, sent to enquire after the Herse. Wee divert the time in conversacion and good wine which Sir Richard Vernon brought from Dumfrees.

12 I read the 2d Book of the Tusculane Qs. Mr. Thornley and Mr. Ashton of Milnrow are added to the Company. Mr. Thornley after dinner plays the Tankard so much that he becomes an ungratefull companion and Figure, after supper, hee occasions the company to part sooner to their Chambers.

13 No informacion yet of the Herse, wee continue in idle and uneasy Expectacion. Mr. Vaudrey and Mr. Patten come to Mr. Cholmley. I am, after noon, in Mr. Okes Chamber. At supper Mr. Thornley renews his language and reputacion, wee with Art evade him, but late. After which Sir Richard, Mr. Banks, Mr. Eckersal and my self take 2 Bottles cheerfully.

14 From sitting late rise so. Sir Richard gos for Chester but leaves Dumfrees behind him. After dinner, indisposd take a walk with Geo Bate to his house where his very old wife and homely 2 daughters. Hee shews mee his house and mencion his estate (as considerable), returning thro the meadows, I miss my way come near the house but hinderd by Water, return half a mile back. A Messenger brings the Herse is at Bartington and will bee at Warrington at 11 to morrow. Mr. Banks, Eckersall, Ashton and myself solace in 2 Bottles.

15 The weather has bin alternate Frost and Thaw, the daies of this week, now on the gentle Thaw. About 11 the company meets at the 3 Crowns, is treated with meat, wine, Gloves. They are at a difficulty about Bearers. Mr. Molyneux, Mr. Culcheth tho papists, Mr. Finch, Rector of Wigan, Ld. Kilmory Mr. Cholmley of Vale Royal, Mr. Case are fixt on. About 100 Horse attend far as Winwick, after fall off. Mr. Banks, Mr. Peake and I call at Hall of Kenyon, are treated here by Mr. Ayde with Ale. Overtake the Herse near Leigh, the town and church crowded, wee come about 5. Mr. Shaw[38] has a good sermon with difficulty pronounced on Rev. [?] Hee gives a good and grave Character of the good Lady. The office is ended before 7. I go to the Swan, meet with Mr. Shaw, am doubtfull whether to go to Winwick, Wigan or Beausee, but determine on the last. It is dark and rainy for an hour. Mr. Shaw and I come readily on, I reach Beausee about 9.

16 About 9 I sett to Winwick Church. Mr. Ed. Finch has a very good discourse

38 L.R.O., Exhibit Book DCh.1 1691,f.23.

on 1 Peter 4 v.19. Mr. Blackburn and I go down to dinner. After at Church where Mr. Alanson preaches on this subject (so run that ye may obtain). After sermon wee return to the Hall, the Brothers by variety of discourse invite and conspire my stay. Mr. Blackburn go's early, Mr. Alanson and I stay supper, drawn on by a Dream at Horwich and Wigan affairs, wee stay till 10. I am at the Gates, shutt at Beausee at 11, knock and indevor, half an hour to enter the House in vain. I come to Warrington about 12 and after a pint of Sack burn't, to Bed about 1.

17 After a rainy night a fair day. I go to Beausee about 9, acquaint Mr. Cholmley with my Adventures last night, drink Tea, mount about 11 and by a constant easy rate reach (D.G.) Home safe about 3. After a full supper and refreshment to bed about 10.

18 After something of Busienes and dinner, examine 2 Wittnesses on Mercer Will. In the Evening at the Bacchus with Arch Deacon Thane, Mr. Hulton, Mr. Starkie, Atturny, wee drink our pints part about 9.

19 In the Town. After a walk of 4 Turns on roodee, My sister Jones comes I lend her 3^{li} and pay Mrs. Whaley besides 50^{s} two daies ago 5^{li}. Am with Mr. Chancellor, ArchDeacon Thane and Henry Hough at the Bacchus a few Glasses, wee part before 9.

20 First Court day this Term, the Busienes competent and easy. After Noon I discourse Mr. Tetloe on an intended pleading against him and take Aspinwalls answer to a Libel. After a full pint of good domestic Claret, to bed about 10.

21 The weather still Frosty. I send by Mr. Mercer a new Almanack to Mr. Vaudrey. Hen. Hough calls on mee, wee go to the Coffee house, discourse Mr. Proby, indevor to see young Holmes, hee comes not tho he promisd. Hen. Hough dines and stays with mee till 6. Then to the Coffee house where I meet Mr. Egerton. After sent to, I and Henry H. go to the Chancellor & Archdeacon at the Bacchus, drink our pints.

22 I draw a scheme of the primary Visitacion[39] and inclose it in a Letter to my Lord. After dinner correct the Articles against Ellison. In the Evening see Lady Soames. After that a domestic pint and to bed about 10.

23 The Frost returns with Severity and the News gives amazing Accounts of its effects in Germany, Poland, France, Flanders. Mr. Aubrey preaches in the Quire on Psalm 51 v 3. I receive a Letter of pacific proposals in order to accommodate the Visitacion of the other Archdeaconry from the Commissary and after prayers communicate that and my scheme of the Visitacion to the Chancellor, hee is pleasd with both. The Archdeacon and I visit him about 6. Hee treats us and Dr. Norris with 2 Bottles of excellent Claret wee part about 8.

24 I write to Mr. Le Neve and John Crosse. About a Quarter after 10 Drs. Thane and Norris and I with Jack set out on Foot and come to Eaton readily before 12, wee walk the Gardens with Sir Richard Grosvenor who receives with

39 By canon law a new bishop must undertake a visitation of his diocese within three years of his election.

great Civility. I see Mr. Cholmley in his Chamber, hee tells mee of the Bill about Beausee affairs, was by negligence of the Solicitor, rejected in the House of Lords. Wee dine in the Great Hall and are very sensible of the stone Floor. The Lady sitts in her rideing dress, a habit disagreeable to her sex and those present. Wee sit after dinner till 4 and are returnd well home (the journy well performd) before 6. I solace in a domestic pint.

25 St Pauls day, cold to extremity, the Frost more vehement. I go to the Quire where Mr. Lancaster has a sermon on the day (not regarding the coldness of the day) an hour long. I see the News which has more of Frost than Action. Ned Roberts, his wife, her sister and his mother, dine with us. After prayers Dr. Thane and I rebound to T. Hatfeilds, Mr. Egerton follows, wee try the rich Lisbon and mix it with turning French. Wee reckon more than pints. Dr. Thane comes with mee home, wee find the company at supper after that gon, I treat him to a domestic pint of excellent wine.

26 About 10 I go to Roodee a sharp and Frosty Ayr scarce admitts of warmth by 4 full turns, hence I call on Lady Soames where my Suzy meets mee. Wee are treated with good Coffee, thence to dinner, after that Busienes. Mr. France of Little Eccleston in Kirkham parish brings mee Letters from Mr. Hornby and Mr. Robinson. I apply to a special Administracion on his behalf. In the Evening, Dr. Thane, Mr. France and I go to T. Hatfeilds. Mr. Hulton comes to us, wee are tolerably cheerfull and drink our Bottles and part after 9.

27 The weather still frosty and cold. A Court day, the busienes easy without much noise. I am indisposd from the nocturnal Bottle. I write to Mr. Hornby by Mr. France. I examine 2 Wittnesses on Mr. Breers Will, relax about 8 in a domestic pint.

28 The Frost on the dissolucion. I write and inclose Mr. Callys Receipt to Sir Wm. Gerard. I after take 4 (2 shorter) Turns on roodee. Hen. Whaley comes before dinner with his old complaint, desires mee to consider him, begs my pardon of his former rude behavior. Speaks of, but does not produce the Counterpart. I promise him nothing, hee recedes abruptly. After Dinner, one Lee, a Sailer and Quaker calls on Tom Birchal. I entertain him with my strong Ale. After some recess and reading and after a long visit made to us by Mrs. Margaret Lloyd and her coz. Mostyn, wee go invited to Mr. Boucher's chamber. After 7 hee brings out a Bottle left by Coll. Vescy, magnifies the Wine and entertains after his manner. Tis good but strong Claret, wee stay till 10.

29 The Frost recedes without rain, but not insensibly. I write to Mr. Lambert, Jebb, Topping, draw a submission and peticion for Aspinwal and order a Monicion to the Churchwardens of Weverham.[40] After a domestic pint to bed before 11.

30 The sensible thaw continues. The News has it that the 2 Houses are about joining in an Address to her Majesty to lay aside her sorrow for the Prince and resume Thoughts of a second Marriage. ArchDeacon Thane has a good sermon

40 C.R.O.,EDC1/103 n.f.

in the Quire on 4 Phil.v.6. After Even prayers Mr. Howard (painter) sees & drinks a dish of Tea with mee. My Suzy begins Dr. Sherlock on Death. After a domestic pint, to bed about 10.
31 The Frost plainly gon, the weather warmer. King Charles 1st his Martyrdom celebrated. Mr. Lancaster has a sermon on 1st Sam. Cap. 24;5 wherein he revives the antiquated Doctrine of Passive Obedience.[41] I apply to Salmasius his Defensio regie. In the Evening Dr. Thane calls on mee, wee go to T. Hatfeild's and drink a Bottle of indifferent wine and part about 9.

FEBRUARY 1 I see the News wherein the Queens answer to the Commons adress about her 2nd Marriage, she saies it is of such a Nature, shee believes they doe not expect a particular Answer. I proceed in Salmasius. Mr. Vaudrey sends, I go to the Bull and Dog, to him. Hee tells mee how hee is prest by the Stamp Commissioner. I go after to Mr. Chancellor, Archdeacon Thane and Capt. Breholt where wee drink more than our pints and part before 10.
2 It blows a severe storm when in the Church, St. Oswalds, where Mr. Fogg preaches Mr. Vernon's Charity Sermon on St. Matt. 6 v. 19,20. The Storm continues most of the day. After repose I return to Salmasius. After prayers Mrs. Thane comes to see us. About 8 wee are surprizd with a fearfull Noise of a Fire in the neighborhood, the Barn and Stables on the back of the old White Lyon (Madocks) all in Flames, the whole Town amazd with the light and terror, I go by way of Crooks Lane, and see the dreadful Flame spread on 2 Haystacks and threatning if not the whole street, that part from Parsons Lane to Mr. Kingstons with destrucion, togeather with the new Hall, the wind being very high from the West, I see most of the Houses near, hot under the Influence and the Owners in Consternacion. Hands, Engine, water are brought in confusion, the Fire layes but dos not proceed, wett sheets and the Engine interpos'd twixt the Hay stacks and the Houses, and the Hands dispers'd into better order. The common Fear abates, the frightened neighborhood remove their Goods with great precipitancy. Jack conducts Mrs. Worger to my House. I mostly out till 12 observing the scenes of hope and danger, this then seems over and the fire, tho glowing and flameing high in the stacks, stopt in its progress. And what is no less than wonder, tho a vehement storm blows all the Night, it recovers not but subsides in its own Ashes. I conclude that an Almighty providence interpos'd and checkt those Flames which in human probability by the means of so high a west wind and so much combustible matter and houses near it, might in this Night, have spread and devourd a great part of the City, this street especially. Therefore to God alone be ascribed all the Honor and Glory as well as the Mercy of so great a Deliverance, Amen. I paid Mr. Vaudrey 2^{li};10s.
3 I see the remains of the Fire, the stacks are burnt to 2 dull heaps of Ashes, so that, tho within 6 yards of each other, I past betwixt them, they are sunk below a

41 The doctrine of Non Resistance and Passive Obedience was the common theme preached in almost every church between 1660 and 1689.

brick wall to the W. where they stood, and that is now a Shelter. The buildings where the fire prevaild afford a horrid prospect. The unaccountable Stop of its progress in so stormy a Night and morning, a matter of admiracion and thanksgiving, to that Great God who gave so narrow limits to its threatening power and accordingly Thanksgiving is returnd in the Quire. I write to Mr. Gilibrand about the interest mony. I send Mrs. Whaley $1^{li};10^{s}$. Sir Wm. Meredith about 12, comes to desire mee lend what Guineas I have by mee, in order only to make tender, After noon promising to return them at 4 a clock. I lend him 20 Guineas. I examine Mr. Birkenhead on Gilberts Will. A tollerable easy Court. Sir Wm. Meredith returns mee the 20 Guineas about 6. I recreate in Aul. Gell. & domestic pint till 9.

4 A warm morning, yet windy. After this little News seen, I betake mee to 4 full turns on roodee. Mr. Ingham brings Mr. Cliftons Nominacion and Testimonials in order to the Curacy of Litham[42]. Connivence is promis'd him. Hee returns with Mr. Cliftons Steward by whom I write to Jeffrey Prescott. I drink a Bottle of good Claret with them at the Mermaid. After prayers and turning in Agellius, Dr. Thane and Mr. Morrey calling on mee, wee go to the Mermaid approve the wine excellent tho not yet settld and ripe in the Bottles, wee drink 3 bottles, pay ½ Crown which wee think too much especially for the measure and part about 10.

5 A fair brisk morning, tho indispos'd, I take not the advantage of it. I write fully to my Lord Bishop and give him an Account of the late Fire, and to my coz. Parre. After dinner, repose and recover. After prayers I turn over Dean Booths Collecion of Articles of 58 Bishops and ArchDeacons. Divert in Agellius and about 9 recreate in a domestic pint.

6 A delicate brisk morning. Mr. Hale has a sermon in the Quire on St. John 6 v 54, a good discourse, modestly, fast and less laudably deliver'd. The papers are at the lowest ebb, invent and repeat dull News. I see a Letter from Mrs. Whaley, send the inclosd to Her. After prayers I see Mrs. Whaley, shee is poor woman, peevish, indiscreet, confusd by temper and adversity. The Queens birthday celebrated by Noise of Bells, not by the Mayor as usuall. I retreat to my Corner and wish all success to her Majesty in my domestic pint.

7 A heavy morning. I draw the Case betwixt Mr. Ellis and myself and apply to other Busienes. At 2 invited as in Favor by Mr. Cholmley. Go down to Mr. Egertons, where only Mr. Wilbraham, Mr. Cholmley and Mr. Okes besides dine with him. After dinner wee retreat to a Bottle good Claret. Mr. Cholmley in good humor, hee returns before 5. Mr. Wilbraham before 6. I stay, an Irish Capt. Brereton comes, wee drink another bottle in Jockey discourse and part about 8.

8 After indisposicion recover. The weather very sharp and frosty. The News still scanty. I pay off Mr. Hodgsons Bill $2^{li};10^{s}$. After a good dinner repose. I visit

42 L.R.O., Richmond Call Book ARR 1709.

Lady Soames about 5 stay near 8. My Lord enters on the 2nd year of his Consecracion. Paid Alderman Ince for rent & Hay 13^{li};$12^{s}0^{d}$.

9 This day sharp and severely cold. I write to Sir Henry Bunbury and in close my Case about Mr. Ellis. I write to my Lord Bishop and to Mr. Feilding. Hen. Whaley comes a 3rd Time submissively to know what I will, in his difficulty, do for him – hee makes it out that his brother brought him into securitys for him for 55^{li} besides the 65^{li} hee lent him – hee brings his sister in law along. I give him a Guinea as a Gift and 5^{s} towards his Charges. About an hour after hee returns and prays mee to make it up to 5^{li}, so insensible this man is of my Circumstances and his rude behavior to mee. Apply to Busienes of Transmission. About 6 Dr. Thane and Mr. Morrey call on mee, wee dispatch 3 of the 4 Bottles of excellent wine which Mr. Morrey brought along with him, wee part about 9.

10 Another as sharp and severe day. A Court day of small Busienes. After prayers I see Lady Soame, Mrs. Mary Oldfeld with her for an hour, return and first read then send the Harwich Dream to her Ladyship. After my domestic pint, apply to and finish the three short Acts in the Transmission betwixt Hartley and Stephenson, Appellants and the Chapellwardens of Colne.[43] I pay 10^{li} to Mr. Vaudrey's Man on Account.

11 Still freezing and excessively cold, the wind N.E. The News brings That the difference betwixt the Emperor and Pope is accommodated. I finish the Certificate of the Transmission (dated as of the 9th) write to Tom Stringer. After Dinner, Lady Soame and Mrs. Mary Oldfeld come to us, and kindly stay with us, till 5. After which, sent for, I go to the Bacchus where the Chancellor, Drs. Wroe, Thane & Norris, much of this time is taken up in opposite Sentiments of the Chancellor and Dr. Norris, about the proceedings of this Parliament as to eleccions and the design of a general Naturalisacion, it holds, ingratefull enough to the rest till 9.

12 Yet very thin sharp cold Ayr. Apply to busienes and preparacion for my Journy. After Noon, I call and see Sir Peter Soame, return'd last night; hee staies mee till 5, treats with indifferent wine. At 6 Mr. Egerton and Archdeacon Thane come to mee, wee in my warm corner dispatch the 2 remaining Bottles of Neston wine, 1 from the Bear and a 4th Bottle of my Good wine; wee pass these and the time, liberally till 11. Twixt 5 & 6 I took 2 short & 2 longer Turns on roodee.

13 Indisposd from the Quantity, I keep home all day till Evening prayer. The public gives an Account of the Popes compliance with the Emperors Terms and the private News of a proposal to trade with France and exchange our imported Goods, Tobacco especially, for their wines. After Book and domestic pint to bed about 9.

14 A great Snow falls and occasions Mr. Hulton and Mr. Stratford to alter a week longer, the time of the intended Commissions. I am pleasd with it. At 6 I

43 C.R.O., EDC1/103 n.f.

go down to the Bear. Dr. Thane, Mr. Hulton & Stratford meet mee there, wee drink 3 Bottles, come back in a deep Thaw about 9. I pay Mr. Cartwright 1^{li};10^{s};6.

15 A brisk frost returnd makes the roads unsafe for man and Horse. Before prayers, I take 2 longer and 2 shorter Turns. I pay Mr. Vaudreys Man, Davies 10^{li} on the Stamp Account. I write to Mr. Styth and Mr. Markland. About 6 call on Mr. Hodgson, hee gos with mee to Mr. Hatfeild's; wee dispatch 3 pints of indifferent Claret parting about 9.

16 The weather excessive cold, a frost more severe and pinching than has yet bin felt this winter. I write to Mr. Le Neve and Mr. Hough on the same subject. I pay Mr. Stringer, Haberdasher, 4^{li};6s. I dine with the Warden of Manchester at Dr. Thanes nice Dinner. About five after prayers send Mrs. Whaley by her daughter 1^{li}. Apply to Books & relax in a domestic pint about 9.

17 The season still severe and obstinate. A Thanksgiving celebrated for the success of the last Campaign. The Warden of Manchester preaches before the Magistracy and City on 25 Prov.25, hee forms an historical and political discourse of the War and our Successes, it is popular and gratefull to the Hearers. I am invited by the Mayor, to his dinner but desire his Excuse. I write to Mr. Lambert fully and to John Crosse. After prayers Dr. Thane calls, wee go to the Mermaid, Mr. Glasier comes to us, fills us with Accounts of Mr. Bennet's managry; wee drink 2 Bottles, pay 5^{s} part about 9.

18 The weather still cold yet the frost (the wind S.W.) rebuts. The Gazet confirms the intimated Victory of the Swedes over the Moscovites, in which Battle the Czar is wounded. I turn over many Titles in the Canon Corpus, till 8 at night when I relax in a domestic pint.

19 A considerable snow fallen in the Night and the Frost recover'd. I proceed in some Titles of the Corpus. Send Mrs. Whaley about 9 by her daughter 1^{li}. The Frost relents after Noon. I divert in Agellius. After prayers Dr. Thane calls, wee try a Bottle of Tom Hatfeilds, it does not please mee, wee part before 9.

20 The Snow and Frost dissolvd insensibly save a small. My S. gos to Wrexham to visit my mother Puleston and returns at Night. The News affords nothing of moment. Mr. Lancaster preaches in the Quire on 2 Ep. St. Peter 3.18 the words, Grow in Grace, the discourse not very clear. After prayers, I apply to 5th Book of Hooker and relax in a domestic pint at 9.

21 The Frost seems vanisht, small rain succeeds, the day clearer after 11. I perform 4 shorter Turns. After a small repose and prayers, I write to Mr. Styth and to Mr. Whaley recur to domestic refreshment at 8.

22 The Frost seems spent for this year. The News is considerable. Apply to Books and Busienes. After prayers at the Bacchus with the Chancellor, Mr. Davies and coz. Kendrick, wee dispose of 6 pints of indifferent wine of several sorts. Church Antiquity takes up the Time past 9. I sent (about 1) 5 Guineas.

23 Indispos'd from the wine last night. I write to Sir Tho. Hanmer and Mr. Harvie about the Charrs[44] I have orderd to them. After morning prayer take 2

44 Chars were fish related to salmon that were found in Morecambe Bay.

full Turns. After Even prayer go with Dr. Thane to the Barrs, but in vain, (Mr. Egerton absent). Wee returning drink a Tankard of Mr. Woods Ale. After the Dr. comes to my Corner, I treat him with a Bottle of good domestic, and over this give him a full account and charg of my 2 Concerns with Mr. Ellis & the Charter House, hee stays past 9.

24 St. Matthias, at early prayers. I attend after 9 Archdeacon Thane to the Coach, Mr. Higgins of Ireland is one of the Company. Hee gives mee 3 pamphlets (Letters) about the Test. I write to Jeffrey Prescott about the Interest mony. After 10 I and Jack sett out on Foot, come to Eaton before 12. It is the Ladys 19th birthday and celebrated in an elegant dinner and a full Glass. I stay with Mr. Cholmley & Breerwood past 5. Wee return home (quickly after my Suzy from Wrexham) after 6 harrasd with wine and walk, to bed before 9.

25 After an indisposd Night a dull morning. The News affords no diversion. I draw out the day in idle indisposicion, dip in Books and finish in domestic pint. I pay Mrs. W. 2 Guineas.

26 The Thaw continues till Noon. I write to my Lord Bishop and to Mr. Lambert. After Dinner it snows and is cold. After prayers apply to Books and recreate in domestic about 9.

27 A severe Frost with snow, a third winter. The News has random proposals of a peace, particion menciond, not complyd with. Mr. Fogg preaches in the Quire on Gen. 16 v.25. After prayers retreat to my warm Corner, reading and domestic pint.

28 The Frost continues but the weather milder. I take 4 full Turns on roodee, tho hinderd with the gathering snow. Refresht turn 1st part of the Monasticon, write to Mr. Green of Prescott, pay John Cross, Joyner, in full $5^{li};17^{s}6^{d}$. After prayers return to Books, receive the Repertorim Londinense, recreate in that and domestic pint till 10.

MARCH 1 A very sharp and severe Frost. I am at early prayers, receive my Lords answer to my former 3 Letters. The News affords no diversion. I take 4 full Turns, in a delicate brisk ayr on Roodee, return to my Books. After prayers with Mr. Hodson, after that to Books and domestic pint till 10.

2 A very severe Morning of Chads Day. I write to my Lord the alteracion of the scheme after Whitehaven. About 11 the Chancellor, Coll. Proby, Mr. Boucher, Mr. Proby and myself sett out in a cold Ayr and thoro the meadows come to Eyton Boat after 12. Sir Richard Grosvenor favors us with his Company. Wee have a full and elegant dinner, good Ale, indifferent wine, to celebrate our Anniversary Chad Feast (the first I remember out of Lent). The weather alters to Storm and Snow. The time spent much at Tables and hazard, a little of policy. About 6, tho wee have horses, wee return (the road way) on Foot. The Chancellor, 2 Probys and I call at the Bear. Here is good Claret. Mr. Chancellor stays till 9, I am an hour longer with the Probys.

3 A cold but thawing day. A Court of easy Busienes. Mr. Vaudrey, Fearnhead comes takes Account of our Blanks in Stock which amounts only to 35^{li}. Wee state the Account, I pay him 20^{li} and give him my Note for 109^{li} on Ballance.

After prayers I return to Books cheifly the Repertorium Londinense, till 10.
4 A severe cold Thaw. I dip in Hospinian. The News brings the D. of Marlborough to Court on Tuesday. After dinner I go with Mrs. Crompton to discourse her Brother T. Brock about the 300^{li}. I move him for payment of it or further security by Judgment in a short Time. Hee is very averse to the later, but promises to pay (if not 2) yet 100^{li} at Michaelmas next. After prayers I go on in Books and divert into domestic pint. About 9 Mrs. Whaley is with us this Evening.
5 A tollerable calme day. I take 4 shorter Turns, am recreated, return to Books not Busienes. After prayers, I go down to Mr. Chancellor and the 2 Probys at the Bear. Here I see Sir Richard Grosvenor and Sir Richard Vernon, wee drink our Bottles. After which, Jack Wright comes in and adds his, wee part about 9. I sent Mrs. Whaley before noon 10s. I write to Mr.Morrey about Wine.
6 Indispos'd from the Quantity last night. Mr. Fogge has a Sermon in the Quire on St.Matt. 11 v. 28. The News makes great Mencion of proposals of peace, by France and of an Address from both Houses concerning it. After prayers and a visit to Mr. Boucher proceed in Hookers 5th Book. I send, at Night, another 10s to Mrs. Whaley, after domestic pint to bed about 10.
7 A dull not rainy day. I apply to the Monasticon and in it particularly to the Monasterys of St. Werbergh and Vale Royal, these take up most of the day. About 4 my coz. Kendrick calls, I go with him to see Mr. Bennet in the Northgate. Hee is cheerful under his Charge and Confinement, wee stay 2 hours with him. After wee go to Alderman Allen confind by the Gout. Hee treats us with a Bottle of good Claret, wee part about 8.
8 Shrove Tuesday and the Queens Day, dull, fair yet cold. I go to early prayers, after return to Books and examine Dr. Chetwode on Cranstons Will. Lend Mrs. Whaleys daughter 2s 6d. The News mencions a probability of the Bishop of Worcesters, and a certainty of the Earl of Meaths, deaths. Before prayers Wee see Mrs. Thane. After those Mr. Chancellor, my coz. Kendric and I go to the Pentice. Here with the Mayor a Company about 30 in number, each has his Bottle before him which is exhausted by these Healths viz. The Queen, to the Church, her Majesties Forces, her Allyes, the Dukes of Hanover, Marlborough, Prince Eugene, Lord High Admiral, Lord Treasurer, Lord Bishop, Lord Lieftenant of the County, prosperity to the City, begun by the Mayor, little of Conversacion in so great a number; wee part about 8.
9 Ash Wednesday, a sharp but not bright day. I write to my Coz. Parre. Mr. Lancaster has a long discourse in the Quire on Jere.3 v 25. Apply to Books. After prayers and Dinner I examine 2 Wittnesses on Cranstons Will. I receive a Letter and 2 Guineas from Jeffrey Prescott on Mr. Clifton of Lytham his Account.
10 A very sharp Frost, my Suzy gos to Wrexham. After 2 shorter Turns on roodee, I call on Mr. Vice Chamberlain Starkie, principally on the affair of my Bond for 100^{li} due for interest of the 500^{li}. I drink a dish of Coffee with him. I pay Mr. Damald for a whole years interest of 80^{li} due 5 of this month 4^{li};16s. A Court day easy in Busienes. After prayers I follow Mr Chancellor and Mr. Vice

Chamberlain to the Bear. Wee dispatch 3 Bottles indifferent Claret in free and freindly Conversacion and part about 8. Mr. Otty comes tells mee the story twixt him & Mrs. A Swift.

11 A very brisk Frost and clear day. The News of the Bishop of Worcesters death contradicted. About 8 Mr. Starkey the Vice Chamberlains Man calls pays mee 10^{li} from Mr. Gilibrand. I execute the Bond for the 100^{li} interest bearing Date of Yesterday. The Vice Chamberlain comes after 9 to see mee, drinks Coffee & stays an Hour. Mr. Alanson comes then on the matter of Dilapidacions at Grapenhale. I receive from Mr. Ayde 5^{li};1^{s} for 6 Licences. After prayers I write to Jeffrey Prescott my Thoughts in Mr. Cliftons Case of Litham Church and recreate in domestic pint about 9.

12 A considerable Snow falls but lies not. I write to my Lord Bishop and to the Commissary. The Chancellor comes in opportunely reads and approves them. After prayers I write to Mr. Whaley and return to Books, these are succeeded by a domestic pint about 9. I pay (about this day) 5^{li} to Mr. Cartwright for drawing a Discharge for my sister Jones.

13 The weather wett and cold. I receive a kind Letter from Mr. Herne. Mr. Fogg has a good sermon on his last Text here, Matt. 11 v 28. The News is full of Warr and Peace. After prayers I go with Mr. Hulton and Mr. Mosse of Manchester to Mr. Pickmore's, thence to T. Hatfeilds, wee drink above our pints. Thence about 8 to Mr. Thane's where my Suzy; wee are entertaind with a Bottle of good Claret and civility, wee stay past 11.

14 A cold morning, I write to Mr. Peirson of the Commons and to Dr. Thane (now at Mr. Richardsons in King Street near St. James's Square) bestow most of the day on Latinus Leitinius and till hee meet, my domestic pint about 9.

15 Still cold and moist. My S. gos to visit my mother Puleston. I see Mrs. Thane, shee reads mee the Drs. Letter hence to the Coffee house, where more noise at the Tables than news. Mrs. Worgers papers give a great victory to the Swede, over the Moscovite. About 4 Mr. Hales calls. I go with him to his chamber, where to Dr. Foulks of Llanbeta Mr. Davis, Dean Booth Mr. Aubrey and myself, hee shows us the Curiosity of a Discection of a Frogg and thoro a microscope the Circulacion of the blood, the admirable texture of his lungs, the poor Animal stretcht cross ways; it is a barbarous Experiment and gives mee very sensible and melancholy reflections. Wee part at 8. I return to domestic pint.

16 A dull cold day bestowd rather on Books than Busienes. After prayers Mr. Clopton ingages Mr. Callis & myself, wee go to T. Hatfeilds and chuse white wine, dispose of 6 pints in various desultory talk, his Lady and Coach call and wee part about 11.

17 A rainy day. I am unhappily affected with the wine last Night, yet go to Court where short busienes, pleases my distempers. Before prayers I attend Mr. Pickness (my old Friend's) corps to the Church followd by 8 children and a freindly company, after prayers he is interrd. About 7 Mrs. Thane comes, staies with us (wee empty 1 Bottle) till 10.

18 A moist day. My Suzy and I sett for Wrexham about 8, come thither about 10. I see my mother Puleston, shee is very weak, apprehensive of her change cheerfully submitting. Shee gives mee and mine her blessing, with the good advice to serve God with Truth and Sincerity, and so to live in this world as not to bee afraid to dye into the next. I see Mr. Grosvenor and discourse my sister Jones, her busienes with him and write to him fully on the subject, to Mr. Jones of Llanlothian. My brother and sister Puleston are freindly here. I wait on my uncle Eyton, hee is satyrical on his son William and not without cause. I go into the end of the Fair and furnish mee with 3 ounces of good snuff. My brother Puleston treats mee with a pint of Claret. Wee remount at 5, and come safe thoro the road full of water in the worst condicion, safe to our Corner (D.G.) ½ hour after 7. I conclude the night with a domestic pint.

19 A dull cold day, less rain. I write to Sir Wm. Robinson and Mr. Hadgood, the D. of Ormonds servant about 2 potts of Charrs, and to John Crosse. About 5 I visit Lady Soame, after Alderman Allen, hee calls for a Bottle of very good Claret, in the beginning of which, Newall, a Seaman comes in, rudely interrupts our discourse, sharing equally of the Bottle, Impatient of this I leave 'em about 8 and after write to the Bishop of Meath.

20 A cold dull day. The News retracts the Swedish victory, some private Letters mencion another invasion on Scotland. I wait on Lord Charlemont. Mr. Lancaster has a more agreeable sermon on psalm. . . After prayers my Suzy and I wait on Lord and Lady Charlemont at the Coach and Horses, are well entertaind by her ingenious Account of the difference betwixt the Duchess of Ormond and Lady Betty Southwell, and the History of my Lord's Spanish expedicion. I return about 7 to my domestic pint.

21 The wind high with sleet of snow. I receive a Letter from Mr. Whaley communicate it to his wife, who receives it very unkindly with indecent reflecions. I thence take 4 shorter Turns in sharp weather on roodee am recreated, write to Mrs. Brockbank of Cartmel incloseing a copy of John Brockbanks Will which comes to 10s and to Mr. Lambert. Mrs. Thane dines with us and in the Evening repeats her kindness in sitting with us and sharing our domestic pint about 9.

22 A brisk but calmer day. I repeat 4 shorter Turns on roodee. After 9 My S. and I drink Tea and Coffee with Mrs. Thane, shee reads out of the Drs. Letter that my Lord Rochester has promisd him his Warrant of Election of my son William to a scholarship in the Charterhouse. Wee heartily congratulate the good News, I go to the Coffee house, but meet with little Entertainment but that ungrateful one of the Tables. After prayers to the Coffee house to speak to Mr. Egerton on Dr. Thanes Account. Hee draws mee and Mr. James Egerton to his Barrs treats us plentifully with good wine and Charrs, about 8 Jack Shakerley comes, adds to the mocion of the Conversacion. Wee part about 11.

23 Indisposicion from the wine last night naturally follows. I write yet to my Lord Bishop and Dr. Thane. I send Mrs. Whaley 13s;3d the last sum of the 50^{li} I gave her, shee gives mee an acknowledgment of the whole sum. After prayers H. Hough calls on mee, I go with him to Mr. Egerton, at the Coffee house,

thence with Mr. Davies and him to the Bacchus. Mr. Davies is full and warm of the Bishop of Worcester. Wee dispatch 3 pints bad wine & part about 9.
24 A calm and warmer day, the wind Westerly. I go and wish Lady Soame a good journy by the Coach, to London. H. Hough sees mee, I advise him to go to London and sollicit his own Affair with Norroy. Hee takes a Week to deliberate. The Busienes of the Court is breifly dispatcht, I examine 3 Wittnesses on Eaton's Will, recreate in my domestic pint and to bed about 10.

1709

MARCH 25 Lady Day, a cold brisk E. wind, I go to early prayers. The News very dull in repecticion. About 9, Jack with mee, I sett for Christleton, come to Mr. Clapton's about 10, stay drink Coffee near an hour with Mrs. Thane, thence proceed to Warton, meet with Mr. Brett in a scandalous Night Gown and Cap in the Lane overseeing his ditches. Hee seems to be glad and gratefull, leads mee to an out building, very infirm and ruinous, tells mee his design to take down an Oven and build a hogstye and over it, a place for his poultry. Hee shews & magnifies the improvement of his orchard, affirms hee dos all for the Honor of the Church, takes us into his house, sends for Ale from an adjoining Ale House, shews the remains of a Veal pye and is noisy and comical in his Invitacion. Wee part with him and return to Mr. Clapton at 12.[1] Wee sitt down to a clearly Lent dinner, the liquor good, his method despotical. Wee pass the time till 5 cheerfully with the Ladys. Thence wee call at Mr. Townsend's, the scene here an elegant dwelling House and Garden furnisht and kept with extraordinary Ayr and fancy. Wee return safe home before 7.
26 A calm morning, I take 4 shorter Turns on roodee. I divert in Books. Mr. Davies comes & gives mee a fragment of an Hypocauston. After prayers wee step to the Coffee House, thence I return to my domestic pint. Mr. Worger our good old Neighbor died this morning about 5 a clock.
27 A calmer day, Mr. Fogg has a good discourse on, "It is the Lord's doing. Let him do what he pleaseth." Hee has a very strong Argument for our Resignacion to the Will of God. The News dos not yet improve. After prayers I take 2 shorter Turns on roodee. After visit Mrs. Thane return'd from Christleton, shee treats mee with 3 Glasses of white wine. I add at home a pint of Claret. About ½ hour after 4 this evening dies, that very tender, charitable and religious person, My good mother Puleston.
28 A calme and pleasant morning, I refresht with 4 shorter Turns on roodee. My Suzy gos to Wrexham. I write to Mr. Waite, Turn Pliny's Epistles. My Suzy returns after 7.
29 A delicate morning but cold. I wait on Mrs. Thane at her Tea, wee complain of the Dr's. silence. The News affords no informacion nor divercion. Apply to

1 C.R.O., EDP1/81, Christleton Parish Papers. Thomas Clopeton, rector, deacon and priest at Bangor on the same day 1673, and presented by Sir Richard Brook.

Busienes and prepare for my mother Puleston's Funeral. After prayers I see Mrs. Thane at and after takeing of her vomit. I drink there my pint of Claret and stay till 9.

30 A delicate brisk morning, equip for Wrexham. I write to Mr. Welham and inclose a Copy of Hughson's Will amounting to 9s. I write to the Bishop of St. Asaph, Mr. Lambert and Mr. Jebbe. About 2 Harry with mee I sett for Wrexham, come thither about 4. The company comes with leasure and make up a considerable number. About 6 the Funeral then proceeds without pomp or indeed the decent solemnities due to the merit and quality of the person. Shee is interr'd close to the North Wall and the end of the Oratory; the vicar (Mr. Price) performing the Office. About 8 I go to Bryn y Funan to see my uncle Eyton, stay an hour and return to my Sister Jones.

31 A pleasant morning. After Tea discourse with my sister Jones, my Suzy and I go visit my cozen Moreton, wee drink a pott of good Coffee, hee receives us with his civility. Hence to prayers and thence to Bryn y Funan where Mr. Richard Davies and Mr. Price are invited. After some time at the Inn (Fox and Goose) and some stay with my sister Jones, wee take horse after 4 come easily and safe D.G. home about 7.

APRIL 1 A soft rain falls almost all the day. About 9 I wait on Mrs. Thane. Wee have both Letters from Dr. Thane but of slender Contents (as to my Affairs). I stay till 11 and then to the Coffee house, where the News reduces the Swede into utmost difficulty and danger. Many persons (no great ones) are here from Ireland. After prayers I see Mr. Egerton at the Coffee house. After that with Capt. Byron over one pint of bad wine at the Mermaid thence to my Corner where I reconcile my stomach with ½ pint of domestic.

2 After a rainy night a moist morning. I am at early prayers. After at the Falcon see a Spanish Bishop (a man of no venerable aspect, of a black and swarthy complexion, midle size, slender, about 40) take Horse under the Custody of a pursuivant, who brought him from Ireland. I write to Dr. Thane inclosing Mr. Hough's Certificate and to Mr. Lambert, Mr. Hough dines with us. After prayers in Books, after domestic to bed about 10.

3 A moist rainy day. Mr. Fogg has a good sermon on Rom. 6 v. 5, 6 Cenae Sanctissimae particeps sum vitam residuam det puriorem.[2] I read part of Bishop Beveridge his excellent discourse of frequent Communion. After prayers at the Coffee house where France is mencion'd with contempt and its King reduc'd to the last, and begging a peace. Dr. Norris is sanguine on this subject. Capt. Byron comes sitts 2 hours with mee. I treat him with Ale & domestic pint.

4 Disposicion to rain continues. I am at early prayers. Apply to Busienes, most of the day recreate in Pliny and a domestic pint in the Evening.

5 A delicate morning. I receive Letters from the Bishop of St. Asaph, Sir Wm. Robinson, Mr. Howard. I take 4 short Turns drink Tea with Mrs. Thane, thence

2 Trans: 'I partake of the most Holy Supper; may [God] grant that the rest of my life be purer.'

to the Coffee house where only imaginary News. I pay the later half years Tax 40s for the Office, the after Noon rainy. After prayers Lord and Lady Charlement setting forward for Neston (tomorrow) visit us. End the day in domestic pint.
6 Indispos'd, uneasy. Disposicion with the day, clears up about noon. I write to my Lord Bishop and to Dr. Stratford. Mrs. Whaley calls on mee and gives mee a History of her journey to Holland. there is a doubt betwixt us about the Lays[3] and Taxes on the Bank the last year. After prayers Mr. Hurst (of Manchester) comes and drinks Tea with mee. About 7 I go to Mr. Davies, Mr. Hurst along. He receives us in his Study and entertains us with indifferent Claret but with gratefull variety of Books and learning especially Ecclesiastical Antiquity, wee part about 9.
7 After a dull interrupted Night, I rise to early prayers, after fly to my solace in 4 shorter Turns on roodee, by which (D.G.) extremely refresht. I write to John Crosse. A Court day of very slender Busienes. I rejoice & repose. In the Evening I wait on Mrs. Thane, shee treats mee with a pint of good Claret. I stay past 9.
8 After uneasy Night, A fine morning. I recurr to 4 shorter Turns on roodee. After drink Tea with Mrs. Thane, shee reads a short mention of mee in the Dr's Letter. Thence to the Coffee House where the papers are still full of peace and preparacions for Warr. After prayers Mr. Crofton (who was left to my care when in the small pox . . .) returns and calls on us. Hee tells me after above 2 years in Christ Church, hee went into Holland, went into Germany, saw the Courts of Prussia and Hanover, was at Hamburgh, Amsterdam and in his return Lisle, before the Citadel was surrender'd. His Account tho ready, seems suspicious. Mrs. Thane comes at the same time to sitt with us. They stay past 9. I pay Philip Bateman for hay 3^{li}.
9 A delicate cool morning. I am at early prayers. After take 4 shorter Turns on roodee, write to the Commissary inclose a copy of the Inhibicion and a Commission to him. I write to Mr. Hugh Howard, to be left at Wills Coffee House, Covent Garden. After prayers at T. Hatfeild's with Lord Charlemont, Mr. Chancellor, Coll, & Mr. Proby where cheerfull in song till 9.
10 A fine morning, I rise early, receive Dr. Thane's Letter refresh in 2 shorter Turns on roodee. Mr. Fogg has a good discourse on Hewbrews 5.v.9. The News yet imaginary. After prayers my Lord and I make visits but fix with Mrs. Thane where we try the Lancashire wine, it proves fine and gratefull; wee part about 11.
11 After an uneasy night, I recover by 4 shorter Turns on roodee. I write to Dr. Thane and John Cross and in the Evening to the Bishop of Meath and Sir William Parsons. After variety in Books, solace in domestic pint about 10.
12 A cool and pleasant morning. At early prayers. After take 4 shorter Turns on roodee, see Mrs. Thane. Thence to the Coffee House where nothing certain

3 Lays were local rates, e.g. poor rates, church rates, etc.

or diverting. After Evening prayers my coz. Kendrick and I go to the Mermaid (Dandy's) try the wine, send to Mr. Davies who comes, wee dispose of 3 Bottles pay 3s the small Bottle, take leave of this wine and return home about 10.

13 Extremely unhappy and indispos'd. I betake mee to roodee where at an high Tide I take 4 full Turns. I write to Mr. Lambert, by his servant, and send the process and 200 printed Notes to him. Mr. Morrey dines with us. I pay Mr. Gamul for Mr. Vaudrey 30^{li}. Indispos'd still, repose. In the Evening Mr. Wells calls on mee, desires my company with the 2 Coopers, Aldersey, Partington, Puleston and Mr. Lee at Pickings. I go there past 6, we are 11 in company have variety of indifferent conversacion drink 13 Bottles & a pint. Wee part about 12.

14 My unhappy disposicion is aggravated. Mrs. Whaley sends for 20s. I lend her 10s. A Court day ending this Term of easy Busienes tho not without noise and disrespect. After dinner and repose, I apply to the Deaneries and enter 7 very barren in Detections. About 8 lend Mrs. Whaley 5s. more, refresh in a domestic pint.

15 A very cold day. I finish the Entry of the Deanaries, divert in Books. The News is full of the misery of France from scarcity of mony and Corn. I draw a Monicion to the Chapelwardens and Sidesmen of Litlebrough to lay a Tax for the Font.[4] Mrs. Thane comes, sitts and sups with us, wee divert in a domestic pint till 10.

16 After Elixir tollerably easy. I pay John upon a running Account 20s. I write to Mr. Adams of Holt. About 4 Lord Wharton, Lord Lieftenant of Ireland, enters the City on Horseback. His retinue of Coaches and dependents with some Gentlemen who mett him, make up a number. The Mayor and Aldermen on a Gallery in the East Gate Street receive him; the Recorder has a speech of Complement – hee returns it in half as many words. In the Evening my sister Partington, my Suzy and myself visit Mrs. Thane, she treats them with a Carp, mee with a pint of Claret.

17 A pleasant morning. I take 2 shorter Turns on roodee and am refresht as well as diverted with the Spring. The Quire is crowded by the Irish Court and spectators. Mr. Fogg has a good sermon on Matt. 27. Lord Wharton appears no good Example of Devotion, tantam reintam negligenter agendo, yet is at both Morning and Evening prayers. After the later, I see Mr. Hulton and visit the Chancellor, indispos'd of a rheumatic Fever. I write to Dr. Stratford, Mr. Pilkington of Croston & Capt. Richard Fitzpatrick.

18 I prepare from journy, write to Mr. Whaley. About 2 Mr. Hulton, Stratford and my self, in a fair day, set out, come to the Rock about 5 and after a very fair, calme and long passage over, come to Liverpool, about 7. Wee go directly to Mr. Swarbreck's run thoro his Cellar, try 6 or 8 Hogsheads and that chosen by Mr. Egerton for my Lord Bishop. Wee drink besides 2 Bottles. About 9 wee come to our Inn, the Georg, Mr. Furnivall's, and after another Bottle here to bed about 11.

4 The Consistory Court Act Book from April 1709-March 1710 is lost.

19 I am indispos'd from the Quantity and variety, last night, At 9 to prayers. Past 10 wee open the Commission in the old Chapel before Mr. Styth who adjourns the Execucion to the Georg where about 20 Wittnesses are produc'd and sworn among whom Mr. Marsden. I examine 13. About 3 wee go to Mr. Swarbreck's where in a company wee while away 2 hours and drink near our Bottles.

20 Recover'd of the indisposition I begin to examine about 8. The Clerk of Formby (Johnson) is tedious in examinacion. I dispatch about 8 a clock 10 Wittnesses today. Wee recurr to Mr. Swarbreck's, drink above our pints and return about 10 to our Quarters.

21 I draw a Bill of this Commission (vidlt betwixt the Chapel wardens of Formby and the Curate Mr. Ellison) which are paid mee. I write to my Suzy. Mr. Hulton and Stratford return. Before Dinner I visit Mr. Houghton and my Shee Cosen Prescott's Family. After Lady Johnson, Mrs. Goderick, Alderman Cleaveland, Mr. Clayton and Mrs. Proctor (a difficult Gantlet) Mr. Styth all along with mee. I return, I fear with too much variety, about 10.

22 Good Friday. I am inexpressibly indispos'd & tortur'd with unhappy reflecions. Go to the old Chapell where Mr. Welsh the Curate preaches. After sermon walk on the Strand meet there the Mayor Mr. Seacome, hee tells mee the Tide at Full moon advances about 15 yards perpendicular above the Level of the Chanell; hee imparts his News and hopes of peace. After this I call on Mr. Swarbreck, wee go to the New Church to prayers about 2.[6] After these take a smal refreshment of pruen Tarts at my Quarters, set hence before 5, come to Holland about 8.

23 I stay till prayers over. After a small Dinner in a cold East Wind, go to Ayrfeild and the Bank. They yet afford not much satisfaction. I return about 6, visit Sam Prescot and Mr. Birchall. Go to bed about 10.

24 Easter Day. I rise at 7, the morning brisk from the East Wind. I take a thoughtful walk round the rough park, return about 9 and am refresht. About 10 wee go to the Church. I sit in my seat in the Chancel. I receive the Holy Sacrament among my native Neighbors. Deus O.M. det vitam novam puram faelicem.[7] Lewis Holland dines with mee. After noon I sitt with Mr. Ashurst in his seat. After service Mrs. Ashurst, Hulm, Prescott, Birchall come to the Inn with mee, stay till 8, after which a short walk and to bed about 9.

25 The Tenant of the Green house, a widow Corles and Matthew Molineux of Whitley Hall come to mee, make up their rents and Accounts for last year. About 11 wee go to prayers, after these ended the Accounts of the late Churchwardens are heard and allow'd. New ones, William Naylor and Boardman of Orrell are chosen. I subscribe first to both. After the Electors (near 20) go to Midletons, where Ale, Buns & Cheese are the repast. I go to my dinner hence about 2. After, company is with mee till 7. I then go and sit with my Coz. S. Prescott near

6 Liverpool old chapel is that of St.Nicholas & Our Lady; the new one was the church of St. Peter.
7 Trans: 'May God the best and greatest grant [me] a new, pure, fruitful life.'

2 hours, return to my lodgings and to bed before 10.[8]

26 The weather alter'd to rainy. John Walmsley comes and Accounts for last years rent, leaving 7^{li} only unpaid. My charges here 20s. I write to Ralph Whaley. About 9 I go and come to Wigan about 10. I meet with my coz. Holt and Mr. Brown at the Coffee House. I am at Morning prayers. I dine with the Rector, where the Dean of York, Mr. Ashton of Prestwich, Mr. Banks, Mr. Bowyer, Lew Walley. About 2 wee go to the Church and into the Vestry, where wee find the Mayor (vid. Mr. Thomas Banks) Justices Herle & Walmsley, some Aldermen and a numerous Mobb. The Rector takes his place on the right hand of the Mayor, his Friends sitt down and mix in the company. The Mayor begins, tells that according to Custom they mett in the Hall and chose Sir Roger Bradshaigh. The Rector interrupts, tells him hee is president of this meeting and that the Accounts of the present Wardens are to be heard before new Wardens chosen. The Accounts are read and approv'd. The Rector orders the Clerk to read the 89 & 90th Canons. Mr. Walmsley interposes says they ought not to be read. That Custom and Law overrule them. The Rector is instant saies, hee will stand and fall by the Canons and that they shall be read. Mr. Walmsley saies, but wee may chuse whether wee hear 'em or no. The Clerk begins to read. Mr. Walmsley makes a motion with his head and hand and forces a Cough or Screatum loud to the party or Mobb, who imediately make a nauseous and rude noise, the Clerk is not heard. At the Rector's request the Mayor calls Silence, which succeeds. The 89th Canon and first clause of the 90th is read. The Mayor as before, tells Sir Roger is chosen in the Hall, a debate and difference happen, about the Choice. The Rector names and chuses Mr. Banks of Winstanley. A Note is offer'd by the present Wardens wherein Mr. Markland, Mr. Hulme and H. Orrett are written of whom one to be chosen by the parishioners. Mr. Markland first nam'd is chosen, unanimously, the Mayor also giving his vote for him. The Mayor and his company the rest proceed to the choice of the sidesmen. The Accounts and elecions are Signd (by mee also as a parishioner) about 4 wee leave the Vestry imediately go from the Vestry into the Church to prayers. After these I attend the present and new chosen Churchwardens to the Clerk's house where Ale, Simlins & Cheese.[9] About 7 I go to Ince to see my coz. Holt, stay till 9 with her, call in my return on Mr. Bowyer. Hee treats mee with a Bottle of good Claret. Wee have free and various discourse. I part and go to my coz. Holt about 11.

27 In a fair morning I go to Mr. Bowyer's about 8 stay till 9 when the Rector, Dean of York and their retinue, to near 20 horse, go by for York. I take my leave here with them. I return to coz. Holts, shee is come from Ince. I stay an hour and drink Tea with her. About 11 I set out on Foot come to Winstanley

8 Easter Monday was the traditional day for church wardens to be nominated for the coming year, and the accounts of the present wardens approved.

9 An authentic account of the troublesome election of churchwardens at Wigan which was held on Easter Tuesday.

about 11. After come Mr. Bowyer and Lowe. Mrs. Banks treats us with an elegant dinner, welcome good ale & wine; past 5 wee return call with Mr. Lowe, stay an hour there, then proceed to my coz. Holt where Mr. Bowyer, with a Bottle in his hand, follows mee wee are here free in conversacion. My uncle Herle comes in, Mr. Bowyer censures Mr. Walmsleys behavior sharply us'd in the vestry. Mr. Herle offended recedes. My shee coz. and I only left, a friendly conversacion is produc'd to 12. I was witness to day at Winstanley of a Bond of 120^{li} given by George Leigh to Mr. Bowyer and of a Discharge wherein Samuel Byrom Esq is concern'd.

28 The weather fair, wind at East and brisk. I struggle with my unhappy indisposicion, set out, call on Mr. Legh at Haydock about 10. Hee shews mee his House and Garden a sweet retreat in excellent soil. I stay above an hour, drink Tea with him. In this space comes Sir William Gerard and Master Molyneux. I leave them, come to Warrington about 1, pay Mr. Fearnhead on the great Account 20 Guineas. I see the new Chapell, school and buildings to the Street. Mr. Patten treats mee and Mr. Golborn with 2 Bottles strong Ale and free discourse on the Chapell.[10] I set hence about 4 reach my corner (D.G.) safe about 8. I with joy receive a Letter from my Lord and one from Dr. Stratford by which hee directs mee to send Jack upon its receipt to Oxford Q.B.E.

29 I communicate the Dr's Letter to Jack, hee receives the News with Joy and Gratitude. I wait on Mrs. Thane thence to the Coffee house where I impart the Letter to the Chancellor, hee advises mee to pursue it. My Suzy and Jack go to Wrexham. After repose about 5, the Chancellor calls. Hee, Mr. Hulton and I go to the Bacchus, the 2 Probys meet us, wee drink above our pints of good but dear wine; part about 8, after which I visit Mrs. Thane, part there also about 10.

30 Hott, unhappy and indispos'd from the wine. I apply to Busienes, write to Mr. Colly of Christ Church, order preparacion of Necessarys for Jack's journy, this imploys my Suzy and Family, I end in domestic about 10.

MAY 1 A fair morning the wind yet at East. Mr. Lancaster preaches in the Quire, the sermon sacramentall. The News scarce answer the pains to the Coffee house. After prayers see Mr. Boucher, consult him about the way to Oxford. Intent on Jack's journy retire home with my Suzy and Jack refresh in domestic about 9.

2 I rise to early prayers in a sweet morning. I take 2 Turns on roodee Jack with mee the later. I drink Tea & Coffee at Home. After at the Coffee House. After prayers I go to Eaton, Jack and Harry with mee. Mr. Cholmley receives us very freindly and kindly. Hee generously gives Jack a Guinea with his good wishes of Success in the University. Mr. Okes expresses his friendly concern. Wee return home about 8. Mrs. Thane sees us and staies with us till 10. After Dinner I went with Jack to Mr. Lancaster's who on the occasion of his going to Oxon gave him good & proper advice.

10 This is the new church of Holy Trinity, Warrington.

3 After early prayers, in a sweet Ayr, take 4 Turns on Roodee. After I drink Tea with Mrs. Thane, thence to the Coffee House. After Dinner indispos'd and interrupted. I write in the Evening to Mr. Vaudrey and later to Mr. Hearne, Keeper of the Bodleian Library, retreat in domestic with my Suzy & Jack about 11.

4 At early prayers, the wind is high and westerly. I write to Dr. Stratford, Dr. Fowks and Mr. Colly. I send 10 Guineas by him to be plac'd in such hands as the Dr. shall think fitt, I give him 3^{li} for his, my Man and Horses expences, in the Journy. Mr. Roberts lends mee 6 Guineas. Jack takes about 8^{li} of his own mony, most of it given him by Freinds, on this occasion. About 3 hee takes his leave with cheerfulness yet affected with Concern. His mother and my self are not insensible of naturall aversion to part with him Q.F.F.F.Q.E. After prayers about 5 the Stage Coach brings back Sir Henry Bunbury, my Lady B. and Dr. Thane. I visit them imediatly. And after in the Evening, stay with Sir Henry Bunbury and his Coach company till 11.

5 My Brother Puleston sends early a Letter and a present of 2 Guineas to Jack. I answer and thank him for them. Tis a Court day of indifferent Busienes. James Barrett and his wife who sues him for restitucion & Alimony are reconcil'd and judicially admonish'd obsequia invicem praestare.[11] I write to Mr. Lambert. After prayers (at which were the Ladies Warrington and Grosvenor) my Suzy and I visit Lady Otway and her Family, wherein particularly Mr. Lambert's daughter: wee are kindly treated & stay till 8. After this I am with Sir Henry Bunbury, Sir Richard Grosvenor is with him, they promote the Glass of very good Claret, the discourse free and cheerfull. Sir Richard hansomly expresses his Gratitude to Mr. Cholmley. I part with Sir Henry after 11.

6 I am indispos'd from the quantity of above a Bottle, see the News yet in Nubibus and prepare for my Journy. I (Will. Willoughby with mee) on Sir Henry's Sorril Mare sett out ½ hour after 3. Near the Foot of Barn hill, the Mare's hinder foot being ingag'd twixt 2 larg stones over a Gutter, I throw myself off on the right side, no harm (D.G.) happens but the shoo pinckt off. I proceed uneasily, wee come to Whitchurch ½ hour after 7. My Lord Bishop and his company in 2 Coaches, come ½ hour before us. His Lordship is pleas'd with my coming, promotes discourse on his Affairs. I stay supper and after that a Bottle or 2 of white wine with his Lordship, Clutterbrook, Maryon, and after I go to the Old Crown past 10.

7 About 7 I rise well refresht, at 8 drink Tea with his Lordship and Mrs. Pierrpont. At 9 in a cool morning wee sett out and makeing a short halt at Hanley come to Chester about 2. The Dean, Archdeacon, Mr. Callis in Coaches, Mr. Hulton and some others on Horseback, meet very near the Town. My Suzy and I dine about 4 with my Lord, hee trys all his liquors and likes them very much; wee stay till 6. I take a Turn with Dr. Thane to the Coffee House, return home & after Mr. Clutterbrook receded there to bed about 10.

11 Trans: 'to discharge their duty towards one another.'

8 The weather is still brisk and cold. I wait on my Lord to Church. Dr. Thane has a good sermon on [?]. My Suzy and I dine with my Lord. Go to St. Oswald's afternoon. After prayers I introduce Mr. Robert Davies & Ned Puleston to my lord, after this I take 4 Turns on roodee, recreate in domestic and with indevor to recover lost rest to bed about 9.

9 Well recover'd in a cold morning, after early prayers I take 4 Turns on roodee which extremely improves, I apply to Busienes especially to the Collection of Instruments and Decrees to bee registr'd. In the Evening Dr. Thane is here, I treat him with a larg pint of Domestic wherein I remember my Charterhouse Benefactors, this produces the Time past 10.

10 After early prayers (the weather still very cool and brisk the wind N.W.) I take 4 Turns on roodee. I draw a Note out of the Heads of my late Lord Bishops Charg to the Clergy. After Dinner I wait on the Bishop, hee has company which part about 3. I write and inclose Directions for Confirmacion to Mrs. Marsden, Styth, Markland. Mrs. Whaley is here in her constant querulous temper against her husband, very unnaturally. I tell her of it and of her reflecions on mee when last at Holland, shee denys. After 6 invited I go to my Lord, with whom Sir Henry Bunbury, Mr. Egerton Mr. Brook. After come the Chancellor and Archdeacon. My Lord receives with excellent wine and free conversacion. I drink my Bottle wee part about 10. After which I write to Tom Gorst about a pad for my Lord.

11 The weather still cold and windy. After the good wine and company, not indispos'd. I rise to early prayers. I apply to Letters to the Bishop of St. Asaph, Mr. Le Neve, Howard and my coz. Parre. I send Sir Thomas Bellott's Will & probat by Bruce of Boughton to Mr. Jebbe, for which & Commission 2^{li}.0.6. About 7 John returns from Oxford with a Letter and Account from Jack of his safe comeing thither on Saturday about 4 a clock, his health and satisfaction in the place for which Hee as well as my self render all praise and glory to God.[12] My Suzy and I visit Dr. Thane & his Lady. They receive us civilly with a Bottle of good Claret and free Conversacion, wee part after 10.

12 The weather still very cold, windy and rainy. After early prayers apply to Busienes. At the meeting in Mr. Boucher's Chamber, a sharp altercacion betwixt Mr. Bouchier and Hulton in the case of Gee & Richardson wherein the former seems blameable. The Busienes brief at Court. I examine one Witnes on Gees part. I write to Mr. Vaudrey for stamps. After prayers about 6 The Mayor and Aldermen about 10 in number visit my Lord. I am present, I after stay with his Lordship hee discourses on the Busienes of the secretary's Fees and of the visitacion. I continue with his Lordship. Mrs. Pierrpont and my Suzy coming to us, wee drink 3 pints of his best wine & stay after domestic prayers.

13 After a rainy night a cold and wett morning. I am at early prayers, after to Busienes. Mr. Woods – Vicar of Bowden consults mee about the Tith of potatoes. After 9 the Chancellor sends to come quickly to him and Sir Roger

12 By the efforts of Canon Stratford, Jack was awarded a place at Christ Church, Oxford.

Bradshaigh. I find Sir Roger instant with him, to give him his oath as Churchwarden of Wigan. The Chancellor tells him since hee is inform'd there is a controversy about the choice of a Churchwarden at Wigan, hee can't regularly do it, and refuses to give the oath, upon which Sir Roger speaks to the Town Clerk (Banks) then present to take notice of the Chancellor's answer, or so in effect. Upon further debate, the Chancellor promises not to swear the other opposite Warden, Mr. Banks, till the matter be judicially heard. Sir Roger seems satisfy'd. The Affairs betwixt Mr. Finch and Sir Roger, vidt. about his Chapell and the Gallery lately taken down is discoursed of but without Concurrence, save that in some things Mr. Finche's proceeding was disapprov'd. After Noon Mr. Lambert calls on mee. After prayers (about 6) I go with my Lord in his coach and Dr. Thane to Mr. Egerton's where Sir Henry Bunbury, the Chancellor, Mrs. Thelwal, Conway, James Egerton, Mr. Egerton entertains with variety of good wine the conversacion free, sometimes grave and more that by mention of Mr. Lancaster's danger from a Fevor hee now is ill of, wee (vid. Mr. Chancellor, Archdeacon & my self) return with my Lord about 9 leaving the rest of the company.

14 A warmer morning yet dull Mr. Lambert calls about 8. I go to the Coffee House, hee after takes horse for Cambridge and London. I recurr to my 4 Turns on roodee, where Mr. Lancaster's danger much affects mee. I lend Mrs. Whaley 10s. After prayers I write to Mr. Whaley. In the Evening, desir'd, go with Mr. Henchman, Aubry and Hodgson to Mr. Holland's, here poor Mr. Lancaster is the subject of our discourse and pity and about 8 Mr. Henchman begins his Health, the rest of the time more cheerfully till about 9 the Maid brings in word, that Mr. Lancaster dyd about 3 Quarters of an hour ago: affected with the News wee part immediatly.

15 The weather grown calme and warm. The Bell for Mr. Lancaster makes all its Hearers melancholy. The Quire is crowded with an Audience and the South Isle with Lord Mountjoy's and another Regiment. My Lord has an excellent sermon on St. John 20 v. 21 "And the Disciples were glad to see the Lord".[13] I call at the Coffee House where still more Expectacion of peace. After prayers I wait on Mr. Egerton and Banks to my Lord. Hee receives generously with good wine, the Affair of Mr. Finch and Sir Roger Bradshaigh, of the Chapel in Warrington and the Advowson of Torpurley much handled. After Mr. Egerton and my self speak to his Lordship about the void prebend on Mr. James Egerton's behalf. His answer is very civil, mencioning his design of such preferment for Mr. Clutterbrook.[14] My good friend Mr. Cartwright dyd of the malignant Fevor about 12 today. Of Mr. Wetenhall who was reported to bee dead there are some small glimmer hopes of recovery.

16 The weather continues warm & springing. Mr. Peter Williams, Attorney is

13 See R.V.H. Burne, *Chester Cathedral*, (London, 1958), p.167, for a biography of Preb. Peter Lancaster.

14 *Ibid.*, p.177, for a biography of Preb. Richard Clutterbrook or Clutterbuck.

dead of the like fatal Fevor. I apply to Letters to Drs. Branston, Pope, Cozen Parre and my son Jack, finish but send 'em too late to the post office. About 3 Afternoon Dr. Thane and I go with my Lord Bishop in his Coach to Eaton. Wee come after some danger of an Overturn about 4 thither, find Lord Gower, Sir Richard Grosvenor, Mr. Francis Cholmondly &c in the Hall. I see Mr. Okes in the parlor. Wee are generously receiv'd, stay 2 hours. My Lord Gower at parting kindly tells mee hee has not had an oportunity of chideing mee for not comeing to him at Trentham. Wee return safe about 7. I drink a pint with Dr. Thane and at home about 10. Mr. Wetenhall dies today about 9.

17 I take a Turn on roodee in fine springing weather. Invited last night, dine with my Lord Bishop, a select number, Lord Gower, Sir Richard Grosvenor, Roger Mostyn, Sir Henry Bunbury, Mrs. Cholmley, Egerton, Dr. Thane &c fill the Table, here is an elegant Dinner, good wine and free conversacion. About 4 my Lord recedes to Mr. Lancaster's Funeral and stays the sermon had by Mr. Henchman.[15] I am not admidst this company unmindfull of the deplorable loss of Mr. Lancaster, my Lord returns about 5 and the Conversacion improves very cheerfully expecially twixt Sir Henry and Mr. Cholmley. They part full and cheerfull about 7.

18 I am indispos'd from the Quantity. Poole's wittnesses come inseasonably. Yet I examine them about 4. About 6 sent for, I go over to Sir Henry Bunbury, where the same company is with Addicion, Healths and the same conversacion is renew'd. My Lord Bishop comes from Utkinton to it about 7. Dr. Thane comes in merrily advanc'd about 8. When the Coaches go off the rest stay liberally, an hour longer. I pay Mr. Morrey 5^{li}.8s for 6 doz. Bottles of Irish Claret, yet to be sent for at 18s the dozen. I receive from Dr. Thane 36s for 2 doz. pay that sum for Mr. Chancellor and as much for myself.

19 My distemper is extremely aggravated and confines mee (tho on a Court day) to my bed till Noon, the Busienes does not require mee. In the Evening I step out into the town & return to a domestic pint.

20 Still indispos'd. I give a Bond of 200^{li} to Mr. Foulks to pay him the Stamp Mony as it accrews or hee calls for it. I write to Mr. Hulme and Mr. Hough. After Evening prayers the Dean speaks to mee to draw a representacion of the Case of Mr. Lancaster's Family. I take 2 long and 4 shorter Turns on Roodee. My Suzy and sister Jones meet mee there. I receive a Letter from Dr. Stratford still at London telling mee he had recommended Jack to the best Tutor and that hee sends him word hee is much pleas'd with him for which D.G. Dr. Thane calls, wee empty a domestic pint before 9.

21 A cool pleasant day, not yet recover'd. I write to the Bishop of St. Asaph and Mr. Le Neve. I lend to Mr. Chapman on Account 10s. Invited I, my Suzy, and sister Jones dine with my sister Partington. Wee have an elegant dinner. After prayers I write to the Bishop of Killala and Sir Wm. Parsons. After this my

15 *Ibid.*, p.191, for a biography of Preb. Charles Henchman.

Suzy and I go to the palace. Wee see the end of a Bottle of good Claret, and return before 9.

22 The weather yet cool, my Blood hott and stomach in disorder. I draw about 9 ounces of Blood, keep in doors till Evening prayers, after which direct my Lord's Direcions for Confirmacion at Warrington to the adjacent parishes and write with 'em. I receive a Letter from Jack by Mr. P. Lancaster. Mrs. Thane comes & after the Dr., wee try a Neston Bottle hee approves not of it.

23 A Warmer, yet windy day. I pay my sister Jones, on Account of the Interest 1^{li}:10s: which with 3^{li} paid her about Christmas last makes ½ years Interest 4^{li}:10s I write to Mr. Colly and my son Jack, pay Sarah the Maid 10s in part of her Wages. About 11 My Lord Bishop, Dr. Thane and myself sett out in my Lord's Coach for Eaton, come thither about 12. My Lord walks and sees the Gardens. Wee dine with my Lord and Lady Gower, Sir Richard Grosvenor & his Lady, Mr. Cholmley, Mr. Stanley, Mr. Levison, Crompton &c. After Dinner the port gos freely round. A discourse is mov'd about Liturgy and the writers upon them, twixt my Lord, Mr. Cholmley, Mr. Okes wherein his Lordship with great clearnes, understanding and readines. Wee part hence about 5, reach Chester about 6. After which I with my Suzy wait on my Lord, hee treats with a Glass of his good wine. The Formality of a Visitacion is much the discourse. Wee part at 9 and to bed imediatly.

24 After a Night disturb'd with melancholy reflexions, I draw the Case of Mr. Lancaster's Family, [16] wait on & drink Tea past 7 with his Lordship where the formalities are setl'd. I prepare Matters for the Court (Chester & Wirral Deaneries in the Consistory) Mr. Clopton has a good discourse before the Clergy on [?]. Past 11 my Lord gos into Court, many of the Clergy of this Visitacion are absent & excus'd yet there is a great audience. My Lord has a nervous and pious Charg, advising the Clergy to preserve their people from Atheism, Socianism to beware of the popish and protestant dissenters, distinguishes betwixt Toleracion and Establishment, says the Schism is Schism still. Advises to own the Queen's Supremacy by their prayer before Sermon according to the Canon, to preach against the growing immortalities to read the Queen's proclamacion and to observe strictly the State daies particularly 5 November as the day of the happy Revolucion, advises to sober, pious and exemplary Lives, and solemnly admonishes them not to give their Testimonials to unworthy Candidates for orders, and concludes with further Exhortacions to a good Life. The Court rises about one. My Lord approves the Case, I gett it ingross'd and bring it to my Lord before hee rises from Dinner. His Lordship, Mr. Chancellor, Dr. Thane, Mrs. Clutterbrook, Clopton subscribe it. I return and apply myself to Exhibicions of Orders &c till 7. After recreate in a domestic pint of which Mrs. Thane comes in for a small Share.

16 *Ibid.*, p. 182, for a reference to Mrs.Lancaster receiving part of the communion alms as relief in her poverty.

25 A calm and temperate morning. I take 2 longer and 2 shorter Turns on roodee. I write to Mr. Lambert (now at London) to see Dr. Pope and pay him (if hee can) 20^{li} for mee. Accounts are stated betwixt Mr. Foulks and mee, I give him a Note of Acknowledgement for 154^{li}.11.3¾. Mr. Morrey dines with mee. I apply most of the Day to Exhibicions of such Instruments as should have bin enter'd yesterday, till 7. After which Dr. Thane, Mr. Jones of Bangor and myself go to the Mermayd (Dandies) wee drink 2 Bottles of excellent wine, ½ Crown the Bottle, part at 9. My Suzy went to Lady Bunbury, to day to visit my Uncle Eaton (who is in a dangerous state of Health) and return'd about 8.

26 A cool & kindly morning, I wait on my Lord Bishop at 8 for his comands. Wee have a Consistory Court about 10. After to the Church where Mr. Leigh of Aldford, has a very grave discourse on Acts 20 v. 28.[17] Thence to the Court a competent Appearance of the Clergy of Frodsham, Malpas, and Bangor Deaneries. My Lord has the same Charg today. After dinner I apply to the Exhibicions which imploy mee strictly till 7. Mr. ArchDeacon Shore, Mr. Dod and Mr. Jones and Mr. Leigh of Aldford call on mee. Wee go to the White Bull. Mr. Dod[18] is chagrin, takes up the Time of 2 Bottles with reflection on the sharpness and frett of the wine and commendacion of his own palat. Wee part at 9. After I go to Dr. Thanes where my Suzy. Wee stay an hour there entertain'd by his wine.

27 A rainy day. I am busy in Exhibicions till 11. I then go to the Coffee house, where the News of Peace is possitive and more particular. After prayers my Lord and Mrs. Pierrpont come to us, they stay freely and cheerfully till 8. Dr. Thane and his Lady come in the Time and make up the Conversacion.

28 Saturday. My Lord (cum Deo Bono)[19] sets out with the Chancellor and the rest of his company. I following at an hours distance, they take Olton in the way are generously receiv'd at dinner. In the Even about 5 proceed, are mett 2 or 3 miles by the Rector and others of Namptwich. Mr. Wilbraham of Derefold chiefly, who brings my Lord to his House where the rest leave him.

29 Sunday. My Lord in the morning gos to Acton Church, the Chancellor, my self &c attend him there. Mr. Edgley[20] reads the prayers and preaches, both stiffly imperfectly. My Lord and his company are receiv'd at a plentiful dinner at Derefold. Hee preaches after noon in a throng Congregacion at Namptwich. I wait on Mr. Wettenhall and Mr. Church.

30 Munday. Namptwich and Midlewich Deaneries. Mr. Oliver has an elegant and sound discourse.[21] My Lord desires him to print it. My Lord sees Mr.

17 L.R.O., Exhibit Book DCh.1 f.10v. Peter Leigh, rector (deacon Chester 1674, priest Chester 1675), presented to Aldford by Lord Charles Gerard, gentleman of the bedchamber 1677.

18 L.R.O., *ibid*, f.10, William Dod M.A. rector (deacon Oxford 1676, priest Oxford 1677), instituted on the presentation of Thomas Dod by assignation from Esther and Adrian Dod, late of Edge, 1680.

19 Trans: 'in company with the Good God.'

20 C.R.O., EDP1/1, Acton Parish Papers.

21 R.V.H. Burne, *op.cit.*,p.178, for a biography of Preb. John Oliver.

Wilbraham's Bride not yet come to her Lares at Derefold. After exhibicions, I examine 3 Wittnesses betwixt Poole and Wettenhal.

31 About 8 the company setts out, wee go the nearer way by Crewe, tis hott, my horse is lame, wee call at Rode, drink Tea. I walk thence to Astbury where my Lord is liberally entertain'd. By Congleton wee go to Macclesfield, the Corporacion meet us in a Body, my Lord lodges at the Mayor's, Mr. Thompson's. I stay late here & lodg at Alderman Johnson's.

JUNE 1 Wednesday. Macclesfield Deanery. Sir Roger Bradshaigh & Mr. Kenyon come here to my Lord with a peticion against Mr. Finch with a mandamus to the Chancellor, the 2nd time to swear Sir Roger Churchwarden. My Lord orders a monicion to bee made to Mr. Finch to desist in the matter of the Gallery.[22] Mr. Hulme preaches,[23] after 6 my Lord gos to Lyme, I am at the Mayor's with Mr. Collebrand.

2 Holy Thursday. Mr. Boucher, myself and some others go to Lyme, come to prayers. A noble dinner & entertainment succeeds. After these wee go on call on Mr. Nichols at Stockport where Tea. The company thickens, the people of Manchester at the bridge about 100 horse bring my Lord to the Wardens. I write to Mr. Holland on Mr. Finch's busienes about 9 a clock.

3 Friday. The Collegiate Church of Manchester in the Chapter House. After that wee dine elegantly at the Warden's. Wee visit several Freinds, are warm in warm weather and Dr. Holbrook is generous to the Chancellor & myself his Guests.

4 Saturday. The deanery of Manchester. Mr. Copley one of the Fellows of the Church preaches.[24] The day fill'd with Busienes, the Evening eases with relaxacion.

5 Sunday. My Lord preaches in a most frequent Congregacion and confirms at Night. After prayers I wait on Mr. Pigot, hee is absent in London placeing his son with an Atturney.

6 Munday. About 10 my Lord setts for Dunham, hee takes the prospect of Bowden by way of Altringham. Wee come to Dunham about 12, here Mr. Nicols & Mr. Simon. My Lord is nobly entertain'd by my Lord Warrington, it Rains. About 4 wee set out, come over Hollingfair, Mr. Legh with about 60 horses, meets my Lord, hee comes to Mr. Shaw's, is receiv'd affectionately.

7 Tuesday. My Lord preaches the Charity Sermon, an extraordinary number of the Clergy, and after dinner such a Collection about 70^{li}.[25] I part with my

22 C.R.O., Consistory Court files EDC.5 (1709) No.2, Wigan gallery and organ.

23 L.R.O., Exhibit Book 1691, DCh.1 f.14. Adam Hulme M.A. (deacon Bishop of Kildare 1679, priest Bishop of Meath 1682), presented to Prestbury on deprivation of George Newton (non juror) by Sir John Legh. The deprivation cause is in the Borthwick Institute of Historical Research, York, Cause Papers H. series.

24 F.R. Raines, *Fellows of the Collegiate Church of Manchester*, Chetham Society, N.S. Vol. 23, *passim*.

25 It was customary for annual sermons to be preached in order to raise funds for the Charity Schools. These were usually preached by bishops and archdeacons.

Freinds and return (D.G.) safe to my Corner about 9.
8 Wednesday. I recreate and repose at home. My Lord confirms at Warrington.
9 Thursday. My Lord, by way of Speake, gos to Liverpoole – My Birthday D.O.M.
10 Friday. St. Barnabas. Hee confirms at Liverpoole.
11 Saturday. Hee returns to Chester.
[No entries 12,13]
14 Tuesday. My Lord visits the Dean and Chapter and adjourns to the 1st September.
[No entries 15 and 16]
17 Friday. My Lord gos to Eaton to see Sir Richard Middleton there. I follow him. Wee have a easy conversacion. About 5 his Lordship reads Even prayers in the Chapell. After these I go on to Wrexham, wait on the Bishop of St. Asaph, his Lady & Son at the Red Lyon, bring in my sister Jones. After with her at the Fox and Goose.
18 Saturday. I and my sister take leave of the Bishop, his Lady invites her to St. Asaph. I visit my brother Puleston at Havod-y-wern, indevor to borrow a horse for my sister Jones, but succeed not, in my return acquaint her with the insuccess and return home about 9.
19 Sunday. Trinity Sunday. My Lord ordains.
[No entry Monday]
21 Tuesday. About 8 my Lord setts out with his company (Hee and Dr. King of Chelsea in the Coach) wee come to Warrington about 12, dine there. About 5 proceed. Hee is met by the Wigan Gentlemen of Sir Roger Bradshaigh's party. Hee comes to Mr. Bowyers about 8.
22 Wednesday. My Lord confirms at Wigan. After gos to Winstanley where hee is receiv'd at a hansom Dinner. returns about 6. The Mayor and Aldermen see and treat him with bad wine and sweet meats at Mr. Bowyer's. Here the matter of the Gallery is disscuss'd. Mr. Boucher on Mr. Finche's part, a Grant is produc'd by the Corporacion under Bishop Pearson's Seal. My Lord shews an Inclination, gratefull to the Corporacion, to give a Process to setting up the Organs in the place of the Galery.[26]
23 Thursday visit the Deanery of Warrington in the Church of Wigan. My Lord confirms in the morning. Mr. Styth has an excellent sermon, the Busienes is very full.
24 St. John Baptist. My Lord admonishes Mr. Holland to forbear (as before) to proceed to the Erection of an Organ or Galery for it in the place of the late one. Hee setts out about 9 and by the way of Chorley and Brindle, comes to Blackburn (the vicarage) about 1. Hee and his company well receiv'd. I see Mr. Gellibrand & Sherburne, drink some potts with them.
25 Blackburn & Lealand Deaneries at Blackburn. Mr. Pilkington has a very

26 C.R.O., EDC.5 (1709) No. 2, Wigan.

feeble discourse on Matt 5.[27] The Busienes is here too considerable.
26 Sunday. My Lord preaches in the Afore and Dr. King the Afternoon. A great Confirmacion in the Evening, among the Candidates Mr. Hesketh of Pulford.
27 Munday. About 10 wee sett for Preston. Mrs Commissary Lambert, Close, Farmer and Thwait meet my Lord at Walton le Dale, Gentlemen out of the Town join us. My Lord lights, and dines (on a dinner from the Black Bull) at Alderman Siddal's.
28 Tuesday. Amounderness Deanery. Mr. Peploe has a long and tedious sermon.[28] The Busienes small, I divert most of the afternoon with Mr. Powell and Jeffrey Prescott. I wait on Lady Greenfield, shee tells mee the History of Hickman's matrimonial Cheat of her and gives or lends mee a Book of his Character.
29 Wednesday. St. Peter's day. After prayers and Confirmacion, My Lord and his company invited, go to Mr. Fleetwood's (Penwortham) on foot. It rains briskly and almost constantly. Here are Sir Christopher Musgreave and Mr. Crowford. Mrs. Fleetwood entertains generously with a good dinner, excellent wine & engageing modesty. Wee return over the Boat (as we came) about 7. After this my Lord is entertain'd by Mr. Franks. I step thither & am at the later end of the Entertainment.
30 Thursday. About 8 wee set for Lancaster, the weather proves favorable. My Lord stops not, is mett about 2 Miles, by the Mayor and Corporacion and Dr. Fenton. The Dr. engrosses the Bishop, carrys him to his house, where hee forces him, the Chancellor, Dr. King & myself to stay 3 hours on a mean pittifull dinner.[29] The Mayor &c send their Wine, Sturgeon &c and treat my Lord in the Vicarage.

JULY 1 Friday, visit Lonsdale Deanery and confirm at Lancaster. Dr. Fenton preaches, the weather rainy with storm, the Busienes not very tedious. The Chancellor & Commissary's company dine togeather. In the Evening, Mr. Foxcroft, Landlord (not Keeper) of the House treats both Companies, over the way, with good wine – plentifully, my Lord is told, till 1.
2 Saturday. About 9 wee set out and thoro Burton to Levins. Invited by Coll. Graham, a fine retreat with larg Gardens, good Ayr, the House well built on the South Bank of the Kent. Here the Earl of Berkshire and his fine Lady, the Coll's elder daughter. Wee are neatly & fully entertain'd. About 6 sett forward, several from Kendal meet. My Lord go's to Mr Crosby's and is treated there by

27 *Ibid.*, EDV2/14. John Pilkington was curate of Brindle.
28 L.R.O., Exhibit Book ARR 1708 f.26. Samuel Peploe junior followed his father as vicar of Preston. His father Samuel was a staunch Whig who resisted the Jacobite rebellion of 1715 and became bishop of Chester.
29 W.R. Roper, *Materials for the History of the Church of Lancaster,* Chetham Society, N.S. Vol. iv. p.59 for details of Dr. Fenton S.T.P., vicar of Lancaster.

the Corporacion. The Chancellor, Commissary and their Company to the Queen's Arms.
3 Sunday. A constant and severe rain. My Lord preaches in the morning, a vast Church and Auditory. Wee dine crowded at Mr Crosby's. After noon Dr. King preaches a numerous Confirmacion. Mr. Crosby (tho no peticion or preparacion to that purpose) solicits my Lord to consecrate Selside Chapell. My Lordship refers the matter very much to mee. Mr. Fryth treats the Chancellor, Commissary and myself at Duke Lamberts with a Bowl of Punch. Wee part about 10, the Chancellor slips down in the street.
4 Munday. The visitacion held for the Deanery of Kendale. I am, beside the Busienes of the day, extremely intent on the previous instrument to, and the Sentence of, the Consecracion of the Chapell of Selside and tho very much indispos'd (D.G.) finish them. I shew my Lord at Night, my rude Draught of the Sentence, hee approves. Mr. Heblethwaite takes it to engross.
5 Tuesday. Very easy D.G. dischrg'd of the Concern the Consecraction gave mee. About 9 my Lord and his company set for Selside, come there before 11. The Trustees at the door offer their Deed and peticion. I read 'em, my Lord alone enters the Chapell, after some prayers, the people follow. Hee proceeds to the Sentence, Mr. Crosby reading the prayers. After Consecraction, Sacrament at which I am one is administered. My Lord appoints the mony offer'd (about 3^{li}) to be laid out on a silver Salver & Chalice.[30] After this and a small repast, my Lord gos to Coll. Grahme's, wee return to Kendal about 1, dine, after to Wattsfeild, Mr. Lambert. Hee in his decent firm house entertains the company with punch and good wine and good ale. Wee part about 9, it rains briskly.
6 Wednesday. The Chancellor and I call at Mr. Lambert's, I drink Tea. Wee go to Levins, where the Company again dine liberally, After my Lord makes a short stay at Dalton Towers[31], thence over the sands to Cartmel, there are in firm order & pleasant. Sir Thomas Lowther meets my Lord on them conducts him into Holkar where wee are generously receiv'd.
7 Thursday. Visit and confirm at Cartmel. The short Busienes over, wee return to a good dinner at Holkar where Strawberries in plenty. The afternoon passes in company mixt. I write at Night to my Suzy.
8 Friday. Wee early up ready at 5. Wee take leave of this plentiful House, cross Ulverston Sands and come to Conishead, Mr. Braddyll's by 8; an ancient religious retreat in a plentifull Situacion. Here the company loyters, indispos'd of the early riseing till Noon. After dinner wee proceed 6 miles to Dudden or Millom Sands, thence along the seaside to Muncaster 12 miles. Sir William Pennington meets my Lord conducts him to his House, a venerable one in a horrid situacion.

30 C.R.O., EDA2/4 f.95, for details of the consecration of Selside Chapel.
31 i.e. Dalham Towers.

9 Saturday. After prayers I make a step into the park to the promontory. My Lord confirms the youth of neighboring parishes, a great crowd fills the House. After dinner Mr. Lambert along, I go before call on Mr. Stanley at Ponsonby, 5 miles from Muncaster, with wine and brandy. Wee hasten and reach my Lord fore Egremond, (6 miles), thence 4 to Whitehaven, hee lodges at the Flatt.
10 Sunday. The rain still follows but dos not accompany Us. My Lord preaches here to a throng'd Auditory in the morning, Dr. King after noon. Mr. Lowther invites us to a hansom, plenty and excellent wine. Mr. Yates is grown asthmatical and hypocondriac.[32] In the Even with Mr. Lambert I go up to the sea prospect, the thickness of the Ayr hinders the sight of the Isle of Man. Here is good wine at the Inn. After a pint to my private Lodging, Mr. Goodwin a Seaman.
11 Munday. Visit Copeland Deanery. Mr. Dalton, Rector of Dean,[33] has a good and grave discourse. The Busienes from the Number tedious. After it wee recreate at the Inn in a Glass of excellent Claret, the weather continues rainy and cold.
12 Tuesday. About 8 wee set out by way of Distington (where Mr. Teasdale offers a smal Entertainment)[34] and by where Mr. Fleming of more generous Character, to Cockermouth. My Lord views the ruinous Chappell. After dines on cold Meat with Mr. Jefferson.[35] About 2 wee proceed his Lordship and Domestics to Rose Castle.[36] Mr. Chancellor, myself &c to Carlisle, the post office about 8.
13 Wednesday. The weather fair. The Chancellor, Dr. Todd and I go to Rose Castle. The Bishop of Carlisle receives us here in his plentiful recess very liberally.[37] Hee with great affability treats mee, takes mee into his Study shews mee his Collection which is cheifly Scotch, Saxon and English. I meet there with Archdeacon Fleming, wee revive acquaintance & come togeather to Carlisle.
14 Thursday. After prayers and psalm 89 well perform'd by a Boy, My Lord and company are entertain'd at a Dinner in the Deanary by the Vice Dean and prebendaries in a Hansom Room where the words, "Loth to Offend" are often repeated on the Ceiling. The Mayor & Corporacion pay their Civility. About 1 wee part, pass the Pict's Wall near Poltross. My Lord, Dr. King & I stay at the Spittle, the Chancellor, offended with my stay, gos a mile further to Haltwisle. My Lord is pleas'd with his clean but narrow Quarters.
15 Friday. About 8 wee mount, severe Showers fall before wee reach Hexam,

32 L.R.O., Exhibit Book ARR 1698, f.34. Francis Yeates (Yates) M.A., priest Gloucester 1687, vicar of Whitehaven 1694.
33 C.R.O., EDV2/14.
34 L.R.O., Exhibit Book ARR 1698, f.32. Lancelot Teasdale M.A. (deacon Oxford 1685, priest Winchester 1686), presented by Lord Lowther to Distington 1692.
35 *Ibid.*, Exhibit Book ARR 1709, f.26. Thomas Jefferson B.A. (deacon Carlisle 1703, priest Chester 1705), presented to Cockermouth 1705.
36 Rose Castle is the residence of the bishops of Carlisle.
37 William Nicholson was bishop of Carlisle at this date.

which wee pass and go to Crossbridge[38] 14m. Here a sordid Inn, not meat nor Ale to refresh. With Mr. Crosby I go to see Mrs. Guy and her comley Daughter. Wee set out about 2, come to Newcastle about 5. Wee see the Key, the Fleet and the Town then to supper. Dr. Ellison the vicar waits on my Lord. In the way Mr. Swainston overtakes us & discovers his Ale by free applicacion to my Lord.
16 Saturday. The weather fair, wee sett hence about 9, come to Durham about 12. The Chancellor and I intend to lodg at the Post Office. The Bishop of Durham sends Mr. Stonyer, Express wee come to the Castle.

AUGUST 14 At the Quire, tho deaf of my Cold. Dr. Thane preaches.
18 Thursday. Lady Bunbury sends to Dr. Thane and myself to dine with her and the Duchess of Grafton, my Suzy is there, the Freedom easy. I gett in 6 Loads, my Hay Harvest this year.
20 Saturday. About 7 I sett out in a fair day, and by Northop, over the Mountain to Brickhill & come to St. Asaph ½ hour after 12. Before Dinner The Bishop receives mee with welcome and Freedom. After Dinner Conversacion holds till prayers. After these Tea and diversion till supper. After this a bottle of Claret & Conversacion till prayers and to bed.
21 Sunday. The Bishop preaches in the Choir on, "I have sinned in that I betray'd innocent Blood." I because deaf hear little of the sermon. Mr. Davies and Mr. Carter dine with the Bishop. After prayers I go with Mr. Davies and Mr. Lloyd to a little Ale House. Thence to see Mr. Lloyd the Registrar and in his house Miss Price who has a room & closet very neat & trim. Paid my sister Jones this Morning upon Account of Interest due to her 4^{li}:10^{s}.
22 Munday. About 8 I walk, Mr. Moulding with mee, to Bodillwythin, Mrs. Humphreys, a good seat in a fine prospect, a delicate Spring in the larg Field before the House is a great Convenience & Ornament to this Seat. Mrs. Humphreys seems to live below the condicion of this Estate. Shee entertains mee with Tea, wee return about 12. After dinner my sister Jones & I in the Coach go to Havord. Wee find Mr. Davies alone, he entertains us kindly, shews mee the fine additions his House and mee his Library.
28 Sunday. A fair day. Mr. John Wright preaches in the Quire, the News confirms the Fate of the King of Sweden. I receive from Mr. Colly a Letter from Jack, In the Evening Dr. Yarborough is with mee. I tell him of Mr. Aynsworth & my ambicion of his Coins. Anthony Close sees mee too at Night I deliver all the presentments of that Archdeaconry to him.
29 Munday. After a walk I apply to busienes and Books. My sons Ken and Will very much indispos'd, the small pox appears in the former, the other weakness and Hectick symptoms.
30 Tuesday. After a Walk and the Coffee house I invite Mr. Colly, he dines with us and makes a domestic Celebracion of my son Jack's Birthday the 19th Det D.O.M. multos et Faelices.[38a]

38 i.e. Corbridge.

31 Wednesday, I intended for Lancashire today but from the Circumstances of my children and my own deafness forbear. In the Evening Dr. Thane calls wee drink an Irish Bottle at Dandies and part about 10.

SEPTEMBER 1 Thursday. My Lord comes from Broxon, hither before 9. The Mayor Recorder & my brother Partington acquaint him, That they have a design to build a receptacle for the Engines, within the Rayles near the palace Wall claiming the whole ground rail'd in as belonging to the City and so rail'd at the request of Bishop Pearson, at his charg, by consent of the then Mayor and magistrates. My Lord deliberates on it for some Time. After prayers My Lord gos to the Chapter House, the Body is call'd over & the Visitacion adjourned to First of May next. A difference then is warmly discust by Mr. Henchman & Mr. Dennis about the rules and Government of the school, some short orders are read, my Lord corrects some, pronounces the Head Master to have compleat authority over all the scholars at all Times. The Usher to have so in the Master's absence. He orders that a Catalogue bee immediately taken of all the scholars, that such a one bee kept carefully in the school. And that the Names of the Boys to bee entered with the Usher bee writt down in the presence of the Master or communicated to Him, that hee may know their Numbers & absences. 2dly since the Scholars are as yet few in the upper part vidt about 50 and more vidt above 70 under the Usher, Hee orders that for the incouragement of the Master the number of the scholars bee equally divided and tho such a number bee taken by the Master as will make him equal to the Ushers, he orders that the Usher bee paid for this Quarter ending at Michaelmas.[39] About 1 his Lordship return'd to Broxon. I write to the Bishop of St. Asaph and send some of Jack's poems to Mr. Kinaston. After domestic pint to bed about 10.

2 At early prayers thence to the Coffee House where I meet the good News of the surrender of the Citadel of Tournay. I take 4 Turns on Roodee. Apply to Books and recollection till 8 at Night and recurr to domestic pint.

3 After early prayers and 4 Turns on roodee, call on Mr. Colly, discourse him in Jack's Circumstance, what Allowances, what Sciences, what Books. I write to Mr. Sherburne.

4 Dr. Fogg has an excellent discourse on the Sacrament which is today administer'd et cuius Ego particeps Det D.O. vitam meliorem.[40] Mr. Collys dines with us And in the Evening I sitt over 2 Bottles (good wine) with him till 10. The Affairs and Customs of the College much the Discourse.[41]

5 Indispos'd from the Heat of the wine, Divert the pain by Act Books and repose. I lend Mr. Whaley on his Letter 20^{s} and I write to Him. In the Evening I

38a Trans: 'May God the best and greatest grant [him] many happy ones.'
39 The King's School, Chester.
40 Trans: 'of which I partake; may God the best grant [me] a better life.'
41 Christ Church, Oxford.

am entertain'd with 2 pints good Claret by Dr. Thane and his Lady till 10. I pay Mr. Danald 80^{li} & Interest & the Bond is cancell'd.

6 The acceptable News of the Defeat of the French Army by the Allyes is early intimated by the Bells and great Guns, a universal Joy in the City.[42] After 4 I indispos'd, take 6 short Turns on roodee & end the day in a domestic pint.

7 The weather disswades still from my Lancashire journy but more the uncertain Condicion & weakness of my son Will. I apply to and Turn Dr. Taylor Ductor Dubitantium till 8.

8 The weather still rainy. Mr. Moulding calls on mee. I draw an Allegacion apud Acta on my cosen Moretons part.[43] I write to my Sister Jones, Mr. Crosby my cosen Parr now in Lancashire and my cosen Holt. I send to Dr. Griffith hee comes to see my son Will. I give him his Fee xs. I turn Suarer de Legibus and Dr. Taylors Ductor Dubitantium till 8 and refresh in domestic pint. I write to Mr. Jones of Llanlothian.

9 The weather clear the rain intermitted. I at the Coffee house see the News confirm'd to a complete Victory after an obstinate dispute, the French fled several waies, the Allies in campt in the place of Battell and detachment of Horse pursuing the scatter'd Troops gives expectacion of Accounts of greater and fuller success. After 5 my Suzy and I see as relacions Tom Kendric & his wife at Mr. Kelsalls after, wait on Sir John Werden. After on Mr. Wood and my sister Partington. After solace in domestic pint and to Bed about 11.

10 Tho a small rain, I go down to roodee am taken and very wett with Showers yet perform 2 full and 2 shorter Turns. I pay to Mr. Dod 53^{li} the principal and Interest of Mr. Whaley's Bond which is thereupon cancell'd. My Cosens Will and Nelly Eyton come to see their sister Moreton. I write to my sister Jones, Mr. Earl's last rates, about 4 Coach Horses to London vidt 24s a day when they travail, 10s when they rest.

11 The weather clear and fair except a small rain about 3. Mr. Cowper has a good discourse in the Quire quickly delivered. The particular successes & losses of the Battle are yet expected. In the Evening I send to Mrs. Whaley, by her eldest daughter, for her son Thomas's equipping and journy to London, 30 shillings. Dr. Thane (which is rare) comes and invites mee to a pint of his wine. I go wee with his Lady have a Bottle in his Study, hee is dull & almost speechless conversacion. Mrs. Mary Oldfield is marry'd today to Mr. Thomas Yates.

12 A delicate Morning, after I had writt to Mrs. Marsden, Brockbank, Dr. Holbrook and George Lyon, invites mee down to Roodee where 4 short Turns relieve my head and stomach. After dinner apply to Busienes and propose a scheme of the next visitacion.

13 About 7 I sett out in a fair cool morning. I light not till near 2 at Holland, a

42 The Battle of Malplaquet.

43 This Consistory Cause between Mr. & Mrs. Moreton was heard in the St. Asaph Consistory. The articles alleging gross brutality, cruelty and abuse of his wife by Moreton are in the Prescott family archives.

small dinner is provided, my expected Freinds come not, from Wigan. Mr. Birchal and S. Prescott come to mee. I set hence about 5 and come to my coz. Holt's about 6.

14 A dull and wett day. My shee cosen Holt and I in the morning pay a visit to Mrs. May over Banks. After noon to Misses Entwisles at their uncles. In the Evening take a Walk. My Cosen Holt returns from Leverpool. Wee conclude the day with a Bottle of his port Claret.

15 My 2 Cosens and I take Horse to Ince, stay 2 hours, a severe shower falls in our return. After dinner wee go to see Mr. Haydock, hee treats us with cheerfull recepcion and 2 Bottles of good Claret, wee return about 6. My Uncle Herle is very much indispos'd of Gravel & Gout.

16 About 8 (the morning fair) I, my daughter Lidia and little Loveday sett out, half an Hour at Holland, thence (S. Prescott with us) wee by way of the Green House, come to Aryfeild where my coz. Parre presently overtakes us. Wee take a walk in the prospect and thence to the Bank where hee spoils some Coffee, the favourable day and the walk gratifys. About 2 wee return to Holland where wee dine on Mutton. I see Mr. Roby's seat in the Church where Knight's wife is solicitous to sitt with Mrs. Roby. I consider the matter & believe it neither decent nor practicable they should sitt together. Ralph Whaley is importunate and assumeing. Mrs. Roby dejected yet averse. I can't yet reconcile the difference which stays mee and the child till near 6 which brings us in twilight to Wigan. Before 8 my coz. Holt & I go to Mr. Bowyer, Hee gives us 2 Bottles indifferent wine and staies us past 10.

17 About 8 I receive Mr. Chancellor's Letter signifying my Lord's resolucion to consecrate the new Chapell in Warrington on Tuesday. I write to my coz. Parr, the Accounts. About 10 call on Mr. Bowyer drink Tea, sett thence about 11 come to Warrington about 1, dine, sett hence about 3 and come safe home (D.G.) before 7. Refresht in my own domestic pint yet very weary.

18 I see the Chancellor before 9, discourse on the Confirmacion of the Chapell finish the first draughts of the peticion and sentence, Mr. Clotterbrook has a good Discourse in the Quire. The News magnifies the success of the conquered French. My Coz. Kendrick promises to go St. Asaph. I write to Mr. Moulding by him.

19 About 10 in a fair morning Mr. Chancellor, his Lady, his son, Mr. Clotterbrook and I sett out, come to Frodsham at 12, stay an hour and refresh too much on cold Beef. Mrs. Wainwright gos to Speak, wee proceed and come to Warrington twixt 3 & 4. My Lord, Mr. Legh &c are at the Golden Lyon, wee hasten and dine with them. In the Even the Clauses of the Sentence, Mr. Legh and Mr. Shaw present, are setl'd. I indeavor to do some service as in Justice and Gratitude engagd to the Family at Beausee. My Lord is positive that the patron of the Church has no Interest, as such, in this Chapell. Hee saves particular rights to the Rector. After Busienes wee retire to our Inn and with Mr. Clotterbrook and Marryon conclude in a tollerable Bottle.

20 I rise about 6 refresht and (D.G.) easy, bring the Instrument prepard, to my

Lord Bishop. Mr. Patten undertakes to procure subscriptions to the peticion; it is showry but not constant. About ½ hour after 9 My Lord and the company (yet small on the occasion) go to the Chapell after habited in the school, hee returns to the Chapell door where Mr. Legh delivers the peticion and Deed of Donacion. I read the peticion. His Lordship, by Mr. Legh, is put in possession of the Chapell. After a short stay opens the door and in sight of persons there kneels and says 2 prayers, rises calls in the company, gos to a Cathedral prepar'd in the upper end on the Northside over against the pulpit. The Morning prayer and office of the Consecracion proceed, proper psalms and Lessons, Epistle and Gospel and (after the Nicene Creed) the sentence, is read. Mr. Shaw has a sermon on 'It is written My House shall be call'd a House of Prayer' the matter not very happily composed, but very disadvantagiously deliverd, about 12 Clergy & as many of the Laity (of which myself one) stay and receive the Sacrament. 5^{li};15s is offerd. My Lord appoints the 5^{li} to bee laid out on a silver Cupp and patin, for this Altar & the 15s to the poor. Hee puts the mony into Mr. Patten's hands. Wee return before 2 to the Golden Lyon where a good dinner is prepar'd, venison seems the Head of the Feast. The sentence is attested by several wittnesses of the Solemnity.[44] Mr. Gelibrand and Sherburn (going for Chester) call mee to the 3 Crowns. My Lord going to Evening prayer, I follow. After these return with Mr. Legh and others, I go with Mr. Eckersall to the Coffee House, after an Hour, return to the Lyon, thence to Mr. Patten's (next door) my Lord's Lodgings, where the company is cheerfull till 10. After this, Mr. Legh, Chancellor, Ward, Mr. Tho. Legh, Swettenham and I stay at Mr. Golbern's 2 Hours & 2 Bottles. Mr. Alanson enters, is noisy from his Ale, upon the subject of his Fasting. Wee part and after a Gill at our Quarters to bed about 1.

21 St. Matthew. I am call'd about 6, hasten with Mr. Chancellor to my Lord. After Tea Hee returns for Broxon. The Chancellor, Mr. Tho. Legh and I go to the Coffee House, here I draw a Bill of the Fees of the Consecracion which (amounting to 13^{li};12;10) Mr. Patten pays mee. About 10 the Chancellor and I, in a dull day, sett out, wee turn and see the Chancel & Churchyard Wall of Backford. Mr. Birkenhead gives each of us an Hare, wee come about 3 safe (D.G.) to my corner & dine about 4. Lord Wharton Leiftenant of Ireland landed 2 daies ago at Hylake, comes to the Falcon this Evening.

22 First Court of this Term competent Busienes and a number of Causes entr'd. I examine Mr. Gilibrand, Mr. Sherburne and 2 other Wittnesses on George Talbot's Will. About 7 ended am with Mrs. Gelibrand, Sherburn, Hulton and Morrey at Mr. Holfield's, the wine good the discourse various, wee stay late past 11.

44 C.R.O., EDA2/4 f.109, for consecration of Holy Trinity, Warrington. Samuel Shaw was rector. (Deacon Chester June 1674, priest Chester Sept. 1674, presented to living by James Holt, 1690. Appointed one of the four King's Preachers for Lancashire 1682. Master of the Grammar School, 1686–90).

23 Extremely indispos'd from last Night's late wine. I am with my bro. Partington on the sad occasion of my sister's Funeral. Dr. Thane desir'd, declines the Funeral sermon. The News brings no more particulars but proceeds with Mons. After repose in the Evening with my Lord, Mrs. Clotterbrook, Maryon, Callis at Dr. Thane's, wee are treated with 6 Bottles good Claret, conversacion easy and ends after 9.

24 After a rainy night a bright day. Upon uncertain news of the Health of young Mr. Fleetwood & the occasion of my Sister Partington's death, I send John to St. Asaph and write, by him, to my sister Jones & Mr. Moulding. In the Evening, invited, am with the Candidates to Orders, 18 in number, my particular Acquaintance among them Mr. Offley, the Conversacion merry on punning stories, the wine good, the Reckoning near 3^{li}, wee part after 9. I receive 13 presentacions from Mr. Couche & 12^{li}.

25 A dull morning and indisposicion keep mee late in Bed. Mr. Colly dines with us. At 5 I go to my Brother Partington's where the House is full, about 6 the Funeral proceeds, attended by the Bishop, Mayor, Magistracy, the better sort, and a great number crowd the Church St. Peter's. Dr. Fogg has a good Sermon on..In it hee gives a hansom full and true character of the good deceas'd person. After the Funeral wee return to my brother Partington's where a company stays togeather past 9.

26 A rainy day, I wait on my Lord at the palace, take leave of Him. About 10 hee setts out for Broxon, from thence to proceed tomorrow towards Southwell. After dinner invited over, I go to Sir Henry Bunbury where my uncle Peck moves his Affair with Mr. Trevor, it is handl'd over 2 Bottles. In the Evening Dr. Thane comes and suddainly returns out of Humor. I follow him to his House where a pint with difficulty to him, is lugg'd out, the rest of the Quart tho mencion'd by his Lady, deny'd by the Dr. The rest of the Evening past with Mrs. Moreton & Sister Jones, pay Alderman Ince for rent, Hay and Coals 16^{li}.5s.

27 After an unhappy night, a better morning. I perform 4 full Turns on roodee & am refresht. My coz. Moreton having staid in my Corner a refugee from her cruel Husband, returns to Wrexham. I go to the Coffee House. Silence about the particular Losses in the Battle, progress in the Seige of Mons. I pay 10s Harry's Minerval; 2^{li} the Tax for the office for ½ year. After dinner apply to busienes, in the Evening treat with Mr. Earle, about 4 Coach horses & write to the Bishop of St. Asaph.

28 A very rainy day. I proceed in Mrs. Moretons Diary write to Mr. Hammond about Mr. Young the nominated Curat of Haslingden.[45] In the Evening Dr. Thane calls, wee go to Dandy's drink one Bottle of French wine and return about 8.

29 Michaelmas a clear day. I go to early prayers. After apply to Busienes. The Fair empty from the wett Season. I go into it about 3, meet with Mr. Colly and Aldersey. In the Evening go to his brother Merchant Colly's where Dr. Thane,

45 C.R.O., EDV2/14.

the said Oxford Colly, Mr. Aldersey and myself are liberally entertain'd by the Merchant with what hee call'd French wine till 10 a clock.
30 After early prayers I write to the Bishop of St. Asaph, to my coz. Parr at Rainford. After take 2 short and 2 longer Turns on roodee. After dinner I write to Mr. Styth on T. Birchall's Account and apply till 9 to Mrs. Moreton's Busienes.

OCTOBER 1 A rainy night and morning. After early prayers return to Mrs. Moreton's papers and after Noon draw some QQs to Dr. Boucher. Pay Mr. Boucher for him a Guinea, to the Washwoman 1^{li};10s for 3 Measures of Wheat 18s 6d one of Barley 3[s]. Lend Mrs. Whaley 2s 6d. After prayers go to Biggin's of the Yatcht where Mr. Chancellor, Dr. Thane, Mr. Callis my Coz. Kendrick & I drink 3 Bottles, the wine port, but pretended to bee French – wee part at 7.
2 The morning rainy. Dr. Fogg has an excellent Sermon on 'God is a spirit and is to bee worshipp'd in spirit and in Truth'. Mr. Colly and his (Merchant) brother dine with us. At prayers a full Quire, Earl of Lincolne, Lord Mohun, their Company beside that the Fair afforded. Stay at home the rest & end in domestic pint.
3 After early prayers in a fair day perform 4 Turns on roodee, proceed in my Coz. Moreton's papers. In the Evening Mr. Murrey calls. Wee go to the Mermaid (Dandy's) drink 2 Bottles good wine part about 10.
4 Indispos'd from the Bottle. Ease the indisposicion by 4 Turns, return after Noon to Books and Mrs. Moreton's Busienes, finish her case, include it in a Letter to Dr. Bouchier. After, recreate in a domestic pint.
5 A delicate morning after prayers I take 4 full Turns after and before Dinner read with great pleasure as intention the 1st of the Tusculan Qs de Morte contemuenda.[46] After Noon and till 9 Turn in the II & Valerius Max.
6 Another delicate morning, a Court day easy of Busienes, bestow the Afternoon on Books. In the Evening at Mr. Hatfield's. The Chancellor, Drs. Thane and Norris and I drink 3 Bottles, dear but indifferent wine.
7 The weather still pleasant, after early prayers Letters to Mr. Sudell and Kippax. I take 4 full Turns on Roodee. The News gives expectacion of Mons but makes the late victory not preferable to their defeat. After dinner in Books and Busienes, save call'd an hour over to Sir Henry Bunbury where Hee, my coz. Kendrick and my self drink one Bottle good Claret; a domestic pint concludes the day.
8 The weather cool pleasant sweet. After prayers I take 4 Turns on roodee. After apply to Books. In the Evening Dr. Thane, Mrs. Colly, Callys, Stratford and I at the White Bull, solace in good wine and cheerfull Conversacion to a Frolick, wee drink our Bottles and stay till 10.
9 Indispos'd from the Quantity of good wine, confin'd at home till Evening prayers. After these the Bishop of Kilaloe invites the Chancellor, Sir Henry

46 Trans: 'concerning death disdained.'

Bunbury, Capt. Steward & myself to the Falcon, hee treats us with 2 or 3 Bottles of Irish Claret, wee part at 8.
10 The weather holds fair. The Chancellor, Dr. Thane, Mr. Jack Wainwright & I about 10 sett for Eaton on foot, wee dine there, receiv'd liberally. Sir Henry Bunbury diverts the Company after dinner. Wee wait on Mr. Cholmley in his Chamber where hee receives us after his free manner. The Chancellor & I walk back and about 6 come to the Bear where wee meet Dr. Thane (who rid back) wee stay till 8 after 3 Bottles of good Irish cheerfully empty'd.
11 Indisposicion renew'd. I see the News which has little of Mons but tells the E. of Pembrook resigns the Admiralty and is to have a pencion of £3000 p.A. In the Evening The Chancellor, Dr. Thane and I return to the Bear, drink 2 Bottles of good wine. I write to Mr. Le Neve and my Cosen Parr.
12 About 10 a Clock in a fair day, I set out with my Suzy, wee come to Wrexham before 1, dine with my coz. Eyton at the office. After prayers about 4 the Bishop of St. Asaph & his Lady come to the Red Lyon, wee, my sister Jones and my coz. Moreton go to wait on them. Wee stay supper and longer with them. After wee drink a Glass of Wine with Mr. Colly the Merchant, thence to our Inn, the Fox and Goose and to bed about 12.
13 Wee take leave with the Bishop who takes coach about 9. Mr. Price and I walk to the Vicarage of Gresford come there before 12, wee find the Chancellor ready to sett out for Gwersilt, Mr. Shakerley's and go along and dine there with him. Mrs. Shakerley receives generously with excellent Claret and other good Liquids. Mr. Robinson comes after dinner, wee stay and the Glass passes freely till 6 when with reluctancy Mr. Shakerley letts mee go. Mr. Price and I come to Wrexham about 7. Wee sitt up at the office till 1. and lodg there.
14 About 10 indispos'd, I set out with Mr. Price on Foot, meet in the way a Messenger with my papers and my coz. Moreton's case from Oxford. I communicate these to Mr. Chancellor of St. Asaph and leave the Case with him. Wee dine at the vicarage, the dinner plentifull, the Beer and Ale good the wine indifferent. Mr. Robinson is at dinner. Mr. Shakerley and Mr. Lloyd of Horsley come after it. I at 4 gett off, call on my Suzy at Borras, wee go to Cornish and stay there.
15 Very much recover'd here and easy had it not bin for the difficult Circumstances of this Family which they fully relate. A short Demand for a great Arrear comes about 11 a clock from Mr. Blackburn. Wee stay dinner after call at Holt, see the new Uniform'd seats in the Church proceed then and come safe (D.G.) to our Corner About 6.
16 After Elixir easy. The new Mayor Alderman Allen and Sheriffs (young Mr. Benett and Mr. Bingley) come to the Quire but I am not there. In the Evening after prayers Philip Bateman is bury'd and Ned Robert's daughter Christen'd. Mr. Chancellor calling on me I go to the solemnity where are the Recorder, Foulks, Stratford and others. I stay to the end of the Entertainment haveing drunk my full Bottle of white wine beside the formal Glasses and part about 10.
17 About 6 rise indispos'd and in still fine weather come to Wrexham about 9. Mr. Williams schoolmaster of Wem and a vicar elsewhere comes to my coz.

Moreton as a Mediator. After prayers about 11 the Court sitts. Mr. Moreton, Mr. Kendrick, the Lawyer Mr.Rode and Mr. David Lloyd enter it with him. Moulding desires the previous Allegacion to be admitted and the proctor answers. Moreton loco ronsi et sine revocacione procuratis gives his allagacion promises to receive and treat his wife Sicut ante recepisset et tractasset affectu maritali and to have William, Collier, Dean (Clergymen) his Fidejussores,[47] this is earnestly and bodly presst by Kendrick. Moulding and I desire it may be rejected & the Allegacion previous admitted. The Chancellor is dubious in inclinacion meanly indeavors to please both sides, and in feeble Terms advises reconciliacion, admitts both Allegacions but Moreton's only quatenus[48] &c. Mr. Price and my coz Kendrick are producd on the Allegacion, prove the marriage and reputed value of his Estate and her Fortune. Kendrick insists on Moreton's Allegacion and Conciliacon, wee object. At length by the Chancellor's motion A Conference begins about securing to Her a certain Alimony. The offer first 23^{li}, after 30^{li} per A, Wee adjourn this till Dinner over, then renew it at the Red Lyon, wee insist on 35^{li} besides a share of the contigent Estates when they fall by his mother's death. Wee desire one of the children and 10^{li} consideracion of its Educacion. Moreton utterly denys her the Child and at last offers 32^{li}10s p.A. wherein contingencies to be included. Shee consulted, rejects it. Hence to the Court agen about 5 by candles, Kendrick harangues on the generous offer and diminishes Moreton's present Estate by 90^{li} p.A. (tho 130^{li}) and the contingent of 40^{li} (tho 120^{li}) much Time spent. The Chancellor computes, find the proposal of 32^{li};10s near the matter but is pessiti about the contingency. At last takes time to deliberate on the Alimony to be allowed & Moreton's Allegacions and Moulding's desires ad Libellandum in proxime[49] which for Kendrick's conveniency is put to 11th Nov. After Court I am with the Chancellor and Registrar and Mr. Price at the Sun, the matter is menciond and the Chancellor seems to have better Sentiments at the Allocacion of Alimony and to resolve to reject Moreton's Allegacion. From the Sun, I go to the office where the transaccions are rememberd by mee with greatest regret. Wee pass the Time in a Bottle of good wine after a bad one and part about 12.

18 I rise before 7 see the News at the Red Lyon where I have some discourse with David Lloyd & Mr. Williams. About 9 Will. Eyton & I sett out, walk to Mr. Hill's fine House, see the inside so too, thence a narrow unfrequented way to Pentry Vellin. Wee come to Havord y wern, walk about in the wood and Field, are kindly and liberally entertain'd, set out thence before 3 and before 4 from Wrexham, my sister Jones comes along with mee. About 6 in a fine day come safe to my Corner. Mr. Whaley comes almost at the same time, interrupts us with his History and affects mee as formerly with his difficulties. Hee comes to borrow mony to carry him & his son to London. Stays here all night.

47 Trans: 'as he had previously taken and treated her with marital affection.' Fidjussores= sureties.
48 Quantenus – lit. 'in so far as.'
49 Trans: 'to bring the charges at the next Court session day.'

19 A delicate morning (after early prayers) tempts mee to roodee. My Bro. Partington in the way falls into my walk, interrupts my purpose. Tells mee of the probability of the Recorder's Knighthood by the E., of Cholmley's interest and this quickly. The design to make a Terras about Roodee, wee perform 6 shorter Turns. I solace in Books. About 6 Mr. Whaley after I had lent him 2^{li} for his and his son's viatica setts out in the dark. This revives the troublesome transactions in our Affair the last Year. D.O.M. det his quaque Finem.[50] After domestic pint to bed about 10.

20 The weather still cool and serene. I am at early prayers after perform 4 full Turns, recurr to my recreacion in Books, write to Mr. Stratford and to Dr. Holbrook. After prayers at the Coffee House. After that Dr. Thane and I at the White Bull, drink our Bottle of good Claret, part at 8, to bed before 10.

21 The weather happily continuing in a sharp morning at early prayers. After take 4 full Turns, call on Mr. Colly, discourse Jack's Circumstance fully with him over his good Tea. Hee dines with us. After dinner my coz. Kendrick and I drink a Bottle with Sir Hen. Bunbury. In the Evening Mr. Colly my coz. Kendrick and I wait on the Mayor who going out orders Mr. Allen to entertain us, hee dos so with excellent Claret, wee stay 5 Bottles and till 10 when the Mayor returns, wee stay a short time with him.

22 Indisposicion from the quantity scares and keeps me in all day till 7 when Sir Henry Bunbury sends. Here is Mrs. Egerton, Dove, Booth, Walley at a short elegant supper. After that variety of Claret gos about, Freedom and cheerfulness along. The Company parts about 1.

23 Extremely indispos'd, confin'd till prayers. After these J. Wainwright takes his leave of mee. I give him half a Guinea. After I go to Mr. Colly, deliver to him 10^{li} for Jack. His Merchant Bro. and hee putt some writeings seal'd up into my custody. After Sir Henry Bunbury, Mrs. Egerton, Brook, Done, Peak &c discourse and good wine go briskly round till past 10.

24 My indisposicion is extremely aggravated, repent with remorse, dispatch some Busienes but with difficulty, I repose and am diverted by reading. To bed before 10.

25 The Fevor something abated. After the Coffee house where the News sends the Troops to their Winter Quarters. I recreate in a fair day in 4 Turns on roodee. After dinner apply to a draught of my coz. Moreton's Libel, finish and write with it to Dr. Bouchier.

26 After early prayers draw the Case of my Coz. Moreton's Libel, send it to Mr. Pierson and desire his answer with expedicion. After take 2 full and 2 shorter Turns am well refresh't. After noon apply to the speculator and other Books of practice till 9 at Night.

27 The weather still fair. After early prayers take 4 full Turns on roodee am extremely recover'd. After Dinner Dr. Griffith calls on us and purposing for Dublin, takes in leave with design to return with the Spring. The Chancellor

50 Trans: 'May God the best & greatest grant an end to these also.'

comes back out of the visitacion from Wigan. Solace in a domestic pint.

28 St. Simon and St. Jude. After early prayers I perform 4 full Turns in a most delicate bright & sweet morning am D.G. extremely refresht. Turn and divert in Books. After 3 wait on the Chancellor, wee go to prayers after with Dr. Thane to the Bear where wee solace in 3 Bottles of excellent Claret part at 8.

29 Indispos'd from the Claret, I take 4 full Turns on roodee before 12, bestow the rest of the day on Books, am extremely affected in my Head and stomach above the relief of a share of good wine at Sir Hen. B's where my uncle Peck is under visible and melancholy impressions of his difficulties with Mr. Trevor. Mr. Acton and my Coz. Peck are of the company, wee part before 9.

30 The weather is yet favorable and happy. Dr. Fogg has an excellent discourse on the Omniscience of God. The News affords nothing but repeticion. Mr. Roberts and the rest of the company return from Wigan. I end the day in Books and the Evening in domestic pint.

31 After early prayers my stomach pains and reflections return. I contend with 'em on roodee in more than four full Turns. For Medecin return to Books which alleviate the pains of reflexion. After Evening prayers Dr. Thane, Mr. Kendrick and I go to the Bear dispatch 2 Bottles, return before 9.

NOVEMBER 1 The month begins with the Auspices the last ended. I go to early prayers and thence with my pains to roodee, perform with industrious Endevor to help & repel my pains above four full Turns. I drink Coffee with my S. at my bro. Partington's shop. After at the Coffee house which affords no news yet diverts. The Citizens celebrate the day with scarlet, musick and solemnity. After dinner at the Charity meeting in the palace where 5 persons make a Committee. After at prayers and thence with Mr. Chancellor and Dr. Thane to Dandy's where wee drink 2 Bottles. Sir Hen. B. comes to us My Coz. Moreton's Affair is the subject of the Conversacion. My daughter Lidia after 4 months entertainment there comes from Wigan.

2 After a disturb'd night I rise to now very early prayers. A thick Fog incubates the City. I hasten to Roodee where I meet a sweet serenity, labor under stomach pains and reflections, perform 6 full Turns and return refresht. Write to Dr. Boucher, the Caution offer'd and the authority quoted Godolp. p. 509. I return to my Books. Mr. Jones of Bangor and my coz. Will Eyton dine with us. I draw some Articles of my Coz. Moreton's Libel and at 8 recreate in domestic pint.

3 After the same disorder in the Night at early prayers, the morning moist and dull. I write to John Cross about the Bank. A Court day, slender and easy of Busienes. Before Court the Cause of Mrs. Moreton is talk't on in Mr. Bouchier's room. Mr. Hulton denys hee drew the Allegacion about the Caution &c., declares hee has done with the Cause, tho' some present believe hee prevaricates and is behind the Curtain. In the Evening I write fully to Jack. After go over to Sir Hen.Bunbury, whilst with Him my Lady is happily deliver'd of a Son about a quarter past 9. On this occasion wee rejoice in a Bottle of good Wine and part past 12.

4 The Night was not without Inquietude. Mr. Roberts &c. go to keep a Court at Frodsham. I recurr to my relief on Roodee, strive with pains and am refresht in 6 Turns. I receive a full & welcome answer from Mr. Pierson, apply to Books and drawing of Mrs. Moreton's Libel. After prayers (about 6) Dr. Thane comes in a moody temper, wee go to Dandy's find the wine above expectacion, venture on the 2nd Bottle, the Dr's. Spirits and humor clear up grow gay and cheerfull, wee part improv'd about 9.

5 A very thick Fogg sitts on the Town, about 9 I go thoro it to Roodee, filld with palpable Ayr but at the river side rarified and pleasant, the sun presently exhales the thick medium and a cheerfull serenity succeeds. I struggle with my pain thoro 4 short and 2 long Turns, am refresht. I write to Mr. Alexander and to my coz. Parr (now at Rainford). The day is solemnly kept. After noon, I apply to Mrs. Moreton's Libel. Mr. Kendrick in the Evening interrupts mee. I end in domestic pint.

6 A moist day with some rain. Dr. Thane on Eph. 5 v 6 has a good discourse Sanctissimae Synaxis participes sumus Ego et S. mea Det D.O.M. vitam puriorem.[51] After Evening prayer apply to Books in Mrs. Moreton's cause. Go over and see her at Sir H. Bunbury, the yong child has private Baptism and is call'd William. Wee come home about 10.

7 I rise to early prayers, go on with Moreton's Libel. I proceed in the Libel which is ingross'd at the same time: at Night relax in a domestic pint.

8 I apply diligently to the Libel advance it to Michaelmas 1708 and refresh late in a domestic pint.

9 I with obstinate diligence proceed with and finish the Libel, about 9, Mr. Moulding calls on mee. Wee with Mrs. Moreton conclude on our practice at Wrexham.

10 I write to John Cross about the Bank. A court easy and calme. Before dinner wee compare the 2 ingross't and original draught of the Libel together it consisting of 51 Articles. About 3 Mrs. Moreton, Mr. Moulding and I take Horse in a fair but dark Evening, wee hasten and come to the office at Wrexham about 5. Mr. Kendrick comes to us there, where over a Glass of wine, I plainly tell him of the necessity of assisting Mrs. Moreton in this Cause and without expense, I would incurre were I able rather than shee should fall in so just a complaint. Hee makes no generous reply.

11 I rise about 7 wait on Mr. Price, after, wee see the News. After morning prayer about 11 The Court sitts. Mrs. Williams, Kendrick, Lloyd and Rhodes take their places on the other side. Friends, Relacions and spectators crowd the place (Sir Hen. Bunbury on the Bench). I desire to kno how the Assignacion is entr'd, the Registrar reads it. Mr. Williams begins a decent and persuasive applicacion to the Judg to admitt the Allegacion and Caucion. Mr. Kendrick

51 Trans: 'My Suzy and I are partakers of the most Holy Eucharist; may God the best and greatest grant [me] a purer life.'

urges it with vehemency, reflection, indecency. Rhodes is rude in desultory sayings. Lloyd is obstreperous, irregular, audacious, clamorous. The Chancellor hears all and reproves no invasion of the practice. I indeavor, with some success to object against the Allegacion which is therefore rejected. Mrs. Moreton appears, gives in propria manu[52] the Libel, desires to bee and is admitted to the Oath of Calumny. I desire proceedings judicial may mangre, the noise & opposicion pass according to Law and practice. Lloyd threatens the Court with a prohibicion.[53] I reprove him for it. They on the other side interrupt mee in every mocion. The Chancellor ad informandum Animum suum – calls for and examines a Witnes, Mrs. Eliz. Cole upon the Saevitia viva voce,[54] Shee deposes that shee saw him strike her with his whip and to throw her from him so that she stumbl'd cross the Kitchen and shee had heard from others of many of his severities to her. The Chancellor taxes Alimony to 11^{li} trepdemadis and the Expenses to 6^{li} admits the Libel and assigns the adverse proctor, ad condemum eidem in proxime. Lloyd protests de appellando.[55] After Court wee dine (1s 6d Ordinary) at the Fox and Goose. Sir Henry Bunbury meets the Lawyer and Atturney on the other side at Dick Jones' (Mr. Chancellor and Mr. Price present). They agree on 33^{li} for separate maintenance at present to which 7^{li} is to be added upon Mrs. Moreton's or Mrs. Beales death and that Mr. Moreton pay the 6^{li} tax't for Expences – About 6 (the Lawyer gon to Chester). Mr. Lloyd (the Registrar) Mr. Moulding and I enter into the Room where a considerable company of Sir Henry's pleas'd with the success of the day promotes Mirth and (white) wine till 12.

12 Warm of last Night I go to the Red Lyon to see Mr. Moreton not indeed as a Friend. I find him by the Kitchen Fire, step close to him and in a louder Accent ask him how hee dos – hee looks downward and makes no answer. I take some turns cross the Kitchen and meeting with Mr. Registrar speak to him about drawing up the Acts, in Mr. Moreton's hearing. Sir Hen. Bunbury and Mr. Hugh Foulks are indispos'd. Wee all sett out from the office before 1 and come to Chester about 3. In the Evening at 6 I go to Sir Henry where my coz. Kendrick, Mr. Foulks and I stay with Sir Hen. at his good Claret, past 9.

13 After Elixir, cool'd and recover'd stay at home till Evening prayers after which Mr. Allen treats with a Bottle of good wine at Mr. Bouchier's, wee part about 9.

14 The weather fair I take 5 gratefull Turns on roodee. Mr.Lambert's daughter dines with us. After prayers Mr. Chancellor Mr. Sewell, Collector, my coz. Kendrick and I, go to the Bear, drink our Bottles cheerfully and have a 5th our Landlords in at the Bargain.

52 Trans: 'by his own hand.'

53 A prohibition was a document terminating the cause in the Consistory Court and transferring it on appeal to the provincial Court (in this case Canterbury) for St. Asaph diocese.

54 Trans: 'for informing his mind'; *and* 'orally on the ferocity.'

55 Trans: 'to sentence him at the next session' *and* 'on appeal'.

15 The season still favorable, I warm from the Quantity. I recurr to roodee perform 5 Turns am invited to dine (with some of the Clergy) at the Mayor's, but beg excuse. In the Evening I am call'd over to Sir Henry B's where Mrs. Hanmer of Fenns, Booth, Walley, Foulks, Linsack, wee have good Claret and good Musick. I take about a pint of the 1st and come home before 10.

16 I still return to roodee, am extremely refresht by 5 Turns. I dine at the Xtning dinner at Sir Henry B's a select company of about 10 fill the table. Mr. Booth moves some philosophical discourse about acquivocal and univocal Generacion is not profound but peevish. Wee go to church about 3. The Child is declar'd and receiv'd into the Church. Mr. Hanmer and Mr. Hurleston are Godfathers. My coz. Moreton (for Mr. Wm. Bunbury's Lady) is Godmother. After wee return to good wine and Cheerfulness till 8.

17 The weather threatens alteracion. I write to Mr. Gilibrand about the interest mony. At Mr. Boucher's Chamber I acquaint Mr. Hulton with the Fate of his Allegacion and falacious Case of Tattenhall,[56] hee suggested to the other side at Wrexham, his confidence tho shock't was not enough confounded. Wee have a Court of small busienes. I examine 1 wittness. After prayers I am with Mr. Chancellor, Dr. Thane and Mr. Whitehead (of Rachdale) at Dandy's, wee are cheerfull, drink each a Bottle part about 10.

18 Indispos'd from the Quantity, stay at home in Books and repose.

19 I perform 5 turns on roodee, apply to Busienes. At Night invited to Sir Hen. B's take more than a pint with him and part about 10.

20 Dr. Fogg has a very good sermon in the Quire. I see her Majesties Speech at the Coffee house, the News tells the K. of Denmark has invaded Schonen. After prayers I read Dr. Blackhall's sermon of Trying of prophets. End the day in domestic pint.

21 The weather tempting, I return to 5 full Turns on roodee, thence to Busienes & Books.

22 I take the invitacion of a calm & fair morning and perform 4 full Turns, about 9. A General Thanksgiving for the success of the last campaign is solemnis'd in St. Oswald's Church. Dr. Fogg has a sermon on psal. 3; 8. The Town is full of joy and noise. My coz. Kendrick comes after dinner, my coz. Moreton's busienes is our common Theme. I with some warmth & freedom reprehend the penurious assistance of her Friends, particularly himself, who had the largest obligacions from her Father, and Family. Hee hears mee but makes no answer. I go in to the pentice which is fill'd with voluntary Company, the public Healths are proclaim'd by the praeces and go briskly round till the remaining company grow warm and cheerfull. I return thence home about 9.

23 I am about 9 with Sir Hen. Bunbury on my coz. Moreton's Deed of separate Maintenance, after that with my coz. Moreton, my Suzy, my sister Jones and Mrs. Mary Vanbrugh at Mrs. Broughton's Coffee. After dinner am indispos'd

56 C.R.O., EDC1/103 n.f.

repose and still, Dr. Thane comes, wee send for a Bottle of Dandy's & drink it about 9.

24 A very brisk weather and frost begun, the Ayr very serene, the sun glorious. I write to my coz. Parr and John Cross. A Court Day and the Busienes easy and run over with expedicion. I divert in Books and at night, still further in domestic pint.

25 The weather very cold, freezing, brisk. At the glorious rising of the Sun I go to roodee perform 5 Turns am refresht, return to Books. I receive an Account of Mrs. Whaley's necessitys, wee send meat & 6d to supply her. In the Evening at Mr. Dandie's, with the Warden of Manchester, Archdeacon Thane and Mr. Hulton. Wee talk the last campaign over, drain our Bottles and part about 9.

26 The weather cold tho not freezing, the wind South: disturb'd by the full Bottles have some relief by 4 short Turns. Apply to Books till 8, when for my stomach I venture to chaw a leaf of Tobacco, it makes mee sick to both motions. Recover'd by time, heat and help to bed before 10.

27 A considerable snow fell in the Night and continues to fall till noon. I stay at home in Books. After evening prayers I return to Books, recreate in domestic pint and to bed about 10.

28 The weather still severe. I write to Mr. Alexander inclose an Abstract of the presentacions of Bedal (Bedale),[57] tell him I owe Mrs. Peirson 13s 4d and desire him to pay as much of that sum as he thinks such a search deserves. I write too to Mrs. Peirson. Indispos'd most of the cold and wet day. I recreate in Lipsius & at 9 domestic pint.

29 The weather wett and dull. I stay at home in Books and Busienes. After Evening prayer I call on Mr. Hodgson, wee go to T. Hatfield's where wee drink a Bottle of his French part about 9.

30 Tho a dull morning I recreate with 2 longer and 2 shorter Turns on roodee. I procure from the Mayor a Bill of 40^{li} and inclose it to Dr. Pope, pay John on Account 6s. Apply to Lipsius. I remember Lady Charlott Cornwallis her birth day (now 31) in a domestic Celebracion. About 4 send by Mr. Roberts 84^{li};16s to T. Hatfeild, hee pays it and brings back Mr. Whaley's Bond (D.G.) About 5 The Chancellor and Dr. Thane send to meet 'em at the Bear. I do so, wee drink 3 Bottles of excellent wine very cheerfully and part before 9. After this I go over and sitt an hour with Lady Bunbury and return to Bed about 10.

DECEMBER 1 The weather rainy, I write to Mr. Banks of Winstanley an answer to his about Bury. Mrs. Morgan's Funeral about 10, proceeds to Stoak. The last Court of this Term easily finish't, I examine 3 Wittnesses on Barnett's Will. Mr. Lambert calls on mee about 7, wee go to the White Bull drink 1 Bottle & part about 9.

2 A clear and brisk morning draws mee down to 4 full Turns on roodee. After I

57 L.D.A., CD/PP/2, Bedale Parish Papers, for a list of presentations since 1637 to the benefice.

am at the Coffee House where Mr. Holland finds & discourses mee on his Master's and young Mr. Morgan's affairs. After dinner Dr. Thane and Mr. Lambert call on mee. Mr. Lloyd (Hugh) from Gwersilt calls and desires my Letter on his behalf to the Bp. of St. Asaph in respect to Marchwaal. After prayers Mr. Chancellor, Dr. Thane, Mr. Lambert and I go to the Bear where wee drink each his Bottle and Part about 8. My Suzy, sister Jones and my self give several matters in charge to Mr. Lambert to buy for us. I give him in order 4 Carolus's (4^{li}; 14s) I after go with him to Lady Otway, thence returning call at Dandy's and after a Bottle part about 11, direct to Mr. Lambert at Mr. Stephen Husband's in Grays Inn.

3 Indispos'd from last night's wine, yet write to the Bp. of St. Asaph. Apply to or rather recreate in Books till Night and then recurr to Elixir.

4 Stay at home, read the service psalms and Chapters for the day and after prayers finish Dr. Scott's excellent discourse on 1 Tim. 4.6. My Suzy and I visit my sister Puleston of Havord-y-w. at Bro. Partington's.

5 A dull and cold day. I write fully to Mr. Rigby in Cannon Street about Mr. Whaley, to Mr. Lambert about 4 potts of Charrs and to James Bradshaw in Shoredich. After dinner, several see mee, yet I repose. In the Evening, Mr. Dockeril invites me and Mr. Roberts to Dandie's, wee drink 2 Bottles & part after 9.

6 A brisk and rainy morning yet I venture on roodee but am driven off in my 2nd turn by a brisk shower, am refresht by the hast, apply to Heinsius and other praelegomeno, to Terence; write and to each inclose 6 Licences to Mr. Styth and Mr. Markland. Divert in Lipsius & Livy and end in a domestic pint about 10.

7 A bright but cold morning. I take 4 full Turns on roodee and am recreated, turn Lenius de Institia and Grotius de Tyre B. et p. After prayers with the Chancellor & Dr. Thane at Dandy's – wee drink 2 Bottles and part at 8. At this time, some refleccions are made on Mr. Hulton and his Mrs. Fox.

8 A brisk and bright day, my Suzy and I prepare for Wrexham. I write to my Ld. Bps. of Chester and St. Asaph, on Mr. Francis Cholmley's Account and to Dr. Boucher on my coz. Moreton's. After 2 wee sett out for Wrexham. At the end of Hanbridge, John has a severe stroke from the Kick of a Horse. Wee come to Wrexham in the dark after 5. About 9 wee drink a Bottle of my sister Jones wine, in variety of company. I grow faint from the heat of the parlour, to bed at 10.

9 About 9 (Peter Massy my Guide) I sett out to place Gronno, come there before they are dres't to receive. Stay 2 hours, am entertain'd with Tea, return hence about 12, a bridg in the way troublesom. Wee dine at the office, leave the Family in a melancholy, Mrs. Beale in a desperate condicion from her Cancer, about 3 wee leave the place come to Cornish about 4, find a disconsolate Family, indevor to divert it till 10 then to bed.

10 About 12 a rainy day wee sett out, come about 1 to Eaton Boat, the storm and rain togeather make the passage difficult and not without danger, wee stay till the storm spent, come safe home D.G. before 3 dine before 4. Wee are too much entertain'd with the misfortunes & ill manners of Mr. Whaley's Family. To bed about 10.

11 Indispos'd stay at home bestow the time till Evening prayer in reading especially Dr. Scott's discourses and Dr. Isha's Funeral Sermon on Dr. Scott's Death.

12 A windy and cold morning yet take 4 Turns on roodee, refresht for Books and Busienes. About 5 (after prayers) the 2 Rectors of Winwick and Wigan send, I go to them at the Falcon, after supper I guide 'em to the Bear, where the Chancellor, Mr. Wright, Subdean, and Dr. Thane, wee drink each a Bottle of good wine, part about 10. I return to the Falcon with the Rectors stay there at ill wine till 12.

13 Extremely indispos'd from the wine and unseasonable time. Stay, repose and repent at Home.

14 After Elixir recover'd. I write to Mr. Lambert now at Mr. Husbands Chambers, Grays Inn, London, apply to Books. After dinner Mr. Chancellor calls tells mee wee are invited by Mr. Sewel the Collector. After prayers wee go thither where in a nice room wee are elegantly entertain'd with Brandy good Clarett, Oysters, Ale, Monks Ale, Ham &c. Hee is very genteel his Lady simply indevors to bee a Gentlewoman. Mr. Allen comes towards the end about 9 and about 10 wee part. I call at Mr. Allen's and part in severall tipps of Brandy.

15 To carry off inconvenient Heat and humor I venture on 4 Turns on roodee, tho the weather very cold apply to Busienes and Books and at Night to Elixir.

16 About 6 in the morning Mr. Newton of St. Peter's dies, about 10 my brother Partington with the Churchwardens of the parish come and desire mee to write to Mr. Oliver. I do that in pursuance of my Lord Bishop's commands and add their Invitacion. I receive 10^{li} from Mr. Moulding by One, Green of Wigan. The 2 Rectors return from Mostyn, I am with them and Dr. Thane at Mr. Chancellor's where wee take each a Bottle of good Claret part about 10.

17 A cool frosty morning. I take 25^{li} with design to pay Mr. Starkie for interest, hasten to the Feathers, his Inn, whence hee had just took Horse. I write to my Ld. of Mr. Newton's death &c. After dinner repose. After prayers vidt. at 6 call'd on to Mrs. Ickens where Sir Henry Bunbury, Mr. Davies, Mr. Chancellor, Dr. Norris, Dr. Thane, Mr. Kendrick. The time is cheerfully spent over good wine, save the last Bottle, till 10. Borrow'd of my sister Jones in order to pay Mr. Starkie the said sum 10 Guineas.

18 At the Choir where Dr. Fogg has a very good discourse on ps. 34 v. 9 After prayers apply close to reading till 9 then relax in a domestic pint.

19 A calme morning. I write to the Earl of Rochester repeat my thanks and give him notice of the Charrs I send him. I write order to John Cross to pay Mr. Starkie 25^{li} interest, to Jeffrey Prescott and Mr. Hayhurst. In the Evening taken with the Latin tho I suspect the truth of the History, read 3 Dialogues . . . recreate in domestic pint.

20 ..Mr. Oliver comes to mee. I send for and leave him in the hands of my Bro. Partington..about 11 (Will. Willoughby with mee) I go to Eaton shew Mr. F.

Cholmley my Ld. Bp's letter..discourses on his own Affair fully & freely (injoyning secrecy) I dine and stay till 4, return home about 9..Wee send for a Bottle to the Bear drink that & part about 9 *[damaged entry]*
21 In a calm fair morning, I take 4 Turns on Roodee, after write to my Ld. Bp. on Mr. Cholmley's, Mr. Oliver and Sir Wm.Meredith's Account. After dinner apply to Books & papers. Compute the Apparitor's Fees for Exhibicions in the Episcopal Visitacion this year to 12^{li};0s;8d.
22 A rainy cold morning. I write to Mr. Piget of Manchester. Apply to Books. In the Evening Sir Hen. Bunbury and Mr. Kendric come over to see mee, they acquaint mee of the finishing of Mr. Moreton's Deed by the Lawyers in a Council of 'em and of the striking out the Clauses which relate to the Ecclesiastical Court. I dissent with some warmth. Mr. Ed. Wright and Mr. Philip Brook come in and break off the discourse which turns to Dr. Sacheveril. I receive a very humble Letter from Mrs. Whaley begging my Charity &c.
23 The mild morning invites mee down to 4 long 2 shorter Turns on roodee, they extremely refresh mee. After Evening prayers invited by Mr. Chancellor I am at his House with Sir Henry Bunbury, Mr. Davies, Dr. Norris, Mr. Bruen and Dr. Thane. The Chancellor treats with punch, Claret and old Beer, the Conversacion is easy and wee part before 9.
24 Under complaints from the varieties of last night, the day cold and rainy. I write to Mr. Rider & Mr. James Bradshaw. After dinner Mrs. Whaley comes, complains of her desolate condicion, wee pity & help her. I give her ½ a Crown, my S. some Xtmas provision. I continue in Books particularly Severus till 10.
25 The weather opens calme yet cold. Dr. Thane has a good discourse in the Quire on . . . Cenae sanctissimae Det D.O.M. bene et recte vitam agere particeps sum.[58] After prayers about 6 Dr. Holbrook comes, stays, sups and drinks a glass of wine with us till 10. Wee entertain with Lancashire Newes.
26 The wind high and cold diverts mee from roodee. Dr. Fogg has a good discourse on the Martyrdom of St. Stephen. I dine with Sir Hen. B., Mr. Chancellor, Archdeacon, Drs. Holbrook & Chetwood & Mr. Done at Mr. Davies who receives us with a full and fine Feast. After that the punch, Claret and Beer with cheerfull Conversacion gos freely about. I chuse the last and come with my share home before 9. I find my coz. Kendric and talkt (I fear too) warmly to Him about my coz. Moreton's Affair.
27 A cold raw day. I go tho fevorish to Church. Dr. Fogg has a good discourse on St. John c. 21. vv. 21,22. Dr. Holbrook dines with us. After dinner wee relaps into Ale. Hee receds, I repose. About 7 the Dr. returns and stays with us till 10. Mr. Whaley's youngest son Jack dies of the small pox.
28 After Elixir cool and easy. The weather hail, snow and severely cold. I write to Dr. Yarborough and inclose Mr. Aynsworth's Letter to him and offer him 25^{li} for his Coins . . . John Cross comes this Evening brings 20^{li} from Ayrfeild, 20^{li}

58 Trans: 'I partake of the most Holy Supper. May God the best and greatest grant [me] to lead [my] life honourably & properly.'

from the Bank, 6^{li} from the Green house..which hee had paid, 25^{li} Dunkenall interest, there remains then only 24^{li}.

29 The Snow continues and gos to about 9 inches deep. Invited my Suzy and I dine with . . . the Foulks Family consisting of 3 Generacions fill the Table . . . Mr. Whaley's 3d son William dies of the small pox.

30 The snow very deep yet John Cross returns. My Suzy and I dine at my brother Alderman Puleston's where wee are receiv'd with Sir Hen. Bunbury, Mr. Bruen their Ladies and a full good company at a hansom dinner. Some drink punch others among whom I drink Ale till 6 then part of a Bottle of Claret, wee pass the Time cheerfull till 10.

31 Indispos'd from the variety of the liquor, I keep my bed till 10. I write to Mr. Rider. After repose and prayers I apply to Chaucer who diverts mee fully till 10.

1709/10

JANUARY 1 Q.F.F.F.Q.S. Dr. Fogg has a good discourse on St. John 3ch 16th. After dinner call'd over, I am some short time with Sir Henry Bunbury So after prayers. The rest in Books at home till 10.

2 Mr. Lambert who return'd last night calls on us this morning. I pay him 2^{li}.1.6, the sum hee laid out above the mony I paid him when hee went for London. I write to my cozen Parr an Invitacion to us, and to Dr. Bramston an Account of the Charrs sent to him. I give Mr. Anthony ½ a Guinea with direction to buy 2 pair of Shoos in Fleet Street. After prayers I meet Mr. Chancellor and Dr. Thane at Hadfield's, wee drink 3 Bottles before 9.

3 I am surpris'd with a small Casket of Coins, they were delivered to the Messenger by Mr. Brayn, when Mr. Ives (his new Father in Law) was present, therefore I suspect this the Donor and write to him accordingly. I perform only 2 Turns on roodee. After prayers my S. sister Jones and I visit Mrs. Jones and Mrs. Middleton. Mrs. Beale our good and old Acquaintance and relacion dies of a Cancer today about 8 at night.

4 A calme day, Mrs. Whaley comes after her begging Letter, shee professes to go to day from Chester with her 2 daughters into Lancashire. I still mov'd with her Circumstances give her 20 shillings, shee is greatefull thinks the Gift considerable and wee part in Freindship. I after 2 longer & 2 shorter Turns on roodee, I write to Mr. Oliver to come hither, to Mrs. Horton to buy mee a pair of Stockings. After prayers apply to Wooton's History of Rome.

5 A dull moist day. I send Capt. Hurleston an old Cheese for a New Year's Gift, apply to papers & for the greater part to Wooton's Life of Marcus Antonius and Commodus. Stay after prayers at home.

6 A fair but sharp day. Dr. Fogg has a good sermon on Hosea 1;10. After dinner, I am present (not a writeing) wittness to Mr. Nichols his payment of 22^{li}15s for Mr. Hen. Bunbury's Annuity due from Sr. Henry (at Midsummer and Martinmas last. 3^{li}5s being deducted for Taxes) to Mr. Geo. Birch brother to

Mrs. Bunbury. Divert in reading and the rest in Christmas entertainment till 10 at Night.
7 I take 4 Turns on roodee. Our Freinds and relacions Lady Bunbury, Alderman Partington, his 2 daughters, Mr. Kendrick, my sister Puleston, dine with us.I receive from Mr. Kendrick 5^{li} tax'd for my Cozen Moreton, After Evening prayer, I go to enquire after Mr. Oliver, meet with him in Mr. Hodgson's Shop. After I am with my bro. Partington, Dr. Chetwood &c. at Mr. Gill till 9, return and find my company at home at Supper. after which to bed about 11.
8 A mild winter day. I go to St. Peter's Church, hear with difficulty Mr. Olivers very excellent discourse on St.John 1:12. Hee has a deep and musical voice, but do's not exert it and is not heard by half the Congregacon. After dinner I go down and into the Pentice, where aside, I tell Mr. Oliver of his insuccess in the morning, and desire him to advance his voice. Hee promises and do's so but not high enough on the same Text.[59] After sermon I go with him to the Chancellor. After that, 2 hours, meet him at Sheriff Bingley's, where in a good company of his parishioners, I am free and plain yet cheerful with him upon the subject of his voice.
9 I take but 2 Turns on roodee,meet Lady Bunbury at her Treat of Freinds at Mrs. Broughton's Coffee. I bestow the rest of the day on Petavius Mediobarbus Helvicus.
10 I take 4 Turns on roodee, write in the morning to Mr. Moulding. After Noon return to Books and in the Evening write to Dr. Stratford, Jack and the Registrar of Hereford.
11 A fair calm day. About 11 sett out on horseback come to Eaton before 12 Mr. Cholmley is pleas'd with my Visit, talks his Family cares freely and fully to mee. Tells mee that the last week Mrs. Whaley was there with a peticion, and sent it into the House by an ill woman, her Companion, who stole a silver spoon out of the pantry. After dinner I am with Mr. Cholmley till 5, at home before 6. After this sent for to the Bear, find the Chancellor and Dr. Thane there, Mr. Walley and Mr. Kendrick come after, wee drink 4 Bottles good wine part about 9.
12 A very brisk freezing morning. I take 4 Turns and recreated, meet Lady Bunbury with her Company at Mrs. Broughton's, where Mr. Kendrick treats with Coffee. After Evening prayers I divert in Sir Walter Rawleigh's History till 9.
13 About 11 Dr. Thane, Will. Massie and I set from the Coffee house come to Newton before 12. Mr. Hurleston has his Dependants, Capt. Pennington, Mr. Glasier and others, wee dine not till 2. After, the strong roapy Ale go's round past 4. Wee return to Will. Willoughby's stay there past 8 correcting by Brandy, the crudity of the Ale.
14 Some Snow faln in the Night. I take 4 full Turns, write to the Bishop of St.

59 R.V.H. Burne, *op.cit*, p. 178, for a biography of John Oliver.

Asaph & Mr. James Pinfold of the Commons. Apply to Godwin de Praesulibus, read his discourse On the first Conversion of the Island to the Xtian Religion.
15 A cold day; snow yet melting. Dr. Fogg has a sermon in the parish church St. Oswald's on 1 Cor 11 v. 26 where wee with the parishioners receive the Sacrament. After prayers I apply to Usher's Primordiae and continue in them till 10.
16 Indispos'd from my stomach apply to various reading, begin but finish not an answer to Mr. Whaley, repose after dinner. In the Evening (on invitacion) Mr. Chancellor, Archdeacon, Dr. Norris, their Ladies, Mr. Boucher and Mrs. Crompton with Lady Bunbury come to end our Xtmas, the Ladies at Cards, the Men at Wine, divert till 9 when supper enters. After this return to the severall divercions which last till 12 a clock.
17 The weather wett the snow melting, I from some discourse last night apply to Camden's H. of Queen Eliz. till near 6 when sent for, I go down to the Chancellor and Archdeacon, at the Bear, here fond of the fine wine, wee drink 3 Bottles of it. Wee return about 8. I find Ned Roberts his wife and her sister at Supper with us. After that, they return to Cards, I to Camden, they stay till 12.
18 A dull day adds to indisposicion. I finish & send my Letter to Mrs. Whaley. After dinner some busienes and repose – divert in Sr Walter Rawleigh's History till 10.
19 A severe cold day with Frost. The first Court (Q.B.E.) of this Term, the Busienes small and easy. I return to History. After prayers The Chancellor Dr. Thane, Mr. Davies and I go to the Bear, wee are temted by the Conversacion and good wine, to venture on 4 Bottles and part about 9.
20 The weather continues very severe and freezing. I (after the Coffee house) perform 4 long & 2 shorter Turns on roodee, return to Rawleigh, read his Comparison of the Macedonian, Roman & Brittish Bravery in Warr. After noon Mr. Smalshaw comes and offers mee his Estate (about 12 acres) in Holland for 280^{li} Mr. Shaw, Steward at Beausee, calls on, and thanks, mee for the Care I us'd in the behalf of the Patron at the Consecracion of the Chapell in Warrington. In the Evening Lady Bunbury calls & Stays with us, tells of a Frolic of Sir Hen. Bunbury and Mr. Harvie at Pontacks. I treat with a domestic pint.
21 The weather still very sharp and severe. I write to Mr. Alanson and Mr. Pigot of Manchester. Apply – After prayers to Livy, till 10 at Night. Mrs. Whaley came to mee about 6, shee took occasion to bee very rude, loud & violent upon my telling her of her suspected Companion to Eaton (whose name shee said is Mary Larg, of Nicols Street) shee rail'd at some words given out by Peggy Birchall, and by my Man John. Shee behav'd her without any sense of Gratitude or Civility, till I at last told her I had order from Mr. Gilibrand to pay her 5^{li} then shee was calm more civil and rather desir'd to have the 5^{li} paid at Ormskirk than here.
22 The weather extreme peircing. Dr. Fogg has in the Quire an excellent discourse on Rom. 12.16 against revenge. After prayers Mr. Stone over a dish of Tea, resolves to go with mee (on foot) tomorrow to Wrexham. I write to Mr. Styth on my cozn Lloyds Seat, and T. Birchall's behalf, to bed before 10.

23 The frost continues sharp, Mr. Stone and I sett out, on Foot, ½ hour after 7 come to Wrexham before 11. Wee call at the Office, refresh an hour in Tea, come to Havodywern before 1, dine, and rest an hour. Then to Wrexham. I wait on the Ladies at the Mount: thence to the King's head where I stay about an hour with my bro. Puleston, Gerard Eyton, Mr. Jones (the Curate) and Mr. Stone. My Bro. and I return over the deep Snow to Havodywern about 7. After a pott of Ale and free Chat to bed about 10.
24 The weather milder and relenting, about 9 my Bro. and I come to Wrexham. I visit Mr. Geo. Langford who had bin sometime sick at the Red Lyon. After Tea at the office, Mr. Stone and I sett out, quickly My Cozn Moreton follows on my black Horse, the way is wett, slippery and dirty from the Thaw, so wee perform the journey with less Ease, return at 3. After Dinner sent to, I go down about 6 (Mr. Stone along) to Mr. Chancellor Dr. Thane and Mr. Harris an Oxfordshire Atturney, to the Bear. Wee drink our Bottles and part about 9.
25 A delicate bright St. Paul's day. Dr. Fogge has a good discourse on St. Paul's Life, vocacion, Apostolate. After dinner and repose, I pay Mrs. Whaley 1^{li}:10s part of 5^{li} order'd by Mr. Gilibrand. After that apply to Usher's Primordia till 9.
26 A mild and dusky day. A Court easy in Busienes. I write to Mr. Pigot of Manchester my Cozen Holt and John Cross. After prayers Mr. Chancellor Dr. Thane, my cozn. Kendrick and I try Dandy of the Bull, his wine, find it inferior to the Bear, drink only 2 Bottles & part at 7.
27 Another mild day draws mee to roodee where I dispatch 4 Turns. After this at my sister Jones her Entertainment of my Lady Bunbury and relacions with Coffee in the office. I pay Mr. Chapman, upon Account 2 Guineas. After prayers Mr. Morrey calls on mee, wee go to the Coffee House, thence to Mr. Hodgson's Shop, hee thence gos with us to the White Bull where wee empty 3 Bottles of very good Claret and part after 10.
28 I indevor to alleviate my indisposicion by 4 shorter Turns on roodee. In the Evening about 5 go to Mrs. Kendrick's in St. John's Church Yard where my brother Partington treats Lady Bunbury and the company invited with Coffee, Chocolate, Cinnamon & Wormwood-water. The rest of the Evening in Books.
29 A very sharp day. Dr. Thane has an affectionate sermon . . . After prayers I apply to Dr. Stillingfleet's Origines Brittannicae for severall hours, after wee wait on Lady Bunbury about 9.
30 In a brisk morning I take 4 shorter Turns on roodee. This day is solemnis'd, Dr. Fogge has a sermon on . . . I apply to reading on occasion of the day. I write to Mr. Hayhurst, to Mrs. Denham and Mr.Shawe and prepare for my Journy tomorrow.
31 About 10 my daughter Lydia with mee, I set out the day fair and calm. I come to Warrington about 2. And after 2 hours respite, take Horse and come before 7 to my cozn. Holt's, where wee are kindly receiv'd. My old Freind Mr. Monnier by his Letter, letts mee kno that a Lord Strange was born this morning 55 minuits after 12. I receiv'd the acceptable News with great Joy.

FEBRUARY 1 It is a dull day with rain, stays mee within. My Cozn Parre now in Wigan is invited and dines with us. After dinner I go to the parsonage, my cozn Holt with mee. Wee stay some Time in discourse with the 2 Rectors, who are full of the present subject, the Controversies betwixt the rector & the Town.
2 I take a walk and go near Standish, am refresht by it. After my cozn Holt, my cozn Parr & I dine at the parsonage. Here the Gentlemen and Ladies take notice of my cozn Parr's Cap made of a Calfs skin and a hood with Flapps under it, an odd and provoking dress, tho against cold and Toothache. It putts 'em into laughter and reflections which they, with difficulty, suppress, yet hee takes notice of it. Wee go to prayers. After these I go to Tootell's, to Mr. Mawdesley the Governor of the Isle of Man. Discourse on his seat in Croston Church, the House of Derby and some mencion of Mrs. Whaley stay us over indifferent Ale and very bad wine, till 8.
3 I repeat my walk towards Standish which refreshes. After dinner about 2, go to the Church which to amazement, is crowded by parishioners. The Rector in a sharp speech (wherein hee satyrically relates the opposicion some of the Corporacion have given him) acquaints them of the occasion of the meeting, tells them of Mr. Wells, his Benefaction (200^{li}) and his own addicion, to compleat & sett up an Organ, proposes this organ to their Acceptance, with promise that the repair and maintenance of it, shall not bee of any (the least) Charg to them or theirs. Mr. Kenion objects against the manner of the Notice given, saying it did not express the Occasion: This is easily answer'd. Hee then objects, That an Organ, once set up will bring a Charg on the parish, to maintain it. And therefore security ought to bee given by the Rector for its maintenance, before the parish consent to its erection. This is abundantly answer'd by the Rector's Assumpcion wherein he shows so much warmth, That his brother, the Dean of York, with hand, perswasion and difficulty dos scarce repress a passion provok'd by their rudeness, resisting such a Benefaction upon the Terms of the rector's word and honor so publickly ingag'd. The Question is put publickly whether the parishioners will accept the Organ, on the Rector's Terms declar'd in his speech and is answer'd with an unanimous Affirmacion, the people expressing great forwardness and affection on the Rector's side, and no person (save Mr. Kenyon and Mr. Walmesley) is heard plainly to contradict it. My cozn Hulm, on this occasion is too severe on Mr. Walmesley's person and mean Family. A paper of Thanks to the rector and acknowledging the candor and justice of his proceeding is publickly read and after (by way of poll) signd, by the majority, I happen to sign it the 2d vidt, after Mr. Banks.[60] The Inhabitants of Holland Chapelry make a considerable Figure in this meeting. The Dean of York & I with difficulty, struggle thoro the Crowd to the Church door. Wee hast thoro a severe shower to the parsonage, sit there an hour. Mr. Bowyer comes and after another hour hee and I return to the Church (find the Rector in a throng of subscribers). Wee leave him and go to Tootell's, where I meet a

60 C.R.O., EDC.5 (1709) No.2, Wigan.

Company of Neighbors and Freinds, some from Holland, stay cheerfully till 9, After which my cozn Holt and I go down to the parsonage, congratulate the success of the day and discourse on the controversy of the Town till 12.

4 Because of the indisposcion, I advance my walk further, and stretch it to a view beyond the school of Standish and am reliev'd by it. Dr. Holbrook here ingages mee to dine with him at the parsonage. In the way I meet with my cozn Parr booted, tho he intended to stay till Tuesday. Hee tells mee hee will go no more to my proud Rector's, resenting their observacions on his Cap and Hood. Hee desires and I pay him a Guinea upon our Account. Mr. Allanson and Ayde, Bowyer and Lowe beside the Doctor and myself are at dinner. After which and a pipe, I am with the 4 Curates an hour at Tootells. After this go to Mrs. Lees house, but find her not, thence to my cozn. Holt where I sit with Dr. Holbrook till 10.

5 In a fair morning I take a walk beyond the Bore's head and am refresht. About 11 my cozn Holt and I take Horse and come to Winstanley before 12. Wee find Cornet Richard Legh here, wee stay along after dinner, supper and the riseing of the Moon, kindly entertain'd with good Ale – and 2 Bottles of the Cornet's wine and come in a dim light, home after 10.

6 I sally out agen on my walk to the highest Feild betwixt Wigan and Standish. After dinner at my cozn Holt's, I go to the parsonage. After this I meet Mr. Hayhurst at Alderman Mason's and deliver Dr. Stratford's Letter to him. Hee consults Tho. Rigby and enters on the Busienes. About 4 Mr. Bowyer and I sett out to the parsonage of Standish, stay more than an hour freely with Mr. Haydock who had bin lately sick and return before 8.[61]

7 About 9, my cozn Holt and I sett for Holland, I go to Ayrfeild and the Bank, walk about near 2 hours, drink here at Ayrfeild Ld. Strange's health in my reserve of Brandy, return to Holland about 2 where a pittifull dinner dissappoints mee and my Freinds. I agree with Geo. Molineux for the Bank for 3 years at 45^{li} p.A. the lower House &c reserv'd, & instructions are given to my cozn Prescot to draw the writeings. I receive Wm. Nayler's yearly rent vid 20s. Wee return to Wigan before 7. After I go to the parsonage, am detain'd in writeing the Forms of the Churchward[ens] oath and a Certificate for the Gallery at the west end and their inportunity till 9.

8 About 9 wee sett from Wigan pass thoro Warrington about 12 come to Frodsham about 2 recreate till 4 and reach home (D.O.M.L.) very safe and well (finding my Family so) about 6.

9 A Court day easy of Busienes. After noon and evening prayers, Coffee house & Books till 10.

10 In a calm morning I go down to roodee, find my old walk there, by above 60 men at work about makeing a Bank or Cop to keep out the Tide, disguis'd, interrupted and almost obliterated yet perform 4 full Turns. In the Evening apply to Busienes and Books. Write to Mr. Morrey about wine. I receive from

61 L.R.O., Exhibit Book DCh.1 1691. William Haydock was rector of Standish.

my sister Jones 10 Guineas more on her Account.

11 In a fair morning take 6 shorter equal to 4 full Turns on roodee. I write to Mr. Empson, Mr. Peirson and the Dean of York, to Dr. Stratford, Mr. Morrey and Mr. Okes. I lend Unise Walmesley by my Suzy ten shillings. I receive by Mr. Morrey's procurement 2 doz. Bottles of wine from Robert Turner.

12 In a fair morning take 4 Turns on roodee. After at St. Peter's where I hear Mr. Oliver's excellent discourse on 3 St. Matt 8. After dinner Dr. Thane and Mr. Oliver come to see mee, stay till prayers after which retreat to domestic reading &c till 10.

13 I speak to Mr. Bouchier on Mr. Hulton's account to deferr Sr Ed. Coke's[62] wittnesses, this occasion brings on the mencion of my Arrears in Visitacion Accounts, wee fix on a method, I am well pleas'd with it. I after make four full Turns on roodee in a fine day & air. After write to Mr. Monnier congratulatorily about Ld. Strange's Birth. In the Evening, the Chancellor & Dr. Thane come to mee, they send for 1 Bottle of Dandy's wine and receded about 8 I pay Peggy Birchall on Account 40s.

14 A calm fair morning, at early prayers. About ½ hour after 10 Mr. Aubray and I sett out in a brisk day come on foot thoro the medows to Eaton after 11. Mr. Cholmley consults mee on Sr Tho. Grosvenors Will particularly on the Trust of Gardianship. Hee is pleas'd with my opinion and forces a Guinea upon mee for Jack. Hee has many reflections on the unhappy Economy of this House and particularly Mr. Brerewood's misfortune. From his Chambers I go down to the Boat house, where there is a good company Archdeacon Thane, Mrs. Okes, Leigh, the 2 Cowpers, Mr. Parker, Pigot and myself at a good Dinner. Wee after continue merrily at the strong Ale till 5. I come to the Bear, The Archdeacon and 2 Cowpers follow, wee dispatch 3 Bottles cheerfully and part about 9. I pay Jonathon Pickering the Carpenter 19s.

15 Indispos'd from the Ale and wine, after 10 in a fine morning take 2 longer and 2 shorter Turns on roodee in which Time, the workmen there are all at dinner on the place. After dinner and repose My Suzy and I go to visit Mr. Tho. Yates and his Lady (Mrs. Mary Oldfield) shee was abroad. After I apply to Busienes till 9. I give Harry 5s, Ken ½ a Crown, Will 1s for the Cock mony.[63]

16 A very cold and rainy day. A Court easy of Busienes. I draw up the Acts in the Wigan Cause, apply to Books. About 8 at night Dr. Thane sends, I go and wee drink in his Chamber a Bottle of his Wine, Hee uses a Chagrin, return to his Lady's obliging behavior. Wee have melancholy reflections on the present violent proceedings of the H. of Comons as to the Church and Monarchy. I part hence before 10.

17 At early prayers in a cold morning. After I perform 4 full Turns. The News of peace with circumstances is gratefull under the Apprehensions the Comons give. In the Evening apply to Swinburn &c till 10.

62 C.R.O., EDC.5 (1709) No.4, Title to a seat in Reddish Chapel, Manchester.
63 Cock money was paid by schoolboys on Shrove Tuesday for the annual cockfight.

18 After early prayers I take 4 full Turns thoro the work, in a very cold Morning, on Roodee. After apply to Books. In the Evening I write to Mr. Fr. Cholmley (who had sent mee yesterday by Mr. Parker 10s for the pains) on the Guardianship constituted by Sr Tho. Grosvenor's Will. After enter on the Unhappy prosperity or the History of Sejanus till 10.

19 A sharp day. Dr. Fogge has, in the Quire, a good discourse on 24 Act. 16. After dinner Lady Bunbury and my cozn Moreton come to see us. After prayers I read the Articles against Dr. Sacheveril and his Answers add other readings till 10.[64]

20 Early prayers ended in a sharp morning perform 4 full Turns on roodee, observe the work notably advancing. I am afterwards at a dish of Coffee with my Suzy and sister Jones. After that at the Coffee house. I acquaint Mr. Mather That the Chancellor desires that Chad Feast may bee on Chad-day at Eaton Boat.[65] The Evening in Books.

21 After early prayers in such a morning the like Turns perform'd on roodee. The matter of the Coffee and Coffee house mencion'd yesterday are to bee referr'd to this. After Books, Horace especially and Evening prayers I meet with Mr. James Egerton, wee agree to go to the Bear, call at the Coffee House for a third Man. Mr. Done occurrs, but is not willing, wee go down tho in a shower. Before 7 Mr. Done and Mr. Robt. Warburton follow us. The wine and discourse go fast and freindly round, wee empty 6 Bottles, carry the Carnival high and part not before 12.

22 Extremely indispos'd and unhappy this Ashwednesday, therefore in Fevor and repentance. Stay in till Evening prayers. After these recur to reading and at Night to Elixir.

23 A Court day favorable to my indisposicion because very easy in Busienes. I examine only one witnes on Articles of Diffamation on the part of Leigh against Ratcliffe.[66] I recreate in reading till 9.

24 A cold rainy morning of St. Matthias. I am at early prayers and after, in a small rain, take 4 Turns on roodee, see the work but not the Men by reason of the wett (or Holy) day. I pay Mr. Cook, Master of the blew Boys 5^{s} due at Candelmas and to Mr. Hatton the Chandler $2^{li}:1^{s}:0^{d}$. The rest of the Day in Books, particularly Lord Clarendon till 10.

25 A milder morning at early prayers. After take 4 Turns on roodee to which the workmen are return'd. I write to the Bishop of St. Asaph, Mr. Whaley, Mr. Alanson and Mr. Bird. I pay Robert Turner for his 24 Bottles of Irish Claret $2^{li}:8^{d}$. After prayers return to Books especially Horace till 10.

26 In a mild morning, to help my stomach, I take 2 Turns on roodee before Church where Dr. Fogg has another sermon on 25 Acts 16. At Noon Lady Bunbury sees us and from Sir Henry's Letter tells mee the main design in

64 G. Holmes, *The Trial of Dr. Sacheverill* (London 1973).
65 March 2nd is the feast of St. Chad.
66 C.R.O., EDC.5 (1709) No.5, Gorton, Manchester.

parliament after Dr. Sacheveril's Tryal is to make a new Test whereby it is to be declar'd, That resistance against the King de Facto or de Iure is lawfull and consentaneous to Scripture (in Animam penetrat)[67]. After prayers Mrs. Hurleston, Mrs. Thane and Mrs. Parry (from Wrexham) visit us.

27 After early prayers (at which the psalms appointed seem very propitious) may God grant they may prove so to the Church in the Tryal of Dr. Sacheveril, to begin this day. I take 4 Turns on roodee in a fair brisk morning, I deposit in Mr. Hiccock's hands 5^{s} as a Gift to the Workmen. I write to Mr. Commissary Waite about my not accepting his son John for my Clerk, and to Mrs. Hutching (at Mr. Linning's a Grocer at the Black Boy and Camel near Little St. Helen's, Bishopgate Street) about her daughter's Ear Rings and Rings. After prayers return to Books. I pay Mr. Golborn, Apothecary $2^{li}:1^{s}:0^{d}$. Draw a recipt for Mrs. Whaley to sign for $3^{li}:10^{s}$ and deliver it to her daughter.

28 After early prayers in a dull morning, I take 4 Turns on roodee. I pay the $3^{li}:10^{s}$ to her daughter, after receive a very scurrilous Letter from her. After Noon Mr. Chancellor comes and considers Mr. Finch's Letter and peticion to my Lord with my Lord's Fiat upon it, but concludes not to send out a Faculty because of the Appeal. After prayers at the Coffee house where Tables and dissagreeable company fill the room. I return to Books till 10.

MARCH 1 In a fairer morning, after early prayers I take 4 Turns on roodee after recreate in Coffee and write to Mr. Whaley some Account of his wife's behaviour. After Evening prayers The Chancellor, Dr. Thane, Mr. Proby and my self go to the Bear where is excellent Claret. Wee drink ½ a Guinea, a Token sent by Mr. Charles Proby, the Clergy man.

2 In a fair morning tho akeing head, I rise to early prayers. After, write to my cozn. Holt and Mr. Bowyer. About 11 wee set out to our Anniversary Chad Feast at Eaton Boat. Mr. Roberts and I only on Foot, there is a good dinner, part of it 2 dishes of Fish, After this Mr. Chancellor and Mr. Mather fall warmly into the Argument of resistance, it ends but abruptly, in Tables. Then do I and Mr. Roberts go to the Hall, I am with Mr. Cholmley an hour in his chamber receiv'd kindly. I divert (by John) a MS directed to the Bp. of St. Asaph to Mr. R. Piget who hopes to bee at London this day 7 night and promises to deliver it to the Bp. Wee set hence after 5 and about ½ hour after 6 are safe at home. Expectacions are uneasy in Dr. Sacheveril's Case.

3 I take 4 Turns on roodee. After hear the Drs. Tryal begun on Munday, continu'd the next day and yet not proceeded thoro the 4 Articles. I apply to Books till 9.

4 After early prayers I take 4 Turns, call on Mr. Callys acquaint him with the Building begun under the palace in the Street and with Dr. Stratford's Letter. After prayers I meet with Mr. Tho. Cowper, wee take 1 Bottle at the Bacchus,

67 Trans: 'it sinks into the mind.'

make up the wine with the Conversacion. I send 12 Bottles Irish Claret to Mr. Cross.
5 After a stormy night, a high wind and tide which threaten the work on roodee. Men and Carts are rais'd to advance the Bank a Foot. Dr. Fogg has a good discourse on 15 St. Matt. 28. The News brings Accounts of an Affectionate Company of 3000 still attending the Dr. from the Temple to Westminster of their honest Comprecacions & Deprecacions and of their pulling down meeting houses and burning their Furniture &c. Tho' this is a Mobb on the Churches side tis fear'd it may suffer by their zeale.
6 The weather wett and windy. I write to the Bp. of St. Asaph about the MS. and send a Form of prayers to bee 15th current, to my cozn Parr. After Evening prayers Mr. Davies sees us, after that to Books. I pay Mr. Dentith for a Gallon of Brandy 12s.
7 The weather continues Stormy. After early prayers I see Dyers Letter which gives Account of a learned and magnanimous Defence made by Sr Simon Harcourt and the rest of the Drs. Council on Friday to the 1st Article, the Queen present, the whole takes a better Aspect, gives hope of Success & inspires a common Alacrity. After prayers I buy Beveridge his private Thoughts on Religion for 1s 6d. I state the Arrears of 7 Visitacions twixt the Chancellor and mee the Balance to the Chancellor is 25^{li}:15^{s}:8. I am desireous in a pint to congratulate the reasonable expectacion of good News. Dr. Thane & Mr. Hodgson declining to go down to the Bear with mee, I rejoice as happily in a pint by my own Fireside till 10.
8 The Queen's day, I am at early prayers and after them, tho the wind high, I take 4 Turns on roodee. After begin on Dr. & Bishop Beveridge his excellent Thoughts. I write to Mr. Whaley & in that Letter desire Mr. Ashurst to give mee credit for a Guinea which I add (with my good wishes) to the rest I have given Mrs. Whaley. After Dinner I state his particular Account with Mr. Bouchier. After prayers Dr. Thane calls, wee go down to the Bear and there in 2 Bottles of excellent Claret, wish well to the Queen, the Nobility, Episcopacy and Commonalty who are patrons, Freinds and Advocates to the Cause of the Church and Crown now ventilated in the highest Tribunal in the Case of Dr. Sacheveril. Wee return ½ hour after 9. This Day the Account is stated and finisht (D.O.M.G.) betwixt the Chancellor and mee and I pay him 25^{li}:15^{s}:8^{d}.
9 In a fine tho windy morning, to relieve my head take, after early prayers, 4 Turns on roodee. Give the Masons as distinct workmen 1s, return about 9 refresht. A Court day of indifferent Busienes. After dinner and a short repose, I examine 4 Wittnesses on Sir Edward Coke's part against the Churchwardens of Manchester. At Night recreate in a domestic pint of Wine and to bed about 10.
10 After early prayers at the Coffee House where Accounts are, That Dr. Sacheveril's Councel have finisht his Defence and answer'd all the 4 Articles. After which hee himself had a Speech above an hour long, wherein hee defends himself with a clearness, decency, yet resolucion and learning, that drew compassion and Tears from the Auditory (The Queen being present) this on Tuesday and the Court adjourn'd to the Thursday. I examine the 4 Wittnesses of

yesterday on Interrogatries and 2 more on the whole. I hear (from the public print) the unwelcome News of my young Lord Strange his death. This and other ingratefull parts of News make the day conclude very melancholy.

11 After early prayers in a doubtfull morning I take 4 Turns on roodee, write to my Lord Bishop about my not observing his Fiat Licentia for Mr. Finch and about the Building begun under the palace to the street. The Inhibicion and Monicion in the Cause betwixt Mr. Finch, the Rector, & the Town of Wigan, are executed upon the Appeal.[68]. After the Busienes and the satisfaction of a Letter from Jack and domestic pint, to bed about 10.

12 In a fair morning rise before 6, see the News that Sir Joseph Jekill, and others the Managers have made their reply to the Drs. defence on the 1st Article. After I take 4 Turns on roodee, And then go to the Quire, where the Warden of Manchester has a discourse on 1st Coll. v. 28 which seems meaner and lower than his Character. Mr. Rosingreave late of Xtchurch, Jack's Acquaintance, calls on mee. I at 7 go to him at the Yatcht (Biggins). Wee are full of Christ Church, dispatch 3 Bottles of good Wine and part after 11.

13 Tho very much indispos'd, apply with resolucion to Busienes, examine the Warden of Manchester on Sir Edward Coke's Libel, write to my Lord about 2 Caveats enter'd by the Earl of Derby and Mr. Banks about the Institucion to Bury on Mr. Gipp's death which happen'd Saturday last.[69] I write to Mr. Banks inclose his Grant and a Form of presentacion in it and to the Rector of Wigan and inclose a paper from Dr. Bouchier. After some rest and Evening prayers I go with Mr. Robert Davies and Mr. Lloyd of Pena Gwern, near St. Asaph, to Dandies where with loyal and affectionate Healths wee empty 4 Bottles of good Claret at 3s the Bottle and part about 9.

14 The pain is doubl'd with the Fever from the wine last Night. The Great Cause has mett with a shock as to manner of the Impeachment not reciteing the very words whereof the party accus'd. This is as a Nullity, objected by the E. of Nottingham in the House, argu'd and confirm'd, by the Judges. Upon this a Vote by the Lords That Dr. Sacheveril shall be try'd according to the Laws of this realm and practice of Parliaments and the Event of the vote is expected with impatience. After an unhappy day, indevor to relieve myself by Elixir.

15 Not yet recover'd the Disturbance, a little Wine gave mee. A Day of Humiliacion is kept. Mr. Shaw (prebendary) has his sermon 5 St. Matt v 4. Wee receive (with a Box to bee sent to the revd. Mr. Wm. Jackson at Mr. Acton's in St. Michael's Lane, Dublin) two small potts of Carp from Mr. Gorst. I write to him. I read Dr. Scot's 2d discourse vidt on National repentance, the Text 18 Ezek. v. 30. After prayers & Meat Turn Pufendorf de Iure Naturae et Gentium, till 9. I the 3d successive Night take Elixir.

16 The wind very strong and very cold confines mee home tho a Court day. I apply to Books of Divercion Pliny's N.H. Aerodius de Rebus Iudicatis and Pufendorf till 9.

68 The documents concerning the appeal to York Chancery Court are lost for this cause.
69 C.R.O., Caveat Book 1709.

17 In a brisk morning at early prayers. After at the Coffee House where I am amaz'd with the prodigious Advancement of Sir Tho. Parker (a strennuous Manager on the Commons side, against Dr. Sacheveril), to the cheif justiceship of the Queen's Bench, and from hence and the mention of Mr. Hoadly to be a prebendary of Westminster,[70] the present Cause of the Church before that great Tribunal, takes a melancholy aspect. I perform 4 Turns on roodee. After dinner the Chancellor calls. I pay him 5^{li} the remnant of my Bond of 30^{li} which hee thereupon delivers cancell'd to mee (D.G.) After prayers upon Mr. Chancellor's Invitacion, Dr. Thane, Mr. Proby and I go with him to the Bear where hee treats with 4 Bottles of good Claret, wee part about 9. After at Lady Bunburys, when Sr T. Parker's Exaltacion is warmly considered on.

18 Indispos'd from the Bottle last Night, much more from the News. I write to my Lord Bishop about the Institucion to Tilston and to John Cross. I state Account to Mr. Bouchier, the Balance of which to him is 16^{li}, whereof I pay him 8^{li}. Wee are entertain'd with News said to come from my Ld Cholmley that Dr. Sacheveril is acquitted meets with more wishes than credit. I am in the Evening at Mr. Bouchers Chamber, return to my Corner and to Books till 10.

19 With a small Dose of Elixir last Night much easier this morning, the wind high and cold confines to my Corner and Books. The News seems to bee possitive. That upon long Debate in the Lords House 58 votes for Sentence against 53 for the Dr. So all hope of a good Event of this great Cause vanishes. I write to Mr. Cholmley and send John with a Box of Caviers which was sent mee by Mr. Thornley to him. After prayers I step down to take leave with the Chancellor. I read Dr. Sacheveril's proper Defence which is very full strong, brave yet very artificial and moveing, and in the Evening Dr. Smalridge, his sermon before the House of Commons 30 Janry. 1701.

20 After early prayers I write to Dr. Stratford and to Jack, include from Mr. Cholmley a Guinea and from myself 5^{s} which Letters are deliver'd to Mr. Chancellor with whom I take leave at the Coffee house about 11, and afterwards to Mr. Broughton where Mr. Robert Davies treats Lady Bunbury and 6 other Ladies with Coffee. Apply in the Evening, to various reading till 10, pay Hugh for looking after my Horse 4^{s}.

21 After early prayers to the Coffee House where the Letters are more particular about the Numbers of the peers and Bishops against Dr. Sacheveril upon all the Articles. I am surpris'd and astonish'd by Mrs. Whaley's Letter which gives the Character of Chester amongst the Bishops against him, but am satisfy'd of the Error before Night, yet certify'd that St. Asaph is one of them. I take 4 melancholy Turns on roodee and can't apply to Busienes. After prayers Dr. Thane and I find Mr. Egerton at Mr. Whishaw's when hee follows us to the Bear where wee drink very cheerfully, rais'd by honest politicks and more benign Aspect of our Affairs, our 5 Bottles of excellent Claret. Mr. Brampton

70 See G. V. Bennett, *Tory Crisis in Church and State 1688–1730* (Oxford 1975), pp 105–112, for the character of Benjamin Hoadly.

and after him Mr. Wishaw, comeing in. Wee stay on the subject and Wine till 12.
22 I am extremely fevorish from the wine and the Times of it, confin'd to my bed, the House, repose and tormented by my malady and the News. I while away the Day in great pain. I pay Mr. Vaudrey on Account 20^{li}. Turn Books and to bed about 9.
23 After Elixir easier yet indispos'd. Therefore tho a Court day, stay at Home, Turn Books and particularly the Origin of Laws by Dawson, extremely affected with the News and to bed about 10.
24 After early prayers I meet at the Coffee house an End of the Great and formidable cause very disproporcionate to it vidt. suspension from preaching only for 3 years, the Dr. being at Liberty to execute his other Clerical offices and capable of preferment but his Books to be executed by Illuminacion. The number against him is 69, for him 52. I find to the confirmacion of my trouble, St. Asaph in the former. I after ruminate on these in 4 Turns on roodee, where recreated, return to the Origin of Laws. After prayers Drs. Thane and Norris and my cozn. Kendrick send to mee from Pickin's. I go thither. Wee drink 3 Bottles of indifferent wine and have the Argument of the Sentence against Dr. S. and of Non resistance calmly discuss'd. Wee part before 9.

1710

MARCH 25 In a fine Morning I take 5 Turns on roodee and refresht return to Grotius De I.B. et P. I write to Mr. James Banks and inclose a Transcript of the presentacion to Bury.[1] Mr. Denis pays mee 3^{li} for half a Year's rent for my house in the Abby Court, due this day After prayers I see Mr. Bunbury fresh come in the stage Coach from London. Hee gives a particular and satisfactory Account of the passages at Dr. Sacheveril's Tryal, having bin an Eye-Wittnes of it. After this I go to wait on my Lord Buckley at the Hope & Anchor, from whence (the wine bad) hee and his company, Mrs. Davies, Done, Griffiths, Pennant, a lame Sea Captain (Jackson) and myself adjourn to the Yacht (Pickin's) where they drink two Bowls of punch, I so many Bottles of Claret. Lord Buckley is obliging and entertains the company with the late transacions in parliament, the rest is freedom, but that loose (in yong Griffith of Cleene) wee stay till 12.
26 From excess of inseasonable wine, too much indispos'd for the Church or Books till prayers. After which I meet with Morecroft, Archdeacon of Kells, his Lady and Mrs. Cliff, daughter to the Bishop of Killala. I wait on them at their Inn the White Bull and attempt to sup with them. Wee have the Busienes of Dr. Sacheveril's Tryal affectionatly mencioned nor are our Friends in Ireland forgott. Wee drink two Bottles of Claret. The Archdeacon and his Lady express great Gratitude to my offices for them & I stay past 10.

1 C.R.O., EDV2/15, for new licences.

27 Tho' I us'd last night Elixir, still fevorish and repineing. Upon Mr. Holland's Letter I engage a place in the Coach of Thursday next for Mr. James Banks and write to Mr. Banks of it. Tho' invited, I decline to go to Lady Bunbury's recepcion of Mr. Morecroft & divert in Books till 9.

28 Recover'd so as to be at early prayers, after at the Coffee House where the News makes the Commons very warm about condemning & burning of the passages pleaded by the Dr. and Decretum Oxoniense. I after take 4 Turns on roodee & am refresht. Mr. Morecroft &c take leave of us (they go to Leverpool). I apply to Busienes and Books, Grotius de I. Bet. P. especially. After prayers Dr. Thane and I go down to the Bear and recreate in one Bottle of good Claret. I and Mr. Boucher are Wittnesses to Sir Wm. Meredith, his signing a presentacion to the Church of Abington in Northamptonshire in the diocese of Peterborough.

29 After early prayers and 5 Turns on roodee in variety of Hale and Sunshine, I apply to the Theodosian Code. After Noon and prayers to Busienes. Mr. Davies calls on mee, after prayers wee receive (as Gifts) the Bishop of St. Asaph's Articles of Visitacion and his late Sermon and condole his vote against Dr. Sacheveril. I return to Busienes and the Code till 10.

30 After early prayers I write to the Rector of Wigan an answer to his objections to the Grant for the Galery at the West end of the Church. After I go to Mr. James Banks at the White Talbot, stay with him till hee take Coach. Mr. Roberts gos to the Court for mee, the last of this Term. I apply to various parts in the Theodosian Code. Mr. Mcylrea from the Isle of Man, consults mee in the Case of Robt. Corlett's Will who dy'd in Barbados. Hee stays tediously till 8 after I return to the Codes till 10.

31 The public papers continue a Heat in the House of Commons and tell of Dr. S's 2 sermons, some parts of Grotius and the Decretum Academiae Oxon burnt in company of pernicious Books, vidt. Rights of the Church &c. After I take 4 Turns on roodee and return to Books. I draw a Case about Corlett's Will late of Barbados. Mr. Mcylrea of the Isle of Man calls on mee for it, about 7, wee go down to the Bear drink 2 Bottles of good wine wherein the House of Derby is remember'd and return after 10.

APRIL 1 Indispos'd stay at home, read the Bishop of St. Asaph, his Charg to his Clergy. Pay for Harry's Quarterage 10s., for Ken and Will's 5s for Peggy's 20[d?] After prayers return to Books till 10.

2 A calme day. Dr. Fogge has a sermon on 24 Matt. 3,4. The News brings a lesse prospect of peace, variety of Humors in the Country upon the late Great Tryal. After prayers Wee visit Mrs. Jones. After that I carefully read Dr. Sacheveril's Sermon before the Lord Mayor, to bed after 10.

3 At early prayers and in a delicate warm morning, I take 5 Turns on roodee (which succeed well D.G.) I write to the Bishop of St. Asaph tell him of the Corrections in his Diocese, of the cool recepcion by the Gentry and of the Affronts by the Mobb at Wrexham, offer'd to the Judg (Jekell) and venture to advise him to putt off his Visitacion to the next year.[2] I draw a scheme of our next visitacion. I pay the Maid Sarah who leaves us today her wages for a year and about a week 2^{li}4s and give her 1s. I draw a scheme Q.E.B. of our next visitacion and state Accounts of principle and Interest betwixt myself and my sister Jones. After read the Case of Dr. Sacheveril in a Letter to a noble Lord. My Suzy receives one Gwen Williams in Sarah's place.

4 After early prayers and the News which gives Account of the death of Sir John Coke, Dean of the Arches, I take 4 Turns on roodee, read Dr. Sacheveril's Speech of Defence with Attencion. After dinner and prayer apply to Busienes, particularly to the Acts to be transmitted in the Wigan Cause, till 9.

5 After early prayers in a sharp wind, I take 4 Turns on roodee, after apply to Books. After Noon to Busienes and the Acts, which I finish in the Wigan Cause. After prayers, return to Books till 10.

6 The morning mild, moist and springing. I after early prayers take 4 Turns on roodee and return to Books and Busienes. I draw the Certificate to the Transmission, and revise the Acts. After Evening prayers I begin the Origin of Laws and almost go thoro the 1st Book.

7 Good Friday – before 7 see the News, in it an aggravated representacion of Mr. Cornwall's sermon before Sir Joseph Jeckill at Welshpool. After take 3 Turns in a sharp cold ayr on Roodee. I go after to the Quire where Dr. Fogg has a sermon on 24 Luke v.25. I return to the Origin of Laws and read almost 4 Ch. I pay to the Collectors of the Tax 2^{li} the last payment of the last year for the Office. After eating, am indispos'd.

8 A fine sharp Air. I go in the Origin. After 10 a clock prayers I write to John Cross, Mrs. Whaley sends a silver Tobacco Box to mee with her Letter, tells mee it cost 3^{li} and is pawn'd for 26s, desires mee to lend her what I think fitt above that sum. I send it to the Goldsmith, who writes that it weighs only 3 Ounces. 16 pwt. and is worth only 16s 6d. Shee over valu's it because her Husband's Coat (a Chevron twixt 3 Whales heads) is ingrav'd upon it, this (with Consideracion of her Ingratitude to mee) does not move mee to lend the money upon it, being a clumsey unfashionable thing. I pay John 4 Guineas upon Account of his Wages. After prayers I return but indisposedly to my Books. I pay Samuel Walmesley 14s for work about the office.

9 Easter Day. About 7 I see the Letter which tells Her Majesty proroug'd the parliament on Thursday, but (in Expectacion of Events from the Treaty) to the 18th of this month. After in a most delicate Ayr, I take 2 Turns on roodee. Dr. Thane has a good and grave discourse (in the Choir) on 14 Rom. 9. Post sanctissimae Eucharistiae particeps sumus. Det D.O.M. sancte Sobrie et iuste vivere.[3] After prayers (intending to send John tomorrow) I write to John Cross and Mr. Bowyer.

2 There was a strong reaction in the strong Tory area of Chester against the sentence on Dr. Sacheverell.

3 Trans: 'afterwards we partake of the most Holy Eucharist. May God the best and greatest grant [me] to live a holy, sober and just life.'

10 In a delicate morning, I rise to early prayers. After write to my cozen Parr the case of Corlett who dyd in Barbados. After seal a Bond dated the 17th current to my sister Jones for 300[li] for 6 months, read a Chapter in the Origin. After 10 (Will. Willoughby with mee) sett out and come to Eaton before 12. I am with Mr. Cholmley in his Chamber before, and after Dinner, with Him Sir Richard G[rosvenor] and a company in the parlor till 5, when Mr. Brerewood, Aubrey, Alderman Ed. Puleston & I thoro the medowes, come hence after 6.
11 The News gives nothing but Expectacion from Flanders. Mr. Oliver has in the Quire, a grave discourse, before the Judg on . . . where in hee gives a Character of a sincere upright Man, but touches not on Occasion. After Noon, I apply to the Origin of Laws, confin'd in 'em till 10. I receive the News of the Rector of Wigan on his success against Incroachers [4]and 22[li] 16s from John Cross upon Account.
12 Upon a note from Mr. Vernon, I go down to the Hall to depose (if call'd) that I observ'd the Duttons Coat (quarterly A & G, a Fret Or upon the 2nd & 3rd Quarters) in a Cause there betwixt Mr. Warburton and Mr. Fleetwood. I stay there 2 hour before, and 2 h after dinner, to which I return,but am not call'd. The verdict passes altogeather in Warburton's Favor. After I go to the Golden Talbot to Mr. Taylor, Steward, & Mr. Moreton, Atturney to my Lord Derby. Mr. Hulton comes to us. Wee have politicks up & I take occasion to declare as well my resolucion about voteing, as Affection to my Lord Derby and his Family. After 3 Bottles & 4 a Clock wee part. I call at Mr. Hodgsons where I meet with Dr. Foulks of Lamedert. Hee, Ned Puleston and I, go down to the Bear. Ned Wright, Mr. Aldersey and Mr. Davie (of Tattenhale) follow. Wee with 5 Bottles, good wine, are warm on the public subject and part about 11.
13 My sister Jones go's hence to Bodley Withens today. I pay her 20s on Account. After 10 I take 5 Turns on roodee. After dinner & repose return to the Origin of Laws, till 10. I send the Wigan Transmission to York by means of Sherlock, the Manchester Carrier.[5]
14 After Elixir easier, not restor'd. I write to Mr. Ayde and send him 3 Licences and Bonds. The News do's not give any expectacion of peace. I pay now (or 2 daies ago) 40s for the Land Tax and to the Maid Charlotte (on Account) 17s;6d. I return to the Civil Law till 10.
15 In a brisk fine morning, I take 4 Turns on roodee. I read the Bishop of Salisbury's speech upon the 1st Article against Dr. Sacheveril and Mr. Wm. Bunbury's Diary of his Tryal. I receive a Letter from Mr. Egerton requesting mee to Oulton, and answer it. After prayers I read Mr. Greenshields (A Clergyman prisoner in the Tolbooth at Edinborough) his deplorable Case.
16 A very clear but sharp day. Mr. Hinchman has a sermon (this morning) in the parish Church on . . . Mr. Mcylrea of the Isle of Man dines with us. After

4 C.R.O., EDC.5(1709) No 3, Wigan intruders.
5 This appeal has not survived in the York Transmissions on Appeal.

prayers I draw direcions about an Administrationem cum Testamento annexo[6] for him.

17 After early prayers and Letters dispatcht, I sett hence in a fine morning about 11 and come to Oulton about 1, Mr. Egerton receives mee kindly. After dinner, at which one Bottle (good Claret), wee walk about his plantacions, studd, and his further projects. Wee go to the school where a very yong boy reads Latin, Greek & Hebrew – but knows not the sense or Grammar. In the Evening wee take each a Bottle of good wine & to bed about 11.

18 A very sharp Air. Mr. Egerton's pacquet brings that the Ally's have easily and without opposicion past the French Lines. Mr. Cholmley of Vale Royal calls, and about 9 Hee and I sett out and come to Chester about 11. Wee find the Bells ringing for the good News of passing the Lines. Mr. Cholmley proposes an Address to the Justices at the Sessions today, but it is rejected. Indispos'd all day, recurr to Elixir at Night.

19 I write to the Bishop of St. Asaph about his refusal to admit Dr. Sacheveril to Sallatyn.[7] About 11 I sett hence and come to Broxton about 1. I find my Lord and his Family come about an hour before. Hee receives mee with welcome and Freedom. After dinner Mr. Davie of Tattenhalle and Mr. Bird come thither. My Lord entertains with good wine and good informacions of the late Tryal. Wee part with him about 5. Mr. Davie, Couché and I call at Mr. Bird's, take some Glasses of his strong Beer, and thence in an hour come briskly to Chester. About 9, I go over with my S. to Lady Bunbury where wee find Dr. Thane and his Lady. Hee in his Hype asks mee if I told Mr. Blake that the prebend was worth nothing. I am more warm'd at this and answer accordingly.

20 Indispos'd from yesterday. Dr. Thane comes to mee and takes notice of my (correption) of him last night. About 10, my Suzy go's into the Stage Coach, I quickly follow, wee come to Broxon about one. Mr. Egerton and Mr. Cholmley dine here at an elegant dinner. After which elegant and rich wine, free & full discourse, about 3 they go out to Bowls for an hour, return to the good wine for more than another. My Suzy and I sett out about 7 and come safe home (D.G.) about 9.

21 Extremely fatigu'd from the Motions of the week. I keep and repose at home, till after Evening prayers. Dr. Thane calls on mee, wee go to the Globe (Charles Nicols) the first Time. Hee seems rather to forget and reconcile, my Correption Wednesday night, than remember it. Wee drink 1 Bottle & part about 9.

22 Mr. Blake, Dr. Thane and Mr. Maryon come from Broxon, and dine with us. I wait on Mr. Blake to the Deane with the Mandate to induct Mr. Blake into the prebend void by Mr. Clutterbook's death. The Dean indicts and installs him with great Formality in the beginning of Evening prayer. After these ended, the

6 Trans: 'Administration with will annexed.'

7 Prescott's letter has not survived, but Bishop Fleetwood's reply will be printed in an appendix to Vol.II.

Dean, Archdeacon, Dr. Fogg and I sign a Certificate of the Installacion, the stall being the 2nd from the Deanes.[8] After some Busienes particularly the vamping up of an Address and a domestic Glass of wine with Mr. Blake, my Guest, to Bed about 10.

23 After seeing a thin Letter at the Coffee House, in a very sharp morning, I take 3 Turns on roodee. Dr. Fogg has a good sermon on Prov. 9 v. 10. Mr. Blake, my Suzy and I dine at Dr. Thane's at a very spruce dinner. Mr. Blake reads the Morning and Evening prayers, his Assent to them and the 2 Episcopall Certificates. In the Evening Dr. Thane comes over to us and wee end it in a Glass of my domestic wine.

24 I direct a Certificate to bee drawn of Mr. Blake's reading the prayers (yesterday and 'tis sign'd by the Dean, Archdeacon, Dr. Fogg & myself. (Mr. Blake in his conduct here, behav'd himself very laudably, civilly and as a scholar). After dinner and repose, I go down to roodee where Sir Richard Grosvenor and Mr. Pigott's horses are only competitors to the plate which falls by precedency to Sir Richard, dureing the race, I take 6 Turns on roodee (the Copp) in view of it. After visit Dr. Thane, hee sends for a bottle promoted by his generous Lady, this abdicates the Hypo at present, wee part about 10.

25 A calmer day. I see little in the News save 4 W. Indian Kings come over to solicite her Majestie to an Alliance and to invoke her Assistance to drive the French out of their Coterminate Country, Canada. I apply to Sir Walter Raleigh. After Noon the Bishop of Cloyn (Dr. Crow) and his Lady see us. I lend my Mare and Horses to Dr. Norris to bring him & his Family to Speak. After domestic to bed at 10.

26 In a fine morning at early prayers. I write to Mr. Alexander, Registrar about Mr. Manley, and to Mr. Corker and Tom Gorst. The Visitacion held for Chester and Wirral Deaneries. I bye Dr. Bingham's Antiquities of the Christian Church 2 vol, for 9s and Brett LL. D. his Account of Church Government for 5s. After prayers Dr. Thane and I walk over the Walls to the Bear. Wee take one Bottle of the newer sort and return before 9.

27 After early prayers and some Busienes, After 9 sett out in a cool, dry morning and come to Broxon about 12. Mr. Egerton and his Lady come there to Dinner. Wee prevail with my Lord to forbear coming into Chester 2 hours longer than hee intended, hee now determines on 12 a Clock. The weather alters to rain, very much desir'd. Wee stay with my Lord till 6. Mr. Egerton gos to Oulton, I reach Chester about 8.

28 The News yet improves not. I examine 3 Wittnesses on Erlains Will. The Mayor moves the Corporacion in Council to Address, proposes one full and high, but the Recorder, trims and reduces it to lean and languid. After prayers, the Bishop of Cloyn calls on mee, wee go over the Walls to the Bear, talk the late Affair and particularly the Bishop of St. Asaph's part, over a Bottle of good wine and return before 9.

8 See R.V.H. Burne, *op.cit.*, p.178, for a biography of Preb. Charles Blake.

29 After a larg dose of Elixir, indispos'd and at Home. Apply to the Acts of the visitacion of the Dean and Chapter. I write to Mr. Shakerley of Gwersylt about my Lord's coming, and to Gerard Eyton.

30 In a fine cool morning, I take 3 Turns on roodee, send John to Gwersilt, who brings an answer before 12. The Warden of Manchester has a grave, stout and substancial Discourse in the Quire on 1 Peter 3:15, the sermon is condemn'd justly, and the different phrase from the last hee had in that place is admir'd, but not by all. The News carrys on Circumvallacion about Doway. After prayers and a visit of the Bishop of Cloyn, I write to Dr. Stratford and Jack dateing of To Morrow. I inclose to him 7^{li}:3s:6d which ballances our Account of this year, as hee is my Creditor. I send 6 Guineas & Luid'Or which is 7^{li}:6s. Upon supputacion I find I have paid this Year, on his Account 41^{li}:19s.

MAY 1 The Bishop comes and visits the Dean & Chapter.

2 To Eaton, after at the Bear.

3 Mr. Rye, Coll. Harman, Bishop Allen, pay 5^{li} to Mr. Boucher.

4 Not at Court, pay John 20s, Lord Wharton at Golden Talbot with Alderman Puleston.

5 Mrs. Moorcroft morning and evening.

6 To Tom B. and Mr. Styth Busienes; pay Mr. Cholmley's man 4^{li} & Mr. Hornby &c.

7 Lord Bishop preaches before, Mr. Rye after, noon. Wee dine with my Lord with Mr. Hornby &c at the Bear.

8 I draw the extracts of presentacions to Bury. Write to Mr. Banks & Barbon. After dinner at Sir H.B.'s with my Lord Bishop &c till prayers. After three at Sir H.B. after that at the Talbot.

9 I take 2 Turns on roodee, after draw about 9 ozs of Blood, prepare for my Journy. My coz. Moreton is with us in the Evening.

10 Come to Midlewich to dinner at 1, at the 2 Yates, late at Mr. Cowpers, ly at Mr. Yates.

11 Rise early, wee all call at Sir Wm. M[eredith']s. In the Even, Mr. B. and I drink a Bottle with Mr. Hulme.

12 After Busienes with Mr. Swetenham, see Mr. Shawcross, wee come about 7 to Manchester.

13 Good Busienes. After dinner with Mr. Ashton and Mr. Holland. At night with Dr. Holbrook.

14 Mr. Sedgwick preaches. After dinner Tea at Mr. Pigot's. Sup at Strangwaies. Mr. Toulis gives mee Ottio.

15 Wee come to Bolton about 12, have some busienes, set out at 5, come to Blackburn about 8.

16 Busienes considerable, after dinner with Mr. Rishton. In the Even at the vicarage. Mr. Hulme repeats a pint.

17 Hot day, competent busienes at Chorley, come to Wigan about 7 find coz. Holt weak.

18 Holy Thursday. After dinner to Winstanley, stay till 7, walk to Wigan with

Mr. Holland till 10; a Meteor.

19 Several Wardens offer'd for Wigan, swear the Rector, the busienes considerable, with Friends at night, Mr. Lever, Mr. Bowyer.

20 The rest go to Ormskirk. I stay draw a sentence & presentacion. In the Evening drink a Bottle with Mr. W.

21 The company returns. At Church forenoon Mr. Bowyer preaches. After noon with Friends at coz. Holt's Ale.

22 Drink Tea with Mr.Heawood, call at Haydock, thence to Frodsham, meet with Mr. Legh & Banks, home about 9.

23 About 10 set out, come to Broxon about 12, towards Even with my S. walk up to the Maiden's Tower.

24 After Tea sett out, wee come to Oulton about 11, dine with a great company, then to Bowls, return about 9.

25 Walk with Dr. Thane and Mr. Maryen, dine and relax, after to Chester about 8 with Mr. Chancellor.

26 My Lord comes about 9. After prayers hears the Lawyers on both sides resolves on a Commission, reads a sentence of vacancy of Claughton[9] Mr. B. entertains at the Bear with 6 Bottles good wine.

27 Mr. Blake & Couché dine, after at Sir H.B. After prayers Mr. Allen treats Mr. B. & mee. I write to Mr. Jos. Birchall.

28 Mr. Blake preaches in the Quire. Wee receive the sacrament. After E. prayers wee walk, after a domestic.

29 Mr. Blake preaches in St. O[swald's] on Ps. 111 v4. In the Even, at the Bear where Mr. Blake treats.

30 The news not considerable. After dinner with Sir H. pay Mr. B. 10^{li}. In the Even with Mr. Bann at the Bear.

31 Write by Mr. Bann to Mr. Pigot and to the Bishop of St. Asaph, Busienes. At night with Mr. Yates at the Bear.

JUNE 1 About 10 Mr. Yates and I set for and come to Eaton before 12. Wee find Mr. C. alone, dine and stay with him till 5. I wait on my Lord at the palace, stay with him past 9.

2 The News gives less expectacion of a Battle. Candidates to Ordinacion and Dr. Fenton see mee. In the Evening Mr. Chancellor, Dr. Thane and I go to the Bear with indifferent success in 2 Bottles.

3 I write to Mr. Peirson of the Commons and to Mr.Bowyer. Dr. Fenton sees mee after prayers. After which the Chancellor, Dr. Thane and I drink 2 Bottles of Pickin's wine which has approbacion. To Tom Birchall 5s.

4 Dr. Fogg has a sermon on, "Let no man despise you". The Ordinacion great near 20 Candidates. Dr. Fenton preaches in St. Oswald's, after noon. After prayers with him, his son and Mr. Gibson till 10.

9 L.R.O., Richmond Call Book ARR 1712 f.3v. Thomas Holme (deacon Carlisle 1698, priest Chester 1701) collated to Claughton 1711.

5 About 9 my Lord sitts in the Chapter house. Mr. Stratford appears for Mr. Otty, my Lord hears the Arguments for Mr. Otty's continuance in the Master of the Choiristers place with patience, but interprets the Statutes to imply that the Organist shall be Master of the Choiristers and therefore pronounces Mr. Otty not duly elected but decrees that hee receive the salary till Edmund White bee elected according to the Statutes.[10] Mr. Otty appeals. Mr. Stratford advances several complaints not very considerable, his Lordship gives his judgment along, directs the School Masters to wear Surplices in the Choir & relaxes the visitacion, After dines at Eaton. After prayers Mrs. Hurleston and her sister Williams visit. Mrs. Shakerley & Hurleston call on them about 9 and help to end my last domestic Claret.

6 After early prayers and 4 Turns on roodee, apply to Books. My Lord go's and returns from Warrington. After prayers Dr. Thane, Mrs. Callis, Maryon, Couché and I go to the Mermaid, drink 4 Bottles of good Claret. After I see my Lord and drink white wine, after call on Mr. Boucher who treats with 2 Tipps of his good Brandy, to bed at 11. I write to Jack.

7 After early prayers wait on my Lord who with Mr. Egerton, takes Coach for Mostyn about 8. I write to Mr. Waite Commissary about the Commission of Bury. In the Evening examine 3 Wittnesses about Mr. Hartley's Administracion. After at the Golden Talbot with Mr. Chancellor, Archdeacon and Mr. Shrigley. After with my Lord, Sir H.B. and Mr. Egerton at the palace till past 10.

8 After Tea at Dr. Thane's, my Lord, Sir H. Bunbury, Mr. Egerton and I set out about 10. Come to Gwersilt at 12 where Sir Richard Middleton, Mr. Hanmer, Mr. Robinson &c a good company. Mr. Shakerley entertains with great plenty, elegancy and Urbanity. The wine circles quick about the table till 6 when my Lord, Sir R.M., Sir H.B., &c take horse, I mount at the same Time and come to Havord-y-wern about 8, sitt up cheerfull till 11.

9 D.O.M.G. dies oritur natalis lx.[11] About ½ hour after 8, the morning cool and the roads fair and pleasant. I set on foot and in less than an hour come to Eaton. I find my coz. Moreton alone in great solitude, wee drink green Tea before and after dinner. I stay with her till 4 and in a fine Even return (D.G.) safe at 7.

10 After early prayers recreate in 4 Turns on roodee. After procure a Bill of 40^{li} from Alderman Murrey and inclose it to Dr. Pope. I write to my S. now at Wigan. The Chancellor is with mee about the Writ, Quare non admisit[12] serv'd on my Lord yesterday by Mr. Moreton. I lend Mr. Whaley upon his Letter xx sh. After prayers Mr. Chancellor, Dr. Thane and I go down to the Bear, where wee empty 2 Bottles. I write to my sister Jones.

11 The News and Doway go slowly on. Dr. Thane has a good Discourse in the Choir on "Hee that exalteth himself shall be debased and hee that humbleth

10 See R.V.H. Burne, *op.cit*, p175, for case involving Edmund White.

11 Trans: 'Thanks to God the best and greatest the day of my 60th birthday dawns.'

12 Trans: 'whereby it is not admitted.'

himself shall be exalted". After dinner I am at Sir H.B.'s for an Hour & after Even prayers at Dr. Thane's. I write to Mr. Peirson, Aynsworth & Le Neve and prepare for my Lancashire journy.

12 After 6 in a cool morning thoro frequent flying showers come (passing Warrington) to Haydock about 11. Find Mr. Leigh, his brother Thomas and Mr. James Banks, ready to sitt down to Cutletts, dine with 'em. Mr. Legh takes Coach (for Lyme) about 12. I stay with Mr. Legh and the other 2 till 4. Wee drink our Bottles cheerfully. I come to Wigan about 5. My coz. Holt is more cheerfull not stronger. My Suzy repeats the story of her Journy, wee pass the Time till 11.

13 Solace till and after dinner. After this, my S. and I make visits to Mr. Bowyer's house, Mrs. Leigh, Mrs. Brown. I pay for a new Wigg here 1^{li};12s;6d, the rest of the time with my coz. Holt.

14 It rains briskly till 12. After which my coz. Holt and I sett out and come to Ayrfeild about 1. Mrs. Birchal, Holme and Prescott meet mee. Wee have a Leg of Mutton well gott. I treat with 6 Bottles of Ale and 4 of Claret. My coz. Holt, taken with a Fitt of Gravel, retires. Mr. James Banks comes to us and shares in 2 Bottles. I receive from Geo. Mollineux more of his rent 5^{li};5s (5^{li} now only remains). Wee part cheerfully about 8. I find my coz. Holt's indisposicions mutually aggravat'd from each others indisposicions, this makes a dull Evening till 12.

15 Wee set not hence till 12, come to Winwick and stay an hour with Mr. Crane. Hee diverts with Freindship & very mean poetry, wee come to Warrington about 4, indispos'd, I lay down till a neck of mutton boyld, wee sett hence about 7 and in the night by Glow-worms, sometimes refresht with rain, come safe home D.O.M.G. about 11.

16 I rest and stay at Home, the News gives nothing but expectacion.

17 Apply to Busienes and Books, after noon with Sir Henry Bunbury, pay Alderman Partington 13^{li}.

18 Sunday, stay at home in Tertullian. Mr. Bell late of Cambridg has a good sermon afternoon.

19 Munday, after 4 Turns on roodee at Home in books and Busienes. The Bishop of St. Asaph comes to the Coach & Horses, wee attend him and his Lady till 11.

20 Wee go in a fine day to Broxon where wee meet Dr. King, Mr. Lech, Legh of Aldford, Mr. Bird are there. Wee come home at 9. The News proceeds with Doway and leaves the Armys in the same posture.

21 At home in Busienes till Noon. In the Evening I pay Mr. Crosby 6^{li};7s;4d, Mr. Lawrence 4^{li};19s;11d. Mr. Bateman (1^{li};1s;6d for straw). Alderman Partington, Mrs. Crosby & Lancaster entertain mee freely with Claret. Wee dispatch 5 Bottles at the Golden Talbot part about 11 to Platt & Taylor 6s.

22 Indispos'd from the Claret and Time, yet attend at Court, examine 4 Wittnesses ex parte Mason. In the Even drink a pint of Claret with Mr. Hulton and Peter Mason, pay Mr. Hincks 2^{li};2;10.

23 The News yet uncertain, the hints are given of a new parliament, people flock to the Fair. I pay Mr.Boucher for Bottles 11s.

24 After early prayers indispos'd take 4 Turns on roodee. After apply strictly to Dispatches, particularly Licences today, considerable in Number. In the Evening solace with domestic pint. To Mr. Boucher 5^{li}, Washwoman 1^{li};10s, for a pillion 8s;6d.

25 Dr. Fogg has a good sermon on "Judg and thou shalt not be judged". Many persons go to see Dr. Sacheveril now at Gresford Church and entertain'd greatly by Mr. Shakerley.[13] Invited, in the Evening at Mr. Tho. Yates on Account of the christning of his daughter, where the Chancellor, Mr. Hurleston, the Mayor of Leverpool (Mr. Earle), Dr. Fogg, Mr. Hulton. Wee are freely receiv'd with good wine and stay till 11.

26 I examine 2 more wittnesses for Mason, stay, save divercion into the Fair, at home in Busienes. Take a pint at the Bear with Mr. Proby.

27 About 10 the Chancellor and I sett out and come to Broxon about 12. Wee find only Dr. King and Mr. Maryon with the Bishop. I impart Dr. Stratford's and Mr. Waite's Letters to him, they divert at Bowls till 7, wee return about 9.

28 I stay at home in Busienes, write to my coz. Parr, that I have had some weeks 50^{li} for him. In the Evening after inspection into the Fair, I go to Mrs. Dod, Gamul, and Cowper at the Ship. I lay down 5s there, an old Token from Mr. Cholmley, wee drink 5 Flasks of Florence and part about 11.

29 Tho indispos'd (after taking leave with Sir Hen. B. takeing coach for Bettisfeild) about 11, I set out and come to Wrexham before 1. Dine and stay with Mrs. Moreton till 5. After to the vicarage where with the vicar, brother Puleston, Gerard Eyton and Tom. Pulford, I stay freely till 9 and come safe home (D.G.) in a sweet Evening before 11.

30 After Elixir, releiv'd of the Heat and weariness of yesterday's journy. The News brings little but want of Mailes. In the Evening Mr. Wells of Sanbach calls, I go down with him to the Bear. Dr. Hancock comes to Us. Wee are free and cheerfull over 3 Bottles which holds us to 12 a clock.

JULY 1 About 9 Mr. Wells calls. I go to the office and try with him a Bottle of the Ale hee gave mee 2 years ago. This adds to my indisposicion which I indevor to reconcile by repose after noon. My Lord Bishop comes from Broxon about 8. I wait on him, hee lodges in my corner.

2 My Lord has an excellent discourse on 1 Cor. c7;31. Sanctissimae Eucharistiae particeps det D.O.M. vitam agere puriorem.[14] After Evening prayers Capt. Clayton drinks a dish of Tea with mee. I go with him to my Lord where wee stay till 8.

3 I take 4 Turns on Roodee and am recreated. After morning prayers wee

13 Prescott's correspondence contains reference to large crowds going to Gresford church to listen to Dr. Sacheverell, who had been suspended from preaching for three years.

14 Trans: 'I partake of the most Holy Eucharist. May God the best and greatest grant [me] to live a purer life.'

drink a pott of Coffee at Mrs. Newtons. I pay Mr. Davies for the Cow 1^{li}. To the Churchwardens for Dr. Fogg 3s. After noon to Busienes. In the Evening I go to the Chancellor where my Lord Bishop, Sir Richard Leving, Dr. King, Mr. Maryon. Sir Richard gives a particular and severe Character of Lord Wharton's person and Administracion of his province. My Lord &c gos at 9, Sir Richard and I stay the other Bottle.

4 Apply in the Morning to Busienes. Ned Roberts gos with my Lord to the office, hee sees it in disorder, from my sister Jones goods. At 2 Mr. Yates and I sett for Eaton, come thither before 3. Mr. Cholmley tells mee of his Aversion to Sir Richard Grosvenor, his competicion for Citizen against Mr. Shakerley.[15] Hee entertains us with 1 Bottle of excellent wine. Wee return before 7. I write to Jack. About 8 my Lord, Dr. King, Mr. Chancellor and Mrs. Pierrpont call on us. They accept of a Bottle or 2 and part about 10.

5 At early prayers, after at Tea with my Lord, it rains till 9. My Lord and Dr. King consider 3 parts of the Bishop of St. Asaph's Articles. My Lord takes horse about 9, Dr. King discourses, on his Defence of Bishop Atherton (of Waterford) which hee gave mee. Hee, Mrs. Pierrpont &c take Coach after 10 for Broxon. I apply to Books. In the Evening Alderman Banks and Peter Greene from my Coz. Holt call on mee. Wee go to the Bear, drink 2 Bottles of good Claret and part about 9.

6 Court day of moderate Busienes. I examine Mr. Banks and Peter Green on my uncle Herl's Will and by Peter send my watch to Mr. Darbishire, near Hacokley, Watchmaker. After prayers, Mr. Leigh of Aldford and I go down to the Bear. Wee are freindly over 3 pints and part before 9. Paid Alderman Ince for Rent till Midsummer 8^{li};5s;0d.

7 After early prayers I see the News which tells that the States have interpos'd their Request to her Majesty not to alter the Ministry or to dissolve the parliament. I take 4 Turns on roodee and take Notice that one Turn takes 1340 of my ordinary steps there. Mr. Richard Davies and Mrs. Ann Thelwal dine with us. After dinner wee are alarm'd with the danger of Mr. Davies Case. My S. desir'd by 2 messengers hastens down. I write to Mr. Jas. Banks and John Cross &c, about 9 give Sir Hen. B. (now at Bettisfeild) an Account of Mr. Davies's danger.

8 I turn Burnets 2nd part of the Reformacion and particularly read Sir Fr. Walsinham's excellent Letter (p.418) about Q. Elizabeth's proceeding against papists and puritans. I draw an Account of Collett's Administracion and sent it inclos'd in a Letter to Mr. Sayer (9s;2d). I write to my coz. Parr about the 50^{li} and to Mr. Morrey about wine. Mr. Davies dies about 9 this morning after 12 days affected with the small pox. So good and so learned a person falls not unlamented by Mankind in common, the shock to his Family and to those admitted to a nearer prospect of his worth, is great and amazeing, not curable but by the gentle Applications of Time and patient submission to the almighty

15 Sir Richard Grosvenor was attempting to replace one of the two M.P.s for Chester.

hand which has withdrawn him into an infinit sphere of Knowledge and happiness. The News of a new parliament upon Applicacion of the States seems to dwindle.

9 Mr. Oliver's Curate has a good and zealous discourse in St. Oswald's in the morning on . . . .After prayers I finish Tertulliam de Pudicitia, turn St. Paul's 2 Epistles to the Corinthians till 9.

10 I write to Mr. Commissary Waite about the Ius patronatus of Bury and to Mr. Peirson. After noon apply to Books and Busienes. About 6 I go with Mr. Lloyd of Tongray and Mr. Pennat to the Bear. Wee drink 2 Bottles. Mr. Pennat acquaints mee that the Bishop of St. Asaph collated him Friday last to LlanArman and thanks mee for my recommendacion. About 8 I go to Mr. Davies's and in melancholy reflections pass an hour in the room with the Corps, after this about 12 Gentlemen come in, are serv'd and presented with Gloves. The Corps gos about 10 severall accompanying them to Mold. I call on the little News at Exchange Coffee house, to bed about 12.

11 Apply to Morellii Specimen rei nummariae. After 10 a clock prayers to the Countess Coffee house. The Allies diverted by the French from Arras invest Bethune. Lord Anglesey to bee Treasurer of Ireland succeeding Lord Coningsby, the place said to be worth 6000^{li} p.A. Will Eyton dines with us. After apply to examine the process betwixt the Churchwardens of St. Oswald and Nickals in 1663 and after prayers finish it.[16] Divert in a domestic pint and to bed about 10.

12 I apply to Books especially to the Titles de Usuris till Evening prayers. After at Pickins the Golden Talbot where Mr. Chancellor, Mr. Proby and I drink each our Bottle of smaller French. Sir Tho. Grosvenor, Sir Henry Bunbury and Mr. Shakerley (as Sir Hen. told mee) settle the Election of Citizen for the next parliament (vidt Sir Hen. and Mr. Shakerley to stand for the next parliament and after that one of them to resign and both give their Interests to Sir Richard Grosvenor.[17])

13 About 8 I step down and take 3 brisk Turns on roodee which effectually discurs my last night's Bottle. About 9 I send to inquire how Mr. Wood of St. John's is in health (haveing heard last night hee was in danger from Asthma). John brings back that hee dy'd about 7 this morning. I heartily condole the loss of so good a Man & so old an Acquaintance.[18] Sir Hen. Bunbury sees us and tells us as above, the reconcilliacion last night. A Court day of small busienes. I examine 2 Wittnesses in Mason's busienes. Mr. and Mrs. Couché and her mother Waine, dine with us. After prayers (about 6) I go to Mr. Stratford invited. Hee gives mee a bottle of French but on the decay, wee secure the acidity with a full Dram of good Brandy. Hee shows mee his Labors vidt

16 C.R.O., EDC.5(1710) No. 11, Churchwardens, etc.
17 Sir Henry Bunbury resigned as M.P. in 1727 and was replaced by Sir Richard Grosvenor.
18 L.R.O., Exhibit Book DCh.1 f.2. Laurence Wood, vicar of St. John and St. Bridgett, Chester, priest Lichfield 1673, collated to St. Bridgett by Bishop Cartwright, and to serve St. John's in 1689.

Common places and other Colecions consisting of 6 Quartos.

14 After early prayers to the Coffee House. The News gives a good prospect of alteracions at Court and in other great and beneficial posts. I intended but go not, to Broxon the day being rainy and myself indispos'd. I apply to Books particularly to Morelii Specimen nummariae antiquae. Invited I go with Sir Wm. Meredith & Mr. Boucher to Mr. Woods funeral, the company proceeds with it from Mr. Spark's house thoro the Orchyard. About 9 wee 3 see the company and corps in the Church of St. John and return about 10. Indispos'd of a Cold I apply to Elixir salutis.

15 I am reliev'd by Elixir. From 6 till 1, it is very stormy with rain not usual at this time of the year. I return to Books, receive a Gallon of Brandy from Mr. Hen. Wolsenholme and pay the fatt woman who brought it 10s. I proceed in Morelii Specimen and (with pleasure) turn Alexander ab Alex. till 9. Affected with a cold & headache take Elixir.

16 I stay the Forenoon at Home. After noon to St. Peter's where Mr. Oliver has an excellent discourse on 4th psalm. After prayers my Suzy and I visit Mr. & Mrs. Yate. Hee and I empty a Bottle, thence to Alderman Partington's where another is emptied, thence home when I write to Dr. Stratford and desire him to sitt to Mr. Ottey for his picture and to Jack, Mr. Stratford designing (but obliquely) for Oxford tomorrow early, calls, I treat him with a pint. ArchDeacon Higgins of Ireland had a remarkable & high sermon this Afternoon in St. Oswalds.

17 I write to the Rector of Wigan now at York, take tho' it blows, 3 Turns on roodee. Will. Eyton dines with us, wee have after, reflections on his brother Eyton and our cozen Kendrick's ungenerous and sordid disposicions. After repose I divert in Alex. ab Alex. till 6. After I see Mr. Higgins and his Lady (sister to Sir William Glyn) hee tells mee of the Queen's answer to Mr. Hagenon the Dutch resident &c. Wee go to the Coffee House where the News gives Account of altering the Leiftenancy of London to some of the most rich and loyal Aldermen. Mr. Vaudrey's Man Fearnihead (about 9) makes a sudden demand of mee, bringing the Account stated, the ballance a surprising sum. I pay him 30 Guineas, and hee seems well pleas'd with it. Among other Changes at Court Lord Hide is said to be made Cofferer, in place of Lord Rialton.

18 About 10 from the Coffee house in blowing weather, Mr. Chancellor and I sett out and come to Broxon about 12. Wee entertain and please my Lord and Dr. King with the good News of the Alteracions at Court. Here are Mr. Oliver, Mr. L. his Curate, Mr. Wright of Stretton and Mr. Leche Rector of Tilston at dinner.[19] After which I am drawn to Bowls, boul 2 Rubbers and come off save to the Greenkeeper 6th equally. I perform in that exercise especially the said games, to surprize. Mr. Oliver, his Curate & I leave Broxon at 6 and come home D.G. safe at 8. John Burrow Apparitor at Kendal, comes with Testimonials and

19 C.R.O., EDV2/14.

desires my Lord's Recommendacion to repair his losses by Fire, but succeeds not. I write to Mr. Lambert, Barton & Holt by & give him 4s.

19 Extremely indispos'd and fevorish, keep in doors and in Books. Mr. Bryer of Bolton le Sands and Mr. Kirks now of St. Bridgetts, call on mee after dinner. In the Evening I return to Books till 9.

20 The last Court day of this Term, the Busienes moderate and quick. I examine 3 Wittnesses in the 2 Causes of Holt.[20] In the Evening Mr. Lowndes and Mr. Yate call on mee, wee go down, about 6 to the Bear where Mr. Gardner is added to us, wee pass the 4 Bottles of good wine and so many hours freely.

21 I take 3 Turns twixt 10 and 11 on roodee, the weather hott and sunny. I return to Books and in them consult the Titles of Simony and repairs of Churches. In the Even my S. and I go to visit Sir John Warden (but find him not at home). Wee call on Mrs. Woods. After at Mr. Bouchers room where hee treats the Chancellor and mee with 1 and Mr. Roberts treats with 2 Bottles, which carry the Time up to 10 a clock.

22 Not very clear or easy, I refuge to roodee take 3 Turns and the 2nd time number my ordinary paces which I find agree with my last curiosity and to amount to 1340 in one length (the 3 Turns makeing 4020). Mr. Gregory is with us from the Bishop of St. Asaph. I write to Mr. Shrigley and inclose a Copy of the Decree for Mrs. Foulkes in it. I proceed in Books. After prayers I go with Mr. Hughes of Frodsham, Mr. Henchman and Mr. Aubrey to the Bear, Mr. Kirks comes to us, wee empty 3 Bottles of good wine & part about 10.

23 Mr. Hughes has a good sermon but not happily deliver'd in the Quire on St. John 15 v. 12; the Earl of Warrington being there. The Letters are silent in further Alteracions and about the parliament. After prayers my S. and I visit Mrs. Jones. I read 4 Chapters of Dr. Stearn's Dissertacione de Morte. I recurr to my domestic pint about 9.

24 I turn Camden and Giraldus Cambrensis. I procure from Alderman Morrey a Bill for 50^{li} (at 6 daies) to my cozen Parre directed to Sir Alex and Mr. Henry Cairnes . . . which I inclose it to my cozen Parre. I receive from Ermin Urmston of Neston 12 Bottles of Claret and the little oldish woman who brought them 24s according to a late letter from Mr. Morrey. I pay Alderman Morrey for the Exchequer 12s;6d. In the Evening Mr. Mercer and Oulton call on mee, wee go down to the Bear and over 2 Bottles discourse of the Title & presentacions or Nominacions to St. Johns. Mr. Mercer tells how Sir Ed. Chisnal was affronted at the late Celebracion of Lord Derby's birth day.

25 I direct a Nominacion and presentacion to be made of Mr. Oulton, hee is instituted today at Broxon as vicar on the later.[21] Mr. Gibson preaches on the subject of the St. in the Quire. The News of Alteracion and parliament revives. Mr. Bowyer and Alderman Markland call on us after dinner. Wee step to the Bear where 1 Bottle of Claret, thence to the Talbot where a Bottle of white: they

20 *Ibid.*, EDC1/104.
21 *Ibid.*, EDP1/73, St. John Chester Parish Papers.

go to Warrington. I write to Mr. Fazakerley of Hillhouse about Mr. Ellison. My Lord returns about 8, wee wait on him, stay an Hour. After I call on Mr. Mercer and Oulton at Willoughby's, to bed about 11.
26 About 8 I wait on my Lord Bishop, hee signs his Confirmacion of Tattenhall Assessment according to the pound rate. Hee with Mrs. Pierrpont set for Holywell about 10. I take 4 Turns on roodee. After a divertion in Books, in the Evening I go with Mr. Mercer, Olton and Will. Eyton to the Bear where wee drink 4 Bottles & part past 10.
27 Indispos'd, yet apply to Busienes, I write a Catalogue of the Clergy of Cheshire and direct it to Mr.Egerton in order to circulate Letters on the part of Sir Geo. Warburton and Mr. Cholmley. In the Evening at the Chancellor's with my cozen Kendrick and Mr. Proby. After at a Bottle with them at the Golden Talbot till 9.
28 The News has a sharp sally repuls'd at Bethune and the Armies entring the Feild of Battle. I wait on Sir. Geo. Warburton and Mr. Cholmley at the Yatcht. After take 3 Turns on roodee and am recreated. After dinner I go with Peter Rawlinson to Mr. Chancellor and drawn an Act of his confession. I write to Mr. Haydock and inclose to him 6 Licences and Bonds and a Copy of Pilkington's Will (5s). The Chancellor, Mr. Boucher and Mr. Roberts drink 2 Bottles here of mine and 1 of Mr. Boucher's wine. I write to Mr. John Shaw successor to Mr. Empson.
[No further entries until November.]

NOVEMBER 7 After 2 Turns, to Court the last of this Term, easy & quiet. After dinner repose. In the Even, Lady B. and Mrs. Lloyd at supper. I divert in the Commentators on Tully.
8 Reliev'd by Elixir and a walk of 4 Turns. The News keeps Spain in the Dark. After prayers I apply to Tully de Signis: am affected as his Auditor. N. Roberts tells mee of a providential delivery of the Office from Fire D.O.M.G.
9 In a calmer morning 4 Turns. I pay Harry's Minerval 10s. Apply to Tully visit my sister P[uleston] of Havod – return about 7 to Siciltoniis Iurisdicione.
10 After a walk of 3 Turns, I go to St. P[eter], hear Mr. Oliver's excellent sermon on 3 Phil. 20. In the Evening, I apply to Lord Strange his Alliance.
11 A high wind prevents my walk. I apply to Bonfinius de rebus Hungarieis and especially to the History of Andrew 2nd. In the Even with Mr. Hinchman, Stone and Hodgson at Ale. After read a pamphlet of a Curat of Salop on 13 Rom.
12 After 11 go to Eaton, dine and stay with Mr. Fr. Cholmley till 4. I read a pamphlet left with mee by Lady Greenford.
13 Begin, not finish, another pamphlet, return both to Lady Gr. Send by Axton, 6 Licences to Mr.Bradshaw, proceed in Bonfinius. In the Even at my bro. Neds with Bro. Puleston &c till 11.
14 I take 4 full turns, dip still in Bonfinius. My bro. Puleston dines with us. In the Even 2 men, Empsons from Yorkshire call, with 'em at the Yatcht.
15 After the news call on the Empsons, in the way to my Walk. Mr. Egerton

sends, I dine with him, Mr. Done & Oldfield. After Mr. Spencer comes, discourse on Lord Wharton, stay till 6, return to Bonfinius.
16 I call on Mrs. Lloyd in Barn Lane take 4 Turns. Mr. Massie dines with us. I am with him, the Chancellor & ArchDeacon at Ale at Mr. Hollands till 9.
20 Tho' a rainy morning I go to Wrexham to see Mr. M.
21 I pay a visit to Mr. Cholmley; after at 6 with Mr. R. at the Bull.
22 In the Even with Mr. Sowaby and Lambert at the Pyde Bull till 11.
23 I recreate in a Walk; in the Even at the Yatcht. Mr. S. with his Munck.
24 Mr. Lambert gos for London. I send ½ C. to be drunk with cozen Heyes.
25 I refresh on roodee and wish well to the parliament which meets today; they return from the Visitacion.
26 I hear Mr. Oliver at St. Peters. In the evening Dr. Hawkshaw sends to mee, his Friend Mr. Proby & I drink 7s:6d in tokens at the Yatcht.
27 Indispos'd, walk but am not refresht.
28 Recover'd, at Early prayers, thence to the News, roodee and Books, the men from Salop come, I write to Jack.
29 After a walk Coffee at M.P.'s with Ladys & Sandby. After Even prayers with the Warden of Manchester at Mr. Hinchman's, thence to the Talbot.
30 Dr. Fogg preaches in the Quire. I write to John Crosse, wee remember Lady Cornwallis now in her 32nd year. In the Even invited, entertain'd at Dr. Norris very gentiley with Fowl and wine.

DECEMBER 1 reliev'd by Elixir. The News brings good omens of Parliament, in Books and repose till prayers. After sent for to the Royal Oak with the Chancellor, ArchDeacon, Mr. Hinchman & Proby. There happens betwixt Mr. H. and myself altercacion about Mr. B. & W. A violent storm to Night till Morn.
3 Dr. Fogg has a good sermon on Matt. 5. Wee receive the H.S. the Evening in reading and domestic wine.
4 At early prayers. After 5 Turns to Books, recreated for Busienes, read pro Caelio and Ligario.
5 At early prayers. After 4 Turns to Books. The Address of Commons very compleat. After noon a Game Bull baited. In the Even at Lady B. a storm high. Mr. Egerton sends, with him Dr. Thane &c at the Royal Oak, each a Bottle, return to Lady B.
6 Tho ly till 9, go take almost 4 Turns. After at Coffee with Mrs. Lloyd. After dinner busienes and after prayers procem in Actionii in Varem.
[No further entries until 17th.]
17 So indispos'd that I stay at home. Read Mr. Oliver his Assize sermon against Atheism. And at Night read the 2nd time the pamphlet on 13 to the Romans.
18 In a brisk morning take 4 Turns, write to Dr. Pope and inclose from Alderman Murrey a Bill of 40^{li}. I write to John Cross to pay the 30^{li} interest, and about my bargain with T. Holland. After dinner Mr. Whitehal sees us. I read the pamphlet. Faults on both sides.
19 The weather too stormy for walk. The news tells of Dr. Aldrich's death the

14th of this month. I pay Dr. Fogg 7[li], 2 years rent for my house in the Abby Court. For Ken and Wills quarterage 5s. Most of the day spent in Cluverius, Descripcion of Germany.

20 I take 4 Turns. After write fully to my cozen Parr about the 2 Hon. Brothers, to Mr. Jebbe & Newman. In the Even with Mr.Stone and Hodgson at T. Holland's Ale.

21 Indispos'd take 5 Turns in a bright day, read variously. After prayers at the Bear with Mr. Chancellor, Archdeacon, the Irish and Chester Bouchers, Mr. Allen. Judg Upton's token of 5s to the Chancellor bought us to gain 2 Tunn of Hay of Alderman Ince.

22 A rainy morning prevents my walk, divert at the Coffee House, then in Coins of Constantius, Magneratus and Decentius. Pay Mrs. Lea, Lydia's Governess 13[li]. I read The Thoughts of a Country Gentleman on Dr. Sacheveril's Tryal.

23 I take 3 Turns. I pay Mr. Chapman for his Fees of the last year 5[li];4s;6d, to Mr. Holland for a Bobb wigg 1[li];15s;9d in Gold. I read Tully in Caecilium.

24 I take 3 Turns, after to St. Peter's, Mr. Oliver has an excellent discourse on Acts 17;31. In the Even in Lord Strange, his Alliance, St. Paul's Ep. the Phil. St. Peter & St. John's Epistles.

25 I take 3 early Turns, Dr. Fogge has a good Sermon on the day. Sanctissimam coenam celebro.[23] After prayers, I read the Acts of the Holy Apostles. Dr. Thane shews great melancholy.

26 After 4 Turns in a fine morning recreate in Coffee, hear the service for the day, read the Ep. to the Romans. After prayers J. Cross comes with 2 Hares & 2 woodcocks from Ayrfeild. I drink my domestic Ale with Him and Mr. Willoughby.

27 I take 4 Turns, after wee drink Coffee at Mrs. Plumleys. I dine with Mr. Chancellor and Dr. Thane at Mr. Egertons. After dinner Sir Wm. Meredith comes into the Circle for an hour. Wee go hence about 6. After at home with John Cross.

28 John and I settle Accounts. Hee leaves with mee 24[li]. I give him for 2 years his Service his Letters and some small expences included 4 Guineas. I direct him to try F. Naylor and of 120 or 130[li] for his 2 Feilds. I took full 3 Turns, pay Mr. Heathleson, Mr. Barbley's Accounts 5s. After I am with Mr. Hodgson & Bassano at Mr. Hollands, thence prayers, after indispos'd at home.

29 The papers bring ill News from Spain, the defeat of K. Charles army. I take 4 Turns on roodee, after read 1st Ep. to the Corinthians. I give my sister Jones on Account a Guinea. In the Even at Dr. Thane's with Mr. Egerton & the Chancellor. Wee drink 5 Bottles, good wine. The Dr. is extremely dull, wee part about 10.

30 In a fine cool morning, I take 4 Turns. I read to divert. After prayers Wee visit Lady Otway and Mrs. Upton. The 3 Ropemakers come to us and are fully

23 Trans: 'I partake of the most Holy Supper.'

entertain'd with Beef and Ale.

31 A brisk and wholesome day. I go to St. Peter's where Mr. Oliver has an excellent discourse on 2 Luke 14. The News of Spain and of a War proclaim'd by the Turk against the Muscovite confirm'd. After prayers Mr. Pool of Oswestry sees mee, hee presents mee with the Coins hee had left with mee. I read 2 Ep. to the Cor. and that to the Gal. After in Caves Historia Literata.

1710/11

JANUARY 1 Q.B.E. a brisk frosty morning, at early prayers, after take 5 Turns on roodee, read the Eps. to the Eph., Phil., Coll., and Thess, write to the Dean of York at Winwick. I apply to Christianas Decis and Menochius. In the Evening see Fireworks well perform'd in the Bridge Street. I am at the Bacchus, with Mr. Henchman and young Mr. Otty, wee drink sack.

2 In a clear, not frosty, morning take 4 Turns. Lady Bunbury, Alderman Partington and his family, dine with mee, they stay till 10 at night. I write to my son Jack.

3 In a duller morning, take 3 Turns. Mrs. Margaret Lloyd and her neice Mary drink Coffee with us. After dinner Mr. Dennis pays mee for the last Quarter's Rent 30s. I pay Mr. Jackson for Ken's writeing 10s, Mr. Roberts states Accounts to mee of last year & pays mee the remaining sum $4^{li}5s$. At 6 I go to the Chancellor where Mr. Egerton, Dr. Thane, yong Mr. Meredith & Wainwright. Wee drink our Bottles. I invite them to mee Sat. night.

4 In a clear brisk morning, I take 3 Turns. Wee dine at Alderman Partingtons, after drink freely his Ale. At 6 Mr. Hodgson and I go to the Bear. I send for Mr. Stone, hee comes, wee drink more than our Bottles of good Claret & return full about 10. I write to Mr. Mallory.

5 Indisposicion keeps mee all day, at Home. I turn Covorruvias Sigonius &c till 10.

6 A sweet calm day tempts mee to 3 Turns on roodee, tho' later I pay Mr. Boucher on his Account Ten pound. I write to the Dean of York, Wee dine with Sir. W. Meredith & his neighbours of the Abby Court, stay after 5 and find Mr. Egerton, the Chancellor & Archdeacon at my House. Mr. Meredith & Mr. Wainwright come after, I treat 'em with their Bottles apeece, they part after 10.

7 A very sick day after so many Feasts. I stay at home till Even prayers. After I write to my son Jack and inclose 3 Guineas by Mr. Crosby and gives besides ½ Crown to him to bee melted with Mr. Colly and Jack.

8 After a sick night, an happier morning rises, I take 4 Turns in a white Frost and glorious sunshine. I pay Peggy Birchal 40s. After dinner Mrs. Whitehall comes and sitts an hour with us. I lend Slater the plasterer towards making his son free 10s. I apply to Books and the women keep to their Cards late.

9 I take a walk of 4 Turns, recurr to Books. After prayers I turn Woods Historia Universitatis Oxoniensae till 10.

10 After a painful night, reliev'd by 4 Turns, I begin an Epitaph on Mr. Okes. About 6 to the Golden Talbot where the Bishop of Man, Dean of York, Rector

of Wigan who intended tomorrow to take Coach for London. The Chancellor, ArchDeacon & I stay till 9.
11 I write and send 4 Licences to Mr. Alanson who has now 8. I write to Mr. Fazakerly of Hill House and Mr. Fletcher, Schoolmaster of Wilmslow. Wee dine at Alderman Pulestons in the same Clan as this day 7 night. I give the Waites 2s 6d.
12 I take 4 Turns. Apply to Gruterus his Inscripcions, at the last finish an Epitaph on Mr. Okes and write fully to my Lord about the Commendams of his predecessors.[24]
13 Mr. Egerton, the Chancellor, Archdeacon and I go to Eaton to Mr. Cholmley, hee entertains us liberally. His Nephew's Health begun by the Chancellor ruffles the old Gentleman and damps the Conversacion. I leave the Epitaph with him. Wee return about 6. Mr. Egerton, ArchDeacon & I drink our Bottles at the Golden Talbot and part about 11. 5s 6d to day.
14 At home indispos'd all the day. After prayers wait on Sir Constantine Phipps Lord Chancellor of Ireland with Mr. Egerton, the number 9, the Glass go's round. After, wee visit Lady B. till 11.
15 Helpt by Elixir apply but uneasily to Books. To busienes after prayers, Dr. Thane & I go to the Bear, drink 1 Bottle of excellent Claret betwixt us.
16 A cold and windy morning. After news I take 3 Turns, after to Books. I send Mr. Styth 6 Licences & Bonds by the Leverpoole Carrier. In Books and Busienes till about 7. Mr. Morrey comes, stays till 9, mostly the Discourse on the seating Neston Church.
17 I take 4 Turns in a brisk morning, write to my Cozn. Parr. After dinner Mr.Morrey comes. After prayers wee seek (meet not) the Chancellor. My cozen Kendrick Mr. Morrey & I drink 2 Bottles at the Bear, return about 9.
18 A brisk frost. The first Court of this Term Q.B.E. I pay the Chancellor for repeticions of Wittnesses for the last year 1^{li}:8s and for his Fees of Institucions to 19 Sept. 1709, 8^{li}. The practice proceeds quietly. After Court I take 2 Turns & return home in ½ hour. After prayers Ned Wright & his brother Tom see us and stay near 9.
19 In a fine clear morning, I take 4 Turns. After wee drink Coffee with Mrs. Lloyd in Barn Lane. I finish the Allegacions on behalf of the Church Wardens of Manchester against Sir E. Coke.[25] In the Even at the Golden Talbot with Mr. Chancellor, ArchDeacon and Mr. Hulton. Wee drink 3 Bottles and part at 8.
20 The Frost continues severely. I take 4 Turns, after stay at home in Books especially in Stow of London.
21 The weather now excessive cold. Mr. Sub Dean Wright has a good but very long sermon for the cold day. I read the 2d Spira and in the Even the Epistles to Timothy, Titus and Philemon.

24 In order that the Bishops could have a reasonable stipend, they were allowed to hold another living, such as Wigan, in commendam.
25 C.R.O., EDC.5(1710) No. 9. This file contains a great deal of information on the growth of Manchester.

22 I take 4 Turns in a brisk and frosty morn. Turn Ushers Annalls. After Even prayers with Dr. Thane, & my Cozen Kendrick at the Golden Talbot. Wee drink 2 Bottles and part before 9.
23 Alderman Partington, Puleston, Mr. Bingley and I walk to Eaton, dine and stay with Mr. Cholmley till 5. After go to Mr. Pigott's where wee find the Mayor & Mr. Stringer. Wine and Beer go briskly round. Wee stay till 7, come fast home by the Moon. Alderman Puleston, Mr. Bingley and I drink a Bottle at the Bear and home before 10.
24 I take only 2 Turns in a fine morning, return to Books. After prayers and 6 Wee are at supper at Dr. Thane's, the Ladys play at Cards, wee drink 1 Bottle.
25 St. Paul. In a delicate morning take 4 Turns. Examine 1 Wittness ex parte Jones & Gee contra Mason. Mrs. Mary Lloyd dines with us. After a Busienes of many years despatcht betwixt Mr. David Wynne & sister Jones. Mr. Griffith of Rhyall consults mee in his Case 1^{li}:1s:6. I writt to John Cross about the Lease &c.
26 The weather still frosty & delicate. I take 4 Turns, recreate in Books. After prayers I apply to Letters to my Lord Bishop (send inclos'd Mr. Morrey's case of Neston Church)[26] to Sir Henry Bunbury & Dr. Pope, draw a Monicion to the Churchwardens of Neston. Wee have the bad news of Dr. Fowk's death.
27 In the like weather take 4 Turns, write to Mr. Monnier and return the draught of a Surrender to Sam. Prescott. After Noon attend on Mr. Barber's Funeral, Mr. Oliver has an excellent sermon at it in the Quire.
28 An excessive cold day. Dr. Thane has a good sermon on Prov . . . .In the Evening at Mr. Hulton from 6 to 9, the female family fill the room. Wee drink several sorts of Ale.
29 The cold and fine weather continues. I take 4 Turns, write to Mr. Hayhurst about Whittley, search 2s 6d, In Books. After prayers with Mr. Seddon of the Isle of Man at the Golden Talbot. Wee remember and condole the Derby family, drink 2 Bottles & part about 10.
30 In the sharp morn take 3 Turns. The King's Martyrdom solemnis'd, Wee hear an excellent discourse by Mr. Oliver on Ps. 51.3. In the Even at the Talbot agen with Mrs. Seddon, Hulton, Allen, Wee drink 3 Bottles. After I write to Mr. Morrey on the Commission.
31 Still a severe Frost and fine weather. I take 5 Turns. I turn Demosthenes. After Noon I go to Newton, Mr. Hurleston gives Mr. Lancaster sack and mee a Bottle of Claret, Wee come home before 6.

FEBRUARY 1 A brisk frost, I take 2 Turns before Court which is easy today. I examine 4 Wittnesses in 3 Causes of Tattenhal,[27] after in the Even go with Mrs. Egerton, Done, Walley & Cottinham to the Golden Talbot, wee stay till 2 in the morning at wine and punch, pay about 4s a peece.

26 *Ibid.*, EDC1/104 n.f.
27 *Ibid.*

2 Candelmas day, very fevorish and unhappy from the unseasonable wine last night, stay at home till Evening when I go to the Chancellor, ArchDeacon and Mr. Ed. Wright to the Golden Talbot, the wine pleases not. Wee part at 8 indispos'd to bed before 10.
3 Not perfectly recover'd, in a fine brisk frost, take 4 Turns on roodee. I write to Geo. Bate for Mr. Egerton about Manks and Scotch Bullocks and to Mr. Morrey on the subject of the Seats. I turn Berties Geography.
4 Well recover'd, but more perfectly by 2 Turns. I send a Messenger to Mr. Morrey with a Letter from the Bishop. Dr. Fogg has a good sermon on psal. 51.3 Wee receive the Holy Sacrament. After prayers read the Epistle of St. Paul to the Hewbrews. The Frost begins to relent.
5 The Frost gon in a fine soft rain, I write to Mr. Peirson, my coz. Parr & Sam. Prescott, I inclose 2 Licences by the post to Mr. Bradshawe, am indispos'd yet after noon examine David Parry. In the Even, wee go to Mr. Roberts, Mr. Boucher comes thither, wee are entertain'd with three Bottles good Wine.
6 Tho' a Snow 2 Inches deep on the place, I take 4 Turns on roodee. The Queen's Birth day (now 46) celebrated. After prayers I celebrate the day in a pint at Home and at Lady B's. Read 3 Acts of Phormio.
7 The snow much dissolv'd. I take 4 Turns. Apply to Books. After prayers begin Enuchus, pay Mr. Foulks on Account 15^{li}, pay the Boys' Cock mony 7s.
8 The snow and cold reviv'd. End Enuchus, an easy Court day. I write to Sam. Prescott. Examine 3 Wittnesses on the part of the Churchwardens of St. Oswald's.[28] Write to my son Jack.
9 More snow with cold wind. I inclose 4 more Licences to Mr. Bradshaw, divert in Books, till six at Night when with Dr. Thane I go to Mr. Egerton's, the Chancellor comes after, wee are plentifully entertain'd with wine and supper. Wee jointly advise Dr. Thane to a London journy but without success. Wee part about 10.
10 The Frost dissolv'd. I from the cold contracted last night, extremely indispos'd. I inclose a Licence for Parish Clerk to Wm. Grice of Ormskirk by the post (for which and postage 14s). I turn thoro Brissonius de Formuliis. I pay 53s for Linnen for Jack and 20s for 2 loads of Coales.
11 The weather cold and thawing. I stay indispos'd at home. I read the Revelations of St. John and some of Dr. Hammond's Notes upon them.
12 The Frost seems wholy gon, my indisposicion diminish'd. Mrs. M. Lloyd dines with us. I apply to Books particularly to Bishop Sanderson's Episcopacy not prejudicial to Royal power. In the Even go to Mr. Hulton's, hee gives mee a Bottle of Claret and sends another to my House.
13 The weather sharp and freezing. Indispos'd of my Cold. I examine 1 Wittness ex parte Calkin contra Coulson, return to Books especially Sanderson.

28 *Ibid.*, EDC.5 (1710) No 11, contains information on the origin of St. Oswald's church in the cathedral.

Mr. Hulton comes here in the Even. Wee open the 2d Bottle, it proves ill, wee drink Ale.

14 A brisk frost, I venture to perform 4 Turns on roodee, am extremely refresh'd, turn some of Plato and Alex. ab Alex., thoroly, celebrate the day, Ash Wednesday, at home.

15 More snow, little Frost, I venture not (for my Cold) to Court. The Fore Noon in Books. I examine 1 Wittness ex parte Guardiani de Bowden contra Frith, [29] return to Books till 9.

16 The [?thaw] and (yet) the snow continue. I turn in the Fore noon Quintilians Declaracions, in the After, Montanus de Iure Tutelarum, with pleasure write and inclose a Commission to swear Ld. Haversham to Mr. Jones and to my cozn. Parr about Jacksons search for Mr. Greenley (2s 6d.)

17 The weather and my cold continuing severe, I stay at Home in Books proper to the Day.

18 My indisposicion aggravating. I take about 8 Ounces of Blood, at 7 at night, by Cupping (pay the Operator 2s;6d) I turn with difficulty (not without some pleasure) Aulus Gellius.

19 A dull snowy day. I turn Fornerius his Decisiones quotidianae. A Gun curious & ancient (formerly Lord Molineux's) is propos'd to mee for a Guinea. I write and commend it, to Mr. Egerton, towards Night very much recover'd of the pain of my Head.

20 I send to see Mr. Fr. Cholmley, continue in Fornerius, examine 1 Wittness on the behalf of the Churchwardens of St. Oswald's; read the Book of Tobit. An extraordinary fall of Snow, After noon.

21 I apply to Books and to Busienes.

22 The weather still Cold. I stay from Court, examine 2 Wittnesses ex parte Marbury contra Tomkinson.[30] In the Even, Mr. Oliver and Mr. Deane have some discourse about the Disposicion of Mr. Moreton's Children, wherein the later tempted by Advantage, is inflexible in his pretended Opinion. Writt to John Cross.

23 After the News the weather more mild. I take the Ayr on the Walls and a Turn and half on Roodee. I apply afternoon to Menochius de Arbitriis particularly.

24 St. Matthew [*sic*] [Matthias] a fine Frost cold and brisk. I venture not out. I send the Administracion of Thompson to Lord Haversham. Write to Mr. Jones and inclose Account of 2^{li};3s about it. I write to Mr. Cholmley of Holford and to my Cozn. Holt and in the Evening to Jack.

25 The weather and my cold still confine mee. I read Dr. Whitby on the Millenium and on several parts of the Epistles.

26 In a fine Frost, I venture 3 Turns on roodee. Apply to Busienes & Read

29 C.R.O., EDC1/104 n.f.
30 *Ibid.*

Plutarch De Liberis educandis and several Titles in the Code to that purpose. I send my Man & Horse to Halghton for Mrs. M. Lloyd.
27 A brisk and frosty Ayr, yet venture to take 3 Turns, Thence to Books. I examine Dr. Fogg & Dunbabin on Interrogations against the Churchwardens of St. Oswald's. Mrs. Margaret Lloyd dies tonight about 9 a clock.
28 In another brisk morning, I take 3 Turns, indispos'd very much to busienes. Wee send by the Oxford Carrier to Jack, 6 new Shirts, 6 Guineas and 2 sugar loaves to him & Mr. Colly either. I pay the Carriages 2s 2d the rest amount near 10^{li}. I writt my cozn Parr. Mrs. Fox with whom Mr. H. is said to have had scarr'd conversacion bury'd today.

MARCH 1 I stay at home from the Court, where the Busienes is very small. Turn Omphalius, De Usurpacione Jurii. After noon Mr. Chancellor comes, I go to Evening prayers. Write to Mr. Shaw (by W. Plumb) and inclose three Licences and Bonds to him. I write to Jack an Account of things directed to him by the Oxford Carrier. A great profusion of scandal breaks out today about Mr. Hulton & Mrs. Fox.
2 About 11 the Chancellor, Dr. Thane and I set out to Eaton, wee visit Mr. Cholmley and after go to the Boat house where wee have our Chad Feast. Mr.Mather in our return invites us to his house, wee stay about an hour, his Liquids not tempting.
3 In a fair morning, I take three Turns. I apply to Books. I write to Mr. Watkinson of Winwick, Mrs. Margaret Lloyd bury'd at 5. After with Mr. Jones of Bangor and Mr. Clopton at the Raven. After visit the House of Mourning in Barn Lane.
4 In the Forenoon, at St. Peter's where Mr. Laitwood the Curat has a Sermon on Lent and Fasting. Aunt Peck is with us, returns home. After prayers I turn Ficinus his Plato.
5 In a fair morning I take 3 Turns on roodee. Afternoon rainy. In the Even return to Plato, Mr. Boucher of Dublin and Mr. Allen come & interupt. Wee drink in my Corner 2 Bottles of Mr. Allen's good Claret.
6 A brisk and fair morning invites to 3 Turns. I read Patin de Cultura Horti. In the Evening turn the Antiquities of Westminster.
7 I draw a negative Certificate about the Gallery in the Chancel of Wigan Church. I send 4 Licences to Mr. Watkinson from whom I receiv'd on Saturday for 4 Licences 3^{li};17s;8d. Mr. Ware comes to see my Coins. Apply to Books particularly to Fabri Semestisa.
8 In a fair morning, I take 3 Turns on roodee. The Queen's Anauguration is celebrated. I write to my sister Jones going to Wrexham, to Mr. Davies about Lealand & Itinerary. Mr. Williams of Mold advises mee about his Answer to a Mre exceptus,[31] hee gives mee a Carolus 1^{li};3;6d.
9 The weather turn'd rainy. The Fore noon taken up with Mr. Williams about

31 i.e. Articles of Exception.

his Answer. The rest with indisposicion.

10 After 3 Turns, I write to John Crosse. After dinner apply agen to Mr. Williams answer and finish Peter Knight's Confirmacion. I write to Mr.Moulding.

11 The weather very sharp, confines us home. In the Evening I turn Plato.

12 I take in a cold wind one Turn and thence round the Walls. Apply to Books particularly Diodorus Siculus by Mr. Booth. I write to Dr. Stratford about Mr. Ellis.

13 The News is full of the Assassinacion of Mr. Harley by Guiscard.[32] I take 3 Turns on roodee, receive my Cosn. Hayes Letter wherein hee presents mee with Cujacius. I apply to Books. In the Even Dr. Thane and I invited drink 3 Bottles of Irish Claret with Mr.Boucher. I pay John today 20s upon Account besides 6s hee had laid down.

14 A snowy sharp morning, I send John to Wrexham for my sister Jones. I write to my Cozen Hayes and my Cozen Parr. The rest variously in Books.

15 A very sharp morning inclines mee to write to John Cross that I have not yet determin'd a Day for our comeing to Holland. I am at Court, I examine 3 Wittnesses against Mr. Lowe, Mr. Raymond the Chancellor of Meath sees mee.

16 After a walk of 3 Turns in a brisk Ayr and the News, I return to Books. After Even prayers and 6 a clock Go with Mr. Egerton, Chancellor, ArchDeacon and Cozn. Kendrick to the Yatcht, where wee cheerfully drink 4 Bottles of good Claret.

17 I write fully to Sir Hen. Bunbury on Mr. Morry's busienes & on my own concern with Mr. Ellis. And to Mr.Monnier & in his Letter to Mr. Seddon. After prayers I borrow 25^{li} of Dr. Thane and immediately pay it (as part of the Bond) to Mr. Boucher. I visit Mr. Whiteall this Evening with my S.

18 The weather is so sharp as still to keep mee at Home. I apply to Books.

19 The weather rainy, alters my design for Ruabon. I write (for my sister Jones) to Mr. Grosvenor & Gerard Eyton.

20 After 3 Turns in a sharp morning, I return to Books and turn the Titulus de Legatis till Night. With Mr. Peters & Mr. Hulton at the Talbot 2 hours.

21 In a calmer morning I take 3 Turns. I write to my cozn. Parre. After return to Books. In the Evening (past 9) step over to see Mr. Bunbury from London, Hee tells the News stirring, stay near 2 hours.

22 The weather rainy. A Court day of some Busienes the Term ending. I write and send by the Carrier six Licences and Bonds to Mr. Ashton of Manchester.

23 After the News and 3 Turns in doubtfull weather in Books. Invited dine with Mr. Egerton. After dinner Mr. Wm. Bunbury, Dr. Thane, Mr. Egerton of Shaw and myself secede with him, Wee are treated freely with good Claret and part about 7.

24 I am indispos'd from the wine last night and the weather today, It rains constantly, towards Night return to Books especially Swinburne.

32 J.R. Jones, *Country and Court 1658–1714* (London, 1978) p.345.

APPENDIX

Translation of longer Latin passages

While every effort has been made to translate the whole of Prescott's often difficult and idiosyncratic Latin, it has seemed advisable to admit defeat over certain particularly obscure words or phrases, or to offer a suggested general paraphrase. Italics have been used in such instances.– General Editor.

A. 8–14 July 1704 (see p. 15)

8 . . . . My Susanna, as the saying goes, invokes Lucina (goddess of birth): Mrs. Anderton the mayor's wife is present as midwife, recalled after leaving the house, the pains come more often, the day is taken up with waiting, night seems to accelerate the birth.
9 About six o'clock in the morning, thanks be to God the best and greatest, with the mother safe, a son is born to me. I stay at home indisposed. Mrs. Anderton and Mrs. Partington lunch with me. The public news gives further assurance of victory against the Bavarians. Messrs Bouchier and Bowyer visit me in the evening.
10 After a dose of elixir, I improve. I write to the Bishop of Chester, the archdeacon of Richmond, John Cross and Mr. Samuel Prescott. I pay 10^{li} to Mr. Partington on account. In the evening for the first time I recover from my sickness. To the Fountain with Messrs Peake and Bouchier, drink red wines moderately. I write to the Bishop of Kildare.
11 I sample the fine weather on the Roodee with Mr. Minshall, it turns out well enough. The public news is somewhat scarce. After Evening Prayers I ask Mr. Egerton, clerk, to be godfather to my little son, not yet baptised, he promises freely. In the evening he and I visit Mr. Cowper, he treats us generously with ale for a little while.
12 Indisposed from the ale. The heat keeps me at home. I write to Mr. Gorst, I send the family insignia of Moreton of Moreton. After prayers, Messrs Bowyer, Minshall and I meet at the Fountain; we consume wine and time freely and cheerfully *nisi quod de Filio Ranulpho Ds. Minshall retulit.*
13 Court day not without clamour. I write firstly to Mr. William Holland about placing his son with me, I keep this private matter to myself. I examine four witnesses for Harrison.
14 Walk a little on the Roodee in warm weather. Public news from the Danube is desired. From Portugal they relate that [?the commander at Castle David], engaged in battle and fighting stubbornly in defence, was brought into the utmost danger.

1–12 October 1705 (see pp. 72–3)

1 After prayers and after completing four turns on the Roodee, I devote myself to Camden's *Annalium Jacobi Apparatum*. I go to the Bishop. The fair continues. Mr. Jones of Mold and his wife are with us. I write to the Chancellor. After lunch with Mr. Jones, I go down to the horse fair, where there is a lack of variety; after Evening Prayers, Archdeacon Booth attracts me to the Fountain. Messrs Thane and Bowyer, invited, are there, we each consume a bottle, afterwards to Mr. Bunbury's with Mr. Jones, [?the day is concluded only in night].
2 Rather indisposed from the wine, I hasten to the Roodee, I am refreshed after completing five turns. [?No public news of the twin boys born on 27 September to Mr. Stephen Fox in his eightieth year]. I examine two witnesses for Hurleston, after lunch apathy takes over. I write to T. Gorst, I remain at home here and there in books, half *carnatus* and after drinking elixir I go to bed.
3 After rain in the night, the day brightens, the suffering vanishes. Two other witnesses undergo examination in the case of Hurleston. Mr. Jones and his wife return. In the evening, keeping out of the way, I meet by chance Mr. Paton, Edward Puleston, and the brothers Pigot at the Fountain. We get together, we each drink a bottle.
4 Suffering as a result of yesterday. I both receive and reply to a letter from Mr. Lambert, having first consulted the bishop. Court day, the business slight, *fuanus* and refreshed by rest. I descend to the Roodee, John with me, [*obscure and incomplete passage on the disposal of human bones found by the city walls*], walk round four times. On my return, Dr Thane summons me to the Fountain, we pass three hours drinking red wine.
5 Not yet [?sufficiently well], I go out, the weather fine and mild, I complete five turns. The public dispatches are silent concerning military actions. [?Spend a little time on the accounts]; after prayers I devote the rest of the day to reading Cornclius Ncpos' Lives of the Six Emperors.
6 After prayers, I spend the day at home. I write to the Chancellor and Messrs Pope and Vaudrey. I pass the rest of the day more intently in books.
7 Rising early from bed, I attend Morning Prayers. I receive a letter from Mr. Parr in which both the Chancellor, now in London, and Dr Pope are mentioned. Mr. Egerton, in the choir, has a short but vigorous sermon on 1 Corinthians 11 v.20. We are partakers of the Holy Eucharist, may God the best and greatest grant me a pious, just, sober life. After Evening Prayers, Mr Bunbury comes, I am in attendance on Mr. Ludlow of Dublin, who I see at the Falcon; Captain Phillips is there. Mr. Ludlow, a generous man upon whom Fortune has breathed long and bountifully, entertains us freely with both dinner and wine.
8 Sick from the unhealthy night and wine. I go early to prayers, then to the bishop, he shows me Dr Pope's letter to him. Messrs Bouchier, Hulton and Roberts go to Malpas. A little shower does not keep me from the Roodee. I complete four turns, rest after lunch, am refreshed. In the evening invited to Mr.

Bunbury's, *dine cheerfully with Messrs Ludlow, Allen and Morgan*, the state of the country is the guests' topic of conversation.

9 After taking a little elixir, I recover. Summoned by the bishop [*?concerning a reply to Dr Pope and business concerning Wigan*]. From then on, the day mostly in books. The public dispatches report that Prince Henry of Darmstadt has been killed in the attack on Barcelona *selopo*. I read Nepos' Lives of the Emperors.

10 A clearer day dawns, I attend prayers. The appointed day for the deaneries of Chester and Wirral. [?Wait on the bishop]. He accuses the Chancellor, in his absence, of great neglect of duty. I write and describe the business. The bishop holds court, he shows weighty, mild and careful judgement. He examines denunciations, everything is done in the proper manner. After Evening Prayers, I devote myself to Peck's Commentaries and the Lives of Nepos.

11 I attend Matins, clear and pleasant weather draws me to the Roodee, where I perform five turns. After lunch I [?return] to Nepos, I pay the quarterly tax of 10^{s} levied on the office. Two witnesses in the case of Hurst undergo examination under oath outside the Court. In the evening Messrs Thane, Allen, Crassus and I each drink [?our pints] at the Fountain.

12 After prayers, I go down to my field the Roodee, I complete four turns. The whole town is intent on choosing the Mayor, Edward Puleston 410, William Starkey 457, Mr. Williams 310 . . . .